ATHENAZE

An Introduction to Ancient Greek

Second Edition

Book I

Maurice Balme

and

Gilbert Lawall

with drawings by Catherine Balme

New York | Oxford
OXFORD UNIVERSITY PRESS
2003

Oxford University Press, Inc., publishes works that further Oxford University's objective of excellence in research, scholarship, and education.

Oxford New York
Auckland Cape Town Dar es Salaam Hong Kong Karachi
Kuala Lumpur Madrid Melbourne Mexico City Nairobi
New Delhi Shanghai Taipei Toronto

With offices in
Argentina Austria Brazil Chile Czech Republic France Greece
Guatemala Hungary Italy Japan Poland Portugal Singapore
South Korea Switzerland Thailand Turkey Ukraine Vietnam

Copyright © 2003 by Oxford University Press, Inc.

Published by Oxford University Press, Inc.
198 Madison Avenue, New York, New York 10016
http://www.oup.com

Oxford is a registered trademark of Oxford University Press

Library of Congress Cataloging-in-Publication Data

Balme, M. G.
    Athenaze : an introduction to ancient Greek, Book I / Maurice Balme and Gilbert Lawall;
with drawings by Catherine Balme.-- 2nd ed.
        p. cm.
    Includes index.
    ISBN-13: 978-0-19-514956-2
    ISBN 0-19-514956-4
      1. Greek language--Grammar. 2. Greek language--Readers. I. Lawall, Gilbert. II. Title.

PA258.B325 2003
488.2'421--dc21

                                                                        2002045015

Printing number: 9 8 7 6 5

Printed in the United States of America
on acid-free paper

PREFACE

This second edition of *Athenaze* was produced on the basis of suggestions made by anonymous reviewers contacted by Oxford University Press and with inspiration from L. Miraglia and T. F. Bórri's Italian edition of *Athenaze*. We are grateful to these teachers and professors and also to the following, who read versions of the revised edition at various stages, offered innumerable helpful suggestions, and caught many errors, typographical and other: Elizabeth Baer of the Berkshire Country Day School, Jessica Mix Barrington of the Northfield Mount Hermon School, James Johnson of Austin College, Cynthia King of Wright State University, Rosemary Laycock of Dalhousie University, Mark Riley of California State University at Sacramento, Kolbeinn Sæmundsson of the Menntaskólinn í Reykjavík, and Rex Wallace of the University of Massachusetts at Amherst. Thanks also go to Latin teachers in Sunday afternoon Greek classes who used preliminary versions of the revised chapters and made many useful observations.

The new features of the revised textbooks include the following:

- Short passages from Classical and New Testament Greek in virtually every chapter
- A strand titled Greek Wisdom, with sayings of the seven wise men of Archaic Greece at various points throughout Book I and fragments of Heraclitus at various points throughout Chapters 18–28 in Book II (Greek Wisdom in Chapter 29 contains material on Socrates)
- Some rearrangement of the sequence in which grammar is introduced, so that the future tense and the passive voice are now introduced in Book I and the first three principal parts of verbs are now listed from Chapter 10, with full sets of principal parts being given in Book II, as before
- Fuller grammatical and linguistic explanations throughout, including material on accents provided along the way, as needed for completing exercises accurately
- New, descriptive terminology used for the tenses of verbs
- Many new exercises, including periodic requests for students to photocopy blank Verb Charts at the ends of Books I and II and to fill in forms of requested verbs, adding new forms as they are learned
- New insertions in Book I titled PRACTICE, requesting that students write out sets of nouns or sets of nouns and matching adjectives
- Presentation of most of the new grammar by Chapter 28 and consolidation of the extracts from Thucydides and Aristophanes' *Acharnians* in the last two chapters, 29 and 30

The purposes of the course remain as they were in the first edition, as they are spelled out in the Introduction. We hope that inclusion of Classical and New Testament passages will attract more students to the study of Greek and that this revised edition will help expand interest in the study of Greek in North America.

—Maurice Balme and Gilbert Lawall

CONTENTS

i

INTRODUCTION

Part I:
About This Course

The aim of *Athenaze* is to teach you to read ancient Greek as quickly, thoroughly, and enjoyably as possible, and to do so within the context of ancient Greek culture. This means within the context of the daily life of the ancient Greeks as it was shaped and given meaning by historical developments, political events, and the life of the mind as revealed in mythology, religion, philosophy, literature, and art. The stories that you will read in Greek provide the basic cultural context within which you will learn the Greek language, and most of the chapters contain essays in English with illustrations drawn from ancient works of art and with background information to deepen your understanding of some aspects of the history and culture of the Greeks.

The course begins with the story of an Athenian farmer named Dicaeopolis and his family; they live in a village or deme called Cholleidae, located north of Athens. The events are fictitious, but they are set in a definite historical context—autumn 432 B.C. to spring 431. The Athenian democracy, led by Pericles, is at its height; the Athenians rule the seas and control an empire, but their power has aroused the fears and jealousy of Sparta and her allies in the Peloponnesus, especially Corinth. By spring 431, Athens and the Peloponnesian League are engaged in a war, which leads twenty-seven years later to the defeat and downfall of Athens.

The story begins with life in the country, but with Chapter 6 a subplot of mythical narrative begins with the story of Theseus and the Minotaur. This mythological subplot continues in Chapter 7 with the story of Odysseus and the Cyclops and runs through Chapter 10 with further tales from the *Odyssey* briefly told at the end of each chapter. The main plot continues in Chapter 8 as the family visits Athens for a festival, and the tempo quickens.

A terrible misfortune that strikes the family in Athens in Chapter 10 precipitates a plot that is interwoven with narratives of the great battles of the Persian Wars, based on the accounts of the historian Herodotus. As the main plot reaches its resolution in Chapters 18–20 of Book II, the family becomes embroiled in the tensions between Athens and Corinth that triggered the Peloponnesian War, and this sets the stage for the remaining chapters.

The experiences of the family of Dicaeopolis at the beginning of the Peloponnesian War in Chapters 21–23 are based on the accounts of the war written by the historian Thucydides. When the son Philip is left behind in Athens to further his education, we hear something of Plato's views on education (Chapter 24) and then read stories from a book of Herodotus's histories that Philip's teacher gives to him (Chapters 25–28). These are some of the most famous tales from Herodotus, including those dealing with Solon the Athenian and his encounter with Croesus, king of Lydia. In Chapter 28 you will read the account by the lyric poet Bacchylides of Croesus's miraculous rescue from the funeral pyre. Chapter 29 returns us to the Peloponnesian War with Thucydides's descriptions of naval battles and the brilliant victories of the Athenian general Phormio. The course concludes with extracts from Aristophanes showing us Dicaeopolis the peacemaker. From there you will be ready to go on to read any Greek author of your choice with considerable confidence in your ability to comprehend what the ancient Greeks had to say.

The Greek in much of the main story line has been made up to serve the instructional purposes of this book. Most of the subplots, however, are based on the ancient Greek writings of Homer, Herodotus, and Thucydides. They move steadily closer to the Greek of the authors themselves. The extracts from Bacchylides and Aristophanes are unaltered except for cuts.

The readings in the early chapters are simple in content and grammatical structure. They are so constructed that with knowledge of the vocabulary that is given before the reading passage and with help from the glosses that are given beneath each paragraph, you can read and understand the Greek before studying the formal elements of the grammar. After you have read the story out loud, understood and translated it, and discovered the new elements of its grammar for yourself, you will study formal presentations of the grammar that usually incorporate examples from the reading passage. There are then exercises of various sorts to help you consolidate your understanding of the grammar and give you skill in manipulating the new forms and structures of the language as you learn them.

Grammar is introduced in small doses to start with and should be reviewed constantly. We also recommend frequent rereading of the stories themselves—preferably out loud—as the best way to reinforce your fluency of pronunciation, your knowledge of the grammar, and your skill in reading new Greek at sight—which is the main goal of any course in Greek.

At the beginning of each section of the narrative is a picture with a caption in Greek. From the picture you should be able to deduce the meaning of the Greek caption. Pay particular attention to these captions, since each has been carefully written to include and reinforce a basic grammatical feature or features of the Greek language that you will be learning in that particular chapter. It may help even to memorize the captions!

The vocabulary given in the lists before the reading passages is meant to be learned thoroughly, both from Greek to English and from English to Greek. Learning the vocabulary will be easier if the words are always studied aloud, combining the advantages of sight *and* sound. The words given in glosses beneath the paragraphs in the readings are not meant to be mastered actively, but you should be able to recognize the meaning of these words when you see them again in context. Fluency of reading depends on acquiring a large, working vocabulary as soon as possible.

Important words are continually reintroduced in the readings in this course to help you learn them. Your skill in recognizing the meaning of Greek words that you have not met will be greatly enhanced by attention to some basic principles of word building. We have therefore laid out some of these basic principles and incorporated a coherent set of word building exercises in this course.

One of the widely recognized goals of classical language study is attainment of a better understanding of English. With regard to the study of Greek, this means largely a knowledge of Greek roots, prefixes, and suffixes that appear in English words. The influence of Greek on English has been especially notable in scientific and medical terminology, but it is also evident in the language of politics, philosophy, literature, and the arts. We have accordingly incorporated word study sections in the chapters of this course, highlighting the influence of Greek on English vocabulary and providing practice in deciphering the meaning of English words derived from Greek elements.

Finally, at the end of almost every chapter and sometimes in the middle of a chapter you will find passages from a wide variety of Classical Greek authors and from the gospels of Luke and John in the New Testament. These have been carefully chosen and are accompanied by glosses that will allow you to read the passages at the points in the course where they are located. We have also included sayings of the seven wise men of Archaic Greece at various points throughout Book I. You will thus be reading authentic Greek from the very beginning of the course and gaining access to the wisdom and the style of writing and thinking of the ancient Greeks and of the writers of the gospels. This is the icing on the cake, and we hope that you will enjoy it thoroughly and learn much from it.

Myrrhine and her daughter Melissa,
two characters from our story, and their dog Argus

Part II:
The Greek Alphabet

Many of the letters of the Greek alphabet will already be familiar to you.

Letter		Name	Transliteration	Pronunciation
A	α	ἄλφα	alpha	α (short alpha), as the sound in *top;* ᾱ (long alpha), as the sound in *top,* but held longer
B	β	βῆτα	bēta	= *b*
Γ	γ	γάμμα	gamma	= *g* (but before γ, κ, ξ, or χ = the sound in *sing*)
Δ	δ	δέλτα	delta	= *d*
E	ε	ἒ ψῑλόν	epsīlon	as the sound in *get*
Z	ζ	ζῆτα	zēta	= σ + δ = *sd* as in *wisdom*
H	η	ἦτα	ēta	as the sound in *bed*, but held longer
Θ	θ	θῆτα	thēta	= aspirated *t* as in *top*
I	ι	ἰῶτα	iōta	ι (short iota), as the sound in *it;* ῑ (long iota), as the sound in *keen*
K	κ	κάππα	kappa	= the sound of *k* (without aspiration), as in *sack*
Λ	λ	λάμβδα	lambda	= *l*
M	μ	μῦ	mū	= *m*
N	ν	νῦ	nū	= *n*
Ξ	ξ	ξῖ	xī	= κ + σ = the sound of *x* in *axe*
O	ο	ὂ μῑκρόν	omīcron	as the sound in *boat* or *goat*
Π	π	πῖ	pī	= *p* (without aspiration), as in *sap*
P	ρ	ῥῶ	rhō	= a trilled *r*
Σ	σ, ς	σίγμα	sigma	= *s* as in *sing*, but = *z* before β, γ, δ, and μ (written ς when last letter of a word)
T	τ	ταῦ	tau	= *t* (without aspiration), as in *sat*
Y	υ	ὒ ψῑλόν	upsīlon	υ (short upsilon), as the sound in French *tu;* ῡ (long upsilon), as the sound in French *tu*, but held longer
Φ	φ	φῖ	phī	= aspirated *p* as in *pot*
X	χ	χῖ	chī	= aspirated *k* as in *kit*
Ψ	ψ	ψῖ	psī	= π + σ = *ps* as in *lips*
Ω	ω	ὦ μέγα	ōmega	as the sound in *caught*, but held longer

The symbol ˘ will occasionally be used over a Greek vowel to indicate a vowel of short quantity. The symbol ‾ indicates a vowel of long quantity (see ᾱ, ῑ, and ῡ in the right-hand column in the list above). Normally short vowels have neither mark above them (see α, ι, and υ in the right-hand column above). When these three vowels are long, they will usually be printed in *Athenaze* with long marks over them (ᾱ, ῑ, and ῡ). The long mark is referred to as a macron (Greek μακρόν, *long*). A long vowel is held approximately twice as long as a short vowel. The vowels η and ω are always long and are therefore not marked with macrons. The digraphs ει and ου represent two additional long vowels in Greek (see Long Vowel Digraphs below). The vowels ε and o are always short.

All vowels marked with a circumflex accent (˜) or with an iota subscript (see below) are always long and will usually not be marked with macrons.

In the Greek names for the letters of the alphabet given on the previous page, identify all long and all short vowels. Practice pronouncing the names of the letters, paying special attention to proper pronunciation of the long and short vowels. Hold the long vowels for twice the length of time as the short vowels.

Breathings

There is no letter *h* in the Attic alphabet, but this sound occurs at the beginning of many Greek words. It is indicated by a mark called a *rough breathing* or *aspiration*, written over the first vowel of a word (over the second vowel of a diphthong), e.g.:

ἑν (pronounced *hen*)   οὑ (pronounced *hou*)

When an *h* sound is not to be pronounced at the beginning of a word beginning with a vowel or diphthong, a *smooth breathing* mark is used, e.g.:

ἐν (pronounced *en*)   οὐ (pronounced *ou*)

Thus, every word beginning with a vowel or a diphthong will have a rough or smooth breathing. Initial ρ always has a rough breathing, e.g., ῥάβδος, *wand*.

Diphthongs

Diphthongs are glides from one vowel sound to another within the same syllable. Attic Greek has the following diphthongs:

Diphthongs	*Words*	*Pronunciation*
αι	αἰγίς	as the sound in *high*
αυ	αὐτοκρατής	as the sound in *how*
ευ	εὐγενής	ε + υ pronounced as one syllable
ηυ	ηὕρηκα	η + υ pronounced as one syllable
οι	οἰκονομίᾱ	as the sound in *foil*
υι	υἱός	υ + ι pronounced as one syllable

Long Vowel Digraphs

Digraphs are combinations of letters that represent a single sound. Two long vowel sounds are represented in Greek by the following digraphs:

Digraphs	*Words*	*Pronunciation*
ει	εἴκοσι	as the sound in *they*
ου	οὔτις	as the sound in *mood*

Iota Subscript

Sometimes the letter ι (*iōta*) is written under a vowel, e.g., ᾳ, ῃ, and ῳ (these combinations are referred to as *long diphthongs*); when so written it is called *iota subscript*. In classical Greek this iota was written on the line after the vowel and was pronounced as a short iota. Its pronunciation ceased in post-classical Greek, and we usually do not pronounce it now. When it appears in a word that is written entirely in capital letters (as in the titles to the readings in this book), it is written on the line as a capital iota. Thus πρὸς τῇ κρήνῃ > ΠΡΟΣ ΤΗΙ ΚΡΗΝΗΙ. Note that accents and breathing marks are not used when all letters are capitalized.

Paired Consonants

Paired consonants such as λλ, μμ, ππ, and ττ should be pronounced double and held approximately twice as long as the single consonant, e.g., the μμ in γάμμα.

Exceptions are γγ, γκ, γξ, and γχ (where the first γ is pronounced as the *ng* in *sing*), as in ἄγγελος, *messenger*, and ἄγκῡρα, *anchor*.

Double Consonants

Three consonants represent combinations of other sounds and are called *double consonants*:

ζ = σ + δ
ξ = κ + σ or γ + σ or χ + σ
ψ = π + σ or β + σ or φ + σ

Aspirated Consonants

Three consonants represent certain sounds followed by an *h* sound or aspiration:

θ = an aspirated τ
φ = an aspirated π
χ = an aspirated κ

Consonant Sounds

Nasals	μ ν	and γ when followed by γ, κ, ξ, or χ
Liquids	λ ρ	
Spirant	σ	

Stops	Voiceless	Voiced	Voiceless Aspirated
Labial	π	β	φ
Dental	τ	δ	θ
Velar	κ	γ	χ
Double	ζ ξ ψ		

Stops Followed by σ

Labial: β or π or φ, when followed by σ, becomes ψ.
Dental: δ or ζ or θ or τ, when followed by σ, is lost.
Velar: γ or κ or χ, when followed by σ, becomes ξ.

Compare what is said about the double consonants ξ and ψ above. These linguistic phenomena will be very important in understanding certain forms of nouns and verbs.

Punctuation

The period and the comma are written as in English. A dot above the line (·) is the equivalent of an English semicolon or colon. A mark that looks like an English semicolon (;) is used at the end of a sentence as a question mark.

Accents

Nearly every word in Greek bears an accent mark: an acute (τίς), a grave (τὸ), or a circumflex (ὁρῶ). These marks seldom affect the sense. They were invented as symbols to provide written aid for correct pronunciation; originally they indicated a change in *pitch*, e.g., the acute accent showed that the syllable on which it fell was pronounced at a higher pitch than the preceding or following syllables. Later *stress* replaced pitch, and now ancient Greek is usually pronounced with stress on the accented syllables (with no distinction among the three kinds of accents) instead of varying the pitch of the voice. For those who wish to use the pitch accent, we recommend the recording of Stephen Daitz, mentioned below.

Note that the grave accent stands only on the final syllable of a word. It usually replaces an acute accent on the final syllable of a word when that word is followed immediately by another word with no intervening punctuation, e.g., instead of τό δῶρον, we write τὸ δῶρον.

Transliteration

Note the following standard transliteration of Greek into English letters:

α = a	η = ē	ν = n	τ = t
β = b	θ = th	ξ = x	υ = u *or* y
γ = g	ι = i	ο = o	φ = ph
δ = d	κ = k	π = p	χ = ch
ε = e	λ = l	ρ = r	ψ = ps
ζ = z	μ = m	σ, ς = s	ω = ō

Remember the following: γγ = ng; γκ = nk; γξ = nx, and γχ = nch; αυ, ευ, ηυ, ου, υι = au, eu, ēu, ou, ui, but when υ is not in a diphthong it is usually transliterated as y. And note that ᾳ, ῃ, and ῳ are transliterated āi, ēi, and ōi, to distinguish them from the short diphthongs, αι, ει, and οι, transliterated ai, ei, and oi.

[The recommendations for pronunciation given above (the *restored pronunciation*) are based on W. Sidney Allen, *Vox Graeca: A Guide to the Pronunciation of Classical Greek*, Cambridge University Press, 3rd ed., 1988, pages 177–179. For demonstration of the restored pronunciation, including the pitch accents, students should consult the cassette recording of Stephen G. Daitz, *The Pronunciation and Reading of Ancient Greek: A Practical Guide*, 2nd ed., 1984, Audio Forum, Guilford, CT 06437 (U.S.A.).]

Part III:
Writing Greek Letters

Certain conventions may be observed in writing Greek letters. With practice one can write them with ease and speed. There should be no difficulty in imitating the printed forms of the capitals; the small letters may be written as indicated below. A small "s" indicates the point where each letter should be begun ("s₁," "s₂," etc., are used if it is necessary to lift the pen or pencil), and an arrowhead (--->) indicates the direction in which the pen or pencil should move. For convenience, the letters may be divided into four groups:

(1) Eleven of the Greek small letters do not extend below the line of writing,and are approximately as wide as they are high (cf. English *a, c, e*, etc.). (The corresponding capitals are given first, then the printed forms of the small letters, then the "diagrams" for imitation.)

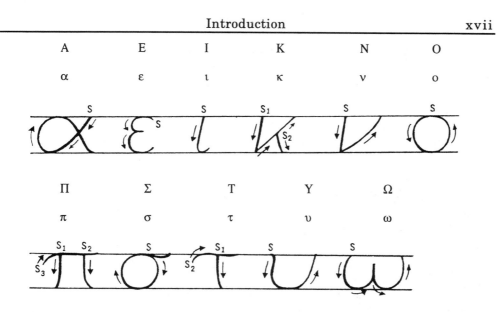

Note that ν has a point at the bottom, whereas υ is round.

(2) Three of the Greek small letters rest on the line of writing but are twice as high as the letters in group 1:

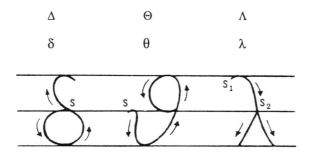

(3) Seven of the Greek small letters rest on the line of writing and extend below it, but do not extend above the letters of group 1:

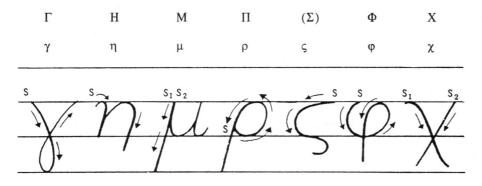

(4) Four of the Greek small letters extend both above and below the line of writing:

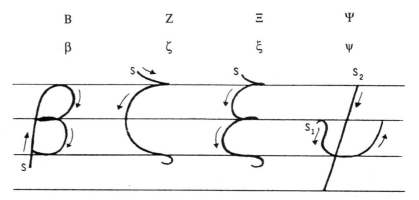

Students will, of course, develop their own writing style, and slight variations from the method of forming the letters that has just been described will not, in general, cause confusion.

[Most of the material in the above section is taken from *The Language of the New Testament* by Eugene Van Ness Goetchius, © Reprinted by permission of Pearson Education, Inc., Upper Saddle River, NJ.]

Part IV:
Practice in Pronunciation and Writing

Practice pronouncing the following words, imitating your teacher. Then copy the Greek words onto a sheet of paper; write the English transliteration of each Greek word, and give an English derivative of each.

1. αἴνιγμα	11. δόγμα	21. μάθημα	31. ῥεῦμα
2. ἀξίωμα	12. δρᾶμα	22. μίασμα	32. στίγμα
3. ἄρωμα	13. ἔμβλημα	23. νόμισμα	33. σύμπτωμα
4. ἄσθμα	14. ζεῦγμα	24. ὄνομα	34. σύστημα
5. γράμμα	15. θέμα	25. πλάσμα	35. σχῆμα
6. δέρμα	16. θεώρημα	26. πνεῦμα	36. σχίσμα
7. διάδημα	17. ἰδίωμα	27. πρᾶγμα	37. σῶμα
8. διάφραγμα	18. κῑνημα	28. ποίημα	38. φλέγμα
9. δίλημμα	19. κλίμα	29. πρίσμα	39. χάσμα
10. δίπλωμα	20. κόμμα	30. πρόβλημα	40. χρῶμα

Copy the following names, practice pronouncing the Greek, imitating your teacher, and write the standard English spelling of each name:

The Twelve Olympians

Ζεύς	Ἄρτεμις	Ἥφαιστος
Ἥρᾱ	Ποσειδῶν	Ἄρης
Ἀθηνᾶ	Ἀφροδίτη	Διόνῡσος
Ἀπόλλων	Ἑρμῆς	Δημήτηρ

The Nine Muses

Κλειώ	Μελπομένη	Πολύμνια
Εὐτέρπη	Τερψιχόρᾱ	Οὐρανίᾱ
Θάλεια	Ἐρατώ	Καλλιόπη

The Three Graces

Ἀγλαΐᾱ	Εὐφροσύνη	Θάλεια

The Three Fates

Κλωθώ	Λάχεσις	Ἄτροπος

Practice reading the following passage of Greek, imitating your teacher, and then copy the first two sentences. In writing the Greek, it will be helpful always to insert the macron over the vowel to which it belongs. As with the accent and breathing mark, the macron should be considered an integral part of the spelling of the word.

ὁ Δικαιόπολις Ἀθηναῖός ἐστιν· οἰκεῖ δὲ ὁ Δικαιόπολις οὐκ ἐν ταῖς Ἀθήναις ἀλλὰ ἐν τοῖς ἀγροῖς· αὐτουργὸς γάρ ἐστιν. γεωργεῖ οὖν τὸν κλῆρον καὶ πονεῖ ἐν τοῖς ἀγροῖς. χαλεπὸς δέ ἐστιν ὁ βίος· ὁ γὰρ κλῆρός ἐστι μῑκρός, μακρὸς δὲ ὁ πόνος. ἀεὶ οὖν πονεῖ ὁ Δικαιόπολις καὶ πολλάκις στενάζει καὶ λέγει· "ὦ Ζεῦ, χαλεπός ἐστιν ὁ βίος· ἀπέραντος γάρ ἐστιν ὁ πόνος, μῑκρὸς δὲ ὁ κλῆρος καὶ οὐ πολὺν σῖτον παρέχει." ἀλλὰ ἰσχῡρός ἐστιν ὁ ἄνθρωπος καὶ ἄοκνος· πολλάκις οὖν χαίρει· ἐλεύθερος γάρ ἐστι καὶ αὐτουργός· φιλεῖ δὲ τὸν οἶκον. καλὸς γάρ ἐστιν ὁ κλῆρος καὶ σῖτον παρέχει οὐ πολὺν ἀλλὰ ἱκανόν.

Part V:
Date Chart

BRONZE AGE

| | Minos, king of Crete; Theseus, king of Athens |
| Ca. 1220 B.C. | Sack of Troy by Agamemnon of Mycenae |

DARK AGE

| Ca. 1050 B.C. | Emigration of Ionians to Asia Minor |

RENAISSANCE

Ca. 850 B.C.	Formation of city states (Sparta, Corinth, etc.)
776 B.C.	First Olympic Games
Ca. 750–500 B.C.	Trade and colonization
Ca. 725 B.C.	Composition of *Iliad* and *Odyssey* by Homer (Ionia)
Ca. 700 B.C.	Composition of *Works and Days* by Hesiod (Boeotia)
Ca. 657–625 B.C.	Cypselus, tyrant of Corinth
Ca. 594 B.C.	Solon's reforms in Athens

PERSIAN INVASIONS

546 B.C.	Defeat of Croesus of Lydia and Greeks in Asia Minor by Cyrus of Persia
507 B.C.	Foundation of democracy in Athens by Cleisthenes
490 B.C.	Expedition sent against Athens by Darius of Persia; battle of Marathon
480 B.C.	Invasion of Greece by Xerxes: Thermopylae (480), Salamis (480), Plataea (479)
	Simonides, poet

IMPERIAL ATHENS

478 B.C.	Foundation of Delian League, which grows into Athenian Empire
472 B.C.	Aeschylus's *Persians*
461–429 B.C.	Pericles dominant in Athens: radical democracy and empire
	War between Athens and Sparta
446 B.C.	Thirty Years Peace with Sparta
	Parthenon and other buildings
	Herodotus, *History*

PELOPONNESIAN WAR

431 B.C.	Outbreak of war between Athens and the Peloponnesian League
430–429 B.C.	Plague at Athens; death of Pericles
425 B.C.	Aristophanes' *Acharnians*
421 B.C.	Temporary peace between Athens and Sparta
415 B.C.	Athenian expedition to Sicily
413 B.C.	Sicilian expedition defeated; war between Athens and Sparta
404 B.C.	Surrender of Athens
	Thucydides, *Histories*

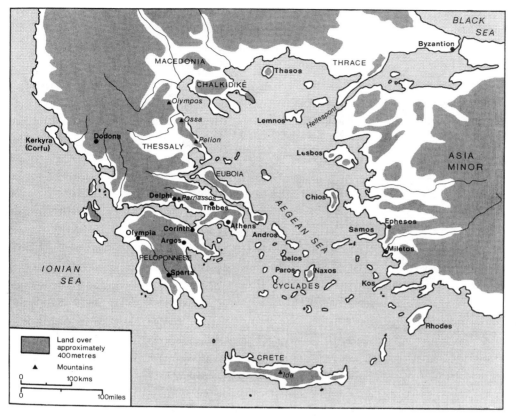

BLACK SEA

Byzantion

MACEDONIA

THRACE

Thasos

CHALKIDIKĒ

▲Olympos

▲Ossa

Lemnos

Hellespont

Kerkyra (Corfu)

Dodona

▲Pelion

THESSALY

Lesbos

ASIA MINOR

EUBOIA

Chios

Delphi ▲▲Parnassos

Thebes

AEGEAN SEA

Olympia

Corinth

Athens

Samos

Ephesos

Argos

Andros

PELOPONNESE

IONIAN SEA

Delos

Miletos

Sparta

Paros

Naxos

Kos

CYCLADES

Rhodes

CRETE

▲Ida

Land over approximately 400 metres

▲ Mountains

0   100 kms

0   100 miles

Greece and the Aegean Sea

1
Ο ΔΙΚΑΙΟΠΟΛΙΣ (α)

ὁ Δικαιόπολις αὐτουργός ἐστιν· φέρει δὲ τὸν μόσχον.

VOCABULARY

Verbs
ἐστί(ν), *he/she/it is*
λέγει, *he/she says; he/she tells;*
he/she speaks
οἰκεῖ, *he/she lives; he/she*
dwells
πονεῖ, *he/she works*
φιλεῖ, *he/she loves*
χαίρει, *he/she rejoices*
Nouns
ὁ ἀγρός,* *field*
ὁ ἄνθρωπος, *man; human be-*
ing; person
ὁ αὐτουργός, *farmer*
ὁ οἶκος, *house; home; dwelling*
ὁ πόνος, *toil, work*
ὁ σῖτος, *grain; food*
Adjectives
καλός, *beautiful*
μακρός, *long; large*
μῑκρός, *small*
πολύς, *much;* pl., *many*
Prepositional Phrase
ἐν ταῖς ᾿Αθήναις, *in Athens*

Adverbs
οὐ, οὐκ, οὐχ,** *not*
οὖν, a connecting adverb, postpositive,*** *so* (i.e., because of
this); *then* (i.e., after this)
Conjunctions
ἀλλά, *but*
γάρ, postpositive,*** *for*
καί, *and*
Particle
δέ, postpositive,*** *and, but*
Proper Names and Adjectives
᾿Αθηναῖος, *Athenian*
ὁ Δικαιόπολις, *Dicaeopolis*

*ὁ is the definite article, *the;* when
the noun is used as an object, the
article becomes τόν. Sometimes
the article need not be translated in
English; sometimes it can best be
translated as a possessive adjective,
e.g., *his.* There is no indefinite
article in Greek.
**οὐ before consonants, οὐκ before
vowels or diphthongs, and οὐχ be-

fore aspirated vowels or aspirated diphthongs (e.g., οὐχ αἱρεῖ, he / she does not take)

***These words are always "placed after" and never occur first in their clause.

ὁ Δικαιόπολις Ἀθηναῖός ἐστιν· οἰκεῖ δὲ ὁ Δικαιόπολις οὐκ ἐν ταῖς Ἀθήναις ἀλλὰ ἐν τοῖς ἀγροῖς· αὐτουργὸς γάρ ἐστιν. γεωργεῖ οὖν τὸν κλῆρον καὶ πονεῖ ἐν τοῖς ἀγροῖς. χαλεπὸς δέ ἐστιν ὁ βίος· ὁ γὰρ κλῆρός ἐστι μῑκρός, μακρὸς δὲ ὁ πόνος. ἀεὶ οὖν πονεῖ ὁ Δικαιόπολις καὶ πολλάκις στενάζει καὶ λέγει· "ὦ Ζεῦ, χαλεπός ἐστιν ὁ βίος· 5 ἀπέραντος γάρ ἐστιν ὁ πόνος, μῑκρὸς δὲ ὁ κλῆρος καὶ οὐ πολὺν σῖτον παρέχει." ἀλλὰ ἰσχῡρός ἐστιν ὁ ἄνθρωπος καὶ ἄοκνος· πολλάκις οὖν χαίρει· ἐλεύθερος γάρ ἐστι καὶ αὐτουργός· φιλεῖ δὲ τὸν οἶκον. καλὸς γάρ ἐστιν ὁ κλῆρος καὶ σῖτον παρέχει οὐ πολὺν ἀλλὰ ἱκανόν. 10

[ἐν τοῖς ἀγροῖς, in the country (lit., in the fields) γεωργεῖ, he farms, cultivates τὸν κλῆρον, the (= his) farm χαλεπὸς, hard ὁ βίος, the (= his) life ἀεὶ, always πολλάκις, often στενάζει, groans ὦ Ζεῦ, O Zeus ἀπέραντος, endless παρέχει, provides ἰσχῡρός, strong ἄοκνος, energetic ἐλεύθερος, free ἱκανόν, enough]

WORD STUDY

Many English words are derived from Greek. Often these derivatives are scientific and technical terms formed in English from Greek stems because the precision of the Greek language makes it possible to express a complex concept in a single word.

What Greek words from the story at the beginning of this chapter do you recognize in the following English words? Define the words, using your knowledge of the Greek:

1. anthropology
2. polysyllabic
3. philosophy
4. microscope

English words such as those above often contain more than one Greek stem. Which of the words above contain stems of the following Greek words?

1. σκοπεῖ, *he/she looks at, examines*
2. σοφίᾱ, *wisdom*
3. λόγος, *word; study*

GRAMMAR

1. Verb Forms: Stems and Endings

Greek verbs have *stems*, which give the meaning of the word, and variable *endings*, which show such things as *number* and *person*. In addition to *singular* and *plural* number, Greek has *dual* number, used when referring to two people or things; it is fairly rare, however, and will not be taught in this course.

Number:		Singular	Plural
Person:	**1st**	I	we
	2nd	you	you
	3rd	he, she, it	they

This chapter introduces only the third person singular of the present tense, e.g., *he/she/it is.*

The Greek verb for *loosen, loose* will serve as an example of a regular Greek verb; the verb for *love* will serve as an example of a contract verb (a type of verb in which the vowel at the end of the stem contracts with the initial vowel of the ending). The irregular verb for *be* is also given.

Stem: λῡ-, *loosen, loose*

3rd singular   λῡ́-ει   *he/she loosens, is loosening, does loosen*

Stem: φιλε-, *love*

3rd singular   φιλέ-ει > φιλεῖ   *he/she loves, is loving, does love*
                   Note that > means "becomes."

Stem: ἐσ-, *be*

3rd singular   ἐστί(ν)*   *he/she/it is*

*ἐστίν is used when followed by a word beginning with a vowel or when coming as the last word in a clause. The -ν is called *movable ν.* The word ἐστί(ν) is *enclitic,* which means that it "leans upon" the previous word and often loses its accent. The rules for accenting enclitics and the words that precede them will be presented as needed for writing Greek in the exercises.

2. Nouns: Genders, Stems, Endings, Cases, and Agreement

a. *Grammatical Gender*

Greek nouns are usually *masculine* or *feminine* or *neuter* (neither masculine nor feminine) in gender. Some words such as Δικαιόπολις, which is masculine, have *natural gender;* the gender of other words such as ἀγρός is not determined by the gender of the thing referred to. Such words have what is called *grammatical gender*, this one being masculine. In learning vocabulary, always learn the article with the noun; this will tell you its gender: ὁ for masculine; ἡ for feminine; and τό for neuter. In this chapter all the nouns listed in the Vocabulary are masculine and are therefore accompanied by the masculine definite article, ὁ.

b. Stems, Endings, and Cases

Greek nouns, pronouns, and adjectives have *stems*, which give the meaning of the word, and variable *endings*, which show the function of the word in the sentence. The endings of nouns, pronouns, and adjectives are called *cases*.

There are five cases in Greek (nominative, genitive, dative, accusative, and vocative); in this chapter we focus on the use of two of them—the *nominative* and the *accusative*.

Stem: κληρο-, *farm*

Nominative Ending: -ς. κληρο- + -ς > κλῆρος. This case is used for the *subject* of the verb and the *complement* after the verb "is," e.g.:

Subject	Verb	Complement
ὁ κλῆρός	ἐστι	μῑκρός.
The farm	*is*	*small.*

Accusative Ending: -ν. κληρο- + -ν > κλῆρον. This case is used for the *direct object* of the verb, e.g.:

Subject	Verb	Direct Object
ὁ ἄνθρωπος	γεωργεῖ	τὸν κλῆρον.
The man	*cultivates*	*the farm.*

Note that it is the endings of the words and not the order in which they are placed in the sentence that builds the meaning of the sentence. The first sentence above could be written μῑκρός ἐστιν ὁ κλῆρος (the definite article marks ὁ κλῆρος as the subject). The second sentence could be written τὸν κλῆρον γεωργεῖ ὁ ἄνθρωπος, with a change in emphasis but no change in basic meaning.

c. Agreement

Definite articles and adjectives agree with the nouns they go with in gender, number (singular or plural), and case, e.g.:

ὁ καλὸς ἀγρός: masculine singular nominative
τὸν μῑκρὸν οἶκον: masculine singular accusative

3. Labeling Functions of Words in Sentences

In exercises you will be asked to label the functions of words in sentences. Label the subject S, the complement C, and the direct object DO. Label linking verbs such as ἐστί(ν) LV. Verbs that take direct objects, such as γεωργεῖ in the sentence above, are *transitive* and are to be labeled TV (Transitive Verb); verbs that do not take direct objects, such as οἰκεῖ in the sentence below, are *intransitive* and are to be labeled IV (Intransitive Verb):

S   IV

ὁ Δικαιόπολις οἰκεῖ ἐν τοῖς ἀγροῖς.

Note that the complement can be either an adjective as in the sentence ὁ κλῆρός ἐστι μῑκρός above or a noun as in the following sentence:

S   C   LV

ὁ Δικαιόπολις αὐτουργός ἐστιν.

4. Use of the Definite Article

The definite article is sometimes used in Greek where it is not used in English, e.g., ὁ Δικαιόπολις = *Dicaeopolis*, and sometimes it can be translated with a possessive adjective in English, e.g.:

ὁ ἄνθρωπος γεωργεῖ **τὸν** κλῆρον.

*The man cultivates **his** farm.*

Exercise 1α

Copy the following sentences and label the function of each noun and verb by writing S, C, DO, LV, TV, or IV above the appropriate words (do not label words in prepositional phrases). Then translate the sentences into English:

1. ὁ πόνος ἐστὶ μακρός.
2. καλός ἐστιν ὁ οἶκος.
3. ὁ Δικαιόπολις τὸν οἶκον φιλεῖ.
4. πολὺν σῖτον παρέχει ὁ κλῆρος.
5. ὁ ἄνθρωπος οὐ πονεῖ ἐν τοῖς ἀγροῖς.

The Athenian Farmer

Dicaeopolis lives in a village in Attica called Cholleidae, about ten miles or sixteen kilometers north of Athens. Although Athens and its port, the Piraeus, formed a very large city by ancient standards, the majority of the Athenian people lived and worked in the country. The historian Thucydides (2.14) says that when Attica had to be evacuated before the Peloponnesian invasion of 431 B.C. "the evacuation was difficult for them since the majority had always been accustomed to living in the country."

Most of these people were farmers like Dicaeopolis. Their farms were small; ten to twenty acres would be the average size. What they grew on their farms would depend partly on the district in which they lived. On the plain near Athens no doubt the staple products would have been vegetables and grain, but most of Attica is hilly; this poorer land would be more suitable for grape vines, olive trees, sheep, and goats (cows were not kept for milk). All farmers aimed at self-sufficiency, but few would have attained it (two-thirds of the grain consumed by the Athenians was imported). If they had a surplus, e.g., of olive oil or wine, they would take it to the market in Athens for sale and buy what they could not produce themselves.

For purposes of administration, the Athenian citizens were divided into four classes, based on property. The top class, the *pentacosiomedimnoi* or "millionaires," a very small class, were those whose estates produced five hundred *medimnoi* of grain a year (a *medimnos* = about one and a half bushels or fifty-two to fifty-three liters). The second class, also small, were the *hippeis*, "knights," whose estates could support a horse (ἵππος); these provided the cavalry for the army (see illustration, page 162). The third and largest class were the farmers like Dicaeopolis, called the *zeugitai,* who kept a team of oxen (ζεῦγος). These provided the heavy infantry of the army. The fourth class were the *thetes*, "hired laborers," who owned no land or not enough to support a family.

Our sources represent the farmers as the backbone of the Athenian democracy—sturdy, industrious, thrifty, and simple, but shrewd. In the comedies of Aristophanes they are often contrasted with self-seeking politicians, decadent knights, and grasping traders. The name of our main character, Dicaeopolis, contains the concepts δίκαιο-, *just*, and πόλις, *city*, and means something like *honest citizen*. He is taken from a comedy of Aristophanes called the *Acharnians;* the play was produced in 425 B.C., and at the end of this course you will read extracts from it.

Scenes of plowing and sowing on a Greek vase

Ο ΔΙΚΑΙΟΠΟΛΙΣ (β)

ὁ Δικαιόπολις μέγαν λίθον αἴρει καὶ ἐκ τοῦ ἀγροῦ φέρει.

VOCABULARY

Verbs
αἴρει, *he/she lifts*
βαδίζει, *he/she walks; he/she goes*
καθίζει, *he/she sits*
φέρει, *he/she carries*
Nouns
ὁ ἥλιος, *sun*

ὁ χρόνος, *time*
Pronoun
αὐτόν, *him*
Adjectives
ἰσχῡρός, *strong*
χαλεπός, *difficult*
Preposition
πρός + acc., *to, toward*

ὁ Δικαιόπολις ἐν τῷ ἀγρῷ πονεῖ· τὸν γὰρ ἀγρὸν σκάπτει. μακρός ἐστιν ὁ πόνος καὶ χαλεπός· τοὺς γὰρ λίθους ἐκ τοῦ ἀγροῦ φέρει. μέγαν λίθον αἴρει καὶ φέρει πρὸς τὸ ἕρμα. ἰσχῡρός ἐστιν ὁ ἄνθρωπος ἀλλὰ πολὺν χρόνον πονεῖ καὶ μάλα κάμνει. φλέγει γὰρ ὁ ἥλιος καὶ κατατρίβει αὐτόν. καθίζει οὖν ὑπὸ τῷ δένδρῳ καὶ ἡσυχάζει οὐ πολὺν χρόνον. δι' ὀλίγου γὰρ ἐπαίρει ἑαυτὸν καὶ πονεῖ. τέλος δὲ καταδῡνει ὁ ἥλιος. οὐκέτι οὖν πονεῖ ὁ Δικαιόπολις ἀλλὰ πρὸς τὸν οἶκον βαδίζει.   5

[**ἐν τῷ ἀγρῷ**, *in the field*   **σκάπτει**, *he is digging*   **τοὺς...λίθους**, *the stones*   **ἐκ τοῦ ἀγροῦ**, *out of the field*   **μέγαν**, *big*   **τὸ ἕρμα**, *the stone heap*   **πολὺν χρόνον**, *for a long time*   **μάλα κάμνει**, *he is very tired*   **φλέγει**, *is blazing*   **κατατρίβει**, *wears out*   **ὑπὸ τῷ δένδρῳ**, *under the tree*   **ἡσυχάζει**, *he rests*   **δι' ὀλίγου**, *soon*   **ἐπαίρει ἑαυτόν**, *he lifts himself, gets up*   **τέλος**, adv., *finally*   **καταδῡνει**, *sets*   **οὐκέτι**, *no longer*]

WORD BUILDING

What is the relationship between the words in the following sets? You have not yet met two of these words (φίλος and γεωργός). Try to deduce their meanings (they both refer to people) from studying the relationship between the words in each set:

1. οἰκεῖ   ὁ οἶκος
2. πονεῖ   ὁ πόνος
3. γεωργεῖ   ὁ γεωργός
4. φιλεῖ   ὁ φίλος

GRAMMAR

5. Accents

Attic Greek has three kinds of accent marks: acute ´, grave `, and circumflex ˆ. The acute accent will be found only on one of the last three syllables of a word, e.g.: ἄνθρωπος, λέγει, μακρός. An acute accent on the final syllable of a word will be changed to a grave accent if it is followed immediately by another word with no punctuation (comma, semicolon, or period) in between, thus ἀλλά + καλός > ἀλλὰ καλός.

An important exception to this rule occurs when *enclitics*, words such as ἐστί(ν), which usually lose their accent and instead "lean upon" the previous word for their accent, follow words with an acute accent on their final syllable, e.g.:

χαλεπός + ἐστί(ν) becomes χαλεπός ἐστι(ν).
The acute on the final syllable of χαλεπός does not change to a grave when the word is followed by an enclitic, and the enclitic loses its accent.

Note also what happens when words accented like ἄνθρωπος, πόνος, and οἶκος are followed by enclitics:

ἄνθρωπος + ἐστί(ν) becomes ἄνθρωπός ἐστι(ν).
An acute accent is added to ἄνθρωπος, and the enclitic loses its accent.

πόνος + ἐστί(ν) remains πόνος ἐστί(ν).
The enclitic keeps its accent.

οἶκος + ἐστί(ν) becomes οἶκός ἐστι(ν).
An acute accent is added to οἶκος, and the enclitic loses its accent.

Exercise 1β

Copy the following Greek sentences and label the function of each noun and verb by writing S, C, DO, LV, TV, or IV above the appropriate words (do not label words in prepositional phrases). Then translate the pairs of sentences. When translating from English to Greek, keep the same word order as in the model Greek sentence. Pay particular attention to accents, following the rules given above. Do not forget to add the movable ν where necessary (see Grammar 1, page 4).

1. ὁ Δικαιόπολις οὐκ οἰκεῖ ἐν ταῖς Ἀθήναις.
    The farmer walks to the field.

2. μακρός ἐστιν ὁ ἀγρός.
    The house is small.

3. ὁ αὐτουργός ἐστιν ἰσχῡρός.
    Dicaeopolis is a farmer.

4. ὁ κλῆρος πολὺν σῖτον παρέχει.
    The man carries the big stone.

5. ὁ ἄνθρωπος τὸν σῖτον παρέχει.
    Dicaeopolis lifts the small stone.

Ο ΚΛΗΡΟΣ

Read the following passage and answer the comprehension questions:

μακρός ἐστιν ὁ πόνος καὶ χαλεπός. ὁ δὲ αὐτουργὸς οὐκ ὀκνεῖ ἀλλ' ἀεὶ γεωργεῖ τὸν κλῆρον. καλὸς γάρ ἐστιν ὁ κλῆρος καὶ πολὺν σῖτον παρέχει. χαίρει οὖν ὁ ἄνθρωπος· ἰσχῡρὸς γάρ ἐστι καὶ οὐ πολλάκις κάμνει.

[ὀκνεῖ, *shirks*]

1. What is the farmer not doing? What does he always do?
2. What does the farm provide?
3. Why does the man rejoice?

Exercise 1γ

Translate into Greek:

1. Dicaeopolis does not always rejoice.
2. He always works in the field.
3. So he is often tired; for the work is long.
4. But he does not shirk; for he loves his home.

Classical Greek

Heraclitus

Heraclitus of Ephesus (fl. 500 B.C.) was a philosopher who maintained that, despite appearances, everything was in a continual state of change. Plato (*Cratylus* 402a) quotes him as saying "You cannot step into the same river twice."

In the same passage of the *Cratylus*, Plato reports that Heraclitus said:

πάντα χωρεῖ καὶ οὐδὲν μένει.

[πάντα, *everything*   χωρεῖ, *is on the move*   οὐδὲν, *nothing*   μένει, *stays (unchanged)*]

New Testament Greek

Title of the Gospel of Luke

The New Testament readings in Book I of *Athenaze* are taken from the Holy Gospel according to Luke. Here is the title of this gospel in Greek:

ΤΟ ΑΓΙΟΝ ΕΥΑΓΓΕΛΙΟΝ ΤΟ ΚΑΤΑ ΛΟΥΚΑΝ

or

τὸ ἅγιον εὐαγγέλιον τὸ κατὰ Λουκᾶν

[τὸ, *the*   ἅγιον, *holy*   εὐαγγέλιον, *good news, gospel* (= Old English *gōd*, "good" + *spel*, "news")   κατὰ, *according to*]

A farmer in contemporary Greece, carrying a kid

Ο ΞΑΝΘΙΑΣ (α)

ὁ μὲν Δικαιόπολις ἐλαύνει τὸν βοῦν, ὁ δὲ δοῦλος φέρει τὸ ἄροτρον.

VOCABULARY

Verbs
ἐκβαίνει, *he/she steps out;*
he/she comes out
ἐλαύνει, *he/she drives*
ἐλθέ, *come!*
καθεύδει, *he/she sleeps*
καλεῖ, *he/she calls*
πάρεστι(ν), *he/she/it is pre-*
sent; he/she/it is here;
he/she/it is there
σπεύδει, *he/she hurries*

Nouns
τὸ ἄροτρον, *plow*
ὁ δοῦλος, *slave*

Pronoun
ἐγώ, *I*

Adjective
ἀργός, *lazy*

Adverbs
μή, *not;* + imperative, *don't...!*
οὕτως, before consonants,
οὕτω, *so, thus*
τί; *why?*

Particles
μέν...δέ..., postpositive, *on*
the one hand...and on the
other hand...; on the one
hand...but on the other hand

Proper Name
ὁ Ξανθίᾱς, *Xanthias*

ὁ Δικαιόπολις ἐκβαίνει ἐκ τοῦ οἴκου καὶ καλεῖ τὸν Ξανθίᾱν. ὁ
Ξανθίᾱς δοῦλός ἐστιν, ἰσχῡρὸς μὲν ἄνθρωπος, ἀργὸς δέ· οὐ γὰρ
πονεῖ, εἰ μὴ πάρεστιν ὁ Δικαιόπολις. νῦν δὲ καθεύδει ἐν τῷ οἴκῳ. ὁ
οὖν Δικαιόπολις καλεῖ αὐτὸν καὶ λέγει· "ἐλθὲ δεῦρο, ὦ Ξανθίᾱ. τί
καθεύδεις; μὴ οὕτως ἀργὸς ἴσθι ἀλλὰ σπεῦδε." ὁ οὖν Ξανθίᾱς 5

βραδέως ἐκβαίνει ἐκ τοῦ οἴκου καὶ λέγει· "τί εἶ οὕτω χαλεπός, ὦ
δέσποτα; οὐ γὰρ ἀργός εἰμι ἀλλὰ ἤδη σπεύδω." ὁ δὲ Δικαιόπολις
λέγει· "ἐλθὲ δεῦρο καὶ συλλάμβανε· αἶρε γὰρ τὸ ἄροτρον καὶ φέρε
αὐτὸ πρὸς τὸν ἀγρόν. ἐγὼ γὰρ ἐλαύνω τοὺς βοῦς. ἀλλὰ σπεῦδε·
μῑκρὸς μὲν γάρ ἐστιν ὁ ἀγρός, μακρὸς δὲ ὁ πόνος."   10

[ἐκ τοῦ οἴκου, *out of the house*   εἰ μὴ, *unless*   νῦν, *now*   ἐν τῷ οἴκῳ, *in the house*
δεῦρο, *here = hither*   μὴ . . . ἴσθι, *don't be!*   βραδέως, *slowly*   δέσποτα, *master*
ἤδη, *already*   συλλάμβανε, *help!*   αὐτὸ, *it*   τοὺς βοῦς, *the oxen*]

WORD STUDY

1.   What do *despotic* and *chronology* mean? What Greek words do you find
     embedded in these English words?
2.   What does a *dendrologist* study?
3.   Explain what a *heliocentric* theory of the universe is.
4.   What is a *chronometer*? What does τὸ μέτρον mean?

GRAMMAR

1. Verb Forms: Indicative Mood; 1st, 2nd, and 3rd Persons Singular

The *moods* indicate whether an action is viewed as being real or
ideal. The *indicative* mood is used to express statements and questions
about reality or fact:

ἐλαύνω τοὺς βοῦς. *I am driving the oxen.*
τί καθεύδεις; *Why are you sleeping?*

The different endings of the verb show not only who or what is per-
forming the action (I; you; he/she/it; we; you; they) but also how the action
is being viewed (mood). In the following examples we give only the singular possibilities (I; you; he/she/it) in the indicative mood:

Stem: λῡ-, *loosen, loose*

1st singular	λῡ́-ω	*I loosen, am loosening, do loosen*
2nd singular	λῡ́-εις	*you loosen, are loosening, do loosen*
3rd singular	λῡ́-ει	*he/she loosens, is loosening, does loosen*

Stem: φιλε-, *love*

1st singular	φιλέ-ω > φιλῶ	*I love, am loving, do love*
2nd singular	φιλέ-εις > φιλεῖς	*you love, are loving, do love*
3rd singular	φιλέ-ει > φιλεῖ	*he/she loves, is loving, does love*

Stem: ἐσ-, *be*

1st singular	εἰμί*	*I am*
2nd singular	εἶ	*you are*
3rd singular	ἐστί(ν)*	*he/she/it is*
*enclitic		

Since the endings differ for each person, subject pronouns need not be expressed in Greek, e.g.:

ἐλαύνω = *I drive.*
ἐλαύνεις = *you drive.*
ἐλαύνει = *he/she drives.*

But they are expressed if they are emphatic, e.g.:

ἐγὼ μὲν πονῶ, **σὺ** δὲ καθεύδεις. *I am working, but **you** are sleeping.*

Exercise 2α

Read aloud and translate into English:

1. τὸν δοῦλον καλῶ.
2. ὁ δοῦλος ἐν τῷ οἴκῳ πονεῖ.
3. τί οὐ σπεύδεις;
4. οὐκ εἰμὶ ἀργός.
5. ἰσχῡρὸς εἶ.
6. τὸ ἄροτρον φέρει.
7. πρὸς τὸν ἀγρὸν σπεύδω.
8. τί καλεῖς τὸν δοῦλον;
9. ὁ δοῦλος οὐκ ἔστιν ἀργός.
10. ὁ δοῦλος ἐκβαίνει ἐκ τοῦ οἴκου.

2. Proclitics

The negative adverb οὐ, οὐκ, οὐχ is called a *proclitic*. Proclitics normally do not have accents but "lean forward" onto the following word (cf. enclitics, page 4), e.g., τί οὐ σπεύδεις; (Exercise 2α, no. 3, above). When the proclitic οὐ is followed by the enclitic εἰμί (1st person singular), the enclitic retains an accent on its second syllable, e.g., οὐκ εἰμὶ ἀργός (Exercise 2α, no. 4, above). When οὐκ is followed by the enclitic ἐστί(ν) (3rd person singular), the enclitic receives an acute accent on its first syllable, e.g., ὁ δοῦλος οὐκ ἔστιν ἀργός (Exercise 2α, no. 9, above).

Exercise 2β

Translate into Greek. Do not begin your Greek sentence with an enclitic. When necessary, apply the rules for proclitics and enclitics given above and in Chapter 1, Grammar 5, page 9.

1. He/she is not hurrying.

2.   Why are you not working?
3.   I am carrying the plow.
4.   You are hurrying to the field.
5.   He is lazy.
6.   I am not strong.
7.   You are not a slave.
8.   The slave is not working.
9.   The slave is carrying the plow to the field.
10. He is not lazy.

3. The Imperative

The *imperative* mood is used to express commands:

σπεῦδ-ε *hurry!*   φίλε-ε > φίλει *love!*   ἴσθι *be!*

In prohibitions (negative commands), μή + the imperative is used:

μὴ αἶρε τὸ ἄροτρον. *Don't lift the plow!*
μὴ ἀργὸς ἴσθι. *Don't be lazy!*

Exercise 2γ

Copy the following sentences and write C, DO, or IMP for imperative above the appropriate words. Then translate the sentences into English:

1.   ἔκβαινε ἐκ τοῦ οἴκου, ὦ Ξανθία, καὶ ἐλθὲ δεῦρο.
2.   μὴ κάθευδε, ὦ δοῦλε, ἀλλὰ πόνει.
3.   μὴ οὕτω χαλεπὸς ἴσθι, ὦ δέσποτα.
4.   αἶρε τὸ ἄροτρον καὶ σπεῦδε πρὸς τὸν ἀγρόν.
5.   κάλει τὸν δοῦλον, ὦ δέσποτα.

Slavery

The adult male population of the city-state of Athens in 431 B.C. has been calculated as follows: citizens 50,000, resident foreigners 25,000, slaves 100,000. The resident foreigners (*metics*, μέτοικοι) were free men who were granted a distinct status; they could not own land in Attica or contract marriages with citizens, but they had the protection of the courts, they served in the army, they had a role in the festivals, and they played an important part in commerce and industry.

Slaves had no legal rights and were the property of the state or individuals. The fourth-century philosopher Aristotle describes them as "living tools." They were either born into slavery or came to the slave market as a result of war or piracy. They were nearly all barbarians, i.e., non-Greek (a document from 415 B.C. records the sale of fourteen slaves—five were from Thrace, two from Syria, three from Caria, two from Illyria, and one each from Scythia and Colchis). It was considered immoral to enslave Greeks, and this very rarely happened.

The whole economy of the ancient world, which made little use of machines, was based on slave labor. Slaves were employed by the state, e.g., in the silver mines; they worked in factories (the largest we know of was a shield factory, employing 120 slaves); and individual citizens owned one or more slaves in proportion to their wealth. Every farmer hoped to own a slave to help in the house and fields, but not all did. Aristotle remarks that for poor men "the ox takes the place of the slave."

It would be wrong to assume that slaves were always treated inhumanely. A fifth-century writer of reactionary views says:

> Now as to slaves and metics, in Athens, they live a most undisciplined life. One is not permitted to strike them, and a slave will not stand out of the way for you. Let me explain why. If the law permitted a free man to strike a slave or metic or a freedman, he would often find that he had mistaken an Athenian for a slave and struck him, for, as far as clothing and general appearance go, the common people look just the same as slaves and metics. (Pseudo-Xenophon, *The Constitution of the Athenians* 1.10)

Slaves and citizens often worked side by side and received the same wage, as we learn from inscriptions giving the accounts of public building works. Slaves might save enough money to buy their freedom from their masters, though this was not as common in Athens as in Rome.

In the country, the slaves of farmers usually lived and ate with their masters. Aristophanes' comedies depict them as lively and cheeky characters, by no means downtrodden. We have given Dicaeopolis one slave, named Xanthias, a typical slave name meaning "fair-haired."

Greek Wisdom

See page 70

μέτρον ἄριστον.   Κλεόβουλος (of Lindos)

A farmer on his way to market; he is followed by a slave carrying
two baskets of produce and accompanied by a pig and a piglet.

Slaves working in a clay pit

Women picking apples–slave and free

Ο ΞΑΝΘΙΑΣ (β)

ὁ Δικαιόπολις λέγει· "σπεῦδε, ὦ Ξανθίᾱ, καὶ φέρε μοι τὸ ἄροτρον."

VOCABULARY

Verbs

ἄγω, *I lead; I take*
  εἰσάγω, *I lead in; I take in*
βαίνω, *I step; I walk; I go*
βλέπω, usually intransitive,
  I look; I see
λαμβάνω, *I take*
  συλλαμβάνω [= συν-, *with*
  + λαμβάνω], *I help*

Nouns

ὁ βοῦς, *ox*
τὸ δένδρον, *tree*
ὁ δεσπότης, *master*
Preposition
εἰς + acc., *into; to; at*
Adverbs
βραδέως, *slowly*
ἔπειτα, *then, thereafter*
ἤδη, *already; now*

ὁ μὲν οὖν Δικαιόπολις ἐλαύνει τοὺς βοῦς, ὁ δὲ Ξανθίᾱς ὄπισθεν
βαδίζει καὶ φέρει τὸ ἄροτρον. δι' ὀλίγου δὲ ὁ Δικαιόπολις εἰσάγει
τοὺς βοῦς εἰς τὸν ἀγρὸν καὶ βλέπει πρὸς τὸν δοῦλον· ὁ δὲ Ξανθίᾱς οὐ
πάρεστιν· βραδέως γὰρ βαίνει. ὁ οὖν Δικαιόπολις καλεῖ αὐτὸν καὶ
λέγει· "σπεῦδε, ὦ Ξανθίᾱ, καὶ φέρε μοι τὸ ἄροτρον." ὁ δὲ Ξανθίᾱς   5
λέγει· "ἀλλ' ἤδη σπεύδω, ὦ δέσποτα· τί οὕτω χαλεπὸς εἶ;" βραδέως δὲ
φέρει τὸ ἄροτρον πρὸς αὐτόν. ὁ οὖν Δικαιόπολις ἄγει τοὺς βοῦς ὑπὸ
τὸ ζυγὸν καὶ προσάπτει τὸ ἄροτρον. ἔπειτα δὲ πρὸς τὸν δοῦλον
βλέπει· ὁ δὲ Ξανθίᾱς οὐ πάρεστιν· καθεύδει γὰρ ὑπὸ τῷ δένδρῳ.

[**ὄπισθεν**, *behind*   **δι' ὀλίγου**, *soon*   **μοι**, *(to) me*   **ὑπὸ τὸ ζυγόν**, *under the yoke*
προσάπτει, *attaches*]

ὁ οὖν Δικαιόπολις καλεῖ αὐτὸν καὶ λέγει· "ἐλθὲ δεῦρο, ὦ   10
κατάρᾱτε. μὴ κάθευδε ἀλλὰ συλλάμβανε. φέρε γὰρ τὸ σπέρμα καὶ
ὄπισθεν βάδιζε." ὁ μὲν οὖν δοῦλος τὸ σπέρμα λαμβάνει καὶ
ἀκολουθεῖ, ὁ δὲ δεσπότης καλεῖ τὴν Δήμητρα καὶ λέγει· "ἵλεως ἴσθι, ὦ
Δήμητερ, καὶ πλήθῡνε τὸ σπέρμα." ἔπειτα δὲ τὸ κέντρον λαμβάνει
καὶ κεντεῖ τοὺς βοῦς καὶ λέγει· "σπεύδετε, ὦ βόες· ἕλκετε τὸ ἄροτρον   15
καὶ ἀροῦτε τὸν ἀγρόν."

[ὦ κατάρᾱτε, *you cursed creature*   τὸ σπέρμα, *the seed*   ἀκολουθεῖ, *follows*   τὴν
Δήμητρα, *Demeter* (goddess of grain)   ἵλεως, *gracious*   πλήθῡνε, *multiply*   τὸ
κέντρον, *the goad*   κεντεῖ, *goads*   ἕλκετε, *drag*   ἀροῦτε, *plow*]

WORD BUILDING

In the readings you have met the following prepositions: εἰς, *into;* ἐκ, *out of;* ἐν, *in;* and πρός, *to, toward.* These prepositions may be prefixed to verbs to form compound verbs, e.g.:

βαίνει, *he/she walks, steps*   ἐκβαίνει, *he/she steps **out***

Deduce the meaning of the following compound verbs:

1. προσφέρει
2. ἐκφέρει
3. προσελαύνει

4. προσβαίνει
5. ἐκκαλεῖ
6. εἰσελαύνει

You can easily deduce the meanings of many more compound verbs of this sort, which are very frequent in Greek. Right from the start of your study of Greek you should begin to recognize the meaning of many new words from your knowledge of ones with which you are already familiar. To encourage you to develop and use this skill, the meaning of compound verbs will not be given in the chapter vocabularies when the meaning is clear from the separate parts of the word. When compound verbs have *special* meanings, they will be given in the vocabulary lists.

GRAMMAR

4. Articles, Adjectives, and Nouns; Singular, All Cases

	Masculine			Neuter		
Nominative	ὁ	καλὸς	ἀγρός	τὸ	καλὸν	δένδρον
Genitive	τοῦ	καλοῦ	ἀγροῦ	τοῦ	καλοῦ	δένδρου
Dative	τῷ	καλῷ	ἀγρῷ	τῷ	καλῷ	δένδρῳ
Accusative	τὸν	καλὸν	ἀγρόν	τὸ	καλὸν	δένδρον
Vocative	ὦ*	καλὲ	ἀγρέ	ὦ	καλὸν	δένδρον

N.B. The endings for the neuter nominative, accusative, and vocative cases are the same.

*Not a definite article, but an interjection used with the vocative.

5. Uses of the Cases

The subject of the sentence and the complement of the verb "to be" are in the *nominative case*, e.g., ὁ ἀγρὸς καλός ἐστιν = **The field is beautiful.** ὁ Δικαιόπολις αὐτουργός ἐστιν. **Dicaeopolis is a farmer**.

The *genitive case* is at present used only after certain prepositions, including those that express motion from a place, e.g., ἐκβαίνει **ἐκ τοῦ οἴκου** = *He/She steps/comes **out of the house***.

The *dative case* is also at present used only after certain prepositions, including those that indicate the place where someone or something is or something happens, e.g., καθεύδει **ἐν τῷ οἴκῳ** = *He/She sleeps **in the house***.

The *accusative case* indicates the direct object of a transitive verb (e.g., καλεῖ τὸν δοῦλον) and is used after certain prepositions, including those that indicate motion toward someone or something, e.g., **πρὸς τὸν οἶκον** βαδίζει = *He/She walks **toward the house***.

The *vocative case* is used when addressing a person, e.g., ἐλθὲ δεῦρο, ὦ δοῦλε = *Come here, **slave**!* It is usually preceded by ὦ, which need not be translated.

6. Persistent Accent of Nouns and Adjectives

The accents of nouns and adjectives are *persistent*, i.e., they remain as they are in the nominative case unless forced to change because of one of several rules. One such rule is that nouns and adjectives such as those in the chart above, if they are accented in the nominative with an acute on the final syllable, change their accent to a circumflex on the final syllable in the genitive and dative cases. Note how this rule applies to the adjective καλός/καλόν and to the noun ἀγρός above. (Of course, the adjective καλός/καλόν as written above in the nominative, accusative, and vocative cases has changed its acute to a grave because of the nouns immediately following.) Note also that the definite article follows a similar rule and has a circumflex accent on the genitive and dative.

Exercise 2δ

Give the correct form of the article to complete the following phrases; be careful with the accents:

1. ___ δοῦλον
2. ἐν ___ ἀγρῷ
3. ___ ἄνθρωπος
4. ἐκ ___ οἴκου
5. ___ ἄροτρον
6. ὑπὸ ___ δένδρῳ
7. ἐν ___ οἴκῳ

Exercise 2ε

Complete the following sentences by giving correct endings to the verbs, nouns, and adjectives, and then translate the sentences into English:

1. ὁ δοῦλος σπεύδ__ πρὸς τὸν ἀγρ__ .
2. ὁ Δικαιόπολις τὸν ἀργ__ δοῦλον καλ__ .
3. ἐλθ__ δεῦρο καὶ συλλάμβαν__ .
4. ἐγὼ ἐλαύν__ τοὺς βοῦς ἐκ τοῦ ἀγρ__ .
5. μὴ χαλεπ__ ἴσθι, ὦ δοῦλ__ , ἀλλὰ πόν__ .

7. Recessive Accent of Verbs

More will be said about accents on verbs later in this course (e.g., Chapter 5, Grammar 2, pages 56–57), but for now observe that the forms ἐλαύνω, ἐλαύνεις, and ἐλαύνει have accents on the next to the last syllable, because the final syllable has a long vowel or diphthong. When the final syllable is short, as in the imperative, the accent recedes to the third syllable from the end, thus, ἔλαυνε. In the second paragraph of story β, find six verbs accented on the third syllable from the end.

Exercise 2ζ

Translate the following pairs of sentences:

1. ὁ δοῦλος οὐκ ἔστιν Ἀθηναῖος.
   Xanthias is not strong.
2. ὁ Δικαιόπολις ἐκβαίνει ἐκ τοῦ οἴκου καὶ καλεῖ τὸν δοῦλον.
   The slave hurries to the field and carries the plow.

3.   ὁ δοῦλος οὐ συλλαμβάνει ἀλλὰ καθεύδει ὑπὸ τῷ δένδρῳ.
    The man is not working but walking to the house.

4.   εἴσελθε εἰς τὸν οἶκον, ὦ Ξανθίᾱ, καὶ φέρε τὸν σῖτον.
    Come, slave, and lead in the oxen.

5.   μὴ πόνει, ὦ Ξανθίᾱ, ἀλλὰ ἐλθὲ δεῦρο.
    Don't sleep, man, but work in the field.

Ο ΔΟΥΛΟΣ

Read the following passage and answer the comprehension questions:

ὁ αὐτουργὸς σπεύδει εἰς τὸν ἀγρὸν καὶ καλεῖ τὸν δοῦλον. ὁ δὲ δοῦλος οὐ
πάρεστιν· καθεύδει γὰρ ὑπὸ τῷ δένδρῳ. ὁ οὖν δεσπότης βαδίζει πρὸς αὐτὸν καὶ
λέγει· "ἐλθὲ δεῦρο, ὦ δοῦλε ἀργέ, καὶ πόνει." ὁ οὖν δοῦλος βαδίζει πρὸς αὐτὸν καὶ
λέγει· "μὴ χαλεπὸς ἴσθι, ὦ δέσποτα· ἤδη γὰρ πάρειμι ἐγὼ καὶ φέρω σοι τὸ ἄροτρον."
ὁ οὖν δεσπότης λέγει· "σπεῦδε, ὦ Ξανθίᾱ· μῑκρὸς μὲν γάρ ἐστιν ὁ ἀγρός, μακρὸς δὲ ὁ   5
πόνος."

[σοι, *to you*]

1. What is the farmer doing?
2. What is the slave doing?
3. When told to come and help, what does the slave do?
4. Why is the slave urged to hurry?

Exercise 2η

*Translate into Greek. When you need to use μέν and another postpositive
word together, always put μέν before the other postpositive (see line 5 of the
story above):*

1. Dicaeopolis no longer (οὐκέτι) works but loosens the oxen.
2. And (*use* δέ, *postpositive*) then he calls the slave and says: "Don't
    work any longer (μηκέτι) but come here and take the plow.
3. "For I (*use personal pronoun*) on the one hand am driving the oxen to
    the house, you (σύ) on the other hand carry (*imperative*) the plow."
4. So on the one hand Dicaeopolis drives the oxen out of the field, and on
    the other hand the slave takes the plow and carries (it) toward the
    house.

Classical Greek

Callimachus

Callimachus of Alexandria (fl. 250 B.C.) was a poet who rejected traditional genres such as epic and advocated the writing of short, light poems. The following saying based on fragment 465 (Pfeiffer) makes his preference clear:

μέγα βιβλίον μέγα κακόν.

[βιβλίον, *book;* supply ἐστί κακόν, *evil, trouble*]

New Testament Greek

Luke 3.22

The context is: "And it happened that when all the people had been baptized and Jesus had been baptized and was praying, the heaven opened, the Holy Ghost came down upon him in bodily form like a dove, and a voice came from heaven." The voice said:

"σὺ εἶ ὁ υἱός μου ὁ ἀγαπητός. . . ."

[ὁ υἱός μου, *my son* ὁ ἀγαπητός, *the beloved*]

See Acknowledgments, page 356.

Youth with cow in a sacrificial procession

3
Ο ΑΡΟΤΟΣ (α)

ὁ μὲν Δικαιόπολις ἐλαύνει τοὺς βοῦς, οἱ δὲ βόες τὸ ἄροτρον ἕλκουσιν.

VOCABULARY

Verbs
  μένω, *I stay* (in one place);
    I wait; I wait for
  πίπτω, *I fall*
  προσχωρέω + dat., *I go toward,*
    approach
  φησί(ν), postpositive enclitic,
    he / she says
Noun
  ὁ λίθος, *stone*
Pronouns
  αὐτό, *it*
  αὐτόν, *him; it*
Adjectives
  αἴτιος, *responsible (for); to*
    blame

  δυνατός, *possible*
  μέγας, *big, large; great*
Preposition
  ἐκ, ἐξ before words beginning
    with vowels + gen., *out of*
Adverbs
  αὖθις, *again*
  δεῦρο, *here,* i.e., *hither*
  ἔτι, *still*
  οὐκέτι, *no longer*
Particle and Conjunction
  τε . . . καί or **τε καί,** the **τε** is
    postpositive and enclitic, *both*
    . . . and
Expression
  ὦ Ζεῦ, *O Zeus*

ὁ μὲν Δικαιόπολις ἐλαύνει τοὺς βοῦς, οἱ δὲ βόες ἕλκουσι τὸ
ἄροτρον, ὁ δὲ Ξανθίᾱς σπείρει τὸ σπέρμα. ἀλλὰ ἰδού, μένουσιν οἱ
βόες καὶ οὐκέτι ἕλκουσι τὸ ἄροτρον. ὁ μὲν οὖν Δικαιόπολις τοὺς
βοῦς καλεῖ καί, "σπεύδετε, ὦ βόες," φησίν· "μὴ μένετε." οἱ δὲ βόες ἔτι
μένουσιν. ὁ οὖν Δικαιόπολις, "τί μένετε, ὦ βόες;" φησίν, καὶ βλέπει 5

πρὸς τὸ ἄροτρον, καὶ ἰδού, λίθος ἐμποδίζει αὐτό. ὁ οὖν Δικαιόπολις
λαμβάνει τὸν λίθον ἀλλ' οὐκ αἴρει αὐτόν· μέγας γάρ ἐστιν. καλεῖ
οὖν τὸν δοῦλον καί, "ἐλθὲ δεῦρο, ὦ Ξανθίᾱ," φησίν, "καὶ
συλλάμβανε· λίθος γὰρ μέγας τὸ ἄροτρον ἐμποδίζει, οἱ δὲ βόες
μένουσιν."   10

[ἕλκουσι, (they) are dragging   σπείρει, is sowing   τὸ σπέρμα, the seed   ἰδού,
look!   ἐμποδίζει, is obstructing]

ὁ οὖν Ξανθίᾱς βραδέως προσχωρεῖ ἀλλ' οὐ συλλαμβάνει· βλέπει
γὰρ πρὸς τὸν λίθον καί, "μέγας ἐστὶν ὁ λίθος, ὦ δέσποτα," φησίν·
"ἰδού, οὐ δυνατόν ἐστιν αἴρειν αὐτόν." ὁ δὲ Δικαιόπολις, "μὴ ἀργὸς
ἴσθι," φησίν, "ἀλλὰ συλλάμβανε. δυνατὸν γάρ ἐστιν αἴρειν τὸν
λίθον." ἅμα οὖν ὅ τε δεσπότης καὶ ὁ δοῦλος αἴρουσι τὸν λίθον καὶ   15
φέρουσιν αὐτὸν ἐκ τοῦ ἀγροῦ.

[ἅμα, together]

ἐν ᾧ δὲ φέρουσιν αὐτόν, πταίει ὁ Ξανθίᾱς καὶ καταβάλλει τὸν
λίθον· ὁ δὲ λίθος πίπτει πρὸς τὸν τοῦ Δικαιοπόλιδος πόδα. ὁ οὖν
Δικαιόπολις στενάζει καί, "ὦ Ζεῦ," φησίν, "φεῦ τοῦ ποδός. λάμβανε
τὸν λίθον, ὦ ἀνόητε, καὶ αἶρε αὐτὸν καὶ μὴ οὕτω σκαιὸς ἴσθι." ὁ δὲ   20
Ξανθίᾱς, "τί οὕτω χαλεπὸς εἶ, ὦ δέσποτα;" φησίν· "οὐ γὰρ αἴτιός εἰμι
ἐγώ· μέγας γάρ ἐστιν ὁ λίθος, καὶ οὐ δυνατόν ἐστιν αὐτὸν φέρειν." ὁ
δὲ Δικαιόπολις, "μὴ φλυάρει, ὦ μαστῑγίᾱ, ἀλλ' αἶρε τὸν λίθον καὶ
ἔκφερε ἐκ τοῦ ἀγροῦ." αὖθις οὖν αἴρουσι τὸν λίθον καὶ μόλις
ἐκφέρουσιν αὐτὸν ἐκ τοῦ ἀγροῦ. ἔπειτα δὲ ὁ μὲν Δικαιόπολις ἐλαύνει   25
τοὺς βοῦς, οἱ δὲ βόες οὐκέτι μένουσιν ἀλλὰ ἕλκουσι τὸ ἄροτρον.

[ἐν ᾧ, while   πταίει, stumbles   καταβάλλει, drops   πρὸς τὸν τοῦ Δικαιοπόλιδος πόδα, upon Dicaeopolis's foot   στενάζει, groans   φεῦ τοῦ ποδός, oh, my poor
foot!   ὦ ἀνόητε, you fool   σκαιὸς, clumsy   φλυάρει, talk nonsense!   ὦ μαστῑγίᾱ,
you rogue (deserving of a whipping)   μόλις, with difficulty]

WORD STUDY

1. What does *lithograph* mean? What does γράφω mean?
2. What is a *monolith*? What does μόνος mean?
3. What does *megalithic* mean?
4. What is a *megaphone*? What does ἡ φωνή mean?

GRAMMAR

1. Verb Forms: 3rd Person Plural, Imperatives, and Infinitives

a. In Chapter 2 you learned the 1st, 2nd, and 3rd person singular indicative forms of λύω, φιλέω, and εἰμί. Here are the 3rd person plural indicative forms:

> **Stem:** λῡ-, *loosen, loose*
> **3rd plural**   λύ-ουσι(ν)   *they loosen, are loosening, do loosen*

> **Stem:** φιλε-, *love*
> **3rd plural**   φιλέ-ουσι(ν) > φιλοῦσι(ν)   *they love, are loving, do love*

> **Stem:** ἐσ-, *be*
> **3rd plural**   εἰσί(ν)*   *they are*
> *enclitic

Locate twelve 3rd person plural verb forms in the reading passage at the beginning of this chapter.

b. In Chapter 2 you learned some forms of the *imperative* mood. These were the singular forms, used to address a command to one person:

> σπεῦδε   *hurry!*
> φίλει   *love!*
> ἴσθι   *be!*
> ἐλθέ   *come! go!*
> Note the accent of ἐλθέ, which is irregular.

In the reading at the beginning of this chapter you have met plural forms of the imperative (see also Chapter 2β, lines 15–16), used to address a command to more than one person (or animal!). The plurals of the imperatives given above are:

> σπεύδετε
> φιλέ-ετε > φιλεῖτε
> ἔστε
> ἔλθετε

Note the accent of ἔλθετε; compare ἐλθέ above.

Locate two plural imperatives in the reading passage at the beginning of this chapter. To whom (or what) are the commands addressed?

c. The *infinitive* is the form of the verb that we create in English by using the word *to*. Greek forms the infinitive by use of an ending:

Stem: λῡ-, *loosen, loose*
Infinitive   λῡ́-ειν   *to loosen, to be loosening*

Stem: φιλε-, *love*
Infinitive   φιλέ-ειν> φιλεῖν   *to love, to be loving*

Stem: ἐσ-, *be*
Infinitive   ἐσ- + -ναι > εἶναι   *to be*

Locate three infinitives in the reading passage at the beginning of this chapter.

Exercise 3α

Copy the first five of the following Greek sentences and label the function of each noun and verb by writing S, C, DO, LV, TV, IV, IMP, or INF for infinitive above the appropriate words (do not label adverbs, conjunctions, particles, words in prepositional phrases or the exclamatory ἰδού). Then translate all of the sentences.

1. οἱ βόες οὐκέτι ἕλκουσι τὸ ἄροτρον.
2. ὅ τε Δικαιόπολις καὶ ὁ δοῦλος προσχωροῦσι καὶ βλέπουσι πρὸς τὸ ἄροτρον.
3. ὁ Δικαιόπολις, "ἰδού," φησίν· "λίθος μέγας τὸ ἄροτρον ἐμποδίζει.
4. "αἶρε τὸν λίθον καὶ ἔκφερε ἐκ τοῦ ἀγροῦ."
5. ὁ δὲ δοῦλος, "ἰδού," φησίν· "μέγας ἐστὶν ὁ λίθος· οὐ δυνατόν ἐστιν αἴρειν αὐτόν."
6. ὅ τε Δικαιόπολις καὶ ὁ δοῦλος τὸν λίθον αἴρουσι καὶ ἐκφέρουσιν ἐκ τοῦ ἀγροῦ.
7. μὴ μένετε, ὦ βόες, ἀλλὰ σπεύδετε.
8. οἱ βόες οὐκέτι μένουσιν ἀλλὰ τὸ ἄροτρον αὖθις ἕλκουσιν.

Exercise 3β

Translate into Greek:

1. The oxen are sleeping in the field.
2. Come here and drive out (*use* ἐξελαύνω)* the oxen, slaves (ὦ δοῦλοι).**
   * I.e., use the correct form of the word given in parentheses.
   ** I.e., use the words given in parentheses without changing them.
3. They take the goad (τὸ κέντρον) and slowly approach the oxen (τοῖς βουσί(ν)).

4. Hurry, oxen; don't sleep in the field.
5. It is not possible to drive out (*use* ἐξελαύνω) the oxen; for they are
   strong (ἰσχῦροί; begin your clause with this word).

The Deme and the Polis

As we have seen, Dicaeopolis lives in a village about ten miles or sixteen
kilometers north of Athens called Cholleidae, situated between Mount Parnes
and Mount Pentelicon. Such districts were called demes, and at the time of
our story there were about 170 of them in Attica, differing greatly in size and
population. Each deme had its own assembly, to which all adult male citizens
belonged. This assembly elected a *demarch* (δήμαρχος, *mayor* or *sheriff*) and
passed decrees on local affairs, both secular and religious. It kept a record of
all births; a man's rights as a citizen depended on his being registered in a
deme when he reached adulthood. In all official contexts a man gave his
name together with that of his father and deme, e.g., Περικλῆς Ξανθίππου Χο-
λαργεύς (Pericles, son of Xanthippus, of the deme of Cholargus).

The houses that composed these villages were mostly small and unpreten-
tious, as far as our evidence goes. A typical house would consist of a courtyard surrounded by single-story rooms, and in one corner a storage-tower
with an upper floor; this upper floor would form the women's quarters, to
which women would retire if strangers called. There would be no source of
water within the house itself; it had to be fetched every day from a public
fountain. Light would be provided by clay lamps fired by olive oil, which was
also used for cooking and washing. We may assume that the majority of the
farmers lived in the village and went out to work on their farms every day, as
farmers still do in parts of Greece and Italy today, where houses are as a general rule not in the fields but clustered together in hilltop villages.

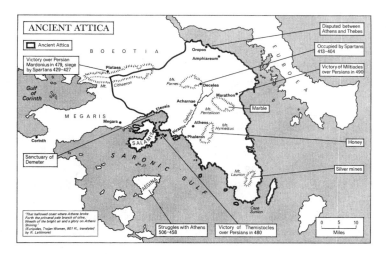

Attica and surroundings

The men worked most of the day in the fields, and no doubt in the evenings they spent their time in the wineshop in the agora or marketplace, discussing farming and politics with their friends. Life was enlivened by a succession of religious festivals. An inscription from the deme of Ercheia records a list of over fifty public sacrifices performed annually, and a public sacrifice usually entailed a public feast. In the winter, at the festival of the Rural Dionysia, touring companies from Athens even brought plays out to the demes. There were also private functions performed with traditional rituals, especially celebrations of birth, marriage, and death.

The farmer's horizon was by no means bounded by the deme. When he produced a surplus of any product such as wine or olives, he would go to Athens to sell it and to buy necessities he could not produce himself. There were religious festivals at regular intervals throughout the year at Athens (see Chapter 10), which he could attend with his wife and family; these included musical, dramatic, and athletic competitions.

There were important political functions that, as an Athenian citizen, the farmer was bound to perform. Forty times a year there were regular meetings of the Athenian Assembly, attended by all adult male citizens. The farmer would in fact have been prevented by his work from attending all of these, but he would certainly have gone to some of them. Every year the assembly of the deme chose representatives for the Council of 500, which was the executive committee of the Assembly. Councilors had to be over thirty years old, and no man could serve more than twice in his lifetime. It has been calculated that sooner or later nearly every farmer would have to take his turn in this office. This might involve residence in the city since the Council met every day.

Lastly, the farmers provided the heavy armed infantry, the *hoplites* (ὁπλῖται), of the army. On reaching manhood they would have to do military training, since fighting in a hoplite line involved much practice and good discipline. In the fourth century every citizen did two years military service from the age of eighteen and thereafter was liable to be called up in an emergency.

At the end of the first year of the great war between Athens and Sparta (about a year after our story begins), the Athenian leader Pericles made a funeral oration over those who had been killed in the war. Most of his speech was devoted to praise of the ideals of Athenian democracy for which they had died. In the course of this he says: "The same people [i.e., the whole citizen body] are concerned not only with their domestic affairs but also with politics [i.e., the affairs of the city]; and although employed in different occupations, they are adequately informed on political matters. We alone consider a man who plays no part in these not as one who minds his own business but as useless" (Thucydides 2.40). The farmer's life under the Athenian democracy, despite primitive physical conditions, was far from drab.

Ο ΑΡΟΤΟΣ (β)

"οὐ δυνατόν ἐστιν, ὦ δέσποτα, τοσούτους λίθους ἐκφέρειν."

VOCABULARY

Verbs
  λείπω, *I leave*
  λύω, *I loosen, loose*
Nouns
  τὸ δεῖπνον, *dinner*
  ὁ or **ἡ παῖς** (ὦ παῖ), *boy; girl;*
    son; daughter; child
  ὁ πατήρ (τὸν πατέρα, ὦ πάτερ),
    father
Pronoun
  σύ, sing., *you*
Adjectives
  ἀνδρεῖος, *brave*

πολλοί, *many*
τοσοῦτος, *so great;* pl., *so great;*
  so many
Preposition
  ἐν + dat., *in; on*
Adverb
  μηκέτι + imperative, *don't . . .*
    any longer!
Conjunction
  ἐπεί, *when*
Proper Name
  ὁ Φίλιππος, *Philip*

ἐν δὲ τούτῳ προσχωρεῖ ὁ Φίλιππος· ὁ Φίλιππός ἐστιν ὁ τοῦ
Δικαιοπόλιδος υἱός, παῖς μέγας τε καὶ ἀνδρεῖος· φέρει δὲ τὸ δεῖπνον
πρὸς τὸν πατέρα. ἐπεὶ δὲ εἰς τὸν ἀγρὸν εἰσβαίνει, τὸν πατέρα καλεῖ
καὶ λέγει· "ἐλθὲ δεῦρο, ὦ πάτερ· ἰδού, τὸ δεῖπνον φέρω. μηκέτι οὖν
πόνει ἀλλὰ κάθιζε καὶ δείπνει."   5

[ἐν . . . τούτῳ, *meanwhile* ὁ τοῦ Δικαιοπόλιδος υἱός, *Dicaeopolis's son* δείπνει, *eat!*]

ὁ οὖν πατὴρ λείπει τὸ ἄροτρον καὶ καλεῖ τὸν δοῦλον.
καθίζουσιν οὖν ἅμα καὶ δειπνοῦσιν. μετὰ δὲ τὸ δεῖπνον ὁ
Δικαιόπολις, "μένε, ὦ παῖ," φησίν, "καὶ συλλάμβανε. φέρε τὸ σπέρμα
καὶ σπεῖρε. σὺ δέ, ὦ Ξανθίᾱ, σκάπτε τοὺς λίθους καὶ ἔκφερε ἐκ τοῦ
ἀγροῦ. πολλοὶ γάρ εἰσιν οἱ λίθοι καὶ μόλις δυνατόν ἐστιν ἀροῦν." ὁ   10
δὲ Ξανθίᾱς, "ἀλλ' οὐ δυνατόν ἐστι τοσούτους λίθους ἐκφέρειν." ὁ δὲ
Δικαιόπολις, "μὴ φλυάρει, ὦ Ξανθίᾱ, ἀλλὰ πόνει." πονοῦσιν οὖν ὅ τε
πατὴρ καὶ ὁ παῖς καὶ ὁ δοῦλος. τέλος δὲ καταδύνει μὲν ὁ ἥλιος, οἱ δὲ
ἄνθρωποι οὐκέτι πονοῦσιν ἀλλὰ λύουσι μὲν τοὺς βοῦς, τὸ δὲ
ἄροτρον λείπουσιν ἐν τῷ ἀγρῷ καὶ πρὸς τὸν οἶκον βραδέως   15
βαδίζουσιν.

[μετά, *after* σκάπτε, *dig!* μόλις, *with difficulty, scarcely* ἀροῦν, *to plow* τέλος,
adv., *finally* καταδύνει, *sets*]

WORD BUILDING

Here are more verbs with prepositional prefixes. Give the meaning of each:

1. εἰσπίπτω 2. ἐκπίπτω 3. εἰσάγω 4. προσάγω 5. προσβλέπω

GRAMMAR

2. Articles, Adjectives, and Nouns; Singular and Plural, All Cases

In Chapter 2 you learned the singular forms of masculine and neuter
articles, adjectives, and nouns. Here are the singulars and plurals:

	Masculine			Neuter		
Nominative	ὁ	καλὸς	ἀγρός	τὸ	καλὸν	δένδρον
Genitive	τοῦ	καλοῦ	ἀγροῦ	τοῦ	καλοῦ	δένδρου
Dative	τῷ	καλῷ	ἀγρῷ	τῷ	καλῷ	δένδρῳ
Accusative	τὸν	καλὸν	ἀγρόν	τὸ	καλὸν	δένδρον
Vocative	ὦ	καλὲ	ἀγρέ	ὦ	καλὸν	δένδρον
Nominative	οἱ	καλοὶ	ἀγροί	τὰ	καλὰ	δένδρα
Genitive	τῶν	καλῶν	ἀγρῶν	τῶν	καλῶν	δένδρων
Dative	τοῖς	καλοῖς	ἀγροῖς	τοῖς	καλοῖς	δένδροις
Accusative	τοὺς	καλοὺς	ἀγρούς	τὰ	καλὰ	δένδρα
Vocative	ὦ	καλοὶ	ἀγροί	ὦ	καλὰ	δένδρα

Note:

1. In the neuter singular the nominative, accusative, and vocative of adjectives and nouns all end in -ον; in the plural these cases all end in -α. The other neuter case endings are the same as for the masculine.

2. The genitive and dative, singular and plural, of the definite article have circumflex accents.

3. When adjectives and nouns of the type seen above are accented on the final syllable in the nominative case (e.g., καλός and ἀγρός), they change that accent to a circumflex in the genitive and dative, singular and plural (see Chapter 2, Grammar 6, page 20).

3. Accent Shifting

Note what happens with the accents in the nouns ἄνθρωπος and οἶκος:

Nominative	ὁ	ἄνθρωπος	ὁ	οἶκος
Genitive	τοῦ	ἀνθρώπου	τοῦ	οἴκου
Dative	τῷ	ἀνθρώπῳ	τῷ	οἴκῳ
Accusative	τὸν	ἄνθρωπον	τὸν	οἶκον
Vocative	ὦ	ἄνθρωπε	ὦ	οἶκε
Nominative	οἱ	ἄνθρωποι	οἱ	οἶκοι
Genitive	τῶν	ἀνθρώπων	τῶν	οἴκων
Dative	τοῖς	ἀνθρώποις	τοῖς	οἴκοις
Accusative	τοὺς	ἀνθρώπους	τοὺς	οἴκους
Vocative	ὦ	ἄνθρωποι	ὦ	οἶκοι

The acute accent can normally stand on the third syllable from the end of a word only when the final syllable has a short vowel (not a long vowel or a diphthong), thus, ἄνθρωπος, ἄνθρωπον, and ἄνθρωπε. The accent of nouns and adjectives is persistent (see Chapter 2, Grammar 6, pages 20–21), which means that the accent remains as it is in the nominative case unless forced to change because of one of several rules. One such rule is that when the final syllable of a word with its accent on the third syllable from the end in the nominative, such as ἄνθρωπος, becomes long (i.e., has a long vowel or a diphthong), the accent shifts one syllable toward the end of the word, thus the genitive and dative singulars, ἀνθρώπου and ἀνθρώπῳ, and the genitive, dative, and accusative plurals. However, the masculine nominative plural ending -οι, although a diphthong, is counted as *short* in determining the accent, and therefore the nominative plural is ἄνθρωποι.

If a word is accented on the next to the last syllable and that syllable is long and the final syllable is short, then the accent is a circumflex, as in οἶκος, οἶκον, etc. When the final syllable becomes long, the accent changes to an acute, as in οἴκου, οἴκῳ, οἴκων, οἴκοις, and οἴκους. Note οἶκοι.

What is said above about οἶκος applies to verbs as well. Thus we have σπεύδει with an acute accent but the imperative σπεῦδε with a circumflex, since the final syllable is now short.

PRACTICE: Write complete sets of the forms of ὁ ἀνδρεῖος δοῦλος and of τὸ μακρὸν ἄροτρον.

Exercise 3γ

Give the correct form of the article to complete the following phrases:

1. ___ ἀνθρώπους
2. ___ δοῦλοι
3. ἐν ___ οἴκοις
4. ἐκ ___ ἀγρῶν
5. πρὸς ___ δένδρα
6. ___ Ἀθηναίων
7. ___ ἄροτρον
8. ___ χρόνον
9. ___ πόνοι
10. ___ δούλους

Exercise 3δ

Complete the following sentences by giving correct endings to the verbs and nouns, and then translate:

1. οἱ δοῦλ__ πον__ ἐν τοῖς ἀγρ__.
2. οἱ ἄνθρωπ__ σπεύδ__ πρὸς τὸν οἶκ__.
3. ὅ τε Δικαιόπολις καὶ ὁ δοῦλ__ μέν__ ἐν τ__ ἀγρῷ.
4. λείπ__ τὰ ἄροτρ__, ὦ δοῦλοι, ἐν τῷ ἀγρ__.
5. αἴρ__ τοὺς λίθ__, ὦ δοῦλοι, καὶ ἐκφέρ__ ἐκ τῶν ἀγρ__.
6. οὐ δυνατόν ἐστι τοὺς λίθους αἴρ__ καὶ ἐκφέρ__.

Exercise 3ε

Translate the following pairs of sentences:

1. ὁ μὲν Δικαιόπολις ἐλαύνει τοὺς βοῦς, οἱ δὲ βόες οὐκέτι ἕλκουσι τὸ ἄροτρον.
   The master calls the slaves, but the slaves do not drive the oxen.
2. μὴ καθίζετε ἐν τῷ οἴκῳ, ὦ παῖδες, ἀλλὰ ἔλθετε δεῦρο καὶ συλλαμβάνετε.
   Don't stay in the fields, boys, but walk to the house and sleep.
3. οἱ παῖδες ἰσχῡροί εἰσιν· λίθους γὰρ μεγάλους φέρουσιν.
   The slaves are lazy; for they are no longer working.
4. λαμβάνετε τὰ ἄροτρα, ὦ δοῦλοι, καὶ σπεύδετε πρὸς τοὺς ἀγρούς.
   Loosen the oxen, slaves, and leave the plows in the field.

5.   μὴ ὀκνεῖτε (*shirk*), ὦ παῖδες. ἀνδρεῖοι ἔστε.
     Don't wait, boys. Don't be so lazy.

ΟΙ ΒΟΕΣ

Read the following passage and answer the comprehension questions:

ὅ τε δεσπότης καὶ ὁ δοῦλος βαδίζουσι πρὸς τὸν ἀγρόν. ὁ μὲν δοῦλος τὸ ἄροτρον
φέρει, ὁ δὲ δεσπότης ἐλαύνει τοὺς βοῦς. ἐπεὶ δὲ τῷ ἀγρῷ προσχωροῦσιν, οἱ βόες
οὐκέτι βαίνουσιν. ὁ οὖν δεσπότης καλεῖ αὐτοὺς καί, "μὴ μένετε, ὦ βόες," φησίν,
"ἀλλὰ σπεύδετε εἰς τὸν ἀγρόν." οἱ δὲ βόες ἔτι μένουσιν. ὁ οὖν δεσπότης τὸν δοῦλον
καλεῖ καί, "ἐλθὲ δεῦρο, ὦ Ξανθία," φησίν, "καὶ συλλάμβανε. οἱ γὰρ βόες μένουσιν,   5
καὶ οὐ δυνατόν ἐστιν ἐλαύνειν αὐτοὺς εἰς τὸν ἀγρόν." ὁ μὲν οὖν δοῦλος προσχωρεῖ
καί, "ἀλλὰ δυνατόν ἐστιν," φησίν· "ἰδού," καὶ κεντεῖ τοὺς βοῦς. οἱ δὲ οὐκέτι
μένουσιν ἀλλὰ σπεύδουσιν εἰς τὸν ἀγρόν.

[αὐτούς, *them*   κεντεῖ, *he goads*   οἱ δέ, *and they*]

1.   What are the master and slave doing?
2.   What happens when they approach the field?
3.   What does the master do and with what result?
4.   What does the master do in his helplessness?
5.   What does the slave do that the master did not do? With what result?

Exercise 3ζ

Translate into Greek:

1.   The master hurries into the field.
2.   He looks at (toward) the field and says, "So many stones are in the
     field! It is not possible to plow (ἀροῦν).
3.   "Come here, slave, and carry the stones out of the field."
4.   But the slave says, "It is not possible to carry so many stones out of the
     field. So *you* help!"

Classical Greek

Menander

Menander of Athens (344–ca. 292 B.C.) wrote over 100 comedies of the type now called New Comedy, concerned with the every-day life of ordinary Athenians. One of his most famous sayings is the following (*Twice a Swindler*, fragment 4):

ὃν οἱ θεοὶ φιλοῦσιν, ἀποθνῄσκει νέος.

[ὃν, *(He) whom*   οἱ θεοὶ, *the gods*   ἀποθνῄσκει, *dies*   νέος, *young*]

New Testament Greek

Luke 6.46

Early in his ministry Jesus said to his disciples:

"τί δέ με καλεῖτε, 'κύριε, κύριε,' καὶ οὐ ποιεῖτε ἃ λέγω;"

[με, *me*   κύριε, *Lord*   ποιεῖτε, *you do*   ἃ, *(the things) that, what*]

The passage continues with the contrast between the man who hears Jesus' words and acts on them, like a man who builds a house with solid foundations, and the man who hears and does not act, like a man who builds his house without foundations.

Dog and cow in a field with a tree

4
ΠΡΟΣ ΤΗΙ ΚΡΗΝΗΙ (α)

αἱ κόραι πληροῦσι τὰς ὑδρίας πρὸς τῇ κρήνῃ.

VOCABULARY

Verbs

    ἀκούω, *I listen;* + gen. of person, acc. of thing, *I listen to; I hear*

    ἐθέλω + infin., *I am willing; I wish*

    ἔχω, *I have; I hold*

    θεωρέω, *I watch; I see*

    ποιέω, *I make; I do*

    χαίρω, *I rejoice*

      χαῖρε; pl., **χαίρετε,** *greetings!*

Nouns

    ὁ ἄγγελος, *messenger*

    ὁ ἀνήρ (τὸν ἄνδρα, ὦ ἄνερ), *man; husband*

    ἡ γυνή (ὦ γύναι, αἱ γυναῖκες, τὰς γυναῖκας), *woman; wife*

    ἡ ἑορτή, *festival*

    ἡ θυγάτηρ (ὦ θύγατερ), *daughter*

    ὁ καιρός, *time; right time*

    ἡ κρήνη, *spring*

    ἡ μήτηρ, *mother*

    ἡ ὑδρίᾱ, *water jar*

    ὁ χορός, *dance; chorus*

Adjectives

    ἀργός [= ἀεργός = ἀ-, *not* + ἐργ-, *work*], **ἀργόν,*** *not working, idle, lazy*

    φίλος, φίλη, φίλον, *dear;* as noun, ὁ φίλος or ἡ φίλη, *friend*

Prepositions

    ἀπό + gen., *from*

      ἀπο-, as a prefix in compound verbs, *away*

    πρός + dat., *at, near, by;*** + acc., *to; toward*

Adverbs

    ἰδού, *look!*

    καί, *even; also, too*

    μάλα, *very*

    μόλις, *with difficulty; scarcely; reluctantly*

    πρῶτον, *first*

    ταχέως, *quickly, swiftly*

Particle

    ἆρα: introduces a question

Expression

    ἐν νῷ ἔχω + infin., *I have in mind; I intend*

Proper Names
τὰ Διονύσια, *the festival of Dionysus*

τὰ Διονύσια ποιῶ, *I celebrate the festival of Dionysus*

ἡ Μέλιττα [= *bee*], *Melissa* (daughter of Dicaeopolis and Myrrhine)

ἡ Μυρρίνη [= *myrtle*, a shrub or tree], *Myrrhine* (wife of Dicaeopolis)

*Compound adjectives do not have separate feminine forms; the masculine serves for feminine as well; thus, ἀργός can be either masculine or feminine.

**Note that new meanings of prepositions are underlined and that previously given meanings are repeated.

τῇ δὲ ὑστεραίᾳ ἐπεὶ πρῶτον ἀνατέλλει ὁ ἥλιος, ἡ γυνὴ τὸν ἄνδρα καλεῖ καί, "ἔπαιρε σεαυτόν, ὦ ἄνερ," φησίν· "ὁ γὰρ ἥλιος ἀνατέλλει, ὁ δὲ δοῦλος ἤδη ἄγει τοὺς βοῦς πρὸς τὸν ἀγρόν, ἐγὼ δὲ καὶ ἡ θυγάτηρ ἐν νῷ ἔχομεν βαδίζειν πρὸς τὴν κρήνην. ἔπαιρε σεαυτόν· καιρὸς γάρ ἐστι βαδίζειν πρὸς τὸν ἀγρόν." ὁ δὲ Δικαιόπολις μάλα   5
κάμνει καὶ οὐκ ἐθέλει ἐπαίρειν ἑαυτόν· λέγει οὖν· "μὴ χαλεπὴ ἴσθι, ὦ γύναι· μάλα γὰρ κάμνω καὶ ἐθέλω καθεύδειν." ἡ δὲ γυνή, "ἀλλ' οὐ δυνατόν ἐστιν," φησίν, "ἔτι καθεύδειν· καιρὸς γάρ ἐστι πονεῖν. ἔπαιρε σεαυτόν, ὦ ἀργέ."

[τῇ ... ὑστεραίᾳ, *the next day*   ἀνατέλλει, *is rising*   ἔπαιρε σεαυτόν, *lift yourself! = get up!*   κάμνει, *is tired*   ἑαυτόν, *himself*]

ὁ μὲν οὖν Δικαιόπολις μόλις ἐπαίρει ἑαυτὸν καὶ βαδίζει πρὸς τὸν   10
ἀγρόν, ἡ δὲ Μυρρίνη καὶ ἡ Μέλιττα πρὸς τὴν κρήνην βαδίζουσιν (ἡ Μέλιττα θυγάτηρ ἐστίν, κόρη μάλα καλή). ἥ τε οὖν μήτηρ καὶ ἡ θυγάτηρ βραδέως βαδίζουσιν· ὑδρίας γὰρ φέρουσιν· μεγάλαι δ' εἰσὶν αἱ ὑδρίαι, ὥστε οὐ δυνατόν ἐστι σπεύδειν.

[κόρη, *girl*   ὥστε, *so that*]

ἐπεὶ δὲ τῇ κρήνῃ προσχωροῦσιν, ἰδού, ἄλλαι γυναῖκες ἤδη   15
πάρεισι καὶ τὰς ὑδρίας πληροῦσιν. ἡ οὖν Μυρρίνη τὰς γυναῖκας καλεῖ καί, "χαίρετε, ὦ φίλαι," φησίν· "ἆρα ἤδη πληροῦτε τὰς ὑδρίας;" αἱ δὲ λέγουσιν· "χαῖρε καὶ σύ· ναί, ἤδη πληροῦμεν τὰς ὑδρίας· πρῲ γὰρ πάρεσμεν. ἀλλ' ἐλθὲ δεῦρο ταχέως καὶ ἄκουε· ἄγγελος γὰρ ἥκει ἀπὸ τοῦ ἄστεως· λέγει δὲ ὅτι οἱ Ἀθηναῖοι τὰ Διονύσια ποιοῦσιν. ἡμεῖς   20

οὖν ἐν νῷ ἔχομεν βαδίζειν πρὸς τὸ ἄστυ· τοὺς γὰρ χοροὺς ἐθέλομεν θεωρεῖν καὶ τοὺς ἀγῶνας καὶ τὰ δράματα. ἆρα ἐθέλεις καὶ σὺ τὴν ἑορτὴν θεωρεῖν;"

[ἄλλαι, *other*   πληροῦσιν, *are filling*   πληροῦτε, *are you* (pl.) *filling?*   αἱ δὲ, *and they*   ναί, *yes*   πρῴ, *early in the day*   ἥκει, *has come*   τοῦ ἄστεως, *the city*   ὅτι, *that*   ἡμεῖς, *we*   τοὺς ἀγῶνας, *the contests*   τὰ δράματα, *the plays*]

WORD STUDY

Identify the Greek stems in the English words below and give the meanings of the English words:

1. acoustics
2. angel
3. gynecology
4. choreographer
5. tachometer
6. philanthropist
7. polyandry
8. misogynist

GRAMMAR

1. Verb Forms: All Persons, Singular and Plural

The reading passage at the beginning of this chapter introduces 1st and 2nd person plural verb forms, so you have now met verbs in all three persons, singular and plural. The following chart contains imperatives and infinitives as well. Be sure to learn all of the following forms thoroughly:

Stem: λῡ-, *loosen, loose*

	Indicative	Imperative	Infinitive
Singular			
1st	λύ-ω		λύειν
2nd	λύ-εις	λῦε	
3rd	λύ-ει		
Plural			
1st	λύ-ομεν		
2nd	λύ-ετε	λύετε	
3rd	λύ-ουσι(ν)		

Stem: φιλε-, *love*

	Indicative		Imperative	Infinitive
Singular				
1st	φιλέ-ω >	φιλῶ		φιλέ-ειν > φιλεῖν
2nd	φιλέ-εις >	φιλεῖς	φίλε-ε > φίλει	
3rd	φιλέ-ει >	φιλεῖ		
Plural				
1st	φιλέ-ομεν >	φιλοῦμεν		
2nd	φιλέ-ετε >	φιλεῖτε	φιλέ-ετε > φιλεῖτε	
3rd	φιλέ-ουσι(ν) >	φιλοῦσι(ν)		

Stem: ἐσ- (with some changes in some of the forms), *be*

Singular

	Indicative	Imperative	Infinitive
1st	εἰμί*		εἶναι
2nd	εἶ	ἴσθι	
3rd	ἐστί(ν)*		

Plural

	Indicative	Imperative	Infinitive
1st	ἐσμέν*		
2nd	ἐστέ*	ἔστε	
3rd	εἰσί(ν)*		

*enclitic

N.B. Verbs with stems ending in -ε- (e.g., φιλε-) are called *contract verbs*, because the vowel of the stem contracts with the vowel of the ending (remember that ει and ου represent long vowels; see page xiv). You have observed this with verbs such as φιλέω from the beginning of the course. The following rules for contractions may be observed:

1. ε + ω > ω
2. ε + ει > ει
3. ε + ε > ει
4. ε + ο > ου
5. ε + ου > ου

The reading passage above contains the following -ε- contract verbs: καλεῖ, προσχωροῦσιν, and θεωρεῖν. Locate all examples of these verbs in the reading.

The reading passage also contains examples of a contract verb of another type, with stem ending in -ο-, namely, the verb πληρόω, *I fill*. Locate three examples of this verb in the reading. For another example of a verb with its stem in -ο-, see ἀροῦτε (2β:16). There are few verbs of this type, and their forms need not be learned now but will be presented in Chapter 15.

A third type of contract verb, with stem ending in -α-, e.g., τῑμάω, *I honor*, will be presented in Chapter 5.

Exercise 4α

Make two photocopies of the Verb Chart on page 282 and fill in the present indicative, imperative, and infinitive forms of ἔχω *and* θεωρέω. *Keep these charts for reference.*

2. Declensions of Nouns and Adjectives

Greek nouns and adjectives are divided into three groups or *declensions*. In the reading passage at the beginning of this chapter are three feminine nouns (ἡ κρήνη, ἡ ὑδρίᾱ, and ἡ Μέλιττᾰ), which are said to belong to the *1st declension*, which has nouns with stems that originally ended in -ᾱ or -ᾰ (this group of nouns is therefore sometimes called the *alpha declension*). In nouns like ἡ κρήνη, the original ᾱ of the stem has been changed to η in the singular in Attic Greek.

In Chapters 2 and 3 you saw charts of masculine and neuter nouns and adjectives (καλὸς ἀγρός and καλὸν δένδρον) that are said to belong to the *2nd* or *omicron declension*.

Nouns such as ἀνήρ, γυνή, θυγάτηρ, and μήτηρ, which you have met in the reading at the beginning of this chapter, are said to belong to the *3rd declension*. The endings of 3rd declension nouns will be presented in Chapter 7; for the time being you can identify their case and number by observing the article that accompanies them.

3. Feminine Nouns and Adjectives of the 1st Declension

Most nouns of the 1st declension are feminine in gender. It is convenient to divide them into the following four types (masculine nouns of the 1st declension will be presented in the second half of this chapter).

Type 1: ἡ κρήνη

The original ᾱ of the stem has been changed to η in the singular in Attic Greek:

	Singular			Plural		
Nom.	ἡ	καλὴ	κρήνη	αἱ	καλαὶ	κρῆναι
Gen.	τῆς	καλῆς	κρήνης	τῶν	καλῶν	κρηνῶν
Dat.	τῇ	καλῇ	κρήνῃ	ταῖς	καλαῖς	κρήναις
Acc.	τὴν	καλὴν	κρήνην	τὰς	καλὰς	κρήνᾱς
Voc.	ὦ	καλὴ	κρήνη	ὦ	καλαὶ	κρῆναι

Note:

1. The genitive and dative, singular and plural, of the feminine definite article have circumflex accents, just as do those forms of the masculine and neuter (see Chapter 3, Grammar 2, pages 31–32).
2. When adjectives and nouns of the 1st declension are accented on the final syllable in the nominative case (e.g., καλή), they change that accent to a circumflex in the genitive and dative, singular and plural (again, see Chapter 3, Grammar 2, pages 31–32, for the same thing with masculine and neuter adjectives and nouns).
3. The accent of nouns and adjectives is persistent (see Chapter 2, Grammar 6, pages 20–21). However, in any Greek word, when the next to the last syllable is long and receives the accent and the final syllable is short, the next to the last syllable will have a circumflex instead of an acute accent (see Chapter 3, Grammar 3, page 32). The nominative plural ending -αι, although a diphthong, is counted as *short* in determining the accent, thus κρῆναι has a circumflex accent. Remember that the nominative plural ending of masculine nouns and adjectives of the 2nd declension, -οι, is also counted as short (see Chapter 3, Grammar 3, page 32).
4. The genitive plural of all 1st declension nouns has a circumflex accent on the final syllable; the original -άων ending contracted to -ῶν.

Type 2: ἡ ὑδρίᾱ

After ε, ι, or ρ, the original -ᾱ of the stem was retained in Attic Greek:

Nom.	ἡ	ὑδρίᾱ	αἱ	ὑδρίαι
Gen.	τῆς	ὑδρίᾱς	τῶν	ὑδριῶν
Dat.	τῇ	ὑδρίᾳ	ταῖς	ὑδρίαις
Acc.	τὴν	ὑδρίᾱν	τὰς	ὑδρίᾱς
Voc.	ὦ	ὑδρίᾱ	ὦ	ὑδρίαι

The word κόρη, *girl,* is an exception to this rule; it has the same endings as κρήνη above.

Type 3: ἡ μέλιττᾰ

A third group consists of nouns ending in -ᾰ, as Μέλιττᾰ; as a common noun meaning *bee,* this noun is declined as follows:

Nom.	ἡ	μέλιττᾰ	αἱ	μέλιτται
Gen.	τῆς	μελίττης	τῶν	μελιττῶν
Dat.	τῇ	μελίττῃ	ταῖς	μελίτταις
Acc.	τὴν	μέλιττᾰν	τὰς	μελίττᾱς
Voc.	ὦ	μέλιττᾰ	ὦ	μέλιτται

Note the forms with η in the genitive and dative singular.

Type 4: ἡ μάχαιρᾰ

If the -ᾰ is preceded by ε, ι, or ρ, long α appears in the genitive and dative, as in μάχαιρᾰ, *knife*:

Nom.	ἡ	μάχαιρᾰ	αἱ	μάχαιραι
Gen.	τῆς	μαχαίρᾱς	τῶν	μαχαιρῶν
Dat.	τῇ	μαχαίρᾳ	ταῖς	μαχαίραις
Acc.	τὴν	μάχαιρᾰν	τᾱς	μαχαίρᾱς
Voc.	ὦ	μάχαιρᾰ	ὦ	μάχαιραι

Note that all 1st declension nouns decline alike in the plural.

PRACTICE: Write complete sets of the forms of ἡ ἑορτή, *festival*; ἡ οἰκίᾱ, *house*; ἡ θάλαττα, *sea*; and ἡ μοῖρα, *fate*.

Exercise 4β

Give the genitive of the following phrases:

1. ἡ Μυρρίνη
2. ἡ Μέλιττα
3. ἡ καλὴ ὑδρίᾱ
4. ἡ καλὴ ἑορτή
5. ἡ καλὴ κρήνη
6. ὁ μακρὸς πόνος
7. ἡ καλὴ μέλιττα
8. τὸ καλὸν δένδρον

Exercise 4γ

Supply the correct form of the definite article in the following phrases:

1. ____ καλαὶ γυναῖκες
2. ἐν ____ ἀγρῷ
3. πρὸς ____ κρήνῃ
4. ____ ἄλλων ἀνδρῶν
5. ἐκ ____ γῆς (*earth*)
6. ἐν ____ ὑδρίαις
7. ____ μεγάλα δένδρα
8. ____ ἄγγελοι

Exercise 4δ

Copy the following Greek sentences and label the function of each noun and verb by writing S, C, DO, LV, TV, IV, IMP, or INF above the appropriate words (do not label other words). Then put into the plural and translate:

1. ἡ κόρη ἄγει τὴν φίλην ἐκ τοῦ ἀγροῦ.
2. ἡ δούλη τὴν ὑδρίᾱν φέρει πρὸς τὴν κρήνην.
3. καλή ἐστιν ἡ κόρη· ἆρ' οὐκ ἐθέλεις αὐτὴν (*her*) καλεῖν;

4. χαῖρε, ὦ κόρη· ἆρα βαδίζεις πρὸς τὴν οἰκίαν; (ἡ **οἰκίᾱ**, *house, home*)

5. ἐν νῷ ἔχω λείπειν τὴν ὑδρίαν ἐν τῇ οἰκίᾳ καὶ συλλαμβάνειν.

Exercise 4ε

Put into the singular and translate:

1. αἱ φίλαι μένουσι πρὸς ταῖς κρήναις.
2. οἱ ἄνθρωποι φέρουσι τὰ ἄροτρα ἐκ τῶν ἀγρῶν.
3. ἀκούετε, ὦ φίλοι· ἐν νῷ ἔχομεν βαδίζειν πρὸς τὰς οἰκίας.
4. τί (*what*) ποιεῖτε, ὦ δοῦλοι; μὴ οὕτω σκαιοὶ (*clumsy*) ἔστε.

Women

When Pericles drew to the end of his funeral oration, he finally had a word for the widows of the dead: "If I should say a word on the duties of the wives who will now be widows, I will sum up the whole in a short piece of advice: your great glory is not to fall beneath the nature you have been given, and hers is the greatest glory who is least talked about among the men for praise or for blame." Women lived in the shadows of their men. This is clearly seen from their legal position; they were treated in law as minors, being under the tutelage of their fathers or guardians until they were married and thereafter under the tutelage of their husbands. They could not own property in their own right; they had no place in public life, no vote in the Assembly, and no seat on the juries.

Their life centered on the *oikos*, and here they were important and respected figures. The fourth century Athenian writer Xenophon in a work called *Oikonomikos* (which means "management of the *oikos*," not "economics" in its modern sense) gives this advice to a young bride:

Two girls, one holding a writing tablet

Your business will be to stay indoors and help to dispatch the servants who work outside, while supervising those who work indoors. You will receive incoming revenue and allocate it to any necessary expenditure; you will be responsible for any surplus and see that the allocation for the year's expenses is not spent in a month. When wool is delivered to you, you will see that garments are made for those who need them, and you will take care that the dried grain is kept fit for consumption. And there is another of your duties that I'm afraid may seem to you rather thankless— you will have to see that any of the servants who is ill gets proper treatment. (*Oikonomikos* 7.35–37)

The duties of a farmer's wife were similar, though instead of organizing slaves she had to do the work herself. The work was endless and gave women little leisure.

Marriages took place early; a girl might be betrothed at five and married at fifteen, and marriages were arranged by parents, often with considerations of property in mind.

Nevertheless, Athenian art shows us many scenes of contented domestic life, and inscriptions testify to happy marriages: "In this tomb lies Chaerestrate: her husband loved her while she was alive and grieved for her when she died" (G. Kaibel, *Epigrammata Graeca ex lapidibus conlecta*, 44, 2–3, Piraeus, fourth or third century B.C.). The husband was his wife's protector and kept her safe from the dangers of life that lay outside the *oikos*. Even in the house she had no contact with men outside the family; if strangers called, she would retire to the women's quarters. In the opening scene of Euripides' tragedy, *Electra,* Electra is talking to women of the village outside her house, when two strange men appear. She immediately says to the women: "You flee down the path and I will take refuge in the house." Later her husband, a farmer, appears when she is talking to the men who claim to have brought news of her brother; he says: "Who are these strangers at our door? Why have they come to our country dwelling? Do they want me? (*to Electra*) It's a disgrace, you know, for a woman to stand around with young men."

But women's lives were not as confined as we have so far suggested. They attended the religious festivals in both deme and city, including, probably, the dramatic festivals. They had important functions in religious rites; they were priestesses in more than forty public cults, and they formed choruses and played a leading role in processions. Some of the most powerful figures in Greek tragedy are women, and all three of the great tragedians, especially Euripides, show deep insight into the character of women and portray them sympathetically. Despite the restrictions that hedged her around, the Athenian woman was no cipher. The sixth-century poet Semonides writes of the good woman:

The gods made her of honey, and blessed is the man who gets her. His property flourishes and is increased by her. She grows old with a husband she loves and who loves her, the mother of a handsome and reputable family. She stands out among all women, and a godlike beauty plays around her. She takes no pleasure in sitting among women where they tell stories about love. (Semonides 7.83–91)

Greek Wisdom

See page 70

καιρὸν γνῶθι.   Πιττακός (of Mitylene)

Women drawing water at a fountain

ΠΡΟΣ ΤΗΙ ΚΡΗΝΗΙ (β)

ἡ Μέλιττα, "οὐκ αἰτίᾱ ἐγώ," φησίν· "μεγάλη γάρ ἐστιν ἡ ὑδρίᾱ."

VOCABULARY

Verbs
    πείθω, *I persuade*
    στενάζω, *I groan*
Noun
    ἡ γῆ, *land; earth; ground*
    ἡ ὁδός, *road; way; journey*
Adjectives
    ἄλλος, ἄλλη, ἄλλο, *other, an-
    other*
    ῥᾴδιος, ῥᾳδίᾱ, ῥᾴδιον, *easy*

Adverbs
    ἀεί, *always*
    μάλιστα, *most, most of all;
    very much; especially*
    οἴκαδε, *homeward, to home*
Expressions
    ἑορτὴν ποιῶ, *I celebrate a festi-
    val*
    τί; *adv., why?* pronoun, *what?*

ἡ δὲ Μυρρίνη, "τί λέγετε, ὦ φίλαι; ἆρα ἀληθῶς ἑορτὴν ποιοῦσιν οἱ
Ἀθηναῖοι; ἐγὼ μὲν μάλιστα ἐθέλω αὐτὴν θεωρεῖν· σὺ δέ, ὦ Μέλιττα,
ἆρα καὶ σὺ ἐθέλεις θεωρεῖν; ἀλλ' οὐ δυνατόν ἐστιν· χαλεπὸς γάρ
ἐστιν ὁ ἀνήρ· ἀεὶ γὰρ πονεῖ καὶ σπανίως ἐθέλει ἰέναι πρὸς τὸ ἄστυ."

[**ἀληθῶς**, *truly, really*   **αὐτὴν**, *it*   **σπανίως**, *rarely*   **ἰέναι**, *to go*]

ἡ δὲ Μέλιττα, "ἀλλ' οὐ μάλα χαλεπός ἐστιν ὁ πατήρ· ῥᾴδιον γάρ   5
ἐστι πείθειν αὐτόν." ἡ δὲ Μυρρίνη, "μὴ οὕτω φλυάρει ἀλλὰ τὴν
ὑδρίᾱν ταχέως πλήρου· καιρὸς γάρ ἐστιν οἴκαδε ἐπανιέναι."

[**φλυᾱρει**, *talk nonsense*   **πλήρου**, *fill!*   **ἐπανιέναι**, *to come back, return*]

ἥ τε οὖν μήτηρ καὶ ἡ θυγάτηρ τὰς ὑδρίας ταχέως πληροῦσι καὶ
οἴκαδε βαδίζουσιν. ἐν δὲ τῇ ὁδῷ πταίει ἡ Μέλιττα καὶ καταβάλλει
τὴν ὑδρίᾱν πρὸς τὴν γῆν καὶ θραύει αὐτήν. στενάζει οὖν καί, "οἴμοι,"   10
φησίν, "οὐκ αἰτίᾱ εἰμὶ ἐγώ· μεγάλη γάρ ἐστιν ἡ ὑδρίᾱ, καὶ οὐ δυνατόν
ἐστι φέρειν αὐτήν." ἡ δὲ μήτηρ, "τί λέγεις, ὦ θύγατερ; μὴ φλυᾱρει
ἀλλὰ οἴκαδε σπεῦδε καὶ ἄλλην ὑδρίᾱν φέρε."

[**πταίει,** *stumbles* **καταβάλλει,** *drops* **θραύει,** *breaks* **οἴμοι,** *alas!*]

ἡ μὲν οὖν Μέλιττα οἴκαδε σπεύδει, ἡ δὲ Μυρρίνη βραδέως βαδίζει·
μεγάλη γάρ ἐστιν ἡ ὑδρίᾱ, καὶ ἡ Μυρρίνη οὐκ ἐθέλει καταβάλλειν   15
αὐτήν.

WORD BUILDING

*Deduce the meaning of the words at the right from your knowledge of those at
the left:*

1.	ὁ χορός	χορεύω		4.	ὁ ἵππος (*horse*)	ἱππεύω
2.	ὁ δοῦλος	δουλεύω		5.	ὁ κίνδῡνος (*danger*)	κινδῡνεύω
3.	τὸ ἄροτρον	ἀροτρεύω		6.	ὁ ἰᾱτρός (*doctor*)	ἰᾱτρεύω

GRAMMAR

4. Masculine Nouns of the 1st Declension

Some nouns of the 1st declension are masculine in gender and end in
-ης or -ᾱς in the nominative singular, in -ου in the genitive singular,
and in -ᾰ or -ᾱ (or sometimes -η, not shown here) in the vocative singular. The ending -ᾱς occurs after stems ending in ε, ι, or ρ. Otherwise they
have the same endings as κρήνη and ὑδρίᾱ. As examples, we give ὁ δεσπότης in the singular and plural and ὁ Ξανθίᾱς in the singular:

	Singular		**Plural**		**Singular**	
Nom.	ὁ	δεσπότης	οἱ	δεσπόται	ὁ	Ξανθίᾱς
Gen.	τοῦ	δεσπότου	τῶν	δεσποτῶν	τοῦ	Ξανθίου
Dat.	τῷ	δεσπότῃ	τοῖς	δεσπόταις	τῷ	Ξανθίᾳ
Acc.	τὸν	δεσπότην	τοὺς	δεσπότᾱς	τὸν	Ξανθίᾱν
Voc.	ὦ	δέσποτα	ὦ	δεσπόται	ὦ	Ξανθίᾱ

Remember that all 1st declension nouns have a circumflex accent on
the final syllable of the genitive plural.

The accent of the vocative singular of ὁ δεσπότης is irregular in that it is not persistent, i.e., it does not stay on the same syllable as in the nominative. Usually the accent is persistent, as in the vocative of ὁ πολίτης, *citizen*, which is ὦ πολῖτα.

Here is the full declension of ὁ νεᾱνίᾱς, *young man*, a 1st declension masculine noun like ὁ Ξανθίᾱς above:

	Singular		**Plural**	
Nom.	ὁ	νεᾱνίᾱς	οἱ	νεᾱνίαι
Gen.	τοῦ	νεᾱνίου	τῶν	νεᾱνιῶν
Dat.	τῷ	νεᾱνίᾳ	τοῖς	νεᾱνίαις
Acc.	τὸν	νεᾱνίᾱν	τοὺς	νεᾱνίᾱς
Voc.	ὦ	νεᾱνίᾱ	ὦ	νεᾱνίαι

PRACTICE: Write complete sets of the forms of ὁ πολίτης, *citizen*, and of ὁ ἀργὸς νεᾱνίᾱς, *the lazy young man.*

Exercise 4ζ

Locate all examples of the words ὁ δεσπότης and ὁ Ξανθίᾱς in the stories in Chapters 2 and 3.

5. Feminine Nouns of the 2nd Declension

Some nouns of the 2nd declension decline like ἀγρός but are feminine in gender, e.g., ἡ ὁδός, *road; way; journey,* and ἡ νῆσος, *island.*

Exercise 4η

Locate one example of the noun ἡ ὁδός in the reading passage above.

6. 1st and 2nd Declension Adjectives

Many Greek adjectives have 1st and 2nd declension endings, e.g., the adjective καλός, καλή, καλόν, *beautiful*, which we have shown along with the nouns ἀγρός, δένδρον, and κρήνη on pages 20, 31, and 40. Here are all the forms of this typical 1st and 2nd declension adjective:

	Singular			**Plural**		
	M.	**F.**	**N.**	**M.**	**F.**	**N.**
Nom.	καλός	καλή	καλόν	καλοί	καλαί	καλά
Gen.	καλοῦ	καλῆς	καλοῦ	καλῶν	καλῶν	καλῶν
Dat.	καλῷ	καλῇ	καλῷ	καλοῖς	καλαῖς	καλοῖς
Acc.	καλόν	καλήν	καλόν	καλούς	καλάς	καλά
Voc.	καλέ	καλή	καλόν	καλοί	καλαί	καλά

Note that adjectives with ε, ι, or ρ preceding -ος have feminine endings that show ᾱ instead of η in the singular (like the noun ἡ ὑδρίᾱ), e.g., ῥᾴδιος, ῥᾳδίᾱ, ῥᾴδιον:

Nom.	ῥᾴδιος	ῥᾳδίᾱ	ῥᾴδιον	ῥᾴδιοι	ῥᾴδιαι	ῥᾴδια
Gen.	ῥᾳδίου	ῥᾳδίᾱς	ῥᾳδίου	ῥᾳδίων	ῥᾳδίων	ῥᾳδίων
Dat.	ῥᾳδίῳ	ῥᾳδίᾳ	ῥᾳδίῳ	ῥᾳδίοις	ῥᾳδίαις	ῥᾳδίοις
Acc.	ῥᾴδιον	ῥᾳδίᾱν	ῥᾴδιον	ῥᾳδίους	ῥᾳδίᾱς	ῥᾴδια
Voc.	ῥᾴδιε	ῥᾳδίᾱ	ῥᾴδιον	ῥᾴδιοι	ῥᾴδιαι	ῥᾴδια

Remember:

1. The accent of adjectives is persistent, i.e., it stays where it is in the nominative masculine singular unless forced to move.
2. 1st and 2nd declension adjectives with an acute accent on the final syllable circumflex the genitive and dative singular and plural.
3. Unlike nouns of the 1st declension, these adjectives do not circumflex the final syllable of the genitive plural (e.g., ῥᾳδίων) unless the accent is already on that syllable (e.g., καλῶν).

In future vocabulary lists adjectives with 1st and 2nd declension endings will be given in abbreviated form, e.g., καλός, -ή, -όν or ῥᾴδιος, -ᾱ, -ον (remember the accent shift in the feminine: ῥᾳδίᾱ).

Two common Greek adjectives, μέγας, μεγάλη, μέγα, *big*, and πολύς, πολλή, πολύ, *much*, pl., *many*, have forms from two different stems:

Stems: μεγα- and μεγαλ-

Nom.	<u>μέγα</u>-ς	μεγάλη	<u>μέγα</u>	μεγάλοι	μεγάλαι	μεγάλα
Gen.	μεγάλου	μεγάλης	μεγάλου	μεγάλων	μεγάλων	μεγάλων
Dat.	μεγάλῳ	μεγάλη	μεγάλῳ	μεγάλοις	μεγάλαις	μεγάλοις
Acc.	<u>μέγα</u>-ν	μεγάλην	<u>μέγα</u>	μεγάλους	μεγάλᾱς	μεγάλα
Voc.	μεγάλε	μεγάλη	<u>μέγα</u>	μεγάλοι	μεγάλαι	μεγάλα

Stems: πολυ- and πολλ-

Nom.	<u>πολύ</u>-ς	πολλή	<u>πολύ</u>	πολλοί	πολλαί	πολλά
Gen.	πολλοῦ	πολλῆς	πολλοῦ	πολλῶν	πολλῶν	πολλῶν
Dat.	πολλῷ	πολλῇ	πολλῷ	πολλοῖς	πολλαῖς	πολλοῖς
Acc.	<u>πολύ</u>-ν	πολλήν	<u>πολύ</u>	πολλούς	πολλάς	πολλά
Voc.	none					

Exercise 4θ

Locate all examples of the adjectives μέγας and πολύς in the stories in Chapters 1, 2, 3, and 4.

7. Formation of Adverbs

Many adverbs may be formed in Greek by changing the last letter of the genitive plural of the corresponding adjective from ν to ς, e.g.:

καλῶν > καλῶς, *beautifully; well*

Exercise 4ι

Find five adverbs ending in -ως in the reading passage on pages 46–47.

8. The Definite Article as Case Indicator

Along with your study of 1st and 2nd declension nouns on pages 31 and 40 you have learned all the forms of the definite article. Review them in the following chart:

	Singular			**Plural**		
	M.	**F.**	**N.**	**M.**	**F.**	**N.**
Nom.	ὁ	ἡ	τό	οἱ	αἱ	τά
Gen.	τοῦ	τῆς	τοῦ	τῶν	τῶν	τῶν
Dat.	τῷ	τῇ	τῷ	τοῖς	ταῖς	τοῖς
Acc.	τόν	τήν	τό	τούς	τάς	τά

In your reading of Greek you should take full advantage of the definite article as a case indicator, which enables you to determine the case of nouns that you have not yet learned to decline. For example in the phrase τοῦ ἀνδρός the definite article τοῦ tells you that ἀνδρός is genitive singular. Remember that the vocative, which is not accompanied by the definite article, is usually preceded by ὦ.

Exercise 4κ

Give the case and number of each of the following phrases:

1. τοὺς ἄνδρας
2. τῇ μητρί
3. τῷ παιδί
4. τὴν ναῦν
5. ὦ πάτερ
6. τὸν βασιλέᾱ
7. τῆς πόλεως
8. τοῦ δεσπότου
9. ταῖς γυναιξί(ν)
10. τοῦ κυνός
11. οἱ κύνες
12. τῆς μητρός
13. τοῖς παισί(ν)
14. τὸν πατέρα
15. ὦ γύναι

ΑΙ ΓΥΝΑΙΚΕΣ ΤΟΥΣ ΑΝΔΡΑΣ ΠΕΙΘΟΥΣΙΝ

Read the following passage and answer the comprehension questions:

πολλαὶ γυναῖκες ἥκουσιν εἰς τὴν κρήνην. ἐν ᾧ δὲ πληροῦσι τὰς ὑδρίας, ἄγγελος προσχωρεῖ. ἐπεὶ δὲ πάρεστιν, "ἀκούετε, ὦ γυναῖκες," φησίν· "οἱ γὰρ Ἀθηναῖοι ἑορτὴν ποιοῦσιν. ἆρ' οὐκ ἐθέλετε αὐτὴν θεωρεῖν; πείθετε οὖν τοὺς ἄνδρας ὑμᾶς ἐκεῖσε ἄγειν." αἱ δὲ γυναῖκες χαίρουσι καὶ λέγουσιν· "μάλιστα ἐθέλομεν θεωρεῖν, καὶ ἐν νῷ ἔχομεν τοὺς ἄνδρας πείθειν." τὰς οὖν ὑδρίας ταχέως ⁵ πληροῦσι καὶ οἴκαδε σπεύδουσιν. ἐπεὶ δὲ ἥκουσιν οἱ ἄνδρες ἐκ τῶν ἀγρῶν, ἑκάστη γυνὴ λέγει· "ἄκουε, ὦ φίλε ἄνερ· ἄγγελος γὰρ πάρεστι καὶ λέγει ὅτι οἱ Ἀθηναῖοι ἑορτὴν ποιοῦσιν. ἆρ' οὐκ ἐθέλεις με ἐκεῖσε ἄγειν;" καὶ ῥᾳδίως πείθουσιν αὐτούς· οἱ γὰρ ἄνδρες αὐτοὶ ἐθέλουσι τὴν ἑορτὴν θεωρεῖν.

[ἐν ᾧ, *while*　ὑμᾶς, acc. pl., *you*　ἐκεῖσε, *there = thither*　ἑκάστη, *each*　με, *me* αὐτούς, *them*　αὐτοὶ, *themselves*]

1. What are the women doing when the messenger approaches?
2. What are the Athenians doing?
3. What does the messenger tell the women to do? (Quote his words.)
4. How do the women react to the messenger's announcement?
5. What do the women do with haste?
6. What do the women do when their husbands return from the fields?
7. Why do they succeed in persuading their husbands?

Two women are folding up a finished piece of cloth over a stool, on which lies another finished piece. On either side a woman stands spinning. On page 112 there is a scene of weaving from the same vase.

Exercise 4λ

Translate into Greek:

1. Dicaeopolis approaches Myrrhine and says, "Greetings, dear wife (γύναι). What are you doing?"
2. "*I* am hurrying to the spring. For I wish to carry water (τὸ ὕδωρ) to the house. But what are *you* doing?"
3. "The slave and I are hurrying to the field. But listen.
   (*Reverse the polite order of the subjects in the English and put the 1st person pronoun first in the Greek.*)
4. "The Athenians are celebrating a festival. Do you wish to see it?"
5. "*I* very much wish to see it. So don't go (μὴ ... ἴθι; *put μή first in your sentence*) to the field but take me to the city (τὸ ἄστυ)."

Four dancing girls on a sheep's knucklebone in ceramic

Classical Greek

Callimachus

For Callimachus, see page 23. His work included a number of funerary epigrams, including the following (21), in which a father laments his dead son.

δωδεκέτη τὸν παῖδα πατὴρ ἀπέθηκε Φίλιππος

ἐνθάδε, τὴν πολλὴν ἐλπίδα Νῑκοτέλην.

[δωδεκέτη, *twelve year old* ἀπέθηκε, *laid to rest* ἐνθάδε, *here* ἐλπίδα, *hope*]

New Testament Greek

Luke 6.45

The following comes from a collection of the sayings of Jesus.

"ὁ ἀγαθὸς ἄνθρωπος ἐκ τοῦ ἀγαθοῦ θησαυροῦ τῆς καρδίᾱς προφέρει τὸ ἀγαθόν,

καὶ ὁ πονηρὸς ἐκ τοῦ πονηροῦ προφέρει τὸ πονηρόν."

[ἀγαθός, *good* θησαυροῦ, *treasure* τῆς καρδίᾱς, *of his heart* προφέρει, *brings forth* πονηρὸς, *evil*]

Jesus concludes: "For his mouth speaks from the abundance of his heart."

5
Ο ΛΥΚΟΣ (α)

ὁ Φίλιππος λαγὼν ὁρᾷ ἐν τῷ ἀγρῷ τρέχοντα καὶ βοᾷ, "ἴθι δή, Ἄργε, δίωκε."

VOCABULARY

Verbs

ἄπειμι, *I am away (from)*
  Cf. **πάρειμι**
βοάω, *I shout*
διώκω, *I pursue, chase*
ζητέω, *I seek, look for*
ἴθι; pl., **ἴτε**, *go!*
  ἴθι δή, *go on!*
ὁράω, *I see*
τῑμάω, *I honor*
τρέχω, *I run*
φεύγω, *I flee; I escape*
φυλάττω, *I guard*

Nouns

ὁ or **ἡ κύων** (τὸν or τὴν κύνα, ὦ
  κύον), *dog*
ὁ λαγώς (τὸν λαγών), *hare*
ὁ λύκος, *wolf*
ἡ οἰκίᾱ, *house; home; dwelling*
τὸ ὄρος (τοῦ ὄρους, τοῖς ὄρεσι(ν)),
  mountain; hill

ὁ πάππος, *grandfather*
τὰ πρόβατα, pl., *sheep*

Adjective

ἄκρος, -ᾱ, -ον, *top (of)*
  ἄκρον τὸ ὄρος, *the top of the
    mountain / hill*
ῥᾴθῡμος [= ῥᾷ, *easily* + θῡμός,
  spirit], **-ον**, *careless*

Prepositions

ἀνά + acc., *up*
κατά + acc., *down*

Adverb

ποῦ; *where?*

Conjunctions

οὐδέ, *and . . . not; nor; not even*
οὔτε . . . οὔτε, note the accent,
  neither . . . nor
ὥστε, note the accent + indicative or infinitive, introducing
  a clause that expresses result,
  so that, that, so as to

Expression
δι' ὀλίγου, *soon*

Proper Name
ὁ Ἄργος, *Argus* (name of a dog;
cf. ἀργός, -ή, -όν, *shining;
swift*)

ἐν ᾧ δ' ἄπεισιν ἥ τε Μυρρίνη καὶ ἡ Μέλιττα, ὁ μὲν πάππος πονεῖ ἐν
τῷ κήπῳ, ὁ δὲ παῖς καὶ ὁ Ἄργος βαδίζουσι πρὸς τὸ αὔλιον· ὁ Ἄργος
κύων ἐστὶ μέγας τε καὶ ἰσχῡρός· τήν τ' οἰκίᾱν φυλάττει καὶ τὰ
πρόβατα. ἐν ᾧ δὲ βαδίζουσιν ὅ τε παῖς καὶ ὁ κύων ἀνὰ τὴν ὁδόν, ὁ
Φίλιππος λαγὼν ὁρᾷ ἐν τῷ ἀγρῷ τρέχοντα· λῡει οὖν τὸν κύνα καί,   5
"ἴθι δή, Ἄργε," φησίν· "δίωκε." ὁ μὲν οὖν Ἄργος ὑλακτεῖ καὶ διώκει
τὸν λαγών, ὁ δὲ φεύγει ἀνὰ τὸ ὄρος. οὕτω δὲ ταχέως τρέχουσιν ὥστε
δι' ὀλίγου οὐ δυνατόν ἐστιν ὁρᾶν οὔτε τὸν κύνα οὔτε τὸν λαγών.

[ἐν ᾧ, *while*   τῷ κήπῳ, *the garden*   τὸ αὔλιον, *the sheepfold*   τρέχοντα, *running*
ὑλακτεῖ, *barks*]

ὁ οὖν Φίλιππος σπεύδει μετ' αὐτοὺς καὶ βοᾷ· "ἐλθὲ δεῦρο, Ἄργε·
ἐπάνελθε, ὦ κύον κατάρᾱτε." ἀλλ' ἔτι διώκει ὁ κύων. τρέχει οὖν ὁ   10
Φίλιππος εἰς ἄκρον τὸ ὄρος ἀλλ' οὐχ ὁρᾷ τὸν κύνα. μέγα οὖν βοᾷ
καὶ καλεῖ, ἀλλ' οὐκ ἀκούει ὁ Ἄργος. τέλος δ' ἀθῡμεῖ ὁ παῖς καὶ
καταβαίνει τὸ ὄρος.

[μετ(ὰ) αὐτούς, *after them*   ἐπάνελθε, *come back!*   κατάρᾱτε, *cursed*   μέγα,
loudly   τέλος, *finally*   ἀθῡμεῖ, *despairs*]

ἐπεὶ δὲ προσχωρεῖ τῷ κήπῳ, ὁρᾷ αὐτὸν ὁ πάππος καί, "τί ποιεῖς, ὦ
παῖ;" φησίν· "πόθεν ἥκεις καὶ ποῦ ἐστιν ὁ Ἄργος;" ὁ δὲ Φίλιππος,   15
"ἀπὸ τοῦ αὐλίου ἥκω, ὦ πάππε. ὁ δ' Ἄργος ἐστί που ἐν τοῖς ὄρεσιν·
λαγὼν γὰρ διώκει." ὁ δὲ πάππος, "ἴθι δή, ὦ παῖ· τί οὐ ζητεῖς αὐτόν;
μὴ οὕτω ῥᾴθῡμος ἴσθι." ὁ δὲ Φίλιππος, "οὐ ῥᾴθῡμός εἰμι, ὦ πάππε,
οὐδὲ αἴτιος ἐγώ. μέγα γὰρ βοῶ καὶ καλῶ, ἀλλ' οὐκ ἀκούει ὁ κύων."
ὁ δὲ πάππος, "ἐλθὲ δεῦρο, ὦ παῖ," φησίν. οὕτω λέγει καὶ τὴν   20
βακτηρίᾱν λαμβάνει καὶ σπεύδει ἅμα τῷ παιδὶ ἀνὰ τὴν ὁδόν.

[πόθεν ἥκεις, *from where have you come?*   που, *somewhere*   τὴν βακτηρίᾱν, *his
stick*   ἅμα + dat., *together with*]

WORD STUDY

Identify the Greek stems in the English words below and give the meanings of the English words:

1. geology
2. geography
3. geometry (what was the original meaning of geometry?)
4. geocentric

GRAMMAR

1. Contract Verbs in -α-

In the story at the beginning of this chapter you have seen two contract verbs, βοάω and ὁράω, with stems in -α- instead of in -ε-, as were the contract verbs presented in earlier chapters. Contract verbs in -α- show their endings as follows (we use the verb τῑμάω, *I honor*, as a model):

Stem: τῑμα-, *honor*

	Indicative		Imperative		Infinitive
Singular					
1st	τῑμά-ω >	τῑμῶ			τῑμά-ειν > τῑμᾶν
2nd	τῑμά-εις >	τῑμᾷς	τῑμα-ε >	τῑμᾱ	
3rd	τῑμά-ει >	τῑμᾷ			
Plural					
1st	τῑμά-ομεν >	τῑμῶμεν			
2nd	τῑμά-ετε >	τῑμᾶτε	τῑμά-ετε >	τῑμᾶτε	
3rd	τῑμά-ουσι(ν) >	τῑμῶσι(ν)			

The following rules for these contractions may be observed:

1. α + ω, ο, or ου > ω.
2. α + ει > ᾳ (the infinitive is an exception to this rule).
3. α + ε > ᾱ.

The third type of contract verbs, having stems in -ο-, like πληρόω, *I fill*, will be presented in Chapter 15. There are few verbs of this type.

2. Recessive Accent of Finite Verbs

While the accents of nouns and adjectives are *persistent* (see Chapter 2, Grammar 6, pages 20–21), the accents of finite forms of verbs (i.e., forms limited by person and number) are *recessive* (see Chapter 2, Grammar 7, page 21). This means that the accent of these forms recedes to the third syllable from the end of the word if the final syllable is short, but only to the second syllable from the end of the word if the final syllable is long.

Thus, in the uncontracted form τῑμά-ω the accent cannot stand on the third syllable from the end because the final syllable is long; it therefore stands on the second syllable from the end. In the uncontracted form τῑμά-ομεν, however, the final syllable is short, and the accent recedes to the third syllable from the end. The uncontracted form of the singular imperative clearly shows how the rule operates; this is the only form on the chart in which the accent falls on the first syllable of the verb: τίμα-ε.

When forms contract (as they do in the Attic dialect), an acute accent over the first of the vowels to contract becomes a circumflex over the resulting contracted vowel, thus τῑμά-ω > τῑμῶ.

Study the charts of verbs in Chapter 4, Grammar 1, pages 38–39, and observe how these rules operate in the forms presented there, except in the enclitic forms of the verb *to be*, which by convention receive an acute on the final syllable in charts of forms.

Exercise 5α

1. *Locate seven -α- contract verb forms in the reading passage at the beginning of this chapter.*
2. *Make two photocopies of the Verb Chart on page 282 and fill in the present indicative, imperative, and infinitive forms of βοάω and ὁράω. Keep these charts for reference.*

Exercise 5β

Read and translate the following forms, and then give the corresponding singular forms:

1. τῑμᾶτε (2 ways)   5. ποιοῦμεν
2. φιλοῦσι(ν)   6. βοῶσι(ν)
3. ὁρῶμεν   7. ὁρᾶτε (2 ways)
4. οἰκεῖτε (2 ways)   8. πονοῦσι(ν)

Exercise 5γ

Read and translate the following forms, and then give the corresponding plural forms:

1. τῑμᾷ   5. βοᾷς
2. φιλεῖς   6. οἰκεῖ
3. ζητῶ   7. φίλει
4. ὁρῶ   8. τίμᾱ

Exercise 5δ

Copy the following Greek sentences and label the function of each noun and verb by writing S, C, DO, LV, TV, IV, IMP, or INF above the appropriate words (do not label other words). Then translate the pairs of sentences:

1. ὁ κύων τὸν λαγὼν ὁρᾷ καὶ διώκει πρὸς ἄκρον τὸ ὄρος.
    Father shouts loudly (**μέγα**) and calls the slave out of the house.
2. ἆρ' ὁρᾶτε τὸν λαγών; τί οὐ λύετε τὸν κύνα;
    What are you doing, friends? Why are you silent (*use* **σῑγάω**)?
3. οὕτω κωφός (*deaf*) ἐστιν ὁ ἀνὴρ ὥστε ἀεὶ μέγα βοῶμεν.
    The boy is so brave that we honor him greatly (**μέγα**).
4. ἐν νῷ ἔχομεν πρὸς τὸ ἄστυ (*the city*) βαδίζειν καὶ τοὺς χοροὺς ὁρᾶν.
    We wish to walk to the temple (**τὸ ἱερόν**) and honor the god (*use* **ὁ θεός**).
5. μὴ οὕτω ῥᾴθῡμος ἴσθι, ὦ παῖ· ἴθι πρὸς τὸ ὄρος καὶ ζήτει τὸν κύνα.
    Don't be so difficult, grandfather; for *I* am not to blame.

3. Article at the Beginning of a Clause

The article + δέ is often used at the beginning of a clause to indicate a change of subject; the article is translated as a pronoun, e.g.:

ὁ μὲν οὖν ῎Αργος ὑλακτεῖ καὶ διώκει τὸν λαγών, **ὁ δὲ** φεύγει ἀνὰ τὸ ὄρος.
*And so Argus barks and pursues the hare, **but it** (i.e., the hare) flees up the hill.*

ὁ δεσπότης τὸν δοῦλον καλεῖ, **ὁ δὲ** οὐ πάρεστιν.
*The master calls the slave, **but he** is not present.*

ὁ πατὴρ τὴν κόρην καλεῖ, **ἡ δὲ** ταχέως προσχωρεῖ.
*The father calls the girl, **and she** approaches quickly.*

4. Elision

If a word ends in a short vowel, this vowel may be *elided* (cut off) when the following word starts with a vowel, e.g., διὰ ὀλίγου > δι' ὀλίγου. Note that the elision is marked by an apostrophe. Further examples;

ἆρα ἐθέλεις > ἆρ' ἐθέλεις
ἀλλὰ ἰδού > ἀλλ' ἰδού

If the following word begins with an aspirated vowel (i.e., a vowel with a rough breathing), the consonant left after elision is itself aspirated if possible, i.e., π becomes φ, and τ becomes θ. Thus:

ἀπὸ Ἑλλάδος (*from Greece*) > ἀφ᾽ Ἑλλάδος

μετὰ ἡμῶν (*with us*) > μεθ᾽ ἡμῶν

κατὰ ἡμέρᾱν (*by day = day by day, daily*) > καθ᾽ ἡμέρᾱν

κατὰ ὅλου (*on the whole, in general*) > καθ᾽ ὅλου or καθόλου, which gives English *catholic*, "comprehensive, universal."

Elision usually occurs when a compound verb is formed by prefixing a preposition that ends in a vowel to a verb that begins with a vowel, e.g.:

ἀνα- + αἴρω > ἀναίρω   ἀπο- + ἐλαύνω > ἀπελαύνω

ἐπι- + αἴρω > ἐπαίρω   ἀπο- + αἱρέω > ἀφαιρέω

παρα- + εἰμί > πάρειμι   κατα- + ὁράω > καθοράω

Exceptions: περι- and προ-, prefixes that you will meet later, do not elide, e.g., περι- + ὁράω > περιοράω, *I overlook, disregard*, and προ- + ἔρχομαι > προέρχομαι, *I go forward, advance*.

Gods and Men

When Dicaeopolis was about to start plowing, he first made a prayer to Demeter, goddess of grain. When he is about to take his family to Athens to the festival of Dionysus, god of wine, he first goes to the altar in the courtyard

Life-size bronze statue of Zeus hurling a thunderbolt

of his house and pours a libation (drink offering) to Zeus, father of gods and men. Religion permeated Greek life; prayer and offerings were daily obligations. Hesiod, the eighth-century poet, says:

> Appease the immortal gods with libations and sacrifices, when you go to bed and when the holy light returns, so that they may have a kindly heart and spirit toward you, and you may buy other people's land and not have someone else buy yours. (*Works and Days,* 338–341)

The Greeks were polytheists (that is, they worshiped many gods), and their religion was an amalgam of many elements. For instance, when Greek speakers first entered Greece from the north about 2,000 B.C., they brought with them as their principal deity Zeus the Father (Ζεὺς πατήρ = Latin *Iuppiter*). The religion of the older inhabitants of Greece centered around a goddess, the Earth Mother, worshiped under various names, including Demeter. Eventually the various deities of different localities and different origins were united into the family of the twelve Olympian gods. They were called Olympian because they were thought to live on the top of the heavenly mountain Olympus, and each god had his (or her) special sphere of influence. Zeus was lord of the thunderbolt and father of gods and men; Hera was his wife and the patron goddess of women; Athena was his daughter and the goddess of wisdom and crafts; Apollo was the god of light, prophecy, and healing; Artemis, his sister, was a virgin huntress and goddess of the moon; Poseidon, Zeus' brother, was god of the sea; Aphrodite was goddess of love; Hermes was the messenger of the gods and bringer of good luck; Hephaestus was the god of fire and smiths; Ares was the god of war; Dionysus was the god of wine; and Demeter was the goddess of grain (for the Greek names, see page xix). Besides the great Olympians, there were many lesser gods, such as Pan and the nymphs, and many foreign gods whose worship was introduced to Greece at various times and who joined the pantheon.

There were in Greek religion no church, no dogma, and no professional full-time priests. Temples were built as the homes of the deity to which they were dedicated; no services were held inside, and the altar at which offerings were made stood in the open outside the temple. The gods were worshiped with prayer and offerings, both privately by the family and publicly by the deme and state at regular festivals recurring throughout the year. The usual offering in private worship was a libation of wine poured over the altar or a pinch of incense burnt in the altar fire. Public ritual culminated in animal sacrifice by the priest of the cult, often on a large scale, followed by a public banquet.

The gods were conceived in human form, and human characteristics were attributed to them. They were immortal, all powerful, and arbitrary. They were primarily interested not in the behavior of humans toward each other (morality) but in the maintenance of the honors due to themselves, and in this respect they were demanding and jealous. If you gave the gods the honors and offerings that were their due, you could expect them to repay you with their help and protection. At the beginning of Homer's *Iliad*, Chryses, whose daughter the Greeks have captured and refuse to return for ransom, prays to Apollo:

> Hearken to me, God of the Silver Bow, protector of Chryse and holy Cilla, mighty ruler of Tenedus, Smintheus, if ever I have built a temple pleasing to you, if ever I have burned the rich thighs of a bull or a goat for you, fulfill now my prayers: may the Greeks pay for my tears through your arrows.

Chryses prays to Apollo by two of his cult titles (the meaning of the second, Smintheus, is not known for certain) and three of the centers of his worship (the gods were not omnipresent, and Apollo might be resident in any one of these places). Chryses reminds Apollo of past services and only then makes his request, that Apollo may punish the Greeks by striking them down with disease (Apollo's arrows brought sickness and death—since he was the god of healing, he was also the god who sent sickness). The prayer was answered, and the Greeks were struck by a plague.

Woman pouring a libation

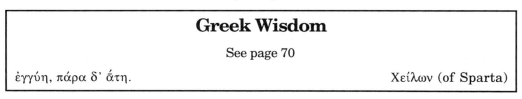

Greek Wisdom

See page 70

ἐγγύη, πάρα δ᾽ ἄτη.   Χείλων (of Sparta)

Ο ΛΥΚΟΣ (β)

ὁ Ἄργος ὁρμᾷ ἐπὶ τὸν λύκον.

VOCABULARY

Verbs

ἀποφεύγω, *I flee away, escape*

γιγνώσκω, *I get to know, learn*
    Cf. Latin *cognōscō* and English
    know

ἥκω, *I have come*

θαυμάζω, intransitive, *I am
    amazed;* transitive, *I wonder
    at; I admire*

πάσχω, *I suffer; I experience*

τύπτω, *I strike, hit*

Noun

ὁ μῦθος, *story*

Pronouns

ἡμεῖς, *we*

ὑμεῖς, pl., *you*

Adjectives

ἀγαθός, -ή, -όν, *good*

ἄγριος, -ᾱ, -ον, *savage; wild;
    fierce*

πρῶτος, -η, -ον, *first*

Adjective or Pronoun

αὐτός, -ή, -ό, intensive adjec-
    tive, *-self, -selves;* adjective,
    same; pronoun in gen., dat.,
    and acc. cases, *him, her, it,
    them* (see Grammar 6 and
    Grammar 9)

Prepositions

ἐπί + dat., *upon, on;* + acc., *at;
    against*

ὑπό + dat., *under;* + acc., *under*

Adverbs

ἐνταῦθα, *then; here; hither;
    there; thither*

    ἐνταῦθα δή, *at that very
        moment, then*

νῦν, *now*

Conjunctions

καί ... καί, *both ... and*

ὅτι, *that*

ἐπεὶ δὲ τῷ αὐλίῳ προσχωροῦσιν ὅ τε Φίλιππος καὶ ὁ πάππος,
πολὺν ψόφον ἀκούουσιν· ὑλακτεῖ γὰρ ἀγρίως ὁ Ἄργος, τὰ δὲ
πρόβατα πολὺν θόρυβον ποιεῖ. σπεύδουσιν οὖν· βούλονται γὰρ

γιγνώσκειν τί πάσχει τὰ πρόβατα. πρῶτος οὖν πάρεστιν ὁ παῖς, καὶ
ἰδού, ὁ μὲν ῎Αργος μένει πρὸς τῇ ὁδῷ καὶ ἀγρίως ὑλακτεῖ, καταβαίνει   5
δὲ ἐκ τοῦ ὄρους πρὸς τὸ αὔλιον λύκος μέγας. ὁ μὲν οὖν Φίλιππος
μέγα βοᾷ καὶ λίθους λαμβάνει καὶ βάλλει τὸν λύκον· ὁ δὲ ῎Αργος
ὁρμᾷ ἐπ' αὐτὸν καὶ οὕτως ἀγρίως ἐμπίπτει ὥστε ἀναστρέφει ὁ λύκος
καὶ ἀποφεύγει. διώκει μὲν οὖν ὁ κύων, ὁ δὲ Φίλιππος σπεύδει μετ'
αὐτόν.   10

[ψόφον, noise   θόρυβον, uproar   βούλονται, they want   βάλλει, pelts   ὁρμᾷ,
rushes   ἐμπίπτει (ἐν- + πίπτει), falls upon, attacks   ἀναστρέφει, turns back
μετ(ὰ) αὐτόν, after him]

ὁ δὲ πάππος ἤδη εἰς ἄκρον τὸ ὄρος ἥκει καὶ τὸν λύκον ὁρᾷ καὶ
βοᾷ, "ἐλθὲ δεῦρο, Φίλιππε· μὴ δίωκε ἀλλ' ἐπάνελθε." νῦν δὲ ὁ
῎Αργος τὸν λύκον ὀδὰξ λαμβάνει καὶ κατέχει, ὁ δὲ Φίλιππος αὐτὸς
ἤδη πάρεστι καὶ τὴν μάχαιραν λαμβάνει καὶ τύπτει τὸν λύκον. ὁ δὲ
ἀσπαίρει καὶ καταπίπτει πρὸς τὴν γῆν.   15

[ὀδὰξ, with his teeth   κατέχει, holds (it) fast   τὴν μάχαιραν, his knife   ἀσπαίρει, struggles]

ἐνταῦθα δὴ προσχωρεῖ ὁ πάππος καὶ τὸν λύκον ὁρᾷ ἐπὶ τῇ γῇ
κείμενον. θαυμάζει οὖν καί, "εὖ γε, ὦ παῖ," φησίν· "μάλα ἀνδρεῖος εἶ.
μέγας γάρ ἐστιν ὁ λύκος καὶ ἄγριος. σὺ δέ, ὦ ῎Αργε, ἀγαθὸς εἶ κύων·
εὖ γὰρ τὰ πρόβατα φυλάττεις. νῦν δέ, ὦ Φίλιππε, οἴκαδε σπεῦδε· ἡ
γὰρ μήτηρ δήπου ἐθέλει γιγνώσκειν ποῦ εἶ καὶ τί πάσχεις."   20

[κείμενον, lying   εὖ γε, well done!   εὖ, well   δήπου, I suppose]

ἐπεὶ δὲ τῇ οἰκίᾳ προσχωροῦσιν, τὴν μητέρα ὁρῶσιν. ὁ μὲν οὖν
πάππος σπεύδει πρὸς αὐτὴν καὶ πάντα λέγει. ἡ δέ, "ἆρα τὰ ἀληθῆ
λέγεις;" φησίν. "εὖ γε, ὦ παῖ· μάλα ἀνδρεῖος εἶ. ἀλλ' ἰδού—προσχωρεῖ
ἡ Μέλιττα ἀπὸ τῆς κρήνης. ἐλθὲ δεῦρο, ὦ Μέλιττα, καὶ ἄκουε· ὁ γὰρ
Φίλιππος λύκον ἀπέκτονεν." ὁ μὲν οὖν πάππος πάντα αὖθις λέγει, ἡ   25
δὲ Μέλιττα μάλα θαυμάζει καὶ λέγει ὅτι καὶ ὁ ῎Αργος καὶ ὁ Φίλιππος
μάλα ἀνδρεῖοί εἰσι καὶ ἰσχῡροί.

[πάντα, all things, everything   τὰ ἀληθῆ, the true things, the truth   ἀπέκτονεν, has
killed]

ἔπειτα δὲ ἡ μήτηρ, "νῦν δὲ ἐλθὲ δεῦρο, ὦ φίλε," φησίν, "καὶ κάθιζε
μεθ' ἡμῶν ὑπὸ τῷ δένδρῳ· μάλα γὰρ κάμνεις. σὺ δέ, ὦ Μέλιττα,
κάθιζε καὶ σύ. ἀκούετε οὖν· ἐγὼ γὰρ μέλλω καλὸν μῦθον ὑμῖν   30
λέγειν."

[μεθ' ἡμῶν, *with us*   κάμνεις, *you are tired*   μέλλω + infin., *I am about* (to)   ὑμῖν,
to you]

ὁ μὲν οὖν πάππος καθεύδει—μάλα γὰρ κάμνει—οἱ δὲ παῖδες
καθίζουσιν ὑπὸ τῷ δένδρῳ καὶ ἀκούουσιν· ἐπιθῡμοῦσι γὰρ ἀκούειν
τὸν μῦθον.

[ἐπιθῡμοῦσι, *they desire*]

WORD BUILDING

*From your knowledge of the verbs at the left, deduce the meaning of the nouns
at the right:*

1. βοάω   ἡ βοή
2. τῑμάω   ἡ τῑμή
3. ὁρμάω (*I rush*)   ἡ ὁρμή
4. νῑκάω (*I defeat; win*)   ἡ νίκη
5. τελευτάω (*I end; die*)   ἡ τελευτή

GRAMMAR

5. Agreement of Subject and Verb

Note that in Greek neuter plural subjects take singular verbs, e.g.:

τὰ πρόβατα πολὺν θόρυβον **ποιεῖ**.
τὰ ἄροτρα μῑκρά **ἐστιν**.

Translate the examples above.

6. Personal Pronouns

In previous chapters you have met the nominative singular personal
pronouns ἐγώ, *I*, and σύ, *you*, and you have met the accusative singular
pronouns αὐτόν, *him* or *it*, αὐτήν, *her* or *it*, and αὐτό, *it*. Personal pronouns
in the genitive and dative cases (ἡμῶν and ὑμῖν) appear in the next to the
last paragraph of the reading passage above (locate five personal pronouns in that paragraph).

The full declensions of the personal pronouns are given below:

1st Person Singular		
Nom.	ἐγώ	*I*
Gen.	ἐμοῦ μου	*of me*
Dat.	ἐμοί μοι	*to* or *for me*
Acc.	ἐμέ με	*me*

1st Person Plural	
ἡμεῖς	*we*
ἡμῶν	*of us*
ἡμῖν	*to* or *for us*
ἡμᾶς	*us*

2nd Person Singular		
Nom.	σύ	*you*
Gen.	σοῦ σου	*of you*
Dat.	σοί σοι	*to* or *for you*
Acc.	σέ σε	*you*

2nd Person Plural	
ὑμεῖς	*you*
ὑμῶν	*of you*
ὑμῖν	*to* or *for you*
ὑμᾶς	*you*

Note: the accented forms ἐμοῦ, ἐμοί, ἐμέ and σοῦ, σοί, σέ are emphatic and are used at the beginning of clauses and in expressing contrasts, e.g.:

ἐμὲ οὐ **σὲ** ἡ Μέλιττα φιλεῖ. *Melissa loves **me** not **you**.*

These forms are usually used after prepositions, e.g.:

ὁ λύκος ὁρμᾷ ἐπ' **ἐμέ**. *The wolf rushes at **me**.*   Exception: πρός με

The unaccented forms are unemphatic and enclitic.

3rd Person

The following forms are used as genitive, dative, and accusative 3rd person pronouns:

	Masculine		**Feminine**		**Neuter**	
Singular						
Gen.	αὐτοῦ	*of him* or *it*	αὐτῆς	*of her* or *it*	αὐτοῦ	*of it*
Dat.	αὐτῷ	*to* or *for him* or *it*	αὐτῇ	*to* or *for her* or *it*	αὐτῷ	*to it*
Acc.	αὐτόν	*him* or *it*	αὐτήν	*her* or *it*	αὐτό	*it*
Plural						
Gen.	αὐτῶν	*of them*	αὐτῶν	*of them*	αὐτῶν	*of them*
Dat.	αὐτοῖς	*to* or *for them*	αὐταῖς	*to* or *for them*	αὐτοῖς	*to* or *for them*
Acc.	αὐτούς	*them*	αὐτάς	*them*	αὐτά	*them*

Note that these words can refer to either persons or things. When they refer to things, the gender of the pronoun depends on the gender of the noun to which it refers, e.g.: ὁ Ξανθίας αἴρει τὸν λίθον. αἴρει **αὐτόν** (*He lifts **it***). The word αὐτόν is translated *it*, but it is masculine because it refers to the masculine noun λίθον. Translate the following examples:

ὁρῶ τὴν οἰκίαν. ὁρᾷς **αὐτήν**; φέρω τὸ ἄροτρον. σὺ **αὐτὸ** οὐ φέρεις.

Exercise 5ε

Look back through story α in Chapter 3 and story β in Chapter 5 and locate at least eight examples of personal pronouns and forms of αὐτός in each story.

7. Attributive and Predicate Position

a. *Attributive Position*

Note the position of the adjective in the following phrases:

ἡ καλὴ οἰκίᾱ   ἡ οἰκίᾱ ἡ καλή

Both phrases mean *the beautiful house*. The adjective is said to be in the *attributive* position in these examples, in which it is placed either between the article and the noun or after the repeated article.

b. *Predicate Position*

In the following examples the adjective stands outside the article-noun group. The following examples constitute complete sentences (note that the verb "to be" may be omitted in simple sentences of this sort), and the adjective is said to be in the *predicate* position. Both sentences mean *The house is beautiful.*

καλὴ ἡ οἰκίᾱ.   ἡ οἰκίᾱ καλή.

8. Possessives

The following possessive adjectives correspond to the personal pronouns above:

1st Person Singular
ἐμός, -ή, -όν *my, mine*

1st Person Plural
ἡμέτερος, -ᾱ, -ον *our, ours*

2nd Person Singular
σός, -ή, -όν *your, yours*

2nd Person Plural
ῡ̔μέτερος, -ᾱ, -ον *your, yours*

Here are some examples:

ὁ μὲν **ἐμὸς** κύων τὸν λύκον διώκει, ὁ δὲ κύων ὁ **σὸς** πρὸς τῇ ὁδῷ καθίζει.
My *dog is pursuing the wolf, but* ***your*** *dog is sitting by the road.*

ὁ μὲν **ἡμέτερος** πατὴρ πονεῖ ἐν τῷ ἀγρῷ, ὁ δὲ **ῡ̔μέτερος** ἀργός ἐστιν.
Our *father works in the field, but* ***your*** *(father) is lazy.*

ὁ κύων **ἐμός** ἐστιν, οὐ **σός**.
The dog is ***mine***, *not* ***yours***.

In the first two examples the possessive adjectives occupy the attributive position, while in the third they occupy the predicate position.

There is no possessive adjective for the 3rd person, but instead the genitive of αὐτός is used:

Masculine	αὐτοῦ	*of him, his; of it, its*
Feminine	αὐτῆς	*of her, her; of it, its*
Neuter	αὐτοῦ	*of it, its*
M., F., N. (Plural)	αὐτῶν	*of them, their*

These possessive genitives occupy the predicate position, i.e., they stand outside the article-noun group to which they belong, and they refer to someone other than the subject of the verb (they are not reflexive), e.g.:

ὁ πάππος πρὸς τὸν παῖδα τρέχει, ὁ δὲ τὴν μάχαιραν **αὐτοῦ** λαμβάνει.
*Grandfather runs to the boy, and he (the boy) takes **his** (the grandfather's) knife.*

ἡ κόρη μάλα κάμνει· ἡ οὖν μήτηρ τὴν ὑδρίαν **αὐτῆς** φέρει.
*The girl is very tired; and so her mother carries **her** (i.e., the girl's) water jar.*

οἱ μὲν παῖδες ἐν τῷ ἀγρῷ μένουσιν, οἱ δὲ πατέρες τοὺς κύνας **αὐτῶν** οἴκαδε ἄγουσιν.
*The boys stay in the field, but the fathers lead **their** (i.e., the boys') dogs home.*

The genitives of the personal pronouns (see above, Grammar 6, page 65), used to indicate possession, also occupy the predicate position, e.g.:

"σὺ εἶ ὁ υἱός **μου** ὁ ἀγαπητός." (Luke 3.22; see page 23)

Note that Greek frequently does not use possessives if the possessor is the same as the subject of the verb, e.g.:

ὁ Φίλιππος τὴν μάχαιραν λαμβάνει καὶ τύπτει τὸν λύκον.
*Philip takes **his** knife and strikes the wolf.*

Exercise 5ζ

Read aloud and translate:

1. ἐλθὲ δεῦρο, ὦ παῖ· ὁ γὰρ ἡμέτερος δεσπότης ἡμᾶς καλεῖ.
2. τί ποιεῖτε, ὦ δοῦλοι; ἐγὼ μὲν γὰρ ὑμᾶς καλῶ, ὑμεῖς δὲ οὐκ ἀκούετε.
3. ἆρ' οὐκ ἀκούετέ μου; φέρετέ μοι τὸ ἄροτρον.
4. ἀλλ', ὦ δέσποτα, νῦν φέρομεν αὐτό σοι.
5. ἡμῖν προσχώρει, ὦ παῖ, καὶ λέγε μοι τί πάσχεις.
6. τὸν ἐμὸν κύνα ζητῶ, ὦ πάτερ· ὁ δὲ φεύγει ἀνὰ τὴν ὁδὸν καὶ οὐκ ἐθέλει ἐπανιέναι (*to come back*).

7. θάρρει (*cheer up*), ὦ παῖ· ἐγὼ γὰρ ἀκούω αὐτοῦ ὑλακτοῦντος (*barking*). ζήτει οὖν αὐτόν.

8. ὁρῶ αὐτὸν ἐπὶ ἄκρῳ τῷ ὄρει μένοντα (*waiting*)· ἰδού, νῦν τρέχει πρὸς ἡμᾶς.

9. ἄγριος μὲν ὁ λύκος καὶ μέγας, ὁ δὲ παῖς τὴν μάχαιραν λαμβάνει καὶ τύπτει αὐτόν.

10. ὁ μὲν πάππος ἤδη πάρεστιν, ὁ δὲ Φίλιππος τὴν μάχαιραν αὐτοῦ λαμβάνει καὶ ἀποκτείνει (*kills*) τὸν λύκον.

9. The Adjective αὐτός, -ή, -ό

The same word that is used in the genitive, dative, and accusative cases as the 3rd person pronoun (see above, Grammar 6) may be used in any case as an *intensive adjective*, meaning *-self* or *-selves*, e.g.:

μάλα ἀνδρεῖοί ἐστε **αὐτοί**. *You **yourselves** are very brave.*

Here are all of its forms:

	Masculine	**Feminine**	**Neuter**
Singular			
Nom.	αὐτός	αὐτή	αὐτό
Gen.	αὐτοῦ	αὐτῆς	αὐτοῦ
Dat.	αὐτῷ	αὐτῇ	αὐτῷ
Acc.	αὐτόν	αὐτήν	αὐτό
Plural			
Nom.	αὐτοί	αὐταί	αὐτά
Gen.	αὐτῶν	αὐτῶν	αὐτῶν
Dat.	αὐτοῖς	αὐταῖς	αὐτοῖς
Acc.	αὐτούς	αὐτάς	αὐτά

There is no vocative.

This adjective may be used to intensify or emphasize the implied subject of a verb or to intensify or emphasize a noun, e.g.:

ὁ δοῦλος πάρεστιν· **αὐτὸς** αἴρει τὸν λίθον.
*The slave is present; he **himself** lifts the stone.*

ὁ πάππος τὸν λύκον **αὐτὸν** ὁρᾷ.
ὁ πάππος **αὐτὸν** τὸν λύκον ὁρᾷ.
*The grandfather sees the wolf **itself**.*

αἱ μὲν κόραι τὰς ὑδρίας πληροῦσιν, αἱ δὲ γυναῖκες **αὐταὶ** οὔ.

αἱ μὲν κόραι τὰς ὑδρίας πληροῦσιν, **αὐταὶ** δὲ αἱ γυναῖκες οὔ.

*The girls fill their water jars, but the women **themselves** do not.*

When used to intensify a noun, this adjective occupies the *predicate* position, as in the second and third examples above.

This same adjective when placed in the *attributive* position means *same*, e.g.:

τὸν **αὐτὸν** λύκον   *the **same** wolf*

αἱ **αὐταὶ** γυναῖκες   *the **same** women*

δὶς ἐς τὸν **αὐτὸν** ποταμὸν οὐκ ἂν ἐμβαίης.
*You couldn't step into the **same** river twice.* —Heraclitus

Exercise 5η

Read aloud and translate:

1. αὐτὸς ὁ πάππος ἡμᾶς κελεύει (*orders*) σπεύδειν πρὸς τὸ αὔλιον· ὁ γὰρ αὐτὸς λύκος καταβαίνει ἀπὸ τοῦ ὄρους.

2. τὸν κύνα αὐτοῦ καλεῖτε· ἀνδρεῖος γάρ ἐστι καὶ τὰ πρόβατα εὖ φυλάττει.

3. σπεύδετε, ὦ παῖδες· τὰ γὰρ πρόβατα αὐτὸν τὸν λύκον ὁρᾷ καὶ πολὺν θόρυβον ποιεῖ.

4. ὁ κύων οὐ διώκει τὸν λύκον ἀλλὰ αὐτὸς ἀποφεύγει· ἄγριος γάρ ἐστιν ὁ λύκος καὶ μέγας.

5. νῦν δὲ ὁ αὐτὸς κύων τὸν λύκον διώκει· ὁ δὲ ἀποφεύγει πρὸς τὸ ὄρος.

Ο ΑΡΓΟΣ ΤΑ ΠΡΟΒΑΤΑ ΣΩΙΖΕΙ

Read the following passages and answer the comprehension questions:

ὅ τε Φίλιππος καὶ ὁ πατὴρ βραδέως βαδίζουσιν ἀνὰ τὴν ὁδόν· ζητοῦσι γὰρ τὰ πρόβατα. ἐπεὶ δὲ εἰς ἄκρον τὸ ὄρος ἥκουσιν, τὰ πρόβατα ὁρῶσιν· μένει γὰρ τὰ πρόβατα πρὸς τῇ ὁδῷ καὶ πολὺν θόρυβον ποιεῖ. ὁ οὖν Δικαιόπολις, "τί πάσχει τὰ πρόβατα;" φησίν· "σπεῦδε κατὰ τὴν ὁδόν, ὦ παῖ, καὶ γίγνωσκε τί τοσοῦτον θόρυβον ποιεῖ." ὁ οὖν Φίλιππος αὐτὸς σπεύδει κατὰ τὴν ὁδόν. ἐπεὶ δὲ τοῖς προβάτοις   5
προσχωρεῖ, μέγαν λύκον ὁρᾷ· τὸν οὖν πατέρα καλεῖ καὶ βοᾷ· "ἐλθὲ δεῦρο, ὦ πάτερ, καὶ βοήθει· μέγας γὰρ λύκος πάρεστι καὶ μέλλει τοῖς προβάτοις ἐμπίπτειν."

[**βοήθει,** *come to the rescue! come to (my) aid!*]

1. What are Philip and his father seeking?
2. When do they see the flocks? What are the flocks doing?
3. What does Philip see when he approaches the flocks?
4. What does he urge his father to do?

ὁ οὖν Δικαιόπολις τὸν κύνα λύει καί, "ἴθι δή, "Αργε," φησίν· "τὸν λύκον δίωκε·
σὺ δέ, ὦ παῖ, μένε ἐνταῦθα." ὁ μὲν οὖν Φίλιππος μένει πρὸς τῇ ὁδῷ, ὁ δὲ "Αργος
ὑλακτεῖ καὶ οὕτως ἀγρίως ὁρμᾷ ἐπὶ τὸν λύκον ὥστε ὁ λύκος ἀποφεύγει. ὁ δὲ   10
Φίλιππος καὶ ὁ πατὴρ τρέχουσι μετ' αὐτοὺς καὶ βοῶσι καὶ λίθους βάλλουσιν.
ἐνταῦθα δὴ τὸν κύνα καλοῦσι καὶ τὰ πρόβατα οἴκαδε ἐλαύνουσιν.

[βάλλουσιν, throw]

5. What does Dicaeopolis do?
6. Does Philip obey his father?
7. What does Argus do? With what result?
8. What do Philip and his father do at the end of the story?

Exercise 5θ

Translate into Greek:

1. We no longer see many wolves in the hills, and they rarely
    (σπανίως) come down (*use* καταβαίνω) into the fields.
2. So we are amazed that Philip has killed (ἀπέκτονε(ν)) a wolf.
3. The same boy guards the flocks well (εὖ), but he does not always speak
    (say) the truth (τὰ ἀληθῆ).
4. So we ourselves intend to hurry to the hill and look for the body (*use* ὁ
    νεκρός).

Greek Wisdom

The Seven Wise Men

The Greeks recognized seven "wise men" or "sages" (σοφοί), who lived in
the early decades of the sixth century B.C. To each was attached a piece of
proverbial wisdom, which is quoted on the page of this book to which reference
is made opposite each name in the following list (the names are given in the
order in which they were listed in antiquity):

Θαλῆς (of Miletus)	page 111
Σόλων (of Athens)	page 230
Περίανδρος (of Corinth)	page 127
Κλεόβουλος (of Lindos)	page 16
Χείλων (of Sparta)	page 61
Βίας (of Priene)	page 211
Πιττακός (of Mitylene)	page 45

Classical Greek

Anacreon

Anacreon of Teos (fl. 535 B.C.) was a lyric poet, whose work included many love poems. Long after his death, a collection of poems was published that were written in his style and called *Anacreontea*, including the following (no. 34), written to a cicada (τέττῑξ), a type of Mediterranean grasshopper.

μακαρίζομέν σε, τέττῑξ.

ὅτε δενδρέων ἐπ᾽ ἄκρων

ὀλίγην δρόσον πεπωκὼς

βασιλεὺς ὅπως ἀείδεις.

σὰ γάρ ἐστι κεῖνα πάντα,

ὁπόσα βλέπεις ἐν ἀγροῖς

χὠπόσα φέρουσιν ὗλαι.

[**μακαρίζομεν**, *we regard* X *as blessed*   **ὅτε**, *when*   **δενδρέων** = δένδρων   **ἐπ(ὶ)** + gen., *on*   **ὀλίγην δρόσον**, *a little dew*   **πεπωκὼς**, *after drinking*   **βασιλεὺς ὅπως**, *like a king*   **ἀείδεις**, *you sing*   **κεῖνα πάντα**, / ὁπόσα, *all those things*, *as many as*   **χὠπόσα** = καὶ ὁπόσα, *and as many as*   **ὗλαι**, *the woods*]

New Testament Greek

Luke 4.22 and 24

When Jesus went to his home village of Nazareth and taught in the synagogue, the people were amazed and said:

"οὐχὶ υἱός ἐστιν Ἰωσὴφ οὗτος;"

[**οὐχὶ**, emphatic οὐ   **υἱός**, *son*   **Ἰωσήφ**, *of Joseph*   **οὗτος**, *this man*, subject of the sentence]

They told him to perform a miracle in his home village, but he said:

"ἀμὴν λέγω ὑμῖν ὅτι οὐδεὶς προφήτης δεκτός ἐστιν ἐν τῇ πατρίδι αὐτοῦ."

[**ἀμὴν**, *in truth*   **οὐδεὶς**, *no*   **προφήτης**, *prophet*   **δεκτός**, *acceptable*   **τῇ πατρίδι αὐτοῦ**, *his own country*]

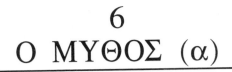

6
Ο ΜΥΘΟΣ (α)

ὅ τε Θησεὺς καὶ οἱ ἑταῖροι ἀφικνοῦνται εἰς τὴν Κρήτην.

VOCABULARY

Verbs
ἀποκτείνω, *I kill*
ἀφικνέομαι [= ἀπο- + ἱκνέομαι],
  I arrive; + εἰς + acc., I arrive
  at
βασιλεύω, *I rule*
βοηθέω, *I come to the rescue;*
  + dat., I come to X's aid;
  I come to rescue/aid X
βούλομαι + infin., *I want;*
  I wish
γίγνομαι, *I become*
  γίγνεται, *he/she/it becomes;*
  it happens
δέχομαι, *I receive*
ἐκφεύγω, *I flee out, escape*
ἔρχομαι, *I come; I go*
  ἀπέρχομαι [= ἀπο- + ἔρχομαι],
  I go away
πείθομαι + dat., *I obey*
πέμπω, *I send*
πλέω, *I sail*
σῴζω, *I save*
φοβέομαι, intransitive, *I am*
frightened, am afraid; transitive, *I fear, am afraid of*
(something or someone)

Nouns
ὁ βασιλεύς, *king*
ὁ ἑταῖρος, *comrade, companion*
ἡ ἡμέρᾱ, *day*
ἡ ναῦς (τῆς νεώς, τῇ νηΐ, τὴν
  ναῦν), *ship*
ἡ νῆσος, *island*
ἡ νύξ, *night*
ὁ πάππας (ὦ πάππα), *papa*
  Cf. **ὁ πάππος**, *grandfather*
ἡ παρθένος, *maiden; girl*

Adjective
δεινός, -ή, -όν, *terrible*

Preposition
μετά + gen., *with;* + acc., *after*

Adverb
ἐκεῖ, *there*

Proper Names
αἱ Ἀθῆναι, *Athens*
ὁ Αἰγεύς, *Aegeus (king of
  Athens)*

72

ἡ Ἀριάδνη, *Ariadne* (daughter of King Minos)
ὁ Θησεύς (τὸν Θησέα, ὦ Θησεῦ), *Theseus* (son of King Aegeus)
ἡ Κνωσός, *Knossos*

ἡ Κρήτη, *Crete*
ὁ Μίνως (τοῦ Μίνω), *Minos* (king of Crete)
ὁ Μῑνώταυρος, *Minotaur*

"ὁ Μίνως οἰκεῖ ἐν τῇ Κρήτῃ· βασιλεὺς δέ ἐστι τῆς νήσου. καὶ ἐν τῇ τοῦ Μίνω οἰκίᾳ ἐστὶν ὁ λαβύρινθος· ἐκεῖ δ' οἰκεῖ ὁ Μῑνώταυρος, θηρίον τι δεινόν, τὸ μὲν ἥμισυ ἄνθρωπος, τὸ δ' ἥμισυ ταῦρος. ὁ δὲ Μῑνώταυρος ἐσθίει ἀνθρώπους. ὁ οὖν Μίνως ἀναγκάζει τοὺς Ἀθηναίους ἑπτά τε νεανίᾱς πέμπειν καὶ ἑπτὰ παρθένους κατ' ἔτος 5 πρὸς τὴν Κρήτην καὶ παρέχει αὐτοὺς τῷ Μῑνωταύρῳ ἐσθίειν.

[ὁ λαβύρινθος, *the labyrinth*   θηρίον τι, *a certain beast*   τὸ ... ἥμισυ, *half* ταῦρος, *bull*   ἐσθίει, *eats*   ἀναγκάζει, *compels*   ἑπτά, *seven*   νεανίᾱς, *youths* κατ' ἔτος, *each year*   παρέχει, *hands over, provides*   τῷ Μῑνωταύρῳ, *to the Minotaur*]

"ἐν δὲ ταῖς Ἀθήναις βασιλεύει ὁ Αἰγεύς· ἔστι δὲ αὐτῷ παῖς τις ὀνόματι Θησεύς. ὁ δὲ ἐπεὶ πρῶτον ἡβᾷ, τοὺς ἑταίρους οἰκτίρει καὶ βούλεται βοηθεῖν αὐτοῖς. προσχωρεῖ οὖν τῷ πατρὶ καί, 'ὦ πάππα φίλε,' φησίν, 'τοὺς ἑταίρους οἰκτίρω καὶ βούλομαι σῴζειν. πέμπε με 10 οὖν μετὰ τῶν ἑταίρων πρὸς τὴν Κρήτην.' ὁ δ' Αἰγεὺς μάλα φοβεῖται ἀλλ' ὅμως πείθεται αὐτῷ.

[ἔστι ... αὐτῷ, *there is for him, he has*   παῖς τις, *a child*   ὀνόματι, *by name* ἡβᾷ, *grows up*   οἰκτίρει, *pities*   ὅμως, *nevertheless*]

"ὁ οὖν Θησεὺς εἰς ναῦν εἰσβαίνει μετὰ τῶν ἑταίρων καὶ πλεῖ πρὸς τὴν Κρήτην. ἐπεὶ δὲ εἰς τὴν νῆσον ἀφικνοῦνται, ὅ τε βασιλεὺς αὐτὸς καὶ ἡ βασίλεια καὶ ἡ θυγάτηρ αὐτῶν, ὀνόματι Ἀριάδνη, δέχονται 15 αὐτοὺς καὶ ἄγουσι πρὸς τὴν Κνωσόν (οὕτω γὰρ τὴν τοῦ Μίνω πόλιν ὀνομάζουσιν) καὶ φυλάττουσιν ἐν τῷ δεσμωτηρίῳ.

[ἡ βασίλεια, *the queen*   τὴν ... πόλιν, *the city*   ὀνομάζουσιν, *they call*   τῷ δεσμωτηρίῳ, *the prison*]

"ἡ δ' Ἀριάδνη, ἐπεὶ πρῶτον ὁρᾷ τὸν Θησέα, ἐρᾷ αὐτοῦ καὶ βούλεται σῴζειν. ἐπεὶ οὖν νὺξ γίγνεται, σπεύδει πρὸς τὸ δεσμωτήριον καὶ τὸν Θησέα καλεῖ καί, 'σίγᾱ, ὦ Θησεῦ,' φησίν· 'ἐγώ, Ἀριάδνη, 20 πάρειμι. ἐρῶ σοῦ καὶ βούλομαι σῴζειν. ἰδού, παρέχω γάρ σοι τοῦτο

τὸ ξίφος καὶ τοῦτο τὸ λίνον. μὴ οὖν φοβοῦ ἀλλὰ ἀνδρείως εἴσβαινε
εἰς τὸν λαβύρινθον καὶ ἀπόκτεινε τὸν Μῑνώταυρον. ἔπειτα δὲ
ἔκφευγε μετὰ τῶν ἑταίρων καὶ σπεῦδε πρὸς τὴν ναῦν. ἐγὼ γὰρ ἐν νῷ
ἔχω πρὸς τῇ νηὶ μένειν· βούλομαι γὰρ ἀπὸ τῆς Κρήτης ἀποφεύγειν   25
καὶ μετὰ σοῦ πρὸς τὰς Ἀθήνᾱς πλεῖν.' οὕτω λέγει καὶ ταχέως
ἀπέρχεται πρὸς τὴν πόλιν. ὁ δὲ Θησεὺς μάλα μὲν θαυμάζει, δέχεται
δὲ τὸ ξίφος καὶ μένει τὴν ἡμέρᾱν."

[ἐρᾷ αὐτοῦ, *loves him*   σῖγα, *be quiet!*   τοῦτο τὸ ξίφος, *this sword*   τοῦτο τὸ
λίνον, *this thread*   μὴ ... φοβοῦ, *don't be afraid!*]

WORD STUDY

*Identify the Greek stems in the English words below and give the meanings
of the English words:*

1. phobia
2. acrophobia
3. agoraphobia
4. entomophobia
5. triskaidekaphobia
6. Anglophobia

GRAMMAR

1. Verb Forms: πλέω

In the two-syllable contract verb πλέω, ε does not contract with ο or ω, thus:

Stem: πλε-, *sail*

Indicative			Imperative	Infinitive
Singular				
1st	πλέ-ω >	πλέω		πλέ-ειν > πλεῖν
2nd	πλέ-εις >	πλεῖς	πλέ-ε > πλεῖ	
3rd	πλέ-ει >	πλεῖ		
Plural				
1st	πλέ-ομεν >	πλέομεν		
2nd	πλέ-ετε >	πλεῖτε	πλέ-ετε > πλεῖτε	
3rd	πλέ-ουσι(ν) >	πλέουσι(ν)		

2. Verbs: Voice

a. Active Voice

You have met many verbs that are *active* in voice and take direct objects, e.g.:

ὁ Μῑνώταυρος **ἐσθίει** ἀνθρώπους.
*The Minotaur **eats** men.*

b. Passive Voice

Sentences of this sort can be turned around so that the direct object becomes the subject, e.g.:

*Men **are eaten** by the Minotaur.*

The verb is now said to be *passive* in voice, and the subject of the sentence is acted on rather than being the actor. The passive voice of Greek verbs will be presented later in this course.

c. Middle Voice

In Greek, verbs may be in a third voice termed *middle*. The middle voice is often reflexive, denoting that the subject acts *on* or *for* itself, e.g.:

Active: ὁ παῖς τὸν κύνα **λούει**.
            *The boy **washes** the dog.*

Middle: ὁ παῖς **λούεται**.
            *The boy **washes himself** or The boy **washes**.*

In this case the subject is thought of as acting *on* itself, and the verb in the middle voice implies a reflexive direct object in the accusative case, *himself*. The middle voice verb here can also be translated as *intransitive*, with no direct object, simply, *The boy **washes***.

Here is another set of similar examples:

Active: ἡ Μυρρίνη τὸν ἄνδρα **ἐγείρει**.
            *Myrrhine **wakes up** her husband.*

Middle: ὁ Δικαιόπολις **ἐγείρεται**.
            *Dicaeopolis **wakes himself up/wakes up**.*

In the above examples, the middle voice verbs are *reflexive with accusative sense*.

Verbs in the middle voice, however, may also be *transitive* and take direct objects:

Active: ὁ παῖς τὸ ἄροτρον **φέρει**.
            *The boy **carries** the plow.*

Middle: ὁ παῖς τὸ ἆθλον **φέρεται.**
           *The boy **carries off** the prize **for himself.***
           *The boy **wins** the prize.*

Here the subject is thought of as acting *for itself, in its own interests, to its own advantage,* and the verb, which takes a direct object, is reflexive with an implied dative of reference, *for himself.*

In the above example, the middle voice verb is *reflexive with dative sense.*

Verbs in the middle voice may occasionally have a *causative sense.* Here the subject of the verb causes someone else to do something. Compare the following sentences:

Active: ὁ παῖς **λύει** τοὺς βοῦς.
           *The boy **looses/frees** the oxen.*

Middle: ὁ πατὴρ τὸν παῖδα **λύεται.**
           *The father **causes** his son **to be set free.***
           *The father **ransoms** his son.*

3. Verb Forms: Middle Voice

Verbs in the middle voice can easily be recognized from their endings, which are different from the endings of the active voice that you learned in Chapters 1–5. Almost any verb can be used in the middle voice, and as samples of verbs in the middle, we will use our familiar λύω and φιλέω. As shown above, λύω in the middle voice may mean *I ransom.* In the case of the verb φιλέω there is no real difference in meaning between the active and middle voices; they are both transitive, and they both mean *I love* (someone or something). The verb τῑμάω is used in the middle voice as a legal term in estimating or proposing a penalty; you may meet it later when reading Plato's *Apology.*

In the following sets of forms note the *thematic* or *variable* vowels (o or ε) between the verb stem and the endings. In the second person singular indicative and the singular imperative, the σ between the two vowels (*intervocalic sigma*) is lost, and the vowels then contract: ε + αι > ει or ῃ, and ε + o > ου. The diphthong αι in the endings below is counted as short in determining placement of accents, e.g., λύ-ο-μαι.

Middle Voice

λύομαι

Stem: λῡ-, *loosen, loose*

Indicative	Imperative	Infinitive
Singular		
λύ-ο-μαι		λύ-ε-σθαι
λύ-ε-σαι > λύει* or λύῃ	λύ-ε-σο > λύου	
λύ-ε-ται		
Plural		
λῡ-ό-μεθα		
λύ-ε-σθε	λύ-ε-σθε	
λύ-ο-νται		

φιλέομαι

Indicative	Imperative	Infinitive
Stem: φιλε-, *love*		
Singular		
φιλέ-ο-μαι > φιλοῦμαι		φιλέ-ε-σθαι > φιλεῖσθαι
φιλέ-ε-σαι > φιλεῖ* or φιλῇ	φιλέ-ε-σο > φιλοῦ	
φιλέ-ε-ται > φιλεῖται		
Plural		
φιλε-ό-μεθα > φιλούμεθα		
φιλέ-ε-σθε > φιλεῖσθε	φιλέ-ε-σθε >φιλεῖσθε	
φιλέ-ο-νται > φιλοῦνται		

*The endings in -ει and -εῖ are more common in Attic prose and are used in this book.

τῑμάομαι

Indicative	Imperative	Infinitive
Stem: τῑμα-, *honor*		
Singular		
τῑμά-ο-μαι > τῑμῶμαι		τῑμά-ε-σθαι > τῑμᾶσθαι
τῑμά-ε-σαι > τῑμᾷ	τῑμά-ε-σο > τῑμῶ	
τῑμά-ε-ται > τῑμᾶται		

Plural

τῑμα-ό-μεθα > τῑμώμεθα
τῑμά-ε-σθε > τῑμᾶσθε   τῑμά-ε-σθε > τῑμᾶσθε
τῑμά-ο-νται > τῑμῶνται

Remember that when contraction takes place, an acute accent over the first of the vowels to contract becomes a circumflex over the resulting contracted vowel (see Chapter 5, Grammar 2, page 57), and remember that ει and ου represent long vowels (see page xiv); thus in the chart above φιλέ-ο-μαι > φιλοῦμαι. An acute accent over the second of two vowels that contract remains acute in the contracted form, thus in the chart above φιλε-ό-μεθα > φιλούμεθα.

Explain the accents in each of the forms above. Remember that the diphthong αι is counted as short in these forms.

4. Deponent Verbs

There are many Greek verbs that have some of their forms *only* in the middle voice; they are said to be *deponent*, as if they had "put aside" (Latin *dēpōnere*) or lost their active forms. In the vocabulary list and the first reading passage in this chapter you have met the following deponent verbs:

> ἀφικνέομαι, *I arrive;* + εἰς + acc., *I arrive at*
> βούλομαι + infin., *I want; I wish*
> γίγνομαι, *I become*
> > γίγνεται, *he / she / it becomes; it happens*
> δέχομαι, *I receive*
> ἔρχομαι, *I come; I go*
> > ἀπέρχομαι, *I go away*

These verbs have no active forms. The verbs πείθομαι and φοβέομαι, however, which have similar endings, do not belong in this list because they *may* be used in the active voice and therefore are not deponent: πείθω = *I persuade* X, and φοβέω = *I put* X *to flight; I terrify* X.

Exercise 6α

Locate thirteen verbs in the middle voice in the reading passage at the beginning of this chapter, and translate the sentences in which they occur. Identify the verbs that are deponent.

Exercise 6β

Make three photocopies of the Verb Chart on page 282 and fill in the present indicative, imperative, and infinitive forms of the deponent verbs γίγνομαι *and* ἀφικνέομαι *and the forms of the verb* ὁρμάομαι, *I hasten, which you will meet in the next chapter. Write only the contracted forms. Keep these charts for reference.*

Exercise 6γ

Read aloud and translate the following sets of sentences containing verbs in the active and middle voices (the middle voice verbs are all reflexive with accusative sense):

1. τὸν κύνα λούω (*wash*).
   ἡμεῖς λουόμεθα.
2. ἡ μήτηρ τὸν παῖδα ἐγείρει (*wakes up*).
   ὁ παῖς ἐγείρεται.
3. ὁ δεσπότης τὸν δοῦλον τοῦ πόνου παύει (*stops from + gen.*).
   τοῦ πόνου παύομαι.
4. ὁ δοῦλος τοὺς λίθους αἴρει.
   ὁ δοῦλος ἐγείρεται καὶ ἐπαίρει ἑαυτόν (*himself*).
5. οἱ παῖδες τὸν τρόχον (*the wheel, hoop*) τρέπουσιν (*turn*).
   ὁ δοῦλος πρὸς τὸν δεσπότην τρέπεται.

Exercise 6δ

Read aloud and translate the following sets of sentences containing verbs in the active and middle voices (the middle voice verbs are all reflexive with dative sense or causative):

1. τί οὐ λύεις τοὺς βοῦς;
   ὁ ἱερεὺς (*the priest*) τὴν παῖδα λύεται.
2. τὸ ἄροτρόν μοι φέρετε.
   ὁ νεᾱνίᾱς τὸ ἆθλον φέρεται.
3. οἱ ναῦται ναῦν μεγάλην ποιοῦσιν.
   οἱ Ἀθηναῖοι ἑορτὴν ποιοῦνται.
   (N.B. Either the active or the middle voice may be used here with little difference in meaning.)
4. ὁ βασιλεὺς τοὺς νεᾱνίᾱς αἱρεῖ.
   ὁ Θησεὺς τοὺς ἑταίρους αἱρεῖται.
      (αἱρέω = *I take*; αἱροῦμαι = *I take for myself* = *I choose*)
5. ὁ βασιλεὺς οὐκ ἐθέλει τοὺς Ἀθηναίους λύειν.
   ἡ βασίλεια βούλεται τοὺς Ἀθηναίους λύεσθαι.

Exercise 6ε

Change the following forms to their corresponding plurals and translate the plurals:

1. λύομαι	3. δέχει	5. ἀφικνεῖται
2. βούλεται	4. φοβοῦμαι	6. γίγνομαι

Exercise 6ζ

Change the following forms to their corresponding singulars and translate the singulars:

1. λύεσθε (2 ways)   3. βούλονται   5. φοβούμεθα
2. πειθόμεθα   4. ἀφικνεῖσθε (2 ways)   6. ἀφικνοῦνται

Exercise 6η

Read aloud and translate the following sentences containing deponent verbs:

1. ὅ τε Θησεὺς καὶ οἱ ἑταῖροι ἀπὸ τῶν Ἀθηνῶν ἀποπλέουσι καὶ δι᾽ ὀλίγου εἰς τὴν Κρήτην ἀφικνοῦνται.
2. ὅ τε βασιλεὺς αὐτὸς καὶ ἡ βασίλεια αὐτοὺς δέχονται.
3. αἱ μὲν παρθένοι μάλα φοβοῦνται, ὁ δὲ Θησεὺς οὔ φοβεῖται.
4. ἆρ᾽ οὐ φοβεῖ τὸν Μινώταυρον; θήριον γὰρ δεινόν ἐστιν.
5. οὐ βουλόμεθα εἰς τὸν λαβύρινθον εἰσιέναι (*to go into*).
6. ἀνδρεῖοι γίγνεσθε. ἐγὼ γὰρ βούλομαι ὑμᾶς σῴζειν.
7. ἐπεὶ νὺξ γίγνεται, ἡ Ἀριάδνη πρὸς τὸ δεσμωτήριον προσέρχεται.
8. ἐπεὶ δὲ ἀφικνεῖται, τὸν Θησέα καλεῖ. βούλεται γὰρ αὐτὸν σῴζειν.
9. "μὴ φοβοῦ," φησίν· "ἐγὼ γὰρ βούλομαί σε σῴζειν."
10. ὁ Θησεὺς τὸ ξίφος δέχεται καὶ ἀνδρείως εἰς τὸν λαβύρινθον εἰσέρχεται.

Exercise 6θ

Translate into Greek:

1. We want to stay.
2. I am not afraid of you.
3. They arrive at the island.
4. Don't be frightened, friends.
5. They are becoming lazy.

Theseus slays the Minotaur.

Myth

The Greek word μῦθος means *story*, and the Greeks were great story-tellers. Many of the stories were of immemorial antiquity, told to all children at their mothers' knees. There were stories about the times before man existed at all, about times when men and gods were on much closer terms than they are today, and about the gods and the heroes of old. The myths included stories of widely differing types. Some, like the creation myths, were concerned exclusively or primarily with the gods. For instance, Hesiod (*Works and Days* 53–68) relates how the demigod Prometheus, in pity for mankind, stole fire from heaven and gave it to man:

> Zeus the Cloud-Gatherer, angry with Prometheus, said to him: "Prometheus, wise beyond all others, you are very pleased to have stolen fire and to have deceived me, but it shall be a cause of suffering both to you and to men to come. In return for the theft of fire, I shall give them a great evil, in which they shall all rejoice, hugging to themselves their own trouble." So spoke the Father of men and gods and laughed aloud. He ordered Hephaestus with all speed to mix earth and water, to put in it the speech and strength of a human, and in face to give it the fair, delightful form of a young girl like the immortal goddesses. He told Athena to teach it crafts to enable it to weave the rich web on the loom; he told golden Aphrodite to pour over its head grace and troublesome desire and pains that melt the limbs; but he bade Hermes put in it the mind of a dog and a deceitful character.

The gods and goddesses did as they were told, and Hermes called the woman Pandora, "because all (πάντες) the gods who live on Olympus each gave (ἐδώρησαν) her a gift (δῶρον), a calamity for men who eat bread." (81–82)

> The Father sent the swift messenger of the gods, who took the gift to Epimetheus (Prometheus's brother). Epimetheus did not reflect on how Prometheus had told him never to accept a gift from Olympian Zeus but to send it back, lest it bring some evil to mortals. After he had received the evil, he remembered. (84–89)

Athena decks out Pandora before sending her to Epimetheus.

Before this men lived on earth free from troubles and hard toil and the grievous diseases that bring destruction.

> But the woman took the lid off the great jar and scattered the contents, and so she brought suffering on the people. Hope alone remained inside in her indestructible home beneath the rim of the jar and did not fly out, for Pandora put the lid back before Hope could escape, through the will of Zeus the Cloud-Gatherer. Countless troubles roam among the people. The earth is full of evils, and full is the sea. Diseases come upon men in the day and others come at night, bringing suffering to mortals, silently, since Zeus has taken from them the power of speech. It is impossible to escape the will of Zeus. (94–105)

This myth offers an explanation of why men suffer diseases and other troubles. (Why, for instance, should men have to work for their food? In the Golden Age earth produced all manner of food spontaneously.) The story is told in allusive style: Pandora takes the lid off a great jar, from which all troubles fly out, but we are told nothing about this jar or about how it got there and why Pandora took the lid off. Hesiod's audience presumably knew the story, and he had no need to tell them. Nor is it clear why Hope is said to remain in the jar. Is the human condition hopeless?

Other myths are based on history or what the Greeks believed to be history. The story of Theseus and the Minotaur falls into this class. Theseus was an early king of Athens, around whom a whole cycle of myths crystalized. He belonged to the generation before the Trojan War and was thought to be responsible for the unification of Attica. Minos, king of Knossos in Crete, was also believed to be a historical figure. Thucydides discusses the extent of his sea-power in the introduction to his history. *Labyrinthos* means in the ancient Cretan language *House of the Double Axe*, which may have been the name of the great palace at Knossos, where the double axe frequently appears as a religious symbol. The large size and complicated plan of this palace may account for the change in meaning of the word *labyrinth* to its later sense of "maze." Bull-jumping played an important part in Cretan ritual and is often portrayed in works of Cretan art. The bull-jumpers may well have been young captives taken from Athens and other places. We thus find in the myth of Theseus historical elements strangely transmuted in the course of time.

In another foreign adventure, Theseus is said to have accompanied Heracles on an expedition to fight the Amazons, a race of female warriors living north of the Black Sea; according to some accounts, Theseus led the expedition himself. He captured the queen of the Amazons and brought her back to Athens, but the Amazons came in pursuit and laid siege to Athens. They were defeated, but the queen of the Amazons bore Theseus a child, named Hippolytus, who was destined to be the cause of much sorrow for Theseus.

The myth of Odysseus and the Cyclops (Chapter 7) is taken from Homer's *Odyssey,* which is concerned in part with the adventures of Odysseus during his journey home to Ithaca from Troy. It illustrates a third strand often found in Greek myth: folk tale. The story of the little man who outwits a one-eyed man-eating giant is found in the folk tales of many other peoples, and the whole structure of the story as told by Homer shows the symmetry common in folk tales.

The making of myths seems to be a universal human activity, and myths are said to enshrine the corporate wisdom of primitive peoples. Their interpretation remains a vexed question, on which no two scholars agree. The strands that go to form the corpus of Greek myth are so many and various that any attempt to form general rules for their interpretation seems doomed to failure. However we look at them, they are stories that have caught the imagination of Western humanity throughout recorded history.

An Amazon in combat with a Greek warrior

Ο ΜΥΘΟΣ (β)

ὁ Θησεὺς οὐ φοβεῖται ἀλλὰ ἀνδρείως μάχεται καὶ τὸν Μῑνώταυρον ἀποκτείνει.

VOCABULARY

Verbs

ἐξέρχομαι + ἐκ + gen., *I come
out of; I go out of*
ἡγέομαι + dat., *I lead*
μάχομαι, *I fight*
παρέχω, *I hand over; I supply,
provide*
πορεύομαι, *I go; I walk;
I march; I journey*
προχωρέω, *I go forward; I come
forward, advance*
Cf. προσχωρέω + dat., *I approach*
φᾱσί(ν), postpositive enclitic,
they say

Noun

αἱ πύλαι, pl., *double gates*

Adverbs

οὐδαμῶς, *in no way, no*
πολλάκις, *many times, often*
ὡς, in exclamations, *how . . . !*

Particles

γε, postpositive enclitic; restrictive, *at least;* intensive, *indeed*
δή, postpositive; emphasizes that
what is said is obvious or true,
indeed, in fact

"ἐπεὶ δὲ ἡμέρᾱ γίγνεται, ὁ Μίνως ἔρχεται πρὸς τὸ δεσμωτήριον καὶ
καλεῖ τόν τε Θησέᾱ καὶ τοὺς ἑταίρους καὶ ἄγει αὐτοὺς πρὸς τὸν
λαβύρινθον. ἐπεὶ δὲ ἀφικνοῦνται, οἱ δοῦλοι ἀνοίγουσι τὰς πύλᾱς καὶ
τοὺς Ἀθηναίους εἰσελαύνουσιν. ἔπειτα δὲ τὰς πύλᾱς κλείουσι καὶ
ἀπέρχονται· οὕτω γὰρ τῷ Μῑνωταύρῳ σῖτον παρέχουσιν εἰς πολλὰς   5
ἡμέρᾱς. οἱ μὲν οὖν ἑταῖροι μάλα φοβοῦνται, ὁ δὲ Θησεύς, 'μὴ
φοβεῖσθε, ὦ φίλοι,' φησίν· 'ἐγὼ γὰρ ῡ̔μᾶς σώσω. ἕπεσθέ μοι οὖν
ἀνδρείως.' οὕτω λέγει καὶ ἡγεῖται αὐτοῖς εἰς τὸν λαβύρινθον.

[ἀνοίγουσι, *open*   κλείουσι, *they shut*   εἰς πολλὰς ἡμέρᾱς, *for many days*   σώσω, *I will save*   ἕπεσθέ μοι, *follow me!*]

"ὁ μὲν οὖν Θησεὺς ἐν μὲν τῇ ἀριστερᾷ ἔχει τὸ λίνον, ἐν δὲ τῇ δεξιᾷ
τὸ ξίφος, καὶ προχωρεῖ εἰς τὸν σκότον. οἱ δὲ ἑταῖροι μάλα φοβοῦνται, 10
ἀλλ' ὅμως ἕπονται· ἡ γὰρ ἀνάγκη αὐτοὺς ἔχει. μακρὰν οὖν ὁδὸν
πορεύονται καὶ πολλάκις μὲν τρέπονται, πολλάκις δὲ ψόφους
δεινοὺς ἀκούουσιν· ὁ γὰρ Μῑνώταυρος διώκει αὐτοὺς ἐν τῷ σκότῳ
καὶ μάλα δεινῶς βρῡχᾶται. ἐνταῦθα δὴ τὸν τῶν ποδῶν ψόφον
ἀκούουσι καὶ τὸ τοῦ θηρίου πνεῦμα ὀσφραίνονται, καὶ ἰδού, ἐν τῇ 15
ὁδῷ πάρεστιν ὁ Μῑνώταυρος. δεινῶς δὴ βρῡχᾶται καὶ ἐπὶ τὸν Θησέᾱ
ὁρμᾶται.

[τῇ ἀριστερᾷ, the left hand   τῇ δεξιᾷ, the right hand   τὸν σκότον, the darkness
ἡ... ἀνάγκη, necessity   τρέπονται, they turn   ψόφους, noises   βρῡχᾶται,
roars   τῶν ποδῶν, of feet   τὸ τοῦ θηρίου πνεῦμα, the breath of the beast   ὀσφραίνονται, they smell   ὁρμᾶται, rushes]

"ὁ δὲ Θησεὺς οὐ φοβεῖται, ἀλλὰ μάλα ἀνδρείως μάχεται· τῇ μὲν
γὰρ ἀριστερᾷ λαμβάνεται τῆς τοῦ θηρίου κεφαλῆς, τῇ δὲ δεξιᾷ τὸ
στῆθος τύπτει. ὁ δὲ Μῑνώταυρος δεινῶς κλάζει καὶ καταπίπτει πρὸς 20
τὴν γῆν. οἱ δὲ ἑταῖροι, ἐπεὶ ὁρῶσι τὸ θηρίον ἐπὶ τῇ γῇ κείμενον,
χαίρουσι καί, 'ὦ Θησεῦ,' φᾱσίν, 'ὡς ἀνδρεῖος εἶ. ὡς θαυμάζομέν σε
καὶ τῑμῶμεν. ἀλλὰ νῦν γε σῷζε ἡμᾶς ἐκ τοῦ λαβυρίνθου καὶ ἡγοῦ
ἡμῖν πρὸς τὰς πύλᾱς. μακρὰ γάρ ἐστιν ἡ ὁδὸς καὶ πολὺς ὁ σκότος·
τὴν δ' ὁδὸν ἀγνοοῦμεν.' 25

[λαμβάνεται... τῆς κεφαλῆς, takes hold of the head   τὸ στῆθος, its breast
κλάζει, shrieks   κείμενον, lying   ἀγνοοῦμεν, we do not know]

"ὁ δὲ Θησεὺς οὐ φοβεῖται, ἀλλὰ τὸ λίνον λαμβάνει—οὕτω γὰρ
τὴν ὁδὸν γιγνώσκει—καὶ ἡγεῖται τοῖς ἑταίροις πρὸς τὰς πύλᾱς. ἐπεὶ δ'
ἀφικνοῦνται, τὸν μόχλον διακόπτουσι καὶ μένουσιν ἐκεῖ· ἔτι γὰρ
ἡμέρᾱ ἐστίν. ἐπεὶ δὲ νὺξ γίγνεται, ἐξέρχονται ἐκ τοῦ λαβυρίνθου καὶ
σπεύδουσι πρὸς τὴν ναῦν. ἐκεῖ δὲ τὴν Ἀριάδνην αὐτὴν ὁρῶσιν· μένει 30
γὰρ πρὸς τῇ νηΐ. ταχέως οὖν εἰσβαίνουσι καὶ ἀποπλέουσι πρὸς τὰς
Ἀθήνᾱς. οὕτως οὖν ὁ Θησεὺς τόν τε Μῑνώταυρον ἀποκτείνει καὶ
τοὺς ἑταίρους σῴζει εἰς τὰς Ἀθήνᾱς."

[τὸν μόχλον, the bolt   διακόπτουσι, they cut through   σῴζει εἰς, brings ... safely to]

οὕτω περαίνει τὸν μῦθον ἡ Μυρρίνη, ἡ δὲ Μέλιττα, "καὶ ἡ
'Αριάδνη;" φησίν· "ἆρα χαίρει; ἆρα φιλεῖ αὐτὴν ὁ Θησεύς;" ἡ δὲ   35
Μυρρίνη, "οὐδαμῶς· οὐ χαίρει ἡ 'Αριάδνη οὐδὲ φιλεῖ αὐτὴν ὁ
Θησεύς." ἡ δὲ Μέλιττα, "τί οὐ φιλεῖ αὐτὴν ὁ Θησεύς; τί γίγνεται;" ἡ δὲ
μήτηρ, "ἐκεῖνον τὸν μῦθον οὐκ ἐθέλω σοι λέγειν νῦν γε."

[περαίνει, *ends*   ἐκεῖνον, *that*]

WORD BUILDING

*Describe the relationship between the words in the following sets. From your
knowledge of the words at the left, deduce the meaning of those on the right:*

1. ὁ δοῦλος   ἡ δούλη
2. ὁ φίλος   ἡ φίλη
3. ὁ θεός   ἡ θεά
4. ὁ ἑταῖρος   ἡ ἑταίρᾱ
5. ὁ οἶκος   ἡ οἰκίᾱ

GRAMMAR

5. Middle Voice: Meaning

Note the following verbs in the middle voice in the reading passage above:

φοβοῦνται, etc. (6, 7, 10, 18, 26) = *they are afraid*, etc.

φοβέω, active voice, transitive = *I put X to flight; I terrify* X

φοβέομαι, middle voice, intransitive = *I am frightened, am afraid*
φοβέομαι, middle voice, transitive + acc. = *I fear, am afraid of* X

τρέπονται (12) = *they turn*

τρέπω, active voice, transitive = *I turn* X (direct object)

τρέπομαι, middle voice, intransitive, reflexive with accusative
sense = *I turn myself, I turn*

ὁρμᾶται (17) = *rushes*

ὁρμάω, active voice, transitive = *I set* X (direct object) *in motion*
This verb may also be intransitive in the active voice:
ὁρμάω, active voice, intransitive = *I start; I rush*

ὁρμάομαι, middle voice, intransitive, reflexive with accusative
sense = *I set myself in motion; I start; I rush; I hasten*

λαμβάνεται (19) = *takes hold of*

λαμβάνω, active voice, transitive = *I take* X (direct object in accusative case); *I take hold of* X (direct object in accusative case)

λαμβάνομαι, middle voice, reflexive with dative sense, object in genitive case = *I take hold of* X *for myself / in my own interests*

Note also the meanings of the following verbs in active and middle voices:

καθίζω, active voice, transitive = *I make* X *sit down; I set; I place*

This verb may also be intransitive in the active voice:
καθίζω, active voice, intransitive = *I sit*

καθίζομαι, middle voice, intransitive, reflexive with accusative sense = *I seat myself, sit down*

πείθω, active voice, transitive = *I persuade*

πείθομαι, middle voice, reflexive with accusative sense = *I persuade myself for* + dat. (someone or something) = *I obey* someone or something
πείθομαι αὐτῷ = *I obey him.*
πείθομαι τοῖς νόμοις = *I obey the laws.*

Exercise 6ι

Read aloud and translate the following sentences containing verbs with middle voice forms. Identify deponent verbs, and identify the non-deponent verbs that are used here in the middle voice:

1. οἴκαδε βαδίζειν βουλόμεθα.
2. οἱ νεᾱνίαι καὶ αἱ παρθένοι ἐν τῷ λαβυρίνθῳ μέγα φοβοῦνται.
3. ἀργὸς γίγνει, ὦ δοῦλε.
4. εἰς τὴν Κρήτην ἀφικνούμεθα.
5. ὁ βασιλεὺς ἡμᾶς δέχεται.
6. ὁ κύων ἐπὶ τὸν λύκον ὁρμᾶται.
7. αἱ γυναῖκες πρὸς τῇ κρήνῃ καθίζονται.
8. ὁ Θησεὺς τοῦ ξίφους λαμβάνεται.
9. ἆρ' οὐκ ἐθέλεις τῷ πατρὶ πείθεσθαι;
10. μὴ φοβεῖσθε τὸν λύκον, ὦ παῖδες.

6. Some Uses of the Dative Case

a. The *indirect object* of verbs of giving, showing, and telling is in the dative case, e.g., οὕτω γὰρ **τῷ Μῑνωταύρῳ** σῖτον παρέχουσιν = *In this way they supply food* **to the Minotaur** *or In this way they supply* **the Minotaur** *with food.* Here the word σῖτον is the direct object of the verb παρέχουσιν, and the words τῷ Μῑνωταύρῳ are the indirect object.

b. The dative case may be used with linking verbs, such as ἐστί(ν) and γίγνεται, to indicate the person who *possesses* something, e.g., ἔστιν **αὐτῷ** παῖς τις ὀνόματι Θησεύς, lit., *there is* **for him** *a child.* . . . = *he has a child.* . . . This is called the *dative of the possessor.*

c. The Greek sentence in b above shows another use of the dative case, the *dative of respect*: ὀνόματι Θησεύς, lit., *Theseus* **with respect to his name** = *called Theseus.* ὁ Μῑνώταυρος δεινός ἐστιν ὄψει καὶ φωνῇ = *The Minotaur is terrible* **with respect to/in appearance** *and* **voice.**

d. The dative case may be used to indicate the *means* or *instrument* by which an action is carried out, e.g., **τῇ** μὲν γὰρ **ἀριστερᾷ** λαμβάνεται τῆς τοῦ θηρίου κεφαλῆς, **τῇ** δὲ **δεξιᾷ** τὸ στῆθος τύπτει = **with his left hand** *he takes hold of the head of the beast, and* **with his right hand** *he strikes its chest.*

e. The dative case may be used to indicate the *time when* an action takes place, e.g., **τῇ ὑστεραίᾳ** = **on the next day.** Note that the Greek does not use a preposition here.

f. The dative case is used after certain prepositions, especially those that indicate the *place where* someone or something is or something happens, e.g., ἐν **τῇ ἀριστερᾷ** and πρὸς **τῇ νηΐ.**

g. The dative case is used with *certain verbs*, e.g.: οἱ βόες **τῷ ἀγρῷ** προσχωροῦσιν = *the oxen approach* **the field.**
      Your English translation will use a direct object in the accusative case, e.g., ὁ Αἰγεὺς πείθεται **αὐτῷ** = *Aegeus obeys* **him;** ἔπεσθέ **μοι** ἀνδρείως = *follow* **me** *bravely;* and ἡγεῖται **αὐτοῖς** εἰς τὸν λαβύρινθον = *he leads* **them** *into the labyrinth.*

      Verbs that take the dative case:

        ἕπομαι, *I follow*
        βοηθέω, *I come to* (someone's) *aid*
        ἡγέομαι, *I lead*
        πείθομαι, *I obey*
        προσχωρέω, *I go toward, approach*
        συλλαμβάνω, *I help*

Exercise 6κ

Locate at least twenty words or phrases in the dative case in reading passages α and β and identify each use of the dative case.

Exercise 6λ

Read aloud, translate, and identify each use of the dative case:

1. ὁ ἀνὴρ ὑμῖν οὐ πείθεται.
2. πείθεσθέ μοι, ὦ παῖδες.
3. πάρεχέ μοι τὸ ἄροτρον.
4. τὸν μῦθον τῷ παιδὶ λέγω.
5. ἔστι τῷ αὐτουργῷ ἄροτρον.
6. ὁ αὐτουργός, Δικαιόπολις ὀνόματι, τοῖς βουσὶν εἰς τὸν ἀγρὸν ἡγεῖται.
7. ὁ παῖς τὸν λύκον λίθοις βάλλει (*pelts*).
8. ἡ γυνὴ τῷ ἀνδρὶ πολὺν σῖτον παρέχει.
9. ὁ δεσπότης τοὺς δούλους τοσαύτῃ βοῇ καλεῖ ὥστε φοβοῦνται.
10. ἔστι τῷ παιδὶ καλὸς κύων.

7. Prepositions

While, as seen above, prepositions that take the dative case usually refer to the *place where* someone or something is or *where* some action takes place, prepositions that take the genitive often express ideas of *place from which*, and prepositions that take the accusative often express ideas of *place to which*. Observe the following examples that have been given in the vocabulary lists so far:

With genitive: ἀπό, *from;* ἐκ/ἐξ, *out of;* μετά, *with* (with this last example there is no sense of motion from a place)

With dative: ἐν, *in; on;* ἐπί, *upon, on;* πρός, *at, near, by;* ὑπό, *under*

With accusative: ἀνά, *up;* εἰς, *into; to; at;* ἐπί, *at; against;* κατά, *down;* μετά, *after;* πρός, *to, toward;* ὑπό, *under*

Exercise 6μ

Write out the following sentences, putting the nouns in the correct case, and then translate the sentences:

1. πρὸς (ὁ ἀγρός) ἐρχόμεθα.
2. πρὸς (ἡ ὁδός) καθίζουσιν.
3. ἐκ (ἡ οἰκίᾱ) σπεύδει.
4. ἀπὸ (ἡ νῆσος) πλέουσιν.
5. κατὰ (ἡ ὁδός) πορεύονται
6. μετὰ (οἱ ἑταῖροι) φεύγει.
7. ἐν (ὁ λαβύρινθος) μένετε.

8.   ἡγεῖσθε ἡμῖν πρὸς (ἡ κρήνη).
9.   οἱ παῖδες τρέχουσιν ἀνὰ (ἡ ὁδός).
10. αἱ παρθένοι καθίζονται ὑπὸ (τὸ δένδρον).
11. ὁ κύων ὁρμᾶται ἐπὶ (ὁ λύκος).
12. οἱ ἑταῖροι εἰς (ὁ λαβύρινθος) εἰσέρχονται.

Exercise 6ν

Translate into Greek:

1.   Aren't you willing to obey me, boy? (Use **ἆρα**.)
2.   Tell me the story.
3.   I hand the plow over to you.
4.   The farmer has a big ox. (*Use dative of the possessor; see Exercise 6λ, no. 5, for placement and accent of the verb.*)
5.   The young man (**ὁ νεᾱνίᾱς**), called Theseus, leads his comrades bravely.
6.   The boy strikes (*use* **βάλλω**) the wolf with a stone.
7.   The girl hands over food to her friend.
8.   The slave strikes the oxen with a goad (*use* **τὸ κέντρον**).
9.   The girl approaches the gates.
10. On the next day the Athenians flee out of the labyrinth.

Exercise 6ξ

Translate the following pairs of sentences:

1.   ὁ Θησεὺς βούλεται τοὺς ἑταίρους σῴζειν.
     Aegeus is very afraid but obeys him.
2.   οἱ μὲν Ἀθηναῖοι ἀφικνοῦνται εἰς τὴν νῆσον, ὁ δὲ βασιλεὺς δέχεται αὐτούς.
     The comrades are especially frightened, but Theseus leads them bravely.
3.   μὴ μάχεσθε, ὦ φίλοι, μηδὲ (*and don't*) βοᾶτε ἀλλὰ σῑγᾶτε (*be quiet*).
     Don't fear the Minotaur, friends, but be brave!
4.   ἐπεὶ νὺξ γίγνεται, ἡ παρθένος ἔρχεται πρὸς τὰς πύλᾱς.
     When day comes (becomes), the ship arrives at the island.
5.   ἐπεὶ ὁ Θησεὺς ἀποκτείνει τὸν Μῑνώταυρον, ἑπόμεθα αὐτῷ ἐκ τοῦ λαβυρίνθου.
     When we are journeying to Crete, we see many islands.

Theseus deserts Ariadne.

Ο ΘΗΣΕΥΣ ΤΗΝ ΑΡΙΑΔΝΗΝ ΚΑΤΑΛΕΙΠΕΙ

Read the following passages and answer the comprehension questions:

οὕτως οὖν ὁ Θησεὺς τοὺς ἑταίρους σῴζει καὶ ἀπὸ τῆς Κρήτης ἀποφεύγει. πρῶτον μὲν οὖν πρὸς νῆσόν τινα, Νάξον ὀνόματι, πλέουσιν. ἐπεὶ δ' ἀφικνοῦνται, ἐκβαίνουσιν ἐκ τῆς νεὼς καὶ ἀναπαύονται. ἐπεὶ δὲ νὺξ γίγνεται, οἱ μὲν ἄλλοι καθεύδουσιν· αὐτὸς δὲ ὁ Θησεὺς οὐ καθεύδει ἀλλὰ ἥσυχος μένει· οὐ γὰρ φιλεῖ τὴν Ἀριάδνην οὐδὲ βούλεται φέρειν αὐτὴν πρὸς τὰς Ἀθήνας. δι' ὀλίγου οὖν, ἐπεὶ καθεύδει ἡ Ἀριάδνη,   5 ὁ Θησεὺς ἐγείρει τοὺς ἑταίρους καί, "σῑγᾶτε, ὦ φίλοι," φησίν· "καιρός ἐστιν ἀποπλεῖν. σπεύδετε οὖν πρὸς τὴν ναῦν." ἐπεὶ οὖν εἰς τὴν ναῦν ἀφικνοῦνται, ταχέως λύουσι τὰ πείσματα καὶ ἀποπλέουσιν· τὴν δ' Ἀριάδνην λείπουσιν ἐν τῇ νήσῳ.

[τινα, *a certain*   Νάξον, *Naxos* (an island in the middle of the Aegean Sea, north of Crete)   ἀναπαύονται, *they rest*   ἥσυχος, *quiet(ly)*   ἐγείρει, *wakes up*   τὰ πείσματα, *the cables*]

1. Where do Theseus and his comrades sail first?
2. What do they do first when they arrive there?
3. Why does Theseus not sleep?
4. What does Theseus say to his men when he awakens them?

ἐπεὶ δὲ ἡμέρᾱ γίγνεται, ἀνεγείρεται ἡ Ἀριάδνη καὶ ὁρᾷ ὅτι οὔτε ὁ Θησεὺς οὔτε   10 οἱ ἑταῖροι πάρεισιν. τρέχει οὖν πρὸς τὸν αἰγιαλὸν καὶ βλέπει πρὸς τὴν θάλατταν· τὴν δὲ ναῦν οὐχ ὁρᾷ. μάλα οὖν φοβεῖται καὶ βοᾷ· "ὦ Θησεῦ, ποῦ εἶ; ἆρά με καταλείπεις; ἐπάνελθε καὶ σῷζέ με."

[ἀνεγείρεται, *wakes up*   τὸν αἰγιαλὸν, *the shore*   τὴν θάλατταν, *the sea*   ἐπάνελθε, *come back!*]

5. What does Ariadne see when she wakes up?
6. What does she shout?

Exercise 60

Translate into Greek:

1. While (ἐν ᾧ) Ariadne is calling, the god (ὁ θεός) Dionysus (ὁ Διόνῡσος) looks from heaven (*use* ὁ οὐρανός) toward earth; then he sees Ariadne and loves her.
2. So he flies (πέτεται) from heaven to earth. And when he arrives at the island, he approaches her and says, "Ariadne, don't be afraid. For I, Dionysus, am here. I love you and want to save you. Come with me to heaven."
3. So Ariadne rejoices and goes to him.
4. Then Dionysus carries her up (ἀναφέρει) to heaven; and Ariadne becomes a goddess (θεά) and stays forever (εἰσαεί) in heaven.

Dionysus rescues Ariadne.

Classical Greek

Marriage

The following lines in praise of marriage are attributed to Hipponax (fragment 182), a sixth century B.C. writer of iambic verse, but are probably from a writer of New Comedy:

γάμος κράτιστός ἐστιν ἀνδρὶ σώφρονι

τρόπον γυναικὸς χρηστὸν ἕδνον λαμβάνειν·

αὕτη γὰρ ἡ προὶξ οἰκίαν σῴζει μόνη. . . .

συνεργὸν οὗτος ἀντὶ δεσποίνης ἔχει

εὔνουν, βεβαίαν εἰς ἅπαντα τὸν βίον.

[**γάμος**, *marriage* **κράτιστος**, *best* (translate, *The best marriage . . . is to take. . . .*) **ἀνδρὶ σώφρονι**, *for the prudent man* **τρόπον γυναικὸς χρηστὸν**, *the good character of a woman* **ἕδνον**, *(as) a wedding gift* **αὕτη . . . ἡ προὶξ**, *this dowry* **μόνη**, *alone* **συνεργὸν**, *helpmate* **οὗτος**, *this man* **ἀντὶ δεσποίνης**, *instead of a tyrant* **εὔνουν**, *well-disposed* **βεβαίαν**, *reliable* **εἰς ἅπαντα τὸν βίον**, *for all his life*]

New Testament Greek

Luke 13.10–16

We begin with an English translation of the first verses of the passage:

Jesus was teaching in a synagogue on the sabbath and cured a woman who had been bowed by an infirmity for eighteen years. He laid his hands on her and said, "Woman, you are freed from your infirmity," and immediately she stood up straight. But the ruler of the synagogue, objecting because Jesus had cured her on the sabbath day, said to the crowd:

"ἓξ ἡμέραι εἰσὶν ἐν αἷς δεῖ ἐργάζεσθαι· ἐν αὐταῖς οὖν ἐρχόμενοι θεραπεύεσθε καὶ μὴ τῇ ἡμέρᾳ τοῦ σαββάτου." ἀπεκρίθη δὲ αὐτῷ ὁ κύριος καὶ εἶπεν, "ὑποκρῖταί, ἕκαστος ὑμῶν τῷ σαββάτῳ οὐ λύει τὸν βοῦν αὐτοῦ ἢ τὸν ὄνον ἀπὸ τῆς φάτνης καὶ ἀπαγαγὼν ποτίζει;"

[**ἓξ**, *six* **ἐν αἷς**, *in which* **δεῖ ἐργάζεσθαι**, *(we) should work* **ἐρχόμενοι**, *coming* **θεραπεύεσθε**, *be healed!* **ἀπεκρίθη**, *answered* **ὁ κύριος**, *the Lord* **εἶπεν**, *said* **ὑποκρῖταί**, *hypocrites* **ἕκαστος**, *each* **ἢ**, *or* **τὸν ὄνον**, *his ass* **τῆς φάτνης**, *the stall* **ἀπαγαγὼν**, *having led (it) away* **ποτίζει**, *give (it) water*]

Jesus concludes: "And this woman, a daughter of Abraham, whom Satan bound for eighteen years, should she not have been freed from this bond on the sabbath day?"

7
Ο ΚΥΚΛΩΨ (α)

ὁ Ὀδυσσεὺς τὸν μοχλὸν ἐλαύνει εἰς τὸν ἕνα ὀφθαλμὸν τοῦ Κύκλωπος.

VOCABULARY

Verbs

αἱρέω, *I take*
Cf. αἴρω, *I lift*

ἐπαίρω [= ἐπι- + αἴρω], *I lift, raise*

ἐπαίρω ἐμαυτόν, *I get up*

εὑρίσκω, *I find*

ἰέναι, *to go*

κελεύω + acc. and infin., *I order, tell* (someone to do something)

παρασκευάζω, *I prepare*

Nouns

ὁ or **ἡ αἴξ** (τῶν αἰγῶν, τὰς αἶγας), *goat*

ἡ θάλαττα, *sea*
Declined like ἡ μέλιττα, *bee* (see Chapter 4, Grammar 3, page 41)

τὸ ὄνομα, *name*

ἡ πόλις, *city*

Interrogative Pronoun/Adjective

τίς, nom. pl., τίνες, interroga-tive pronoun, *who?* interroga-tive adjective, *which . . . ? what . . . ?*

Indefinite Pronoun/Adjective

τις, acc. sing., τινά, enclitic pronoun, *someone; some-thing; anyone; anything;* en-clitic adjective, *a certain; some; a, an*

Pronoun/Adjective

οὐδείς, οὐδεμία, οὐδέν, masc. acc. sing., οὐδένα, pronoun, *no one; nothing;* adjective, *no*

Reflexive Pronoun

ἐμαυτοῦ, σεαυτοῦ, ἑαυτοῦ, *of myself, of yourself, of him-, her-, itself*

Adjective

μέγιστος, -η, -ον, *very big, very large; very great; biggest, largest; greatest*
Cf. μέγας, μεγάλη, μέγα, *big, large; great*

94

Prepositions
περί + gen., *about, concerning;*
   + acc., *around*
Proper Names
ὁ Ἀγαμέμνων (τοῦ

Ἀγαμέμνονος), *Agamemnon*
οἱ Ἀχαιοί, *Achaeans; Greeks*
ὁ Ὀδυσσεύς (τοῦ Ὀδυσσέως,
   τῷ Ὀδυσσεῖ), *Odysseus*
ἡ Τροία, *Troy*

ἐπεὶ δὲ περαίνει τὸν μῦθον ἡ Μυρρίνη, ἡ Μέλιττα, "ὡς καλός ἐστιν
ὁ μῦθος," φησίν. "λέγε ἡμῖν ἄλλον τινὰ μῦθον, ὦ μῆτερ." ἡ δὲ
Μυρρίνη, "οὐδαμῶς," φησίν· "νῦν γὰρ ἐν νῷ ἔχω τὸ δεῖπνον
παρασκευάζειν." ἡ μὲν οὖν Μέλιττα δακρύει, ὁ δὲ Φίλιππος, "μὴ
δάκρυε, ὦ Μέλιττα," φησίν· "ἐγὼ γὰρ ἐθέλω σοι μῦθον καλὸν λέγειν   5
περὶ ἀνδρὸς πολυτρόπου, ὀνόματι Ὀδυσσέως.

[**περαίνει,** *finishes*   **δακρύει,** *cries*   **πολυτρόπου,** *much-traveled*]

"ὁ γὰρ Ὀδυσσεὺς ἐπὶ τὴν Τροίαν πλεῖ μετὰ τοῦ τ' Ἀγαμέμνονος
καὶ τῶν Ἀχαιῶν. δέκα μὲν οὖν ἔτη περὶ Τροίαν μάχονται, τέλος δὲ
τὴν πόλιν αἱροῦσιν. ὁ οὖν Ὀδυσσεὺς τοὺς ἑταίρους κελεύει εἰς τὰς
ναῦς εἰσβαίνειν, καὶ ἀπὸ τῆς Τροίας οἴκαδε ἀποπλέουσιν. ἐν δὲ τῇ   10
ὁδῷ πολλὰ καὶ δεινὰ πάσχουσιν. πολλάκις μὲν γὰρ χειμῶνας
ὑπέχουσιν, πολλάκις δὲ εἰς ἄλλους κινδύνους μεγίστους ἐμπίπτουσιν.

[**δέκα . . . ἔτη,** *for ten years*   **τέλος,** adv., *finally*   **χειμῶνας,** *storms*   **ὑπέχουσιν,**
they undergo   **κινδύνους,** *dangers*   **ἐμπίπτουσιν** (ἐν- + πίπτουσιν), *fall into*]

"πλέουσί ποτε εἰς νῆσόν τινα μῑκρᾱ́ν, ἐκβαίνουσι δὲ ἐκ τῶν νεῶν
καὶ δεῖπνον ποιοῦσιν ἐν τῷ αἰγιαλῷ. ἔστι δὲ ἐγγὺς ἄλλη νῆσος·
καπνὸν ὁρῶσι καὶ φθόγγον ἀκούουσι προβάτων τε καὶ αἰγῶν. τῇ οὖν   15
ὑστεραίᾳ ὁ Ὀδυσσεὺς τοὺς ἑταίρους κελεύει εἰς τὴν ναῦν εἰσβαίνειν·
βούλεται γὰρ εἰς τὴν νῆσον πλεῖν καὶ γιγνώσκειν τίνες ἐκεῖ οἰκοῦσιν.

[**ποτε,** *at one time*   **τῶν νεῶν,** *the ships*   **τῷ αἰγιαλῷ,** *the beach*   **ἐγγύς,** *nearby*
καπνόν, *smoke*   **φθόγγον,** *the sound*   **τῇ . . . ὑστεραίᾳ,** *on the next day*]

"δι' ὀλίγου οὖν ἀφικνοῦνται εἰς τὴν νῆσον. ἐγγὺς τῆς θαλάττης
ἄντρον μέγα ὁρῶσι καὶ πολλά τε πρόβατα καὶ πολλᾱ̀ς αἶγας. ὁ οὖν
Ὀδυσσεὺς τοῖς ἑταίροις, 'ὑμεῖς μέν,' φησίν, 'πρὸς τῇ νηΐ μένετε. ἐγὼ δὲ   20
ἐν νῷ ἔχω εἰς τὸ ἄντρον εἰσιέναι.' δώδεκα οὖν τῶν ἑταίρων κελεύει
ἑαυτῷ ἕπεσθαι. οἱ δὲ ἄλλοι πρὸς τῇ νηΐ μένουσιν. ἐπεὶ δὲ εἰς τὸ

ἄντρον ἀφικνοῦνται, οὐδένα ἄνθρωπον εὑρίσκουσιν ἔνδον. οἱ οὖν
ἑταῖροι, 'ὦ Ὀδυσσεῦ,' φασίν, 'οὐδεὶς ἄνθρωπός ἐστιν ἔνδον. ἔλαυνε
οὖν τά τε πρόβατα καὶ τὰς αἶγας πρὸς τὴν ναῦν καὶ ἀπόπλει ὡς   25
τάχιστα.'

[ἄντρον, *cave*   δώδεκα, *twelve*   ἑαυτῷ ἕπεσθαι, *to follow him*   ἔνδον, *inside*
ὡς τάχιστα, *as quickly as possible*]

   "ὁ δ' Ὀδυσσεὺς οὐκ ἐθέλει τοῦτο ποιεῖν· βούλεται γὰρ γιγνώσκειν
τίς ἐν τῷ ἄντρῳ οἰκεῖ. οἱ δὲ ἑταῖροι μάλα φοβοῦνται· ὅμως δὲ τῷ
Ὀδυσσεῖ πείθονται καὶ μένουσιν ἐν τῷ ἄντρῳ."

[τοῦτο, *this*   ὅμως, *nevertheless*]

WORD STUDY

*Identify the Greek stems in the English words below and give the meanings
of the English words:*

1. myth
2. mythology
3. polytheist
   (what does ὁ θεός mean?)
4. pantheist
   (what does πᾶν mean?)

5. monotheist (what does μόνος mean?)
6. atheist (what does ἀ- mean?)
7. theology

GRAMMAR

1. Substantive Use of Adjectives

   Adjectives, especially in the plural, are often used as substantives,
thus functioning as nouns, and can be translated by supplying words such
as "men," "women," or "things," depending on the gender of the adjective,
e.g.:

ἐν δὲ τῇ ὁδῷ **πολλοὺς** ὁρῶμεν.
*We see **many (men)** on the road.*

πρὸς τὴν κρήνην **πολλαὶ** ὑδρίᾱς φέρουσιν.
***Many (women)** are carrying water jars to the spring.*

ἐν δὲ τῇ ὁδῷ **πολλὰ** καὶ **δεινὰ** πάσχουσιν.
*On the journey they suffer **many terrible (things)**.*

Note also that Greek uses the conjunction καί here, while English does not
use a connective.

2. Nouns: Declensions

As you have seen, Greek nouns are divided into three large groups or *declensions*. You have already studied nouns of the *1st* or *alpha declension* (e.g., ἡ κρήνη, ἡ ὑδρίᾱ, ἡ μέλιττα, ἡ μάχαιρα, ὁ δεσπότης, ὁ Ξανθίᾱς, and ὁ νεᾱνίᾱς) and of the *2nd* or *omicron declension* (e.g., ὁ ἀγρός and τὸ δένδρον). Nouns of the 1st declension are feminine, except for those whose nominatives end in -ης or -ᾱς, such as ὁ δεσπότης, ὁ Ξανθίᾱς, and ὁ νεᾱνίᾱς; most nouns of the 2nd declension are masculine (e.g., ὁ ἀγρός), a few are feminine (e.g., ἡ ὁδός, ἡ νῆσος, and ἡ παρθένος), and some are neuter (e.g., τὸ δένδρον).

The *3rd declension* has many nouns of all three genders, and it is not easy to predict the gender from the ending of the nominative singular, as it is with 1st and 2nd declension nouns. Some 3rd declension nouns can be either masculine or feminine, such as ὁ or ἡ παῖς, *boy; girl; son; daughter; child*.

The stems of 3rd declension nouns end in a consonant or in vowels or diphthongs. Nouns of the 3rd declension can be recognized by the ending -ος or -ως in the genitive singular, e.g., παῖς, genitive, παιδός and πόλις, genitive, πόλεως. By removing the genitive singular ending, you find the stem, e.g., παιδ-.

To help you identify the declension to which a noun belongs and to help you determine the stem of 3rd declension nouns, we will henceforth list nouns in the vocabulary lists with their nominative and genitive forms, as follows:

1st Declension: ἡ κρήνη, τῆς κρήνης, *spring*
(stems in -ᾱ or -α) ἡ ὑδρίᾱ, τῆς ὑδρίᾱς, *water jar*
                    ἡ μέλιττα, τῆς μελίττης, *bee*
                    ἡ μάχαιρα, τῆς μαχαίρᾱς, *knife*
                    ὁ δεσπότης, τοῦ δεσπότου, *master*
                    ὁ νεᾱνίᾱς, τοῦ νεᾱνίου, *young man*

2nd Declension: ὁ ἀγρός, τοῦ ἀγροῦ, *field*
(stems in -o)   ἡ ὁδός, τῆς ὁδοῦ, *road; way; journey*
                    τὸ δένδρον, τοῦ δένδρου, *tree*

3rd Declension: ὁ or ἡ παῖς, τοῦ or τῆς παιδός, *boy; girl; son; daughter; child*
                    ἡ πόλις, τῆς πόλεως, *city*

3. 3rd Declension Consonant Stem Nouns: Velar and Dental Stems

The stems of many 3rd declension nouns end in consonants. You find the stem by dropping the -ος ending from the genitive singular. The 3rd declension endings shown in the chart of forms below are then added to the stem.

a. *Stems ending in a velar (γ, κ, χ)*

ὁ φύλαξ, τοῦ φύλακ-ος, *guard*

Cf. φυλάττω, *I guard*

Stem: φυλακ-, *guard*

	Singular		**Plural**	
Nom.	ὁ	φύλακ-ς > φύλαξ	οἱ	φύλακ-ες
Gen.	τοῦ	φύλακ-ος	τῶν	φυλάκ-ων
Dat.	τῷ	φύλακ-ι	τοῖς	φύλακ-σι(ν) > φύλαξι(ν)
Acc.	τὸν	φύλακ-α	τοὺς	φύλακ-ας
Voc.	ὦ	φύλακ-ς > φύλαξ	ὦ	φύλακ-ες

Note that the vocatives are the same as the nominatives. Note that in the nominative and vocative singular and the dative plural the κ of the stem and the ς/σ of the ending produce the combination of sounds represented by the letter ξ (see page xv). And note that, as is the case with most nouns, the accent is persistent; in the genitive plural the accent cannot stand on the third syllable from the end because the final syllable is long (see Chapter 3, Grammar 3, page 32).

ὁ or ἡ αἴξ, τοῦ or τῆς αἰγ-ός, *goat*

Stem: αἰγ-, *goat*

	Singular		**Plural**	
Nom.	ὁ	αἴγ-ς > αἴξ	οἱ	αἶγ-ες
Gen.	τοῦ	αἰγ-ός	τῶν	αἰγ-ῶν
Dat.	τῷ	αἰγ-ί	τοῖς	αἰγ-σί(ν) > αἰξί(ν)
Acc.	τὸν	αἶγ-α	τοὺς	αἶγ-ας
Voc.	ὦ	αἴγ-ς > αἴξ	ὦ	αἶγ-ες

Note that monosyllabic nouns of the 3rd declension usually have an accent on the final syllable of the genitive and dative cases, singular and plural. Note that the vocatives are the same as the nominatives. Note that in the nominative and vocative singular and the dative plural the γ and ς/σ produce the combination of sounds represented by the letter ξ. And note the circumflex accent over the diphthong of the stem when it is accented and followed by a short syllable (see Chapter 3, Grammar 3, page 32).

PRACTICE: Write the complete set of the forms of ὁ ὄνυξ, τοῦ ὄνυχος, *claw; nail* (note that χ and ς/σ produce the combination of sounds represented by the letter ξ).

b. *Stems ending in a dental (δ, θ, τ)*

ὁ or ἡ παῖς, τοῦ or τῆς παιδ-ός, *boy; girl; son; daughter; child*

Stem: παιδ-, *boy; girl; son; daughter; child*

	Singular		**Plural**	
Nom.	ὁ	παῖδ-ς > παῖς	οἱ	παῖδ-ες
Gen.	τοῦ	παιδ-ός	τῶν	παίδ-ων
Dat.	τῷ	παιδ-ί	τοῖς	παιδ-σί(ν) > παισί(ν)
Acc.	τὸν	παῖδ-α	τοὺς	παῖδ-ας
Voc.	ὦ	παῖδ > παῖ	ὦ	παῖδ-ες

Remember that all dental stops are lost before σ (see page xv); thus in the nominative singular and the dative plural of παῖς the δ is lost before the ς/σ of the endings. The vocative singular is the stem without the -δ (all stop consonants are lost in word-final position; the only consonants with which Greek words can end are ν, ρ, ς, or one of the double consonants ξ and ψ). Note that while monosyllabic nouns of the 3rd declension usually have an accent on the final syllable of the genitive and dative cases, singular and plural (see ὁ αἴξ on the opposite page), in this word the accent of the genitive plural is persistent and remains on the first syllable.

PRACTICE: Write the complete set of the forms of ἡ ἐλπίς, τῆς ἐλπίδος, *hope.*

The following is an example of a *neuter* dental-stem noun of the 3rd declension. Note the ways in which it is similar to and different from the masculine/feminine nouns above:

τὸ ὄνομα, τοῦ ὀνόματ-ος, *name*

Stem: ὀνοματ-, *name*

	Singular		**Plural**	
Nom.	τὸ	ὄνοματ > ὄνομα	τὰ	ὀνόματ-α
Gen.	τοῦ	ὀνόματ-ος	τῶν	ὀνομάτ-ων
Dat.	τῷ	ὀνόματ-ι	τοῖς	ὀνόματ-σι(ν) > ὀνόμασι(ν)
Acc.	τὸ	ὄνοματ > ὄνομα	τὰ	ὀνόματ-α
Voc.	ὦ	ὄνοματ > ὄνομα	ὦ	ὀνόματ-α

Remember that in neuter nouns the nominative, accusative, and vocative singular forms are identical, as are the corresponding plural forms, which end in ᾰ as do 2nd declension neuters. Third declension neuter nouns do not add ς to the stem in the nominative singular as do masculine and feminine velar and dental stem nouns. Instead, the τ of the stem is lost (see above), as it also is before the σ of the dative plural ending. The vocative singular is the stem without the -τ (cf. ὦ παῖ).

Exercise 7α

Locate the following 3rd declension nouns in the reading passage at the beginning of this chapter. Identify the case and number of each, and explain why that particular case is being used:

1. ἀνδρός
2. ὀνόματι
3. Ἀγαμέμνονος

4. χειμῶνας
5. αἰγῶν
6. αἶγας

Exercise 7β

The following 3rd declension nouns have been given in the vocabulary lists in Chapters 2–7, in the following order. Declensions of the nouns marked with asterisks have been given above; declensions of other types of 3rd declension nouns will be given in subsequent grammar sections. Give the meaning of each of the following:

ὁ βοῦς, τοῦ βοός
ὁ or ἡ παῖς, τοῦ or τῆς παιδός*
ὁ πατήρ, τοῦ πατρός
ὁ ἀνήρ, τοῦ ἀνδρός
ἡ γυνή, τῆς γυναικός
ἡ θυγάτηρ, τῆς θυγατρός
ἡ μήτηρ, τῆς μητρός
ὁ or ἡ κύων, τοῦ or τῆς κυνός
τὸ ὄρος, τοῦ ὄρους (< ὄρε-ος)

ὁ βασιλεύς, τοῦ βασιλέως
ἡ ναῦς, τῆς νεώς
ἡ νύξ, τῆς νυκτός
ὁ Αἰγεύς, τοῦ Αἰγέως
ὁ Θησεύς, τοῦ Θησέως
τὸ ὄνομα, τοῦ ὀνόματος*
ἡ πόλις, τῆς πόλεως
ὁ Ἀγαμέμνων, τοῦ Ἀγαμέμνονος
ὁ Ὀδυσσεύς, τοῦ Ὀδυσσέως

Using the information supplied in the charts and lists above, give the definite article to accompany each of the following 3rd declension nouns:

1. κυνί (2 ways)
2. πατράσι(ν)
3. ἄνδρα
4. Ὀδυσσεῖ
5. ὀνόματα
6. μητέρες
7. θυγατράσι(ν)
8. γυναῖκας
9. ἀνδρῶν
10. νυκτί

11. νύκτα
12. θυγατρί
13. πόλεσι(ν)
14. ἄνδρας
15. βόες
16. ναυσί(ν)
17. Ἀγαμέμνονι
18. κύνα (2 ways)
19. γυναιξί(ν)
20. παισί(ν) (2 ways)

4. Reflexive Pronouns

In Chapter 4 Myrrhine says to Dicaeopolis ἔπαιρε **σεαυτόν**, ὦ ἄνερ = *Lift yourself, husband!* or *Get up, husband!* Later ὁ Δικαιόπολις μόλις ἐπαίρει **ἑαυτόν**, *Dicaeopolis reluctantly lifts himself (= gets up).* The pronouns σεαυτόν, *yourself*, and ἑαυτόν, *himself*, are called *reflexive* since they are used to refer to or reflect the subject of the verb. Usually in English we use a word ending in -*self* to translate reflexive pronouns, but note the following example in lines 21–22 of the first story in this chapter: δώδεκα οὖν τῶν ἑταίρων κελεύει **ἑαυτῷ** ἕπεσθαι, *and so he orders twelve of his companions to follow* **him**.

Reflexive pronouns combine elements of the personal pronouns (see Chapter 5, Grammar 6, page 65) with the intensive adjective αὐτός (see Chapter 5, Grammar 9, page 68), thus σε, *you* + αὐτόν, *self* > σεαυτόν, *yourself*.

In the 1st and 2nd persons, the reflexive pronouns have masculine and feminine forms only; in the 3rd person there are neuter forms as well. There are no nominatives.

	1st Person		**2nd Person**	
	Masculine	**Feminine**	**Masculine**	**Feminine**
G.	ἐμαυτοῦ	ἐμαυτῆς	σεαυτοῦ	σεαυτῆς
D.	ἐμαυτῷ	ἐμαυτῇ	σεαυτῷ	σεαυτῇ
A.	ἐμαυτόν	ἐμαυτήν	σεαυτόν	σεαυτήν
G.	ἡμῶν αὐτῶν	ἡμῶν αὐτῶν	ὑμῶν αὐτῶν	ὑμῶν αὐτῶν
D.	ἡμῖν αὐτοῖς	ἡμῖν αὐταῖς	ὑμῖν αὐτοῖς	ὑμῖν αὐταῖς
A.	ἡμᾶς αὐτούς	ἡμᾶς αὐτάς	ὑμᾶς αὐτούς	ὑμᾶς αὐτάς

	3rd Person		
	Masculine	**Feminine**	**Neuter**
G.	ἑαυτοῦ	ἑαυτῆς	ἑαυτοῦ
D.	ἑαυτῷ	ἑαυτῇ	ἑαυτῷ
A.	ἑαυτόν	ἑαυτήν	ἑαυτό
G.	ἑαυτῶν	ἑαυτῶν	ἑαυτῶν
D.	ἑαυτοῖς	ἑαυταῖς	ἑαυτοῖς
A.	ἑαυτούς	ἑαυτάς	ἑαυτά

Translate each of the forms above, e.g., ἐμαυτοῦ, *of myself*, ἐμαυτῷ, *to/for myself*, ἐμαυτόν, *myself*.

Exercise 7γ

Read aloud and translate the following sentences:

1. ἐγὼ ἐμαυτὸν ἐπαίρω. τί σὺ σεαυτὸν οὐκ ἐπαίρεις;
2. ἡ παῖς ἑαυτὴν ἐπαίρει.
3. ἑαυτὸν ἐπαίρει.
4. ἡμᾶς αὐτοὺς ἐπαίρομεν.

5. σεαυτὴν ἐν τῷ κατόπτρῳ (*mirror*) ὁρᾷς.
6. ἆρα ὑμᾶς αὐτοὺς ἐν τῷ κατόπτρῳ ὁρᾶτε;

Exercise 7δ

Read aloud and translate (fill in appropriate reflexive pronouns where missing):

1. ὁ παῖς ἑαυτὸν ἐπαίρει καὶ πρὸς τὸν ἀγρὸν σπεύδει.
2. οἱ παῖδες _____ ἐπαίρουσι καὶ πρὸς τὸν ἀγρὸν σπεύδουσιν.
3. ἔπαιρε σεαυτήν, ὦ γύναι, καὶ ἐλθὲ δεῦρο.
4. ἐπαίρετε _____, ὦ γυναῖκες, καὶ ἔλθετε δεῦρο.
5. οὐκ ἐθέλω ἐμαυτὴν ἐπαίρειν· μάλα γὰρ κάμνω (*I am tired*).
6. οὐκ ἐθέλομεν _____ ἐπαίρειν· μάλα γὰρ κάμνομεν.
7. τίνι (*to whom*) λέγει ἡ παρθένος τὸν μῦθον; ἆρ' ἑαυτῇ λέγει;
8. ὁ πατὴρ τὴν θυγατέρα μεθ' ἑαυτοῦ καθίζει (*makes . . . sit down*).
9. οἱ πατέρες τὰς θυγατέρας μεθ' _____ καθίζουσιν.
10. ὁ παῖς τὸν τοῦ πατρὸς κύνα ὁρᾷ ἀλλ' οὐχ ὁρᾷ τὸν ἑαυτοῦ.
11. μὴ εἴσιτε εἰς τὸ ἄντρον, ὦ φίλοι· αὐτοὶ γὰρ ὑμᾶς αὐτοὺς εἰς μέγιστον κίνδῡνον ἄγετε.
12. βοήθει ἡμῖν, ὦ Ὀδυσσεῦ· οὐ γὰρ δῠνάμεθα (*we are able*) ἡμᾶς αὐτοὺς σῴζειν.

Homer

The earliest poems in Western literature (and according to some, the greatest) are the *Iliad* and the *Odyssey*. These are epics, that is to say, long narrative poems; each of the poems contains twenty-four books, the books varying in length from 450 to 900 lines. They tell stories about the age of the heroes, and both center upon the Trojan War.

The *Iliad* tells the story of the wrath of Achilles, the greatest of the Greek heroes who fought at Troy.

Homer

After besieging Troy for nine years, Achilles and Agamemnon, leader of the Greek host, quarrel at an assembly of the army. Agamemnon takes away Achilles' prize, a captive girl whom he loves. Thus insulted, Achilles refuses to fight any longer and stays by his ships, with disastrous consequences for both himself and the rest of the Greeks.

Without his help the Greeks suffer heavy losses and are driven back to their ships. Achilles still refuses to fight but is at last persuaded to allow his closest friend, Patroclus, to lead his men into battle. Only when Patroclus has been killed by Hector, the greatest of the Trojan heroes, does Achilles turn his anger from Agamemnon and fight against the Trojans. To avenge the death of Patroclus, he leads his men into battle, causing terrible carnage. He sweeps the Trojans back into the city and kills Hector in single combat before the walls of Troy, even knowing that with Hector's death his own death is imminent. He then ties the corpse of Hector behind his chariot and drags it in front of the walls of Troy before the eyes of Hector's father, Priam, and his mother and wife.

Achilles' anger does not cease until the aged Priam, alone and at night, makes his way through the Greek camp to Achilles' tent and begs him to return the body of Hector for burial. Achilles, obeying a command from Zeus, consents and allows a truce for his burial.

The *Odyssey* tells the story of the return of Odysseus from Troy to his home in Ithaca. The plot is more complex than that of the *Iliad*. It starts in Ithaca, where Penelope, Odysseus's wife, has been waiting for twenty years for her husband's return (Odysseus was fighting before Troy for ten years and spent another ten on the journey home). She is beset by suitors who are competing for her hand and the kingdom. Her son, Telemachus, sets out to look for his father, who, he believes, is still alive.

Odysseus, meanwhile, is held captive by a nymph, Calypso, on a far-off island. She is at last persuaded by the gods to let him go and helps him build a raft. He sails off, only to be wrecked on the island of Phaeacia. Here the king receives him kindly, and at a banquet given in his honor Odysseus recounts the adventures he has undergone since he left Troy. The Phaeacians load him with gifts and take him home to Ithaca, where they leave him sleeping on the shore. The second half of the *Odyssey* tells how he returned to his palace disguised as a beggar and with the help of Telemachus and a faithful servant slew the suitors and was reunited with Penelope.

The Greeks attributed both of these great poems to Homer. Scholars have shown that the poems are in fact the culmination of a long tradition of oral poetry, that is of poetry composed without the aid of writing. The tradition probably originated in the Bronze Age, and in every succeeding generation poets retold and embroidered the stories about the heroes. Finally, Homer composed these two great poems, which are on a far larger scale than oral poetry usually is, in an age when writing had just been reintroduced to Greece.

The internal evidence of the *Iliad* suggests that it was composed between 750 and 700 B.C. in Ionia. Modern scholars are not agreed on whether the *Odyssey* was composed by the same poet; there are considerable differences in style and tone between the two poems. Both poems show characteristics of oral poetry that make them very different from literary poetry. They were composed to be recited or sung aloud to the accompaniment of the lyre. The stories themselves, the recurrent themes, and a large proportion of the actual lines are traditional, but the structure of the poems, the clear and consistent characterization of the leading figures, and the atmosphere of each poem, tragic in the *Iliad,* romantic in the *Odyssey,* are the creation of a single poet.

Ο ΚΥΚΛΩΨ (β)

ὁ Ὀδυσσεὺς ἐκ τοῦ ἄντρου τοῦ Κύκλωπος ἐκφεύγει.

VOCABULARY

Verbs

ἀποκρίνομαι, *I answer*

βάλλω, *I throw; I put; I pelt; I hit, strike*

μέλλω + infin., *I am about* (to); *I am destined* (to); *I intend* (to)

ὁρμάω, active, transitive, *I set* X *in motion;* active, intransitive, *I start; I rush;* middle, intransitive, *I set myself in motion; I start; I rush; I hasten*

παύω, active, transitive, *I stop* X; middle, intransitive, *I stop doing* X; + gen., *I cease from* **παῦε**, *stop!*

Nouns

ὁ ξένος, τοῦ ξένου, *foreigner; stranger*

ὁ οἶνος, τοῦ οἴνου, *wine*

ὁ ὀφθαλμός, τοῦ ὀφθαλμοῦ, *eye*

τὸ πῦρ, τοῦ πυρός, *fire*

ὁ χειμών, τοῦ χειμῶνος, *storm; winter*

Adjectives

δύο, *two*

εἷς, μία, ἕν (acc. sing. masc., ἕνα), *one*

πᾶς, πᾶσα, πᾶν (nom. pl. masc., πάντες; gen. pl., πάντων; acc. pl. masc. πάντας; nom. and acc. pl. neuter, πάντα), *all; every; whole*

σώφρων, σῶφρον, *of sound mind; prudent; self-controlled*

Adverbs

ἐνθάδε, *here; hither; there; thither*

πόθεν; *from where? whence?*

πῶς; *how?*

Proper Names

ὁ Κύκλωψ, τοῦ Κύκλωπος, *Cyclops* (one-eyed monster)

"δι' ὀλίγου δὲ ψόφον μέγιστον ἀκούουσιν, καὶ εἰσέρχεται γίγᾱς φοβερός· εἷς γὰρ ὀφθαλμὸς ἐν μέσῳ τῷ μετώπῳ ἔνεστιν. ὅ τ' οὖν Ὀδυσσεὺς καὶ οἱ ἑταῖροι μάλα φοβοῦνται καὶ εἰς τὸν τοῦ ἄντρου

μυχὸν φεύγουσιν. ὁ δὲ γίγᾱς πρῶτον μὲν τὰ πρόβατα καὶ τὰς αἶγας εἰς
τὸ ἄντρον εἰσελαύνει, ἐπεὶ δὲ πάντα ἔνδον ἐστίν, λίθον μέγιστον αἴρει   5
καὶ εἰς τὴν τοῦ ἄντρου εἴσοδον βάλλει. ἐνταῦθα δὴ πρῶτον μὲν τὰς
αἶγας ἀμέλγει, ἔπειτα δὲ πῦρ κάει. οὕτω δὴ τόν τ' Ὀδυσσέᾱ καὶ τοὺς
ἑταίρους ὁρᾷ καί, 'ὦ ξένοι,' βοᾷ, 'τίνες ἐστὲ καὶ πόθεν πλεῖτε;'

[**ψόφον**, *noise*   **γίγᾱς φοβερός**, *a terrifying giant*   **μέσῳ τῷ μετώπῳ**, *the middle of
his forehead*   **τὸν τοῦ ἄντρου μυχόν**, *the far corner of the cave*   **τὴν ... εἴσοδον**, *the entrance*   **ἀμέλγει**, *milks*   **κάει**, *lights*]

"ὁ δ' Ὀδυσσεύς, 'ἡμεῖς Ἀχαιοί ἐσμεν,' φησίν, 'καὶ ἀπὸ τῆς Τροίᾱς
οἴκαδε πλέομεν. χειμὼν δὲ ἡμᾶς ἐνθάδε ἐλαύνει.'   10

"ὁ δὲ Κύκλωψ οὐδὲν ἀποκρίνεται ἀλλὰ ὁρμᾶται ἐπὶ τοὺς
Ἀχαιούς· τῶν ἑταίρων δὲ δύο ἁρπάζει καὶ κόπτει πρὸς τὴν γῆν· ὁ δὲ
ἐγκέφαλος ἐκρεῖ καὶ δεύει τὴν γῆν."

[**ἁρπάζει**, *he seizes*   **κόπτει**, *he strikes, bashes*   **πρὸς τὴν γῆν**, *onto the ground*   **ὁ
... ἐγκέφαλος ἐκρεῖ**, *their brains flow out*   **δεύει**, *wet*]

ἡ δὲ Μέλιττα, "παῦε, ὦ Φίλιππε," φησίν, "παῦε· δεινὸς γάρ ἐστιν ὁ
μῦθος. ἀλλ' εἰπέ μοι, πῶς ἐκφεύγει ὁ Ὀδυσσεύς; ἆρα πάντας τοὺς   15
ἑταίρους ἀποκτείνει ὁ Κύκλωψ;"

[**εἰπέ**, *tell*]

ὁ δὲ Φίλιππος, "οὐδαμῶς" φησίν· "οὐ πάντας ἀποκτείνει ὁ
Κύκλωψ. ὁ γὰρ Ὀδυσσεύς ἐστιν ἀνὴρ πολύμητις. πρῶτον μὲν οὖν
πολὺν οἶνον τῷ Κύκλωπι παρέχει, ὥστε δι' ὀλίγου μάλα μεθύει. ἐπεὶ
δὲ καθεύδει ὁ Κύκλωψ, μοχλὸν μέγιστον ὁ Ὀδυσσεὺς εὑρίσκει καὶ   20
τοὺς ἑταίρους κελεύει θερμαίνειν αὐτὸ ἐν τῷ πυρί. ἐπεὶ δὲ μέλλει
ἅψεσθαι ὁ μοχλός, ὁ Ὀδυσσεὺς αἴρει αὐτὸν ἐκ τοῦ πυρὸς καὶ
ἐλαύνει εἰς τὸν ἕνα ὀφθαλμὸν τοῦ Κύκλωπος. σίζει δὲ ὁ ὀφθαλμὸς
αὐτοῦ.

[**πολύμητις**, *cunning*   **μεθύει**, *is drunk*   **μοχλόν**, *stake*   **θερμαίνειν**, *to heat*
ἅψεσθαι, *to catch fire*   **σίζει**, *hisses*]

"ὁ δ' ἀναπηδᾷ καὶ δεινῶς κλάζει. ὁ δ' Ὀδυσσεὺς καὶ οἱ ἑταῖροι εἰς   25
τὸν τοῦ ἄντρου μυχὸν φεύγουσιν. ὁ δὲ Κύκλωψ οὐ δύναται αὐτοὺς
ὁρᾶν. τυφλὸς γάρ ἐστιν."

[ἀναπηδᾷ, *leaps up*   κλάζει, *shrieks*   οὐ δύναται, *is not able, cannot*   τυφλὸς, *blind*]

ἡ δὲ Μέλιττα, "ὡς σοφός ἐστιν ὁ Ὀδυσσεύς. ἀλλὰ πῶς ἐκφεύγουσιν ἐκ τοῦ ἄντρου;"

[σοφός, *clever*]

ὁ δὲ Φίλιππος, "τῇ ὑστεραίᾳ, ἐπεὶ πρῶτον ἀνατέλλει ὁ ἥλιος, ὁ 30
Κύκλωψ τὸν λίθον ἐξαίρει ἐκ τῆς τοῦ ἄντρου εἰσόδου καὶ πάντα τά
τε πρόβατα καὶ τὰς αἶγας ἐκπέμπει. ὁ οὖν Ὀδυσσεὺς τοὺς μὲν
ἑταίρους κρύπτει ὑπὸ τῶν προβάτων, ἑαυτὸν δὲ ὑπὸ κριοῦ μεγάλου.
οὕτω δὴ ὁ Κύκλωψ ἐκπέμπει τοὺς Ἀχαιοὺς μετὰ τῶν προβάτων καὶ
τοῦ κριοῦ, οἱ δὲ πάντα τὰ πρόβατα πρὸς τὴν ναῦν ἐλαύνουσι καὶ 35
ἀποπλέουσιν."

[τῇ ὑστεραίᾳ, *on the next day*   ἀνατέλλει, *rises*   ἐξαίρει, *lifts out*   κρύπτει, *hides*   ὑπὸ + gen., *under*   κριοῦ, *ram*]

WORD BUILDING

From the meanings of the words in boldface, deduce the meaning of the other word in each pair:

1. ἡ παρασκευή   παρασκευάζω
2. **τὸ ὄνομα**   ὀνομάζω
3. τὸ θαῦμα   θαυμάζω
4. **τὸ ἔργον** (*work*)   ἐργάζομαι

GRAMMAR

5. 3rd Declension Consonant Stem Nouns: Nasal Stems

Review the formation of the nominative and vocative singular and the dative plural of 3rd declension velar and dental stem nouns as presented in Grammar 3, pages 97–99 above.

Note what happens when the stem ends in the nasal consonant ν:

ὁ χειμών, τοῦ χειμῶν-ος, *storm; winter*:

Stem: χειμων-, *storm; winter*

	Singular		**Plural**	
Nom.	ὁ	χειμών	οἱ	χειμῶν-ες
Gen.	τοῦ	χειμῶν-ος	τῶν	χειμών-ων
Dat.	τῷ	χειμῶν-ι	τοῖς	χειμῶν-σι(ν) > χειμῶσι(ν)
Acc.	τὸν	χειμῶν-α	τοὺς	χειμῶν-ας
Voc.	ὦ	χειμών	ὦ	χειμῶνες

Sigma is not added to the stem in the nominative and vocative singular, and the ν is lost before the dative plural ending.

PRACTICE: Write the complete set of the forms of ὁ κύων, τοῦ κυνός, *dog*. Remember what happens with the accent in the genitive and dative, singular and plural, when the stem is monosyllabic. Voc. sing.: ὦ κύον.

6. 3rd Declension Consonant Stem Nouns: Labial and Liquid Stems

Some 3rd declension nouns have stems ending in labials (β, π, and φ), e.g., ὁ κλώψ, τοῦ κλωπ-ός, dative plural, τοῖς κλωψί(ν), *thief*, and in liquids (λ and ρ), e.g., ὁ ῥήτωρ, τοῦ ῥήτορ-ος, dative plural, τοῖς ῥήτορσι(ν), *orator*. See Forms, pages 288 and 289.

7. A 3rd Declension Adjective: σώφρων, σῶφρον, *of sound mind; prudent; self-controlled*

Stem: σωφρον-, *of sound mind; prudent; self-controlled*

The stem ends in -ον-, and ς is not added in the masculine/feminine nominative singular. The o is lengthened to ω in the masculine/feminine nominative singular, but not in the neuter. As with χειμών, the ν of the stem is lost before the σ of the dative plural ending.

	Singular		**Plural**	
	M. & F.	**N.**	**M. & F.**	**N.**
Nom.	σώφρων	σῶφρον	σώφρον-ες	σῶφρον-α
Gen.	σώφρον-ος	σώφρον-ος	σωφρόν-ων	σωφρόν-ων
Dat.	σώφρον-ι	σώφρον-ι	σώφρον-σι(ν)>	σώφρον-σι(ν) >
			σώφροσι(ν)	σώφροσι(ν)
Acc.	σώφρον-α	σῶφρον	σώφρον-ας	σῶφρον-α
Voc.	σῶφρον	σῶφρον	σώφρον-ες	σώφρον-α

Note that adjectives such as σώφρων, σῶφρον, which have only 3rd declension forms, have one set of forms for masculine and feminine and one for neuter, thus ὁ σώφρων ἄνθρωπος and ἡ σώφρων κόρη, but τὸ σῶφρον τέκνον (*child*).

Exercise 7ε

Translate into English (1–5) and into Greek (6–10):

1. ἐλθὲ δεῦρο, ὦ παῖ, καὶ τὰς αἶγας πρὸς τὸν ἀγρὸν ἔλαυνε.
2. οἴκαδε σπεύδετε, ὦ δοῦλοι, καὶ σῖτον ταῖς αἰξὶ παρέχετε.
3. κέλευε τοὺς φύλακας τοῖς παισὶ βοηθεῖν.
4. ἆρ' οὐ τὸν χειμῶνα φοβεῖσθε, ὦ φίλοι;
5. ὁ αὐτουργὸς τοῖς κυσὶν ἡγεῖται πρὸς τὸν ἀγρόν.
6. We are leading the goats up the road.
7. The boys are not willing to obey the guards.
8. The guards want to help the boys.
9. The prudent girls fear the storm.
10. We wish to tell the names of the girls to the boy.

8. The Interrogative Pronoun and Adjective

When the Cyclops asks Odysseus and his men τίνες ἐστὲ καὶ πόθεν πλεῖτε; he uses a form of the interrogative pronoun τίς; τί; *who? what?* The same word may be used as an interrogative adjective, e.g.:

εἰς **τίνα** νῆσον πλέομεν;
To **what** island are we sailing?

This pronoun/adjective has 3rd declension endings, and its masculine and feminine forms are the same. It always receives an acute accent on the first syllable (the acute on τίς and τί does not change to grave when another word follows). Its forms are as follows (note in particular the dative plural):

Stems: τιν-/τι

	Singular		**Plural**	
	M. & F.	**N.**	**M. & F.**	**N.**
Nom.	τίς	τί	τίν-ες	τίν-α
Gen.	τίν-ος	τίν-ος	τίν-ων	τίν-ων
Dat.	τίν-ι	τίν-ι	τίν-σι(ν) > τίσι(ν)	τίν-σι(ν) > τίσι(ν)
Acc.	τίν-α	τί	τίν-ας	τίν-α

Locate two occurrences of the interrogative pronoun in the reading passage 7α at the beginning of this chapter.

Remember that τί may mean either *what?* or *why?*

9. The Indefinite Pronoun and Adjective

In the sentence πλέουσί ποτε εἰς νῆσόν **τινα** μῑκρᾱ́ν, the word τινα is an indefinite adjective meaning *a certain, some,* or simply *a, an.* This word may also be used as an indefinite pronoun meaning *someone, something, anyone, anything,* e.g.:

ἆρ' ὁρᾷς **τινα** ἐν τῷ ἄντρῳ;
Do you see anyone *in the cave?*

In all of its forms this word is spelled the same as the interrogative pronoun τίς given above, but it is enclitic (see Enclitics and Proclitics, pages 285–286).

Locate two occurrences of the indefinite adjective in the first two paragraphs of the first reading passage in Chapter 6. Explain their agreement with the nouns they modify and explain the accents.

Exercise 7ζ

Read aloud and translate. Identify any interrogative pronouns or adjectives and any indefinite pronouns or adjectives.

1. τί ποιοῦσιν οἱ ἄνδρες;
2. ὁ ἀνὴρ μῦθόν τινα τῇ παιδὶ λέγει.
3. παῖδές τινες τοὺς κύνας εἰς τοὺς ἀγροὺς εἰσάγουσιν.
4. βούλομαι γιγνώσκειν τίς ἐν τῷ ἄντρῳ οἰκεῖ.
5. τίνα μῦθον βούλεσθε ἀκούειν, ὦ παῖδες;
6. μῦθόν τινα βουλόμεθα ἀκούειν περὶ γίγαντός τινος.
7. τίσιν ἡγεῖσθε πρὸς τὸν ἀγρόν, ὦ παῖδες;
8. ξένοις τισὶν ἡγούμεθα, ὦ πάτερ.
9. τίνος πρόβατα τοσοῦτον ψόφον ποιεῖ;
10. τίνι μέλλεις παρέχειν τὸ ἄροτρον;

Exercise 7η

Read aloud and translate:

1. τίς ἐν τῷ ἄντρῳ οἰκεῖ; γίγᾱς τις φοβερὸς ἐν τῷ ἄντρῳ οἰκεῖ.
2. τίνα ἐν τῇ οἰκίᾳ ὁρᾷς; γυναῖκά τινα ἐν τῇ οἰκίᾳ ὁρῶ.
3. τίσιν εἰς τὴν πόλιν ἡγεῖ; δούλοις τισὶν εἰς τὴν πόλιν ἡγοῦμαι.
4. τίνος ἄροτρον πρὸς τὸν ἀγρὸν φέρεις; τὸ φίλου τινὸς ἄροτρον φέρω.
5. τίνι ἐστὶν οὗτος (*this*) ὁ κύων; ἔστι τῷ ἐμῷ πατρί.

Ο ΤΟΥ ΘΗΣΕΩΣ ΠΑΤΗΡ
ΑΠΟΘΝΗΙΣΚΕΙ

Read the following passages and answer the comprehension questions:

The story of Theseus, concluded. This part of the story begins with a flashback to the time when Theseus left Athens to sail to Crete with the victims to be fed to the Minotaur.

ἐπεὶ δὲ ὁ Θησεὺς πρὸς τὴν Κρήτην μέλλει ἀποπλεῖν, ὁ πατὴρ αὐτῷ λέγει· "ἐγὼ μάλα φοβοῦμαι ὑπὲρ σοῦ, ὦ παῖ· ὅμως δὲ ἴθι εἰς τὴν Κρήτην καὶ τόν τε Μῑνώταυρον ἀπόκτεινε καὶ σῷζε τοὺς ἑταίρους· ἔπειτα δὲ οἴκαδε σπεῦδε. ἐγὼ δέ, ἕως ἂν ἀπῇς, καθ' ἡμέραν ἀναβήσομαι ἐπὶ ἄκρᾱν τὴν ἀκτήν, βουλόμενος ὁρᾶν τὴν σὴν ναῦν. ἀλλ' ἄκουέ μου· ἡ γὰρ ναῦς ἔχει τὰ ἱστία μέλανα. σὺ δέ, ἐὰν τόν τε   5 Μῑνώταυρον ἀποκτείνῃς καὶ τοὺς ἑταίρους σώσῃς, οἴκαδε σπεῦδε, καὶ ἐπειδὰν ταῖς Ἀθήναις προσχωρῇς, στέλλε μὲν τὰ μέλανα ἱστία, αἶρε δὲ τὰ ἱστία λευκά. οὕτω γὰρ γνώσομαι ὅτι σῶοί ἐστε."

[ὑπὲρ, *on behalf of, for*   ὅμως, *nevertheless*   ἕως ἂν ἀπῇς, *as long as you are away* καθ' ἡμέρᾱν, *every day*   ἀναβήσομαι, *I will go up*   ἐπί + acc., *onto*   ἄκρᾱν τὴν ἀκτήν, *the top of the promontory*   βουλόμενος, *wishing*   τὰ ἱστία μέλανα, *sails (that are) black*   ἐᾱν, *if*   ἀποκτείνῃς, *you kill*   σώσῃς, *you save*   ἐπειδὰν ... προσχωρῇς, *when you are approaching*   στέλλε, *take down*   λευκά, *white* γνώσομαι, *I will learn*   σῶοί, *safe*]

1. Where does Aegeus say he will go every day while Theseus is away?
2. What will he watch for?
3. What does Aegeus tell Theseus to do with the sails of his ship on the return voyage?

ὁ οὖν Θησεὺς λέγει ὅτι τῷ πατρὶ μέλλει πείθεσθαι καὶ πρὸς τὴν Κρήτην ἀποπλεῖ. ὁ δ' Αἰγεὺς καθ' ἡμέρᾱν ἐπὶ ἄκρᾱν τὴν ἀκτὴν ἀναβαίνει καὶ πρὸς τὴν   10 θάλατταν βλέπει.

4. What does Theseus promise Aegeus?
5. What does Aegeus do in Theseus' absence?

ἐπεὶ δὲ ὁ Θησεὺς τὴν Ἀριάδνην ἐν τῇ Νάξῳ λείπει καὶ οἴκαδε σπεύδει, ἐπιλανθάνεται τῶν τοῦ πατρὸς λόγων, καὶ οὐ στέλλει τὰ μέλανα ἱστία. ὁ οὖν Αἰγεὺς τὴν μὲν ναῦν γιγνώσκει, ὁρᾷ δὲ ὅτι ἔχει τὰ μέλανα ἱστία. μάλιστα οὖν φοβεῖται ὑπὲρ τοῦ Θησέως. μέγα μὲν βοᾷ, ῥίπτει δὲ ἑαυτὸν ἀπὸ τῆς ἀκτῆς εἰς τὴν   15 θάλατταν καὶ οὕτως ἀποθνήσκει. διὰ τοῦτο οὖν τῇ θαλάττῃ τὸ ὄνομά ἐστιν Αἰγαῖος πόντος.

[τῇ Νάξῳ, *Naxos* (an island in the middle of the Aegean Sea, north of Crete) ἐπιλανθάνεται τῶν ... λόγων, *he forgets the words*   μέγα, *loudly*   ῥίπτει, *he throws*   ἀποθνήσκει, *he dies*   διὰ τοῦτο, *for this reason*   πόντος, *sea*]

6.   What does Theseus forget to do after abandoning Ariadne?
7.   What does Aegeus see when he spots Theseus' ship?
8.   What is his emotional reaction?
9.   What three things does he do?
10. How did the Aegean Sea get its name?

Exercise 7θ

Translate into Greek:

1.   When Theseus arrives at Athens, he learns that his father is dead (τέθνηκεν).
2.   His mother says to the young man (*use* ὁ νεᾱνίᾱς), "You are to blame; for you always forget (*use* ἐπιλανθάνομαι + *gen.*) your father's words."
3.   Theseus is very sad (*use* λῡπέομαι) and says, "I myself am to blame; and so I intend to flee from home."
4.   But his mother tells (orders) him not (μή) to go away (ἀπιέναι).
5.   Soon he becomes king, and all the Athenians love and honor him.

Classical Greek

Sophocles

King Oedipus, old, blind, and in exile, addresses Theseus, son of Aegeus and king of Athens, who has offered him protection (Sophocles, *Oedipus at Colonus*, 607–609):

ὦ φίλτατ' Αἰγέως παῖ, μόνοις οὐ γίγνεται

θεοῖσι γῆρας οὐδὲ κατθανεῖν ποτε,

τὰ δ' ἄλλα συγχεῖ πάνθ' ὁ παγκρατὴς χρόνος.

[φίλτατ(ε), *dearest*   μόνοις, *alone*   θεοῖσι = θεοῖς   γῆρας, *old age*   οὐδέ . . . ποτε, *and never*   κατθανεῖν, *to die*   συγχεῖ, *destroys* (lit., *pours together, confounds*)   πάνθ' = πάντα, *all things* (take with ἄλλα)   παγκρατὴς, *all-powerful*]

Greek Wisdom

γνῶθι σεαυτόν.   Θαλῆς (of Miletus)

8

ΠΡΟΣ ΤΟ ΑΣΤΥ (α)

αἱ γυναῖκες διαλεγόμεναι ἀλλήλαις πέπλον ὑφαίνουσιν.

VOCABULARY

Verbs

διαλέγομαι + dat., *I talk to, converse with*

ἕπομαι + dat., *I follow*
Cf. ἡγέομαι + dat., *I lead*

ἐργάζομαι, *I work; I accomplish*

θεάομαι, *I see, watch, look at*

Nouns

τὸ ἄστυ, τοῦ ἄστεως, *city*

τὸ ἔργον, τοῦ ἔργου, *work; deed*

ἡ ἑσπέρᾱ, τῆς ἑσπέρᾱς, *evening*

ὁ θεός, τοῦ θεοῦ, *god*

ἡ θύρᾱ, τῆς θύρᾱς, *door*

ὁ ποιητής, τοῦ ποιητοῦ, *poet*

Adverbs

ἐκεῖσε, *to that place, thither*

εὖ, *well*

οἴκοι, note the accent, *at home*

ὥσπερ, note the accent, *just as*

Conjunctions

ὅμως, *nevertheless*

Expressions

ἐν ᾧ, *while*

εὖ γε, *good! well done!*

Proper Name

ὁ Διόνῡσος, τοῦ Διονῡσου, *Dionysus*

ἐν δὲ τούτῳ ὅ τε Δικαιόπολις καὶ ὁ δοῦλος οὐ παύονται ἐργαζόμενοι. ἐπεὶ δὲ ἑσπέρᾱ γίγνεται, ὁ μὲν Δικαιόπολις τοὺς βοῦς λύει καὶ οἴκαδε ἐλαύνει, ὁ δὲ δοῦλος τῷ δεσπότῃ ἑπόμενος τὸ ἄροτρον φέρει. ἐπεὶ δὲ τῇ οἰκίᾳ προσχωροῦσιν, τὸν πάππον ὁρῶσιν

112

ἐν τῷ κήπῳ ἐργαζόμενον. ὁ οὖν Δικαιόπολις καλεῖ αὐτὸν καί,　5
"ἑσπέρᾱ ἤδη γίγνεται, ὦ πάππα," φησίν. "παῦε οὖν ἐργαζόμενος καὶ
ἡσύχαζε." ὁ δέ, "εὖ λέγεις, ὦ παῖ," φησίν· "μάλα γὰρ κάμνω."
παύεται οὖν ἐργαζόμενος καὶ πρὸς τὴν οἰκίᾱν σπεύδει.

[ἐν . . . τούτῳ, meanwhile　　τῷ κήπῳ, the garden　　ἡσύχαζε, rest!　κάμνω, I am tired]

οἴκοι δὲ ἥ τε Μυρρίνη καὶ ἡ θυγάτηρ πέπλον ὑφαίνουσιν· ἐν ᾧ δὲ
ὑφαίνουσιν, διαλέγονται ἀλλήλαις. δι' ὀλίγου δὲ ἡ μήτηρ τόν τε　10
ἄνδρα καὶ τὸν δοῦλον καὶ τὸν πάππον ὁρᾷ εἰς τὴν αὐλὴν
ἀφικνουμένους. παύεται οὖν ἐργαζομένη καὶ σπεύδει πρὸς τὴν
θύρᾱν καί, "χαῖρε, ὦ ἄνερ," φησίν, "καὶ ἄκουε. ὅ τε γὰρ Φίλιππος καὶ
ὁ Ἄργος λύκον ἀπεκτόνᾱσιν." ὁ δέ, "ἆρα τὰ ἀληθῆ λέγεις; εἰπέ μοι
τί ἐγένετο." ἡ μὲν οὖν Μυρρίνη πάντα ἐξηγεῖται, ὁ δὲ θαυμάζει καὶ　15
λέγει· "εὖ γε· ἀνδρεῖός ἐστιν ὁ παῖς καὶ ἰσχῡρός. ἀλλ' εἰπέ μοι, ποῦ
ἐστιν; βουλόμενος γὰρ τῑμᾶν τὸν λυκοκτόνον μέλλω ζητεῖν αὐτόν."
καὶ ἐν νῷ ἔχει ζητεῖν τὸν παῖδα. ἡ δὲ Μυρρίνη, "ἀλλὰ μένε, ὦ φίλε,"
φησίν, "καὶ αὖθις ἄκουε. ἄγγελος γὰρ ἥκει ἀπὸ τοῦ ἄστεως· λέγει δὲ
ὅτι οἱ Ἀθηναῖοι τὰ Διονύσια ποιοῦνται. ἆρα ἐθέλεις ἐμέ τε καὶ τοὺς　20
παῖδας πρὸς τὴν ἑορτὴν ἄγειν;" ὁ δέ, "ἀλλ' οὐ δυνατόν ἐστιν, ὦ
γύναι· ἀνάγκη γάρ ἐστιν ἐργάζεσθαι. ὁ γὰρ λῑμὸς τῷ ἀργῷ ἀνδρὶ
ἕπεται, ὥσπερ λέγει ὁ ποιητής· ἐξ ἔργων ἄνδρες 'πολύμηλοί τ' ἀφνειοί
τε' γίγνονται."

[πέπλον, cloth, robe　　ὑφαίνουσιν, are weaving　　ἀλλήλαις, with one another
τὴν αὐλὴν, the courtyard　　ἀπεκτόνᾱσιν, have killed　　τὰ ἀληθῆ, the true things,
the truth　　εἰπέ, tell　　ἐγένετο, happened　　ἐξηγεῖται, relates　　τὸν λυκοκτόνον,
the wolf-slayer　　ἀνάγκη . . . ἐστιν, it is necessary　　ὁ . . . λῑμὸς, hunger
πολύμηλοί τ' ἀφνειοί τε, rich in flocks and wealthy　(Hesiod, Works and Days 308)]

ἡ δὲ Μυρρίνη ἀποκρῑναμένη, "ἀλλ' ὅμως," φησίν, "ἡμᾶς ἐκεῖσε　25
ἄγε, ὦ φίλε ἄνερ. σπανίως γὰρ πορευόμεθα πρὸς τὸ ἄστυ· καὶ πάντες
δὴ ἔρχονται." ὁ δέ, "ἀλλ' ἀδύνατον· ἀργὸς γάρ ἐστιν ὁ δοῦλος· ὅταν
γὰρ ἀπῶ, παύεται ἐργαζόμενος."

[ἀποκρῑναμένη, replying　　σπανίως, rarely　　ἀδύνατον, (it's) impossible
ὅταν . . . ἀπῶ, whenever I'm away]

ἡ δὲ Μέλιττα, "ἀλλὰ μὴ χαλεπὸς ἴσθι, ὦ πάτερ, ἀλλὰ πείθου ἡμῖν.
ἆρ' οὐκ ἐθέλεις καὶ σὺ τὴν ἑορτὴν θεᾶσθαι καὶ τὸν θεὸν τῑμᾶν; ὁ   30
γὰρ Διόνῡσος σῴζει ἡμῖν τὰς ἀμπέλους. καὶ τὸν Φίλιππον—ἆρ' οὐ
βούλει τῑμᾶν τὸν παῖδα, διότι τὸν λύκον ἀπέκτονεν; βούλεται γὰρ
τούς τε ἀγῶνας θεᾶσθαι καὶ τοὺς χοροὺς καὶ τὰ δρᾱματα. ἄγε οὖν
ἡμᾶς πάντας πρὸς τὸ ἄστυ."

[τὰς ἀμπέλους, *the vines*   διότι, *because*   τοὺς ... ἀγῶνας, *the contests*   τὰ
δρᾱματα, *the plays*]

ὁ δὲ Δικαιόπολις, "ἔστω οὖν, ἐπεὶ οὕτω βούλεσθε. ἀλλὰ λέγω ὑμῖν   35
ὅτι ὁ λῑμὸς ἕπεσθαι ἡμῖν μέλλει—ἀλλ' οὐκ αἴτιος ἔγωγε."

[ἔστω, *let it be! very well!*   ἐπεί, here, *since*   ἔγωγε, an emphatic ἐγώ]

WORD STUDY

*Identify the Greek stems in the English words below and give the meanings
of the English words:*

1. politics
2. politburo
3. metropolis (*metr-* is not from μέτρον)
4. necropolis (ὁ νεκρός = *corpse*)
5. cosmopolitan

GRAMMAR

1. Participles: "Present" or Progressive: Middle Voice

In addition to the indicative mood, the imperative, and the infinitive,
which you have studied so far in this course, verbs have adjectival forms
known as *participles* (verbal adjectives). These may be used in several
ways:

a. Participles may describe some circumstance that accompanies the
main action of the sentence, e.g.:

ὁ δοῦλος τῷ δεσπότῃ **ἑπόμενος** τὸ ἄροτρον φέρει.
*The slave, **following** his master, carries the plow.*

τὸν πάππον ὁρῶσιν ἐν τῷ κήπῳ **ἐργαζόμενον**.
*They see the grandfather (**as/while he is**) **working** in the garden.*

This use is called *circumstantial*; the participle is in the predicate position (see Chapter 5, Grammar 7b, page 66), and it agrees with the
noun it modifies in gender, number, and case.

b. Participles in the attributive position (see Chapter 5, Grammar 7a, page 66) may simply modify nouns or pronouns like any other adjective, agreeing in gender, number, and case. When so used, they are called *attributive*, e.g.:

οἱ αὐτουργοὶ οἱ ἐν τῷ ἀγρῷ **ἐργαζόμενοι** μάλα κάμνουσιν.
*The farmers **working** in the field are very tired.*

c. Participles may be used to complete the meaning of a verb, e.g.:

ὁ δοῦλος οὐ παύεται **ἐργαζόμενος**.
*The slave does not stop **working**.*

This use is called *supplementary*, since the participle fills out or completes the meaning of the verb. The participle agrees with the stated or implied subject of the verb in gender, number, and case.

"Present" participles do not refer to time as such but describe the action as in process, ongoing, or progressive.

The sentences above contain participles of deponent verbs, which have their forms in the middle voice. The following charts give the full sets of forms of *present/progressive middle participles*. Each form has a stem, a thematic vowel (o), the suffix -μεν-, and an ending. The endings, which indicate gender, number, and case, are the same as those of 1st and 2nd declension adjectives such as καλός, -ή, -όν (see page 48).

λῡ-ό-μεν-ος

	Masculine	**Feminine**	**Neuter**
Nom.	λῡόμενος	λῡομένη	λῡόμενον
Gen.	λῡομένου	λῡομένης	λῡομένου
Dat.	λῡομένῳ	λῡομένη	λῡομένῳ
Acc.	λῡόμενον	λῡομένην	λῡόμενον
Voc.	λῡόμενε	λῡομένη	λῡόμενον
Nom., Voc.	λῡόμενοι	λῡόμεναι	λῡόμενα
Gen.	λῡομένων	λῡομένων	λῡομένων
Dat.	λῡομένοις	λῡομέναις	λῡομένοις
Acc.	λῡομένους	λῡομένᾱς	λῡόμενα

Recite all the forms of the present participle of ἕπομαι.

φιλε-ό-μεν-ος > φιλούμενος

Nom.	φιλούμενος	φιλουμένη	φιλούμενον
Gen.	φιλουμένου	φιλουμένης	φιλουμένου
Dat.	φιλουμένῳ	φιλουμένη	φιλουμένῳ
Acc.	φιλούμενον	φιλουμένην	φιλούμενον
Voc.	φιλούμενε	φιλουμένη	φιλούμενον

Nom., Voc.	φιλούμενοι	φιλούμεναι	φιλούμενα
Gen.	φιλουμένων	φιλουμένων	φιλουμένων
Dat.	φιλουμένοις	φιλουμέναις	φιλουμένοις
Acc.	φιλουμένους	φιλουμένᾱς	φιλούμενα

τῑμα-ό-μεν-ος > τῑμώμενος

| **Nom.** | τῑμώμενος | τῑμωμένη | τῑμώμενον |
| | etc. | | |

When the accent is on the second of two vowels that contract, the diphthong that results from contraction receives an acute accent, thus φιλε-ό-μενος > φιλούμενος (see Chapter 6, Grammar 3, page 78).

Recite all the forms of the present participle of ἡγέομαι and all the forms of τῑμώμενος.

Exercise 8α

Fill in the present participles on the three Verb Charts on which you entered forms for Exercise 6β. Keep these charts for reference.

Exercise 8β

Read aloud and translate the following sentences. Identify and explain the gender, number, and case of each participle:

1. αἱ γυναῖκες παύονται ἐργαζόμεναι.
2. ὁ Φίλιππος τὸν πατέρα ὁρᾷ εἰς τὴν οἰκίᾱν ἀφικνούμενον.
3. βουλόμενοι τὴν ἑορτὴν θεᾶσθαι, πρὸς τὸ ἄστυ σπεύδομεν.
4. ἆρ' ὁρᾶτε τοὺς παῖδας ταῖς καλαῖς παρθένοις ἑπομένους;
5. αἱ παρθένοι μάλα φοβούμεναι ὡς τάχιστα (*as quickly as possible*) οἴκαδε τρέχουσιν.
6. ἆρ' ἀκούεις τῶν γυναικῶν ἐν τῇ οἰκίᾳ ἀλλήλαις διαλεγομένων;
7. οἱ παῖδες τῷ πατρὶ ἕπονται πρὸς τὸ ἄστυ πορευομένῳ.
8. ἡ κύων τὸν λύκον φοβουμένη ἀποφεύγει.
9. ἡ κύων ἐπὶ τὸν λύκον ὁρμωμένη ἀγρίως ὑλακτεῖ (*barks*).
10. ὁ αὐτουργὸς τὰ πρόβατα εὑρίσκει ἐν τοῖς ὄρεσι πλανώμενα (*wandering*).

Exercise 8γ

Translate into Greek:

1. Do you see the boys fighting in the road?
2. Dicaeopolis stops working and drives the oxen home.
3. Stop following me and go away (**ἄπελθε**)!
4. Obeying Myrrhine, Melissa stays at home.
5. Bravely leading his comrades, Theseus escapes out of the labyrinth.
6. The men (**οἱ ἄνδρες**) rejoice, journeying to the island.

Athens: A Historical Outline

1. The Bronze Age

Athens grew around the Acropolis, the rocky hill that rises precipitously in the middle of the later city. Archaeologists have shown that in the Bronze Age the Acropolis was fortified and was crowned by a palace, which was no doubt the administrative center of the surrounding district, like the palaces at Mycenae and Pylos. Tradition says that Theseus united Attica in the generation before the Trojan War, but in the *Iliad* there is scant mention of Athenian heroes, and this suggests that Athens was not an important center in the Bronze Age.

2. The Dark Age

Bronze Age civilization collapsed soon after the end of the Trojan War, about 1200 B.C. In the troubles that ensued, the so-called Dorian invasions, Athens, according to tradition, was the only city not sacked. In this period Athens grew in size, and we are told that the emigration (ca. 1050 B.C.) that peopled the islands and coast of Asia Minor with Greeks was largely from Athens, which later claimed to be the mother city of all Ionian settlements.

3. The Renaissance of Greece (ca. 850 B.C.)

As Greece slowly recovered from the Dark Age, population increased, and other states sent out colonies that peopled much of the Mediterranean coast from southern France to the Black Sea (750–500 B.C.). Athens played no part in this movement and seems not to have experienced those problems that led to emigration from other parts of Greece.

The Acropolis of Athens

4. The Reforms of Solon

Monarchy had been succeeded by the rule of the nobles, who oppressed the farmers until revolution threatened. In this crisis the Athenians chose an arbitrator named Solon (chief archon in 594/593 B.C., but his reforms may date to twenty years later), who worked out a compromise between the conflicting interests of the nobles and farmers. Solon was not only a statesman but a poet, and in a surviving fragment (5) of his poetry he defends his settlement:

To the people I gave as much power as was sufficient,
Neither taking from their honor nor giving them excess;
As for those who held power and were envied for their wealth,
I saw that they too should have nothing improper.
I stood there casting my sturdy shield over both sides
And allowed neither to conquer unjustly.

His settlement included important economic reforms, which gave the farmer a new start, and constitutional reforms, which paved the way for the later democracy. It was he who divided the citizens into four classes according to property qualifications and gave appropriate rights and functions to each; in this way, wealth, not birth, became the criterion for political privilege, and the aristocratic monopoly of power was weakened.

5. Tyranny—Pisistratus

Solon's settlement pleased neither side, and within half a generation, a tyrant, Pisistratus, seized power and ruled off and on for 33 years (561–528 B.C.). Under his rule Athens flourished; the economy improved, the city was adorned with public buildings, and Athens became a greater power in the Greek world. His son, Hippias, succeeded him but was driven out in 510 B.C.

6. Cleisthenes and Democracy

Three years later Cleisthenes put through reforms that made Athens a democracy, in which the Assembly of all male citizens was sovereign. The infant democracy immediately faced a crisis. Hippias had taken refuge with the King of Persia, whose empire now reached the shores of the Aegean and included the Greek cities of Ionia. In 499 the Ionians revolted and asked the mainland cities for help. Athens sent a force, which was highly successful for a short time, but the revolt was finally crushed in 494 B.C.

7. The Persian Wars

In 490 B.C. the Persian king Darius sent an expedition by sea to conquer and punish Athens. It landed on the east coast of Attica at Marathon. After an anxious debate, the Athenians sent their army to meet the Persians and won a spectacular victory, driving the Persians back to their ships. Athens and Plataea defeated this Persian expedition; it was a day the Athenians never forgot, and it filled the new democracy with confidence. (See map, page 230.)

Ten years later Darius's son, Xerxes, assembled a vast fleet and army with the intention of conquering all Greece and adding it to his empire. The Greeks mounted a holding operation at Thermopylae (August, 480 B.C.), before abandoning all Greece north of the Peloponnesus, including Attica. Athens was evacuated and sacked by the Persians, but in September the combined Greek fleet, inspired by the Athenian general Themistocles, defeated the Persian fleet off the island of Salamis. Xerxes, unable to supply his army without the fleet, led a retreat to Asia, but he left a force of 100,000 men in the north of Greece under the command of Mardonius with orders to subdue Greece the following year. In spring, 479 B.C., the Greek army marched north and met and defeated the Persians at Plataea; on the same day, according to tradition, the Greek fleet attacked and destroyed the remains of the Persian navy at Mycale in Asia Minor.

Persian soldiers

8. The Delian League and the Athenian Empire

These victories at the time seemed to the Greeks to offer no more than a respite in their struggle against the might of the Persian Empire. Many outlying Greek cities, including the islands and the coasts of the Aegean, were still held by the Persians. In 478 B.C. a league was formed at the island of Delos of cities that pledged themselves to continue the fight against Persia under Athenian leadership.

The Delian League under the Athenian general Cimon won a series of victories and only ceased fighting when the Persians accepted humiliating peace terms in 449 B.C. Meanwhile what had started as a league of free and independent states had gradually developed into an Athenian empire in which the allies had become subjects. Sparta was alarmed by the growing power of Athens, and these fears led to an intermittent war in which Sparta and her allies (the Peloponnesian League) fought Athens in a series of indecisive actions. This first Peloponnesian war ended in 446 B.C., when Athens and Sparta made a thirty years' peace.

9. Pericles and Radical Democracy

In this period Pericles dominated Athens; from 443 until he died in 429 he was elected general every year. At home he was responsible for the measures that made Athens a radical democracy. In foreign policy he was an avowed imperialist, who reckoned that the Athenian Empire brought positive benefits to its subjects that outweighed their loss of independence.

After the Thirty Years' Peace, Athens embarked on no more imperial ventures. She controlled the seas, kept a tight hand on her empire, and expanded her economic influence westwards. Sparta and its allies had good reason to fear Athenian ambitions, and Corinth, whose prosperity and very existence depended on her trade, was especially alarmed by Athenian expansion into the western Mediterranean. There were dangerous incidents, as when Corfu, a colony of Corinth, made a defensive alliance with Athens and an Athenian naval squadron routed a Corinthian fleet (434 B.C.). In the autumn of 432 B.C. (when our story of Dicaeopolis and his family begins) there was frantic diplomatic activity, as both sides prepared for war.

Pericles

A reconstruction of two semi-detached houses in Athens

Classical Greek

Archilochus

Archilochus (fl. 650 B.C.), the earliest lyric poet of whom anything survives, proudly claims to be both a warrior and a poet (poem no. 1):

εἰμὶ δ' ἐγὼ θεράπων μὲν Ἐνῡαλίοιο ἄνακτος

καὶ Μουσέων ἐρατὸν δῶρον ἐπιστάμενος.

[θεράπων, *servant*   Ἐνῡαλίοιο ἄνακτος, *of lord Enyalios* (the war god)   ἐρατὸν δῶρον, *the lovely gift*   ἐπιστάμενος, *knowing, skilled in*]

New Testament Greek

Luke 5.20–21

When Jesus was teaching, some men wanted to carry a paralyzed man to him to be cured; when they could not get near, they let him down through the roof. Jesus is the subject of the clause with which our quotation begins.

κὰι ἰδὼν τὴν πίστιν αὐτῶν εἶπεν, "ἄνθρωπε, ἀφέωνταί σοι αἱ ἁμαρτίαι σου."

[ἰδὼν, *seeing*   τὴν πίστιν, *the faith*   εἶπεν, *said*   ἀφέωνταί σοι αἱ ἁμαρτίαι σου, *your sins have been* (= are) *forgiven you*]

The scribes and Pharisees began to debate, saying:

"τίς ἐστιν οὗτος ὃς λαλεῖ βλασφημίᾱς; τίς δύναται ἁμαρτίᾱς ἀφεῖναι εἰ μὴ μόνος ὁ θεός;"

[οὗτος ὅς, *this (man) who*   λαλεῖ, *speaks*   δύναται, *is able, can*   ἀφεῖναι, *to forgive*   εἰ μὴ, *unless, except*   μόνος, *only, alone*]

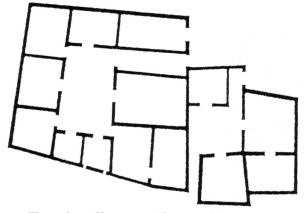

Floor plan of houses on the opposite page

ΠΡΟΣ ΤΟ ΑΣΤΥ (β)

ὁ Δικαιόπολις σπονδὴν ποιούμενος
τὸν Δία εὔχεται σῴζειν πάντας.

VOCABULARY

Verbs

ἀναβαίνω, *I go up, get up;* + ἐπί
+ acc., *I climb, go up onto*

ἐγείρω, active, transitive,
I wake X up; middle, intransitive, *I wake up*

εὔχομαι, *I pray;* + dat., *I pray to;*
+ acc. and infin., *I pray (that)*

καθίζω, active, transitive,
I make X sit down; I set;
I place; active, intransitive,
I sit; middle, intransitive,
I seat myself, sit down

Nouns

ἡ ἀγορά, τῆς ἀγορᾶς, *agora,*
city center, market place

ὁ βωμός, τοῦ βωμοῦ, *altar*

ὁ νεᾱνίᾱς, τοῦ νεᾱνίου, *young*
man

ὁ πολῑτης, τοῦ πολῑτου, *citizen*

ἡ χείρ, τῆς χειρός, *hand*

Preposition

ὑπέρ + gen., *on behalf of, for*

Adverb

τέλος, *in the end, finally*

Expressions

ἐν . . . τούτῳ, *meanwhile*

τῇ ὑστεραίᾳ, *on the next day*

Proper Names

ἡ Ἀκρόπολις, τῆς
Ἀκροπόλεως, *the Acropolis*
(the citadel of Athens)

ὁ Ζεύς, τοῦ Διός, τῷ Διί, τὸν Δία,
ὦ Ζεῦ, *Zeus* (king of the gods)

ὁ Παρθενών, τοῦ Παρθενῶνος,
the Parthenon (the temple of
Athena on the Acropolis in
Athens)

τῇ οὖν ὑστεραίᾳ, ἐπεὶ πρῶτον ἡμέρᾱ γίγνεται, ἐγείρεταί τε ἡ
Μυρρίνη καὶ τὸν ἄνδρα ἐγείρει καί, "ἔπαιρε σεαυτόν, ὦ ἄνερ," φησίν·
"οὐ γὰρ δυνατόν ἐστιν ἔτι καθεύδειν· καιρὸς γάρ ἐστι πρὸς τὸ ἄστυ
πορεύεσθαι." ὁ οὖν ἀνὴρ ἐπαίρει ἑαυτόν· καὶ πρῶτον τὸν Ξανθίᾱν
καλεῖ καὶ κελεύει αὐτὸν μὴ ἀργὸν εἶναι μηδὲ παύεσθαι ἐργαζόμενον. 5

ἐν δὲ τούτῳ ἡ Μυρρίνη τόν τε σῖτον φέρει καὶ τόν τε πάππον ἐγείρει
καὶ τοὺς παῖδας. ἔπειτα δὲ ὁ Δικαιόπολις εἰς τὴν αὐλὴν εἰσέρχεται
καὶ τοῖς ἄλλοις ἡγεῖται πρὸς τὸν βωμόν· σπονδὴν δὲ ποιούμενος τὸν
Δία εὔχεται σῴζειν πάντας πρὸς τὸ ἄστυ πορευομένους. τέλος δὲ τὸν
ἡμίονον ἐξάγει, ὁ δὲ πάππος ἀναβαίνει ἐπ’ αὐτόν. οὕτως οὖν　　10
πορεύονται πρὸς τὸ ἄστυ.

[μηδέ, and not　　τὴν αὐλήν, the courtyard　　σπονδήν, a libation (drink offering)
τὸν ἡμίονον, the mule　　ἐπ(ὶ), onto]

　　μακρὰ δ’ ἐστὶν ἡ ὁδὸς καὶ χαλεπή. δι’ ὀλίγου δὲ κάμνει ἡ
Μυρρίνη καὶ βούλεται καθίζεσθαι· κάμνει δὲ καὶ ὁ ἡμίονος καὶ οὐκ
ἐθέλει προχωρεῖν. καθιζόμενοι οὖν πρὸς τῇ ὁδῷ ἀναπαύονται. δι’
ὀλίγου δ’ ὁ Δικαιόπολις, “καιρός ἐστι πορεύεσθαι,” φησίν· “θάρρει, ὦ　　15
γύναι· μακρὰ γὰρ ἡ ὁδὸς καὶ χαλεπὴ τὸ πρῶτον, ‘ἐπὴν δ’ εἰς ἄκρον
ἵκηαι,’ ὥσπερ λέγει ὁ ποιητής, ῥᾳδίᾱ δὴ ἔπειτα γίγνεται.”

[κάμνει, is tired　　ἀναπαύονται, they rest　　θάρρει, cheer up! μακρά . . . γίγνεται
(Dicaeopolis is again alluding to Hesiod, Works and Days 290–292.)　　ἐπήν . . . ἵκηαι,
when(ever) you arrive/get]

　　προχωροῦσιν οὖν ἀνὰ τὸ ὄρος καί, ἐπεὶ εἰς ἄκρον ἀφικνοῦνται,
τὰς Ἀθήνᾱς ὁρῶσι κάτω κειμένᾱς. ὁ δὲ Φίλιππος τὴν πόλιν θεώμενος,
“ἰδού,” φησίν, “ὡς καλή ἐστιν ἡ πόλις. ἆρ’ ὁρᾶτε τὴν Ἀκρόπολιν;” ἡ　　20
δὲ Μέλιττα, “ὁρῶ δή. ἆρ’ ὁρᾶτε καὶ τὸν Παρθενῶνα; ὡς καλός ἐστι
καὶ μέγας.” ὁ δὲ Φίλιππος, “ἀλλὰ σπεῦδε, ὦ πάππα· καταβαίνομεν
γὰρ πρὸς τὴν πόλιν.”

[κάτω κειμένᾱς, lying below]

　　ταχέως οὖν καταβαίνουσι καὶ εἰς τὰς πύλᾱς ἀφικόμενοι τὸν
ἡμίονον προσάπτουσι δένδρῳ τινὶ καὶ εἰσέρχονται. ἐν δὲ τῷ ἄστει　　25
πολλοὺς ἀνθρώπους ὁρῶσιν ἐν ταῖς ὁδοῖς βαδίζοντας· ἄνδρες γάρ,
γυναῖκες, νεᾱνίαι, παῖδες, πολῖταί τε καὶ ξένοι, σπεύδουσι πρὸς τὴν
ἀγορᾶν. ἡ οὖν Μυρρίνη φοβουμένη ὑπὲρ τῶν παίδων, “ἐλθὲ δεῦρο, ὦ
Φίλιππε,” φησίν, “καὶ λαμβάνου τῆς χειρός. σὺ δέ—Μέλιτταν λέγω—
μὴ λεῖπέ με ἀλλ’ ἕπου ἅμα ἐμοί· τοσοῦτοι γάρ εἰσιν οἱ ἄνθρωποι ὥστε　　30
φοβοῦμαι ὑπὲρ σοῦ.”

[ἀφικόμενοι, *having arrived*   προσάπτουσι, *they tie* X (acc.) *to* Y (dat.)   βαδί-
ζοντας, *walking*   ἅμα ἐμοί, *with me*]

WORD BUILDING

The following sets contain words expressing ideas of place where, place to
which, and place from which. You already know the meanings of the words
in boldface; deduce the meanings of the others. Copy the chart carefully onto a
sheet of paper and write the meanings of the words in the appropriate slots
(note that sometimes the same word can express ideas of place where and
place to which, depending on the context):

	Place Where		**Place to Which**		**Place from Which**	
1.	ποῦ	_____	ποῖ *or* πόσε	_____	πόθεν	_____
2.			δεῦρο	_____		
3.	ἔνθα	*there*	ἔνθα	_____		
4.	ἐνθάδε	_____	ἐνθάδε	_____		
5.	ἐνταῦθα	_____	ἐνταῦθα	_____		
6.	ἐκεῖ	_____	ἐκεῖσε	_____	ἐκεῖθεν	_____
7.	οἴκοι	_____	οἴκαδε	_____	οἴκοθεν	_____
8.	ἄλλοθι	_____	ἄλλοσε	_____	ἄλλοθεν	_____
9.	πανταχοῦ	_____	πανταχόσε	_____	πανταχόθεν	_____
10.	Ἀθήνησι(ν)	_____	Ἀθήναζε	_____	Ἀθήνηθεν	_____

GRAMMAR

2. 3rd Declension Consonant Stem Nouns: Stems in - ρ-

The endings of these nouns are the same as those you learned for 3rd
declension nouns in Chapter 7, but each of these nouns has four stems, as
follows:

πατηρ-	μητηρ-	θυγατηρ-	ἀνηρ-
πατερ-	μητερ-	θυγατερ-	ἀνερ-
πατρ-	μητρ-	θυγατρ-	ἀνδρ-
πατρα-	μητρα-	θυγατρα-	ἀνδρα-

In the following chart, locate the forms with each of these stems:

ὁ	πατήρ	ἡ	μήτηρ	ἡ	θυγάτηρ	ὁ	ἀνήρ
τοῦ	πατρ-ός	τῆς	μητρ-ός	τῆς	θυγατρ-ός	τοῦ	ἀνδρ-ός
τῷ	πατρ-ί	τῇ	μητρ-ί	τῇ	θυγατρ-ί	τῷ	ἀνδρ-ί
τὸν	πατέρ-α	τὴν	μητέρ-α	τὴν	θυγατέρ-α	τὸν	ἄνδρ-α
ὦ	πάτερ	ὦ	μῆτερ	ὦ	θύγατερ	ὦ	ἄνερ
οἱ	πατέρ-ες	αἱ	μητέρ-ες	αἱ	θυγατέρ-ες	οἱ	ἄνδρ-ες
τῶν	πατέρ-ων	τῶν	μητέρ-ων	τῶν	θυγατέρ-ων	τῶν	ἀνδρ-ῶν
τοῖς	πατρά-σι(ν)	ταῖς	μητρά-σι(ν)	ταῖς	θυγατρά-σι(ν)	τοῖς	ἀνδρά-σι(ν)
τοὺς	πατέρ-ας	τὰς	μητέρ-ας	τὰς	θυγατέρ-ας	τοὺς	ἄνδρ-ας
ὦ	πατέρ-ες	ὦ	μητέρ-ες	ὦ	θυγατέρ-ες	ὦ	ἄνδρ-ες

Note that these nouns do not add ς in the nominative singular. Note also the accents on the final syllables in the genitive and dative singulars (regular with monosyllabic stems) and the recessive accent in the vocative singulars. The nominative and vocative plurals all have accents on the next to the last syllable.

3. **Two Important Irregular Nouns: ἡ γυνή, τῆς γυναικός, *woman; wife*, and ἡ χείρ, τῆς χειρός, *hand***

For ἡ γυνή, note that the nominative is not formed from the stem plus -ς, as is usual with velar stem nouns such as φύλακ-ς > φύλαξ; the accent in the genitive and dative, singular and plural, falls on the final syllable; and the vocative singular consists of the stem minus the final κ, since all stop consonants are lost in word-final position. For ἡ χείρ, note the shortened stem in the dative plural.

Singular:

Stem: γυναικ-, *woman; wife*   **Stem:** χειρ-, *hand*

Nom.	ἡ γυνή	ἡ	χείρ
Gen.	τῆς γυναικ-ός	τῆς	χειρ-ός
Dat.	τῇ γυναικ-ί	τῇ	χειρ-ί
Acc.	τὴν γυναῖκ-α	τὴν	χεῖρ-α
Voc.	ὦ γύναικ > γύναι	ὦ	χείρ

Plural:

Nom.	αἱ γυναῖκ-ες	αἱ	χεῖρ-ες
Gen.	τῶν γυναικ-ῶν	τῶν	χειρ-ῶν
Dat.	ταῖς γυναικ-σί(ν) > γυναιξί(ν)	ταῖς	χερ-σί(ν)
Acc.	τὰς γυναῖκ-ας	τὰς	χεῖρ-ας
Voc.	ὦ γυναῖκ-ες	ὦ	χεῖρες

PRACTICE: Write complete sets of forms of ὁ δεινὸς ἀνήρ, *the terrible man*; ἡ φίλη μήτηρ, *the dear mother*; and ἡ σώφρων γυνή, *the prudent woman*.

4. 1st/3rd Declension Adjective πᾶς, πᾶσα, πᾶν, *all; every; whole*

You have met a number of forms of this adjective in the readings. Here are all of its forms. Note that in the masculine and neuter it has 3rd declension endings and that in the feminine it has endings like those of the 1st declension noun μέλιττα (including the circumflex on the final syllable of the genitive plural; see Chapter 4, Grammar 3, page 41).

Stems: παντ- for masculine and neuter; πᾱσ- for feminine

Singular:

	M.	**F.**	**N.**
Nom.	πάντ-ς > πᾶς	πᾶσ-α	πάντ > πᾶν
Gen.	παντ-ός	πᾱσ-ης	παντ-ός
Dat.	παντ-ί	πᾱσ-ῃ	παντ-ί
Acc.	πάντ-α	πᾶσ-αν	πάντ > πᾶν
Voc.	πάντ-ς > πᾶς	πᾶσ-α	πάντ > πᾶν

Plural:

	M.	**F.**	**N.**
Nom.	πάντ-ες	πᾶσ-αι	πάντ-α
Gen.	πάντ-ων	πᾱσ-ῶν	πάντ-ων
Dat.	πάντ-σι(ν) > πᾶσι(ν)	πᾱσ-αις	πάντ-σι(ν) > πᾶσι(ν)
Acc.	πάντ-ας	πᾱσ-ᾱς	πάντ-α
Voc.	πάντ-ες	πᾶσ-αι	πάντ-α

For the nominative and vocative masculine singular forms, the -ντ at the end of the stem is lost because of the ς, and the stem vowel lengthens. Remember that all stop consonants in word-final position are lost; thus the stem παντ- gives πᾶν in the neuter nominative, accusative, and vocative singulars with loss of the τ; the stem vowel was probably lengthened because of the masculine πᾶς and the feminine πᾶσα. In the dative plural the -ντ is lost before the σ of the ending -σι(ν), and the stem vowel lengthens. Note the following uses of this adjective:

Predicate position:	πάντες οἱ θεοί or οἱ θεοὶ πάντες = *all the gods*
	πᾶσα ἡ ναῦς or ἡ ναῦς πᾶσα = *the whole ship*, i.e., all of its parts
Attributive position (rare):	ἡ πᾶσα πόλις = *the whole city* (regarded collectively as the sum total of its parts)
Without definite article:	πᾶς ἀνήρ = *every man*
Used as a substantive:*	πάντες = *all people, everyone*
	πάντα (n. pl.) = *all things, everything*

*See Chapter 7, Grammar 1, page 96.

Locate occurrences of this adjective in the stories in Chapters 7β, 8α, and 8β.

Exercise 8δ

Read aloud and translate:

1. πᾶσαι αἱ γυναῖκες πρὸς τὴν κρήνην σπεύδουσιν.
2. αἱ γὰρ μητέρες τὰς θυγατέρας ζητοῦσιν.
3. ἐπεὶ δὲ εἰς τὴν κρήνην ἀφικνοῦνται, οὐκ ἐκεῖ πάρεισιν αἱ θυγατέρες.
4. οἴκαδε οὖν τρέχουσιν αἱ γυναῖκες καὶ τοῖς ἀνδράσι πάντα λέγουσιν.
5. οἱ οὖν ἄνδρες πρὸς τοὺς ἀγροὺς ὁρμῶνται· μέλλουσι γὰρ τὰς θυγατέρας ζητεῖν.
6. ἀφικόμενοι (*having arrived*) δὲ εἰς τοὺς ἀγρούς, οἱ πατέρες τὰς θυγατέρας ὁρῶσι νεανίαις τισὶ διαλεγομένᾱς.
7. τὰς οὖν θυγατέρας καλοῦσι καί, "ἔλθετε δεῦρο, ὦ θυγατέρες," φασίν· "μὴ διαλέγεσθε νεᾱνίαις."
8. αἱ οὖν θυγατέρες τοῖς πατράσι πειθόμεναι οἴκαδε αὐτοῖς ἕπονται.
9. ἐπεὶ δὲ οἴκαδε ἀφικνοῦνται, οἱ ἄνδρες πάντα ταῖς γυναιξὶ λέγουσιν.
10. αἱ δὲ μητέρες ταῖς θυγατράσι μάλα ὀργίζονται (*grow angry at* + dat.).

Exercise 8ε

Translate into Greek:

1. The mother tells (orders) her daughter to hurry to the spring.
2. But the daughter walks to the field and looks for her father.
3. And she finds her father working in the field with other men.
4. And she says to her father, "Father, mother tells me to bring water (ὕδωρ) from the spring.
5. "But all the other girls are playing (*use* παίζω)."
6. And her father says, "Obey your mother, daughter. Fetch (*use* φέρω) the water."
7. And at the spring the daughter sees many women; they are all carrying water jars.
8. So she says to the women, "Greetings, friends," and she fills (πληροῖ) her water jar.
9. And when she arrives home, she tells her mother everything.
10. And her mother says, "Well done (εὖ γε); go now and play with the other girls."

Greek Wisdom

μελέτη τὸ πᾶν.   Περίανδρος (of Corinth)

5. Numbers

The cardinal adjectives in Greek from one to ten are:

1	εἷς, μία, ἕν	4	τέτταρες, τέτταρα	7	ἑπτά	10	δέκα
2	δύο	5	πέντε	8	ὀκτώ		
3	τρεῖς, τρία	6	ἕξ	9	ἐννέα		

The numbers from five to ten are indeclinable adjectives; that is, they appear only in the forms given above no matter what gender, case, or number the noun is that they modify. For the number *one*, there is a full set of forms in the singular, given at the left below, with the masculine and neuter showing 3rd declension endings, and the feminine showing 1st declension endings similar to those of μάχαιρα (see Chapter 4, Grammar 3, page 42). Compare the declension of πᾶς, πᾶσα, πᾶν above. The word οὐδείς, οὐδεμία, οὐδέν or μηδείς, μηδεμία, μηδέν means *no one; nothing* as a pronoun and *no* as an adjective.

Stems: ἑν- for masculine and neuter; μι- for feminine

	M.	F.	N.	M.	F.	N.
Nom.	ἕν-ς > εἷς	μί-α	ἕν	οὐδείς	οὐδεμία	οὐδέν
Gen.	ἑν-ός	μι-ᾶς	ἑν-ός	οὐδενός	οὐδεμιᾶς	οὐδενός
Dat.	ἑν-ί	μι-ᾷ	ἑν-ί	οὐδενί	οὐδεμιᾷ	οὐδενί
Acc.	ἕν-α	μί-αν	ἕν	οὐδένα	οὐδεμίαν	οὐδέν

Note the accents of the genitives and datives.

The declensions of δύο, τρεῖς, and τέτταρες are as follows:

M. F. N.	M. F.	N.	M. F.	N.
δύο	τρεῖς	τρία	τέτταρες	τέτταρα
δυοῖν	τριῶν	τριῶν	τεττάρων	τεττάρων
δυοῖν	τρισί(ν)	τρισί(ν)	τέτταρσι(ν)	τέτταρσι(ν)
δύο	τρεῖς	τρία	τέτταρας	τέτταρα

The ordinal adjectives (*first, second, third*, etc.) are as follows:

πρῶτος, -η, -ον	ἕκτος, -η, -ον
δεύτερος, -ᾱ, -ον	ἕβδομος, -η, -ον
τρίτος, -η, -ον	ὄγδοος, -η, -ον
τέταρτος, -η, -ον	ἔνατος, -η, -ον
πέμπτος, -η, -ον	δέκατος, -η, -ον

6. Expressions of Time When, Duration of Time, and Time within Which

Ordinal adjectives are used in expressions of *time when* with the dative case (see Chapter 6, Grammar 6e, page 88), and cardinal adjectives are used in expressions of *duration of time* with the accusative case, e.g.:

Time when: τῇ πρώτῃ ἡμέρᾳ = *on the first day*
Duration of time: δύο ἡμέρᾱς = *for two days*

Cardinal adjectives are also used in phrases expressing *time within which* with the genitive case, e.g.:

Time within which: πέντε ἡμερῶν = *within five days.*

Compare the genitives ἡμέρᾱς, *by day*, and νυκτός, *at/by night.*

Exercise 8ζ

Read aloud and translate:

1. αὐτουργῷ τινί εἰσι τρεῖς παῖδες, δύο μὲν υἱεῖς (*sons*), μία δὲ θυγάτηρ.
2. οἱ μὲν παῖδες πᾶσαν τὴν ἡμέρᾱν ἐν τῷ ἀγρῷ πονοῦσιν, ἡ δὲ θυγάτηρ οἴκοι μένει καὶ τῇ μητρὶ συλλαμβάνει. νυκτὸς δὲ πάντες ἐν τῇ οἰκίᾳ καθεύδουσιν.
3. τῇ δ' ὑστεραίᾳ ἡ μήτηρ τῇ θυγατρί, "οὐ πολὺ ὕδωρ ἐστὶν ἐν τῇ οἰκίᾳ· δυοῖν ἡμερῶν οὐδὲν ὕδωρ ἕξομεν (*we will have*). ἴθι οὖν καὶ φέρε μοι ὕδωρ."
4. ἀφικομένη (*having arrived*) δ' εἰς τὴν κρήνην, ἡ παῖς τέτταρας γυναῖκας ὁρᾷ τὰς ὑδρίᾱς πληρούσᾱς (*filling*).
5. ἡ πρώτη γυνή, "χαῖρε, ὦ φίλη," φησίν· "ἐλθὲ δεῦρο καὶ τὴν ὑδρίᾱν πλήρου (*fill!*)."
6. ἡ δὲ δευτέρᾱ, "τί σὺ ἥκεις εἰς τὴν κρήνην; τί ποιεῖ ἡ σὴ μήτηρ;"
7. ἡ δὲ παῖς ἀποκρῑναμένη· "ἡ μήτηρ," φησίν, "περίεργός (*busy*) ἐστιν· πέντε γὰρ πέπλους ὑφαίνει (*is weaving*)."
8. ἡ δὲ τρίτη γύνη, "σπεῦδε, ὦ ἀργὲ παῖ," φησίν· "ἡ γὰρ μήτηρ σε μένει."
9. ἡ δὲ τετάρτη γυνή, "μὴ οὕτω χαλεπὴ ἴσθι," φησίν· "ἡ γὰρ παῖς ἤδη σπεύδει."
10. ἡ οὖν παῖς τὴν πᾶσαν ὑδρίᾱν ταχέως πληροῖ (*fills*) καὶ οἴκαδε σπεύδει.

Exercise 8η

Read aloud and translate:

1. αἱ θυγατέρες τῇ μητρὶ πειθόμεναι τὸν πατέρα ἐγείρουσι καὶ πείθουσιν αὐτὸν Ἀθήνᾱζε πορεύεσθαι.
2. ὁ πατὴρ τοὺς μὲν παῖδας οἴκοι λείπει, ταῖς δὲ θυγατράσιν Ἀθήνᾱζε ἡγεῖται.
3. μακρὰ ἡ ὁδὸς καὶ χαλεπή· τῇ δὲ δευτέρᾳ ἡμέρᾳ ἐκεῖσε ἀφικνοῦνται.
4. πολλοὺς ἀνθρώπους ὁρῶσιν διὰ (*through*) τῶν ὁδῶν πανταχόσε σπεύδοντας (*hurrying*).
5. ἐπεὶ δὲ εἰς τὴν ἀγορὰν ἀφικνοῦνται, πολὺν χρόνον μένουσι πάντα θεώμενοι.
6. δύο μὲν ἡμέρᾱς τὰ (*the things*) ἐν τῇ ἀγορᾷ θεῶνται, τῇ δὲ τρίτῃ ἐπὶ τὴν Ἀκρόπολιν ἀναβαίνουσιν.
7. ἐννέα μὲν ἡμέρᾱς Ἀθήνησι μένουσιν, τῇ δὲ δεκάτῃ οἴκαδε ὁρμῶνται.

8. τέτταρας μὲν ἡμέρᾱς ὁδὸν ποιοῦνται, βραδέως πορευόμενοι, τῇ δὲ πέμπτῃ
    οἴκαδε ἀφικνοῦνται.

Ο ΟΔΥΣΣΕΥΣ ΚΑΙ Ο ΑΙΟΛΟΣ

Read the following passage and answer the comprehension questions:

Odysseus tells how he sailed on to the island of Aeolus, king of the winds,
and almost reached home:

ἐπεὶ δὲ ἐκ τοῦ ἄντρου τοῦ Κύκλωπος ἐκφεύγομεν, ἐπανερχόμεθα ταχέως πρὸς
τοὺς ἑταίρους. οἱ δέ, ἐπεὶ ἡμᾶς ὁρῶσιν, χαίρουσιν. τῇ δ' ὑστεραίᾳ κελεύω αὐτοὺς
εἰς τὴν ναῦν αὖθις εἰσβαίνειν. οὕτως οὖν ἀποπλέομεν.

[τοῦ ἄντρου, *the cave*   ἐπανερχόμεθα, *we return*]

1. What do Odysseus and his men do when they escape from the cave of the
    Cyclops?
2. What does Odysseus order his men to do the next day?

δι' ὀλίγου δὲ εἰς νῆσον Αἰολίᾱν ἀφικνούμεθα. ἐκεῖ δὲ οἰκεῖ ὁ Αἴολος, βασιλεὺς
τῶν ἀνέμων. ἡμᾶς δὲ εὐμενῶς δεχόμενος πολὺν χρόνον ξενίζει. ἐπεὶ δὲ ἐγὼ   5
κελεύω αὐτὸν ἡμᾶς ἀποπέμπειν, παρέχει μοι ἀσκόν τινα, εἰς ὃν πάντας τοὺς
ἀνέμους καταδεῖ πλὴν ἑνός, Ζεφύρου πρᾱ́ου.

[Αἰολίᾱν, *of Aeolus* (king of the winds)   τῶν ἀνέμων, *of the winds*   εὐμενῶς, *kindly*
ξενίζει, *entertains*   ἀσκόν, *bag*   ὅν, *which*   καταδεῖ, *he ties up*   πλὴν + gen.,
except   Ζεφύρου, *Zephyr* (the west wind)   πρᾱ́ου, *gentle*]

3. Where do Odysseus and his men arrive next?
4. How long do Odysseus and his men stay with Aeolus?
5. What does Aeolus give Odysseus at his departure?
6. What wind was not in the bag?

ἐννέα μὲν οὖν ἡμέρᾱς πλέομεν, τῇ δὲ δεκάτῃ ὁρῶμεν τὴν πατρίδα γῆν.
ἐνταῦθα δὴ ἐγὼ καθεύδω· οἱ δὲ ἑταῖροι, ἐπεὶ ὁρῶσί με καθεύδοντα, οὕτω λέγουσιν·
"τί ἐν τῷ ἀσκῷ ἔνεστιν; πολὺς δήπου χρῡσὸς ἔνεστιν, πολύ τε ἀργύριον, δῶρα τοῦ   10
Αἰόλου. ἄγετε δή, λύετε τὸν ἀσκὸν καὶ τὸν χρῡσὸν αἱρεῖτε."

[τὴν πατρίδα γῆν, *our fatherland*   καθεύδοντα, *sleeping*   δήπου, *surely*   χρῡ-
σός, *gold*   ἀργύριον, *silver*   δῶρα, *gifts*   ἄγετε δή, *come on!*]

7. How long do Odysseus and his men sail?
8. When they come within sight of their fatherland, what does Odysseus do?
9. What do his comrades think is in the bag?

ἐπεὶ δὲ λύουσι τὸν ἀσκόν, εὐθὺς ἐκπέτονται πάντες οἱ ἄνεμοι καὶ χειμῶνα
δεινὸν ποιοῦσι καὶ τὴν ναῦν ἀπὸ τῆς πατρίδος γῆς ἀπελαύνουσιν. ἐγὼ δὲ ἐγείρομαι
καὶ γιγνώσκω τί γίγνεται. ἀθῡμῶ οὖν καὶ βούλομαι ῥίπτειν ἐμαυτὸν εἰς τὴν

θάλατταν· οἱ δὲ ἑταῖροι σῴζουσί με. οὕτως οὖν οἱ ἄνεμοι ἡμᾶς εἰς τὴν τοῦ Αἰόλου   15
νῆσον πάλιν φέρουσιν.

[εὐθύς, *at once*   ἐκπέτονται, *fly out*   ἀθυμῶ, *I despair*   ῥίπτειν, *to throw*   πάλιν, *again*]

10. What happens when the men open the bag?
11. How does Odysseus react when he wakes up?
12. Where do the winds carry the ship?

Exercise 8θ

Translate into Greek:

1. When we arrive at the island, I go to the house of Aeolus.
2. And he, when he sees me, is very amazed and says: "What is the matter (= what are you suffering)? Why are you here again?"
3. And I answer: "My comrades are to blame. For they loosed (ἔλῦσαν) the winds. But come to our aid, friend."
4. But Aeolus says: "Go away (ἄπιτε) from the island quickly. It is not possible to come to your aid. For the gods surely (δήπου) hate (*use* μῑσέω) you."

Classical Greek

Sappho: The Deserted Lover: A Girl's Lament

These lines are quoted by a writer on Greek meter (Hephaestion, 2nd century A.D.) without giving the author. Some scholars ascribe them to Sappho of Lesbos (seventh century B.C.), the greatest female poet of Greek literature. The passage (D. A. Campbell, *Greek Lyric Poetry*, page 52) is given at the left as it is quoted by Hephaestion in the Attic dialect and then at the right with Sappho's Aeolic forms restored.

δέδῡκε μὲν ἡ σελήνη   δέδῡκε μὲν ἀ σελάννᾱ
καὶ Πληϊάδες, μέσαι δὲ   καὶ Πληΐαδες, μέσαι δὲ
νύκτες, παρὰ δ᾽ ἔρχεθ᾽ ὥρᾱ,   νύκτες, παρὰ δ᾽ ἔρχετ᾽ ὤρᾱ,
ἐγὼ δὲ μόνη καθεύδω.   ἔγω δὲ μόνᾱ κατεύδω.

[δέδῡκε, *has set*   ἡ σελήνη, *the moon*
Πληϊάδες, *the Pleiades* (seven mythical daughters of Atlas and Pleione, changed into a cluster of stars)
μέσαι, *middle*   μέσαι δὲ νύκτες: supply a form of the verb *to be* in your translation
παρὰ ... ἔρχεθ᾽ = παρέρχεται, *passes*   ὥρᾱ, *time*   μόνη, *alone*]

9
Η ΠΑΝΗΓΥΡΙΣ (α)

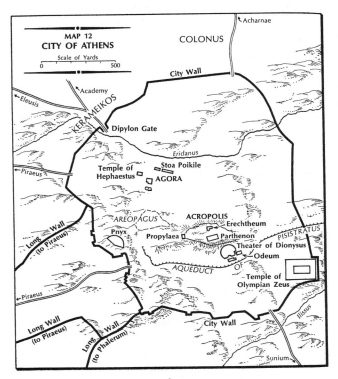

αἱ Ἀθῆναι

ὁρῶσι τὴν εἰκόνα τῆς Ἀθηνᾶς,
ἐνοπλίου οὔσης καὶ Νίκην τῇ δεξιᾷ φερούσης.

VOCABULARY

Verbs

ἄγε; pl., ἄγετε, *come on!*

ἐπανέρχομαι [= ἐπι- + ἀνα- + ἔρχομαι], infinitive, ἐπανιέναι, *I come back, return;* + εἰς or πρός + acc., *I return to*

ἐσθίω, *I eat*

κάμνω, *I am sick; I am tired*

πίνω, *I drink*

Nouns

ἡ ἀριστερά, τῆς ἀριστερᾶς, *left hand*

ἡ δεξιά, τῆς δεξιᾶς, *right hand*

ἡ θεός, τῆς θεοῦ, *goddess*

τὸ ἱερόν, τοῦ ἱεροῦ, *temple*

ὁ κίνδυνος, τοῦ κινδύνου, *danger*

Adjective

κάλλιστος, -η, -ον, *most beautiful; very beautiful*

Preposition

διά + gen., *through*

ἐπί + dat., *upon, on;* + acc., *at; against;* <u>onto, upon</u>

Proper Names

ἡ Ἀθηνᾶ, τῆς Ἀθηνᾶς, τῇ Ἀθηνᾷ, τὴν Ἀθηνᾶν, ὦ Ἀθηνᾶ, *Athena (daughter of Zeus)*

ἡ Νίκη, τῆς Νίκης, *Nike (the goddess of victory)*

ἡ Παρθένος, τῆς Παρθένου, *the Maiden (= the goddess Athena)*

ὁ Φειδίας, τοῦ Φειδίου, *Pheidias (the great Athenian sculptor)*

οὕτως οὖν πορευόμενοι ἀφικνοῦνται εἰς τὴν ἀγοράν. ἐκεῖ δὲ τοσοῦτός ἐστιν ὁ ὅμῑλος ὥστε μόλις προχωροῦσι πρὸς τὴν Ἀκρόπολιν. τέλος δὲ τῷ Δικαιοπόλιδι ἑπόμενοι εἰς στοάν τινα ἀφικνοῦνται, καὶ καθιζόμενοι θεῶνται τοὺς ἀνθρώπους σπεύδοντας καὶ βοῶντας καὶ θόρυβον ποιοῦντας.   5

[ὁ ὅμῑλος, *the crowd*   στοάν, *portico, colonnade*   θόρυβον, *an uproar*]

ἤδη δὲ μάλα πεινῶσιν οἱ παῖδες. ὁ δὲ Φίλιππος ἀλλᾱντοπώλην ὁρᾷ διὰ τοῦ ὁμῑλου ὠθιζόμενον καὶ τὰ ὤνια βοῶντα. τὸν οὖν πατέρα καλεῖ καί, "ὦ πάππα φίλε," φησίν, "ἰδού, ἀλλᾱντοπώλης προσχωρεῖ. ἆρ' οὐκ ἐθέλεις σῖτον ὠνεῖσθαι; μάλα γὰρ πεινῶμεν." ὁ οὖν Δικαιόπολις τὸν ἀλλᾱντοπώλην καλεῖ καὶ σῖτον ὠνεῖται. οὕτως   10 οὖν ἐν τῇ στοᾷ καθίζονται ἀλλᾶντας ἐσθίοντες καὶ οἶνον πίνοντες.

[πεινῶσιν, *are hungry*   ἀλλᾱντοπώλην, *a sausage-seller*   ὠθιζόμενον, *pushing* τὰ ὤνια, *his wares*   ὠνεῖσθαι, *to buy*   ἀλλᾶντας, *sausages*]

μετὰ δὲ τὸ δεῖπνον ὁ Δικαιόπολις, "ἄγετε," φησίν, "ἆρ' οὐ βούλεσθε ἐπὶ τὴν Ἀκρόπολιν ἀναβαίνειν καὶ τὰ ἱερὰ θεᾶσθαι;" ὁ μὲν πάππος μάλα κάμνει καὶ οὐκ ἐθέλει ἀναβαίνειν, οἱ δ' ἄλλοι

λείπουσιν αὐτὸν ἐν τῇ στοᾷ καθιζόμενον καὶ διὰ τοῦ ὁμίλου ὠθι-   15
ζόμενοι ἐπὶ τὴν Ἀκρόπολιν ἀναβαίνουσιν.

ἐπεὶ δὲ εἰς ἄκρᾱν τὴν Ἀκρόπολιν ἀφικνοῦνται καὶ τὰ προπύλαια
διαπερῶσιν, τὸ τῆς Παρθένου ἱερὸν ὁρῶσιν ἐναντίον καὶ τὴν τῆς
Ἀθηνᾶς εἰκόνα, μεγίστην οὖσαν, ἐνόπλιον καὶ δόρυ δεξιᾷ φέρουσαν.
πολὺν οὖν χρόνον ἡσυχάζουσιν οἱ παῖδες τὴν θεὸν θεώμενοι, τέλος   20
δὲ ὁ Δικαιόπολις, "ἄγετε," φησίν, "ἆρ᾽ οὐ βούλεσθε τὸ ἱερὸν
θεᾶσθαι;" καὶ ἡγεῖται αὐτοῖς πόρρω.

[τὰ προπύλαια, the gateway, the Propylaea   διαπερῶσιν, they pass through
ἐναντίον, opposite   τὴν ... εἰκόνα, the statue   οὖσαν, being   ἐνόπλιον, fully
armed   δόρυ, spear   ἡσυχάζουσιν, stay quiet   πόρρω, forward]

μέγιστόν ἐστι τὸ ἱερὸν καὶ κάλλιστον. πολὺν χρόνον τὰ
ἀγάλματα θεῶνται, ἃ τὸ πᾶν ἱερὸν κοσμεῖ. ἀνεῳγμέναι εἰσὶν αἱ
πύλαι· ἀναβαίνουσιν οὖν οἱ παῖδες καὶ εἰσέρχονται. πάντα τὰ εἴσω   25
σκοτεινά ἐστιν, ἀλλ᾽ ἐναντίᾱν μόλις ὁρῶσι τὴν τῆς Ἀθηνᾶς εἰκόνα,
τὸ κάλλιστον ἔργον τοῦ Φειδίου. ἡ θεὸς λάμπεται χρῡσῷ, τῇ μὲν
δεξιᾷ Νίκην φέρουσα τῇ δὲ ἀριστερᾷ τὴν ἀσπίδα. ἅμα τ᾽ οὖν
φοβοῦνται οἱ παῖδες θεώμενοι καὶ χαίρουσιν. ὁ δὲ Φίλιππος
προχωρεῖ καὶ τὰς χεῖρας ἀνέχων τῇ θεῷ εὔχεται· "ὦ Ἀθηνᾶ Παρθένε,   30
παῖ Διός, πολιοῦχε, ἵλεως ἴσθι καὶ ἄκουέ μου εὐχομένου· σῷζε τὴν
πόλιν καὶ σῷζε ἡμᾶς ἐκ πάντων κινδύνων." ἐνταῦθα δὴ πρὸς τὴν
Μέλιτταν ἐπανέρχεται καὶ ἡγεῖται αὐτῇ ἐκ τοῦ ἱεροῦ.

[τὰ ἀγάλματα, the carvings   ἅ, which   κοσμεῖ, decorate   ἀνεῳγμέναι, open
τὰ εἴσω, the things inside, the inside   σκοτεινά, dark   λάμπεται, gleams   χρῡσῷ,
with gold   τὴν ἀσπίδα, her shield   ἅμα, at the same time   ἀνέχων, holding up
πολιοῦχε, holder / protectress of our city   ἵλεως, gracious]

πολύν τινα χρόνον τοὺς τεκόντας ζητοῦσιν, τέλος δὲ εὑρίσκουσιν
αὐτοὺς ὄπισθεν τοῦ ἱεροῦ καθορῶντας τὸ τοῦ Διονῡσου τέμενος. ὁ   35
δὲ Δικαιόπολις, "ἰδού, ὦ παῖδες," φησίν, "ἤδη συλλέγονται οἱ
ἄνθρωποι εἰς τὸ τέμενος. καιρός ἐστι καταβαίνειν καὶ ζητεῖν τὸν
πάππον."

[τοὺς τεκόντας, their parents   ὄπισθεν + gen., behind   καθορῶντας, looking
down on   τὸ ... τέμενος, the sanctuary   συλλέγονται, are gathering]

καταβαίνουσιν οὖν καὶ σπεύδουσι πρὸς τὴν στοάν· ἐκεῖ δὲ
εὑρίσκουσι τὸν πάππον ὀργίλως ἔχοντα· "ὦ τέκνον," φησίν, "τί ποιεῖς; 40
τί με λείπεις τοσοῦτον χρόνον; τί τὴν πομπὴν οὐ θεώμεθα;" ὁ δὲ
Δικαιόπολις, "θάρρει, ὦ πάππα," φησίν· "νῦν γὰρ πρὸς τὸ τοῦ
Διονύσου τέμενος πορευόμεθα· δι᾽ ὀλίγου γὰρ γίγνεται ἡ πομπή. ἄγε
δή." οὕτω λέγει καὶ ἡγεῖται αὐτοῖς πρὸς τὸ τέμενος.

[ὀργίλως ἔχοντα, *being angry, in a bad temper* τέκνον, *child* τὴν πομπὴν, *the
procession* θάρρει, *cheer up!*]

WORD STUDY

*Identify the Greek stems in the English words below and give the meanings
of the English words (ὁ δῆμος = the people):*

1. democracy (what does τὸ κράτος mean?)
2. demagogue
3. demography
4. endemic
5. epidemic
6. pandemic

GRAMMAR

1. Participles: Present or Progressive: Active Voice

In the last chapter you learned the forms of the present, progressive
participle in the middle voice, e.g., λυόμενος, λυομένη, λυόμενον, which has
the same endings for case, number, and gender as the adjective καλός,
καλή, καλόν.

In the reading passage at the beginning of this chapter you have met
many forms of the *present active participle*, e.g., σπεύδοντας, *hurrying*,
βοῶντας, *shouting*, and ποιοῦντας, *making*. Present active participles,
like present middle participles, do not refer to time as such but describe the
action as in process, ongoing, or progressive.

Present active participles, like the adjective πᾶς, πᾶσα, πᾶν (Chapter 8,
Grammar 4, page 126) have 3rd declension endings in the masculine and
neuter and 1st declension endings in the feminine. They have the suffix
-οντ- in the masculine and neuter and the suffix -ουσ- in the feminine.
There is no -ς in the nominative masculine singular. The τ is lost in the
masculine and neuter nominative and vocative singulars, since all stop
consonants are lost in word-final position, and in the masculine the ο is
lengthened to ω; thus for the verb εἰμί the masculine participle (stem, ὀντ-)
is ὤν and the neuter is ὄν. In the masculine and neuter dative plurals, the
ντ is lost before the σ, with a resulting spelling of οὖσι(ν). Present active
participles are declined as follows:

	Masculine	**Feminine**	**Neuter**

The verb εἰμί:

	Masculine	**Feminine**	**Neuter**
Nom., Voc.	ὄντ > ὤν	οὖσ-α	ὄντ > ὄν
Gen.	ὄντ-ος	οὔσ-ης	ὄντ-ος
Dat.	ὄντ-ι	οὔσ-ῃ	ὄντ-ι
Acc.	ὄντ-α	οὖσ-αν	ὄντ > ὄν
Nom., Voc.	ὄντ-ες	οὖσ-αι	ὄντ-α
Gen.	ὄντ-ων	οὐσ-ῶν	ὄντ-ων
Dat.	ὄντ-σι(ν) > οὖσι(ν)	οὔσ-αις	ὄντ-σι(ν) > οὖσι(ν)
Acc.	ὄντ-ας	οὔσ-ᾱς	ὄντ-α

The verb λῡ́ω:

	Masculine	**Feminine**	**Neuter**
Nom., Voc.	λῡ́-ων	λῡ́-ουσα	λῦ-ον
Gen.	λῡ́-οντος	λῡ-ούσης	λῡ́-οντος
Dat.	λῡ́-οντι	λῡ-ούσῃ	λῡ́-οντι
Acc.	λῡ́-οντα	λῡ́-ουσαν	λῦ-ον
Nom., Voc.	λῡ́-οντες	λῡ́-ουσαι	λῡ́-οντα
Gen.	λῡ-όντων	λῡ-ουσῶν	λῡ-όντων
Dat.	λῡ́-ουσι(ν)	λῡ-ούσαις	λῡ́-ουσι(ν)
Acc.	λῡ́-οντας	λῡ-ούσᾱς	λῡ́-οντα

For the participles of contract verbs, we show how the contractions work in the nominative singular but then give only contracted forms:

The verb φιλέω:

	Masculine	**Feminine**	**Neuter**
Nom., Voc.	φιλέ-ων > φιλῶν	φιλέ-ουσα > φιλοῦσα	φιλέ-ον > φιλοῦν
Gen.	φιλοῦντος	φιλούσης	φιλοῦντος
Dat.	φιλοῦντι	φιλούσῃ	φιλοῦντι
Acc.	φιλοῦντα	φιλοῦσαν	φιλοῦν
Nom., Voc.	φιλοῦντες	φιλοῦσαι	φιλοῦντα
Gen.	φιλούντων	φιλουσῶν	φιλούντων
Dat.	φιλοῦσι(ν)	φιλούσαις	φιλοῦσι(ν)
Acc.	φιλοῦντας	φιλούσᾱς	φιλοῦντα

The verb τῑμάω:

	Masculine	**Feminine**	**Neuter**
Nom., Voc.	τῑμά-ων > τῑμῶν	τῑμά-ουσα > τῑμῶσα	τῑμά-ον > τῑμῶν
Gen.	τῑμῶντος	τῑμώσης	τῑμῶντος
Dat.	τῑμῶντι	τῑμώσῃ	τῑμῶντι
Acc.	τῑμῶντα	τῑμῶσαν	τῑμῶν

Nom., Voc.	τῑμῶντες	τῑμῶσαι	τῑμῶντα
Gen.	τῑμώντων	τῑμωσῶν	τῑμώντων
Dat.	τῑμῶσι(ν)	τῑμώσαις	τῑμῶσι(ν)
Acc.	τῑμῶντας	τῑμώσᾱς	τῑμῶντα

Exercise 9α

1. *Locate twelve present active participles in the reading passage at the beginning of this chapter, identify the gender, case, and number of each, and locate the noun, pronoun, or subject of a verb that each participle modifies.*
2. *Fill in the present participles on the four Verb Charts on which you entered forms for Exercises 4α and 5α.*

Exercise 9β

Write the correct form of the present participle of the verb given in parentheses to agree with the following article-noun groups:

1. οἱ παῖδες (τρέχω)
2. τῷ ἀνδρί (βαδίζω)
3. τοὺς νεᾱνίᾱς (τῑμάω)
4. τοῖς παισί(ν) (εἰμί)
5. τῶν νεᾱνιῶν (μάχομαι)
6. τὰς γυναῖκας (λέγω)
7. τὸν Δικαιόπολιν (εὔχομαι)
8. τοῦ δούλου (πονέω)
9. αἱ παρθένοι (ἀκούω)
10. τοῦ ἀγγέλου (βοάω)

Exercise 9γ

Complete each of the following sentences by adding the correct form of a participle to translate the verb in parentheses, and then translate the sentence:

1. οἱ δοῦλοι ἥκουσι τοὺς βοῦς (leading).
2. ὁ πολῑτης ξένον τινὰ ὁρᾷ πρὸς τῇ ὁδῷ (waiting).
3. αἱ γυναῖκες ἐν τῷ ἀγρῷ καθίζονται τοὺς παῖδας (watching).
4. οἱ παῖδες οὐ παύονται λίθους (throwing).
5. οἱ ἄνδρες θεῶνται τὴν παρθένον πρὸς τὴν πόλιν (running).

Exercise 9δ

Translate the following pairs of sentences:

1. οἱ παῖδες ἐν τῇ ἀγορᾷ καθίζονται οἶνον πῑνοντες.
   The slaves hurry home, driving the oxen.
2. ἆρ’ ὁρᾷς τὴν παρθένον εἰς τὸ ἱερὸν σπεύδουσαν;
   The foreigner sees the boys running into the agora.
3. πάντες ἀκούουσι τοῦ ἀλλᾱντοπώλου τὰ ὤνια βοῶντος.
   No one hears the girl calling her mother.

4. οἱ ἄνδρες τὰς γυναῖκας λείπουσιν ἐν τῷ οἴκῳ τὸ δεῖπνον παρασκευα-
ζούσᾱς.
The boy finds his father waiting in the agora.

5. ὁ νεᾱνίᾱς τὴν παρθένον φιλεῖ μάλα καλὴν οὖσαν.
The father honors the boy who is (= *being*) very brave.

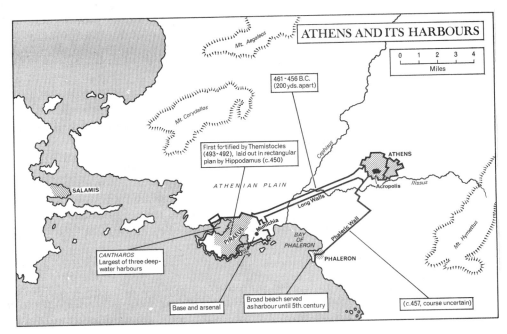

The Piraeus and Athens in the time of Pericles

Reconstruction of the agora at Athens as seen from the southeast, about 400 B.C.

The City of Athens

The city to which Dicaeopolis and his family journeyed was largely built after the battle of Salamis, since the earlier city and its temples were destroyed when the Persians occupied and sacked Athens. A visitor coming by sea would arrive at the Piraeus, the greatest port in Greece and perhaps its finest natural harbor. The fortification of the Piraeus was begun by Themistocles in 493–492 B.C. It was completed after the Greek victory at Plataea, when the city of Athens was rebuilt and connected to the Piraeus by the Long Walls, making Athens virtually impregnable as long as she controlled the seas.

Leaving the harbor quarter, visitors would have made their way through the marketplace and town of Piraeus to the road that led between the Long Walls, and then they would have walked the five miles or eight kilometers to Athens through continuous traffic of mules and ox-carts carrying goods to and from the city. From a distance they would have seen the Parthenon dominating the Acropolis and perhaps the spear of the great statue of Athena in full armor, which stood outside the Parthenon.

Entering the city, they would see on their left close to the city wall the Pnyx, a large open slope where the Assembly met (see map, page 132). They would then pass between the Areopagus (Hill of Ares), a bare outcrop of rock of immemorial sanctity, and the Acropolis into the agora. This was the center of Athens. On the left stood the Strategeion or Generals' Headquarters (to the left of and not shown in the model on the facing page) and then (see model) the Tholos (the round magistrates' clubhouse), the Metroon (Archive), the temple of Apollo Patroos, and the stoa of Zeus; behind the Metroon stood the Bouleuterion (Council Chamber); on the right (not shown in the model) were the law courts. On the hill behind the Bouleuterion there still stands the temple of Hephaestus, the best preserved of all Greek temples. In the agora itself were great altars to Zeus and to the ten eponymous heroes of Athens, and there were also fine marble colonnades (stoas), where people could rest and talk in the shade.

The agora was not only the seat of government but also the market and mercantile center of Athens. Here you could buy anything, as a comic poet of this time wrote:

> You will find everything sold together in the same place at Athens: figs, witnesses to summonses, bunches of grapes, turnips, pears, apples, givers of evidence, roses, medlars, porridge, honeycombs, chickpeas, lawsuits, puddings, myrtle, allotment-machines, irises, lambs, waterclocks, laws, indictments.

Pushing their way eastwards through the crowds of people conducting business or strolling in conversation, our visitors would reach the Panathenaic Way, which led to the Acropolis (see map, page 132, and illustrations, page 141). As they climbed to the top of the steep road, they would see on their right the little temple of Athena Nike, built to commemorate victory over the

Persians (see model, page 141, and photograph, page 280). They would then enter the great monumental gateway, the Propylaea, designed by Mnesicles to balance the Parthenon but never completed, since work was interrupted by the outbreak of war in 431 B.C. Even so, it was a beautiful and impressive building, which included a picture gallery.

On leaving the Propylaea, our visitors face the Parthenon and in front of it the great bronze statue of Athena Promachos. The temple takes the traditional form of a cella, in which stood the statue of the goddess, surrounded by a peristyle of Doric columns. The architect, Ictinus, incorporated many subtleties in the basically simple design, and these give the temple a unique grace and lightness, despite its great size. The sculptures that adorned the two pediments, the 92 metopes, and the frieze running around the cella were designed by Pericles' friend Pheidias. On the frieze was depicted the great Panathenaic procession, in which every fourth year representatives of the whole people of Athens brought the offering of a new robe to their patron goddess. Inside the cella was the great statue of Athena, standing in full armor, made of ivory and gold, so awe-inspiring that none could look on it without fear and admiration (see reconstruction, page 132).

To the north of the Parthenon stood the Erechtheum, sacred to Erechtheus, the founder-king of Athens, and to Poseidon and Athena. The temple is irregular in plan, having three porticoes, each in a different style; it stood on the site of the most ancient shrine on the Acropolis. Here could be seen the sacred olive tree that Athena had given to the people of Athens and the sacred serpent, which embodied the spirit of Erechtheus.

Crossing to the southern edge of the Acropolis, behind the Parthenon, our visitors would look down on the precinct of Dionysus (see photograph, page 144). There was the theater (not built in stone until the following century) and the temple of Dionysus.

All these buildings, and others, were part of Pericles' master program. They were paid for by the tribute of the subject allies. His political opponents said, "The treasure contributed for the necessity of war was being squandered on the city, to gild her all over and adorn her like a harlot, with precious stones and statues and temples." Pericles answered that the people were not obliged to give any account of the money to the allies, provided that Athens maintained their defense and kept off the Persians. His program gave employment to an army of workmen and artists and made Athens a worthy center of her empire, "an education to Greece."

Maidens from the frieze of the Parthenon

Model of the Athenian Acropolis

The Parthenon seen from the Propylaea

Η ΠΑΝΗΓΥΡΙΣ (β)

τῶν παρόντων πολλοὶ μεθύοντες κωμάζουσιν.

VOCABULARY

Verbs
αὐξάνω, *I increase*
καίω or **κᾱ́ω**, κᾱ́εις, κᾱ́ει, κᾱ́ομεν,
κᾱ́ετε, κᾱ́ουσι(ν), active, transitive, *I kindle, burn;* middle,
intransitive, *I burn, am on
fire*
σῑγάω, *I am silent*
τέρπομαι, *I enjoy myself;*
+ dat., *I enjoy* X; + participle,
I enjoy doing X
Nouns
ὁ γέρων, τοῦ γέροντος, *old
man*
ὁ δῆμος, τοῦ δήμου, *the people*
τὸ ἱερεῖον, τοῦ ἱερείου, *sacrificial victim*

ὁ ἱερεύς, τοῦ ἱερέως, *priest*
ὁ κῆρυξ, τοῦ κήρῡκος, *herald*
ὁ οὐρανός, τοῦ οὐρανοῦ, *sky,
heaven*
ἡ πομπή, τῆς πομπῆς, *procession*
Adjectives
ἄριστος, -η, -ον, *best; very
good; noble*
γέρων, γέροντος, *old*
ἕτοιμος, -η, -ον, *ready*
ἵλεως, acc., ἵλεων, *propitious*
μέσος, -η, -ον, *middle (of)*
Proper Name
ὁ Βρόμιος, τοῦ Βρομίου, *the
Thunderer* (a name of Dionysus)

ἑσπέρᾱ ἤδη πάρεστιν. δι' ὀλίγου σῑγῶσι πάντες οἱ ἄνθρωποι· ὁ
γὰρ κῆρυξ προχωρεῖ καὶ βοῶν, "σῑγᾶτε, ὦ πολῖται," φησίν· "ἡ γὰρ
πομπὴ προσχωρεῖ. ἐκποδὼν γίγνεσθε." πάντες οὖν ἐκποδὼν γίγνονται καὶ τὴν πομπὴν μένουσιν.

[**ἐκποδών**, *out of the way*]

ἐνταῦθα δὴ τὴν πομπὴν ὁρῶσι προσχωροῦσαν. ἡγοῦνται μὲν οἱ   5
κήρυκες· ἔπειτα δὲ παρθένοι κάλλισται βαδίζουσι κανᾶ φέρουσαι
βοτρύων πλήρη. ἕπονται δὲ αὐταῖς πολλοί τε πολῖται ἀσκοὺς οἴνου
φέροντες καὶ πολλοὶ μέτοικοι σκάφια φέροντες. ἔπειτα δὲ προχωρεῖ ὁ
τοῦ Διονύσου ἱερεὺς καὶ ἅμ᾽ αὐτῷ νεανίαι ἄριστοι τὴν τοῦ Διονύσου
εἰκόνα φέροντες. τελευταῖοι δὲ οἱ ὑπηρέται ἔρχονται τὰ ἱερεῖα   10
ἄγοντες.

[κανᾶ, *baskets*   βοτρύων πλήρη, *full of grapes*   ἀσκοὺς οἴνου, *skins (full) of wine*
μέτοικοι, *metics* (resident aliens)   σκάφια, *trays* (of offerings)   ἅμ᾽ αὐτῷ, *together
with him*   τελευταῖοι, *last in order*   οἱ ὑπηρέται, *the attendants*]

πάντες οὖν χαίροντες τῇ πομπῇ ἕπονται πρὸς τὸ τοῦ θεοῦ
τέμενος. ἐπεὶ δὲ ἀφικνοῦνται, ὁ μὲν ἱερεὺς καὶ οἱ νεανίαι τὴν τοῦ θεοῦ
εἰκόνα εἰς τὸ ἱερὸν φέρουσιν, οἱ δὲ ὑπηρέται τὰ ἱερεῖα πρὸς τὸν βωμὸν
ἄγουσιν. ἔπειτα δὲ ὁ κῆρυξ τῷ δήμῳ κηρύττων, "εὐφημεῖτε, ὦ   15
πολῖται," φησίν. σῑγᾷ οὖν ὁ πᾶς ὅμιλος καὶ ἥσυχος μένει.

[κηρύττων, *proclaiming*   εὐφημεῖτε, *keep holy silence!*   ἥσυχος, *quiet(ly)*]

ὁ δὲ ἱερεὺς τὰς χεῖρας πρὸς τὸν οὐρανὸν αἴρων, "ὦ ἄναξ
Διόνυσε," φησίν, "ἄκουέ μου εὐχομένου· Βρόμιε, τήν τε θυσίαν δέχου
καὶ ἵλεως ἴσθι τῷ δήμῳ· σὺ γὰρ ἵλεως ὢν τάς τε ἀμπέλους σῴζεις καὶ
αὐξάνεις τοὺς βότρυας ὥστε παρέχειν ἡμῖν τὸν οἶνον."   20

[ἄναξ, *lord*   τήν ... θυσίαν, *the sacrifice*   τάς ... ἀμπέλους, *the vines*]

οἱ δὲ παρόντες πάντες βοῶσιν· "ἐλελεῦ, ἴου, ἴου, Βρόμιε, ἵλεως ὢν
τούς τε βότρυας αὔξανε καὶ πάρεχε ἡμῖν τὸν οἶνον." ἔπειτα δὲ ὁ
ἱερεὺς σφάττει τὰ ἱερεῖα· οἱ δὲ ὑπηρέται ἕτοιμοι ὄντες λαμβάνουσιν
αὐτὰ καὶ κατατέμνουσιν. καὶ τὰ μὲν τῷ θεῷ παρέχουσιν ἐν τῷ βωμῷ
κάοντες, τὰ δὲ τοῖς παροῦσι διαιροῦσιν. ἐπεὶ δὲ ἕτοιμά ἐστι πάντα, ὁ   25
ἱερεὺς οἶνον σπένδει καὶ τῷ θεῷ εὔχεται. ἐνταῦθα δὴ πάντες τόν τ᾽
οἶνον πίνουσι καὶ τὰ κρέα ἐσθίουσι τῷ δαιτὶ τερπόμενοι.

[ἐλελεῦ, ἴου, ἴου: *untranslatable ritual chants*   σφάττει, *slaughters*   κατατέμνουσιν, *cut up*   τὰ μὲν ... τὰ δὲ, *some (parts) ... other (parts)*   διαιροῦσιν,
they divide   σπένδει, *pours ... as a libation*   τὰ κρέα, *the flesh*   τῷ δαιτὶ, *the feast*]

μέση νὺξ νῦν ἐστιν, τῶν δὲ παρόντων πολλοὶ μεθύοντες

κωμάζουσιν. ἡ οὖν Μυρρίνη, φοβουμένη ὑπὲρ τῶν παίδων, "ἄγε δή,
ὦ ἄνερ," φησίν, "ὁ πάππος μάλα κάμνει. καιρός ἐστιν ἐπανιέναι πρὸς   30
τὰς πύλας καὶ καθεύδειν." ὁ δὲ πάππος, "τί λέγεις;" φησίν, "οὐ κάμνω
ἐγώ. βούλομαι κωμάζειν." ὁ δὲ Δικαιόπολις, "γέρων εἶ, ὦ πάππα,"
φησίν· "οὐ προσήκει σοι κωμάζειν. ἐλθέ." οὕτω λέγει καὶ ἡγεῖται
αὐτοῖς πρὸς τὰς πύλας. ἐπεὶ δὲ ἀφικνοῦνται, τὸν ἡμίονον εὑρίσκουσιν, καὶ πάντες χαμαὶ καθεύδουσιν.   35

[μεθύοντες, *being drunk*   κωμάζουσιν, *are reveling*   οὐ προσήκει σοι, *it is not
suitable for you*   τὸν ἡμίονον, *the mule*   χαμαὶ *on the ground*]

WORD BUILDING

*Describe the relationship between the words in the following sets. From your
knowledge of the words at the left, deduce the meaning of those to the right:*

1. ἡ πόλις   ὁ πολίτης   πολῑτικός, -ή, -όν
2. ἡ ναῦς   ὁ ναύτης   ναυτικός, -ή, -όν
3. ποιέω   ὁ ποιητής   ποιητικός, -ή, -όν

The theater of Dionysus

GRAMMAR

2. 3rd Declension Nouns with Stems Ending in -ντ-

In Vocabulary 9β you had the noun ὁ γέρων, τοῦ γέροντος, *old man;* as adjective in the masculine and neuter only, *old*. Nouns and adjectives such as this with stems ending in -ντ- decline the same as present active participles such as λύων, λύοντος (see Grammar 1, pages 135–136). PRACTICE: Write all the forms of ὁ γέρων, τοῦ γέροντος.

3. 3rd Declension Nouns with Stems Ending in a Vowel: ἡ πόλις and τὸ ἄστυ

Stems: πολι-/πολε-, *city*

	Singular		**Plural**	
Nom.	ἡ	πόλι-ς	αἱ	πόλε-ες > πόλεις
Gen.	τῆς	πόλε-ως	τῶν	πόλε-ων
Dat.	τῇ	πόλε-ι	ταῖς	πόλε-σι(ν)
Acc.	τὴν	πόλι-ν	τὰς	πόλεις
Voc.	ὦ	πόλι	ὦ	πόλε-ες > πόλεις

Stems: ἀστυ-/αστε-, *city*

	Singular		**Plural**	
Nom.	τὸ	ἄστυ	τὰ	ἄστε-α > ἄστη
Gen.	τοῦ	ἄστε-ως	τῶν	ἄστε-ων
Dat.	τῷ	ἄστε-ι	τοῖς	ἄστε-σι(ν)
Acc.	τὸ	ἄστυ	τὰ	ἄστε-α > ἄστη
Voc.	ὦ	ἄστυ	ὦ	ἄστε-α > ἄστη

Note that the stems appear as πολι- and αστυ- in the nominative, accusative, and vocative singulars and as πολε- and ἀστε- in the other cases. Note the -ως ending instead of -ος in the genitive singular of both words and ν instead of α in the accusative singular of πόλις. Note where contraction takes place.

Note that nouns of this type accent the third syllable from the end in the genitive singular and plural even though the final syllable is long. Originally the genitive singular was πόληος, and this became πόλεως by *quantitative metathesis*, with the original accent retained. The genitive plural πόλεων accents its first syllable in imitation of the singular.

PRACTICE: Write the complete sets of the forms of ὁ μάντις, τοῦ μάντεως, *seer*, and of ὁ πῆχυς, τοῦ πήχεως, *forearm*.

4. 3rd Declension Nouns with Stems Ending in Diphthongs or Vowels: ὁ βασιλεύς and the Irregular Nouns ἡ ναῦς and ὁ βοῦς

The stem of βασιλεύς was originally βασιληϝ-; for the letter ϝ, see below.

Stems: βασιλευ-/βασιλε-, *king*

	Singular		Plural	
Nom.	ὁ	βασιλεύ-ς	οἱ	βασιλῆς
Gen.	τοῦ	βασιλέ-ως	τῶν	βασιλέ-ων
Dat.	τῷ	βασιλέ-ι > βασιλεῖ	τοῖς	βασιλεῦ-σι(ν)
Acc.	τὸν	βασιλέ-ᾱ	τοὺς	βασιλέ-ᾱς
Voc.	ὦ	βασιλεῦ	ὦ	βασιλῆς

The stem βασιλευ- is used before consonants, and the stem βασιλε-, before vowels. The words ὁ Θησεύς and ὁ ἱερεύς are declined the same as ὁ βασιλεύς.

The stems of ναῦς and βοῦς were originally νηϝ- and βοϝ-. The letter ϝ (digamma) represented a *w* sound (compare Latin *navis* and *bovis*). This sound and letter were lost in the development of the Greek language.

Stems: ναυ-/νε-/νη-, *ship* **Stems:** βου-/βο-, *ox*

	Singular		Plural		Singular		Plural	
Nom.	ἡ	ναῦ-ς	αἱ	νῆ-ες	ὁ	βοῦ-ς	οἱ	βό-ες
Gen.	τῆς	νε-ώς	τῶν	νε-ῶν	τοῦ	βο-ός	τῶν	βο-ῶν
Dat.	τῇ	νη-ΐ	ταῖς	ναυ-σί(ν)	τῷ	βο-ΐ	τοῖς	βου-σί(ν)
Acc.	τὴν	ναῦ-ν	τὰς	ναῦ-ς	τὸν	βοῦ-ν	τοὺς	βοῦ-ς
Voc.	ὦ	ναῦ	ὦ	νῆ-ες	ὦ	βοῦ	ὦ	βό-ες

PRACTICE: Write complete sets of ὁ μέγας βασιλεύς, *the great king*, ἡ καλὴ ναῦς, *the beautiful ship*, and ὁ ἰσχυρὸς βοῦς, *the strong ox*.

Exercise 9ε

In each of the following phrases put the noun and adjective into the correct forms to agree with the article:

1. αἱ (μακρός) (ναῦς)
2. τοῦ (καλός) (ἄστυ)
3. τῶν (μέγας) (βασιλεύς)
4. τῷ (μέγας) (βοῦς)
5. τῆς (μέγας) (πόλις)
6. τοῖς (μέγας) (ἄστυ)
7. (πᾶς) τῶν (ναῦς)
8. τὴν (πᾶς) (πόλις)
9. τοῖς (ἰσχυρός) (βοῦς)
10. τῇ (μῑκρός) (πόλις)
11. τοῦ (μέγας) (βασιλεύς)
12. τὰς (μέγιστος) (ναῦς)
13. οἱ (μέγας) (βοῦς)
14. τὸν (σοφός) (βασιλεύς)

5. Uses of the Genitive Case

a. The genitive is frequently used to show *possession*, e.g., ὁ τοῦ παιδὸς κύων = the **boy's** dog, the dog **of the boy**. Note that the genitive is usually placed in the *attributive position* between the article and the noun (see Chapter 5, Grammar 7a, page 66) or after the repeated article: ὁ κύων ὁ τοῦ παιδός. Exception: the possessive genitives αὐτοῦ, αὐτῆς, and αὐτῶν, *of him / of it, of her*, and *of them* occupy the predicate position (see Chapter 5, Grammar 7b, page 66), e.g., ὁ κύων **αὐτοῦ**, *his dog*.

b. The genitive is used to express the whole of which some part is mentioned; this is the *genitive of the whole* or the *partitive genitive*, e.g., **τῶν παρόντων** πολλοί = many **of those present**.

c. The genitive case is used after certain prepositions, often (but by no means always) expressing ideas of *place from which*, e.g., ἀπό, *from;* διά, *through;* ἐκ, ἐξ, *out of;* μετά, *with;* and ὑπέρ, *on behalf of, for*.

d. The genitive is used with certain verbs, e.g.:

ἡ Ἀριάδνη, ἐπεὶ πρῶτον ὁρᾷ τὸν Θησέα, **ἐρᾷ αὐτοῦ**.
*Ariadne, when she first sees Theseus, **loves him**.*

ὁ Θησεὺς τῇ ἀριστερᾷ **λαμβάνεται τῆς** τοῦ θηρίου **κεφαλῆς**.
*Theseus **takes hold of the head** of the beast with his left hand.*

e. For the genitive of time within which, see Chapter 8, Grammar 6, page 129.

Exercise 9ζ

Translate the following:

1. τί ἐστι τὸ τοῦ ξένου ὄνομα;
2. ὁ βασιλεὺς δέχεται τὸν τῶν Ἀθηναίων ἄγγελον.
3. ἀφικνούμεθα εἰς τὸν τοῦ πατρὸς ἀγρόν.
4. ὁ παῖς κατὰ τὴν ὁδὸν βαδίζων τῆς τοῦ πατρὸς χειρὸς ἔχεται.
5. οἱ πολῖται τοῦ ἀγγέλου ἀκούουσι βουλόμενοι γιγνώσκειν τοὺς τοῦ βασιλέως λόγους (*words / proposals*).
6. We hear the messenger's words.
7. I am going to the house of the poet.
8. They are looking for the girl's father.
9. The mother hears the girl crying (*use* δακρύω) and hurries out of the house.
10. The citizens take hold of the messenger and lead him to the king.
11. Many of the women want to go to the city with their husbands.

6. Some Uses of the Article

a. You have already met the following uses of the article (see Chapter 5, Grammar 3, page 58):

ὁ δέ = *and / but he*   ἡ δέ = *and / but she*

οἱ δέ = *and / but they*   αἱ δέ = *and / but they*

ὁ/ἡ/τὸ μὲν . . . ὁ/ἡ/τὸ δέ = *the one . . . the other*

οἱ/αἱ/τὰ μὲν . . . οἱ/αἱ/τὰ δέ = *some . . . others*

b. The article + an adjective can form a noun phrase, e.g.:

Adjectives: **Noun Phrases:**

ἀνδρεῖος, -ᾱ, -ον = *brave*   οἱ ἀνδρεῖοι = *the brave men*

σώφρων, σῶφρον = *prudent*   αἱ σώφρονες = *the prudent women*

φίλος, -η, -ον = *dear*   οἱ φίλοι or αἱ φίλαι = *the friends*

πολέμιος, -ᾱ, -ον = *hostile*   οἱ πολέμιοι = *the enemy*

c. The article + an adverb, prepositional phrase, or genitive can form a noun phrase, e.g.:

οἱ νῦν = *the now men* = *the men of today* = *the present generation*

οἱ πάλαι = *the men of old*

αἱ ἐν τῇ ἀγορᾷ = *the women in the agora*

αἱ πρὸς τῇ κρήνῃ = *the women at the spring*

ὁ βασιλέως = *the (son) of the king* = *the king's son*

τὰ εἴσω = *the things inside* = *the inside*

τὰ τῆς πόλεως = *the things (i.e., the affairs) of the city* = *politics*

d. The neuter of an adjective + the article is often used as an abstract noun, e.g.:

τὸ καλόν = *beauty*; *virtue*; *honor*

τὸ αἰσχρόν = *dishonor*; *disgrace*; *vice*

τὸ ἀληθές or τὰ ἀληθῆ = *the truth*

τὸ δίκαιον = *justice*

τὸ ἕν = *the one* = *unity*

e. The article + a participle forms a noun phrase that may be translated by a relative clause in English, e.g.:

οἱ παρόντες = *the ones being present* = *those who are present*

οἱ ἐν τῷ ἀγρῷ ἐργαζόμενοι = *the in the field working (men)* = *the men who are working in the field*

ὁ ἱερεὺς ὁ τὴν θυσίᾱν ποιούμενος = *the priest who is making the sacrifice*

These participles are said to be *attributive*, serving as simple adjectives; see Chapter 8, Grammar 1b, page 115.

Exercise 9η

Read aloud and translate:

1. ὁ πατὴρ τὸν παῖδα κελεύει ἐν τῷ ἄστει μένειν· ὁ δὲ οὐ πείθεται αὐτῷ.

2. τῶν πολῑτῶν οἱ μὲν οἴκαδε ἐπανέρχονται, οἱ δὲ μένουσι τὴν πομπὴν θεώμενοι.

3. τῶν παρθένων αἱ μὲν πρὸς τῇ κρήνῃ μένουσιν, αἱ δὲ μετὰ τῶν μητέρων ἤδη οἴκαδε ἐπανέρχονται.

4. αἱ παρθένοι αἱ τὰ κανᾶ φέρουσαι κάλλισταί εἰσιν.

5. οἱ τοὺς χοροὺς θεώμενοι μάλα χαίρουσιν.

6. ἆρ' ὁρᾷς τοὺς ἐν τῷ ἀγρῷ πονοῦντας;

7. οἱ σοὶ φίλοι βούλονται τὰ τῆς πόλεως γιγνώσκειν.

8. οἱ νεᾱνίαι οἱ πρὸς τὸν ἀγρὸν σπεύδοντες μέλλουσι τῷ πατρὶ συλλαμ-βάνειν.

9. μὴ ταῦτά (*this*) μοι λέγε· ἀγνοεῖς (*you do not know*) γὰρ τὰ τῆς πόλεως.

10. πάντες οἱ νῦν τῑμῶσι τοὺς τὴν πόλιν φιλοῦντας.

11. οἱ σοὶ φίλοι βούλονται γιγνώσκειν τί ἐστι τὸ δίκαιον.

12. αἱ ἐν τῇ οἰκίᾳ διαλέγονται ἀλλήλαις περὶ τοῦ καλοῦ.

13. σῷζε τοὺς ἐν τῇ νηΐ· ἐν μεγίστῳ γὰρ κινδῡνῳ εἰσίν.

Ο ΟΔΥΣΣΕΥΣ ΚΑΙ Η ΚΙΡΚΗ

Read the following passages and answer the comprehension questions:

Odysseus comes to the island of Aeaea, where the witch Circe lives:

ἐπεὶ δὲ ἡμᾶς ἀποπέμπει ὁ Αἴολος, ἀποπλέομεν λῡπούμενοι καὶ δι' ὀλίγου ἀφικνούμεθα εἰς τὴν νῆσον Αἰαίᾱν· ἐκεῖ δὲ οἰκεῖ ἡ Κίρκη, θεὸς οὖσα δεινή. ἐγὼ δὲ τοὺς ἑταίρους πρὸς τῇ νηῒ λείπων ἐπὶ ὄρος τι ἀναβαίνω, βουλόμενος γιγνώσκειν εἴ τις ἄνθρωπος ἐν τῇ νήσῳ οἰκεῖ. ἐπεὶ δὲ εἰς ἄκρον τὸ ὄρος ἀφικνοῦμαι, καπνὸν ὁρῶ πρὸς τὸν οὐρανὸν φερόμενον. πρὸς τὴν ναῦν οὖν ἐπανέρχομαι καὶ τῶν ἑταίρων τοὺς   5 μὲν κελεύω πρὸς τῇ νηῒ μένειν, τοὺς δὲ κελεύω πρὸς μέσην τὴν νῆσον πορευομένους γιγνώσκειν τίς ἐκεῖ οἰκεῖ. ὁ δὲ Εὐρύλοχος αὐτοῖς ἡγεῖται.

[λῡπούμενοι, *grieving*   εἴ τις, *if any*   καπνὸν, *smoke*   φερόμενον, *rising* Εὐρύλοχος, *Eurylochus*]

1. With what feelings do Odysseus and his men set sail?
2. How is Circe described?
3. Why does Odysseus climb the hill?
4. What does he see from the top of the hill?
5. With what purpose in mind does Odysseus send some of his men to the middle of the island?
6. Who leads them?

οἱ δὲ τὴν τῆς Κίρκης οἰκίαν εὑρίσκουσιν ἐν μέσῃ ὕλῃ οὖσαν· ἐγγὺς δὲ τῆς οἰκίας πολλούς τε λύκους ὁρῶσι καὶ πολλοὺς λέοντας. τούτους δὲ ὁρῶντες μάλα φοβοῦνται καὶ πρὸς τῇ θύρᾳ μένουσιν. ἔπειτα δὲ τῆς Κίρκης ἀκούουσιν ἔνδον ᾀδούσης. 10 καλοῦσιν οὖν αὐτήν· ἡ δὲ ἐκ τῆς θύρας ἐκβαίνει καὶ εἰσκαλεῖ αὐτούς. οἱ δὲ πάντες ἕπονται αὐτῇ· μόνος δὲ ὁ Εὐρύλοχος ἔξω μένει, φοβούμενος κίνδῡνόν τινα. ἡ δὲ Κίρκη τοὺς ἄλλους εἰσάγει καὶ καθίζεσθαι κελεύει καὶ σῖτόν τε αὐτοῖς παρέχει καὶ οἶνον· φάρμακα δὲ κακὰ τῷ σίτῳ κυκᾷ.

[ὕλη, woods   ἐγγὺς + gen., near   λέοντας, lions   τούτους, them   ἔνδον, inside
ᾀδούσης, singing   μόνος, only   ἔξω, outside   φάρμακα . . . κακὰ, evil drugs
κυκᾷ, she mixes]

7. What do the men see around Circe's house?
8. What feeling prompts the men to wait at Circe's door rather than going in?
9. What do they hear?
10. Why does Circe come out of the door?
11. Who follow her in?
12. Why does Eurylochus not go in?
13. What three things does Circe hand over to the men to eat and drink?

ἐπεὶ δὲ οἱ ἑταῖροι ἐσθίουσι τὸν σῖτον, ἡ Κίρκη τῇ ῥάβδῳ αὐτοὺς πλήττει καὶ εἰς 15 τοὺς συφεοὺς ἐλαύνει· οἱ δὲ εὐθὺς σύες γίγνονται. ἔπειτα δὲ ἡ Κίρκη βαλάνους αὐτοῖς βάλλει ἐσθίειν καὶ λείπει αὐτοὺς ἐν τοῖς συφεοῖς.

[τῇ ῥάβδῳ, with her wand   πλήττει, strikes   τοὺς συφεοὺς, the pigsties   εὐθὺς,
immediately   σύες, pigs   βαλάνους, acorns]

14. How does Circe change the men into pigs?
15. What does she now hand over to them to eat and where does she leave them?

Exercise 9θ

Translate into Greek:

1. When Eurylochus sees what is happening, he flees and runs to the ship.
2. But I, when I hear everything, go to Circe's house, wishing to save my comrades.
3. And Circe hands over to me food and wine; then, striking (*use* πλήττω) me with her wand (*use* ἡ ῥάβδος), she orders (me) to go to the pigsties (*use* οἱ συφεοί).
4. But I do not become a pig (σῦς); and she, being very afraid, is willing to free (λύειν) my comrades.

Classical Greek

Simonides

The following is an epigram (no. LXXVI, Campbell) written by Simonides of Ceos (late sixth to early fifth century B.C.) on sailors lost at sea; they were taking spoils of war (ἀκροθίνια) from Sparta to Delphi as an offering to Apollo (ὁ Φοῖβος). Since the men were lost at sea and the hull of their ship was their tomb, the verb ἐκτέρισεν is used ironically.

τούσδε ποτ᾽ ἐκ Σπάρτᾱς ἀκροθίνια Φοίβῳ ἄγοντας

ἓν πέλαγος, μία νύξ, ἓν σκάφος ἐκτέρισεν.

[**τούσδε,** *these men*　**ποτ(ε),** *once*　**πέλαγος (τό),** *sea*　**σκάφος,** *hull of a ship*
ἐκτέρισεν, *buried with due honors* (τὰ κτέρεα, *funeral gifts, honors*)]

New Testament Greek

Luke 6.31–33
The Sermon on the Mount

"καὶ καθὼς θέλετε ἵνα ποιῶσιν ὑμῖν οἱ ἄνθρωποι ποιεῖτε αὐτοῖς ὁμοίως. καὶ εἰ ἀγαπᾶτε τοὺς ἀγαπῶντας ὑμᾶς, ποίᾱ ὑμῖν χάρις ἐστίν; καὶ γὰρ οἱ ἁμαρτωλοὶ τοὺς ἀγαπῶντας αὐτοὺς ἀγαπῶσιν. καὶ ἐὰν ἀγαθοποιῆτε τοὺς ἀγαθοποιοῦντας ὑμᾶς, ποίᾱ ὑμῖν χάρις ἐστίν; καὶ οἱ ἁμαρτωλοὶ τὸ αὐτὸ ποιοῦσιν."

[**καθὼς,** *as*　**θέλετε** = ἐθέλετε　**ἵνα ποιῶσιν ὑμῖν οἱ ἄνθρωποι,** *that men should do to you*　**ὁμοίως,** *likewise*　**εἰ,** *if*　**ἀγαπᾶτε,** *you love*　**τοὺς ἀγαπῶντας,** *those who love (those loving)*　**ποίᾱ . . . χάρις,** *what thanks?*　**ἁμαρτωλοὶ,** *sinners*
ἐὰν, *if*]

Concluded in Chapter 10α

Odysseus threatens Circe.

REVIEW OF VERB FORMS

The following are full sets of the forms of λύω, φιλέω, τῑμάω, and εἰμί that you have met so far in this course:

λύω: Active Voice

Indicative	Imperative	Infinitive	Participle
λύω		λύειν	λύων,
λύεις	λῦε		λύουσα,
λύει			λῦον,
λύομεν			gen., λύοντος, etc.
λύετε	λύετε		
λύουσι(ν)			

λύω: Middle Voice

Indicative	Imperative	Infinitive	Participle
λύομαι		λύεσθαι	λυόμενος, -η, -ον
λύει *or* λύῃ	λύου		
λύεται			
λῡόμεθα			
λύεσθε	λύεσθε		
λύονται			

φιλέω: Active Voice

Indicative	Imperative	Infinitive	Participle
φιλῶ		φιλεῖν	φιλῶν,
φιλεῖς	φίλει		φιλοῦσα,
φιλεῖ			φιλοῦν,
φιλοῦμεν			gen., φιλοῦντος, etc.
φιλεῖτε	φιλεῖτε		
φιλοῦσι(ν)			

φιλέω: Middle Voice

Indicative	Imperative	Infinitive	Participle
φιλοῦμαι		φιλεῖσθαι	φιλούμενος, -η, -ον
φιλεῖ *or* φιλῇ	φιλοῦ		
φιλεῖται			
φιλούμεθα			
φιλεῖσθε	φιλεῖσθε		
φιλοῦνται			

τῑμάω: Active Voice

Indicative	Imperative	Infinitive	Participle
τῑμῶ		τῑμᾶν	τῑμῶν,
τῑμᾷς	τίμᾱ		τῑμῶσα,
τῑμᾷ			τῑμῶν,
τῑμῶμεν			gen., τῑμῶντος, etc.
τῑμᾶτε	τῑμᾶτε		
τῑμῶσι(ν)			

τῑμάω: Middle Voice

τῑμῶμαι		τῑμᾶσθαι	τῑμώμενος, -η, -ον
τῑμᾷ	τῑμῶ		
τῑμᾶται			
τῑμώμεθα			
τῑμᾶσθε	τῑμᾶσθε		
τῑμῶνται			

εἰμί: Active Voice Only

εἰμί		εἶναι	ὤν,
εἶ	ἴσθι		οὖσα,
ἐστί(ν)			ὄν,
ἐσμέν			gen., ὄντος, etc.
ἐστέ	ἔστε		
εἰσί(ν)			

Odysseus threatens Circe
(a grotesque representation in the Boeotian Cabiran style)

PREVIEW OF
NEW VERB FORMS

Most of the verbs in the stories up to now have been in the present tense. In the stories in the remainder of this course you will also meet verbs in the imperfect, future, aorist, perfect, and pluperfect tenses.

The following is a brief overview of the Greek verbal system. It will give you a framework within which you will be able to place the various new verb forms. Note that only active voice forms are shown in the lists below.

First we give sample forms of λύω, which is typical of many Greek verbs that have past tense formations called *sigmatic 1st aorists*:

Present: λύ-ω = *I loosen, am loosening, do loosen*

Imperfect or Past Progressive: ἔ-λυ-ον = *I was loosening*

Sigmatic Future: λύ-σ-ω = *I will loosen, will be loosening*

Sigmatic 1st Aorist: ἔ-λυ-σα = *I loosened, did loosen*

    Sigmatic 1st Aorist Imperative: λῦ-σον = *loosen!*

    Sigmatic 1st Aorist Infinitive: λῦ-σαι = *to loosen*

    Sigmatic 1st Aorist Participle: λύ-σᾱς = *having loosened, after loosening*, sometimes, *loosening*

-κα 1st Perfect: λέ-λυ-κα = *I have loosened*

-κη 1st Pluperfect: ἐ-λε-λύ-κη = *I had loosened*

Some verbs have past tense formations without a σ as in the aorists above but with a thematic vowel (ο or ε) between the stem and the endings. These are called *thematic 2nd aorists*; here are the present and aorist tenses of such a verb (note the different stem in the 2nd aorist; see Chapter 11, Grammar 1, page 176):

Present: λείπ-ω = *I leave, am leaving, do leave*

Thematic 2nd Aorist: ἔ-λιπ-ο-ν = *I left, did leave*

    Thematic 2nd Aorist Imperative: λίπ-ε = *leave!*

    Thematic 2nd Aorist Infinitive: λιπ-εῖν = *to leave*

    Thematic 2nd Aorist Participle: λιπ-ών = *having left, after leaving*, sometimes, *leaving*

Notes on the lists above:

1. The imperfect or past progressive (e.g., ἔ-λυ-ον) is formed from the present stem, which is augmented by adding the prefix ἐ- or by lengthening the initial vowel, e.g., ἄγ-ω > ἦγ-ο-ν. Augmenting in one of these two ways signals past time. (For the imperfect or past progressive tense, see Chapter 13.)

2. The future tense is usually formed by adding -σ- to the stem and adding the same endings as for the present: e.g., λύ-σ-ω. (See Chapter 10.)

154

3. The sigmatic 1st aorist (e.g., ἔ-λῡ-**σα**) is formed with the suffix -σα and with augment, which shows past time and appears only in the indicative mood. (See Chapter 12.) Augment is absent from the aorist imperative (λῦ-**σον**), which does not refer to past time, from the infinitive (λῦ-**σαι**), which usually does not refer to past time, and from the participle (λῡ́-**σᾱς**), which usually describes an action completed prior to the action of the main verb but may describe an action without reference to time (further details in Chapters 11 and 12).

4. In thematic 2nd aorists (e.g., ἔ-**λιπ**-ο-ν) there is a change in the stem of the verb, a thematic vowel (ο or ε), and no -σα suffix. (See Chapter 11.)

Aspect

Aspect or the way an action is looked upon is very important in Greek. There are three aspects: (1) *progressive*, of action in process or ongoing, e.g., "John runs/is running/was running"; (2) *aorist*, of simple action, sometimes in past time, e.g., "John ran," and sometimes not, e.g., "Run, John!"; and (3) *perfective*, with emphasis on the enduring result of a completed action, e.g., "John has won the race"= "John won the race and is *now* the winner."

Voice

In Chapter 6 you learned that there are three voices in Greek, *active*, *middle*, and *passive*. In the present, imperfect, perfect, and pluperfect tenses, middle and passive forms are spelled the same and are distinguishable only by the context in which they are used (see Chapter 16). In the future and aorist there are different forms for the passive (see Chapter 17, Book II).

Verb Stems and Principal Parts

In many verbs the stem of the present tense is different from the stem or stems from which the other tenses are formed, as in the verb φέρω, *I carry*:

Present tense, φέρ-ω: stem, φερ-
Future tense, οἴ-σ-ω: stem, οἰ-
Aorist, ἤνεγκ-ο-ν: stem, ἐνεγκ-

In order to make it easier for you to learn the *principal parts* of Greek verbs, i.e., the forms that you need to know in order to make the various tenses, we will give in subsequent vocabulary lists the stem or stems when they are different from what is seen in the present tense, e.g.:

φέρω, [οἰ-] **οἴσω**, [ἐνεγκ-] **ἤνεγκον**, *I carry*

We will not give stems when they are the same in the other tenses as they are in the present.

Greek verbs normally have six principal parts, but in the vocabulary lists in the remainder of Book I we will give only the first three, as above. They should be memorized carefully.

10
Η ΣΥΜΦΟΡΑ (α)

ὁ πρῶτος χορὸς προχωρεῖ· τὰ τοῦ Διονύσου ἔργα ὑμνήσει.

VOCABULARY

Verb
ἀφικνέομαι [= ἀπο- + ἱκνέομαι],
[ἱκ-] **ἀφίξομαι, ἀφῑκόμην,** *I
arrive;* + εἰς + acc., *I arrive at*
γίγνομαι, [γενε-] **γενήσομαι,**
[γεν-] **ἐγενόμην,** *I become*
εὑρίσκω, [εὑρε-] **εὑρήσω,** [εὑρ-]
ηὗρον or **εὗρον,** *I find*
θεάομαι, θεάσομαι (note that
because of the ε the α lengthens

to ᾱ instead of η), **ἐθεᾱσάμην,**
I see, watch, look at
νῑκάω, νῑκήσω, ἐνίκησα, *I defeat; I win*
Adverb
καλῶς, *well*
Interjection
φεῦ, often used with gen. of
cause, *alas!*

τῇ δ' ὑστεραίᾳ, ἐπεὶ πρῶτον ἀνατέλλει ὁ ἥλιος, ὁ Δικαιόπολις τήν
τε γυναῖκα καὶ τοὺς παῖδας ἐγείρει· "ἐγείρεσθε," φησίν· "δι' ὀλίγου γὰρ
θεᾱσόμεθα τοὺς χορούς. σπεύδετε. εἰ γὰρ μὴ σπεύσετε, ὀψὲ
ἀφιξόμεθα." ὁ δὲ πάππος ἔτι καθεύδει. ὁ οὖν Δικαιόπολις, "ἐγείρου,
ὦ πάππα," φησίν. "εἰ γὰρ μὴ σπεύσεις, ὀψὲ ἀφίξει. ἄγε, ἡγήσομαί σοι   5
πρὸς τὸ θέᾱτρον." ὁ μὲν οὖν πάππος ἐγείρεται, ὁ δὲ Δικαιόπολις πᾶσι
πρὸς τὸ θέᾱτρον ἡγεῖται. ἐπεὶ δ' ἀφικνοῦνται, πλεῖστοι ἤδη ἄνθρωποι
τὸ θέᾱτρον πληροῦσιν.

[**ἀνατέλλει,** *is rising*   **ὀψὲ,** *(too) late*   **τὸ θέᾱτρον,** *the theater*   **πλεῖστοι,** *very
many*   **πληροῦσιν,** *are filling*]

ὁ οὖν πάππος στενάζει καί, "φεῦ, φεῦ," φησίν, "μεστόν ἐστι τὸ πᾶν
θέατρον· τοὺς οὖν χοροὺς οὐ θεάσομαι.   τί ποιήσομεν;" ὁ δὲ   10
Δικαιόπολις, "θάρρει, ὦ πάππα," φησίν. "ἕπου μοι. θρᾶνον
εὑρήσομεν." καὶ ἡγεῖται αὐτοῖς ἄνω καὶ θρᾶνον εὑρίσκει ἐν ἄκρῳ τῷ
θεάτρῳ. ἡ δὲ Μυρρίνη, "καθίζεσθε, ὦ παῖδες," φησίν. "ἐντεῦθεν
πάντα εὖ θεᾱσόμεθα."

[μεστόν, *full*   θάρρει, *cheer up!*   θρᾶνον, *bench, seat*   ἄνω, *upwards*   ἐντεῦθεν,
from here]

ἐπεὶ πρῶτον καθίζονται, προχωρεῖ ὁ κῆρυξ εἰς μέσην τὴν   15
ὀρχήστρᾱν καί, "εὐφημεῖτε, ὦ πολῖται," φησίν· "νῦν γὰρ γενήσονται οἱ
χοροί." ἐνταῦθα δὴ ὁ πρῶτος χορὸς προχωρεῖ εἰς τὴν ὀρχήστρᾱν,
καὶ τὰ τοῦ Διονύσου ἔργα ὑμνεῖ. θαυμάζει οὖν ἡ Μέλιττα θεωμένη
καὶ χαίρει ἀκούουσα. "ὡς καλῶς χορεύουσιν οἱ νεᾱνίαι," φησίν·
"νῑκήσουσι τοὺς ἄλλους καὶ δέξονται τοὺς στεφάνους."   20

[τὴν ὀρχήστρᾱν, *the dancing circle*   εὐφημεῖτε, *keep holy silence!*   ὑμνεῖ, *praises*
χορεύουσιν, *dance*   τοὺς στεφάνους, *the garlands*]

πέντε χοροὶ παίδων καὶ πέντε ἀνδρῶν ἐφεξῆς ἀγωνίζονται, καὶ
πάντες ἄριστα χορεύουσιν. ἐπεὶ δὲ παύεται ὁ δέκατος χορός, οἱ
νῑκῶντες τοὺς στεφάνους δέχονται, καὶ πάντες οἱ παρόντες
σπεύδουσιν ἐκ τοῦ θεάτρου.

[ἐφεξῆς, *in order*   ἀγωνίζονται, *compete*   ἄριστα, *very well*]

WORD STUDY

*Identify the Greek stems in the italicized words below and give the meanings
of the English words:*

1. He found fulfillment in an *agonistic* way of life.
2. She is studying *macroeconomics*.
3. He suffers from *xenophobia*.
4. He is a dangerous *pyromaniac*. What does ἡ μανίᾱ mean?
5. She is an *ophthalmic* surgeon.

GRAMMAR

1. Verb Forms: Verbs with Sigmatic Futures

Most verbs form the future tense by adding the suffix -σ- and adding the same endings as in the present tense, e.g.:

Future Active

Indicative	Infinitive	Participle
λύ-σ-ω, *I will loosen*	λύ-σ-ειν, *to be*	λύ-σ-ων,
λύ-σ-εις, *you will loosen*	*about to loosen*	λύ-σ-ουσα,
λύ-σ-ει, *he/she will loosen*		λῦ-σ-ον,
λύ-σ-ομεν, *we will loosen*		gen., λύ-σ-οντ-ος, etc.,
λύ-σ-ετε, *you will loosen*		*being about to loosen*
λύ-σ-ουσι(ν), *they will loosen*		

Future Middle

λύ-σ-ο-μαι, *I will ransom*	λύ-σ-ε-σθαι,	λῡ-σ-ό-μεν-ος, -η, -ον,
λύ-σ-ει *or* λύ-σ-ῃ, *you will ransom*	*to be about to*	*being about to*
λύ-σ-ε-ται, *he/she will ransom*	*ransom*	*ransom*
λῡ-σ-ό-μεθα, *we will ransom*		
λύ-σ-ε-σθε, *you will ransom*		
λύ-σ-ο-νται, *they will ransom*		

There is no future imperative.

The diphthong αι in the endings is counted as short for purposes of accentuation.

In the following, note what happens when the stem of the verb ends in a consonant instead of a vowel, as does λύ-ω above:

a. If the stem ends in a *labial* (β, π, φ), the labial + the future suffix -σ- produces the combination of sounds represented by the letter ψ, e.g.:

> βλέπ-ω, *I look; I see,* **βλέψομαι**
> πέμπ-ω, *I send,* **πέμψω**
> γράφ-ω, *I write,* **γράψω**

b. If the stem ends in a *velar* (γ, κ, χ), the velar + the future suffix -σ- produces the combination of sounds represented by the letter ξ, e.g.:

> λέγ-ω, *I say; I tell; I speak,* **λέξω** *or* ἐρῶ
> διώκ-ω, *I pursue,* **διώξομαι** *or,* less commonly, **διώξω**
> φυλάττω, *I guard,* [φυλακ-] **φυλάξω**
> δέχ-ομαι, *I receive,* **δέξομαι**
> Note: ἔχ-ω, *I have; I hold,* has two future forms: **ἕξω** (irregular), *I will have,* and [σχε-] **σχήσω**, *I will get.*

c. If the stem ends in a *dental* (δ, θ, τ) or ζ (= σ + δ), the dental or ζ is lost before the -σ- of the future, e.g.:

σπεύδ-ω, *I hurry*, **σπεύσω**
πείθ-ω, *I persuade*, **πείσω**
πάττω, *I sprinkle*, [πατ-] **πάσω**
παρασκευάζ-ω, *I prepare*, **παρασκευάσω**

2. Verb Forms: The Asigmatic Contract Future of Verbs in -ίζω

If the present tense form of a verb ends in -ίζω, its future stem ends in -ιε-, e.g., κομίζω, future stem, κομιε-. The future suffix -σ- is lost between the vowel at the end of the stem and the vowels of the personal endings. The vowels then contract as in the present tense of -ε- contract verbs such as φιλέω. We call futures formed this way *asigmatic contract futures*, e.g.:

κομίζ-ω, *I bring; I take*, κομιέ-(σ)-ω > **κομιῶ**, κομιεῖς, κομιεῖ, etc.
κομίζ-ο-μαι, *I get for myself, acquire*, κομιέ-(σ)-ο-μαι > **κομιοῦμαι**, κομιεῖ/κομιῇ, κομιεῖται, etc.

3. Verb Forms: The Sigmatic Future of Contract Verbs

Contract verbs lengthen the final stem vowel and then add -σ-, e.g.:

φιλέ-ω, *I love*, **φιλήσω**, φιλήσεις, φιλήσει, etc.
  Exception: καλέ-ω, *I call*, **καλῶ**, καλεῖς, καλεῖ, etc. (an asigmatic contract future with no difference in spelling between the present and the future)
ἡγέ-ο-μαι, *I lead*, **ἡγήσομαι**, ἡγήσει/ἡγήσῃ, ἡγήσεται, etc.
τῑμά-ω, *I honor*, **τῑμήσω**, τῑμήσεις, τῑμήσει, etc.
  Note: θεάομαι, *I see, watch, look at*, **θεᾱσομαι** (note that because of the ε the α lengthens to ᾱ rather than η)

A few verbs lengthen the ε of one form of their stem and add -σ-, e.g.:

γίγνομαι, *I become*, [γενε-] **γενήσομαι**, γενήσει/ῃ, γενήσεται, etc.
ἐθέλω, *I am willing; I wish*, [ἐθελε-] **ἐθελήσω**, ἐθελήσεις, ἐθελήσει, etc.

4. Verb Forms: Verbs with Deponent Futures

Some verbs, active in the present tense, have futures that are middle in form but active in meaning (i.e., deponent), often with a different stem, e.g.:

ἀκούω, *I hear*, **ἀκούσομαι**
βαδίζω, *I walk; I go*, [**βαδιε-**] **βαδιοῦμαι**

βαίνω, *I step; I walk; I go,* [βη-] **βήσομαι**

βλέπω, *I look; I see,* **βλέψομαι**

βοάω, *I shout,* **βοήσομαι**

γιγνώσκω, *I come to know; I perceive; I learn,* [γνω-] **γνώσομαι**

διώκω, *I pursue, chase,* **διώξομαι** or, less commonly, **διώξω**

θαυμάζω, intransitive, *I am amazed;* transitive, *I wonder at, admire,*
    θαυμάσομαι

ὁράω, *I see,* [ὀπ-] **ὄψομαι**

πάσχω, *I suffer; I experience,* [πενθ-] **πείσομαι**
    Note: πενθ-σ- > πενσ- > πεισ-

πίνω, *I drink,* [πῑ-] **πίομαι** (note absence of -σ-)

πίπτω, *I fall,* **πεσοῦμαι** (irregular)

πλέω, *I sail,* [πλευ-] **πλεύσομαι** or [πλευσε-] **πλευσοῦμαι**

τρέχω, *I run,* [δραμε-] **δραμοῦμαι**

φεύγω, *I flee; I escape,* **φεύξομαι**

The future of εἰμί, *I am,* is deponent:

Stem: ἐσ-

Indicative	Infinitive	Participle
ἔσομαι	ἔσεσθαι	ἐσόμενος, -η, -ον
ἔσει or ἔσῃ		
ἔσται (no thematic vowel)		
ἐσόμεθα		
ἔσεσθε		
ἔσονται		

Remember these compounds of εἰμί:

    ἄπειμι, *I am away,* **ἀπέσομαι**
    πάρειμι, *I am present; I am here; I am there,* **παρέσομαι**

Exercise 10α

1. *Make four photocopies of the Verb Charts on pages 282 and 283 and fill in the forms of βλέπω, φυλάττω, σπεύδω, and κομίζω that you have learned to date.*

2. *Make seven copies of the Verb Chart on page 283 and fill in the future indicatives, infinitives, and participles of the verbs for which you entered forms for Exercises 4α, 5α, and 6β. Keep all charts for reference.*

Exercise 10β

Give the 1st person singular of the future of the following verbs:

1. νῑκάω
2. τέρπομαι
3. παύω
4. παρασκευάζω
5. πέμπω
6. ἡγέομαι
7. βοάω
8. πείθω
9. δέχομαι
10. πάσχω

Exercise 10γ

Give the corresponding future form of the following:

1. πέμπει
2. λῡόμενοι
3. τῑμῶμεν
4. φιλεῖτε
5. σπεύδουσι(ν)
6. ζητεῖν
7. βλέπουσα
8. φυλάττομεν
9. βαδίζει
10. ἐσμέν

Exercise 10δ

Read aloud and translate:

1. ἡγήσομαί σοι πρὸς τὸ θέᾱτρον.
2. τὸν πάππον πείσομεν οἴκαδε σπεύδειν.
3. ὁ βασιλεὺς ἄγγελον πέμψει πρὸς τὸ ἄστυ.
4. τοὺς νεᾱνίᾱς φυλάξομεν ἐν τῷ δεσμωτηρίῳ (*prison*).
5. ἡ Ἀριάδνη τῷ Θησεῖ βοηθήσει.
6. δι' ὀλίγου ἑσπέρᾱ γενήσεται, ἀλλ' οὐ παυσόμεθα ἐργαζόμενοι.
7. πρὸς τὸ ἄστυ σπεύσομεν καὶ τοὺς χοροὺς θεᾱσόμεθα.
8. τίς ἡμῖν βοηθήσει; δι' ὀλίγου γὰρ ἐν κινδύνῳ ἐσόμεθα.
9. τὸν πατέρα οὐ πείσεις ἡμῖν πρὸς τὸ ἄστυ ἡγεῖσθαι.
10. αἱ παρθένοι τέρψονται τοὺς χοροὺς θεώμεναι.

Exercise 10ε

Translate into Greek:

1. We will send a messenger to the king.
2. The king will hear the messenger and will come to our aid.
3. What will you do, boys? You will soon be in danger.
4. We will obey father and hurry home.
5. The young men will lead us, and we will follow them.

Festivals

In the course of his praise of the democracy, Pericles says in his funeral oration: "We provide more refreshments for the spirit from toil than any other state, with competitions and sacrifices throughout the year." There were in fact over sixty days in the year that were holidays in Athens, when festivals were held in honor of the gods. These involved all members of the population, citizens and metics, men and women, children and slaves. Many festivals entailed processions, and most culminated in public sacrifice, followed by a feast in which all present joined.

The greatest of all the processions is represented on the Parthenon frieze. Here we see all classes of Athenians playing a part. The knights are shown, at first preparing for parade, then moving off, and later entering the procession at a canter. Stewards are portrayed, marshaling the procession. Next comes a group of elders, led by lyre players and flutists. Ahead of them are young men bearing jugs of holy water and others with trays of offerings. Girls carry wine jars, bowls for pouring libations, and incense burners. The victims are led toward the central scene on the east side, where in the middle stand the priestess and a magistrate with the robe that has been offered to Athena. On either side of them are seated larger figures, looking outward toward the procession; these are the twelve Olympian gods, watching and enjoying the procession.

Sacrifice was performed at the altar, which stood outside every shrine, in accordance with a set ritual. Priest and victims wore garlands. There was a call for holy silence. The altar and participants were sprinkled with water. Then the priest scattered sacred grain over the victim's head and cut a lock of hair from it, which he burnt in the altar fire. The victim was lifted up by attendants and stunned with a blow from a club. Then, while music played, the priest cut the victim's throat and caught the blood in a dish; this was poured as an offering over the altar. Next the victim was skinned and cut up. The inedible parts (the thigh bones wrapped in fat) were burned on the altar for the gods, and the rest was cooked and divided among the people to eat. Thus, gods and men shared the sacrificial banquet.

Knights in the Panathenaic procession on the Parthenon frieze

Every festival had its own ritual. Many, perhaps all, were celebrated with music and dancing. At some there were athletic competitions, notably at the Panathenaea. At the most important festival of Dionysus, the Greater Dionysia, the ten tribes into which the Athenian people were divided each put on a chorus, five of men and five of boys, which sang and danced in competition. Later in the festival, which lasted six days in all, there were three days of drama. On each of these days, three tragedies were performed in the morning, followed in the afternoon by a satyr play (an old form of drama in which the chorus consisted of satyrs, half-man, half-goat) and a comedy. The theater held between 17,000 and 20,000 people, so that a large proportion of the citizens could be present.

Classical Greek

Theognis

Theognis (fl. 550 B.C.) was a noble of Megara; he was exiled when there was a democratic revolution. Several of Theognis's poems, such as the following (lines 567–570) lament the transience of youth and the imminence of death. Indeed, such thoughts are characteristic of much Greek literature.

ἥβῃ τερπόμενος παίζω· δηρὸν γὰρ ἔνερθεν

    γῆς ὀλέσᾱς ψῡχὴν κείσομαι ὥστε λίθος

ἄφθογγος, λείψω δ' ἐρατὸν φάος ἠελίοιο·

    ἔμπης δ' ἐσθλὸς ἐὼν ὄψομαι οὐδὲν ἔτι.

[ἥβῃ, *in youth* παίζω, *I play* δηρὸν, *for long* ἔνερθεν γῆς, *beneath the earth* ὀλέσᾱς ψῡχὴν, *after losing my life* κείσομαι, *I will lie* ὥστε, *as* ἄφθογγος, *mute, dumb* ἐρατὸν φάος ἠελίοιο* (= ἠλίου), *the lovely light of the sun* ἔμπης* . . . ἐσθλὸς ἐὼν* (= ὤν), *although being noble* ὄψομαι, *I will see* ἔτι, *any more*]

New Testament Greek

Luke 6.35–36
The Sermon on the Mount

"πλὴν ἀγαπᾶτε τοὺς ἐχθροὺς ὑμῶν καὶ ἀγαθοποιεῖτε καὶ δανίζετε μηδὲν ἀπελπίζοντες· καὶ ἔσται ὁ μισθὸς ὑμῶν πολύς, καὶ ἔσεσθε υἱοὶ ὑψίστου, ὅτι αὐτὸς χρηστός ἐστιν ἐπὶ τοὺς ἀχαρίστους καὶ πονηρούς. γίνεσθε οἰκτίρμονες καθὼς ὁ πατὴρ ὑμῶν οἰκτίρμων ἐστίν."

[πλὴν, *but* ἀγαπᾶτε, *love* τοὺς ἐχθροὺς, *the enemies* δανίζετε, *lend* μηδὲν ἀπελπίζοντες, *expecting nothing in return* μισθός, *reward* υἱοί, *sons* ὑψίστου, *(the) Highest* (i.e., God) ὅτι, *because* χρηστός, *good, kind* ἐπὶ, *toward* ἀχαρίστους, *unthankful* πονηρούς, *evil* γίνεσθε = γίγνεσθε οἰκτίρμονες, *merciful* καθὼς, *just as*]

Η ΣΥΜΦΟΡΑ (β)

ὁ Φίλιππος νεᾱνίᾱς τινὰς ὁρᾷ ἐν τῇ ὁδῷ μαχομένους.

VOCABULARY

Verbs

αἴρω, [ἀρε-] **ἀρῶ**, [ἀρ-] **ἦρα**,
I lift; with reflexive pronoun,
I get up

ἀποκτείνω, [κτενε-] **ἀποκτενῶ**, [κτειν-] **ἀπέκτεινα**,
I kill

ἀποφεύγω, **ἀποφεύξομαι**,
[φυγ-] **ἀπέφυγον**, I flee away,
escape

δεῖ, impersonal + acc. and infin., it is necessary
δεῖ ἡμᾶς παρεῖναι, we
must be there

ἔξεστι(ν), impersonal + dat.
and infin., it is allowed /
possible
ἔξεστιν ἡμῖν μένειν, we
are allowed to stay, we
may stay; we can stay

καταλείπω, **καταλείψω**,
[λιπ-] **κατέλιπον**, I leave behind, desert

μένω, [μενε-] **μενῶ**, [μειν-]
ἔμεινα, intransitive, I stay

(in one place); I wait; transitive, I wait for

τρέπω, **τρέψω**, **ἔτρεψα**, active,
transitive, I turn X; middle,
intransitive, I turn myself,
turn

τύπτω, [τυπτε-] **τυπτήσω**, no
other principal parts of this
verb in Attic, I strike, hit

Nouns

ἡ βοή, τῆς βοῆς, shout
Cf. βοάω, βοήσομαι, ἐβόησα,
I shout

ἡ κεφαλή, τῆς κεφαλῆς, head

οἱ τεκόντες, τῶν τεκόντων,
pl., parents

τὸ ὕδωρ, τοῦ ὕδατος, water

Preposition

πρό + gen., of time or place, before

Adverbs

εὐθύς, straightway, immediately, at once

ποτέ, enclitic, at some time, at
one time, once, ever

ἡ δὲ Μυρρίνη τοῖς παισὶν ἐκ τοῦ θεάτρου ἡγουμένη τῷ ἀνδρί, "τί
νῦν ποιήσομεν;" φησίν· "ἆρ' ἔξεστιν ἡμῖν ἐν τῷ ἄστει μένειν; αὔριον
γὰρ γενήσονται αἱ τραγῳδίαι. τὴν οὖν νύκτα ἐν τῷ ἄστει μενοῦμεν.
ἀλλὰ ποῦ καθευδήσομεν; ἆρα δέξεται ἡμᾶς ὁ σὸς ἀδελφός;" ὁ δὲ
Δικαιόπολις, "ἀλλ' οὐ μενοῦμεν ἐν τῷ ἄστει ἀλλ' εὐθὺς οἴκαδε   5
πορευσόμεθα. πολὺν γὰρ χρόνον ἀπὸ τοῦ κλήρου ἄπεσμεν· ὁ δὲ
Ξανθίας, ἀργὸς ὤν, οὐδὲν ποιήσει· οἱ οὖν βόες πεινήσουσιν, τὰ δὲ
πρόβατα ἀποφεύξεται, ὁ δὲ οἶκος κατ' εἰκὸς ἤδη κάεται. σπεύσομεν
οὖν πρὸς τὰς πύλᾱς καὶ οἴκαδε πορευσόμεθα. δεῖ γὰρ ἡμᾶς πρὸ τῆς
νυκτὸς ἐκεῖσε παρεῖναι."   10

[αὔριον, *tomorrow*   αἱ τραγῳδίαι, *the tragedies*   ἀδελφός, *brother*   τοῦ
κλήρου, *the farm*   πεινήσουσιν (from πεινάω), *will be hungry*   κατ(ὰ) εἰκὸς,
probably]

οἱ μὲν οὖν παῖδες τῷ πατρὶ πειθόμενοι πρὸς τὰς πύλᾱς
σπεύδουσιν. ὁ δὲ πάππος, "φεῦ, φεῦ," φησίν, "βούλομαι τὰς
τραγῳδίᾱς θεᾶσθαι. ὑμεῖς μὲν οὖν οἴκαδε σπεύδετε, ἐγὼ δὲ ἐν τῷ
ἄστει μενῶ ὡς τὰς τραγῳδίᾱς θεᾱσόμενος." ἡ δὲ Μυρρίνη, "μὴ φλυάρει," φησίν. "οὐ γὰρ καταλείψομέν σε ἐν τῷ ἄστει. ἐλθὲ μεθ' ἡμῶν."   15
καὶ ἡγεῖται αὐτῷ δεινολογουμένῳ πρὸς τὰς πύλᾱς.

[ὡς ... θεᾱσόμενος, *to see*   φλυᾱρεῖ, *talk nonsense*   δεινολογουμένῳ, *complaining loudly*]

ἐν ᾧ δὲ σπεύδουσι διὰ τῶν ὁδῶν, ὁ Φίλιππος νεᾱνίᾱς τινὰς ὁρᾷ ἐν
τῇ ὁδῷ μαχομένους· πολὺν γὰρ οἶνον πεπώκᾱσι καὶ μεθύουσιν. μένει
οὖν ὁ Φίλιππος τὴν μάχην θεώμενος· τέλος δὲ οἱ ἄλλοι νεᾱνίαι ἕνα
τινὰ καταβάλλουσι καὶ οὐ παύονται τύπτοντες αὐτόν. ὁ δὲ   20
Φίλιππος φοβούμενος ὑπὲρ αὐτοῦ προστρέχει καί, "τί ποιήσετε, ὦ
ἄνθρωποι;" φησίν. "παύετε τύπτοντες αὐτόν. ἀποκτενεῖτε γὰρ τὸν
τλήμονα." τῶν δὲ νεᾱνιῶν τις ἀγρίως βοῶν πρὸς τὸν Φίλιππον
τρέπεται καί, "τίς ὢν σύ," φησίν, "οὕτω πολυπρᾱγμονεῖς;" καὶ τύπτει
αὐτόν. ὁ δὲ πρὸς τὴν γῆν καταπίπτει καὶ ἀκίνητος μένει.   25

[πεπώκᾱσι (from πίνω), *they have drunk*   μεθύουσιν, *they are drunk*   τὴν μάχην,
the fight   τὸν τλήμονα, *the poor man*   πολυπρᾱγμονεῖς, *do you interfere?*   ἀκίνητος, *motionless*]

οἱ δὲ τεκόντες τὰς βοὰς ἀκούοντες τρέχουσι πρὸς τὸν παῖδα καὶ
ὁρῶσιν αὐτὸν ἐπὶ τῇ γῇ κείμενον. αἴρουσιν οὖν αὐτόν, ὁ δὲ ἔτι
ἀκίνητος μένει. ἡ δὲ Μέλιττα, "ὦ Ζεῦ," φησίν, "τί ποτε πάσχει ὁ
τλήμων;" ἡ δὲ μήτηρ, "φέρετε αὐτὸν πρὸς τὴν κρήνην." φέρουσιν οὖν
αὐτὸν πρὸς τὴν κρήνην καὶ ὕδωρ καταχέουσι τῆς κεφαλῆς. δι'   30
ὀλίγου οὖν κῑνεῖται καὶ ἀναπνεῖ. ἐπαίρει οὖν ἑαυτὸν καὶ τῆς μητρὸς
ἀκούει λεγούσης. βλέπων δὲ πρὸς αὐτήν, "ποῦ εἶ σύ, ὦ μῆτερ;" φησίν.
"τί σκότος ἐστίν;" ἡ δὲ μήτηρ, "ἀλλ' οὐ σκότος ἐστίν, ὦ παῖ· βλέπε
δεῦρο." ἀλλ' οὐδὲν ὁρᾷ ὁ παῖς· τυφλὸς γὰρ γέγονεν.

[κείμενον, *lying*   καταχέουσι, *they pour* X (acc.) *over* Y (gen.)   κῑνεῖται, *he moves*
ἀναπνεῖ, *he breathes again, recovers*   σκότος, *darkness*   τυφλὸς, *blind*   γέγονεν,
he has become, he is]

WORD BUILDING

*Study the relationships between the words in the following sets, and give defi-
nitions of each word:*

1.	μάχομαι	ἡ μάχη	ἡ νόσος	νοσέω
	εὔχομαι	ἡ εὐχή	(*sickness*)	
	βούλομαι	ἡ βουλή	ὁ φόβος	φοβέομαι
	λέγω	ὁ λόγος		
	πέμπω	ἡ πομπή	4. ὁ βασιλεύς	βασιλεύω
	σπεύδω	ἡ σπουδή	ὁ πολίτης	πολῑτεύω
			ὁ κίνδῡνος	κινδῡνεύω
2.	ἡ θέᾱ	θεάομαι	ὁ παῖς	παιδεύω
	ἡ βοή	βοάω	(παιδ-)	
	ἡ νίκη	νῑκάω		
	ἡ σῑγή	σῑγάω	5. ὁ χρόνος	χρονίζω
			ὁ λόγος	λογίζομαι
3.	σώφρων	σωφρονέω	(*calculation*)	
	(σωφρον-)		ἡ ὀργή	ὀργίζομαι

GRAMMAR

5. Verb Forms: The Asigmatic Contract Future of Verbs with Liquid and Nasal Stems

If the stem ends in a *liquid* (λ, ρ) or a *nasal* (μ, ν), an ε is added to the
stem, the future suffix -σ- is lost between this vowel and the vowel of the
endings, and contraction takes place, e.g., μεν-έ-(σ)-ω > μενῶ. This is
an asigmatic contract future like the future of verbs in -ίζω (page 159).

Here are the present and the future active forms of μένω.

Present Active

Stem: μεν-, *stay; wait; wait for*

Indicative	Imperative	Infinitive	Participle
μένω		μένειν	μένων,
μένεις	μένε		μένουσα,
μένει			μένον,
μένομεν			gen., μένοντος, etc.
μένετε	μένετε		
μένουσι(ν)			

Future Active

Stem: μενε-

Indicative		Infinitive	Participle
μενέ-(σ)-ω >	μενῶ	μενέ-(σ)-ειν > μενεῖν	μενῶν,
μενέ-(σ)-εις >	μενεῖς		μενοῦσα,
μενέ-(σ)-ει >	μενεῖ		μενοῦν,
μενέ-(σ)-ομεν >	μενοῦμεν		gen., μενοῦντος, etc.
μενέ-(σ)-ετε >	μενεῖτε		
μενέ-(σ)-ουσι(ν) >	μενοῦσι(ν)		

The present and future of some liquid and nasal verbs are thus distinguished only by the circumflex accent in the future, except in the 1st and 2nd persons plural and most forms of the participle, where contraction produces a different spelling as well. The future middle forms of liquid and nasal verbs are also contract forms; see ἀποκρίνομαι and κάμνω below.

In most liquid and nasal verbs, however, the stem not only has an ε but is spelled differently in the future, e.g.:

αἴρω, *I lift*, [ἀρε-] ἀρῶ

ἀποκρίνομαι, *I answer*, [κρινε-] ἀποκρινοῦμαι

ἀποκτείνω, *I kill*, [κτενε-] ἀποκτενῶ

βάλλω, *I throw*, [βαλε-] βαλῶ

ἐγείρω, *I wake X up;* middle, *I wake up*, [ἐγερε-] ἐγερῶ

κάμνω, *I am sick; I am tired*, [καμε-] καμοῦμαι

The verb μάχομαι, although not a liquid or nasal stem verb, also has an asigmatic contract future: μάχομαι, *I fight*, [μαχε-] μαχοῦμαι, μαχεῖ/ῇ, μαχεῖται, etc.

The verb ἐλαύνω, *I drive*, is a nasal stem verb but is irregular in the future: ἐλῶ, ἐλᾷς, ἐλᾷ, etc. Compare the present of -α- contract verbs.

Exercise 10ζ

Make two photocopies of the Verb Charts on pages 282 and 283 and fill in
the forms of ἀποκτείνω and of ἀποκρίνομαι that you have learned to date.

Exercise 10η

Read aloud and translate:

1. ἆρα μενοῦμεν ἐν τῷ ἄστει ἢ (*or*) οἴκαδε πορευσόμεθα;
2. οἱ παῖδες τὸν πάππον ἐγεροῦσιν· δι' ὀλίγου γὰρ ὁρμησόμεθα.
3. ὁ αὐτουργὸς τὸν λύκον λίθοις βαλεῖ.
4. ἑσπέρᾱ δι' ὀλίγου γενήσεται· ὁ αὐτουργὸς τὸ ἄροτρον ἀρεῖ καὶ οἴκαδε οἴσει
   (*future of* φέρω).
5. οἱ δοῦλοι τοὺς βοῦς λύσουσι καὶ οἴκαδε ἄξουσιν.
6. ὁ Θησεύς, ἀνδρεῖος ὤν, τὸν Μῑνώταυρον ἀποκτενεῖ.
7. οἱ μὲν παῖδες οἴκοι μενοῦσιν, ἐγὼ δὲ πρὸς τὸ ἄστυ σπεύσω.
8. ἆρ' οὐκ ἐγερεῖς τὸν πάππον; ὀψὲ γὰρ εἰς τὸ θέᾱτρον ἀφιξόμεθα.

6. The Irregular Verb εἶμι

The verb εἶμι in the *indicative* refers to future time and means *I will
go*. In Attic Greek it is used as the future of ἔρχομαι. Thus: ἔρχομαι, *I come;
I go*; future, εἶμι, *I will come; I will go*

Here are the forms of εἶμι. Note that the verb has a long-vowel stem εἰ-
(compare Latin *īre*) and a short-vowel stem ἰ-:

Stems: εἰ-/ἰ-, *come; go*   Compare the verb *to be:*

εἶμι, *I will come; I will go*   εἰμί, *I am*
εἶ   εἶ
εἶσι(ν)   ἐστί(ν)
ἴμεν   ἐσμέν
ἴτε   ἐστέ
ἴᾱσι(ν)   εἰσί(ν)

Sacrifice to Apollo

Here is the verb εἶμι in the indicative, imperative, infinitive, and participle:

Stems: εἰ-/ἰ-, *come; go*

Future	Present	Usually Present	Usually Present
Indicative	**Imperative**	**Infinitive**	**Participle**
εἶμι		ἰέναι	ἰών,
εἶ	ἴθι		ἰοῦσα,
εἶσι(ν)			ἰόν,
ἴμεν			gen., ἰόντος, etc.
ἴτε	ἴτε		
ἴᾱσι(ν)			

As noted above, the indicative forms of εἶμι refer to future time. The imperative, infinitive, and participle, however, are used in Attic Greek in place of the corresponding present forms of ἔρχομαι; the infinitive and participle usually refer to present time, the imperative always. The imperative, infinitive, and participle of ἔρχομαι are not used in Attic Greek.

Here are six common compounds of the verb ἔρχομαι:

ἀπέρχομαι, *I go away*, **ἄπειμι**

εἰσέρχομαι + εἰς + acc., *I come in(to); I go in(to)*, **εἴσειμι**

ἐξέρχομαι + ἐκ + gen., *I come out of; I go out of*, **ἔξειμι**

ἐπανέρχομαι, *I come back, return;* + εἰς or πρός + acc., *I return to,*
   ἐπάνειμι

προσέρχομαι + dat. or πρός + acc., *I approach*, **πρόσειμι**

Exercise 10θ

Read aloud and translate:

1. ἴθι δή, ὦ παῖ, καὶ τῇ μητρὶ εἰπὲ ὅτι πρὸς τῇ θύρᾳ μενῶ.
2. πρὸς τὸν ἀγρὸν ἴμεν καὶ τὸν κύνα ζητήσομεν.
3. τὸν κύνα ὁρῶμεν πρὸς τὰ πρόβατα προσιόντα.
4. ὁ πατὴρ ἡμᾶς κελεύει οἴκαδε ἐπανιέναι.
5. αἱ παρθένοι εἰς τὸ ἄστυ ἴᾱσιν.
6. ἴτε, ὦ παρθένοι· ὁ πατὴρ ὑμῖν εἰς τὸ ἄστυ ἡγήσεται.
7. ἡ μήτηρ πρὸς τὴν κρήνην εἶσιν· τὰς δὲ παρθένους κελεύει ἑαυτῇ συλλαμβάνειν.
8. αἱ παρθένοι πρὸς τὴν κρήνην ἰοῦσαι μεγάλᾱς ὑδρίᾱς φέρουσιν.
9. αἱ γυναῖκες αἱ πρὸς τῇ κρήνῃ ὁρῶσιν αὐτὰς προσιούσᾱς.
10. "χαίρετε, ὦ παρθένοι," φᾱσίν. "πότε (*when*) πρὸς τὸ ἄστυ ἴτε;"

7. Future Participle to Express Purpose

The future participle may be used to express purpose, often preceded by ὡς. In English we use a simple infinitive, e.g.:

ἐν τῷ ἄστει μενῶ **ὡς** τὰς τραγῳδίας **θεασόμενος.**
lit., *I will remain in the city **as being about to watch** the tragedies.*
*I will remain in the city **to watch** the tragedies.*

Exercise 10ι

Read aloud and translate:

1. ἄγγελον πέμψομεν ὡς τοῖς πολίταις πάντα λέξοντα.
2. οἱ πολῖται πρὸς τὴν ἀγορὰν σπεύδουσιν ὡς τοῦ ἀγγέλου ἀκουσόμενοι.
3. εἰς τὸ ἄστυ πορεύονται ὡς τῇ ἑορτῇ παρεσόμενοι.
4. παρασκευάζονται ὡς μαχούμενοι.
5. ὁ Θησεὺς πρὸς τὴν Κρήτην πλεῖ ὡς σώσων τοὺς ἑταίρους.

8. Impersonal Verbs

Greek has a number of verbs that are used in the 3rd person singular with an impersonal subject, often an infinitive or infinitive phrase. They are often translated into English with *it* as subject. You have met the following in the reading passage above:

Impersonal verb with infinitive phrase as subject:

ἆρ᾽ ἔξεστιν ἡμῖν <u>ἐν τῷ ἄστει μένειν</u>;
*Is <u>to stay in the city</u> **allowed/possible** for us?*
*Is it **allowed/possible** for us <u>to stay in the city</u>?*
***May/Can** we <u>stay in the city</u>?*

Impersonal verb with accusative and infinitive phrase as subject:

δεῖ <u>ἡμᾶς πρὸ τῆς νυκτὸς ἐκεῖσε παρεῖναι.</u>
*<u>(For) us to be there before night</u> **is necessary.***
***It is necessary** <u>for us to be there before night.</u>*
*<u>We **must** be there before night.</u>*

Exercise 10κ

Translate the following pairs of sentences:

1. καιρός ἐστιν ἐπανιέναι· δεῖ ἡμᾶς εὐθὺς ὁρμᾶσθαι.
   Don't wait; we must hurry.
2. ἆρ᾽ οὐκ ἔξεστιν ἡμῖν τὰς τραγῳδίας θεάσασθαι;
   Can't I/May I not stay in the city?
3. οὐ δεῖ σε τύπτειν τὸν νεανίαν.
   We must carry the boy to the spring.

4. δεῖ τὸν Φίλιππον τῷ πατρὶ πείθεσθαι.
   Melissa must stay at home.

5. ἆρ' ἔξεστί μοι γιγνώσκειν τί πάσχει ὁ παῖς;
   We are allowed to/We may/We can go to the city; we must start immediately.

9. Review of Questions

ἆρα; introduces a question   πῶς; *how?*

ποῖ; *where to? whither?*   τί; *why?*

πόθεν; *where from? whence?*   τί; *what?*

πότε; *when?*   τίς; *who?*

ποῦ; *where?*

Exercise 10λ

Read aloud and translate:

1. τί βούλεται ὁ Ὀδυσσεὺς εἰς τὴν νῆσον πλεῖν;
2. βούλεται γιγνώσκειν τίνες ἐν τῇ νήσῳ οἰκοῦσιν.
3. ὁ Κύκλωψ τὸν Ὀδυσσέα ἐρωτᾷ (*asks*) πόθεν ἥκει.
4. πῶς ἐκφεύγουσιν ὅ τε Ὀδυσσεὺς καὶ οἱ ἑταῖροι;
5. ἆρα πάντας τοὺς ἑταίρους σῴζει ὁ Ὀδυσσεύς;
6. ἐπεὶ ἐκφεύγει ὁ Ὀδυσσεύς, ποῖ πλεῖ;
7. ὁ Αἴολος τὸν Ὀδυσσέα ἐρωτᾷ τίς ἐστι καὶ πόθεν ἥκει.
8. ὁ Αἴολος τὸν Ὀδυσσέα ἐρωτᾷ πότε ἐν νῷ ἔχει ἀποπλεῖν.

Ο ΟΔΥΣΣΕΥΣ ΤΟΥΣ ΕΤΑΙΡΟΥΣ ΑΠΟΛΛΥΣΙΝ

Read the following passages and answer the comprehension questions:

ὁ δὲ Ὀδυσσεὺς πολλὰ ἔτι καὶ δεινὰ πάσχει σπεύδων εἰς τὴν πατρίδα γῆν νοστεῖν. τὰς γὰρ Σειρῆνας μόλις φεύγει, καὶ παρὰ τὴν Σικελίαν πλέων εἰς τὸν μέγιστον κίνδῡνον ἐμπίπτει. ἔνθεν μὲν γάρ ἐστιν ἡ Σκύλλη, τέρας δεινόν, ἐξ κεφαλὰς ἔχουσα, ἣ ἐξ ἄντρου τινὸς ὁρμωμένη τοὺς παραπλέοντας ἁρπάζει καὶ ἐσθίει· ἔνθεν δ' ἐστὶν ἡ Χάρυβδις, δίνη μάλα φοβερά, ἣ πάντα καταπίνει. ὁ δὲ   5
Ὀδυσσεὺς τὴν Χάρυβδιν φεύγων παρὰ τὴν Σκύλλην παραπλεῖ· ἡ δὲ ἐκ τοῦ ἄντρου ὁρμωμένη ἒξ τῶν ἑταίρων ἁρπάζει· τοὺς δ' ἄλλους σῴζει ὁ Ὀδυσσεύς.

[τὴν πατρίδα γῆν, *his fatherland*   νοστεῖν, *to return home*   τὰς ... Σειρῆνας, *the Sirens*   παρὰ τὴν Σικελίαν, *along/past Sicily*   ἐμπίπτει = ἐν + πίπτει   ἔνθεν ... ἔνθεν, *on one side ... on the other side*   ἡ Σκύλλη, *Scylla (a monster formed of a woman and six dogs)*   τέρας, *a monster*   ἥ, *which*   ἄντρου, *cave*   ἁρπάζει, *snatches*   ἡ Χάρυβδις, *Charybdis*   δίνη, *a whirlpool*   φοβερά, *frightening*   ἥ, *which*   καταπίνει, *drinks/gulps down*]

1. What does Odysseus continue to experience as he hastens to return home?
2. Where does he fall into the greatest danger?
3. How is Scylla described?
4. How is Charybdis described?
5. What does Scylla do as Odysseus sails by?
6. Why did Odysseus have to sail so close to Scylla?

δι' ὀλίγου εἰς ἄλλην τινὰ νῆσον ἀφικνοῦνται· ἐκεῖ δὲ πολλοὺς βοῦς εὑρίσκουσιν.
οἱ οὖν ἑταῖροι, "τί," φασίν, "οὐκ ἀποκτενοῦμεν τοὺς βοῦς; πεινῶμεν γάρ." ὁ δὲ
Ὀδυσσεύς, "μὴ βλάπτετε τοὺς βοῦς· τῷ γὰρ Ἡλίῳ εἰσίν. εἰ δὲ βλάψετε αὐτούς, ὁ   10
Ἥλιος ῡ̔μᾶς τῑμωρήσει." οἱ δὲ οὐ πείθονται αὐτῷ ἀλλ' ἀποκτείνουσι τοὺς βοῦς. ὁ
μὲν οὖν Ἥλιος τῷ πατρὶ Διὶ εὐχόμενος, "ὦ Ζεῦ πάτερ," φησίν, "οἱ τοῦ Ὀδυσσέως
ἑταῖροι τοὺς ἐμοὺς βοῦς ἀποκτείνουσιν. τῑμώρει οὖν αὐτούς. εἰ δὲ μὴ τῑμωρήσεις
αὐτούς, οὐδέποτε αὖθις ἐν τοῖς ἀνθρώποις λάμψω."

[πεινῶμεν, *we are hungry*   βλάπτετε, *harm*   τῷ ... Ἡλίῳ, *Helios (the god of the
sun)*   τῑμωρήσει, *will punish*   εἰ ... μή, *if ... not*   οὐδέποτε, *never*   λάμψω, *I
will shine*]

7. What do Odysseus's comrades find on the island, and what do they want
   to do?
8. Why does Odysseus tell them not to do this?
9. Do they obey?
10. What does the Sun God ask Zeus to do?
11. What threat does the Sun God make?

ὁ δὲ Ζεὺς ἀκούει αὐτοῦ εὐχομένου· ἐπεὶ γὰρ ὅ τε Ὀδυσσεὺς καὶ οἱ ἑταῖροι   15
ἀποπλέοντες τὴν νῆσον λείπουσιν, χειμῶνα δεινὸν πέμπει καὶ τὴν ναῦν κεραύνῳ
βάλλει. πάντες οὖν οἱ ἑταῖροι ἐκ τῆς νεὼς ἐκπίπτουσι καὶ ἀποθνῄσκουσιν· μόνος δὲ
ὁ Ὀδυσσεὺς ἐκφεύγει, τοῦ ἱστοῦ λαμβανόμενος.

[κεραύνῳ, *with a thunderbolt*   ἀποθνῄσκουσιν, *die*   μόνος, *only*   τοῦ ἱστοῦ, *the
mast*]

12. What three things does Zeus do?
13. What happens to Odysseus's comrades? How does Odysseus escape?

Exercise 10μ

Translate into Greek:

1. For nine days the wind (ὁ ἄνεμος) carries Odysseus (τὸν Ὀδυσσέᾱ)
   through the sea, but on the tenth he arrives at another island.
2. The nymph (ἡ νύμφη) Calypso (ἡ Καλυψώ) lives there; she receives
   him kindly (εὐμενῶς).
3. Loving him, she says: "Stay with me always on the island." But

Odysseus wants to return home and to see his wife and child.

4. Finally Zeus sends a messenger and orders the nymph to release (*use* λύω) Odysseus.

5. Calypso tells him to make a raft (*use* σχεδίᾱ) and helps him.

6. When the raft is ready, Odysseus sails away rejoicing.

Classical Greek

Menander

From *The Shield* (417–418)

> ἐν μιᾷ γὰρ ἡμέρᾳ
τὸν εὐτυχῆ τίθησι δυστυχῆ θεός.

[τὸν εὐτυχῆ, *the fortunate man*   τίθησι, *makes*   δυστυχῆ, *unfortunate*]

Archilochus

For Archilochus, see page 121. In the following poem he says that his whole life depends on his spear (poem no. 2):

> ἐν δορὶ μέν μοι μᾶζα μεμαγμένη, ἐν δορὶ δ' οἶνος
> Ἰσμαρικός, πίνω δ' ἐν δορὶ κεκλιμένος.

[ἐν δορὶ: supply ἐστί, *is*, and translate it, *depends*   μοι: take as possessive with δορὶ   μᾶζα μεμαγμένη, *my kneaded bread*   Ἰσμαρικός, *Ismaric* (from Ismarus, in Thrace)   κεκλιμένος, *leaning*]

New Testament Greek

Luke 5.30–32

Jesus had called Levi, a tax collector (τελώνης), to follow him, and Levi had entertained Jesus, his disciples, many tax collectors, and others in his house. The scribes and Pharisees then murmured against Jesus' disciples.

καὶ ἐγόγγυζον οἱ Φαρισαῖοι καὶ οἱ γραμματεῖς αὐτῶν πρὸς τοὺς μαθητὰς αὐτοῦ λέγοντες, "διὰ τί μετὰ τῶν τελωνῶν καὶ ἁμαρτωλῶν ἐσθίετε καὶ πίνετε;" καὶ ἀποκρῖθεὶς ὁ Ἰησοῦς εἶπεν πρὸς αὐτούς, "οὐ χρείαν ἔχουσιν οἱ ὑγιαίνοντες ἰᾱτροῦ ἀλλὰ οἱ κακῶς ἔχοντες· οὐκ ἐλήλυθα καλέσαι δικαίους ἀλλὰ ἁμαρτωλοὺς εἰς μετάνοιᾱν."

[ἐγόγγυζον, *were muttering, complaining*   οἱ γραμματεῖς, *the scribes*   τοὺς μαθητὰς, *the disciples*   διὰ τί, *why*   ἁμαρτωλῶν, *sinners*   ἀποκρῖθεὶς, *answering*   εἶπεν, *he said*   χρείᾱν, *need*   οἱ ὑγιαίνοντες, *the healthy*   ἰᾱτροῦ, *of/for a doctor*   οἱ κακῶς ἔχοντες, *those who are sick*   ἐλήλυθα, *I have come*   καλέσαι, *to call*   δικαίους, *righteous (people)*   ἁμαρτωλοὺς, *sinners*   μετάνοιᾱν, *repentance*]

11

Ο ΙΑΤΡΟΣ (α)

ἐπεὶ ἀφίκοντο εἰς τὴν τοῦ ἀδελφοῦ οἰκίᾱν, ὁ Δικαιόπολις ἔκοψε τὴν θύρᾱν.

VOCABULARY

Verbs

αἰτέω, αἰτήσω, ᾔτησα, *I ask;
I ask for*

**ἀποθνῄσκω, [θανε-] ἀπο-
θανοῦμαι, [θαν-] ἀπέθανον,**
I die

δακρύω, δακρύσω, ἐδάκρῡσα,
I cry, weep

δοκεῖ, impersonal, **[δοκ-] δόξει,
ἔδοξε(ν),** impersonal, *it
seems (good);* + dat., e.g.,
δοκεῖ μοι, *it seems good to me;
I think it best*

**εἰσάγω, εἰσάξω, [ἀγαγ-] εἰσ-
ήγαγον,** *I lead in; I take in*

ἔφη, *he/she said*

**κομίζω, [κομιε-] κομιῶ, [κομι-]
ἐκόμισα,** *I bring; I take*

κόπτω, [κοπ-] κόψω, ἔκοψα,
I strike; I knock on (a door)

**λαμβάνω, [ληβ-] λήψομαι,
[λαβ-] ἔλαβον,** *I take;* middle
+ gen., *I seize, take hold of*

λείπω, λείψω, [λιπ-] ἔλιπον,
I leave

**μανθάνω, [μαθε-] μαθήσομαι,
[μαθ-] ἔμαθον,** *I learn; I understand*

**πάσχω, [πενθ-] πείσομαι,
[παθ-] ἔπαθον,** *I suffer; I experience*

**σκοπέω, [σκεπ-] σκέψομαι,
ἐσκεψάμην,** *I look at, examine; I consider*

Nouns

**ὁ ἀδελφός, τοῦ ἀδελφοῦ,
ὦ ἄδελφε,** *brother*

ὁ ἱᾱτρός, τοῦ ἱᾱτροῦ, *doctor*

ὁ λόγος, τοῦ λόγου, *word; story*

Adjective

σοφός, -ή, -όν, *skilled; wise;
clever*

τυφλός, -ή, -όν, *blind*

Preposition

παρά + acc., of persons only, *to*

Adverb

αὔριον, *tomorrow*

174

Conjunction	*Expressions*
εἰ, *if;* in indirect questions, *whether*	**καλῶς ἔχω**, *I am well*
	πῶς ἔχεις; *How are you?*

ἡ δὲ Μυρρίνη, ἐπεὶ ἔμαθεν ὅτι τυφλός ἐστιν ὁ παῖς, δακρύσασα τῷ ἀνδρί, "ὦ Ζεῦ," ἔφη, "τί δεῖ ἡμᾶς ποιεῖν; ὦ ἄνερ, τοῖς θεοῖς εὔχου βοηθεῖν ἡμῖν." ὁ δὲ Δικαιόπολις, "ἀλλὰ δεῖ ἡμᾶς τὸν παῖδα φέρειν παρὰ ἰατρόν τινα," ἔφη· "ἀλλὰ νὺξ δι' ὀλίγου γενήσεται. νῦν οὖν δεῖ πρὸς τὴν τοῦ ἀδελφοῦ οἰκίαν σπεύδειν καὶ αἰτεῖν αὐτὸν ἡμᾶς   5 δέχεσθαι. αὔριον δὲ ζητήσομεν ἰατρόν."

[**δακρύσασα**, *bursting into tears*]

βραδέως οὖν τῷ παιδὶ ἡγούμενοι βαδίζουσι πρὸς τὴν τοῦ ἀδελφοῦ οἰκίᾱν. ἐπεὶ δ' ἀφίκοντο, ὁ μὲν Δικαιόπολις ἔκοψε τὴν θύρᾱν. ὁ δὲ ἀδελφὸς πρὸς τὴν θύρᾱν ἐλθὼν καὶ τὸν Δικαιόπολιν καὶ τὸν πατέρα ἰδών, "χαίρετε, ὦ πάππα καὶ ἄδελφε," ἔφη· "πῶς ἔχετε; σὺ δέ, ὦ   10 Μυρρίνη, χαῖρε καὶ σύ. ὑμεῖς δέ, ὦ Φίλιππε καὶ Μέλιττα, χαίρετε καὶ ὑμεῖς. ἀλλ' εἴπετέ μοι, τί πάσχετε; τί οὐκ ἐπανέρχεσθε εἰς τοὺς ἀγροὺς ἀλλ' ἔτι μένετε ἐν τῷ ἄστει; ἑσπέρᾱ γὰρ ἤδη γίγνεται." ὁ δὲ Δικαιόπολις, "ἐγὼ μὲν καλῶς ἔχω, ὁ δὲ παῖς, ἰδού, τυφλὸς γὰρ γέγονεν· οὐδὲν ὁρᾷ. πάρεσμεν οὖν αἰτοῦντές σε ἡμᾶς δέχεσθαι." ὁ δὲ   15 ἀδελφὸς ἰδὼν τὸν παῖδα τυφλὸν ὄντα, "ὦ Ζεῦ," ἔφη, "τί ποτε ἔπαθεν ὁ παῖς; εἰσέλθετε καὶ εἴπετέ μοι τί ἐγένετο."

[**ἐλθών**, *having come, after coming, coming*   **ἰδών**, *having seen, after seeing, seeing* **εἴπετέ**, *tell*   **γέγονεν**, *has become, is*]

οὕτως εἰπὼν εἰσήγαγεν αὐτοὺς εἰς τὴν οἰκίᾱν· οἱ δὲ πάντα τὰ γενόμενα εἶπον αὐτῷ. ὁ δὲ τὴν γυναῖκα καλέσᾱς, "ἐλθὲ δεῦρο, ὦ γύναι," ἔφη· "πάρεισι γὰρ ὅ τε Δικαιόπολις καὶ ἡ Μυρρίνη· ὁ δὲ   20 Φίλιππος δεινὸν ἔπαθεν· τυφλὸς γὰρ γέγονεν. κόμιζε οὖν αὐτόν τε καὶ τὰς γυναῖκας εἰς τὸν γυναικῶνα. ἡσυχάσουσι γὰρ ἐκεῖ. σὺ δέ, ὦ πάππα καὶ ἄδελφε, ἔλθετε δεῦρο." ὅ τε οὖν Δικαιόπολις καὶ ὁ ἀδελφὸς καὶ ὁ πατὴρ εἰς τὸν ἀνδρῶνα εἰσελθόντες πολλὰ διαλέγονται σκοποῦντες τί δεῖ ποιεῖν. τέλος δὲ ὁ ἀδελφός, "ἅλις   25 λόγων," ἔφη · "ἐγὼ σοφὸν ἰᾱτρὸν ἔγνωκα καὶ αὔριον, εἴ σοι δοκεῖ, κομιῶ ὑμᾶς παρὰ αὐτόν. νῦν δέ—ὀψὲ γάρ ἐστιν—δεῖ ἡμᾶς καθεύδειν."

[εἰπὼν, *having said, after saying, saying*   τὰ γενόμενα, *the things that (had) happened*   εἶπον, *told*   καλέσᾱς, *calling*   τὸν γυναικῶνα, *the women's quarters*   ἡσυχάσουσι (from ἡσυχάζω), *they will rest*   τὸν ἀνδρῶνα, *the men's quarters*   εἰσελθόντες, *entering, having entered*   ἅλις + *gen.*, *enough*   ἔγνωκα, *I know*   ὀψὲ, *late*]

WORD STUDY

Identify the Greek stems in the English words below and give the meanings of the English words:

1. logic   2. dialogue   3. monologue   4. prologue   5. eulogy

GRAMMAR

1. Verb Forms: Past Tense: The Aorist

Both English and Greek have several different past tenses, e.g., "I was coming," "I came," "I had come." The term *aorist* (= ἀ-, *without* + ὁ ὅρος, *boundary*) means *without boundaries, without limits* and is used to describe forms of verbs that express *simple action*, in contrast, for example, with the present tense, which expresses *progressive, ongoing action*. In the indicative mood, aorist forms usually express simple action in *past time*, e.g., ἦλθον, *I came* or *I went* = the simple past tense in English.

There are two ways of forming the aorist in Greek, corresponding to two ways of forming the simple past tense in English:

1. A suffix is added to the verb stem, e.g.:

    Present: λῡ́-ω, *I loosen*
    Sigmatic 1st Aorist: ἔ-λῡ-**σα**, *I loosen**ed***

2. The verb stem is changed, e.g.:

    Present: λείπ-ω, *I leave*
    Thematic 2nd Aorist: ἔ-**λιπ**-ο-ν, *I left*

Most Greek verbs have sigmatic 1st aorists, some have thematic 2nd aorists, and a few have both.

In the aorist indicative an ε is placed before the stem of verbs that begin with consonants. This is called an *augment*, and it indicates past time. If the stem of the verb begins with a vowel, the stem is augmented by lengthening the vowel, e.g., the aorist stem of ἄγω, namely ἀγαγ-, is augmented to ἠγαγ- (see Grammar 8, pages 190–191). Note in the lists of forms below that the augment is not present in the forms of the imperative, infinitive, and participle.

2. Verb Forms: The Thematic 2nd Aorist

Thematic 2nd aorists have thematic vowels (ο or ε) between the stem and the ending in the indicative. The personal endings for the thematic 2nd aorist indicative active are slightly different from those for the present indicative. The present endings are called *primary*, and the thematic 2nd aorist endings are called *secondary*. The latter should be memorized as follows:

Secondary: -ν, -ς, —, -μεν, -τε, -ν

The endings for the active and middle thematic 2nd aorist imperative, infinitive, and participle are similar to those you have learned for the present tense.

The aorist middle indicative has secondary endings, four of which are different from the primary ones you have learned for the present middle indicative. Memorize both the primary and the secondary middle endings as follows:

Primary: -μαι, -σαι, -ται, -μεθα, -σθε, -νται
Secondary: -μην, -σο, -το, -μεθα, -σθε, -ντο

Thematic 2nd Aorist Active

Present: λείπω, *I leave;* **Aorist Stem:** λιπ-

Indicative	Imperative	Infinitive	Participle
ἔ-λιπ-ο-ν, *I left*		λιπ-εῖν,	λιπ-ών,
ἔ-λιπ-ε-ς	λίπ-ε,	*to leave*	λιπ-οῦσα,
ἔ-λιπ-ε(ν)	*leave!*		λιπ-όν,
ἐ-λίπ-ο-μεν			gen., λιπ-όντ-ος, etc.
ἐ-λίπ-ε-τε	λίπ-ετε,		*having left,*
ἔ-λιπ-ο-ν	*leave!*		*after leaving,*
			sometimes, *leaving*

Thematic 2nd Aorist Middle

Present: γίγνομαι, *I become;* **Aorist Stem:** γεν-

Indicative	Imperative	Infinitive	Participle
ἐ-γεν-ό-μην, *I became*		γεν-έ-σθαι,	γεν-ό-μεν-ος,
ἐ-γέν-ε-σο > ἐγένου	γενοῦ,	*to become*	γεν-ο-μέν-η,
ἐ-γέν-ε-το	*become!*		γεν-ό-μεν-ον,
ἐ-γεν-ό-μεθα			*having become,*
ἐ-γέν-ε-σθε	γέν-ε-σθε,		*after becoming,*
ἐ-γέν-ο-ντο	*become!*		sometimes, *becoming*

Note:

1. Thematic vowels come between the stems and the endings in many of these forms, just as in the present middle forms (see Chapter 6, Grammar 3, pages 76–77).
2. Note the accents of the active infinitive and participles. Compare the accents of the present active infinitive and participles (see page 152).
3. The accent of the singular aorist middle imperative is irregular: γενοῦ.
4. Note that thematic 2nd aorist middle infinitives are always accented on the next to the last syllable, e.g., γενέσθαι. Compare the present and future middle infinitives, λύεσθαι and λύσεσθαι.

Exercise 11α

In the reading passage at the beginning of this chapter, locate two examples of an aorist of the verb πάσχω and two aorist forms of the verb γίγνομαι.

Exercise 11β

1. *Make photocopies of the Verb Charts on pages 282 and 283 and copy the aorist active forms of λείπω given above on the second chart. Then fill in the present active and future active forms of this verb that you have learned to date.*
2. *On the chart that you filled out with the future forms of γίγνομαι (Exercise 10α.2), fill in the aorist indicative, imperative, infinitive, and participle of this verb. Be sure to keep all of your charts for reference.*

Exercise 11γ

1. *Make two photocopies of the Verb Charts on pages 282 and 283 and fill in the present, future, and aorist active forms of πάσχω (aorist ἔ-παθ-ο-ν) that you have learned to date on one set of charts.*
2. *On your second set of charts fill in the present and aorist middle forms of λαμβάνομαι,* I take hold of*, aorist, ἐ-λαβ-ό-μην, that you have learned to date. Keep these charts for reference.*

3. Aspect

a. *Indicatives*

Notice that the indicatives in the charts on the previous page are translated *I left*, *you left*, etc. In the indicative mood the aorist usually designates *simple action in past time*.

Occasionally the aorist indicative is used to express general truths and is translated with a present tense. This is called the *gnomic aorist* (cf. αἱ γνῶμαι, *maxims, aphorisms*), e.g.:

παθὼν νήπιος **ἔμαθεν**. *A fool **learns** by experience.*

b. Imperatives

Notice, however, that with the imperatives, which have no augment, the translations are the same as those for the present tense. This is because the aorist imperative differs from the present not in *time* but in *aspect*, that is, in the way in which the action of the verb is conceived in the mind. The present tense is *progressive* and is used of an *ongoing process;* the aorist is used of *simple action*, e.g.:

Present, progressive imperative:

ἄκουε τὸν μῦθον. **Listen to** *the story!*
(The listening is conceived of as a process that will take place over a period of time.)

Aorist imperative:

λαβοῦ τῆς ἐμῆς χειρός. **Take** *my hand!*
(The reference is to the simple action itself.)

c. Infinitives

Present infinitives express *progressive, ongoing action*, e.g.:

νῦν δέ—ὀψὲ γάρ ἐστιν—δεῖ ἡμᾶς **καθεύδειν**.
*But now—for it is late—it is necessary for us **to be sleeping**.*

Aorist infinitives usually express *simple action* without reference to time, e.g.:

ὁ Δικαιόπολις τὸν πάππον ἔπεισεν οἴκαδε **ἐπανελθεῖν**.
*Dicaeopolis persuaded grandfather **to return** home.*

d. Participles

Present participles express *progressive, ongoing action*, e.g.:

ἡ Μέλιττα **φέρουσα** τὴν ὑδρίαν ἔπταισε καὶ αὐτὴν κατέβαλεν.
*Melissa, **carrying** her water jar, stumbled and dropped it.*

Usually the aorist participle describes a simple action that preceded or was finished before the action of the main verb, e.g.:

οἱ δὲ πάντα τὰ **γενόμενα** αὐτῷ εἶπον.
*They told him all the things **that had happened**.*

Aorist participles sometimes designate *simple action* without reference to time (the following example uses an asigmatic 1st aorist participle, to be introduced in the next chapter):

ἀποκρῑνάμενος εἶπεν. Not **Having answered**, *he said*, but **Answering**, *he said* or *He said **in reply**.*

Here are further examples of aorist participles:

ὁ δὲ ἀδελφὸς πρὸς τὴν θύραν **ἐλθὼν** καὶ τὸν Δικαιόπολιν **ἰδών**, "χαῖρε,
ὦ ἄδελφε," ἔφη.
*And his brother, **having come/after coming/coming** to the door
and **having seen/after seeing/seeing** Dicaeopolis, said, "Greetings, brother."*

Here the actions described by the aorist participles clearly took
place before the brother greeted Dicaeopolis, and so we may translate
them *having come/after coming* and *having seen/after seeing*. But
they are simple actions and so may also be translated simply *coming*
and *seeing*. Present, progressive participles would be inappropriate
here because the actions are not continuous or ongoing.

4. Thematic 2nd Aorist Active and Middle Participles

The thematic 2nd aorist active participle has the same endings as the
present active participle (see Chapter 9, Grammar 1, page 136), but it
differs in accent:

Nom., Voc.	λιπ-ών	λιπ-οῦσα	λιπ-όν
Gen.	λιπ-όντος	λιπ-ούσης	λιπ-όντος
Dat.	λιπ-όντι	λιπ-ούσῃ	λιπ-όντι
Acc.	λιπ-όντα	λιπ-οῦσαν	λιπ-όν
Nom., Voc.	λιπ-όντες	λιπ-οῦσαι	λιπ-όντα
Gen.	λιπ-όντων	λιπ-ουσῶν	λιπ-όντων
Dat.	λιπ-οῦσι(ν)	λιπ-ούσαις	λιπ-οῦσι(ν)
Acc.	λιπ-όντας	λιπ-ούσᾱς	λιπ-όντα

The thematic 2nd aorist middle participle has the same endings as the
present middle participle (see Chapter 8, Grammar 1, page 115):

Nom.   γεν-ό-μεν-ος   γεν-ο-μέν-η   γεν-ό-μεν-ον
etc.

5. Verb Forms: Common Verbs with Thematic 2nd Aorists

Learn the following verbs, paying particular attention to the difference between the verb stems in the present tense and those in the future
and aorist. Remember that some verbs that have active forms in the present tense are deponent in the future (see Chapter 10, Grammar 4, pages
159–160). We give the aorist participles here and in the vocabulary lists
in the remainder of Book I in order to remind you that the augment occurs
only in the indicative forms. Remember that stems beginning with vowels or diphthongs augment in the aorist indicative by lengthening the
initial vowel (see Grammar 8, pages 190–191).

ἄγ-ω, *I lead, take*, ἄξω, [**ἀγαγ-**] ἤγαγ-ο-ν, ἀγαγ-ών

ἀπο-θνῄσκ-ω, *I die*, [θανε-] ἀποθανοῦμαι, [**θαν-**] **ἀπ-έ-θαν-ο-ν**, ἀπο-θαν-ών

ἀφ-ικνέ-ο-μαι, *I arrive*, [ἱκ-] ἀφίξομαι, [**ἱκ-**] **ἀφ-ῑκ-ό-μην**, ἀφ-ικ-ό-μενος

βάλλ-ω, *I throw*, [βαλε-] βαλῶ, [**βαλ-**] **ἔ-βαλ-ο-ν**, βαλ-ών

γί-γν-ο-μαι, *I become*, [γενε-] γενήσομαι, [**γεν-**] **ἐ-γεν-ό-μην**, γεν-ό-μενος

εὑρίσκ-ω, *I find*, [εὑρε-] εὑρήσω, [**εὑρ-**] **ηὗρ-ο-ν** or **εὗρ-ο-ν**, εὑρ-ών

ἔχ-ω, *I have; I hold*, ἕξω (irregular) (*I will have*) and [σχε-] σχήσω, (*I will get*), [**σχ-**] **ἔ-σχ-ο-ν**, σχ-ών

κάμν-ω, *I am sick; I am tired*, [καμε-] καμοῦμαι, [**καμ-**] **ἔ-καμ-ο-ν**, καμ-ών

λαμβάν-ω, *I take*, [ληβ-] λήψομαι, [**λαβ-**] **ἔ-λαβ-ο-ν**, λαβ-ών

λείπ-ω, *I leave*, λείψω, [**λιπ-**] **ἔ-λιπ-ο-ν**, λιπ-ών

μανθάν-ω, *I learn*, [μαθε-] μαθήσομαι, [**μαθ-**] **ἔ-μαθ-ο-ν**, μαθ-ών

πάσχ-ω, *I suffer*, [πενθ-] πείσομαι, [**παθ-**] **ἔ-παθ-ο-ν**, παθ-ών

πίνω, *I drink*, [πῑ-] πίομαι (note absence of -σ-), [πι-] ἔπιον, πι-ών

πί-πτ-ω, *I fall*, πεσοῦμαι (irregular), **ἔ-πεσ-ο-ν** (irregular), πεσ-ών

φεύγ-ω, *I flee*, φεύξομαι, [**φυγ-**] **ἔ-φυγ-ον**, φυγ-ών

Give the forms of the future indicatives, aorist indicative, and aorist participle of the compound verb παρέχω. Note that the aorist imperative singular of ἔχω [aorist stem σχ-] is σχές and that the aorist imperative of παρέχω is παράσχες.

Exercise 11δ

Give the 2nd person singular and the 2nd person plural of the future and the aorist of the following verbs:

1. πίπτω
2. βάλλω
3. λείπω
4. ἀφικνέομαι
5. λαμβάνω
6. μανθάνω
7. ἄγω
8. εὑρίσκω
9. ἔχω
10. γίγνομαι
11. πάσχω
12. φεύγω
13. ἀποθνῄσκω
14. παρέχω

Exercise 11ε

Give the corresponding future and aorist forms of the following:

1. ἀποθνῄσκων
2. εὑρίσκομεν
3. πίπτειν
4. μανθάνουσι(ν) (2 ways)
5. βάλλειν
6. φεύγει
7. ἀφικνούμενος
8. ἄγειν
9. γίγνομαι
10. ἔχομεν
11. πάσχων
12. λαμβάνω
13. παρέχουσι(ν) (2 ways)
14. λείπειν

Exercise 11ζ

Read aloud and translate. Identify all aorist indicatives, aorist participles, and present participles. For each participle, explain why the aorist or the present is being used in the sentence.

1. ἡ γυνή, μαθοῦσα ὅτι τυφλὸς ἐγένετο ὁ παῖς, τῷ ἀνδρί, "ὦ Ζεῦ," ἔφη, "τί δεῖ ἡμᾶς ποιεῖν;"
2. ἀφικόμενοι εἰς τὴν τοῦ ἀδελφοῦ οἰκίαν εἶπον αὐτῷ τί ἔπαθεν ὁ παῖς.
3. οἱ ἄνδρες τὰς γυναῖκας ἐν τῷ οἴκῳ λιπόντες τὸν παῖδα πρὸς τὸν ἰατρὸν ἤγαγον.
4. ὁ αὐτουργὸς τὸν κύνα πρὸς τὸ ὄρος ἀγαγὼν τὸν λύκον ηὗρε τοῖς προβάτοις ἐμπεσούμενον (ἐν + πίπτω).
5. ἡ μήτηρ τὸν σῖτον τῷ παιδὶ παρασχοῦσα κελεύει αὐτὸν σπεύδειν πρὸς τὸν ἀγρόν.
6. εἰς τὸν ἀγρὸν ἀφικόμενος τῷ πατρὶ τὸ δεῖπνον παρέσχεν.
7. ὁ πατὴρ τὸ ἄροτρον ἐν τῷ ἀγρῷ λιπὼν τὸ δεῖπνον ἔλαβεν.
8. ὁ μὲν παῖς τὸν λύκον ἔβαλεν, ὁ δὲ φοβούμενος ἔφυγεν.
9. οἱ νεανίαι ἀπέθανον ὑπὲρ τῆς πόλεως μαχόμενοι.
10. δεινὰ παθόντες οὐκ ἔφυγον ἀλλὰ ἔπεσον ἀνδρείως μαχόμενοι.

Exercise 11η

Translate into Greek:

1. We left grandfather sitting in the agora.
2. The boys pelted the wolf with stones.
3. Did you learn what happened?
4. The doctor soon arrived at the city.
5. Having left the plow in the field, the farmer led the oxen home.
6. The women, having learned what had happened, fled.
7. The boy fell from the tree and suffered terribly (= terrible things).

Healing: divine and secular
The inscription at the bottom of this relief says that it was dedicated by Aeschinus to the
hero healer Amphiaraus. On the right, the patient sleeps in the sanctuary and is visited
by Amphiaraus and his divine serpent, which licks his wound. On the left a doctor (or the
god himself?) operates on the wound.

Greek Science and Medicine

The beginnings of Greek science are to be found in the speculations of the
philosophers who lived in the Ionian city of Miletus in the sixth century B.C.
The first of these thinkers was Thales, one of the seven wise men or sages of
archaic Greece, whose floruit can be dated confidently, since he predicted an
eclipse of the sun that took place on 25 May 585 B.C. He and his successors
were primarily interested in questions of physics. They all sought for a uni-
fying principle underlying the multifarious appearances of the physical
world; in simple terms, they asked, "What is the ultimate constituent of matter?" Thales answered that this was water. He conceived of the earth as a flat
disc floating on water (the ocean), with water above (rain falling from the
sky). Water, when rarefied, becomes steam or mist. He speculated that air,
when rarefied, becomes fire. Water condensed takes on a solid form, ice or
mud; further condensed it becomes earth and stone. The interest in Thales'
theory lies not in its truth or falsehood but in the boldness with which he sought
for an answer in terms of natural causation to questions that had been tradi-
tionally answered in terms of myth.

The speculations of the Ionian philosophers had no practical end in view,
and here they differed from Greek medicine, which had developed from early
time as an art; the doctor (ἰᾱτρός = *healer*) was a craftsman. There were already famous doctors before we hear of any theory of medicine. The best
known is Democedes, whose story as told by the historian Herodotus is given
at the end of this chapter.

The man whom the Greeks looked upon as the founder of medical science belonged to the next century. This was Hippocrates (fl. 430 B.C.), who founded a famous medical school on the little island of Cos (see map, page 272). To him is ascribed a large collection of writings that cover all aspects of medicine including anatomy, physiology, prognostics, dietetics, surgery, and pharmacology. They include a book of precepts on how doctors should behave toward their patients and the famous Hippocratic oath, which was taken by all students of medicine:

> I will pay the same respect to my master in the science as to my parents and share my life with him and pay all my debts to him. I will regard his sons as my brothers and teach them the science, if they desire to learn it, without fee or contract. . . . I will give treatment to help the sick to the best of my ability and judgment. . . . I will not give lethal drugs to anyone if I am asked . . . nor will I give a woman means to procure an abortion. . . . Whatever I see or hear that should not be spoken to any person outside, I will never divulge. . . .

The oath both gives an insight into how the medical schools were organized (a system of apprenticeship) and also shows the ethical principles to which ancient Greek doctors subscribed.

None of the writings can be confidently ascribed to Hippocrates himself, but many, perhaps most, were written in the fifth century and contain some strikingly enlightened features. The case histories recorded in the Hippocratic writings are particularly interesting, showing the close observation and careful recording on which all sound diagnosis must depend. For instance:

> At Thasos, Pythion had a violent rigor and high fever as the result of strain, exhaustion, and insufficient attention to his diet. Tongue parched, he was thirsty and bilious and did not sleep. Urine rather dark, containing suspended matter, which did not settle. Second day: about midday, chilling of the extremities. . . . (*Epidemics* 3.2, case 3)

The patient's condition and symptoms continued to be recorded until the tenth day, when he died.

Greek doctors did not claim to be able to effect cures in many cases. Their remedies were simple. Drugs, usually purgatives, were used sparingly. Surgery made steady advances, although anatomy was held back by reluctance to perform dissection of the human body. Bloodletting was a common remedy, and great importance was attached to diet and exercise. Despite its limitations, Greek medicine was rational in all aspects and rejected the belief that sickness was caused by evil spirits, still current in the Palestine of New Testament times. If a Greek doctor could not cure a patient, the only recourse for the patient was to visit one of the healing sanctuaries, where a combination of medical care and faith healing resulted in some remarkable cures, if the tablets put up by patients are to be believed.

Classical Greek

Theognis

Theognis (see page 163) traveled to Sicily, Euboea, and Sparta during his exile but always longed for his native Megara.　The following are lines 783–788:

ἦλθον μὲν γὰρ ἔγωγε καὶ εἰς Σικελήν ποτε γαῖαν,

　ἦλθον δ᾽ Εὐβοίης ἀμπελόεν πεδίον,

Σπάρτην τ᾽ Εὐρώτα δονακοτρόφου ἀγλαὸν ἄστυ,

　καί μ᾽ ἐφίλευν προφρόνως πάντες ἐπερχόμενον·

ἀλλ᾽ οὔτις μοι τέρψις ἐπὶ φρένας ἦλθεν ἐκείνων·

　οὕτως οὐδὲν ἄρ᾽ ἦν φίλτερον ἄλλο πάτρης.

[ἦλθον, *I went*　ἔγωγε (a strengthened form of ἐγώ), *I indeed*　Σικελήν . . . γαῖαν, *the land of Sicily*　ἀμπελόεν πεδίον, *the vine-clad plain*　Εὐρώτα δονακοτρόφου, *of the Eurotas* (Sparta's river), *which nourishes reeds*　ἀγλαὸν, *glorious*　ἐφίλευν* = ἐφίλουν (imperfect of φιλέω), here, *were welcoming*　προφρόνως, *graciously*　ἐπερχόμενον, *(when) coming to (them)*　οὔτις . . . τέρψις, *no joy*　φρένας, *my heart*　ἐκείνων, *from those things*　οὕτως . . . ἄρ(α), *so true is it that*　οὐδὲν . . . ἦν . . . ἄλλο, translate, *no other thing is (was)*　φίλτερον . . . πάτρης, *dearer (to a man) than his fatherland*]

New Testament Greek

Luke 6.20–21
The Beatitudes

The following comes from the beginning of the Sermon on the Mount:

καὶ αὐτὸς ἐπάρας τοὺς ὀφθαλμοὺς αὐτοῦ εἰς τοὺς μαθητὰς αὐτοῦ ἔλεγεν,

　"μακάριοι οἱ πτωχοί,

　　ὅτι ὑμετέρᾱ ἐστὶν ἡ βασιλείᾱ τοῦ θεοῦ.

　μακάριοι οἱ πεινῶντες νῦν,

　　ὅτι χορτασθήσεσθε.

　μακάριοι οἱ κλαίοντες νῦν,

　　ὅτι γελάσετε."

[αὐτὸς: i.e., Jesus　ἐπάρας, *lifting up*　τοὺς μαθητὰς, *the disciples*　ἔλεγεν, *he was saying*　μακάριοι, *blessed*　οἱ πτωχοί, *the beggars*　ὅτι, *because, for*　ἡ βασιλείᾱ, *the kingdom*　οἱ πεινῶντες, *those who are hungry*　χορτασθήσεσθε, *you will be filled*　οἱ κλαίοντες, *those who weep*　γελάσετε, *you will laugh*]

Ο ΙΑΤΡΟΣ (β)

ὁ ἰᾱτρός, "ἐλθὲ δεῦρο, ὦ παῖ," ἔφη. "τί ἔπαθες; πῶς τυφλὸς ἐγένου;"

VOCABULARY

Verbs

Participles of thematic 2nd aorist verbs are given to remind you that the augment regularly occurs only in the indicative.

αἱρέω, αἱρήσω, [ἑλ-] εἷλον (irregular augment), ἑλών, *I take*

δοκεῖ, impersonal, [δοκ-] δόξει, ἔδοξε(ν), δόξαν, *it seems (good);* + dat., e.g., δοκεῖ μοι, *it seems good to me; I think it best;* + dat. and infin., e.g., δοκεῖ αὐτοῖς σπεύδειν, *it seems good to them to hurry, they decide to hurry*

ἔρχομαι, [εἰ-/ἰ-] εἶμι (irregular), [ἐλθ-] ἦλθον, ἐλθών, *I come; I go*
    προσέρχομαι + dat. or πρός + acc., *I approach*

λέγω, λέξω or [ἐρε-] ἐρῶ, ἔλεξα or [ἐπ-] εἶπον (irregular augment), εἰπών (augment retained), *I say; I tell; I speak*

νοσέω, νοσήσω, ἐνόσησα, *I am sick, ill*

ὁράω, [ὀπ-] ὄψομαι, [ἰδ-] εἶδον (irregular augment), ἰδών, *I see*

ὠφελέω, ὠφελήσω, ὠφέλησα, *I help; I benefit*

Nouns

τὸ ἀργύριον, τοῦ ἀργυρίου, *silver; money*

ἡ δραχμή, τῆς δραχμῆς, *drachma (a silver coin worth six obols)*

ὁ μισθός, τοῦ μισθοῦ, *reward; pay*

ὁ ὀβολός, τοῦ ὀβολοῦ, *obol (a silver coin of slight worth)*

Preposition

πρός + dat., *at, near, by;* + acc., *to, toward;* <u>against</u>

Interjection

οἴμοι, note the accent, *alas!*

Expression

κατὰ θάλατταν, *by sea*

Proper Names

ὁ Ἀσκληπιός, τοῦ Ἀσκληπιοῦ, *Asclepius (the god of healing)*

ἡ Ἐπίδαυρος, τῆς Ἐπιδαύρου, *Epidaurus*

ὁ Πειραιεύς, τοῦ Πειραιῶς, τῷ Πειραιεῖ, τὸν Πειραιᾶ, *the Piraeus (the port of Athens)*

τῇ οὖν ὑστεραίᾳ, ἐπεὶ πρῶτον ἡμέρα ἐγένετο, τὰς γυναῖκας ἐν τῇ
οἰκίᾳ λιπόντες ὅ τε Δικαιόπολις καὶ ὁ ἀδελφὸς τὸν Φίλιππον εἰς τὴν
ὁδὸν ἤγαγον. ὁ δὲ τῆς τοῦ πατρὸς χειρὸς ἐλάβετο ἀλλ' ὅμως πρὸς
τοὺς λίθους πταίων πρὸς τὴν γῆν κατέπεσεν. ὁ οὖν πατὴρ αἴρει
αὐτὸν καὶ φέρει. οὕτως οὖν πορευόμενοι δι' ὀλίγου ἀφίκοντο εἰς τὴν   5
τοῦ ἰᾱτροῦ οἰκίαν. ὁ δ' ἀδελφός, "ἰδού," ἔφη· "εἰς τοῦ ἰᾱτροῦ ἥκομεν.
ἐλθὲ δεῦρο καὶ κόψον τὴν θύρᾱν." τοῦτο εἰπὼν ὁ ἀδελφὸς οἴκαδε
ἐπανῆλθεν.

[**πταίων**, *stumbling*　　**εἰς τοῦ ἰᾱτροῦ**, *to (the house) of the doctor*　　**κόψον**, *knock on*
τοῦτο, *this*　　**ἐπανῆλθεν**, *returned*]

　　ὁ οὖν Δικαιόπολις προσελθὼν ἔκοψε τὴν θύρᾱν, ἀλλ' οὐδεὶς
ἦλθεν. ἐπεὶ δ' αὖθις ἔκοψεν, δοῦλός τις ἐξελθών, "βάλλ' ἐς   10
κόρακας," ἔφη. "τίς ὢν σὺ κόπτεις τὴν θύρᾱν;" ὁ δὲ Δικαιόπολις·
"ἀλλ', ὦ δαιμόνιε, ἐγώ εἰμι Δικαιόπολις· τὸν δὲ παῖδα κομίζω παρὰ
τὸν σὸν δεσπότην· τυφλὸς γὰρ γέγονεν." ὁ δὲ δοῦλος· "ἀλλ' οὐ
σχολὴ αὐτῷ." ὁ δὲ Δικαιόπολις· "ἀλλ' ὅμως κάλει αὐτόν. δεινὰ γὰρ
ἔπαθεν ὁ παῖς· ἀλλὰ μένε, ὦ φίλε." καὶ οὕτως εἰπὼν δύο ὀβολοὺς τῷ   15
δούλῳ παρέσχεν. ὁ δέ· "μένετε οὖν ἐνταῦθα. ἐγὼ γὰρ τὸν δεσπότην
καλῶ, εἴ πως ἐθελήσει ὑμᾶς δέχεσθαι."

[**βάλλ' ἐς κόρακας**, *go to the crows! (= go to hell!)*　　**ὦ δαιμόνιε**, *my dear fellow*　　**οὐ
σχολὴ αὐτῷ**, *he doesn't have leisure (= he's busy)*　　**εἴ πως**, *if somehow, if perhaps*]

　　ὅ τε οὖν πατὴρ καὶ ὁ παῖς ὀλίγον τινὰ χρόνον μένουσιν ἐπὶ τῇ
θύρᾳ. ἔπειτα δ' ὁ δοῦλος ἐξελθών, "εἰσέλθετε," ἔφη. "ὁ γὰρ δεσπότης
ὑμᾶς δέξεται." ὁ οὖν πατὴρ τῷ παιδὶ εἰσηγούμενος τὸν ἰᾱτρὸν εἶδεν ἐν   20
τῇ αὐλῇ καθιζόμενον. προσελθὼν οὖν, "χαῖρε," ἔφη· "ἐγὼ μέν εἰμι
Δικαιόπολις Χολλείδης, κομίζω δὲ παρὰ σὲ τὸν ἐμὸν παῖδα· δεινὰ
γὰρ ἔπαθεν· τυφλὸς γέγονεν." ὁ δὲ ἰᾱτρός, "δεῦρο ἐλθέ, ὦ παῖ. τί
ἔπαθες; πῶς τυφλὸς ἐγένου;" ὁ μὲν οὖν Δικαιόπολις πάντα τῷ ἰᾱτρῷ
εἶπεν, ὁ δὲ τοὺς τοῦ παιδὸς ὀφθαλμοὺς πολὺν χρόνον σκοπεῖ. τέλος   25
δέ· "ἐγὼ μὲν οὐ δυνήσομαι αὐτὸν ὠφελεῖν. οὐδὲν γὰρ νοσοῦσιν οἱ
ὀφθαλμοί. οὐκ οὖν δυνήσονται ὠφελεῖν οἱ ἄνθρωποι, ἀλλὰ τοῖς γε

θεοῖς πάντα δυνατά. δεῖ οὖν σε κομίζειν τὸν παῖδα πρὸς τὴν Ἐπίδαυρον καὶ τῷ Ἀσκληπιῷ εὔχεσθαι, εἴ πως ἐθελήσει αὐτὸν ἰᾶσθαι." ὁ δὲ Δικαιόπολις, "οἴμοι, πῶς γὰρ ἔξεσταί μοι πένητι ὄντι   30
πρὸς τὴν Ἐπίδαυρον ἰέναι;" ὁ δὲ ἰατρός, "σὸν ἔργον, ὦ ἄνθρωπε," ἔφη· "χαίρετε."

[ὀλίγον, *small, short*   τῇ αὐλῇ, *the courtyard*   Χολλείδης, *from Cholleidae* (Dicaeopolis's home village or deme)   δυνήσομαι, *will be able*   ἰᾶσθαι, *to heal* πένητι, *a poor man*   σὸν ἔργον, *(that's) your business*]

ὁ οὖν Δικαιόπολις μάλα λῡπούμενος βαδίζει πρὸς τὴν θύραν καὶ τῷ παιδὶ οἴκαδε ἡγεῖται. ἀφικόμενος δὲ πάντα τὰ γενόμενα τῷ ἀδελφῷ εἶπεν. ἡ δὲ Μυρρίνη πάντα μαθοῦσα, "ἔστω· οὐ δυνάμεθα τῇ   35
ἀνάγκῃ μάχεσθαι. δεῖ σε οὖν τὸν παῖδα πρὸς τὴν Ἐπίδαυρον κομίζειν." ὁ δὲ Δικαιόπολις, "ἀλλὰ πῶς ἔξεσταί μοι, ὦ γύναι," ἔφη, "τὸν παῖδα ἐκεῖσε ἄγειν; δεῖ γὰρ κατὰ θάλατταν ἰέναι· οὐ γὰρ δυνήσεται πεζῇ ἰέναι ὁ παῖς τυφλὸς ὤν. πῶς οὖν ἔξεσται τὸν μισθὸν παρασχεῖν τῷ ναυκλήρῳ; οὐ γάρ ἐστί μοι τὸ ἀργύριον."   40

[λῡπούμενος, *grieving*   ἔστω, *all right!*   τῇ ἀνάγκῃ, *necessity*   πεζῇ, *on foot*   τῷ ναυκλήρῳ, *to the ship's captain*]

ὁ δὲ ἀδελφός, "μὴ φρόντιζε, ὦ φίλε," ἔφη. καὶ πρὸς κυψέλην τινὰ ἐλθὼν πέντε δραχμὰς ἐξεῖλε καὶ τῷ Δικαιοπόλιδι παρέσχεν. ὁ δὲ τὸ ἀργύριον δέχεται καὶ μεγάλην χάριν ἔχων, "ὦ φίλτατ' ἀνδρῶν," ἔφη, "τοὺς θεοὺς εὔχομαι πάντα ἀγαθά σοι παρέχειν οὕτως εὔφρονι ὄντι." οὕτως οὖν δοκεῖ αὐτοῖς τῇ ὑστεραίᾳ πρὸς τὸν Πειραιᾶ σπεύδειν καὶ   45
ναῦν τινα ζητεῖν πρὸς τὴν Ἐπίδαυρον πλευσομένην.

[μὴ φρόντιζε, *don't worry!*   κυψέλην, *chest*   χάριν ἔχων, *giving* (lit., *having*) thanks   φίλτατ(ε), *dearest*   εὔφρονι, *kind*]

WORD BUILDING

Three types of nouns are commonly formed from verb stems:

1. First declension masculine nouns ending in -της express the doer of the action, e.g., ποιε-, *make* > ὁ ποιη-τής, *the maker; the poet.*
2. Third declension feminine nouns ending in -σις express the action of the verb, e.g., ἡ ποίη-σις, *the making; the creation; the composition.*

3. Third declension neuter nouns ending in -μα express the result of the action, e.g., τὸ ποίη-μα, *the thing made; the work; the poem.*

Give the meanings of the following:

1. οἰκέω   ὁ οἰκητής   ἡ οἴκησις   τὸ οἴκημα
2. μανθάνω (μαθ-)   ὁ μαθητής   ἡ μάθησις   τὸ μάθημα

GRAMMAR

6. Verbs with Thematic 2nd Aorists from Unrelated Stems

The thematic 2nd aorists you have studied so far use stems that are related etymologically to the stem seen in the present tense, e.g. λαμβάνω and ἔλαβον, like English *take* and *took.* A few Greek verbs form their aorists from a completely different root, etymologically unrelated to that seen in the stem used for the present tense, as does English with, for example, *I go* (present) and *I went* (past). The following are the most common such verbs in Greek, and you have already seen some of their aorist imperatives and participles in the readings:

αἱρέω, *I take,* αἱρήσω, [ἑλ-] **εἷλον** (irregular augment), ἑλών

ἔρχομαι, *I come; I go,* [εἰ-/ἰ-] **εἶμι** (irregular), [ἐλθ-] **ἦλθον**, ἐλθών

ἐσθίω, *I eat,* [ἐδ-] **ἔδομαι**, [**φαγ-**] **ἔφαγον**, φαγών

λέγω, *I say; I tell; I speak,* λέξω, [ἐπ-] **εἶπον** (irregular augment), εἰπών (augment retained)

ὁράω, *I see,* [ὀπ-] **ὄψομαι**, [**ἰδ-**] **εἶδον** (irregular augment), ἰδών

τρέχω, *I run,* [δραμε-] **δραμοῦμαι**, [**δραμ-**] **ἔδραμον**, δραμών

φέρω, *I carry;* of roads, *lead,* [οἰ-] **οἴσω**, [**ἐνεγκ-**] **ἤνεγκον**, ἐνεγκών

Note that the accent of compound verbs never recedes beyond the augment; thus the aorist of ἐπανέρχομαι is ἐπανῆλθον.

Exercise 11θ

1. *Make photocopies of the Verb Charts on pages 282 and 283 and fill in the forms of ἔρχομαι, future, εἶμι, and aorist, ἦλθον, that you have learned to date.*
2. *On your charts with the future of ἔχω and ὁράω (Exercise 10α.2), fill in the aorist forms that you have learned to date.*

7. Accents on Thematic 2nd Aorist Active Imperatives

The aorist imperatives of most verbs with thematic 2nd aorists have regular recessive accents, e.g., λίπε, λίπετε (see Grammar 2, page 177). The accents of the aorist imperatives of ἔρχομαι, λέγω, ὁράω, εὑρίσκω, and λαμβάνω, however, are irregular in the singular in that they are not recessive. In the plural the accents of all five of these words are recessive:

| Singular: | ἐλθέ | εἰπέ | ἰδέ | εὑρέ | λαβέ |
| Plural: | ἔλθετε | εἴπετε | ἴδετε | εὕρετε | λάβετε |

Note that in the singular the accent of the *compound* forms of these imperatives *is* recessive, e.g., ἐπάνελθε (from ἐπανέρχομαι).

Exercise 11ι

Read aloud and translate:

1. "ἐλθὲ δεῦρο, ὦ ἄδελφε, καί μοι σύλλαβε.
2. "χθὲς (*yesterday*) λύκον εἶδον πρὸς τὸ αὔλιον (*sheepfold*) προσιόντα.
3. "ἴσως (*perhaps*) αὐτὸν ἐν τοῖς ὄρεσιν ὀψόμεθα καὶ αἱρήσομεν."
4. οἱ οὖν παῖδες εἰς τὸ αὔλιον ἀφικόμενοι λύκον εἶδον ἐκ τῶν ὀρῶν κατιόντα.
5. τὸν λύκον ἰδόντες λίθους αἴρουσι καὶ διώκουσιν αὐτόν.
6. ὁ δὲ πάππος τοὺς παῖδας ἰδὼν τὴν βακτηρίᾱν (*his stick*) εἷλε καὶ ἦλθεν ὡς συλληψόμενος.
7. οἱ παῖδες τὸν πάππον εἶδον προσιόντα καὶ εἶπον· "ἐλθὲ δεῦρο, ὦ πάππε· ἡμεῖς σε μενοῦμεν.
8. "σπεῦδε. πρὸς τὰ ὄρη ἴμεν καὶ τὸν λύκον αἱρήσομεν."
9. ὁ δὲ πάππος εἶπεν· "ἐπανέλθετε, ὦ παῖδες· μὴ ἴτε πρὸς τὰ ὄρη· τὸν γὰρ λύκον οὐχ εὑρήσετε."
10. οὕτως εἰπὼν τοὺς παῖδας οἴκαδε ἤγαγεν.

8. Augment

To indicate past time in the aorist indicative, as we saw in Grammar 1 above, Greek puts an ε before the stem of verbs beginning with consonants. This is called a *syllabic augment*. If the stem begins with a short vowel or diphthong, the initial vowel is lengthened in spelling and/or sound. This is called *temporal augment*, because long vowels are held for a longer *time*. The following list compares present and aorist indicatives and shows how the stems of verbs beginning with vowels and diphthongs are augmented. A number of these verbs are sigmatic or asigmatic 1st aorists (to be introduced in the next chapter) and are cited merely as examples of temporal augment.

Present	**Aorist**	
Single vowels:		
ἀκούω	ἤκουσα	(α lengthens to η)
ἐγείρω	ἤγειρα	(ε also lengthens to η)
ἡγέομαι	ἡγησάμην	(no change)
ἱκνέομαι	ἱκόμην	(ῐ lengthens to ῑ)
ὁρμάω	ὥρμησα	(ο lengthens to ω)

| ὑβρίζω | ὕβρισα | (ῠ lengthens to ῡ) |
| ὠφελέω | ὠφέλησα | (no change) |

Diphthongs:

αἰτέω	ᾔτησα	(α lengthens to η, and ι goes subscript)
αὐξάνω	ηὔξησα	(αυ lengthens to ηυ)
εὔχομαι	ηὐξάμην	(ευ lengthens to ηυ)
οἰκέω	ᾤκησα	(ο lengthens to ω, and ι goes subscript)

Remember that the thematic 2nd aorist stems of αἱρέω, λέγω, and ὁράω, namely, ἑλ-, ἑπ-, and ἰδ- augment irregularly to ει, giving εἷλον, εἶπον, and εἶδον and that εἶπον retains its augment in its imperative, εἰπέ/εἴπετε, infinitive, εἰπεῖν, and participle, εἰπών (see Grammar 6, page 189).   Some other verbs may also augment ε to ει, e.g., ἐργάζομαι, *I work*, aorist, ἠργασάμην or εἰργασάμην.

Exercise 11κ

Augment the following stems where possible:

1. κελευ-	4. ἰᾱτρευ-	7. ἠγε-	10. ὀνομαζ-
2. ἐθελ-	5. ἀρχ-	8. ἀμῡν-	11. ἐλθ-
3. ὀτρῡν-	6. λαβ-	9. εὐχ-	12. μαθ-

Exercise 11λ

Turn the following forms into corresponding forms of the aorist and translate both forms:

1. λαμβάνομεν	7. λέγε	13. λέγειν
2. μανθάνει	8. ἔχω	14. ἔρχομαι
3. πάσχουσι(ν) (2 ways)	9. ἀφικνεῖσθαι	15. ὁρᾶν
4. λείπω	10. λείπειν	16. λέγομεν
5. πίπτων	11. λαμβάνουσα	17. ὁρᾷ
6. γιγνόμεθα	12. λείπετε (2 ways)	18. αἱροῦσι(ν) (2 ways)

Exercise 11μ

Read aloud and translate:

1. ὁ αὐτουργὸς εἰς τὸν ἀγρὸν εἰσελθὼν τὴν θυγατέρα εἶδεν ὑπὸ τῷ δένδρῳ καθιζομένην.
2. προσῆλθεν οὖν καὶ εἶπεν· "τί καθίζει ὑπὸ τῷ δένδρῳ δακρύουσα, ὦ θύγατερ;"

3. ἡ δὲ εἶπεν· "τὸ δεῖπνόν σοι φέρουσα, ὦ πάτερ, ἐν τῇ ὁδῷ κατέπεσον καὶ τὸν πόδα (*foot*) ἔβλαψα (*I hurt*)."

4. ὁ δέ, "ἐλθὲ δεῦρο," φησίν, "δεῖ με τὸν σὸν πόδα σκοπεῖν."

5. τὸν οὖν πόδα αὐτῆς σκοπεῖ καὶ ἰδὼν ὅτι οὐδὲν νοσεῖ, "θάρρει (*cheer up*), ὦ θύγατερ," ἔφη· "οὐδὲν κακὸν (*bad*) ἔπαθες. παράσχες οὖν μοι τὸ δεῖπνον καὶ οἴκαδε ἐπάνελθε."

6. ἡ οὖν παρθένος τὸ δεῖπνον τῷ πατρὶ παρασχοῦσα οἴκαδε βραδέως ἀπῆλθεν.

Exercise 11v

Translate into Greek:

1. How did you become blind, boy? Tell me what happened.
2. Where did you see the oxen? Did you leave them in the field?
3. After suffering much (= many things: *use neuter plural adjective*) by sea, they finally arrived at the land.
4. After seeing the dances, the boys went home and told their father (*dative case*) what happened.
5. Falling (*use aorist participle*) into the sea, the girls suffered terribly (= terrible things).

Ο ΔΗΜΟΚΗΔΗΣ ΤΟΝ ΒΑΣΙΛΕΑ ΙΑΤΡΕΥΕΙ

Read the following passage (based on Herodotus 3.129–130) and answer the comprehension questions:

ἐπεὶ δὲ ἀπέθανεν ὁ Πολυκράτης, οἱ Πέρσαι τούς τε ἄλλους θεράποντας τοῦ Πολυκράτους λαβόντες καὶ τὸν Δημοκήδη εἰς τὰ Σοῦσα ἐκόμισαν. δι' ὀλίγου δὲ ὁ βασιλεὺς κακόν τι ἔπαθεν· ἀπὸ τοῦ ἵππου γὰρ πεσὼν τὸν πόδα ἔβλαψεν. οἱ δὲ ἰᾱτροὶ οὐκ ἐδύναντο αὐτὸν ὠφελεῖν. μαθὼν δὲ ὅτι ἰᾱτρός τις Ἑλληνικὸς πάρεστιν ἐν τοῖς δούλοις, τοὺς θεράποντας ἐκέλευσε τὸν Δημοκήδη παρ' ἑαυτὸν ἀγαγεῖν. ὁ   5
οὖν Δημοκήδης εἰς μέσον ἦλθεν, πέδᾱς τε ἕλκων καὶ ῥάκεσιν ἐσθημένος. ὁ οὖν βασιλεὺς ἰδὼν αὐτὸν ἐθαύμασε καὶ ἤρετο εἰ δύναται τὸν πόδα ἰᾱτρεύειν. ὁ δὲ Δημοκήδης φοβούμενος εἶπεν ὅτι οὐκ ἔστιν ἰᾱτρὸς σοφὸς ἀλλ' ἐθέλει πειρᾶσθαι. ἐνταῦθα δὴ Ἑλληνικῇ ἰᾱτρείᾳ χρώμενος τὸν πόδα ταχέως ἰᾱτρευσεν. οὕτως οὖν φίλος ἐγένετο τῷ βασιλεῖ, ὁ δὲ πολὺ ἀργύριον αὐτῷ παρέσχε καὶ μέγα ἐτίμᾱ.   10

[ὁ **Πολυκράτης**, τοῦ **Πολυκράτους**, *Polycrates* (tyrant of Samos, sixth century B.C.; he was captured and put to death by the Persians)   οἱ **Πέρσαι**, *the Persians* **θεράποντας**, *servants*   ὁ **Δημοκήδης**, τὸν **Δημοκήδη**, *Democedes*   τὰ **Σοῦσα**, neuter acc. pl., *Susa*   **ἐκόμισαν**, *brought*   **κακόν τι**, *something bad*   τοῦ **ἵππου**, *his horse*   τὸν **πόδα**, *his foot*   **ἔβλαψεν**, *he hurt*   **ἐδύναντο**, *were able*   **Ἑλληνικὸς**, *Greek*   **ἐκέλευσε**, *he ordered*   **πέδᾱς ... ἕλκων**, *dragging his shackles*   **ῥάκεσιν** ἐσθημένος, *clothed in rags*   ἐθαύμασε, *was amazed*   ἤρετο, *asked*   ἰᾱτρεύειν, *to heal*   πειρᾶσθαι, *to try*   ἰᾱτρείᾳ, *healing, medicine*   χρώμενος + dat., *using*   ἐτίμα, *was honoring*]

1. What happened to the Persian king? Of what help were his doctors?
2. What did the king learn? What did he order his servants to do?
3. In what two ways could Democedes be recognized as a prisoner?
4. How does the Persian king react to the sight of Democedes?
5. What did Democedes say to the king? How did he heal the king's foot?
6. In what three ways did Democedes benefit?

Exercise 11ξ

Translate into Greek:

1. The king, falling (*use aorist participle*) from his horse, suffered something bad, but the doctors said that they could not (οὐ δύνανται; *use this present tense form*) help him.
2. Having learned that there was (*use present tense*) another doctor among the slaves, the servants said: "It is necessary to bring this doctor (τοῦτον τὸν ἰᾱτρόν) to you."
3. And when the doctor arrived, the king said, "Is it possible to heal my foot?"
4. The doctor said that he was willing (*use present tense*) to try (πειρᾶσθαι).
5. And when the doctor cured (ἰᾱτρευσε) his foot, the king became very friendly to him.

New Testament Greek

Luke 6.27–29
The Sermon on the Mount

Jesus is speaking:

"ἀλλὰ ὑμῖν λέγω τοῖς ἀκούουσιν, ἀγαπᾶτε τοὺς ἐχθροὺς ὑμῶν, καλῶς ποιεῖτε τοῖς μῑσοῦσιν ὑμᾶς, εὐλογεῖτε τοὺς καταρωμένους ὑμᾶς, προσεύχεσθε περὶ τῶν ἐπηρεαζόντων ὑμᾶς. τῷ τύπτοντί σε ἐπὶ τὴν σιᾱγόνα πάρεχε καὶ τὴν ἄλλην."

[ἀγαπᾶτε, *love!*   τοὺς ἐχθρούς, *the enemies*   τοῖς μῑσοῦσιν, *those hating*   εὐλογεῖτε, *bless!*   τοὺς καταρωμένους, *those cursing*   περὶ τῶν ἐπηρεαζόντων, *for those mistreating/insulting*   ἐπὶ τὴν σιᾱγόνα, *on the cheek*]

ΠΡΟΣ ΤΟΝ ΠΕΙΡΑΙΑ (α)

προσεχώρησεν ἀνήρ τις ἅμαξαν ἐλαύνων.

VOCABULARY

Verbs
All aorist participles are now
given.
ἀπορέω, ἀπορήσω, ἠπόρησα,
ἀπορήσᾱς, *I am at a loss*
φροντίζω, [φροντιε-] **φροντιῶ,**
[φροντι-] **ἐφρόντισα,** φροντίσᾱς,
I worry; I care

Nouns
ὁ ἡμίονος, τοῦ ἡμιόνου, *mule*
ὁ λιμήν, τοῦ λιμένος, *harbor*
ὁ ὅμῑλος, τοῦ ὁμῑλου, *crowd*
τὸ τεῖχος, τοῦ τείχους, *wall*

Adjectives
γεραιός, -ά, -όν, *old*

κακός, -ή, -όν, *bad; evil*
ὀρθός, -ή, -όν, *straight; right,*
correct

Adverbs
τάχιστα, *most quickly; most*
swiftly
ὡς τάχιστα, *as quickly as*
possible

Conjunction
ἤ, *or*
ἤ ... ἤ, *either ... or*
καίπερ + participle, *although*

Expression
χαίρειν κελεύω + acc., *I bid* X
farewell, I bid farewell to X

τῇ δ' ὑστεραίᾳ ἐπεὶ πρῶτον ἡμέρᾱ ἐγένετο, ὁ Δικαιόπολις πάντας
ἐκέλευσε παρασκευάζεσθαι.   οἱ μὲν οὖν ἄλλοι εὐθὺς παρεσκευάσαντο βουλόμενοι ὡς τάχιστα πορεύεσθαι καὶ δι' ὀλίγου
ἕτοιμοι ἦσαν.   ὁ δὲ πάππος οὐκ ἠθέλησε πορεύεσθαι· οὕτω γὰρ
γεραιὸς ἦν ὥστε οὐκ ἐδύνατο μακρὰν βαδίζειν· ἡ δὲ Μέλιττα οὕτω   5

μακρὰν τῇ προτεραίᾳ βαδίσᾱσα ὑπέρκοπος ἦν· ἔδοξεν οὖν τῇ μητρὶ
καταλιπεῖν αὐτὴν οἴκοι μετὰ τοῦ πάππου. ἐπεὶ δὲ παρῆσαν οἱ ἄλλοι,
ὁ Δικαιόπολις ἡγησάμενος αὐτοῖς εἰς τὴν αὐλὴν τῷ βωμῷ
προσεχώρησε καὶ σπονδὴν ποιησάμενος τὸν Δία ηὔξατο σῴζειν
πάντας τοσαύτην ὁδὸν ποιουμένους.   10

[ἐκέλευσε, ordered   παρεσκευάσαντο, prepared themselves   ἦσαν (imperfect),
they were   ἠθέλησε, wished   ἦν (imperfect), he was   ἐδύνατο (imperfect), he was
able   μακρὰν, a long (way)   τῇ προτεραίᾳ, the day before   βαδίσᾱσα, having
walked   ὑπέρκοπος, exhausted   ἡγησάμενος, having led   τὴν αὐλὴν, the
courtyard   προσεχώρησε, he approached   σπονδὴν, a libation   ποιησάμενος, after making   ηὔξατο (from εὔχομαι), he prayed]

τόν τ' οὖν πάππον καὶ τὴν Μέλιτταν χαίρειν κελεύσαντες
ὥρμησαν, καὶ δι' ὀλίγου, εἰς τὰς τῆς πόλεως πύλᾱς ἀφικόμενοι, τὴν
πρὸς τὸν λιμένα ὁδὸν εἵλοντο. ὀρθὴ δ' ἦν ἡ ὁδός, διὰ τῶν μακρῶν
τειχῶν φέρουσα· πολλοὶ δὲ ἄνθρωποι ἐνῆσαν, πολλαὶ δὲ ἄμαξαι,
πολλοὶ δὲ καὶ ἡμίονοι φορτία φέροντες ἢ πρὸς τὴν πόλιν ἢ ἀπὸ τῆς   15
πόλεως πρὸς τὸν λιμένα. ὁ δὲ Δικαιόπολις σπεύδει διὰ τοῦ ὁμίλου
βουλόμενος ὡς τάχιστα ἀφικέσθαι. ὁ δὲ Φίλιππος καίπερ τῆς τοῦ
πατρὸς χειρὸς ἐχόμενος ἔπταισε καὶ πρὸς τὴν γῆν κατέπεσεν. ἡ δὲ
μήτηρ βοήσᾱσα, "ὦ τλῆμον παῖ," ἔφη, "τί ἔπαθες;" καὶ προσδραμοῦσα ἦρεν αὐτόν. ὁ δὲ οὐδὲν κακὸν παθών, "μὴ φρόντιζε, ὦ   20
μῆτερ," ἔφη· "καίπερ γὰρ πεσὼν ἐγὼ καλῶς ἔχω." ἡ δὲ μήτηρ ἔτι
φροντίζει καὶ τὸν παῖδα σκοπεῖ.

[ὥρμησαν, they set out   εἵλοντο, they chose   ἄμαξαι, wagons   τὰ φορτία, burdens, cargoes   ἐχόμενος + gen., holding   ἔπταισε, stumbled   βοήσᾱσα, shouting,
i.e., in a loud voice   τλῆμον, wretched, poor   προσδραμοῦσα, having run toward
(him)]

ἐν ᾧ δὲ πάντες περιμένουσιν ἀπορόῦντες τί δεῖ ποιεῖν,
προσεχώρησεν ἀνήρ τις ἄμαξαν ἐλαύνων. ἰδὼν δ' αὐτοὺς ἐν τῇ ὁδῷ
περιμένοντας καὶ ἀπορόῦντας, τὸν ἡμίονον ἔστησε καί, "εἴπετέ μοι, τί   25
πάσχετε, ὦ φίλοι;" ἔφη, "τί οὕτω περιμένετε; ἆρα κακόν τι ἔπαθεν ὁ
παῖς;" οἱ μὲν οὖν πάντα ἐξηγήσαντο, ὁ δέ, "ἐλθὲ δεῦρο, ὦ παῖ," ἔφη,
"καὶ ἀνάβηθι ἐπὶ τὴν ἄμαξαν. καὶ σύ, ὦ γύναι, εἰ τῷ ἀνδρὶ δοκεῖ,
ἀνάβηθι. καὶ ἐγὼ γὰρ πρὸς τὸν λιμένα πορεύομαι." οἱ δὲ ἐδέξαντο

τὸν λόγον καὶ οὕτω πορευόμενοι δι᾽ ὀλίγου ἀφίκοντο εἰς τὸν λιμένα.　30

[περιμένουσιν, *are waiting around*　ἔστησε, *he stopped*　ἐξηγήσαντο, *related*
ἀνάβηθι, *get up*　ἐδέξαντο, *received, accepted*]

WORD STUDY

*Identify the Greek stems in the English words below and give the meanings
of the English words:*

1. mathematics
2. polymath
3. orthodoxy (what must ἡ δόξα mean?)
4. orthodontist (what must ὁ ὀδούς, τοῦ ὀδόντος mean?)
5. orthopedics *or* orthopaedics

GRAMMAR

1. Verb Forms: Past Tense: The Sigmatic 1st Aorist

Most Greek verbs have *sigmatic 1st aorists*, rather than the thematic
2nd aorist formations studied in the last chapter. Sigmatic 1st aorists are
formed by adding the suffix -σα to the verb stem, e.g., ἔ-λῡ-σα. (In certain types of verbs the σ is lost and one finds only -α and not -σα; these
asigmatic 1st aorist formations will be studied in the second half of this
chapter.) As with the thematic 2nd aorists, the verb stem is augmented
only in the indicative. Compare the forms below with those of the thematic
2nd aorist (see Chapter 11, Grammar 2, page 177).

Sigmatic 1st Aorist Active

Present: λῡω, *I loosen;* **Aorist Stem:** λῡ-

Indicative	Imperative	Infinitive	Participle
ἔ-λῡ-σα, *I loosened*		λῦ-σαι,	λῡ-σᾱς,
ἔ-λῡ-σα-ς	λῦ-σον,	*to loosen*	λῡ-σᾱσα,
ἔ-λῡ-σ-ε(ν)	*loosen!*		λῦ-σαν,
ἐ-λῡ-σα-μεν			gen., λῡ-σαντ-ος, etc.
ἐ-λῡ-σα-τε	λῡ-σα-τε,		*having loosened,*
ἔ-λῡ-σα-ν	*loosen!*		*after loosening,*
			sometimes, *loosening*

Sigmatic 1st Aorist Middle

Indicative	Imperative	Infinitive	Participle
ἐ-λῡ-σά-μην, *I ransomed*		λύ-σα-σθαι,	λῡ-σά-μεν-ος,
ἐ-λύ-σα-σο > ἐλύσω	λῦ-σαι,	*to ransom*	λῡ-σα-μέν-η,
ἐ-λύ-σα-το	*ransom!*		λῡ-σά-μεν-ον,
ἐ-λῡ-σά-μεθα			*having ransomed,*
ἐ-λύ-σα-σθε	λύ-σα-σθε		*after ransoming,*
ἐ-λύ-σα-ντο	*ransom!*		sometimes, *ransoming*

Note:

1. The letter α is characteristic of sigmatic and asigmatic 1st aorists, and it occurs in all forms except the 3rd person singular of the active indicative (ἔλῡσε(ν)) and the singular imperative (λῦσον).

2. Sigmatic and asigmatic 1st aorist active infinitives are always accented on the next to the last syllable, e.g., λῦσαι and κελεῦσαι (the diphthong -αι is short here for purposes of accentuation).

3. The -αι of sigmatic and asigmatic 1st aorist middle infinitives is also counted as short, and the accent may thus stand on the third syllable from the end, e.g., λύσασθαι (compare γενέσθαι, Chapter 11, Grammar 2, page 177, λύεσθαι, Review of Verbs, page 152, and λύσεσθαι, Chapter 10, Grammar 1, page 158).

When the stem ends in a consonant, the same rules apply as in the formation of the sigmatic future (see Chapter 10, Grammar 1, pages 158–159). Here are the present, future, and aorist of the same verbs given as examples of the future in Chapter 10, Grammar 1, pages 158–159:

a. If the stem ends in a *labial* (β, π, φ), the labial + -σ- produces the combination of sounds represented by the letter ψ in the future and aorist, e.g.:

> βλέπω, *I look; I see*, βλέψομαι, **ἔβλεψα**
> πέμπ-ω, *I send*, πέμψω, **ἔπεμψα**
> γράφ-ω, *I write*, γράψω, **ἔγραψα**

b. If the stem ends in a *velar* (γ, κ, χ), the velar + -σ- produces the combination of sounds represented by the letter ξ in the future and aorist, e.g.:

> λέγω, *I say; I tell; I speak*, λέξω or ἐρῶ, **ἔλεξα** or εἶπον
> διώκ-ω, *I pursue*, διώξομαι or, less commonly, διώξω, **ἐδίωξα**
> φυλάττω, *I guard*, [φυλακ-] φυλάξω, **ἐφύλαξα**
> δέχ-ομαι, *I receive*, δέξομαι, **ἐδεξάμην**

c. If the stem ends in a *dental* (δ, θ, τ) or ζ, the dental or ζ is lost before the -σ- of the future and aorist, e.g.:

> σπεύδ-ω, *I hurry*, σπεύσω, **ἔσπευσα**

πείθ-ω, *I persuade*, πείσω, **ἔπεισα**

πάττω, *I sprinkle*, [πατ-] πάσω, **ἔπασα**

παρασκευάζ-ω, *I prepare*, παρασκευάσω, **παρεσκεύασα**

Note: κομίζ-ω, *I bring; I take*, [κομιε-] κομιῶ, [κομι-] **ἐκόμισα**

Contract verbs lengthen the final stem vowel and then add σ for the future and the aorist, e.g.:

φιλέ-ω, *I love*, φιλήσω, **ἐφίλησα**

Exception: καλέ-ω, *I call*, καλῶ (no difference in spelling between the present and the future tense for this verb), **ἐκάλεσα** (the ε of the stem does not lengthen in the aorist).

ἡγέ-ο-μαι, *I lead*, ἡγήσομαι, **ἡγησάμην**

τῑμά-ω, *I honor*, τῑμήσω, **ἐτίμησα**

Note: θεά-ο-μαι, *I see, watch, look at*, θεάσομαι, **ἐθεᾱσάμην** (note that because of the ε the α lengthens to ᾱ rather than η).

Here are the verbs listed in Chapter 10, Grammar 4, pages 159–160, with deponent futures that have sigmatic 1st aorists:

ἀκούω, *I hear*, ἀκούσομαι, **ἤκουσα**, ἀκούσᾱς

βαδίζω, *I walk; I go*, [βαδιε-] βαδιοῦμαι, [βαδι-] **ἐβάδισα**, βαδίσᾱς

βλέπω, *I look; I see*, βλέψομαι, **ἔβλεψα**, βλέψᾱς

βοάω, *I shout*, βοήσομαι, **ἐβόησα**, βοήσᾱς

διώκω, *I pursue, chase*, διώξομαι or διώξω, **ἐδίωξα**, διώξᾱς

θαυμάζω, intransitive, *I am amazed*; transitive, *I wonder at, admire*, θαυμάσομαι, **ἐθαύμασα**, θαυμάσᾱς

πλέω, *I sail*, [πλευ-] πλεύσομαι or [πλευσε-] πλευσοῦμαι, [πλευ-] **ἔπλευσα**, πλεύσᾱς

Remember that the following verb may have an irregular augment: ἐργάζομαι, *I work; I accomplish*, aorist, ἠργασάμην or εἰργασάμην (see Chapter 11, Grammar 8, page 191).

Exercise 12α

In the second and third paragraphs of the reading passage at the beginning of this chapter, locate eight sigmatic 1st aorist verb forms. Identify each form (mood, person, and number for finite verbs; gender, case, and number for participles).

Exercise 12β

1. *On the second pages of the sets of Verb Charts that you filled out for Exercise 10a.1, fill in the aorist forms that you have learned to date of the four verbs, βλέπω, φυλάττω, σπεύδω, and κομίζω.*

2. *On your charts for* θεωρέω, βοάω, ἀφικνέομαι, *and* ὁρμάομαι, *fill in the aorist forms that you have learned to date.*

Exercise 12γ

Give the future indicative and the aorist indicative, 1st person singular, of the following verbs:

1. δακρύω	6. διώκω	11. βοηθέω
2. βλέπω	7. νῑκάω	12. ἐθέλω
3. θαυμάζω	8. σπεύδω	13. παύω
4. ἀκούω	9. κομίζω	14. φυλάττω
5. δέχομαι	10. ἡγέομαι	15. πέμπω

2. Sigmatic 1st Aorist Active and Middle Participles

The sigmatic 1st aorist active participle is declined like the adjective πᾶς, πᾶσα, πᾶν (see Chapter 8, Grammar 4, page 126), except for the accent:

Stems: λῡσαντ- for masculine and neuter; λῡσᾱσ- for feminine

	Masculine	Feminine	Neuter
Singular:			
Nom.	λῡσαντ-ς > λῡσᾱς	λῡσᾶσα	λῦσαντ > λῦσαν
Gen.	λῡσαντ-ος	λῡσάσης	λῡσαντ-ος
Dat.	λῡσαντ-ι	λῡσάσῃ	λῡσαντ-ι
Acc.	λῡσαντ-α	λῡσᾶσαν	λῦσαντ > λῦσαν
Plural:			
Nom.	λῡσαντ-ες	λῡσᾶσαι	λῡσαντ-α
Gen.	λῡσάντ-ων	λῡσᾱσῶν	λῡσάντ-ων
Dat.	λῡσαντ-σι(ν) > λῡσᾱσι(ν)	λῡσάσαις	λῡσαντ-σι(ν) > λῡσᾶσι(ν)
Acc.	λῡσαντ-ας	λῡσάσᾱς	λῡσαντ-α

The sigmatic 1st aorist middle participle has the same endings as the present middle participle (see Chapter 8, Grammar 1, page 115):

Nom. λῡ-σά-μεν-ος λῡ-σα-μέν-η λῡ-σά-μεν-ον
etc.

Exercise 12δ

Write the forms of the aorist active participles of βλέπω *and* ποιέω.

Exercise 12ε

Change the following present forms into corresponding forms of the aorist:

1. κελεύομεν	6.	οἰκοῦμεν	11.	βοηθεῖν
2. πέμπουσι(ν) (2 ways)	7.	τῑμᾷ	12.	νῑκῶμεν
3. ἀκούετε	8.	δακρῡ́ων	13.	ἡγούμενος
4. λῡ́εται	9.	κομίζω	14.	δέχου
5. εὐχόμενοι	10.	βαδίζομεν	15.	προσχωροῦσι(ν) (2 ways)

Exercise 12ζ

Translate into English. Identify present and aorist participles and explain why the present or the aorist is used in each case.

1. ὁ Δικαιόπολις οὐκ ἠθέλησε τῇ γυναικὶ πρὸς τὸ ἄστυ ἡγήσασθαι.
2. ὁ ξένος εἰσελθὼν εὐθὺς οἶνον ᾔτησεν.
3. ὁ ἱερεὺς σπονδὴν ποιησάμενος τοῖς θεοῖς ηὔξατο.
4. αἱ γυναῖκες, καίπερ τοὺς ἄνδρας ἰδοῦσαι, οὐκ ἐπαύσαντο βοῶσαι.
5. εἴσελθε, ὦ παῖ, καὶ τὸν πατέρα κάλεσον.
6. ἐλθὲ δεῦρο, ὦ παῖ, καὶ εἰπέ μοι τί ἐποίησας.
7. ἡ παρθένος τοὺς χοροὺς θεᾱσαμένη οἴκαδε ἔσπευσεν.
8. ὁ μὲν δεσπότης τοὺς δούλους ἐκέλευσε σῑγῆσαι, οἱ δὲ οὐκ ἐπαύσαντο διαλεγόμενοι.
9. οἱ ναῦται, τὴν ναῦν λῡ́σαντες, ἔπλευσαν ἐκ τοῦ λιμένος.
10. ὁ κῆρυξ τοὺς πολίτᾱς ἐκέλευσε σῑγήσαντας ἀκοῦσαι.

Exercise 12η

Translate into Greek (note that to render the correct aspect of the actions, all verb forms in this exercise—indicatives, imperatives, infinitives, and participles—should be in the aorist):

1. After making a libation (*use* ἡ σπονδή) and praying to the gods, we walked to the city.
2. The father told the boy to send the dog home.
3. I came to your aid, but you led (*use* ἡγέομαι) me into danger.
4. Call your mother, boy, and ask her to receive us.
5. The young man, after winning, received a crown (*use* ὁ στέφανος).
6. Having arrived at the city, we saw many men in the roads.

Trade and Travel

In the late Bronze Age the Achaeans traded extensively throughout the eastern Mediterranean. The Dark Age that followed (ca. 1100–800) was generally a period of isolation, in which there was little overseas trade and during which contacts with the East were broken. Early in the eighth century B.C., two Greek settlements were being made specifically for trade, the first in the East at Al Mina at the mouth of the Orontes River in Syria, the second in the West on the island of Ischia outside the Bay of Naples about 775 B.C. Both were probably made for trade in metals, essential for manufacturing arms (copper and tin from the East; copper, tin, and iron from Etruria in the West).

Al Mina was strategically placed to tap trade both inland up the Orontes to Mesopotamia and down the coast to Phoenician cities and Egypt. Its foundation was followed by a flood of Eastern imports into Greece, not only metals and artefacts, but also craftsmen and ideas, notably the alphabet, adapted by Greeks from Phoenician script about 750 B.C. The period was one of rapid change and development in Greece, a kind of renaissance. The *polis* (city-state) developed from unions of villages. Aristocracy replaced monarchy in most states. There was a revolution in warfare: hoplites (heavy armed infantry fighting in close line) replaced cavalry as the main fighting force. Growth in population led to emigrations; cities sent out colonies that peopled the coasts of the Mediterranean wherever there was no strong power to keep them out. These colonies, though founded primarily to provide land for surplus population, soon grew into prosperous, independent cities (e.g., Syracuse, founded in 733 B.C. by Corinth) and further stimulated trade, especially in grain, to supply the increasing population of the mainland. Italy from the Bay of Naples south and almost the entire coast of Sicily were studded with Greek colonies, and the area became known as Greater Greece. The leading states in this movement were Chalcis and Eretria in Euboea, Aegina, and Corinth. Miletus and other East Greek states were active in the north of the Aegean and the Black Sea.

The story of Colaeus of Samos, who voyaged out through the Straits of Gibraltar and landed at Tartessus in the Bay of Cadiz, was told by Herodotus and is given at the end of this chapter; it shows the enterprise of these traders. The new market in the West opened up by Colaeus was developed by another Ionian state, Phocaea, located on the western coast of Asia Minor (see map, page 272). Phocaeans founded Massilia (Marseilles) about 600 B.C. and soon after entered into profitable trade with the king of Tartessus. This western expansion of Greek trade was curtailed by the Carthaginians, who succeeded in pushing back the Greeks and monopolizing the route through the Straits of Gibraltar to Spain, Brittany, and Britain.

Trade with Egypt developed in the seventh century, encouraged by a friendly pharaoh, Psammetichus I (664–610 B.C.). From Egypt the Greeks imported grain; their exports were olive oil, wine, perhaps silver, and certainly mercenary soldiers. Psammetichus employed a regular force of Greek hoplites, and two reigns later his grandson, Psammetichus II still used Greek mercenaries. A Greek settlement was made at the mouth of the Nile and was named Naucratis. It was given a charter by the pharaoh Amasis (570–526 B.C.). Naucratis developed into the largest port in Egypt, a flourishing center of trade and tourism. Egypt, with a culture of immemorial antiquity, fascinated the Greeks, and many visited it out of curiosity as well as for trade. When the family members of the poet Sappho were exiled from their native Lesbos, she went to Sicily, but her brother went to Egypt, where he fell in love with the most famous courtesan of the day and spent his fortune on her. Sappho's contemporary, the poet Alcaeus, also went to Egypt during his exile, but his brother Antimenidas served as a mercenary in the army of Nebuchadnezzar, king of Babylon, and took part in the campaign that culminated in the capture of Jerusalem (587 B.C.) and the exile of the Jews.

At the time of our story, the Piraeus was the greatest port in Greece and, indeed, in the whole Mediterranean. In Chapter 14 we will explain how Athens came to take the lead from Corinth as a naval and mercantile power. The harbor must have been always crowded with ships both Athenian and foreign, both Greek and barbarian. The most important single item of import was grain, which came from the great grain producing areas of the ancient world: Egypt, Sicily, and the steppes of south Russia (Scythia). Athens had treaties with the princes of Scythia that gave her a monopoly of this trade. Shipbuilding timber was imported in large quantities both for building merchantmen and for the great Athenian navy (300 triremes). Attica did not produce any metals except for silver from the mines at Laurium. She exported olive oil, silver, and fine pottery (her black and red figure vases had driven out all competitors by 550 B.C.).

Although commerce and far-flung trade thrived, we should not forget that only a minority of the people were involved in it. The farmers stuck to their farms, and the attitude of Dicaeopolis to seafaring may have been not unlike that of Hesiod three centuries before. The only voyage he ever made was to cross the straits between Boeotia and Euboea to take part in a poetry competition. You can only sail safely, he says, in the fifty days following the summer solstice (21 June). You might also, he says, risk a voyage in spring:

The perils of seafaring
A pirate ship bears down on an unsuspecting merchant ship;
it is about to ram the merchant ship with its bronze beak.

I don't recommend it. It has no attraction for me—it must be snatched, and you are unlikely to avoid trouble. But men will do it in the foolishness of their hearts; for money is life to unhappy mortals. But it is a terrible thing to die in the waves. (Hesiod, *Works and Days* 682–687)

Classical Greek

Scolion
The Four Best Things in Life

The following is an example of a type of Greek poetry called *scolia*, songs sung during the drinking after dinner parties. The author is unknown. The lines (Campbell, no. 890) incorporate traditional Greek sentiments.

ὑγιαίνειν μὲν ἄριστον ἀνδρὶ θνητῷ,

δεύτερον δὲ καλὸν φυὰν γενέσθαι,

τὸ τρίτον δὲ πλουτεῖν ἀδόλως,

καὶ τὸ τέταρτον ἡβᾶν μετὰ τῶν φίλων.

[ὑγιαίνειν, *to be healthy:* this and the infinitive in the second line are the subjects of their clauses; supply ἐστί in each clause   θνητῷ, *mortal*   φυὰν, accusative of respect, *in physique*   τὸ τρίτον, *the third (best) thing;* subject, supply ἐστί   πλουτεῖν, *to be rich*   ἀδόλως, *without tricks, without treachery, honestly*   ἡβᾶν, *to be young*]

New Testament Greek

Luke 15.3–7
The Parable of the Lost Sheep

εἶπεν δὲ πρὸς αὐτοὺς τὴν παραβολὴν ταύτην λέγων, "τίς ἄνθρωπος ἐξ ὑμῶν ἔχων ἑκατὸν πρόβατα καὶ ἀπολέσας ἐξ αὐτῶν ἕν οὐ καταλείπει τὰ ἐνενήκοντα ἐννέα ἐν τῇ ἐρήμῳ καὶ πορεύεται ἐπὶ τὸ ἀπολωλὸς ἕως εὕρῃ αὐτό; καὶ εὑρὼν ἐπιτίθησιν ἐπὶ τοὺς ὤμους αὐτοῦ χαίρων καὶ ἐλθὼν εἰς τὸν οἶκον συγκαλεῖ τοὺς φίλους καὶ τοὺς γείτονας λέγων αὐτοῖς, 'συγχάρητέ μοι, ὅτι εὗρον τὸ πρόβατόν μου τὸ ἀπολωλός.' λέγω ὑμῖν ὅτι οὕτως χαρὰ ἐν τῷ οὐρανῷ ἔσται ἐπὶ ἑνὶ ἁμαρτωλῷ μετανοοῦντι ἢ ἐπὶ ἐνενήκοντα ἐννέα δικαίοις οἵτινες οὐ χρείαν ἔχουσιν μετανοίας."

[εἶπεν: Jesus is the subject   πρὸς αὐτοὺς, i.e., to the Pharisees and scribes who complained that Jesus was associating with tax collectors and sinners   ταύτην, *this*   ἑκατὸν, *a hundred*   ἀπολέσας (from ἀπόλλυμι), *having lost*   ἐνενήκοντα ἐννέα, *ninety-nine*   τῇ ἐρήμῳ, *the desert*   ἐπὶ + acc., *after*   τὸ ἀπολωλός, *the lost (one)*   ἕως, *until*   εὕρῃ, subjunctive, *he finds*   ἐπιτίθησιν, *he puts (it) on*   τοὺς ὤμους, *shoulders*   αὐτοῦ = ἑαυτοῦ   τοὺς γείτονας, *his neighbors*   συγχάρητέ (from συγχαίρω) + dat., *rejoice with*   ὅτι, *because*   χαρὰ, *joy*   ἐπὶ, *over, at*   ἁμαρτωλῷ, *sinner*   μετανοοῦντι, *repenting*   ἢ, *than, (more) than*   δικαίοις, *just / righteous (men)*   οἵτινες, *who*   χρείαν, *need*   μετανοίας, *of / for repentance*]

ΠΡΟΣ ΤΟΝ ΠΕΙΡΑΙΑ (β)

ὁ Δικαιόπολις τὴν γυναῖκα χαίρειν κελεύσᾱς, τῷ Φιλίππῳ πρὸς τὴν ναῦν ἡγήσατο.

VOCABULARY

Verbs

ἐξηγέομαι [ἐκ- + ἡγέομαι].
ἐξηγήσομαι, ἐξηγησάμην,
ἐξηγησάμενος, *I relate*
ἐρωτάω, ἐρωτήσω, ἠρώτησα,
ἐρωτήσᾱς or [ἐρ-] **ἠρόμην,**
ἐρόμενος, *I ask*
φαίνομαι, [φανε-] **φανοῦμαι,**
(aorist to be presented later),
I appear

Nouns

ὁ ἔμπορος, τοῦ ἐμπόρου, *merchant*
ὁ ναύκληρος, τοῦ ναυκλήρου,
ship's captain

ὁ ναύτης, τοῦ ναύτου, *sailor*

Adjectives

πλείων/πλέων, alternative
forms for either masculine or
feminine, **πλέον,** neuter,
more
πλεῖστος, -η, -ον, *most; very
great;* pl., *very many*

Adverbs

Ἀθήνᾱζε, *to Athens*
μέγα, *greatly; loudly*
τότε, *then*

Expression

μάλιστά γε, *certainly, indeed*

ἐν δὲ τῷ λιμένι πλεῖστος μὲν ἦν ὅμῑλος, πλεῖστος δὲ θόρυβος.
πανταχόσε γὰρ ἔσπευδον οἱ ἄνθρωποι· οἱ μὲν γὰρ ναύκληροι τοὺς
ναύτᾱς ἐκάλουν, κελεύοντες αὐτοὺς τὰ φορτία ἐκ τῶν νεῶν ἐκφέρειν,
οἱ δὲ ἔμποροι μέγα ἐβόων τὰ φορτία δεχόμενοι καὶ εἰς ἁμάξᾱς
εἰσφέροντες· ἄλλοι δὲ τὰ πρόβατα ἐξελάσαντες διὰ τῶν ὁδῶν ἦγον. ὁ   5
δὲ Δικαιόπολις πάντα θεώμενος ἠπόρει τί δεῖ ποιῆσαι καὶ ποῦ δεῖ

ζητεῖν ναῦν τινα πρὸς τὴν Ἐπίδαυρον πλευσομένην· πλείστας γὰρ
ναῦς εἶδε πρὸς τῷ χώματι ὁρμούσας. τέλος δὲ πάντες ἐν οἰνοπωλίῳ
τινὶ καθισάμενοι οἶνον ᾔτησαν.

[θόρυβος, *uproar*   πανταχόσε, *in all directions*   ἔσπευδον, *were hurrying*
ἐκάλουν, *were calling*   ἐβόων, *were shouting*   ἐξελάσαντες, *having driven out*
ἦγον, *were leading*   ἠπόρει, *was at a loss*   τῷ χώματι, *the pier*   ὁρμούσας, *lying
at anchor*   οἰνοπωλίῳ, *wine-shop, inn*]

ἐν ᾧ δὲ τὸν οἶνον ἔπινον, προσεχώρησε ναύτης τις γεραιὸς καί,   10
"τίνες ἐστέ, ὦ φίλοι," ἔφη, "καὶ τί βουλόμενοι πάρεστε; ἄγροικοι γὰρ
ὄντες φαίνεσθε ἀπορεῖν. εἴπετέ μοι τί πάσχετε." ὁ δὲ Δικαιόπολις
πάντα ἐξηγησάμενος, "ἆρ' οἶσθα," ἔφη, "εἴ τις ναῦς πάρεστι
μέλλουσα πρὸς τὴν Ἐπίδαυρον πλεύσεσθαι;" ὁ δέ, "μάλιστά γε,"
ἔφη· "ἡ γὰρ ἐμὴ ναῦς μέλλει ἐκεῖσε πλεύσεσθαι. ἕπεσθέ μοι οὖν παρὰ   15
τὸν ναύκληρον. ἀλλ' ἰδού, πάρεστιν αὐτὸς ὁ ναύκληρος εἰς καιρὸν
προσχωρῶν." καὶ οὕτως εἰπὼν ἡγήσατο αὐτοῖς παρὰ νεανίαν τινὰ ἐκ
νεώς τινος τότε ἐκβαίνοντα.

[ἔπινον, *they were drinking*   ἄγροικοι, *countrymen, rustics*   ἆρ' οἶσθα, *do you
know?*   εἰς καιρόν, *at just the right time*]

ὁ οὖν Δικαιόπολις προσχωρήσας ἤρετο αὐτὸν εἰ ἐθέλει κομίζειν
αὐτοὺς πρὸς τὴν Ἐπίδαυρον. ὁ δέ, "μάλιστά γε," ἔφη, "ἐθέλω ὑμᾶς   20
ἐκεῖσε κομίζειν. ἀλλὰ εἴσβητε ταχέως· εὐθὺς γὰρ πλευσόμεθα." ὁ δὲ
Δικαιόπολις, "ἐπὶ πόσῳ;" ὁ δὲ ναύκληρος, "ἐπὶ πέντε δραχμαῖς," ἔφη.
ὁ δὲ Δικαιόπολις, "ἀλλ' ἄγαν αἰτεῖς. ἐγὼ δύο δραχμὰς ἐθέλω
παρασχεῖν." ὁ δέ· "οὐδαμῶς· τέτταρας αἰτῶ." ὁ δὲ Δικαιόπολις,
"ἰδού, τρεῖς δραχμάς· οὐ γὰρ δύναμαι πλέον παρασχεῖν." ὁ δέ,   25
"ἔστω· παράσχες μοί τὸ ἀργύριον· καὶ εἴσβητε ταχέως."

[εἴσβητε, *get on board*   ἐπὶ πόσῳ; *for how much?*   ἄγαν, *too much*   ἔστω, *all right!*]

ὁ οὖν Δικαιόπολις τὸ ἀργύριον τῷ ναυκλήρῳ παρέσχε καὶ τήν τε
γυναῖκα καὶ τὸν ἀδελφὸν χαίρειν ἐκέλευσεν. ἡ δὲ Μυρρίνη
δακρύσασα, "τὸν παῖδα," ἔφη, "εὖ φύλαττε, ὦ φίλε ἄνερ, καὶ σπεῦδε
ὡς τάχιστα οἴκαδε ἐπανιέναι. σὺ δέ, ὦ φίλτατε παῖ, θάρρει καὶ σὺν   30
θεῷ δι' ὀλίγου νόστησον ὑγιεῖς ἔχων τοὺς ὀφθαλμούς." οὕτως

εἰποῦσα ἀπετρέψατο· ὁ δὲ ἀδελφὸς αὐτῇ ἡγήσατο Ἀθήναζε δακρῦούσῃ.

[δακρύσᾱσα, *bursting into tears*   φίλτατε, *dearest*   θάρρει, *cheer up!*   σὺν θεῷ, *with god's help*   νόστησον, *return home*   ὑγιεῖς, *sound, healthy*   ἀπετρέψατο, *she turned herself away*]

WORD BUILDING

The prefix ἀ- (ἀ-privative) may be attached to the beginning of many verbs, nouns, and adjectives (ἀν- is prefixed to words beginning with vowels) to negate or reverse their meaning or to express a lack or absence, e.g., δυνατός, *possible*, ἀδύνατος, *impossible*. Compare *moral* and *amoral* ("without morals"; compare *immoral*) in English.

From the words at the left, deduce the meaning of those to the right:

1. αἴτιος, -ᾱ, -ον   ἀναίτιος, -ον
2. ἄξιος, -ᾱ, -ον (*worthy*)   ἀνάξιος, -ον
3. δίκαιος, -ᾱ, -ον (*just*)   ἄδικος, -ον
4. ἀνδρεῖος, -ᾱ, -ον (from ὁ ἀνήρ, τοῦ ἀνδρός)   ἄνανδρος, -ον

Note that adjectives compounded with ἀ-privative have no separate feminine forms; the masculine forms are used with either masculine or feminine nouns.

The Piraeus, from the southeast
The large landlocked harbor to the northwest was Cantharus, the main commercial port; the smaller harbors to the south, Zea (left) and Munychia (right), were for warships.

GRAMMAR

3. Verb Forms: The Asigmatic 1st Aorist of Verbs with Liquid and Nasal Stems

You will recall that verbs with stems ending in a *liquid* (λ, ρ) or a *nasal* (μ, ν) have asigmatic contract futures with stems often different from the stem seen in the present tense (see Chapter 10, Grammar 6, pages 166–167). In the aorist of these verbs ε is not added to the stem as it is in the future, and the σ of the -σα aorist suffix is lost; this causes the stem vowel (seen in the future) to lengthen (if it is not long already). Because of the loss of the σ, we call these *asigmatic 1st aorists*.

αἴρω, *I lift*, [ἀρε-] ἀρῶ, [**ἀρ-**] ἦρ-α (ᾱ of the stem does not change)
ἀποκρῑ́νομαι, *I answer*, [κρῑνε-] ἀποκρινοῦμαι, [**κρῑν-**] **ἀπεκρῑν-ά-μην**
  (ῐ lengthens to ῑ)
ἀποκτείνω, *I kill*, [κτενε-] ἀποκτενῶ, [**κτειν-**] **ἀπέκτειν-α**
  (ε lengthens to ει)
ἐγείρω, *I wake (someone) up*; middle, *I wake up*, [ἐγερε-] ἐγερῶ,
  [**ἐγειρ-**] **ἤγειρα** (ε lengthens to ει)
μένω, *I stay; I wait*, [μενε-] μενῶ, [**μειν-**] **ἔμειν-α** (ε lengthens to ει)

As an example, we give the verb αἴρω, *I lift*, which in the middle voice may mean *I carry off for myself; I win* (e.g., a prize).

Asigmatic 1st Aorist Active

Present: αἴρω, *I lift;* **Aorist Stem:** ἀρ-

Indicative	Imperative	Infinitive	Participle
ἦρ-α, *I lifted*		ἆρ-αι,	ἄρ-ᾱς,
ἦρ-α-ς	ἆρ-ον,	*to lift*	ἄρ-ᾱσα,
ἦρ-ε(ν)	*lift!*		ἄρ-αν,
ἤρ-α-μεν			gen., ἄρ-αντ-ος, etc.,
ἤρ-α-τε	ἄρ-α-τε,		*having lifted,*
ἦρ-α-ν	*lift!*		*after lifting,*
			sometimes, *lifting*

Asigmatic 1st Aorist Middle

ἠρ-ά-μην, *I carried off*		ἄρ-α-σθαι,	ἀρ-ά-μεν-ος,
ἤρ-α-σο > ἤρω	ἆρ-αι,	*to carry off*	ἀρ-α-μέν-η,
ἤρ-α-το	*carry off!*		ἀρ-ά-μεν-ον,
ἠρ-ά-μεθα			*having carried off,*
ἤρ-α-σθε	ἄρ-α-σθε		*after carrying off,*
ἤρ-α-ντο	*carry off!*		sometimes, *carrying off*

Exercise 12θ

Fill in the aorist forms of the verbs ἀποκτείνω and ἀποκρίνομαι that you have learned to date on the Verb Charts on which you entered forms for Exercise 10ζ.

Exercise 12ι

Change the following present forms into corresponding forms of the aorist:

1. αἴρειν
2. ἐγείρει
3. μένουσα
4. ἀποκρίνεται
5. ἀποκρῑνόμενος
6. μένε
7. ἀποκτείνειν
8. αἴρων
9. μένειν
10. αἴρομεν
11. ἐγείρων
12. ἀποκρίνου
13. ἀποκρίνεται
14. ἀποκρίνεσθαι
15. ἀποκτείνουσι(ν) (2 ways)

4. Irregular Sigmatic 1st Aorists

Learn the future and aorist of the following verbs, which are irregular:

δοκεῖ, impersonal, *it seems (good)*, [**δοκ-**] **δόξει, ἔδοξε(ν)**, δόξαν

ἐθέλω, *I am willing; I wish*, [**ἐθελε-**], **ἐθελήσω, ἠθέλησα**, ἐθελήσᾱς

ἐλαύνω, *I drive*, [**ἐλα-**] **ἐλῶ, ἐλᾷς, ἐλᾷ**, etc., **ἤλασα**, ἐλάσᾱς

καίω or κᾱ́ω, *I kindle, burn*; middle, intransitive, *I burn, am on fire*, [**καυ-**] **καύσω, ἔκαυσα**, καύσᾱς

καλέω, *I call*, **καλῶ, ἐκάλεσα**, καλέσᾱς

μάχομαι, *I fight*, [**μαχε-**] **μαχοῦμαι, ἐμαχεσάμην**, μαχεσάμενος

πλέω, *I sail*, [**πλευ-**] **πλεύσομαι** or [**πλευσε-**] **πλευσοῦμαι**, [**πλευ-**] **ἔπλευσα**, πλεύσᾱς

Exercise 12κ

Read aloud and translate. Identify liquid, nasal, and irregular aorists:

1. ὁ πάππος ἐπὶ τῇ γῇ κείμενος (*lying*) ἠθέλησε καθεύδειν.
2. ἀλλ' ὁ Φίλιππος προσδραμὼν ἤγειρεν αὐτόν.
3. ὁ δέ, "τί με ἤγειρας, ὦ παῖ;" ὁ δὲ Φίλιππος ἔφη· "λύκος τις ἐπὶ τὰ πρόβατα ὁρμᾶται."
4. ὁ δὲ πάππος, "κάλεσον τὸν Ἄργον," ἔφη, "καὶ ἄμῡνον τὸν λύκον τοῖς προβάτοις." **ἀμῡ́νω**, [**ἀμυνε-**], **ἀμῡνῶ, ἤμῡνα**, *I ward off* X (acc.) *from* Y (dat.)
5. ὁ οὖν Φίλιππος τὸν Ἄργον καλέσᾱς ἀνὰ τὸ ὄρος ἔσπευσεν.

6. ὁ μὲν οὖν Ἄργος ἀγρίως ὑλακτῶν (*barking*) τὸν λύκον ἐδίωξεν, ὁ δὲ Φίλιππος λίθους ἄρας αὐτὸν ἔβαλεν.

7. δι' ὀλίγου δὲ ὁ Ἄργος τὸν λύκον ὀδὰξ (*with his teeth*) ἔσχεν, ὁ δὲ Φίλιππος τῇ μαχαίρᾳ αὐτὸν ἀπέκτεινεν.

8. ὁ δὲ πάππος εἰς ἄκρον τὸ ὄρος ἀφικόμενος, "εὖ γε," ἔφη, "τοῖς προβάτοις τὸν λύκον ἀνδρείως ἠμύνατε.

9. "νῦν δὲ σὺ μὲν ἐνθάδε μεῖνον, ἐγὼ δὲ οἴκαδε ἐπάνειμι· βούλομαι γὰρ τῇ μητρὶ ἀγγεῖλαι τί ἐγένετο." ἀγγέλλω, [ἀγγελε-] ἀγγελῶ, [ἀγγειλ-] ἤγγειλα, *I announce; I tell*

10. τῷ οὖν Φιλίππῳ ἔδοξε τὰ πρόβατα εἰς τὸ αὔλιον (*sheepfold*) εἰσελάσαι.

5. Verb Forms: Augment of Compound Verbs

Verbs with prepositional prefixes attach the syllabic augment to the stem of the simple verb. Observe βάλλω (aorist ἔβαλον) with the following prefixes, and note the changes in the spelling of some of the prefixes in the combined forms:

εἰσ- *into*	εἰσβάλλω, εἰσέβαλον
ἐκ- *out*	ἐκβάλλω, ἐξέβαλον
προσ- *to, toward*	προσβάλλω, προσέβαλον
ἀπο- *away*	ἀποβάλλω, ἀπέβαλον
κατα- *down*	καταβάλλω, κατέβαλον
συν- *together*	συμβάλλω, συνέβαλον

Exercise 12λ

Give the aorist indicative, 1st person singular, of the following verbs:

1. προσχωρέω	4. ἀποκρίνομαι	7. εἰσκομίζω
2. ἐκπέμπω	5. εἰσπέμπω	8. συνέρχομαι*
3. ἀποφεύγω	6. ἀποκτείνω	9. συλλαμβάνω (συν-)

*N.B. The accent of compound verbs never recedes beyond the augment.

Exercise 12μ

Read aloud and translate:

1. οἱ δοῦλοι τοὺς λίθους ἄραντες ἐξέβαλον ἐκ τοῦ ἀγροῦ.
2. ὁ δεσπότης τοὺς βοῦς εἰς τὸν ἀγρὸν εἰσελάσας τοὺς δούλους ἐκάλεσεν.
3. ὁ δεσπότης τοὺς μὲν δούλους ἀπέπεμψεν, αὐτὸς δὲ ἐν τῷ ἀγρῷ ἔμεινεν.
4. οἱ δοῦλοι τὸ ἄροτρον ἐν τῷ ἀγρῷ καταλιπόντες ταχέως οἴκαδε ἐπανῆλθον.
5. ἡ παρθένος τὸν πατέρα ἰδοῦσα ταχέως προσεχώρησε καὶ ἤρετο τί οὐκ οἴκαδε ἐπανέρχεται.
6. ὁ δὲ ἀπεκρίνατο ὅτι δεῖ τὸν ἀγρὸν ἀροῦν (*to plow*).

7. οἱ νεᾱνίαι οὐκ ἀπέφυγον ἀλλὰ ἀνδρείως ἐμαχέσαντο.
8. ὁ ἄγγελος ἤγγειλεν ὅτι πολλοὶ ἐν τῇ μάχῃ (battle) ἀπέθανον.
9. οἱ ναῦται τὴν ναῦν παρασκευάσαντες ἐκ τοῦ λιμένος ἐξέπλευσαν.
10. τῷ ναυκλήρῳ τὸν χειμῶνα φοβουμένῳ ἔδοξε πρὸς τὸν λιμένα ἐπανελθεῖν.

Ο ΚΩΛΑΙΟΣ ΤΟΝ ΤΑΡΤΗΣΣΟΝ ΕΥΡΙΣΚΕΙ

Read the following passages (based on Herodotus 1.163 and 4.152) and answer the comprehension questions:

πρῶτοι τῶν Ἑλλήνων εἰς τὸν Τάρτησσον ἀφίκοντο οἱ Σάμιοι. ἔμπορος γάρ τις, Κωλαῖος ὀνόματι, ἀπὸ τῆς Σάμου ὁρμώμενος πρὸς τὴν Αἴγυπτον ἔπλει, ἀλλὰ χειμὼν μέγιστος ἐγένετο, καὶ πολλὰς ἡμέρᾱς οὐκ ἐπαύσατο ὁ ἄνεμος ἀεὶ φέρων τὴν ναῦν πρὸς τὴν ἑσπέρᾱν. τέλος δὲ ὁ Κωλαῖος καὶ οἱ ἑταῖροι Ἡρακλείᾱς στήλᾱς διεκπεράσαντες εἰς Ὠκεανὸν εἰσέπλευσαν καὶ οὕτως εἰς τὸν Τάρτησσον ἀφίκοντο.   5

[τῶν Ἑλλήνων, *of the Greeks*   Τάρτησσον, *Tartessus*   οἱ Σάμιοι, *the Samians*
Κωλαῖος, *Colaeus*   τῆς Σάμου, *Samos*   τὴν Αἴγυπτον, *Egypt*   ἔπλει, *was sailing*
ὁ ἄνεμος, *the wind*   τὴν ἑσπέρᾱν, *the evening, the west*   Ἡρακλείᾱς στήλᾱς, *the
Pillars of Hercules*   διεκπεράσαντες, *having passed through*   Ὠκεανὸν, *the
Ocean*]

1. Who were the first Greeks to arrive at Tartessus?
2. To what country did Colaeus set out to sail?
3. What happened that made him sail westward?
4. What did he sail through before arriving at Tartessus?

οἱ δὲ ἐπιχώριοι λαβόντες αὐτοὺς ἐκόμισαν παρὰ τὸν βασιλέα, γέροντά τινα, Ἀργαθώνιον ὀνόματι. ὁ δὲ ἤρετο αὐτοὺς τίνες εἰσὶ καὶ πόθεν ἥκουσιν. ὁ δὲ Κωλαῖος ἀπεκρίνατο· "Ἕλληνές ἐσμεν, καὶ πρὸς τὴν Αἴγυπτον πλέοντας χειμὼν ἡμᾶς εἰς τὴν σὴν γῆν ἤλασεν." ὁ δὲ βασιλεὺς πάντα ἀκούσᾱς ἐθαύμασεν, εὐμενῶς δὲ δεξάμενος αὐτοὺς πλεῖστόν τε ἀργύριον καὶ πλεῖστον καττίτερον αὐτοῖς   10 παρέσχεν. οἱ δὲ πολύν τινα χρόνον ἐν τῷ Ταρτήσσῳ μένοντες ἐμπορίᾱν ἐποιοῦντο. τέλος δὲ τὸν Ἀργαθώνιον χαίρειν κελεύσαντες ἀπέπλευσαν καὶ εἰς τὴν Σάμον ἐπανῆλθον οὐδὲν κακὸν παθόντες.

[οἱ ... ἐπιχώριοι, *the natives*   Ἀργαθώνιον, *Argathonius*   εὐμενῶς, *kindly*
καττίτερον, *tin*   ἐμπορίᾱν ἐποιοῦντο, *were carrying on trade*]

5. Where did the natives take Colaeus?
6. What did Argathonius ask Colaeus and his men?
7. What did Colaeus answer?
8. How did Argathonius receive Colaeus and his men and what did he give them?

9.   What did Colaeus and his men do in Tartessus?

10.   Did Colaeus and his men arrive home safely?

Exercise 12v

Translate into Greek:

1.   When Colaeus returned home, he told the Greeks (τοῖς Ἕλλησι(ν)) what happened.

2.   All were amazed, and many, having heard that Argathonius was (*use present tense*) very wealthy (ὄλβιος), wanted (ἐβούλοντο) to sail to Tartessus.

3.   They decided to set out immediately; and having prepared four ships they sailed away.

4.   After suffering many terrible things, they finally arrived at Tartessus.

5.   The king received them kindly and handed over to them much silver and tin (*use* ὁ καττίτερος).

6.   Then the Greeks for a long time were carrying on trade with (πρός) the citizens of Tartessus.

Greek Wisdom

οἱ πλεῖστοι κακοί.   Βίας (of Priene)

An ancient shipwreck; an overturned ship and men in the sea, one being eaten by a fish

13
ΠΡΟΣ ΤΗΝ ΣΑΛΑΜΙΝΑ (α)

στρογγύλη ἦν ἡ ναῦς, ἣ σῖτόν τε καὶ οἶνον ἔφερε πρὸς τὰς νήσους.

VOCABULARY

Verbs
ἐρέσσω, no future, [ἐρετ-]
 ἤρεσα, ἐρέσᾱς, *I row*
ἡσυχάζω, ἡσυχάσω, ἡσύχασα,
 ἡσυχάσᾱς, *I keep quiet; I rest*
Nouns
ὁ ἄνεμος, τοῦ ἀνέμου, *wind*
τὰ ἱστία, τῶν ἱστίων, *sails*
Pronoun
ἀλλήλων, *of one another*

Adjectives
βέβαιος, -ᾱ, -ον, *firm, steady*
λαμπρός, -ά, -όν, *bright; brilliant*
ταχύς, ταχεῖα, ταχύ, *quick,
 swift*
Proper Name
ἡ Σαλαμίς, τῆς Σαλαμῖνος,
 Salamis

ἐν δὲ τούτῳ ὁ ναύτης ὁ γεραιὸς τόν τε Δικαιόπολιν καὶ τὸν παῖδα
εἰς τὴν ναῦν ἀγαγὼν ἐκέλευσε καθίζεσθαι ἐπὶ τῷ καταστρώματι.
ἐνταῦθα δὴ ὁ μὲν ναύκληρος ἐκέλευσε τοὺς ναύτᾱς λῦσαι τὰ
πείσματα, οἱ δὲ ναῦται τὰ πείσματα λύσαντες τὴν ναῦν βραδέως
ἤρεσσον πρὸς τὴν θάλατταν. ἔπειτα δὲ τὴν γῆν καταλιπόντες τὰ   5
ἱστία ἐπέτασαν.

[**τῷ καταστρώματι,** *the deck*   **τὰ πείσματα,** *the cables*   **ἤρεσσον,** *were rowing*
ἐπέτασαν (from πετάννῡμι), *they spread*]

ἐπεὶ δὲ ἡ μὲν ναῦς βεβαίως ἔπλει, οἱ δὲ ναῦται τῶν ἔργων
παυσάμενοι ἡσύχαζον, ὁ Δικαιόπολις πᾶσαν τὴν ναῦν ἐσκόπει.

στρογγύλη ἦν ἡ ναῦς, οὐ μεγάλη οὐδὲ ταχεῖα ἀλλὰ βεβαία, ἣ φορτία
ἔφερε πρὸς τὰς νήσους· σῖτός τε γὰρ ἐνῆν καὶ οἶνος καὶ ὕλη καὶ   10
πρόβατα. πολλοὶ δ᾿ ἐνῆσαν ἄνθρωποι, ἄγροικοι ὄντες, οἳ τὰ φορτία
ἐν ταῖς Ἀθήναις πωλήσαντες οἴκαδε ἐπανῆσαν· ἄλλοι δὲ παρὰ τοὺς
οἰκείους ἐπορεύοντο, οἳ ἐν ταῖς νήσοις ᾤκουν. πάντες δὲ ἐτέρποντο
πλέοντες—οὔριος γὰρ ἦν ὁ ἄνεμος καὶ λαμπρὸς ὁ ἥλιος—καὶ ἢ
διελέγοντο ἀλλήλοις ἢ μέλη ᾖδον.   15

[ἐσκόπει, *began to examine*   στρογγύλη, *round*   ἦν, *was*   ἥ, *which*   φορτία,
cargo   ἐνῆν, *was in (it)*   ὕλη, *timber*   ἐνῆσαν, *were in (it)*   ἄγροικοι, *rustic*   οἵ,
who   πωλήσαντες, *having sold*   ἐπανῆσαν, *were going back, returning*   τοὺς
οἰκείους, *their relatives*   οὔριος, *favorable*   μέλη, *songs*   ᾖδον (*from* ᾄδω), *they
were singing*]

WORD STUDY

*Identify the Greek stems in the English words below and give the meanings
of the English words. Give the meanings of the Greek words in parentheses:*

1. nautical
2. cosmonaut (ὁ κόσμος, τοῦ κόσμου)
3. aeronaut (ὁ *or* ἡ ἀήρ, τοῦ *or* τῆς ἀέρος)
4. astronaut (τὸ ἄστρον, τοῦ ἄστρου)
5. cosmology
6. astrology

GRAMMAR

1. Verb Forms: The Imperfect or Past Progressive Tense

a. *Regular and Contract Verbs:*

For regular and contract verbs, the *imperfect* or *past progressive* tense
is formed by augmenting the verb stem as found in the present tense and
adding the thematic vowels and the secondary personal endings. Compare the formation and endings of the thematic 2nd aorist, which is similar except that it is based on a different stem. The imperfect tense has
forms only in the indicative; there are no imperfect imperatives, infinitives, or participles.

Regular Verbs

Imperfect Active

ἔ-λῡ-ο-ν	*I was loosening, I used to loosen*
ἔ-λῡ-ε-ς	*you were loosening, you used to loosen*
ἔ-λῡ-ε(ν)	*he/she was loosening, he/she used to loosen*
ἐ-λύ-ο-μεν	*we were loosening, we used to loosen*
ἐ-λύ-ε-τε	*you were loosening, you used to loosen*
ἔ-λῡ-ο-ν	*they were loosening, they used to loosen*

Imperfect Middle

ἐ-λῡ-ό-μην	*I was ransoming, I used to ransom*
ἐ-λύ-ε-σο > ἐλύου	*you were ransoming, you used to ransom*
ἐ-λύ-ε-το	*he/she was ransoming, he/she used to ransom*
ἐ-λῡ-ό-μεθα	*we were ransoming, we used to ransom*
ἐ-λύ-ε-σθε	*you were ransoming, you used to ransom*
ἐ-λύ-ο-ντο	*they were ransoming, they used to ransom*

Contract Verbs

Contract verbs follow the rules given above for the formation of the imperfect tense and the rules for contraction given on pages 39 and 56:

Active

ἐ-φίλε-ο-ν >	ἐφίλουν	ἐ-τῑμα-ο-ν >	ἐτῑμων
ἐ-φίλε-ε-ς >	ἐφίλεις	ἐ-τῑμα-ε-ς >	ἐτῑμᾱς
ἐ-φίλε-ε >	ἐφίλει	ἐ-τῑμα-ε >	ἐτῑμᾱ
ἐ-φιλέ-ο-μεν >	ἐφιλοῦμεν	ἐ-τῑμά-ο-μεν >	ἐτῑμῶμεν
ἐ-φιλέ-ε-τε >	ἐφιλεῖτε	ἐ-τῑμά-ε-τε >	ἐτῑμᾶτε
ἐ-φίλε-ο-ν >	ἐφίλουν	ἐ-τῑμα-ο-ν >	ἐτῑμων

Middle

ἐ-φιλε-ό-μην >	ἐφιλούμην	ἐ-τῑμα-ό-μην >	ἐτῑμώμην
ἐ-φιλέ-ε-σο >	ἐφιλοῦ	ἐ-τῑμά-ε-σο >	ἐτῑμῶ
ἐ-φιλέ-ε-το >	ἐφιλεῖτο	ἐ-τῑμά-ε-το >	ἐτῑμᾶτο
ἐ-φιλε-ό-μεθα >	ἐφιλούμεθα	ἐ-τῑμα-ό-μεθα >	ἐτῑμώμεθα
ἐ-φιλέ-ε-σθε >	ἐφιλεῖσθε	ἐ-τῑμά-ε-σθε >	ἐτῑμᾶσθε
ἐ-φιλέ-ο-ντο >	ἐφιλοῦντο	ἐ-τῑμά-ο-ντο >	ἐτῑμῶντο

Here is the imperfect active of πλέω (for the present, see Chapter 6, Grammar 1, page 74): ἔπλεον, ἔπλεις, ἔπλει, ἐπλέομεν, ἐπλεῖτε, ἔπλεον. Only the forms of this verb with ε + ε are contracted in Attic Greek.

b. Irregular Verbs:

Imperfect of εἰμί, *I am:*

ἦ or ἦν	*I was*
ἦσθα	*you were*
ἦν	*he / she / it was*
ἦμεν	*we were*
ἦτε	*you were*
ἦσαν	*they were*

Imperfect of εἶμι [εἰ-/ἰ-], which serves as the future of ἔρχομαι in **Attic Greek** (see Chapter 10, Grammar 6, pages 168–169) and means *I will go:*

ἦα	or	ᾔειν	*I was going*
ᾔεισθα	or	ᾔεις	*you were going*
ᾔειν	or	ᾔει	*he / she / it was going*
ᾖμεν			*we were going*
ᾖτε			*you were going*
ᾖσαν	or	ᾔεσαν	*they were going*

Note that in the imperfect the ε of the long vowel stem (εἰ-) is augmented to η and that the ι becomes subscript. Note that the iota subscript occurs in all the forms of the imperfect of εἶμι but in none of the forms of the imperfect of εἰμί.

Note:

Present, ἔρχομαι, *I come; I go*
Imperfect, ἦα or ᾔειν, *I was coming; I was going*
Future: εἶμι, *I will come; I will go*
Aorist: ἦλθον, *I came; I went*

For the compounds of ἔρχομαι, see Chapter 10, Grammar 6, page 169.

c. Irregular Augment:

ἕλκω, *I drag,* becomes εἷλκον *in the imperfect.*
ἕπομαι, *I follow,* becomes εἱπόμην *in the imperfect.*
ἐργάζομαι, *I work; I accomplish,* becomes ἠργαζόμην *or* εἰργαζόμην *in the imperfect.*
ἔχω, *I have; I hold,* becomes εἶχον *in the imperfect.*
ὁράω, *I see,* becomes ἑώρων *in the imperfect, with double augment.*

Exercise 13α

In the first two paragraphs of the reading passage at the beginning of this chapter locate:

1. Seven imperfects of regular verbs
2. Three imperfects of contract verbs
3. Four imperfects of εἰμί (including compound verbs)
4. One imperfect of εἶμι (compound)

Exercise 13β

Fill in the imperfect forms on all of the Verb Charts on which you have entered forms to date. Keep these charts for reference.

2. Aspect

The imperfect or past progressive indicative usually looks on the action of the verb as an ongoing process in past time, just as the present tense looks on the action as an ongoing process in present time; note that these two tenses use the same stem. The aorist indicative, on the other hand, usually looks on the action as a simple action or event in past time. Note the following uses of the imperfect or past progressive:

a. The imperfect tense usually indicates *continuous or incomplete action in past time.* When so used it can be translated by the English imperfect, e.g.:

ἐπεὶ **προσεχωροῦμεν**, οἱ φύλακες τὰς πύλας **ἔκλειον.**
*When **we were approaching**, the guards **were shutting** the gates.*

Compare the aorist:

ἐπεὶ **εἰσήλθομεν**, οἱ φύλακες τὰς πύλας **ἔκλεισαν.**
*When **we went in**, the guards **shut** the gates.*

The imperfect can also be translated with phrases such as *used to . . . , was/were accustomed to . . .* of repeated or habitual action, e.g.:

οἱ βόες **ἔμενον** ἐν τῷ ἀγρῷ.
*The oxen **used to stay/were accustomed to staying** in the field.*

b. The imperfect may also be used to indicate *the beginning of an action in past time*, e.g.:

εἰς τὸν ἀγρὸν εἰσελθόντες **ἐπόνουν.**
*Entering the field, **they began to work.***

This is called the *inchoative imperfect*, from the Latin verb *incohō*, "I begin."

The aorist may also be used with certain verbs to indicate the entrance into a state or the beginning of an action, e.g., ἡ Μυρρίνη **ἐδάκρῡσε**, *Myrrhine **burst** into tears.* This is called the *ingressive aorist*, from the Latin verb *ingredior*, "I begin."

c. The imperfect may also be used to indicate *an attempt to do something in past time*, e.g.:

τὸν πατέρα **ἐπείθομεν** οἴκαδε ἐπανελθεῖν· ὁ δὲ οὐκ ἠθέλησεν.
*We **tried to persuade** father to return home, but he did not want to.*

This use is called the *conative imperfect* from the Latin verb *cōnor,* "I try, attempt."

Contrast the aorist:

τὸν πατέρα **ἐπείσαμεν**.
We persuaded *father.*

Exercise 13γ

Identify the tense and form (indicative, participle, infinitive, imperative) of the underlined verbs, translate the verb, and explain why each tense is used (use the information given in the discussions of aspect in Chapter 11, Grammar 3, pages 178–180, and in Grammar 2 above. Then translate the sentences.

1. ὁ παῖς τοὺς βοῦς οἴκαδε <u>ἦγεν</u>, <u>καταπεσὼν</u> δὲ τὸν πόδα <u>ἔβλαψεν</u> (from βλάπτω, *I harm, hurt*).
2. πολὺν μὲν χρόνον ἐν τῷ ἄστει <u>ἐμένομεν</u>, τέλος δὲ οἴκαδε <u>ὡρμησάμεθα</u>.
3. αἱ παρθένοι πρὸς τῇ κρήνῃ <u>ἔμενον</u> <u>διαλεγόμεναι</u>, τοὺς δὲ παῖδας <u>ἰδοῦσαι</u> <u>προσχωροῦντας</u> <u>ἀπῆλθον</u>.
4. ὁ ἀνὴρ πολὺν χρόνον τὴν γυναῖκα πρὸς τῇ ὁδῷ <u>ἔμενεν</u>, τέλος δὲ <u>εἶδεν</u> αὐτὴν <u>προσχωροῦσαν</u>.
5. αἱ γυναῖκες αἱ ἐν τῇ οἰκίᾳ μύθους <u>ἔλεγον</u>, τοὺς δὲ ἄνδρας <u>ἰδοῦσαι</u> ἐπαύσαντο <u>λέγουσαι</u> καὶ <u>ἐκάλεσαν</u> αὐτούς.
6. ὁ Φίλιππος τὸν κύνα καθ᾽ ἡμέρᾱν (*every day*) πρὸς τὸ αὔλιον (*the sheepfold*) <u>ἦγεν</u>.
7. ἡ παρθένος τὸν πατέρα <u>ἔπειθεν</u> ἑαυτὴν πρὸς τὸ ἄστυ <u>ἀγαγεῖν</u>, ὁ δὲ οὐκ <u>ἤθελεν</u>. ἡ δὲ μήτηρ ῥᾳδίως <u>ἔπεισεν</u> αὐτόν.
8. <u>σῑγήσατε</u>, ὦ παῖδες, καὶ <u>ἀκούετέ</u> μου.
9. ἡ παρθένος τὴν ὑδρίᾱν <u>καταβαλοῦσα</u> <u>δακρΰσᾱσα</u> τὴν μητέρα <u>ἐκάλεσεν</u>.
10. ἡ μήτηρ τὴν παρθένον <u>ἐκέλευσεν</u> ἄλλην ὑδρίᾱν ἀπὸ τοῦ οἴκου <u>κομίσαι</u>· ἡ δὲ <u>δακρΰουσα</u> οἴκαδε <u>ἔσπευδεν</u>.

Exercise 13δ

Change the following forms first into the corresponding forms of the imperfect, then of the future, and then of the aorist. Watch out for verbs that have deponent futures and ones that have sigmatic 1st aorists or thematic 2nd aorists.

1. λῡ́ομεν	6. ἀκούετε	11. ἀφικνεῖται
2. λῡ́ονται	7. ἡγεῖ	12. νῑκῶμεν
3. ποιοῦσι(ν)	8. γιγνόμεθα	13. βοᾷ
4. φιλεῖ	9. πέμπομεν	14. πῑ́πτει
5. λαμβάνει	10. εὔχονται	15. λείπω

Exercise 13ε

Translate into Greek:

1. The young men were running very quickly to the agora.
2. When the boy returned home, the girl was waiting by the door.
3. He was already sailing through the straits (τὰ στενά) to the harbor.
4. I was staying at home, but you were journeying to the city.
5. When we arrived at the island, no one was willing to come to our aid (*use* βοηθέω + dat.).
6. What were you doing, boy, when I saw you in the harbor?
7. Were you watching the ship sailing out (*use* ἐκπλέω) to sea?
8. The captain was shouting loudly, but we were not afraid of him.

The Rise of Persia

The events that led to the sudden emergence of Persia as a world power are complex, involving the fall of three ancient empires in quick succession. Until the sixth century, the Persians were a wandering mountain tribe, the name of which occasionally crops up in contemporary records as the tribe gradually worked its way southeast from Russia down the mountains of western Iran. By 550 B.C. the Persians were settled east of the mouth of the Tigris as a vassal kingdom of Media. To understand their rapid rise to power it is necessary to go back to the middle of the seventh century, a turning point in the history of the ancient world.

By 650 B.C. the Assyrian Empire, which had ruled Mesopotamia, Egypt, and Syria, began to crumble. In Egypt Psammetichus led a national revival and threw off the Assyrian yoke with the help of Greek mercenaries (ca. 650 B.C.). The Medes, united under King Phraortes (675–653 B.C.), became a formidable power, extending their kingdom on all sides. In Lydia, Gyges (685–657 B.C.) founded a new dynasty and expanded westward to Ionia, where he defeated some of the Ionian Greeks, and eastward to the river Halys (the northeastern border of the Lydian Empire as marked on the map). Babylon, which a thousand years earlier had ruled all of Mesopotamia, revolted from Assyria about 625 B.C. and made an alliance with the Medes. In 612 B.C. the Babylonians and Medes took the Assyrian capital Nineveh and proceeded to divide up their empire. Babylon took the south; their king, Nebuchadnezzar, controlled all of Mesopotamia. He defeated the Egyptians at the great battle of Carchemish (605 B.C.) and drove them from Syria. When the Jews revolted, he took and destroyed Jerusalem (587 B.C.) and carried the tribes of Judah into captivity in Babylon. Assyria itself and the lands to the west up to the borders of Lydia fell to the Medes. On these borders the Medes fought several battles with Lydians, the last of which (28 May 585 B.C.) was broken off when the eclipse of the sun predicted by Thales occurred.

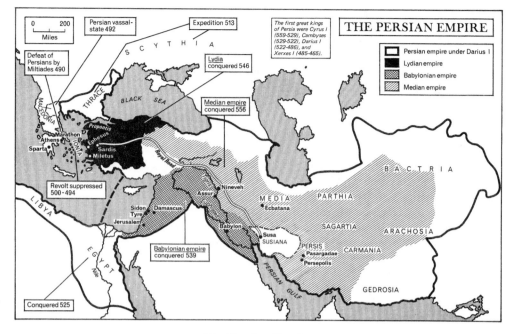

The Persian Empire

The stage was now set for the rise of Persia. In 556 B.C. Cyrus, king of the Persians, defeated the Medes and became king of the Medes and Persians, founding the dynasty of the Achaemenids, who were to rule the greatest empire the world had ever seen, until they were overthrown by Alexander the Great two hundred years later.

Croesus, king of Lydia, alarmed by the growing power of Cyrus, decided to make a pre-emptive strike. He consulted the oracle of Apollo at Delphi, which answered that if he crossed the river Halys, he would destroy a great empire. Thus encouraged, he led his army over the river and was met by Cyrus near the city of Pteria, about 60 miles or 100 kilometers east of the Halys. A bloody but indecisive battle followed, after which Croesus led his troops back to Sardis, intending to invade again the following year with larger forces. Cyrus, however, pursued him hotfoot, defeated him, and took the city of Sardis (546 B.C.). Many of the Greek cities of Asia Minor submitted at once. Those that did not were reduced the following year by the general whom Cyrus left behind when he returned to Persia.

When Cyrus had consolidated his empire in Iran, he was ready to move against Babylon, which was suffering from discord. He came as a liberator, for example, of the Jews: "Comfort ye, comfort ye, my people, saith God. . . . Comfort Jerusalem, for her time of humiliation is ended"—so prophesied Isaiah (xl), welcoming the coming of Cyrus as the savior sent by God. Babylon fell in 539 B.C., and there followed a peaceful and orderly occupation. Cyrus was proclaimed king of Babylon the following year: "I am Cyrus, king of the world, the Great King, the legitimate king, king of Babylon, king of Sumer and Akkad, king of the four corners of the earth" reads an inscription found on a cylinder at Babylon. One of his first decrees allowed the Jews to return to Jerusalem and rebuild the Temple. He died in 530 B.C., much lamented; he had been no mere conqueror but the father of his people.

His son Cambyses consolidated Persian power in the Levant and invaded and defeated Egypt (525 B.C.). In March of 522 B.C., shortly before he died, there was a rebellion led by a Persian who called himself Bardiya, son of Cyrus. By July most of the empire acknowledged him, but in September a conspiracy was formed by seven great Persian nobles, who maintained that Bardiya was a pretender. They murdered him and set on the throne one of their number: Darius. Darius had to put down revolts all over the empire before his position was secure. He consolidated the empire and extended it in the East from Afghanistan into India (the Punjab) and opened up a sea route from the mouth of the Indus to the Persian Gulf and Egypt.

Darius then turned his attention northwest. In 513 B.C. he led his army into Europe across the Hellespont, subdued most of Thrace, and marched north to the mouth of the Danube. He crossed the river by a bridge of boats, built by his Greek engineers, and he disappeared into the steppes of Russia, to deal with the nomad Scythians, who were harassing the northern borders of his empire. He was gone for over sixty days, and the Greeks who were guarding the bridge discussed whether they should break up the bridge and leave him to his fate but decided it was wiser to remain at their post. Eventually he returned with the survivors of his army, having accomplished little against the hit-and-run tactics of the Scythians. He returned to Persia, leaving a general to complete the conquest of Thrace. This was accomplished in one campaign, which brought the Persians up to the borders of Macedonia. By now most of the islands of the Aegean Sea were held by the Persians. The threat to mainland Greece was uncomfortably close.

In 499 B.C. the Ionian Greeks revolted, expelling the tyrants whom the Persians had installed to control them. The revolt was led by Aristagoras, tyrant of Miletus, who was in trouble with the Persian authorities. Aristagoras visited the mainland to beg for support. At Sparta, King Cleomenes refused, but at Athens the assembly of the newly founded democracy was won over by his appeal and voted to send an expedition of twenty ships. These joined the Ionian forces at Ephesus, and the allies marched up country and took and destroyed Sardis, the capital of the satrapy. When a Persian relief force arrived, they retreated rapidly to the coast. The Athenian contingent, satisfied with their exploit, returned to Athens. The Ionians kept up the struggle for four more years with varying success until the Persians eventually crushed all resistance and took Miletus (494 B.C.).

Darius is said to have ordered one of his officials to say to him every day: "Remember the Athenians." Retribution was assured. In 492 B.C. a large force was dispatched by land and sea. Thrace and Macedonia submitted, but, when the fleet was wrecked off Mount Athos, the expedition against Greece was called off. Two years later a second expedition sailed straight across the

Aegean, landed near Eretria in Euboea (Eretria had sent five ships to help the Ionians), and took and destroyed the city. They then landed on the coast of Attica at Marathon. After heated debate, the Athenian Assembly at the urging of Miltiades decided to send their army out to meet the Persians at Marathon rather than to shut themselves up in the city. The Athenians, though greatly outnumbered, faced the Persians alone (apart from a small contingent sent by their ally Plataea). Sparta sent a force to help, but it arrived too late for the battle. By brilliant tactics, the Athenians routed the Persian force and pursued them to the sea, inflicting heavy casualties for small losses (490 B.C.). This day was never forgotten. To have fought at Marathon was an Athenian's proudest boast. Aeschylus, the great tragic poet, makes no mention of his poetry in his epitaph; he simply says: "Of his glorious courage the groves of Marathon could speak, and the long-haired Mede, who knew it well." The dead were buried beneath a great mound still to be seen on the site of the battle.

Darius' preparations to take revenge on the Greeks were thwarted first by a revolt in Egypt and then by his death. It was not until 483 B.C. that his successor, Xerxes, began to assemble the vast force that was intended finally to settle Persia's score with Greece.

Darius, the Persian king, holds an audience.
His son and successor, Xerxes, stands behind his throne.

ΠΡΟΣ ΤΗΝ ΣΑΛΑΜΙΝΑ (β)

ἰδού, τὰ στενὰ ἐν οἷς πρὸς τοὺς βαρβάρους ἐμαχόμεθα.

VOCABULARY

Verbs

ἀμύνω, [ἀμυνε-] **ἀμυνῶ**, [ἀμῡν-]
ἤμῡνα, ἀμῦνᾱς, active, transitive, *I ward off* X (acc.) *from* Y
(dat.); middle, transitive,
I ward off X (acc.); *I defend
myself against* X (acc.)

ὀργίζομαι, [ὀργιε-] **ὀργιοῦμαι**,
no aorist middle, *I grow angry; I am angry;* + dat., *I grow
angry at; I am angry at*

Nouns

ἡ ἀρχή, τῆς ἀρχῆς, *beginning*

ὁ βάρβαρος, τοῦ βαρβάρου,
barbarian

ἡ ἐλευθερίᾱ, τῆς ἐλευθερίᾱς,
freedom

τὸ κῦμα, τοῦ κύματος, *wave*

ἡ μάχη, τῆς μάχης, *fight; battle*

τὸ ναυτικόν, τοῦ ναυτικοῦ,
fleet

τὰ στενά, τῶν στενῶν, pl.,
*narrows, straits; mountain
pass*

ἡ τριήρης, τῆς τριήρους,
trireme (a warship)

Pronoun and Adjective

μηδείς, μηδεμία, μηδέν, used
instead of οὐδείς with imperatives and infinitives, *no one,
nothing; no*

Relative Pronouns

ὅς, ἥ, ὅ, *who, whose, whom,
which, that*

ὅσπερ, ἥπερ (note the accent), **ὅπερ**, emphatic
forms, *who, whose, whom,
which, that*

Adjectives

ἀληθής, ἀληθές, *true*

τὰ ἀληθῆ, τῶν ἀληθῶν, *the
truth*

ἐκεῖνος, ἐκείνη, ἐκεῖνο, *that;*
pl., *those*

Note the predicate position:
ἐκείνη ἡ μάχη or ἡ μάχη
ἐκείνη, *that battle*

ψευδής, -ές, *false*
τὰ ψευδῆ, τῶν ψευδῶν, *lies*
Preposition
ἐγγύς + gen., *near*
Adverbs
ἅμα, *together, at the same time*
ὅτε, *when*
ὡς, *as*

ὡς δοκεῖ, *as it seems*
Expression
τῷ ὄντι, *in truth*
Proper Names
ἡ Ἑλλάς, τῆς Ἑλλάδος, *Hellas, Greece*
ὁ Ποσειδῶν, τοῦ Ποσειδῶνος, *Poseidon*

ἐπεὶ δὲ ὀλίγον χρόνον ἔπλευσαν, δέκα νῆες μακραὶ ἐφαίνοντο, αἳ πρὸς τὸν Πειραιᾶ ἐπορεύοντο ἀπὸ τῶν νήσων ἐπανιοῦσαι. πάντες οὖν τὰς τριήρεις ἐθεῶντο, αἳ ταχέως διὰ τῶν κυμάτων ἔσπευδον. οἱ γὰρ ἐρέται τῷ κελευστῇ πειθόμενοι τὴν θάλατταν ἅμα ἔτυπτον. ἐπεὶ δὲ οὐκέτι ἐφαίνοντο αἱ τριήρεις, μείζων μὲν ἐγίγνετο ὁ ἄνεμος, ἡ δὲ   5
θάλαττα ἐκύμαινεν. οἱ δ᾽ ἄνθρωποι οὐκέτι ἐτέρποντο, ἀλλ᾽ οἱ μὲν ἄνδρες ἐσίγων, αἱ δὲ γυναῖκες μέγα ἔκλαζον εὐχόμεναι τὸν Ποσειδῶνα σῴζειν ἑαυτὰς εἰς τὸν λιμένα.

[ὀλίγον, *small, short*   νῆες μακραὶ, *long ships = warships*   οἱ ... ἐρέται, *rowers* τῷ κελευστῇ, *boatswain* (he beat the time for the rowers)   μείζων, *larger, greater* ἐκύμαινεν, *inchoative, was becoming rough*   ἔκλαζον, *inchoative, began to shriek*]

ἀνὴρ δέ τις, ὃς ἐγγὺς τοῦ Δικαιοπόλιδος ἐκαθίζετο, ἀνέστη καὶ βοήσας, "ὀργίζεται ἡμῖν," ἔφη, "ὁ Ποσειδῶν, ὡς δοκεῖ. κακὸν γὰρ   10
ἄνθρωπον ἐν τῇ νηὶ φέρομεν, ὃν δεῖ ῥίπτειν εἰς τὴν θάλατταν." καὶ τοὺς παρόντας ἐπιφθόνως ἐσκόπει. ὁ δὲ γέρων προσελθών, "σίγησον, ὦ ἄνθρωπε," ἔφη· "οὐδὲν γὰρ λέγεις. ἤδη γὰρ πίπτει ὁ ἄνεμος καὶ οὐκέτι τοσοῦτο κυμαίνει ἡ θάλαττα. κάθιζε οὖν καὶ ἥσυχος ἔχε." τρεψάμενος δὲ πρὸς τὸν Φίλιππον, "μηδὲν φοβοῦ, ὦ παῖ," ἔφη· "δι᾽   15
ὀλίγου γὰρ εἰς τὴν Σαλαμῖνα ἀφιξόμεθα. ἤδη γὰρ πλέομεν διὰ τῶν στενῶν πρὸς τὸν λιμένα. ἰδού, ὦ Δικαιόπολι, τὰ στενά, ἐν οἷς τὸ τῶν βαρβάρων ναυτικὸν ἐμένομεν ὅτε τῇ Ἑλλάδι αὐτοὺς ἠμύνομεν ὑπὲρ τῆς ἐλευθερίας μαχόμενοι."

[ἀνέστη, *stood up*   ῥίπτειν, *to throw*   ἐπιφθόνως, *maliciously, malignantly* τοσοῦτο, *so*   ἥσυχος ἔχε, *keep quiet!*]

ὁ δὲ Δικαιόπολις, "τί λέγεις, ὦ γέρον;" ἔφη. "ἆρα σὺ ἐκείνῃ τῇ   20
μάχῃ παρῆσθα;" ὁ δὲ γέρων, "μάλιστά γε," ἔφη, "ἐγὼ παρῆν, νεανίας

ὢν καὶ ἐρέτης ἐν τριήρει ᾿Αθηναίᾳ." ὁ δὲ Φίλιππος, "ἆρα τὰ ἀληθῆ
λέγεις; μάλα οὖν γεραιὸς εἶ, εἰ τῷ ὄντι ἐκείνῃ τῇ μάχῃ παρῆσθα.
ἀλλ᾿ εἰπὲ ἡμῖν τί ἐγένετο." ὁ δέ, "μακρός ἐστιν ὁ λόγος," ἔφη, "ἀλλ᾿ εἰ
βούλεσθε τὰ γενόμενα μαθεῖν, πάντα ἐξ ἀρχῆς ἐξηγήσομαι. ἐγὼ δέ,   25
ὃς παρῆν, τέρπομαι ἐξηγούμενος. ἀκούετε οὖν."

WORD BUILDING

Give the meanings of the words in the following sets:

1. ἡ ναῦς   ὁ ναύτης   ναυτικός, -ή, -όν   τὸ ναυτικόν
2. ναυμαχέω   ἡ ναυμαχίᾱ   ὁ ναύκληρος   ὁ ναύαρχος

GRAMMAR

3. Relative Clauses

You have now seen a number of relative clauses in the reading passages, e.g.:

a. δέκα νῆες μακραὶ ἐφαίνοντο, **αἳ πρὸς τὸν Πειραιᾶ ἐπορεύοντο.**
   *Ten warships were visible, **which were going to the Piraeus.***

b. κακὸν ἄνθρωπον ἐν τῇ νηὶ φέρομεν, **ὃν δεῖ ῥίπτειν εἰς τὴν θάλατταν.**
   *We are carrying an evil man in the ship, **whom it is necessary to
   throw into the sea.***

Relative clauses are adjectival or descriptive clauses that are introduced by relative pronouns, of which English has the forms *who, whose,
whom, which,* and *that.* In Greek the relative pronoun may appear in any
of the following forms:

	Singular			**Plural**			
	M.	**F.**	**N.**	**M.**	**F.**	**N.**	
Nom.	ὅς	ἥ	ὅ	οἵ	αἵ	ἅ	*who, which, that*
Gen.	οὗ	ἧς	οὗ	ὧν	ὧν	ὧν	*whose, of whom, of which*
Dat.	ᾧ	ᾗ	ᾧ	οἷς	αἷς	οἷς	*to/for whom/which*
Acc.	ὅν	ἥν	ὅ	οὕς	ἅς	ἅ	*whom, which, that*

Be careful not to confuse relative pronouns with definite articles. You
may wish to compare the forms and accents of relative pronouns with
those of the definite article (Chapter 4, Grammar 8, page 50). Note that the
relative pronoun never begins with the letter τ and that the masculine and

feminine nominative singular and plural definite articles do not have accents.

Note the following rule: the relative pronoun, which introduces the relative clause, agrees with the noun, noun phrase, or pronoun to which it refers in the main clause (i.e., its *antecedent*) in gender and number, but its case is determined by its function in the relative clause.

Thus, in sentence a above, the noun phrase δέκα νῆες μακραί (feminine plural) is the antecedent of the relative pronoun, which must accordingly be feminine and plural. The relative pronoun is the subject of the verb in its own clause (ἐπορεύοντο) and must accordingly be in the nominative case; the correct form is therefore αἵ (feminine, plural, nominative).

In sentence b above, the noun phrase κακὸν ἄνθρωπον is the antecedent of the relative pronoun, which must accordingly be masculine and singular. The relative pronoun is the object of ῥίπτειν in its own clause and must accordingly be accusative; the correct form is therefore ὅν (masculine, singular, accusative).

The suffix -περ may be added to the forms of the relative pronoun given above for emphasis, e.g., ὅσπερ = *the very one who*.

Exercise 13ζ

In the first two paragraphs of reading passage β, locate five relative clauses. Identify the antecedent of each relative pronoun, and explain why the relative pronoun is in its gender, number, and case. Two of the five examples have already been analyzed above.

Exercise 13η

Read aloud and translate into English. Explain the gender, number, and case of each relative pronoun:

1. οἱ ἔμποροι, οἳ ἐν ἐκείνῃ τῇ νηῒ ἔπλεον, τὰ κύματα οὐκ ἐφοβοῦντο.
2. ὁ ναύτης, ᾧ τὸ ἀργύριον παρέσχες, ἡμῖν ἡγήσατο εἰς τὴν ναῦν.
3. οἱ ἄνθρωποι, οὓς ἐν τῷ ὄρει εἴδετε, σῖτον Ἀθήναζε ἔφερον.
4. ἐκεῖνοι οἱ δοῦλοι πάντα ἐποίουν ἅπερ ἐκέλευσεν ὁ δεσπότης.
5. αἱ γυναῖκες, αἷς διελεγόμεθα, οὐκ ἔλεγον τὰ ἀληθῆ.
6. πάντας ἐτίμων οἵπερ ὑπὲρ τῆς ἐλευθερίας ἐμάχοντο.
7. ἐκείνη ἡ ναῦς, ἣν ἐθεῶ ἀποπλέουσαν, σῖτον ἔφερεν ἀπὸ τοῦ Πόντου (*the Black Sea*).
8. ὁ ἄγγελος, οὗ ἐν τῇ ἀγορᾷ ἠκούετε, οὐκ ἔλεγε τὰ ψευδῆ.
9. ἆρ' οὐκ ἐφοβεῖσθε τοὺς βαρβάρους οὓς ὁ Ξέρξης ἐπὶ τὴν Ἑλλάδα ἦγεν;
10. ἆρ' εἶδες ἐκείνην τὴν παρθένον, ᾗ οὕτως ὠργίζετο ὁ γέρων;

Exercise 13θ

Translate into Greek:

1. Those young men were journeying to certain friends who live in the city.
2. The young men, whom you saw on the mountains, were looking for their sheep all day.
3. The captain received the money that I handed over to him.
4. He was sailing through the straits, in which the Greeks defeated the barbarians.
5. That priest, with whom we were conversing (*use* διαλέγομαι + dat.), was telling lies.
6. The ship, in which he was sailing, arrived at the harbor within four days.
7. I was listening to the women, who were working in the house at night.
8. On the next day the sailors did all that the captain ordered.
9. Weren't you afraid of that old man, who was shouting so loudly?
10. The foreigners, although hurrying, helped the old man, who was looking for the oxen.

4. 3rd Declension Nouns and Adjectives with Stems in -εσ-

Some 3rd declension nouns and adjectives have stems ending in -εσ-, from which the σ is lost before the endings, allowing the ε of the stem to contract with the vowels of the endings, e.g., τὸ τεῖχος (stem τειχεσ-). The usual contractions occur, as follows:

ε + ε > ει   ε + α > η
ε + ο > ου   ε + ω > ω

Stem: τειχεσ-, *wall*

	Singular			**Plural**		
Nom.	τὸ	τεῖχος		τὰ	τείχεσ-α >	τείχη
Gen.	τοῦ	τείχεσ-ος >	τείχους	τῶν	τειχέσ-ων >	τειχῶν
Dat.	τῷ	τείχεσ-ι >	τείχει	τοῖς	τείχεσ-σι(ν) >	τείχεσι(ν)
Acc.	τὸ	τεῖχος		τὰ	τείχεσ-α >	τείχη
Voc.	ὦ	τεῖχος		ὦ	τείχεσ-α >	τείχη

Neuters with stems in -εσ- have -ος in the nominative, accusative, and vocative singular.

So also τὸ ὄρος, τοῦ ὄρους, *mountain; hill*

Stem: τριηρεσ-, *trireme*

Nom.	ἡ	τριήρης		αἱ	τριήρεσ-ες >	τριήρεις
Gen.	τῆς	τριήρεσ-ος >	τριήρους	τῶν	τριηρέσ-ων >	τριήρων
Dat.	τῇ	τριήρεσ-ι >	τριήρει	ταῖς	τριήρεσ-σι(ν) >	τριήρεσι(ν)
Acc.	τὴν	τριήρεσ-α >	τριήρη	τὰς	τριήρεις	
Voc.	ὦ	τριῆρες		ὦ	τριήρεσ-ες >	τριήρεις

The genitive plural borrows its accent from the other forms, and the accusative plural borrows its form from the nominative plural.

The adjective ἀληθής (stem ἀληθεσ-) has only two sets of forms, the first to go with masculine or feminine nouns and the second to go with neuter nouns. It also loses the σ of the stem before the endings and shows the same contractions as the noun above:

Stem: ἀληθεσ-, *true*

	M. & F.		**N.**	
Nom.	ἀληθής		ἀληθές	
Gen.	ἀληθέσ-ος >	ἀληθοῦς	ἀληθέσ-ος >	ἀληθοῦς
Dat.	ἀληθέσ-ι >	ἀληθεῖ	ἀληθέσ-ι >	ἀληθεῖ
Acc.	ἀληθέσ-α >	ἀληθῆ	ἀληθές	
Voc.	ἀληθές		ἀληθές	
Nom.	ἀληθέσ-ες >	ἀληθεῖς	ἀληθέσ-α >	ἀληθῆ
Gen.	ἀληθέσ-ων >	ἀληθῶν	ἀληθέσ-ων >	ἀληθῶν
Dat.	ἀληθέσ-σι(ν) >	ἀληθέσι(ν)	ἀληθέσ-σι(ν) >	ἀληθέσι(ν)
Acc.	ἀληθεῖς		ἀληθέσ-α >	ἀληθῆ
Voc.	ἀληθέσ-ες >	ἀληθεῖς	ἀληθέσ-α >	ἀληθῆ

So also ψευδής, ψευδές, *false*

PRACTICE: Write all the forms of τὸ μέγα ὄρος, *the big mountain*. Write the forms of ὁ Σωκράτης, *Socrates*, in the singular. Write all the forms of the following phrases: ὁ ψευδὴς λόγος, *the false story*; ἡ ἀληθὴς ἀρετή, *the true virtue;* and τὸ ψευδὲς ὄνομα, *the false name*.

5. 1st/3rd Declension Adjective with 3rd Declension Stems in -υ- and -ε-

As does the adjective πᾶς, πᾶσα, πᾶν (Chapter 8, Grammar 4, page 126), the adjective ταχύς, ταχεῖα, ταχύ, *quick, swift*, has masculine and neuter forms that are 3rd declension, while the feminine is 1st declension (with α, because the stem ends in ι; compare the declension of μάχαιρα, Chapter 4, Grammar 3, page 42). For the 3rd declension forms, compare the declensions of πόλις and ἄστυ, Chapter 9, Grammar 3, page 145.

Stems: ταχυ-/ταχε- for masculine and neuter; ταχει- for feminine, *quick, swift*

| | **Singular** | | | **Plural** | | |
	Masc.	**Fem.**	**Neut.**	**Masc.**	**Fem.**	**Neut.**
Nom.	ταχύ-ς	ταχεῖα	ταχύ	ταχεῖς	ταχεῖαι	ταχέ-α
Gen.	ταχέ-ος	ταχείᾱς	ταχέ-ος	ταχέ-ων	ταχειῶν	ταχέ-ων
Dat.	ταχεῖ	ταχείᾳ	ταχεῖ	ταχέ-σι(ν)	ταχείαις	ταχέ-σι(ν)
Acc.	ταχύ-ν	ταχεῖαν	ταχύ	ταχεῖς	ταχείᾱς	ταχέ-α
Voc.	ταχύ	ταχεῖα	ταχύ	ταχεῖς	ταχεῖαι	ταχέ-α

So also βραδύς, βραδεῖα, βραδύ, *slow*.

PRACTICE: Write all the forms of ὁ ταχὺς κύων, *the swift dog;* ἡ ταχεῖα τριήρης, *the swift trireme;* and τὸ ταχὺ ζῷον, *the swift animal.*

Exercise 13ι

Read aloud and translate:

1. οἱ παῖδες ἐπὶ τὰ τείχη ἀναβαίνουσιν.
2. αἱ τῶν Ἑλλήνων τριήρεις, ταχεῖαι οὖσαι, τὰς τῶν βαρβάρων ναῦς ῥᾳδίως ἔλαβον.
3. ἀεὶ τὰ ἀληθῆ λέγε, ὦ παῖ.
4. ὁ ἄγγελος ψευδῆ τοῖς πολίταις εἶπεν.
5. μὴ τὰ πρόβατα ἀνὰ τὰ ὄρη ἔλαυνε· πολλοὶ γὰρ λύκοι ἐν τοῖς ὄρεσίν εἰσιν.

Ο ΞΕΡΞΗΣ ΤΟΝ ΕΛΛΗΣΠΟΝΤΟΝ ΔΙΑΒΑΙΝΕΙ

Read the following passages (based on Herodotus 7.33–35 and 44) and answer the comprehension questions:

ὁ δὲ Ξέρξης, τοὺς Ἕλληνας καταστρέψασθαι βουλόμενος, στρατὸν μέγιστον παρεσκεύασεν. ἐπεὶ δὲ πάντα τὰ ἄλλα ἕτοιμα ἦν, τοὺς στρατηγοὺς ἐκέλευσε γέφῡραν ποιῆσαι ἐπὶ τῷ Ἑλλησπόντῳ, τὸν στρατὸν ἐθέλων διαβιβάσαι εἰς τὴν Εὐρώπην. οἱ μὲν οὖν στρατηγοὶ γέφῡραν ἐποίησαν, χειμὼν δὲ μέγας γενόμενος πάντα διέφθειρε καὶ ἔλῡσεν.   5

[ὁ . . . Ξέρξης, *Xerxes*   τοὺς Ἕλληνας, *the Greeks*   καταστρέψασθαι, *to overthrow, subdue*   στρατόν, *army*   τοὺς στρατηγούς, *the generals*   γέφῡραν, *bridge*   τῷ Ἑλλησπόντῳ, *the Hellespont*   διαβιβάσαι, *to take across, transport*   τὴν Εὐρώπην, *Europe*   διέφθειρε, *destroyed*]

1. What did Xerxes wish to do?
2. What did he prepare?
3. What did he order his generals to build? With what purpose in mind?
4. What happened?

ἐπεὶ δὲ ἔμαθεν ὁ Ξέρξης τὰ γενόμενα, μάλα ὀργιζόμενος ἐκέλευσε τοὺς δούλους μαστῑγῶσαι τὸν Ἑλλήσποντον καὶ τοὺς τὴν θάλατταν μαστῑγοῦντας ἐκέλευσε ταῦτα λέγειν· "ὦ πικρὸν ὕδωρ, ὁ δεσπότης σε οὕτω κολάζει· ἠδίκησας γὰρ αὐτὸν οὐδὲν κακὸν πρὸς αὐτοῦ παθόν. καὶ βασιλεὺς Ξέρξης διαβήσεταί σε, εἴτε βούλει εἴτε μή."　　10

[μαστῑγῶσαι, to whip　　ταῦτα, these things　　πικρὸν, bitter, spiteful, mean
κολάζει, punishes　　ἠδίκησας, you wronged　　πρὸς αὐτοῦ, from him　　παθόν,
(although) having suffered: note that this aorist participle is neuter to agree with ὕδωρ,
the subject of ἠδίκησας　　διαβήσεταί, will cross　　εἴτε . . . εἴτε, whether . . . or]

5. How did Xerxes react to what had happened?
6. What did he order his slaves to do?
7. To what do the slaves address their speech?
8. What justification is cited for the punishment of the Hellespont?
9. What will Xerxes do?

οὕτω μὲν οὖν ἐκόλασε τὴν θάλατταν, ἐκείνους δὲ οἳ τὴν γέφῡραν ἐποίησαν ἀπέκτεινε, τὰς κεφαλὰς ἀποταμών. ἔπειτα δὲ τοὺς στρατηγοὺς ἐκέλευσεν ἄλλην γέφῡραν ποιῆσαι, μάλα ἰσχῡράν. ἐπεὶ δὲ ἑτοίμη ἦν ἡ γέφῡρα, ὁ Ξέρξης πρὸς τὸν Ἑλλήσποντον προσελθών, πρῶτον μὲν πάντα τὸν στρατὸν ἤθελεν θεᾶσθαι· ἐπὶ ὄχθον οὖν τινα ἀνέβη, ὅθεν πάντα τὸν πεζὸν στρατὸν ἐθεᾶτο καὶ πάσᾱς τὰς ναῦς.　　15 ἔπειτα δὲ τοὺς στρατηγοὺς ἐκέλευσε τὸν πεζὸν στρατὸν διαβιβάσαι εἰς τὴν Εὐρώπην. οὕτως οὖν τῷ στρατῷ ἡγεῖτο ἐπὶ τὴν Ἑλλάδα.

[ἀποταμών (from ἀποτέμνω), cutting off　　ὄχθον, hill　　ἀνέβη, he went up, ascended
ὅθεν, from where, whence　　τὸν πεζὸν στρατὸν, the infantry]

10. What did Xerxes do to those who had built the bridge?
11. What did he order his generals to do?
12. What did Xerxes want to do when he approached the Hellespont?
13. Where did he go and what did he see?
14. What did he order his generals to do?

Exercise 13κ

Translate into Greek:

1. When Philip was sailing to Salamis, the old sailor said that he was present at the battle (*dat. without a preposition*).
2. And Philip, who was very amazed, said, "Unless (εἰ μὴ) you are

3. And the sailor answered: "I was a young man then and was rowing in the fleet.
4. "If you want to listen, I am willing to tell you what happened.
5. "But the story is long, which I must tell from the beginning."

Greek Wisdom

μηδὲν ἄγᾶν.   Σόλων (of Athens)

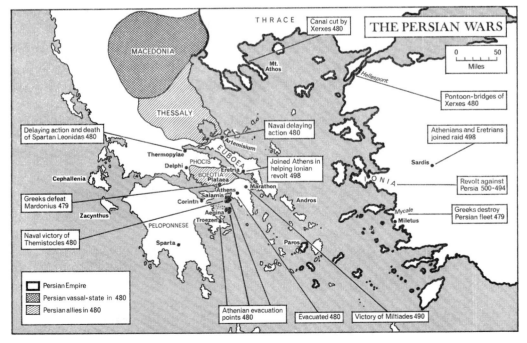

The Persian Wars

Classical Greek

Archilochus

For Archilochus, see pages 121 and 173. After seeing an eclipse of the sun (648 B.C.), he declares that nothing is impossible (fragment 122, Gerber).

χρημάτων ἄελπτον οὐδέν ἐστιν οὐδ' ἀπώμοτον
οὐδὲ θαυμάσιον, ἐπειδὴ Ζεὺς πατὴρ 'Ολυμπίων
ἐκ μεσαμβρίης ἔθηκε νύκτ', ἀποκρύψας φάος
ἡλίου λάμποντος, ὑγρὸν δ' ἦλθ' ἐπ' ἀνθρώπους δέος.

[**χρημάτων** . . . **οὐδέν**, *nothing of things = nothing at all*   **ἄελπτον**, *unexpected*
ἀπώμοτον, *to be sworn impossible*   **ἐπειδὴ**, *since*   **μεσαμβρίης**, *midday*   **ἔθηκε**,
made   **ἀποκρύψας**, *hiding*   **(τὸ) φάος**, *the light*   **λάμποντος**, *shining*   **ὑγρὸν**,
moist, clammy (we print this emendation instead of the unmetrical λυγρὸν, *baneful*, of the
transmitted text)   **δέος**, *fear*]

New Testament Greek

Luke 21.1–4
The Widow's Mite

ἀναβλέψας δὲ εἶδεν τοὺς βάλλοντας εἰς τὸ γαζοφυλάκιον τὰ δῶρα αὐτῶν
πλουσίους. εἶδεν δέ τινα χήραν πενιχρὰν βάλλουσαν ἐκεῖ λεπτὰ δύο, καὶ εἶπεν,
"ἀληθῶς λέγω ὑμῖν ὅτι ἡ χήρα αὕτη ἡ πτωχὴ πλεῖον πάντων ἔβαλεν· πάντες γὰρ
οὗτοι ἐκ τοῦ περισσεύοντος αὐτοῖς ἔβαλον εἰς τὰ δῶρα, αὕτη δὲ ἐκ τοῦ ὑστερήματος
αὐτῆς πάντα τὸν βίον ὃν εἶχεν ἔβαλεν."

[**ἀναβλέψας**: Jesus is the subject   **γαζοφυλάκιον**, *treasury*   **τὰ δῶρα**, *the gifts*
πλουσίους, *wealthy*   **χήραν**, *widow*   **πενιχρὰν**, *poor*   **λεπτὰ**, *small coins*   **αὕτη**
(take with ἡ χήρα), *this*   **ἡ πτωχὴ**, *the poor (one)*   **πλεῖον πάντων**, *more than all*
οὗτοι, *these (men)*   **τοῦ περισσεύοντος αὐτοῖς**, *the more than enough for them,
their abundance*   **αὕτη**, *this (woman)*   **ὑστερήματος**, *need, poverty*   **τὸν βίον**,
the livelihood]

14
Η ΕΝ ΤΑΙΣ ΘΕΡΜΟΠΥΛΑΙΣ ΜΑΧΗ (α)

οἱ Ἕλληνες ἀνδρειότατα μαχόμενοι τοὺς βαρβάρους ἤμῦνον.

VOCABULARY

Verbs

ἐλπίζω, [ἐλπιε-] **ἐλπιῶ**, [ἐλπι-] **ἤλπισα**, ἐλπίσᾱς, *I hope; I expect; I suppose*

ἐπιπέμπω, ἐπιπέμψω, ἐπέπεμψα, ἐπιπέμψᾱς, *I send against; I send in*

πρᾱ́ττω, [πρᾱκ-] **πρᾱ́ξω, ἔπρᾱξα**, πρᾱ́ξᾱς, intransitive, *I fare*; transitive, *I do X*

προσβάλλω, [βαλε-] **προσ-βαλῶ**, [βαλ-] **προσέβαλον**, προσβαλών + dat., *I attack*

συμβάλλω [= συν- + βάλλω], [βαλε-] **συμβαλῶ**, [βαλ-] **συνέβαλον**, συμβαλών, *I join battle*; + dat., *I join battle with*

συνέρχομαι, [εἰ-/ἰ-] **σύνειμι**, [ἐλθ-] **συνῆλθον**, συνελθών, *I come together*

χράομαι (present and imperfect have η where α would be expected: χρῶμαι, χρῇ, χρῆται, etc.), **χρήσομαι** (note that the α changes to η even after the ρ), **ἐχρησάμην**, χρησάμενος + dat., *I use; I enjoy*

Nouns

ὁ ὁπλῑ́της, τοῦ ὁπλῑ́του, *hoplite (heavily-armed foot soldier)*

τὸ πλῆθος, τοῦ πλήθους, *number; multitude*

ὁ στόλος, τοῦ στόλου, *expedition; army; fleet*

ὁ στρατιώτης, τοῦ στρατιώτου, *soldier*

ὁ στρατός, τοῦ στρατοῦ, *army*

Adjectives

ὀλίγος, -η, -ον, *small*; pl., *few*

οὗτος, αὕτη, τοῦτο, *this*; pl., *these*

Note the predicate position: **τοῦτο τὸ ἐπίγραμμα** or **τὸ ἐπίγραμμα τοῦτο**, *this inscription*

στενός, -ή, -όν, *narrow*
Cf. τὰ στενά, *narrows;*
straits; mountain pass
Conjunction
ἤ, with comparatives, *than*
Expressions
ἐν μέσῳ + gen., *between*
κατὰ γῆν, *by land*
Proper Names
ὁ Ἕλλην, τοῦ Ἕλληνος,
Greek; pl., *the Greeks*
ἡ Εὔβοια, τῆς Εὐβοίας, *Euboea*

αἱ Θερμοπύλαι, τῶν Θερ-
μοπυλῶν, *Thermopylae*
ἡ Κόρινθος, τῆς Κορίνθου,
Corinth
οἱ Λακεδαιμόνιοι, τῶν
Λακεδαιμονίων, *the*
Lacedaemonians, Spartans
ὁ Λεωνίδης, τοῦ Λεωνίδου,
Leonidas
ὁ Ξέρξης, τοῦ Ξέρξου, *Xerxes*
οἱ Πέρσαι, τῶν Περσῶν, *the*
Persians

"ἐπεὶ ὁ Ξέρξης, βασιλεὺς ὢν τῶν Περσῶν, τὸν στόλον παρεσκεύαζεν, ἐν νῷ ἔχων πᾶσαν τὴν Ἑλλάδα καταστρέψασθαι, οἱ τῶν Ἑλλήνων πρῶτοι συνῆλθον εἰς τὴν Κόρινθον καὶ ἐσκόπουν τί δεῖ πράττειν. πολὺν δὲ χρόνον ἠπόρουν· μείζονα γὰρ στρατὸν εἶχεν ὁ Ξέρξης ἢ πάντες οἱ Ἕλληνες καὶ πλέονας ναῦς. τέλος δὲ ἔδοξεν 5
αὐτοῖς τοὺς βαρβάρους ἀμύνειν ἐν ταῖς Θερμοπύλαις· ἐκεῖ γὰρ κατὰ μὲν γῆν τὰ ὄρη οὕτω πρόσκειται τῇ θαλάττῃ ὥστε ὀλίγοι πρὸς πολλοὺς δύνανται μάχεσθαι, κατὰ δὲ θάλατταν πόροι εἰσὶ στενοὶ ἐν μέσῳ τῆς τε Εὐβοίας καὶ τῆς ἠπείρου. μαθόντες οὖν οἱ Ἕλληνες ὅτι ὁ Ξέρξης ἤδη πρὸς τὴν Ἑλλάδα πορεύεται καὶ δι' ὀλίγου εἰς τὰς 10
Θερμοπύλας οἱ Πέρσαι ἀφίξονται, τὸν Λεωνίδην ἔπεμψαν, βασιλέα ὄντα τῶν Λακεδαιμονίων, ἑπτακισχῑλίους ἔχοντα ὁπλῑτας. οὗτοι δὲ ἀφικόμενοι εἰς τὰς Θερμοπύλᾱς παρεσκευάζοντο ἀμύνειν τοὺς βαρβάρους τῇ Ἑλλάδι.

[καταστρέψασθαι, *to subdue*   μείζονα, *bigger, larger*   πρόσκειται + dat., note the neuter plural subject, *lie close to*   δύνανται, *are able*   πόροι, *straits*   τῆς ἠπείρου, *the mainland*   ἑπτακισχῑλίους, *seven thousand*]

"ὁ δὲ Ξέρξης ἀφικόμενος εἰς τὰ στενὰ στρατὸν ἔχων μέγιστον δή, 15
τέτταρας μὲν ἡμέρᾱς ἡσύχαζεν· ἤλπιζε γὰρ τοὺς Ἕλληνας ἀποφεύξεσθαι ἰδόντας τὸ πλῆθος τοῦ στρατοῦ. τῇ δὲ πέμπτῃ ἡμέρᾳ—οἱ γὰρ Ἕλληνες ἔτι ἀκίνητοι ἔμενον—τὸν στρατὸν ἐκέλευσεν εὐθὺς προσβαλεῖν. οἱ δὲ Ἕλληνες ἀνδρειότατα μαχόμενοι τοὺς βαρβάρους ἤμῡνον. τέλος δὲ ὁ βασιλεὺς τοὺς Πέρσας ἐπέπεμψεν οὓς 20

'ἀθανάτους' ἐκάλει, ἀνδρειοτάτους ὄντας τῶν στρατιωτῶν, ἐλπίζων τούτους γε ῥᾳδίως νῑκήσειν τοὺς Ἕλληνας. ἐπεὶ δὲ καὶ οὗτοι συνέβαλον, οὐδὲν ἄμεινον ἔπρᾱττον ἢ οἱ ἄλλοι, ἐν τοῖς στενοῖς μαχόμενοι καὶ οὐ δυνάμενοι τῷ πλήθει χρῆσθαι. ὁ δὲ βασιλεὺς τὴν μάχην θεώμενος τρὶς ἀνέδραμεν, ὡς λέγουσιν, ἐκ τοῦ θρόνου, 25 φοβούμενος ὑπὲρ τοῦ στρατοῦ."

[ἤλπιζε . . . τοὺς Ἕλληνας ἀποφεύξεσθαι, *he was hoping that the Greeks would flee* ἀκίνητοι, *unmoved* ἀθανάτους, *Immortals* ἄμεινον, *better* τρὶς, *three times* ἀνέδραμεν (from ἀνατρέχω), *leaped to his feet* τοῦ θρόνου, *his throne*]

WORD STUDY

Using your knowledge of Greek, explain the meaning of the following fore-names:

1. Philip
2. George
3. Theodore (τὸ δῶρον = *gift*)
4. Sophie
5. Dorothea
6. Ophelia

GRAMMAR

1. Comparison of Adjectives

Adjectives have three *degrees*, e.g., "beautiful" (*positive*), "more beautiful" (*comparative*), and "most beautiful" (*superlative*) or "brave" (*positive*), "braver" (*comparative*), and "bravest" (*superlative*).

In Greek the comparative and superlative of adjectives are regularly formed by adding -τερος, -τέρᾱ, -τερον and -τατος, -τάτη, -τατον to the stem of the positive:

Positive	Comparative	Superlative
ἀνδρεῖος, -ᾱ, -ον, *brave*		
Stem: ἀνδρειο-	ἀνδρειό-τερος, -ᾱ, -ον *braver*	ἀνδρειό-τατος, -η, -ον *bravest*
χαλεπός, -ή, -όν, *difficult*		
Stem: χαλεπο-	χαλεπώ-τερος, -ᾱ, -ον *more difficult*	χαλεπώ-τατος, -η, -ον *most difficult*

Note that in 1st and 2nd declension adjectives as in the examples above, the o at the end of the stem of the positive is lengthened to ω if the syllable preceding it is regarded as short (e.g., contains a short vowel that is not followed by two consonants).

Positive	Comparative	Superlative

3rd Declension:

ἀληθής, ἀληθές, *true*
Stem: ἀληθεσ-   ἀληθέσ-τερος, -ᾱ, -ον   ἀληθέσ-τατος, -η, -ον
                         truer   *truest*

Note what happens when the stem ends in -ον-:

σώφρων, σῶφρον, *of sound mind; prudent; self-controlled*
Stem: σωφρον-   σωφρον-έσ-τερος, -ᾱ, -ον   σωφρον-έσ-τατος, -η, -ον
                         more prudent   *most prudent*

The endings -έσ-τερος, -ᾱ, -ον and -έσ-τατος, -η, -ον are constructed by analogy with ἀληθ<u>έσ-τερος</u>, -ᾱ, -ον and ἀληθ<u>έσ-τατος</u>, -η, -ον.

2. Irregular Comparison of Adjectives

Some adjectives are irregular in their formation of comparatives and superlatives and show forms ending in -ίων or -ων (masculine and feminine) and -ῑον or -ον (neuter) for the comparative and -ιστος, -ίστη, -ιστον for the superlative. The comparatives are declined like σώφρων, σῶφρον (see Chapter 7, Grammar 7, page 107), with some alternative forms that will be presented later.

Positive	Comparative	Superlative
ἀγαθός, -ή, -όν *good*	ἀμείνων, ἄμεινον *better*	ἄριστος, -η, -ον *best*
κακός, -ή, -όν *bad*	κακίων, κάκῑον *worse*	κάκιστος, -η, -ον *worst*
καλός, -ή, -όν *beautiful*	καλλίων, κάλλῑον *more beautiful*	κάλλιστος, -η, -ον *most beautiful*
μέγας, μεγάλη, μέγα *big, large, great*	μείζων, μεῖζον *bigger, larger, greater*	μέγιστος, -η, -ον *biggest, largest greatest*
ὀλίγος, -η, -ον *small; pl., few*	ἐλάττων, ἔλαττον *smaller; pl., fewer*	ὀλίγιστος, -η, -ον *smallest (in number); pl., fewest*
πολύς, πολλή, πολύ *much; pl., many*	πλείων/πλέων, πλεῖον/πλέον *more*	πλεῖστος, -η, -ον *most; very great; pl., very many*

PRACTICE: Write the forms of ἡ ἀμείνων γυνή and of τὸ ἄμεινον τέκνον (*child*).

3. Comparison of Adverbs

As you learned in Chapter 4 (Grammar 7, page 50), the positive degree of an adverb is regularly the same in spelling and accent as the genitive plural of the corresponding adjective, but with ς instead of ν at the end, e.g., adjective, gen. pl., καλῶν > adverb, καλῶς. The comparative degree of the adverb is the neuter singular of the comparative adjective, and the superlative degree of the adverb is the neuter plural of the superlative adjective, e.g.:

Positive	**Comparative**	**Superlative**
Regular:		
ἀνδρείως	ἀνδρειότερον	ἀνδρειότατα
bravely	*more bravely*	*most bravely*
ἀληθῶς	ἀληθέστερον	ἀληθέστατα
truly	*more truly*	*most truly*
Irregular:		
εὖ	ἄμεινον	ἄριστα
well =	*better*	*best*
adverb corres-		
ponding to ἀγαθός		
κακῶς	κάκῑον	κάκιστα
badly	*worse*	*worst*
πολύ	πλέον	πλεῖστα
much	*more*	*most*
μάλα	μᾶλλον	μάλιστα
very	*more; rather*	*most, most of all;*
		very much;
		especially

Note the use of μᾶλλον ἤ, *rather than*:

ὁ πάππος ἐβούλετο ἐν τῷ ἄστει μένειν **μᾶλλον ἢ** οἴκαδε ἐπανελθεῖν. *Grandfather was wanting to stay in the city **rather than** to return home.*

4. Uses of Comparatives and Superlatives

a. *Comparatives*

μείζονα στρατὸν εἶχεν <u>ὁ Ξέρξης</u> ἢ <u>πάντες οἱ Ἕλληνες.</u> <u>*Xerxes*</u> *had a **bigger** army **than** <u>all the Greeks</u>.*

Here the conjunction ἤ, *than*, is used; in this construction the two things being compared (underlined in the examples above and below) are in the same case. Here is another example:

ὁ νεανίας <u>τὸν Φίλιππον</u> **ἀγριώτερον** ἔτυψεν ἢ <u>τὸν ἄλλον νεανίαν</u>.
*The young man hit <u>Philip</u> **more fiercely than** (he hit) <u>the other young man</u>.*

The following examples show how the genitive case (*genitive of comparison*) may be used instead of the conjunction ἤ:

ὁ ἀνὴρ **μείζων** ἐστὶ <u>τοῦ παιδός</u>.
*The man is **bigger** <u>than the boy</u>.*

οἱ ἀθάνατοι **οὐδὲν ἄμεινον** ἔπραττον <u>τῶν ἄλλων</u>.
*The Immortals were faring **no better** <u>than the others</u>.*

b.   Superlatives

ὁ Λεωνίδης <u>πάντων τῶν στρατιωτῶν</u> **ἄριστος** ἦν.
*Leonidas was **the best** <u>of all the soldiers</u>.*

The genitive used with superlatives, as above, is a *partitive genitive*.

c.   Strengthened Comparisons

An adjective in the dative case may be used to enhance a comparison, e.g.:

πολλῷ/μακρῷ μείζονα στρατὸν εἶχεν ὁ Ξέρξης ἢ πάντες οἱ Ἕλληνες.
*Xerxes had a **much/far** bigger army than all the Greeks.*

This is called the *dative of degree of difference;* lit., *bigger **by much / by far***. An adverb may also be used, e.g.:

ὁ Λεωνίδης πάντων τῶν στρατιωτῶν **πολὺ** ἄριστος ἦν.
*Leonidas was **by far** the best of all the soldiers.*

d.   Superlatives with ὡς

Note the following:

ὡς τάχιστα, *as quickly as possible*
ὡς ἀνδρειότατα, *as bravely as possible*
ὡς πλεῖστοι, *as many as possible*

e.   Special Meanings of Comparatives and Superlatives

Sometimes comparatives are used when no explicit comparison is being made; the comparative softens the statement, e.g.:

οἱ βάρβαροι **ἀνδρειότεροί** εἰσιν.
*The barbarians are **rather/somewhat** brave.*

Sometimes superlatives are used to indicate a very high degree of a quality when no explicit comparison is being made, e.g.:

οἱ ἀθάνατοι **ἀνδρειότατοί** εἰσιν.
*The Immortals are **very** brave.*

Exercise 14α

Locate six comparatives/superlatives in the reading passage at the beginning of this chapter and explain the constructions in which they occur.

Exercise 14β

Translate into English:

1. τῶν Ἑλλήνων πλεῖστοι ἔπεσον ἄριστα μαχόμενοι.
2. οἱ ὁπλῖται, καίπερ ἀνδρειότατα μαχόμενοι, οὐκ ἐδύναντο (*were able*) τοὺς πολεμίους (*the enemy*) πλέονας ὄντας ἀμύνειν.
3. οἱ Ἕλληνες ἀνδρειότεροι ἦσαν τῶν βαρβάρων καὶ ἄμεινον ἐμάχοντο.
4. τοῖς Ἕλλησι πολλῷ ἐλάττονες νῆες ἦσαν ἢ τοῖς βαρβάροις.
5. ἐν ἐκείνῃ τῇ μάχῃ τῶν μὲν Ἑλλήνων πολλοὶ ἀπέθανον, τῶν δὲ πολεμίων πολλῷ πλέονες.
6. ἡ γυνή, πολλῷ σωφρονεστέρᾱ οὖσα τοῦ ἀνδρός, ἀληθέστερα εἶπεν.
7. οἱ Ἕλληνες, καίπερ ὀλίγιστοι ὄντες, τὰ ὅπλα (*their weapons*) παρεσκεύαζον, ἐν νῷ ἔχοντες ὡς ἀνδρειότατα ἀποθανεῖν.
8. οἱ βάρβαροι, καίπερ ἀγριώτατα προσβάλλοντες, οὐκ ἐδύναντο τοὺς Ἕλληνας νῑκῆσαι.

Exercise 14γ

Translate into Greek:

1. The Persians had (*use imperfect of* ἔχω) a bigger army than we, but we were fighting more bravely.
2. The best soldiers of Xerxes attacked most fiercely but were faring no better than the others.
3. Old men are not always wiser than young men.
4. The hoplites attacked the Persians even (καί) more fiercely.
5. We decided to return home rather than to stay in the city.
6. The messenger, whom we heard in the agora, spoke more truly than you.

The Rise of Athens

Athens played no part in the colonizing movement of the eighth and seventh centuries; she controlled a larger area than any other Greek state except Sparta and so had less need to send out colonies. She was also at this time somewhat backward. An attempt was made to establish a tyranny at Athens by Cylon (632 B.C.), but he failed to win popular support.

Forty years later in the 590s, the discontent of the farmers threatened to lead to civil war in Attica, and Solon was appointed arbitrator to find a solution (see page 118). Although his legislation pleased neither farmers nor nobles, his reforms had a lasting and profound effect both constitutionally and economically. Athens enjoyed a new prosperity. She began to export both olive oil and fine pottery; Attic black figure pottery, which had begun to appear about 600 B.C., gradually drove out Corinthian ware, and achieved a monopoly throughout the Greek world and beyond.

A renewed threat of civil war allowed Pisistratus to establish a tyranny, but Athens continued to grow in prosperity and power throughout his tyranny (546–527) and that of his son, Hippias. Hippias was driven out in 510, and three years later Cleisthenes put through the reforms that established a democracy. Immediately Athens was attacked by enemies on every side. The Spartan king Cleomenes led the army of the Peloponnesian League against her but turned back at the border, because the Corinthians refused to fight in an unjust war. Meanwhile the Boeotians had invaded Attica from the north and the Chalcidians from the east. As soon as Cleomenes had turned back, the Athenian army hurried north, defeated the Boeotians and then crossed to Euboea and inflicted a crushing defeat on the Chalcidians, taking and destroying their city.

When Aristagoras arrived in Athens to ask for help in the Ionian revolt against Persia, the Athenian people were confident enough to accept his appeal (see page 220). Since Hippias had taken refuge with the Persians, their motives were not entirely disinterested. Less than ten years later, Athens faced the might of Persia alone at Marathon, and her victory there filled the democracy with boundless pride and confidence.

Although Athens was now powerful by land, her navy was still inconsiderable. The founder of Athenian sea power was Themistocles, the victor of Salamis, who foresaw that the future of Athens lay by sea and who, as archon in 493/492 B.C., had begun the fortification of the Piraeus. Ten years later an exceptionally rich vein of silver was found in the state mines at Laurium. It was proposed to divide this windfall up among the citizens, but Themistocles persuaded the Assembly to use the money to build a new fleet. Two years later at Salamis we find that Athens had a fleet of 200 triremes, more than half the whole Greek force of 350 ships. Themistocles as admiral of the Athenian contingent had the greatest influence in the allied councils and devised the tactics that won victory at Salamis in 480 B.C. If Sparta remained the greatest land power among the Greeks, from now on there could be no doubt that Athens would take the lead by sea.

When representatives of the thirty-one loyal Greek states had met at Corinth in 481 B.C. to plan resistance to Xerxes' imminent invasion, the allies agreed without dispute to give Sparta command by both land and sea. News of Xerxes' preparations must have reached Greece a good time before this. He had summoned contingents from all over his empire and spent the winter of 481/480 at Sardis assembling and preparing his invasion force. According to Herodotus, his navy consisted of 1,207 ships and his army of

1,700,000 fighting men. The figure for the navy may be approximately correct, but that for the army is absurd. It may have numbered 200,000. To bring this great host into Europe, Xerxes' engineers constructed two bridges of boats across the Hellespont (480 B.C.). When they were destroyed by a storm, two new and stronger bridges were built, and the army crossed the Hellespont and proceeded along the coast, supplied by the navy. At Mount Athos, off which the Persian fleet had been wrecked in 492 B.C., a canal had been dug across the promontory, one and a half miles or two and a half kilometers long, to forestall a similar disaster (see map, page 230). The invading force continued inexorably through Macedonia and into Thessaly. There was no resistance; the Greeks had abandoned any idea of making a stand anywhere north of Thermopylae, the only place where geography made it possible to hold off the Persians by a combined operation by sea and land. The next defensible point was the Isthmus of Corinth, but withdrawal to this would mean abandoning Attica. Even the wall across the Isthmus would not provide effective defense, if the position could be circumvented by a landing of the Persian fleet south of the Isthmus.

Around the outside of this cup four Athenian warships are being rowed, with dolphins leaping beside their prows. They are not triremes, which with 170 oarsmen were too complicated for any artist to draw on a vase. They are penteconters, which had fifty oarsmen. Note the helmsmen holding the steering oars, the high platform in the bows where the lookout stood, and the bronze beaks that were used for ramming the enemy.

Classical Greek

Archilochus

For Archilochus, see pages 121, 173, and 231. In the following epigram (poem 5, Gerber), he defiantly tells the world that in a battle against a Thracian tribe, the Saioi, he threw away his shield and ran:

ἀσπίδι μὲν Σαίων τις ἀγάλλεται, ἣν παρὰ θάμνῳ,

  ἔντος ἀμώμητον, κάλλιπον οὐκ ἐθέλων·

αὐτὸν δ᾽ ἐξεσάωσα. τί μοι μέλει ἀσπὶς ἐκείνη;

  ἐρρέτω· ἐξαῦτις κτήσομαι οὐ κακίω.

[ἀσπίδι (from ἀσπίς), my shield   ἀγάλλεται + dat., enjoys   παρὰ θάμνῳ, by a bush   ἔντος, a weapon   ἀμώμητον, blameless, excellent   κάλλιπον = κατέλιπον   αὐτὸν = ἐμαυτὸν   ἐξεσάωσα = ἐξέσωσα (from ἐκσῴζω, I keep X safe)   τί μοι μέλει ἀσπὶς ἐκείνη, what do I care about that shield?, lit., why is that shield a concern to me?   ἐρρέτω, let it go!   ἐξαῦτις = αὖθις   κτήσομαι (supply ἄλλην), I will get (another)   κακίω = κακίονα]

New Testament Greek

Luke 10.25–29
The Good Samaritan

καὶ ἰδοὺ νομικός τις ἀνέστη ἐκπειράζων αὐτὸν λέγων, "διδάσκαλε, τί ποιήσας ζωὴν αἰώνιον κληρονομήσω;" ὁ δὲ εἶπεν πρὸς αὐτόν, "ἐν τῷ νόμῳ τί γέγραπται; πῶς ἀναγῑνώσκεις;" ὁ δὲ ἀποκριθεὶς εἶπεν, "ἀγαπήσεις κύριον τὸν θεόν σου ἐξ ὅλης καρδίας σου καὶ ἐν ὅλῃ τῇ ψῡχῇ σου καὶ ἐν ὅλῃ τῇ ἰσχύϊ σου καὶ ἐν ὅλῃ τῇ διανοίᾳ σου, καὶ τὸν πλησίον σου ὡς σεαυτόν." εἶπεν δὲ αὐτῷ, "ὀρθῶς ἀπεκρίθης· τοῦτο ποίει καὶ ζήσῃ." ὁ δὲ θέλων δικαιῶσαι ἑαυτὸν εἶπεν πρὸς τὸν Ἰησοῦν, "καὶ τίς ἐστίν μου πλησίον;"

[νομικός, lawyer   ἀνέστη, stood up   ἐκπειράζων, testing   αὐτὸν, i.e., Jesus   διδάσκαλε, teacher   ζωὴν, life   αἰώνιον, eternal   κληρονομήσω, will I inherit   τῷ νόμῳ, the law   γέγραπται, has been/is written   ἀναγῑνώσκεις = ἀναγιγνώσκεις, do you read   ἀποκριθεὶς, aorist passive participle with active meaning, answering   ἀγαπήσεις, you will love   κύριον, the Lord   ὅλης, whole   καρδίας, heart   ἐν, here best translated with   τῇ ψῡχῇ, the soul   τῇ ἰσχύϊ, the strength   τῇ διανοίᾳ, the mind   πλησίον, adv. or prep. + gen., near; τὸν πλησίον σου = your neighbor   ζήσῃ (from *ζάω), you will live   δικαιῶσαι, to justify   μου πλησίον = ὁ πλησίον μου, the one near me, my neighbor]

Concluded at the end of the chapter

Η ΕΝ ΤΑΙΣ ΘΕΡΜΟΠΥΛΑΙΣ ΜΑΧΗ (β)

οἱ Ἕλληνες μνημεῖον ἐποίησαν τῷ Λεωνίδῃ,
ἀνδρὶ ἀρίστῳ, λέοντα λίθινον.

VOCABULARY

Verbs

ἀγγέλλω, [ἀγγελε-] ἀγγελῶ,
[ἄγγειλ-] ἤγγειλα, ἀγγείλᾱς,
I announce; I tell

ἀναχωρέω, ἀναχωρήσω,
ἀνεχώρησα, ἀναχωρήσᾱς,
I retreat, withdraw

ἀντέχω [= ἀντι- + ἔχω],
imperfect, ἀντεῖχον (irregular
augment), ἀνθέξω
(irregular), [σχ-] ἀντέσχον,
ἀντισχών + dat., *I resist*

γράφω, γράψω, ἔγραψα,
γράψᾱς, *I write*

διέρχομαι [= δια- + ἔρχομαι],
[εἰ-/ἰ-] δίειμι, [ἐλθ-] διῆλθον,
διελθών, *I come through; I go
through*

παραγίγνομαι, [γενε-] παρα-
γενήσομαι, [γεν-] παρε-
γενόμην, παραγενόμενος, *I arrive*

φράζω, φράσω, ἔφρασα,
φράσᾱς, *I show; I tell; I tell of,
explain*

Nouns

ὁ πόλεμος, τοῦ πολέμου, *war*

αἱ πύλαι, τῶν πυλῶν, pl.,
double gates; pass (through the
mountains)

Adjectives

ἅπᾱς, ἅπᾱσα, ἅπᾱν, *all; every; whole*

ὅδε, ἥδε (note the accent), τόδε,
this here; pl., *these here*
  Note the predicate position:
  ὅδε ὁ ἄνθρωπος or ὁ
  ἄνθρωπος ὅδε, *this man
  here*

πολέμιος, -ᾱ, -ον, *hostile; enemy*
  οἱ πολέμιοι, τῶν
  πολεμίων, *the enemy*

Adverb
ὅπου, *where*
Conjunctions
ἕως, *until*
ὡς, *when*
Expression
τῇ προτεραίᾳ, *on the day before*
Proper Names
τὸ Ἀρτεμίσιον, τοῦ
Ἀρτεμισίου, *Artemisium*
ἡ Ἀττική, τῆς Ἀττικῆς, *Attica*

ἡ Βοιωτίᾱ, τῆς Βοιωτίᾱς, *Boe-*
otia
ὁ Ἐφιάλτης, τοῦ Ἐφιάλτου,
Ephialtes
ἡ Πελοπόννησος, τῆς Πελο-
ποννήσου, *the Peloponnesus*
ὁ Σπαρτιάτης, τοῦ
Σπαρτιάτου, *a Spartan*
τὸ Φάληρον, τοῦ Φαλήρου,
Phalerum (the old harbor of
Athens)

"τῇ δ' ὑστεραίᾳ οἱ βάρβαροι αὖθις προσβαλόντες οὐδὲν ἄμεινον ἔπρᾱττον ἢ τῇ προτεραίᾳ. ὡς οὖν ἠπόρει ὁ Ξέρξης, προσῆλθε πρὸς αὐτὸν ἀνήρ τις τῶν Ἑλλήνων, Ἐφιάλτης ὀνόματι, ἔφρασέ τε τὴν ἀτραπὸν τὴν διὰ τοῦ ὄρους φέρουσαν εἰς τὰς Θερμοπύλᾱς. ταῦτα δὲ μαθὼν ὁ Ξέρξης τοὺς ἀθανάτους ταύτῃ ἔπεμψεν, κελεύων αὐτοὺς ἐκ   5
τοῦ ὄπισθεν λαβεῖν τοὺς Ἕλληνας. οἱ δὲ Ἕλληνες μαθόντες τί γίγνεται πρῶτον μὲν ἠπόρουν τί δεῖ πρᾶξαι, τέλος δὲ ἔδοξε τῷ Λεωνίδῃ τοὺς μὲν ἄλλους ἀποπέμψαι πρὸς τὴν Ἀττικήν, αὐτὸς δὲ ἔμενεν ἐν ταῖς Θερμοπύλαις τριᾱκοσίους ἔχων Σπαρτιάτᾱς ἐν νῷ ἔχων τὰς πύλᾱς φυλάττειν.   10

[τε, *and*   τὴν ἀτραπὸν, *the path*   φέρουσαν, *leading*   ταύτῃ, *this way*   ἐκ τοῦ
ὄπισθεν, *from the rear*   τριᾱκοσίους, *three hundred*]

"οἱ μὲν οὖν βάρβαροι προσέβαλον, οἱ δὲ Σπαρτιᾶται ἐμάχοντο πρὸς πολεμίους πολλαπλασίους ὄντας καὶ πλείστους δὴ ἀπέκτειναν· τῶν δ' Ἑλλήνων ἄλλοι τε πολλοὶ ἔπεσον καὶ αὐτὸς ὁ Λεωνίδης, ἀνὴρ ἄριστος γενόμενος. τέλος δὲ οἱ Πέρσαι οἱ διὰ τοῦ ὄρους διελθόντες παρεγένοντο καὶ ἐκ τοῦ ὄπισθεν προσέβαλον. τότε δὴ οἱ Σπαρτιᾶται   15
εἰς τὸ στενὸν τῆς ὁδοῦ ἀνεχώρουν καὶ ἐνταῦθα ἐμάχοντο ἕως ἅπαντες ἔπεσον.

[πολλαπλασίους, *many times their number*]

"οἱ δὲ Ἕλληνες μετὰ τὸν πόλεμον τοὺς τριᾱκοσίους ἔθαψαν ὅπου ἔπεσον καὶ μνημεῖον ἐποίησαν τῷ Λεωνίδῃ, λέοντα λίθινον, ὃν καὶ νῦν ἔξεστιν ἰδεῖν. καὶ τοῦτο τὸ ἐπίγραμμα ἐν στήλῃ λιθίνῃ   20
ἔγραψαν·

ὦ ξεῖν᾽, ἀγγέλλειν Λακεδαιμονίοις ὅτι τῇδε

κείμεθα, τοῖς κείνων ῥήμασι πειθόμενοι.

[ἔθαψαν, *they buried*   ἐπίγραμμα, *inscription*   στήλη, *tombstone*   ὦ ξεῖν᾽ = ὦ
ξένε   ἀγγέλλειν: infinitive used as imperative   τῇδε, *here*   κείμεθα, *we lie*
τοῖς κείνων ῥήμασι, *their words*]

"ἐν δὲ τούτῳ κατὰ θάλατταν οἱ Ἕλληνες πρὸς τῷ Ἀρτεμισίῳ
μένοντες τὰ στενὰ ἐφύλαττον καὶ ναυμαχοῦντες τοὺς βαρβάρους   25
ἐνίκησαν καίπερ πλέονας ὄντας καὶ ἤμῡναν. ὡς δὲ οἱ βάρβαροι τὰς
Θερμοπύλᾱς εἷλον, οἱ Ἕλληνες οὐκέτι ἐφύλαττον τὰ στενὰ ἀλλὰ
πρὸς τὴν Σαλαμῖνα ταῖς ναυσὶν ἀνεχώρουν. κατὰ δὲ γῆν οὐκέτι
ἐδύναντο ἀντέχειν τοῖς βαρβάροις ἀλλὰ ἔφευγον πρὸς τὴν
Πελοπόννησον, τήν τε Βοιωτίᾱν καὶ τὴν Ἀττικὴν τοῖς πολεμίοις   30
καταλιπόντες. οὕτως οὖν οἱ βάρβαροι κατὰ μὲν γῆν προχωρήσαντες
ταῖς Ἀθήναις προσβαλεῖν ἐν νῷ εἶχον, κατὰ δὲ θάλατταν εἰς τὸ
Φάληρον πλεύσαντες ἐν τῷ λιμένι ὥρμουν."

[ναυμαχοῦντες, *fighting at sea*   ταῖς ναυσὶν, *with their ships*   ἐδύναντο, *they
were able*   ὥρμουν (from ὁρμέω), *came to lie at anchor*]

WORD BUILDING

Deduce the meanings of the words in the following sets:

1. ὁ στρατός   ἡ στρατιᾱ́   στρατεύω (-ομαι)   τὸ στράτευμα
2. ὁ στρατηγός   στρατηγέω   στρατηγικός, -ή, -όν   ὁ στρατιώτης
3. ὁ πόλεμος   πολέμιος, -ᾱ, -ον   πολεμικός, -ή, -όν   πολεμέω

GRAMMAR

5. Demonstrative Adjectives

Here are three demonstrative adjectives, used when pointing to particular things (cf. the Latin *dēmōnstrō*, "I point out"):

οὗτος, αὕτη, τοῦτο, *this*
ἐκεῖνος, ἐκείνη, ἐκεῖνο, *that*
ὅδε, ἥδε, τόδε, *this here*

In the chart below, note that the demonstrative adjective οὗτος begins
with τ everywhere the definite article does; the feminine has -αυ- instead of -ου- everywhere except in the genitive plural; and the neuter plural nominative and accusative have -αυ-:

| Singular | | | Plural | | |
| **M.** | **F.** | **N.** | **M.** | **F.** | **N.** |

οὗτος, αὕτη, τοῦτο, *this*

Nom.	οὗτος	αὕτη	τοῦτο	οὗτοι	αὗται	ταῦτα
Gen.	τούτου	ταύτης	τούτου	τούτων	τούτων	τούτων
Dat.	τούτῳ	ταύτῃ	τούτῳ	τούτοις	ταύταις	τούτοις
Acc.	τοῦτον	ταύτην	τοῦτο	τούτους	ταύτᾱς	ταῦτα

ἐκεῖνος, ἐκείνη, ἐκεῖνο, *that*

Nom.	ἐκεῖνος	ἐκείνη	ἐκεῖνο	ἐκεῖνοι	ἐκεῖναι	ἐκεῖνα
Gen.	ἐκείνου	ἐκείνης	ἐκείνου	ἐκείνων	ἐκείνων	ἐκείνων
Dat.	ἐκείνῳ	ἐκείνῃ	ἐκείνῳ	ἐκείνοις	ἐκείναις	ἐκείνοις
Acc.	ἐκεῖνον	ἐκείνην	ἐκεῖνο	ἐκείνους	ἐκείνᾱς	ἐκεῖνα

The demonstrative adjective ὅδε is formed from the definite article plus -δε.

ὅδε, ἥδε, τόδε, *this here*

Nom.	ὅδε	ἥδε	τόδε	οἵδε	αἵδε	τάδε
Gen.	τοῦδε	τῆσδε	τοῦδε	τῶνδε	τῶνδε	τῶνδε
Dat.	τῷδε	τῇδε	τῷδε	τοῖσδε	ταῖσδε	τοῖσδε
Acc.	τόνδε	τήνδε	τόδε	τούσδε	τάσδε	τάδε

Note that these demonstrative adjectives require the definite article to be used with the noun and that the adjectives stand outside the definite article-noun group, i.e., in the *predicate position* (see Chapter 5, Grammar 7b, page 66), e.g.:

οὗτος ὁ ἀνήρ or ὁ ἀνὴρ **οὗτος** = *this man*
ἐκείνη ἡ γυνή or ἡ γυνὴ **ἐκείνη** = *that woman*
τόδε τὸ ἔργον or τὸ ἔργον **τόδε** = *this work*

The datives ταύτῃ and τῇδε are used as adverbs, meaning *in this way; here*.

Exercise 14δ

Give the correct form of the demonstrative to fit the following phrases:

1. (οὗτος) αἱ γυναῖκες
2. (ἐκεῖνος) τὸ δένδρον
3. (οὗτος) τὰ ὀνόματα
4. (ὅδε) τῶν νεᾱνιῶν
5. (οὗτος) τῆς παρθένου
6. (οὗτος) οἱ βάρβαροι
7. (ἐκεῖνος) τοῦ στρατοῦ
8. (οὗτος) τῇ πόλει
9. (ὅδε) οἱ γέροντες
10. (οὗτος) τοῦ στρατιώτου

Exercise 14ε

Translate:

1. ἐκεῖνο τὸ δένδρον μέγιστόν ἐστιν· οὐδέποτε (*never*) εἶδον δένδρον μεῖζον.
2. ἆρ' ὁρᾷς τούσδε τοὺς παῖδας, οἳ ἐκεῖνον τὸν κύνα διώκουσιν;
3. ταῦτα μαθοῦσαι αἱ γυναῖκες εὐθὺς τοὺς ἄνδρας ἐκάλεσαν.
4. τί οὐ βούλει τῷ ἀρότρῳ τούτῳ χρῆσθαι; ἄμεινον γάρ ἐστιν ἐκείνου.
5. τί ποιεῖς, ὦ πάτερ; ἆρα ταύτῃ τῇ γυναικὶ διαλέγει;
6. οἱ Ἕλληνες ἀνδρειότεροι ἦσαν τῶν Περσῶν.
7. οἱ Σπαρτιᾶται πάντες ἀπέθανον ἀνδρειότατα μαχόμενοι.
8. This road is worse than that, but that (one) is longer.
9. After seeing this (*use the neuter plural*), that old man was growing very angry.
10. These women are wiser than those young men.

6. Interrogative and Indefinite Pronouns, Adjectives, and Adverbs

In Chapter 7 (Grammar 8 and Grammar 9, pages 108–109) you learned the interrogative pronoun/adjective τίς, τί, *who? what?* and the corresponding indefinite pronoun/adjective τις, τι, meaning *a certain, a,* or *an.* The interrogative pronoun/adjective always has an acute accent, while the indefinite pronoun/adjective is enclitic.

Interrogative adverbs also have corresponding indefinite, enclitic forms:

Interrogative Adverbs		**Indefinite Adverbs**	
ποῦ;	*where?*	που	*somewhere, anywhere*
πόθεν;	*from where? whence?*	ποθέν	*from somewhere*
ποῖ;	*to where? whither?*	ποι	*to somewhere*
πότε;	*when?*	ποτέ	*at some time, at one time, once, ever*
πῶς;	*how?*	πως	*somehow, in any way*

These indefinite adverbs cannot stand first in their clause, and they attach themselves to some important word as enclitics.

If an enclitic is followed by another enclitic, the first receives an accent but the second does not, e.g.: δυνατόν ἐστί ποτε, *it is ever possible.* (Remember that ἐστί is enclitic.) If an enclitic is followed by more than one enclitic, all but the last receive acute accents, e.g.: δυνατόν ἐστί σοί ποτε, *it is ever possible for you.*

Exercise 14ζ

Translate into English. Locate indefinite adjectives and adverbs and explain why the accents are used that accompany them. Consult Enclitics and Proclitics, page 285, if necessary.

1. τίνες ἐλαύνουσι τοὺς βοῦς; γέροντές τινες αὐτοὺς ἐλαύνουσιν.
2. ποῖ πορεύεται ὁ βασιλεύς; ὁ βασιλεὺς πορεύεταί ποι πρὸς τὰ ὄρη.
3. ποῦ εἰσιν οἱ ναῦται; ἐν τῷ λιμένι πού εἰσιν οἱ ναῦται.
4. τί πάσχετε, ὦ παῖδες; ἆρα κακόν τι πάσχετε;
5. πόθεν ἥκεις, ὦ ἄνερ; ἥκω ἀπὸ τῶν ὀρῶν ποθεν, ὦ γύναι.
6. πότε ἐν νῷ ἔχεις εἰς τὸ ἄστυ ἰέναι; δι' ὀλίγου ποτὲ ἐκεῖσε ἰέναι ἐν νῷ ἔχω.
7. πῶς τοῦτο ἐποίησας; τοῦτο ἐποίησα τεχνικῶς (*skillfully*) πως.
8. ποῦ μένει ὁ ἀδελφός; ὁ σὸς ἀδελφὸς μένει που ἐγγὺς τῆς ἀγορᾶς.

ΟΙ ΠΕΡΣΑΙ ΤΑ ΥΠΕΡ ΘΕΡΜΟΠΥΛΩΝ ΣΤΕΝΑ ΑΙΡΟΥΣΙΝ

Read the following passages (based on Herodotus 7.215–219) and answer the comprehension questions:

ὁ δὲ Ξέρξης, μαθὼν ὅτι ἀτραπός ἐστιν ὑπὲρ τὸ ὄρος φέρουσα, μάλα χαίρων ἔπεμψε τὸν Ὑδάρνην, στρατηγὸν ὄντα ἄριστον, καὶ τοὺς ἄνδρας ὧν ἐστρατήγει ὁ Ὑδάρνης. ὡρμῶντο δὲ πρὸς ἑσπέραν ἀπὸ τοῦ στρατοπέδου, ἡγεῖτο δὲ αὐτοῖς ὁ Ἐφιάλτης. αὕτη δὲ ἡ ἀτραπὸς ἄρχεται ἀπὸ τοῦ Ἀσωποῦ ποταμοῦ. οἱ οὖν Πέρσαι τὸν Ἀσωπὸν διαβάντες ἐπορεύοντο πᾶσαν τὴν νύκτα. ἐγίγνετο δὲ ἡμέρα, καὶ οἱ   5
Πέρσαι ἀφίκοντο εἰς ἄκρον τὸ ὄρος. κατὰ δὲ τοῦτο τοῦ ὄρους ἐφύλαττον Ἑλλήνων χίλιοι ὁπλῖται.

[ὑπὲρ + acc., *over*   τὸν Ὑδάρνην, *Hydarnes*   στρατηγόν, *general*   ὧν ἐστρα-τήγει, *of whom (he) was in command*   τοῦ στρατοπέδου, *the camp*   ἄρχεται, *begins*   τοῦ Ἀσωποῦ ποταμοῦ, *the Asopus River*   διαβάντες, *having crossed*   κατὰ . . . τοῦτο τοῦ ὄρους, *on this (part) of the mountain*   χίλιοι, *a thousand*]

1. What had Xerxes learned? Whom did he send?
2. When did they set out? Who led them?
3. Where did the path begin?
4. How long did the Persians march?
5. Who were guarding the top of the mountain?

οὗτοι δὲ οὐκ εἶδον τοὺς Πέρσας ἀναβαίνοντας· πολλὰ γὰρ ἦν δένδρα κατὰ τὸ ὄρος. ψόφον δὲ ἀκούοντες ἔμαθον ὅτι ἀνέβησαν οἱ Πέρσαι. ἔδραμον οὖν οἱ Ἕλληνες καὶ ἐνέδυον τὰ ὅπλα, καὶ εὐθὺς παρῆσαν οἱ βάρβαροι. ἐπεὶ δὲ οἱ Πέρσαι εἶδον   10

ἄνδρας ἐνδύοντας ὅπλα, ἐθαύμαζον· ἐλπίζοντες γὰρ οὐδένα φυλάττειν τὴν
ἀτραπόν, ἐνεκύρησαν στρατῷ. ὁ μὲν οὖν Ὑδάρνης διέταξε τοὺς Πέρσας εἰς μάχην·
οἱ δὲ Ἕλληνες ἐλπίζοντες τοὺς βαρβάρους ἐν νῷ ἔχειν προσβαλεῖν, ἔφυγον εἰς τὸν
τοῦ ὄρους κόρυμβον καὶ παρεσκευάζοντο μαχόμενοι ἀποθανεῖν. οἱ δὲ Πέρσαι τῶν
μὲν Ἑλλήνων οὐδένα λόγον ἐποιοῦντο, κατέβησαν δὲ τὸ ὄρος ὡς τάχιστα.   15

[ψόφον, *noise*   ἀνέβησαν, *had come up, had ascended*   ἐνέδῡον (from ἐνδύω) τὰ
ὅπλα, *began to put on their armor, began to arm themselves*   ἐνεκύρησαν (from
ἐγκυρέω) + dat., *they met, came face to face with*   διέταξε (from διατάττω), *arranged,
marshaled*   εἰς + acc., *for*   τὸν . . . κόρυμβον, *the top, the peak*   οὐδένα λόγον
ἐποιοῦντο + gen., *were taking no notice of*, lit., *were making no calculation of*
κατέβησαν, *they went down*]

6.   Why didn't the Greeks see the Persians approaching?
7.   How did they learn of the Persians' arrival?
8.   What did the Greeks do immediately?
9.   Why were the Persians surprised to see the Greeks?
10. What did Hydarnes do?
11. What was the response of the Greeks?
12. What did the Persians do?

Exercise 14η

Translate into Greek:

1.   When the Persians had taken (*use aorist*) Thermopylae, they went to-
     ward (*use* προσχωρέω) Attica.
2.   The Greeks retreated both by land and by sea, leaving (behind) Attica
     to the enemy.
3.   The Athenians, having sent the women and children and old men to
     the Peloponnesus and Salamis, were preparing to fight by sea.
4.   So they asked the other Greeks to sail to Salamis as quickly as possi-
     ble.
5.   The Peloponnnesians (οἱ Πελοποννήσιοι), who were making a wall
     across (διά + *gen.*) the Isthmus (*use* ὁ Ἰσθμός), were not wishing to
     come to aid the Athenians, but nevertheless sent their ships to
     Salamis.

Classical Greek

Theognis

For Theognis, see pages 163 and 185. In the following lines (1197–1200), while in exile, he hears the crane, which in its autumn migration to Africa is a sign that it is time to plow:

ὄρνῑθος φωνήν, Πολυπαΐδη, ὀξὺ βοώσης

  ἤκουσ᾽, ἥ τε βροτοῖς ἄγγελος ἦλθ᾽ ἀρότου

ὡραίου· καί μοι κραδίην ἐπάταξε μέλαιναν,

  ὅττι μοι εὐανθεῖς ἄλλοι ἔχουσιν ἀγρούς.

[**ὄρνῑθος φωνήν**, *the voice of the bird* (ὄρνῑς) i.e., the crane   **Πολυπαΐδη**, voc., Polypaïdes is the friend to whom Theognis addresses his poetry   **ὀξὺ**, *loudly*   **ἥ τε**, *which*   **βροτοῖς**, *to mortals*   **ἦλθ**(εν), gnomic aorist, translate as present, *comes*   **ἀρότου ὡραίου**, *of plowing (being) seasonable*, i.e., of the season of plowing   **μοι κραδίην**, *my heart*   **ἐπάταξε**, *struck*   **μέλαιναν**, *black*   **ὅττι** = ὅτι, *because*   **εὐανθεῖς**, *fair-flowering*]

New Testament Greek

Luke 10.30–37
The Good Samaritan (concluded)

ὑπολαβὼν ὁ Ἰησοῦς εἶπεν, "ἄνθρωπός τις κατέβαινεν ἀπὸ Ἰερουσαλὴμ εἰς Ἰεριχὼ καὶ λῃσταῖς περιέπεσεν, οἳ καὶ ἐκδύσαντες αὐτὸν καὶ πληγὰς ἐπιθέντες ἀπῆλθον ἀφέντες ἡμιθανῆ. κατὰ συγκυρίαν δὲ ἱερεύς τις κατέβαινεν ἐν τῇ ὁδῷ ἐκείνῃ καὶ ἰδὼν αὐτὸν ἀντιπαρῆλθεν· ὁμοίως δὲ καὶ Λευίτης κατὰ τὸν τόπον ἐλθὼν καὶ ἰδὼν ἀντιπαρῆλθεν. Σαμαρίτης δέ τις ὁδεύων ἦλθεν κατ᾽ αὐτὸν καὶ ἰδὼν ἐσπλαγχνίσθη, καὶ προσελθὼν κατέδησεν τὰ τραύματα αὐτοῦ ἐπιχέων ἔλαιον καὶ οἶνον, ἐπιβιβάσας δὲ αὐτὸν ἐπὶ τὸ ἴδιον κτῆνος ἤγαγεν αὐτὸν εἰς πανδοχεῖον καὶ ἐπεμελήθη αὐτοῦ. . . . τίς τούτων τῶν τριῶν πλησίον δοκεῖ σοι γεγονέναι τοῦ ἐμπεσόντος εἰς τοὺς λῃστάς;" ὁ δὲ εἶπεν, "ὁ ποιήσας τὸ ἔλεος μετ᾽ αὐτοῦ." εἶπεν δὲ αὐτῷ ὁ Ἰησοῦς, "πορεύου καὶ σὺ ποίει ὁμοίως."

[**ὑπολαβὼν**, *answering*   **λῃσταῖς**, *thieves*   **ἐκδύσαντες**, *having stripped*   **πληγὰς ἐπιθέντες**, *having put blows on him*   **ἀφέντες** (from ἀφίημι) **ἡμιθανῆ**, *having left (him) half dead*   **κατὰ συγκυρίαν**, *by chance*   **ἀντιπαρῆλθεν**, *went past on the other side*   **ὁμοίως**, *likewise*   **κατὰ τὸν τόπον**, *to the place*   **ὁδεύων**, *journeying, on a journey*   **ἐσπλαγχνίσθη**, *was filled with pity*   **κατέδησεν**, *he bound up*   **τὰ τραύματα**, *the wounds*   **ἐπιχέων**, *pouring on*   **ἔλαιον**, *olive oil*   **ἐπιβιβάσας**, *having mounted*   **τὸ ἴδιον κτῆνος**, *his own beast*   **πανδοχεῖον**, *inn*   **ἐπεμελήθη** + gen., *he cared for*   (ὁ) **πλησίον** . . . **τοῦ ἐμπεσόντος**, *the neighbor of the one who fell among*   **γεγονέναι**, *to have been*   **ὁ ποιήσας τὸ ἔλεος**, *the one who had* (lit., *who made*) *pity on*   **μετ**(ὰ), *on*]

15

Η ΕΝ ΤΗΙ ΣΑΛΑΜΙΝΙ
ΜΑΧΗ (α)

οἱ Ἀθηναῖοι εἰς τὰς ναῦς εἰσβάντες παρεσκευάζοντο κατὰ θάλατταν μάχεσθαι.

VOCABULARY

Verbs

ἀναγκάζω, ἀναγκάσω, ἠνάγκασα, ἀναγκάσᾱς, *I compel*

διαφθείρω, [φθερε-] **διαφθερῶ,** [φθειρ-] **διέφθειρα,** διαφθείρᾱς, *I destroy*

εἴκω, εἴξω, εἶξα (no augment), εἴξᾱς + dat., *I yield*

Nouns

ἡ ἀπορίᾱ, τῆς ἀπορίᾱς, *perplexity; difficulty; the state of being at a loss*

Cf. ἀπορέω, *I am at a loss*

ὁ ναύαρχος, τοῦ ναυάρχου, *admiral*

ὁ νοῦς, τοῦ νοῦ, *mind*

Cf. ἐν νῷ ἔχω + infin., *I have in mind; intend*

ὁ στρατηγός, τοῦ στρατηγοῦ, *general*

ἡ φυγή, τῆς φυγῆς, *flight*

Adjective

μόνος, -η, -ον, *alone; only*

Adverb

μηκέτι (cf. Vocabulary 3α) + imperative, *don't . . . any longer;* + infin., *no longer*

μόνον, *only*

Conjunctions

οὐ μόνον . . . ἀλλὰ καί, *not only . . . but also*

250

Proper Name
ὁ Θεμιστοκλῆς, τοῦ Θεμισ-
τοκλέους, *Themistocles*

"οἱ μὲν οὖν Ἀθηναῖοι ἐν ἀπορίᾳ ἦσαν πλείστῃ· ὁ δὲ Θεμιστοκλῆς
ἔπεισεν αὐτοὺς μὴ εἴκειν τοῖς βαρβάροις ἀλλὰ ὑπὲρ τῆς ἐλευθερίας
μάχεσθαι. τάς τ' οὖν γυναῖκας καὶ τοὺς παῖδας καὶ τοὺς γέροντας εἰς
τήν τε Πελοπόννησον καὶ τὴν Σαλαμῖνα ἐκόμισαν, τήν τ' Ἀττικὴν
καὶ τὴν πόλιν τοῖς πολεμίοις καταλιπόντες. αὐτοὶ δὲ εἰς τὰς ναῦς   5
εἰσβάντες πρὸς τὴν Σαλαμῖνα προσέπλευσαν καὶ παρεσκευάζοντο
ὡς κατὰ θάλατταν μαχούμενοι.

[εἰσβάντες, *having gotten into, having embarked upon*]

"ἐν δὲ τούτῳ οἱ μὲν τῶν Ἑλλήνων στρατηγοὶ ἐν τῇ Σαλαμῖνι
συνελθόντες οὕτως ἐφοβοῦντο ὥστε ἀποφυγεῖν ἐβούλοντο πρὸς τὴν
Πελοπόννησον· ὁ δὲ Θεμιστοκλῆς ἐν τῷ συνεδρίῳ ἀναστὰς εἶπεν ὅτι   10
ἔτι καὶ νῦν δύνανται τοὺς πολεμίους νῑκῆσαι· ἐν γὰρ τοῖς στενοῖς
μαχόμενοι οὐ δυνήσονται οἱ βάρβαροι τῷ πλήθει χρῆσθαι· δεῖ οὖν
ἀναγκάσαι αὐτοὺς ἐκεῖ συμβαλεῖν.

[τῷ συνεδρίῳ, *the council*   ἀναστὰς, *having stood up*   δύνανται, *they were* (lit.,
are) *able*]

"οὕτως εἰπὼν οὐ μόνον τοὺς ἄλλους στρατηγοὺς ἔπεισε
μάχεσθαι, ἀλλὰ καὶ ἄγγελον παρὰ τὸν Ξέρξην ἔπεμψε λάθρα, ὡς   15
λέξοντα ὅτι οἱ Ἕλληνες παρασκευάζονται εἰς φυγήν. ὁ οὖν Ξέρξης,
ὡς ἔγνω ὅτι ἀποφυγεῖν ἐν νῷ ἔχουσιν οἱ Ἕλληνες, βουλόμενος
αὐτοὺς ὡς τάχιστα διαφθεῖραι, διέγνω αὐτοὺς ἀναγκάσαι ἐν
Σαλαμῖνι μάχεσθαι. τῶν οὖν νεῶν τὰς μὲν ἔπεμψε περὶ τὴν νῆσον,
κελεύων τοὺς ναυάρχους τοὺς ἔκπλους φυλάττειν, τὰς δὲ ἐκέλευσε   20
φυλάττειν τὰ στενὰ ὥστε μηκέτι ἐξεῖναι τοῖς Ἕλλησιν ἀποπλεῖν."

[λάθρα, *secretly*   εἰς + acc., *for*   ἔγνω, *he learned*   διέγνω, *decided*   τῶν . . .
νεῶν τὰς μὲν . . . τὰς δὲ, *some of the ships . . . others*   τοὺς ἔκπλους, *the escape
routes*]

WORD STUDY

Identify the Greek stems in the English words below and give the meanings of the English words:

1. monogamy (what does γαμέω mean?)
2. monologue
3. monochrome (what does τὸ χρῶμα mean?)
4. monosyllable (what does ἡ συλλαβή mean? From what verb is this noun formed?)
5. monograph

GRAMMAR

1. Athematic 2nd Aorists

The following common verbs form their aorist indicatives, imperatives, and infinitives by adding the appropriate endings directly to a long-vowel stem without a thematic vowel in between. The participles are formed on the short-vowel stem. We call these *athematic 2nd aorists*. The aorist of βαίνω is used only in compounds in Attic Greek:

βαίνω, βήσομαι, ἔβην
I step, walk, go
Aorist Stems: βη-/βα-

Indic.	Imper.	Infin.	Partic.
ἔβην		βῆναι	βάς,
ἔβης	βῆθι		βᾶσα,
ἔβη			βάν,
ἔβημεν		gen., βάντος, etc.	
ἔβητε	βῆτε		
ἔβησαν			

γιγνώσκω, γνώσομαι, ἔγνων
I come to know; I perceive; I learn
Aorist Stems: γνω-/γνο-

Indic.	Imper.	Infin.	Partic.
ἔγνων		γνῶναι	γνούς,
ἔγνως	γνῶθι		γνοῦσα,
ἔγνω			γνόν,
ἔγνωμεν		gen., γνόντος, etc.	
ἔγνωτε	γνῶτε		
ἔγνωσαν			

The other tenses of the following verb will be presented in Book II:

ἔστην
I stood; I stopped
Aorist Stems: στη-/στα-

Indic.	Imper.	Infin.	Partic.
ἔστην		στῆναι	στάς,
ἔστης	στῆθι		στᾶσα,
ἔστη			στάν,
ἔστημεν		gen., στάντος, etc.	
ἔστητε	στῆτε		
ἔστησαν			

The participles of ἔβην and ἔστην are declined the same as sigmatic 1st aorist participles (see Chapter 12, Grammar 2, page 199). The participle of ἔγνων is declined the same as the present participle of εἰμί (see Chapter 9, Grammar 1, page 136), except for the masculine nominative singular.

Note the meanings of the following words:

ἀνέβην, *I went up*
ἀνάβηθι, *go up!*
ἀναβῆναι, *to go up*
ἀναβάς, *having gone up, after going up*, sometimes, *going up*

ἔγνων, *I came to know; I perceived; I learned*
γνῶθι, *know!*
γνῶναι, *to know; to perceive; to learn*
γνούς, *having learned, after learning*, sometimes, *learning*

ἔστην, *I stood; I stopped*
στῆθι, *stand! stop!*
στῆναι, *to stand; to stop*
στάς, *having stood, after standing*, sometimes, *standing;*
    having stopped, after stopping, sometimes, *stopping*

Exercise 15α

In the reading passage at the beginning of this chapter, locate four instances of the above verbs or compounds of them; identify each form.

Exercise 15β

Read aloud and translate:

1. ἆρ' οὐ βούλεσθε γνῶναι τί εἶπεν ὁ ἄγγελος;
2. οἱ Ἀθηναῖοι, γνόντες ὅτι οἱ βάρβαροι τάς τε Θερμοπύλας εἷλον καὶ τῇ Ἀττικῇ προσχωροῦσιν, μάλα ἐφοβοῦντο.
3. ὁ Θεμιστοκλῆς, στρατηγὸς ὤν, ἀνέστη καὶ τοὺς Ἀθηναίους ἔπεισε μὴ εἴκειν τοῖς πολεμίοις.
4. οἱ Ἀθηναῖοι τάς τε γυναῖκας καὶ τοὺς παῖδας εἰς τὴν Σαλαμῖνα κομίσαντες εἰς τὰς ναῦς εἰσέβησαν.
5. ὁ Ξέρξης, γνοὺς ὅτι ἐν νῷ ἔχουσιν ἀποφυγεῖν οἱ Ἕλληνες, ἐβούλετο ἀναγκάσαι αὐτοὺς στῆναί τε καὶ πρὸς τῇ Σαλαμῖνι μάχεσθαι.
6. ἔκβηθι ἐκ τῆς νεώς, ὦ παῖ, καὶ στῆθι ἐν τῷ χώματι (*pier*).
7. ὁ ναύκληρος τὸν παῖδα ἐκέλευσεν ἀναστάντα ἐκβῆναι ἐκ τῆς νεώς.
8. αἱ γυναῖκες εἰς τὴν ἀγορὰν εἰσελθοῦσαι ἔστησαν πάντα θαυμάζουσαι.
9. ὁ Ἀπόλλων ἐν τοῖς Δελφοῖς ἔφη· "γνῶθι σεαυτόν."
10. στῆτε, ὦ φίλοι, καὶ ἐμὲ μείνατε.

Exercise 15γ

Translate into Greek, using athematic aorist verbs from page 252 with the prepositional prefixes ἀνα-, εἰσ-, ἐκ-, and ἐπι- as appropriate (check the vocabularies at the end of the book as necessary). Particles and infinitives when compounded with prefixes retain the accent of their uncompounded forms, but the accent of compound indicatives and imperatives is recessive.

1. After going into the house, the women were sitting talking to one another.
2. Be silent, boy; stand up and help me.
3. Having gone into the temple, the priest stood and prayed to the god.
4. After climbing the mountain, we stood and were looking at the city.
5. The old man told the boys to stand up and listen.
6. Having learned what had happened (*use aorist*), the boy went out of the house to look for his father.
7. The women want to know why they must leave their homes behind.
8. Having learned that the barbarians were approaching (*use present tense*), the women embarked on the ships.
9. The soldiers, whom Xerxes sent, climbed the mountain very quickly.
10. When they arrived at the top (τὸ ἄκρον), they saw the Greeks, who did not stand bravely but fled away.

2. More 3rd Declension Nouns with Stems in -εσ-

In Chapter 13, Grammar 4, pages 226–227, you learned the declension of nouns with stems in -εσ-, such as τὸ τεῖχος (stem τειχεσ-) and ἡ τριήρης (stem τριηρεσ-). The noun ὁ Θεμιστοκλῆς, τοῦ Θεμιστοκλέους also has a stem in -εσ-, but with a preceding ε so that the following contractions occur:

Stem: Θεμιστοκλε-εσ-, *Themistocles*

Nom.	ὁ	Θεμιστοκλῆς	
Gen.	τοῦ	Θεμιστοκλέ-εσ-ος >	Θεμιστοκλέους
Dat.	τῷ	Θεμιστοκλέ-εσ-ι >	Θεμιστοκλεῖ
Acc.	τὸν	Θεμιστοκλέ-εσ-α >	Θεμιστοκλέᾱ
Voc.	ὦ	Θεμιστόκλε-εσ- >	Θεμιστόκλεις

As usual, the intervocalic σ is lost. The last two vowels then contract in the usual ways, except that after ε the vowels ε + α > ᾱ, and not η, thus τὸν Θεμιστοκλέᾱ. The names Ἡρακλῆς, Περικλῆς, and Σοφοκλῆς are declined the same way.

Aeschylus's *Persae*

Aeschylus, the first of the three great Athenian writers of tragedy, had fought at the battle of Marathon and probably also at Salamis. He certainly saw the battle, and he has left us an eyewitness account of it. Eight years after the battle, he entered his play *The Persians* (Πέρσαι) in the dramatic contest at the festival of Dionysus in 472 B.C. This is our earliest extant Greek tragedy, and it is unique in that it has an historical theme; all other extant tragedies draw their plots from myth. For Aeschylus, human events were interwoven with the divine; he saw the defeat and humiliation of Xerxes as the supreme example of *hubris* (human pride) punished by *Nemesis* (Divine Vengeance).

The scene of the play is Susa, the Persian capital, where the Elders anxiously wait for news of Xerxes' expedition. Since he left, they have heard nothing, and their hearts are heavy with foreboding as they wonder what has happened to the host that went forth in pride to cast the yoke of slavery on Greece. As they speculate gloomily, they see Atossa, the Queen-mother, approaching. She tells them that ever since her son left, she has been troubled by dreams and that now she has had a dream of unmistakable significance: she saw Xerxes yoke two women to his chariot, one in Asian dress, the other in Greek. The Asian woman was proud of her harness and was obedient to the reins, but the Greek struggled, tore the harness from the chariot, threw off the bridle, and broke the yoke. When Atossa woke and went to the altar to pray for deliverance from evil, she saw another terrible omen: an eagle (the king of birds = Xerxes) flew to Apollo's altar, pursued by a falcon (= the Greeks), which clawed at its head, while it cowered unresisting.

As the Elders attempt to calm and comfort Atossa, a messenger is seen approaching in haste, who without preamble reveals the news they have dreaded: "Cities of all the lands of Asia, by one blow your great prosperity has been destroyed and the flower of the Persians is fallen and gone; the whole host has perished."

While Atossa is stunned to silence, the Elders lament wildly until the queen recovers and with quiet dignity asks the messenger how it could have happened since the Persians surely outnumbered the Greeks. The messenger replies (337–347, tr. Podlecki):

> Be sure of this, that in a matter of sheer numbers,
> The ships on our side would have conquered, for the Greeks'
> Entire total of ships was only three hundred ten. . . .
> But the multitude of ships in Xerxes' fleet—I know
> The facts—were no less than a thousand, those in speed
> Surpassing, two hundred seven. This is the total sum.
> Was it here you think we were surpassed when battle came?
> No, not by numbers, but some Spirit crushed the host,
> Threw in an evil fate against us in the scales.
> The gods are keeping the Goddess Pallas' city safe.

The messenger then describes the battle as follows (386–430, tr. Podlecki):

But when the white-horsed chariot of dawn appeared
And filled the entire earth with radiance to behold,
The first thing was a sound, a shouting from the Greeks,
A joyful song, and to it, making shrill response,
From the island rocks about there came an antiphony
Of echoes; fear stood next to each one of our men,
Tripped up in their hopes: for not as if in flight
Were the Greeks raising then a solemn paean-strain,
But rushing into battle with daring confidence;
A trumpet, too, blazed over everything its sound.
At once, with measured stroke of surging, sea-dipped oar,
They struck the brine and made it roar from one command,
And quickly all of them were visible to sight.
Their right wing first, in order just as they had been
Arranged, led off, and next the whole remaining force
Came out to the attack, and with the sight we heard
A loud voice of command: "O sons of Greeks, go on,
Bring freedom to your fatherland, bring freedom to
Your children, wives, and seats of your ancestral gods,
And your forebears' graves; now the struggle is for all."
Of course, on our side, too, a roar of Persian tongues
Went forth in answer; the moment would not brook delay.
Immediately ship struck its brazen-plated beak
On ship. The ramming was begun by a Greek ship
And it snapped off from one of the Phoenicians the whole
Curving stern, and men on both sides shot their spears.
At first the streaming Persian force withstood the shocks;
But when their crowd of ships was gathered in the straits,
And no assistance could be given one to another,
But they were being struck by their own brazen rams,
They kept on breaking all their equipage of oars,
And the ships of the Greeks, with perfect plan and order, came
Around them in a circle and struck, and hulls of ships
Were overturned; and the sea no longer was visible,
Filled as it was with shipwrecks and the slaughter of men.
The beaches, too, and the reefs around were filled with corpses.
Now every ship that came with the Persian armament
Was being rowed for quick escape, no order left.
And they kept striking us, deboning us, like tunnies
Or a catch of fish, with broken fragments of oars, or bits
Of flotsam from the wrecks; and all this time, moaning
And wailing held control of that area of sea,
Until the eye of black night took it away.
So great a crowd of ills, not even if I took
Ten days in order to tell, could I tell the tale in full.

New Testament Greek

Luke 2.1–14
The Birth of Jesus

ἐγένετο δὲ ἐν ταῖς ἡμέραις ἐκείναις ἐξῆλθεν δόγμα παρὰ Καίσαρος Αὐγούστου ἀπογράφεσθαι πᾶσαν τὴν οἰκουμένην. αὕτη ἀπογραφὴ πρώτη ἐγένετο ἡγεμονεύοντος τῆς Συρίας Κυρηνίου. καὶ ἐπορεύοντο πάντες ἀπογράφεσθαι, ἕκαστος εἰς τὴν ἑαυτοῦ πόλιν. ἀνέβη δὲ καὶ Ἰωσὴφ ἀπὸ τῆς Γαλιλαίας ἐκ πόλεως Ναζαρὲθ εἰς τὴν Ἰουδαίαν εἰς πόλιν Δαυὶδ ἥτις καλεῖται Βηθλέεμ, διὰ τὸ εἶναι αὐτὸν ἐξ οἴκου καὶ πατριᾶς Δαυίδ, ἀπογράψασθαι σὺν Μαριὰμ τῇ ἐμνηστευμένῃ αὐτῷ, οὔσῃ ἐγκύῳ. ἐγένετο δὲ ἐν τῷ εἶναι αὐτοὺς ἐκεῖ ἐπλήσθησαν αἱ ἡμέραι τοῦ τεκεῖν αὐτήν, καὶ ἔτεκεν τὸν υἱὸν αὐτῆς τὸν πρωτότοκον, καὶ ἐσπαργάνωσεν αὐτὸν καὶ ἀνέκλῑνεν αὐτὸν ἐν φάτνῃ, διότι οὐκ ἦν αὐτοῖς τόπος ἐν τῷ καταλύματι.

[δόγμα, *order, decree* παρὰ + gen., *from* ἀπογράφεσθαι, *to be registered, enrolled* (in the census) τὴν οἰκουμένην, *the inhabited world, the Roman Empire* ἡγεμονεύοντος ... Κυρηνίου, *when Quirinius was governor* ἕκαστος, *each* διὰ τὸ εἶναι αὐτὸν, *because of his being* πατριᾶς, *family, nation, people* σὺν + dat., *with* Μαριὰμ: indeclinable τῇ ἐμνηστευμένῃ, *the betrothed* ἐγκύῳ, *pregnant* ἐπλήσθησαν, *were fulfilled* τεκεῖν (from τίκτω), *to give birth* τὸν υἱόν, *the son* πρωτότοκον, *first-born* ἐσπαργάνωσεν, *she wrapped X in swaddling bands* ἀνέκλῑνεν (from ἀνακλῑνω) *she made X recline* φάτνῃ, *manger, feeding-trough* διότι, *because* τόπος, *place* τῷ καταλύματι, *the inn*]

καὶ ποιμένες ἦσαν ἐν τῇ χώρᾳ τῇ αὐτῇ ἀγραυλοῦντες καὶ φυλάσσοντες φυλακὰς τῆς νυκτὸς ἐπὶ τὴν ποίμνην αὐτῶν. καὶ ἄγγελος κυρίου ἐπέστη αὐτοῖς καὶ δόξα κυρίου περιέλαμψεν αὐτούς, καὶ ἐφοβήθησαν φόβον μέγαν. καὶ εἶπεν αὐτοῖς ὁ ἄγγελος, "μὴ φοβεῖσθε, ἰδοὺ γὰρ εὐαγγελίζομαι ὑμῖν χαρὰν μεγάλην ἥτις ἔσται παντὶ τῷ λαῷ, ὅτι ἐτέχθη ὑμῖν σήμερον σωτὴρ ὅς ἐστιν Χρῑστὸς κύριος ἐν πόλει Δαυίδ. καὶ τοῦτο ὑμῖν τὸ σημεῖον, εὑρήσετε βρέφος ἐσπαργανωμένον καὶ κείμενον ἐν φάτνῃ." καὶ ἐξαίφνης ἐγένετο σὺν τῷ ἀγγέλῳ πλῆθος στρατιᾶς οὐρανίου αἰνούντων τὸν θεὸν καὶ λεγόντων,

"δόξα ἐν ὑψίστοις θεῷ
καὶ ἐπὶ γῆς εἰρήνη ἐν ἀνθρώποις εὐδοκίας."

[ποιμένες, *shepherds* τῇ χώρᾳ, *the place* ἀγραυλοῦντες, *living out of doors* φυλάσσοντες = φυλάττοντες φυλακὰς, *watches* ἐπὶ + acc., *over* τὴν ποίμνην, *the flock* ἄγγελος, *angel* κυρίου, *of the Lord* δόξα, *the glory* περιέλαμψεν, *shone around* ἐφοβήθησαν, *they feared* φόβον, *fear* εὐαγγελίζομαι, *I announce* χαρὰν, *joy* τῷ λαῷ, *the people* ἐτέχθη (from τίκτω), *was born* σήμερον, *today* σωτὴρ, *savior* τὸ σημεῖον, *the sign* βρέφος, *baby, infant* ἐσπαργανωμένον, *wrapped in swaddling bands* κείμενον, *lying* ἐξαίφνης, *suddenly* στρατιᾶς, *of an army, host* οὐρανίου, *heavenly* αἰνούντων, *of ones praising* ἐν ὑψίστοις, lit., *among the highest (things), in heaven* εἰρήνη, *peace* εὐδοκίας, *of good will* or *of (His) choice*] Concluded in Chapter 16β

Η ΕΝ ΤΗΙ ΣΑΛΑΜΙΝΙ
ΜΑΧΗ (β)

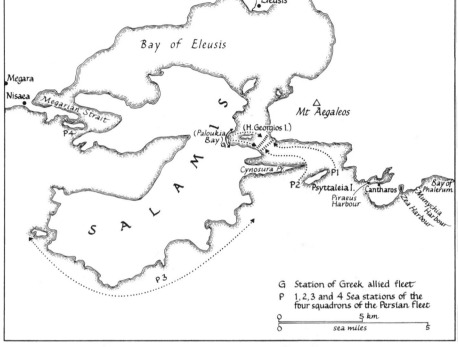

ἡ ἐν τῇ Σαλαμῖνι μάχη

VOCABULARY

Verbs

ἀνέστην, ἀναστάς, *I stood up*

βλάπτω, [βλαβ-] βλάψω,
ἔβλαψα, βλάψᾱς, *I harm, hurt*

δηλόω, δηλώσω, ἐδήλωσα,
δηλώσᾱς, *I show*

ἐλευθερόω, ἐλευθερώσω,
ἠλευθέρωσα, ἐλευθερώσᾱς,
I free, set free

ἐμπίπτω [= ἐν- + πίπτω],
ἐμπεσοῦμαι (irregular),
ἐνέπεσον (irregular),
ἐμπεσών + dat., *I fall into;
I fall upon; I attack*

ἐπιπλέω, [πλευ-] ἐπιπλεύ-
σομαι, ἐπέπλευσα, ἐπιπλεύ-
σᾱς + dat. or + εἰς + acc., *I sail
against*

ναυμαχέω, ναυμαχήσω,
ἐναυμάχησα, ναυμαχήσᾱς,
I fight by sea

πειράω, πειράσω (note that because of the ρ the α lengthens to ᾱ
rather than η), ἐπείρᾱσα,
πειρᾱσᾱς, active or middle,
I try, attempt

πιστεύω, πιστεύσω,
ἐπίστευσα, πιστεύσᾱς + dat.,
*I trust, am confident (in); I be-
lieve; + ὡς, I believe (that)*

συμπίπτω [= συν- + πίπτω],
    συμπεσοῦμαι (irregular),
    [πετ-] συνέπεσον (irregular),
    συμπεσών, I clash; + dat.,
    I clash with

Nouns

ὁ ἀγών, τοῦ ἀγῶνος, struggle;
    contest
ἡ ἀρετή, τῆς ἀρετῆς, excel-
    lence; virtue; courage
ὁ θόρυβος, τοῦ θορύβου, uproar,
    commotion
ὁ κόσμος, τοῦ κόσμου, good or-
    der
    κόσμῳ, in order
τὸ μέρος, τοῦ μέρους, part
ὁ νεκρός, τοῦ νεκροῦ, corpse
ἡ νίκη, τῆς νίκης, victory
ἡ πατρίς, τῆς πατρίδος, father-
    land
ὁ πέπλος, τοῦ πέπλου, robe;
    cloth

ὁ πρόγονος, τοῦ προγόνου, an-
    cestor
ἡ σπουδή, τῆς σπουδῆς, haste;
    eagerness
ἡ τύχη, τῆς τύχης, chance;
    luck; fortune

Adjectives

δεξιός, -ά, -όν, right (i.e., on
    the right hand)
πεζός, -ή, -όν, on foot

Adverb

πανταχοῦ, everywhere

Conjunction

ὡς, that

Proper Names

ὁ Αἰσχύλος, τοῦ Αἰσχύλου,
    Aeschylus
ἡ Ἀσία, τῆς Ἀσίας, Asia (i.e.,
    Asia Minor)
Περσικός, -ή, -όν, Persian
ὁ Σιμωνίδης, τοῦ Σιμωνίδου,
    Simonides

"πᾶσαν οὖν τὴν νύκτα οἱ βάρβαροι ἔνθα καὶ ἔνθα ἤρεσσον τά τε στενὰ φυλάττοντες καὶ τοὺς ἔκπλους, οἱ δὲ Ἕλληνες ἡσύχαζον παρασκευαζόμενοι μάχεσθαι. ἐπεὶ δὲ πρῶτον ἡμέρᾱ ἐγένετο, προὐχώρουν οἱ βάρβαροι εἰς τὰ στενά, πιστεύοντες ὡς ῥᾳδίως μέλλουσι νῑκήσειν τοὺς Ἕλληνας, ἐξαίφνης δὲ βοὴν μεγίστην 5 ἤκουσαν ὥστε μάλα ἐφοβοῦντο. οἱ γὰρ Ἕλληνες, κόσμῳ χρώμενοι εἰς μάχην προὐχώρουν καὶ ἐπὶ τοὺς βαρβάρους πλέοντες τὸν παιᾶνα ἐβόων.

[ἔνθα καὶ ἔνθα, this way and that   ἐξαίφνης, suddenly   τὸν παιᾶνα, the battle song]

"οὕτω δὲ ὁ Αἰσχύλος ὁ ποιητής, ὃς καὶ αὐτὸς τῇ μάχῃ παρῆν, τοὺς Ἕλληνας ποιεῖ ἐπὶ τοὺς βαρβάρους ἐπιπλέοντας·   10

τὸ δεξιὸν μὲν πρῶτον εὐτάκτως κέρας
ἡγεῖτο κόσμῳ, δεύτερον δ' ὁ πᾶς στόλος
ἐπεξεχώρει, καὶ παρῆν ὁμοῦ κλύειν
πολλὴν βοήν, 'ὦ παῖδες Ἑλλήνων ἴτε,

ἐλευθεροῦτε πατρίδ', ἐλευθεροῦτε δὲ　　　　　　　15
παῖδας, γυναῖκας, θεῶν τε πατρῴων ἕδη,
θήκᾱς τε προγόνων· νῦν ὑπὲρ πάντων ἀγών.'

[**ποιεῖ**, here, *describes*　**τὸ δεξιὸν . . . κέρας**, *the right wing*　**εὐτάκτως**, *in an or-*
derly manner　**δεύτερον**, *secondly*　**ἐπεξεχώρει**, *was coming out against* (them)
παρῆν, *it was possible*　**ὁμοῦ**, *together, at the same time*　**κλύειν**, *to hear*　**θεῶν**:
pronounce as one syllable　**πατρῴων**, *ancestral*　(**τὰ**) **ἕδη**, *seats, shrines*　**θήκᾱς**,
tombs　　(The quotation is from Aeschylus, *Persians* 399–405.)]

"οὕτως οὖν οἱ Ἕλληνες τῷ Περσικῷ στρατῷ προσέβαλλον καὶ ἐν
τοῖς στενοῖς συμπίπτοντες ἐναυμάχουν ὀλίγοι πρὸς πολλούς. οἱ δὲ
βάρβαροι, καίπερ πλείστᾱς ἔχοντες ναῦς, οὐκ ἐδύναντο πάσαις ταῖς　　20
ναυσὶν ἅμα χρῆσθαι. καὶ οἱ μὲν Ἕλληνες τὰς πρώτᾱς τῶν
βαρβάρων ναῦς ἢ ἔβλαψαν ἢ κατέδῡσαν τοσαύτῃ σπουδῇ
προσβάλλοντες ὥστε οἱ βάρβαροι μάλα φοβούμενοι ἐτρέποντο καὶ
ἐπειρῶντο ἐκφυγεῖν. ἐνταῦθα δὴ πλεῖστος ἐγένετο θόρυβος. αἱ γὰρ
τῶν βαρβάρων νῆες ἀλλήλαις ἐνέπῑπτον, αἱ μὲν ἐκ τῆς μάχης　　25
πειρώμεναι ἐκφυγεῖν, αἱ δὲ εἰς τὴν μάχην προχωροῦσαι. τέλος δὲ
πάντες οἱ βάρβαροι ἔφευγον οὐδενὶ κόσμῳ χρώμενοι, οἱ δὲ Ἕλληνες
διώκοντες πλείστᾱς δὴ ναῦς κατέδῡσαν· καὶ πανταχοῦ μὲν ἦν
ναυάγια, πανταχοῦ δὲ νεκροί, ὥστε τὴν θάλατταν οὐκέτι ἐξῆν ἰδεῖν.
οὕτως οὖν ἐμάχοντο ἕως νὺξ ἐγένετο.　　　　　　　　　　　　　30

[**ἐδύναντο**, *were able*　**κατέδῡσαν**, *sank*　**ναυάγια**, *shipwrecks*]

"ἐν δὲ τούτῳ ὁ Ξέρξης ἐκαθίζετο ἐπὶ ὄχθῳ τινὶ ἐγγὺς τῆς θαλάττης
τὴν μάχην θεώμενος· ἐπίστευε γὰρ ὡς ῥᾳδίως νῑκήσουσιν οἱ Πέρσαι·
ἠγνόει γὰρ τὰ τῆς τύχης οὐδ' ἔγνω τί ἐν νῷ ἔχουσιν οἱ θεοὶ ἀλλ' ἀεὶ
ὕβρει ἐχρῆτο.

[**ὄχθῳ**, *hill*　**ἠγνόει**, *he was ignorant of*　**τὰ τῆς τύχης**, *the (things) of chance*, i.e.,
that chance rules human affairs　**ὕβρει**, *insolence, pride*]

"γνοὺς δὲ ὅτι νῑκῶσι μὲν οἱ Ἕλληνες οἱ δὲ βάρβαροι ἀπο-　　35
φεύγουσιν, ἀνέστη καὶ τοὺς πέπλους ἔρρηξεν. ἐν ἀπορίᾳ γὰρ μεγίστῃ
ἦν· ἀπολέσᾱς γὰρ τὸ ναυτικὸν οὐκέτι ἐδύνατο σῖτον παρέχειν τῷ
πεζῷ στρατῷ μεγίστῳ ὄντι. τοὺς μὲν οὖν στρατηγοὺς ἐκέλευσε τὸν

πεζὸν στρατὸν ἄγειν κατὰ γῆν πρὸς τὴν Ἀσίαν, αὐτὸς δὲ ἀπέφυγεν
ὀδῡρόμενος.   40

[ἔρρηξεν (from ῥήγνῡμι, *I break*), *he tore*   ἀπολέσᾱς (from ἀπόλλῡμι), *having lost*
ὀδῡρόμενος, *lamenting*]

"οὕτως οὖν οἱ Ἕλληνες τοὺς Πέρσᾱς νῑκήσαντες τὴν Ἑλλάδα
ἠλευθέρωσαν. καὶ δὴ καὶ ἐν τούτῳ τῷ ἔργῳ οἱ Ἀθηναῖοι πλείστᾱς τε
ναῦς παρέσχον τῶν Ἑλλήνων καὶ πλείστην ἐδήλωσαν ἀρετήν, ὥστε
ἔξεστιν ἀληθῶς λέγειν ὅτι οἱ Ἀθηναῖοι τὴν Ἑλλάδα ἔσωσαν, καὶ οὐχ
ἥκιστα ὁ Θεμιστοκλῆς, ὃς στρατηγὸς ὢν Ἀθηναῖος μάλιστα αἴτιος ἦν   45
τῆς νίκης.

[καὶ δὴ καί, *and in particular, and what is more*   ἥκιστα, *least*]

"τοῦτο τὸ ἐπίγραμμα τοῖς Ἀθηναίοις τοῖς ἐν τούτῳ τῷ πολέμῳ
ἀποθανοῦσιν ἔγραψεν ὁ Σιμωνίδης, ποιητὴς ὢν ἄριστος·

εἰ τὸ καλῶς θνῄσκειν ἀρετῆς μέρος ἐστὶ μέγιστον,
    ἡμῖν ἐκ πάντων τοῦτ' ἀπένειμε Τύχη·   50
Ἑλλάδι γὰρ σπεύδοντες ἐλευθερίην περιθεῖναι
    κείμεθ' ἀγηράντῳ χρώμενοι εὐλογίῃ."

[τὸ ἐπίγραμμα, *epigram*   τὸ καλῶς θνῄσκειν, *to die well* (this infinitive phrase is
the subject of the sentence)   ἀπένειμε (from ἀπονέμω), *bestowed, gave*   περιθεῖναι
(from περιτίθημι), *to put around, to put* X (acc.) *on* Y (dat.), as one would put a garland or
a crown on someone's head   κείμεθ(α), *we lie* (in our graves)   ἀγηράντῳ (cf. τὸ
γῆρας, *old age*), *ageless*   εὐλογίῃ, *praise, eulogy*]

WORD BUILDING

*In the following pairs of words, deduce the meaning of the nouns and the ad-
jective from the meanings of the verbs. Note the change in vowels from ε in
the verbs to o in the nouns and the adjective:*

1. λέγω   ὁ λόγος   4. μένω   ἡ μονή
2. τρέπω   ἡ τροπή   5. σπεύδω   ἡ σπουδή
3. πέμπω   ἡ πομπή   6. λείπω   λοιπός, -ή, -όν

GRAMMAR

3. Contract Verbs in -o-

In the vocabulary list and reading passage above, you have seen examples of two contract verbs with stems ending in -o- instead of in -ε- or

-α-, namely, δηλόω, δηλώσω, ἐδήλωσα, and ἐλευθερόω, ἐλευθερώσω, ἠλευθέρωσα. Verbs in -ο- contract as follows:

Stem: δηλο-, *show*

Present Active

Indicative		Imperative	Infinitive	Participle
δηλό-ω>	δηλῶ		δηλοῦν	
δηλό-εις>	δηλοῖς	δήλο-ε >		δηλό-ων > δηλῶν,
δηλό-ει>	δηλοῖ	δήλου		δηλό-ουσα > δηλοῦσα,
δηλό-ομεν>	δηλοῦμεν			δηλό-ον > δηλοῦν,
δηλό-ετε>	δηλοῦτε	δηλό-ετε >		gen., δηλοῦντος
δηλό-ουσι(ν) >	δηλοῦσι(ν)	δηλοῦτε		

Present Middle
Shown here in contracted forms only

δηλοῦμαι		δηλοῦσθαι	δηλούμενος, -η, -ον
δηλοῖ	δηλοῦ		
δηλοῦται			
δηλούμεθα			
δηλοῦσθε	δηλοῦσθε		
δηλοῦνται			

Imperfect Active

ἐ-δήλο-ον >	ἐδήλουν
ἐ-δήλο-ες >	ἐδήλους
ἐ-δήλο-ε >	ἐδήλου
ἐ-δηλό-ομεν >	ἐδηλοῦμεν
ἐ-δήλο-ετε >	ἐδηλοῦτε
ἐ-δήλο-ον >	ἐδήλουν

Imperfect Middle

ἐδηλο-ό-μην >	ἐδηλούμην
ἐδηλό-ε-σο >	ἐδηλοῦ
ἐδηλό-ε-το >	ἐδηλοῦτο
ἐδηλο-ό-μεθα >	ἐδηλούμεθα
ἐδηλό-ε-σθε >	ἐδηλοῦσθε
ἐδηλό-ο-ντο >	ἐδηλοῦντο

The following rules for these contractions may be observed:

1. ο + ε, ο, or ου > ου.
2. ο + ει, οι, or η > οι.
3. ο + η or ω > ω.

There are only a few contract verbs in -ο-; examples are ἀρόω, *I plow*, δηλόω, *I show*, ἐλευθερόω, *I free, set free*, δουλόω, *I enslave*, and πληρόω, *I fill*. The futures and aorists obey the usual rules for contract verbs, lengthening the stem vowel.

Exercise 15δ

Locate four examples of -ο- contract verbs in reading passage β in this chapter and identify the form of each.

Exercise 15ε

Make two photocopies of the Verb Charts on pages 282 and 283 and on one set fill in the forms of δηλόω that you have learned to date in the active voice and on the other, in the middle voice.

4. Contract Nouns of the 2nd Declension

A few nouns of the 2nd declension with stems ending in -oo- show the same process of contraction as is seen in the verbs above.

Stem: νοο-, *mind*

	Singular		**Plural**	
Nom.	ὁ νόο-ς > νοῦς		οἱ νόοι > νοῖ	
Gen.	τοῦ νόου > νοῦ		τῶν νόων > νῶν	
Dat.	τῷ νόῳ > νῷ		τοῖς νόοις > νοῖς	
Acc.	τὸν νόο-ν > νοῦν		τοὺς νόους > νοῦς	
Voc.	ὦ νόε > νοῦ		ὦ νόοι > νοῖ	

Exercise 15ζ

Read aloud and translate:

1. ὁ στρατηγὸς τὰ ἀληθῆ γνοὺς πάντα τῷ δήμῳ δηλοῖ.
2. οἱ πολέμιοι τὴν πόλιν ἑλόντες τοὺς ἐνοίκους (*inhabitants*) δουλοῦσιν.
3. δεῖ ἀνδρείως μάχεσθαι, ὦ ἄνδρες, καὶ ἐλευθεροῦν τὴν πατρίδα.
4. τὴν ἀρετὴν δηλοῦτε ἣν ἀεὶ ἐδήλουν οἱ πρόγονοι.
5. οἱ ὁπλῖται, ταῦτα γνόντες, τοῖς πολεμίοις προσέβαλον καὶ πλείστην ἀρετὴν δηλοῦντες τὴν πόλιν ἠλευθέρωσαν.
6. τί ἐν νῷ ἔχει ὁ Ξέρξης; ἐν νῷ ἔχει πᾶσαν τὴν Ἑλλάδα δουλοῦν.
7. τοῖς Ἕλλησιν ἔδοξε τούς τε βαρβάρους ἀμύνειν καὶ τὴν Ἀσίαν ἐλευθερῶσαι.

5. More Numbers

You have already learned the cardinals 1–10 and the ordinals 1st–10th (see Chapter 8, Grammar 5, page 128). You should learn to recognize the following cardinals and ordinals, including the cardinals on page 264:

11	ἕνδεκα	11th	ἑνδέκατος, -η, -ον
12	δώδεκα	12th	δωδέκατος, -η, -ον
20	εἴκοσι(ν)	20th	εἰκοστός, -ή, -όν
100	ἑκατόν	100th	ἑκατοστός, -ή, -όν
1,000	χίλιοι, -αι, -α	1,000th	χῑλιοστός, -ή, -όν
10,000	μύριοι, -αι, -α	10,000th	μῡριοστός, -ή, -όν

13, etc. = τρεῖς καὶ δέκα, etc. 21, etc. = εἷς καὶ εἴκοσι(ν), etc.

The numbers 30 to 90 are formed from the cardinal numbers for 3 to 9 + -κοντα (with some variations in spelling): τριάκοντα, τετταράκοντα, πεντήκοντα, ἑξήκοντα, ἑβδομήκοντα, ὀγδοήκοντα, ἐνενήκοντα.

The numbers 200 to 900 are formed from the cardinal numbers for 2 to 9 + -κόσιοι, -αι, -α (with some variations in spelling): διᾱκόσιοι, τριᾱκόσιοι, τετρακόσιοι, πεντακόσιοι, ἑξακόσιοι, ἑπτακόσιοι, ὀκτακόσιοι, ἐνακόσιοι.

The word μῡρίοι, -αι, -α is used in the general sense of *numberless, count-less;* note the different accent from that of μῡριοι, -αι, -α, *10,000,* on the previous page.

6. Uses of ὡς and Its Compounds

a. As Adverbs

Exclamatory (*how*): "ὦ Θησεῦ," φᾱσίν, "**ὡς** ἀνδρεῖος εἶ." (6β:22)

Introducing a parenthetical comment (*just as*): **ὥσπερ** λέγει ὁ ποιητής (8α:23)

Expressing purpose with future participle (*to*): "ἐγὼ δὲ ἐν τῷ ἄστει μενῶ **ὡς** τὰς τραγῳδίᾱς θεᾱσόμενος." (10β:13–14 and 10 Gr 7)

With superlatives (*as . . . as possible*): οἱ μὲν οὖν ἄλλοι εὐθὺς παρεσκευάσαντο βουλόμενοι **ὡς** τάχιστα πορεύεσθαι. (12α: 2–3 and 14 Gr 4d)

Introducing a parenthetical comment (*as,* cf. ὥσπερ above): "ὀργίζεται ἡμῖν," ἔφη, "ὁ Ποσειδῶν, **ὡς** δοκεῖ." (13β:10)

b. As Conjunctions

Expressing result (*that*): οὕτω δὲ ταχέως τρέχουσιν **ὥστε** δι᾽ ὀλίγου οὐ δυνατόν ἐστιν ὁρᾶν οὔτε τὸν κύνα οὔτε τὸν λαγών. (5α:7–8)

Expressing time (*when*): **ὡς** οὖν ἠπόρει ὁ Ξέρξης, προσῆλθε πρὸς αὐτὸν ἀνήρ τις τῶν Ἑλλήνων. (14β:2–3)

Introducing an indirect statement (*that*): προὐχώρουν οἱ βάρβαροι εἰς τὰ στενά, πιστεύοντες **ὡς** ῥᾳδίως μέλλουσι νῑκήσειν τοὺς Ἕλληνας. (15β:4–5)

ΟΙ ΠΕΡΣΑΙ ΤΑΣ ΑΘΗΝΑΣ ΑΙΡΟΥΣΙΝ

Read the following passages (based on Herodotus 8.51–53) and answer the comprehension questions:

οἱ Πέρσαι αἱροῦσιν ἔρημον τὸ ἄστυ, καί τινας εὑρίσκουσι τῶν Ἀθηναίων ἐν τῷ ἱερῷ ὄντας, ταμίᾱς τε τοῦ ἱεροῦ καὶ πένητας ἀνθρώπους, οἳ φραξάμενοι τὴν Ἀκρόπολιν ἠμύνοντο τοὺς προσβάλλοντας. οἱ δὲ Πέρσαι καθιζόμενοι ἐπὶ τὸν ὄχθον τὸν ἐναντίον τῆς Ἀκροπόλεως, ὃν οἱ Ἀθηναῖοι καλοῦσιν Ἄρειον πάγον, ἐπολιόρκουν.

[**ἔρημον,** *deserted*   **ταμίᾱς,** *stewards*   **πένητας,** *poor*   **φραξάμενοι,** *having barricaded*
ἐπὶ τὸν ὄχθον, *upon the hill*   **ἐναντίον** + gen., *opposite*

Ἄρειον πάγον, *the Areopagus* (Hill of Ares, the god of war)   ἐπολιόρκουν, *were besieging*]

1. When the Persians take the city, whom do they find in the temple?
2. What had these people done, and what were they doing?
3. How did the Persians situate themselves to besiege the Acropolis?

οἱ δὲ Ἀθηναῖοι, καίπερ κάκιστα πάσχοντες, οὐκ ἤθελον εἴκειν ἀλλὰ ἠμύνοντο,   5
ὥστε πολὺν χρόνον Ξέρξης ἠπόρει, οὐ δυνάμενος αὐτοὺς ἑλεῖν. τέλος δὲ οἱ Πέρσαι
οὕτως εἷλον· ἀνέβησαν γάρ τινες ὅπου ἀπόκρημνος ἦν ὁ χῶρος καὶ οὐκ ἐφύλαττον οἱ
Ἀθηναῖοι ἀλλ᾽ ἐπίστευον ὡς οὐδεὶς δύναται ταύτῃ ἀναβῆναι. ὡς δὲ εἶδον αὐτοὺς
ταύτῃ ἀναβεβηκότας ἐπὶ τὴν Ἀκρόπολιν, οἱ μὲν ἔρριπτον ἑαυτοὺς κατὰ τοῦ τείχους
καὶ ἀπέθανον, οἱ δὲ εἰς τὸ ἱερὸν ἔφευγον. οἱ δὲ Πέρσαι πρῶτον μὲν τοὺς ἱκέτᾱς   10
ἀπέκτειναν, ἔπειτα δὲ τὸ ἱερὸν συλήσαντες ἐνέπρησαν πᾶσαν τὴν Ἀκρόπολιν.

[ἀπόκρημνος, *sheer*   ὁ χῶρος, *the place*   ἀναβεβηκότας (perfect participle of
ἀναβαίνω), *having gone up*   ἔρριπτον (from ῥίπτω), *threw*   κατὰ τοῦ τείχους,
down from the wall   τοὺς ἱκέτᾱς, *the suppliants*   συλήσαντες, *having plundered*
ἐνέπρησαν (from ἐμπίμπρημι), *they set fire to*]

4. How were the Athenians faring and what were their intentions?
5. Why was it possible for the Persians finally to scale the Acropolis?
6. What did the Athenians do when they saw the Persians coming up?
7. What did the Persians do that showed their ignorance of or lack of respect for customary forms of Greek behavior?

Exercise 15η

Translate into Greek:

1. When the Athenians learned that the Persians were advancing (*use present tense*) toward Attica, they sent messengers to Delphi (*use* οἱ Δελφοί).
2. These, having gone into the temple, asked the god what the Athenians must (δεῖ) do.
3. The god, answering (*use aorist participle*), said: "Athena is not able (οὐ δύναται) to save you. The barbarians will take Athens. Only the wooden (*use* ξύλινος, -ον) wall will be unsacked (*use* ἀπόρθητος, -ον)."
4. The messengers wrote these words and having returned to Athens announced them to the people (*dative*).
5. Themistocles, having stood up, said: "Hear, Athenians, what the oracle (τὸ χρηστήριον) means (λέγει); the ships of the Athenians are the wooden wall; for these will save the city."
6. Having spoken thus, he persuaded the Athenians not to yield to the barbarians but to fight by sea.

16
ΜΕΤΑ ΤΗΝ ΕΝ ΤΗΙ ΣΑΛΑΜΙΝΙ
ΜΑΧΗΝ (α)

τάς τε πυραμίδας ἐθεωρήσαμεν καὶ τὴν Σφίγγα καὶ ζῷα ἔκτοπα.

VOCABULARY

Verbs

δύναμαι, imperfect, ἐδυνάμην, **δυνήσομαι**, aorist to be presented later, *I am able; I can*

ἐπίσταμαι, imperfect, ἠπιστάμην, **ἐπιστήσομαι**, no aorist middle, *I understand; I know*

καταλαμβάνω, [ληβ-] **καταλήψομαι**, [λαβ-] **κατέλαβον**, καταλαβών, *I overtake, catch*

κεῖμαι, imperfect, ἐκείμην, **κείσομαι**, no aorist **κατάκειμαι**, *I lie down*

στρατεύω, στρατεύσω, **ἐστράτευσα**, στρατεύσᾱς, active or middle, *I wage war, campaign;* + ἐπί + acc., *I campaign* (against)

συναγείρω, [ἀγερε-] **συναγερῶ**, [ἀγειρ-] **συνήγειρα**, συναγείρᾱς, active, transitive, *I gather* X; middle, intransitive, *I gather together*

τελευτάω, τελευτήσω, ἐτελεύτησα, τελευτήσᾱς, *I end; I die*

Nouns

ὁ ἔνοικος, τοῦ ἐνοίκου, *inhabitant*

ὁ σύμμαχος, τοῦ συμμάχου, *ally*

ἡ συμφορά, τῆς συμφορᾶς, *misfortune; disaster*

Adjectives

διᾱκόσιοι, -αι, -α, *two hundred*

ἑκατόν, indeclinable, *a hundred*

πόσος; πόση; πόσον; *how much?* pl., *how many?*

Preposition

ὑπό + gen., *under;* of agent, by;* + dat., *under;* + acc., *under*

Adverbs

οὐδαμοῦ, *nowhere*

πολλαχόσε, *to many parts*

ὕστερον, *later*

Expressions
καὶ δὴ καί, *and in particular;*
    and what is more
ποῦ γῆς; *where (in the world)?*

Proper Names
For the proper names in this
reading, see the vocabulary at
the end of the book.

* The preposition ὑπό + the genitive case, meaning *by*, will often be found with verbs in
the passive voice, e.g., ὑπὸ τῶν βαρβάρων ἔτι εἴχοντο, *they were still being held by the
barbarians.* In the present and imperfect tenses the passive voice, introduced in this
chapter, has the same forms as the middle voice, which you have seen since Chapter 6.
In the following reading you will find a number of verbs with middle voice endings,
with which you are familiar, but being used in the passive voice. The context will tell
you whether the verb is being used as middle or passive; if it is accompanied by a
prepositional phrase with ὑπό + the genitive case, it is most likely passive.

οὕτως οὖν περᾱνᾱς τὸν λόγον ὁ ναύτης κατέκειτο ἐπὶ τῷ καταστρώματι, ὁ δὲ Δικαιόπολις καὶ ὁ Φίλιππος ἐσίγων, πάντα
θαυμάζοντες ἅπερ εἶπεν. τέλος δὲ ὁ Φίλιππος, "ὡς ἀνδρείως," ἔφη,
"ἐμάχοντο οἱ Ἕλληνες, ὡς λαμπρῶς τοῖς συμμάχοις ἡγοῦντο οἱ
Ἀθηναῖοι. σὺ δὲ τί ἐποίεις μετὰ τὸν πόλεμον; ἆρα ἔμπορος   5
γενόμενος ἐν ὁλκάσιν ἔπλεις;" ὁ δέ, "οὐδαμῶς," ἔφη, "οὐ γὰρ
ἐτελεύτησεν ὁ πόλεμος, ἀλλὰ πολὺν ἔτι χρόνον ἔδει πρὸς τοὺς
βαρβάρους μάχεσθαι. πᾶσαί τε γὰρ αἱ νῆσοι καὶ πᾶσα ἡ Ἰωνίᾱ ὑπὸ
τῶν βαρβάρων ἔτι εἴχοντο.

[**περᾱνᾱς** (from περαίνω), *having finished*   **τῷ καταστρώματι,** *deck*   **ὁλκάσιν,**
merchant ships]

ὁ δὲ Φίλιππος, "ἀλλὰ πόσον χρόνον ἔδει μάχεσθαι; ἆρα πολλαῖς   10
παρῆσθα μάχαις;"

ὁ δὲ ναύτης, "μάλιστά γε, ὦ παῖ," ἔφη, "πλείσταις τε μάχαις παρῆν
καὶ πολλαχόσε τῆς γῆς ἔπλεον μετὰ τῶν συμμάχων. ἀεὶ μὲν γὰρ οἱ
βάρβαροι ἐμάχοντο, ἀεὶ δὲ ἐνῑκῶντο."

ὁ δὲ Φίλιππος, "ἀλλὰ ποῦ γῆς ἐμάχεσθε;"   15

ὁ δέ, "πρῶτον μὲν ἅμα ἦρι ἀρχομένῳ οἱ Ἴωνες ὑφ' ἡμῶν
ἐλευθεροῦνται· πλεύσαντες γὰρ ἑκατὸν ναυσὶ πρὸς τὴν Σάμον καὶ τὸ
τῶν βαρβάρων ναυτικὸν εἰς τὴν Μυκάλην διώξαντες, οὕτω προθύμως
αὐτοῖς προσβάλλομεν ὥστε νῑκᾶταί τε ὁ στρατὸς αὐτῶν καὶ
διαφθείρεται τὸ ναυτικόν. οἱ δὲ Ἴωνες, ὡς ἠπίσταντο ὅτι οἱ βάρβαροι   20

νῑκῶνται, ἡμῖν ἐβοήθουν· οὕτως οὖν πᾶσά τε ἡ Ἰωνίᾱ ἐλευθεροῦται
καὶ πᾶσαι αἱ νῆσοι. οὐδαμοῦ γὰρ δύνανται οἱ βάρβαροι ἡμῖν
ἀντέχειν.

[ἅμα ἦρι ἀρχομένῳ, together with the beginning of spring   ἑκατὸν ναυσὶ, with a
hundred ships   προθΰμως, eagerly]

  "ὕστερον δέ, ὡς οἱ Πέρσαι στρατόν τε μέγιστον καὶ ναῦς διᾱκοσίᾱς
συναγείραντες εἰς τὸν Αἰγαῖον πόντον αὖθις εἰσβιάζεσθαι ἐπειρῶντο,   25
καταλαβόντες αὐτοὺς πρὸς τῷ Εὐρυμέδοντι ποταμῷ ἐνῑκήσαμεν ἐν
μάχῃ μεγίστῃ κατὰ γῆν τε καὶ θάλατταν.

[πόντον, sea   εἰσβιάζεσθαι, to force their way into   ποταμῷ, river]

  "καὶ δὴ καὶ εἰς τὴν Αἴγυπτον ἐστρατεύσαμεν καὶ τοῖς ἐνοίκοις
βοηθοῦντες τοὺς Πέρσᾱς ἐξηλάσαμεν. ἀνά τε γὰρ τὸν Νεῖλον
ἐπλεύσαμεν καὶ τὴν Μέμφιν εἵλομεν, πόλιν μεγίστην ἐπὶ τῷ Νείλῳ   30
κειμένην. ἓξ οὖν ἔτη ἐν τῇ Αἰγύπτῳ ἐμένομεν καὶ πολλὰ θαύματα
εἴδομεν. τάς τε γὰρ πυραμίδας ἐθεωρήσαμεν, σήματα μέγιστα οὔσᾱς
τῶν βασιλέων τῶν ἀρχαίων, καὶ τὴν Σφίγγα, εἰκόνα δεινοτάτην, τὸ μὲν
ἥμισυ λέαιναν, τὸ δὲ ἥμισυ γυναῖκα. καὶ δὴ καὶ ζῷα ἔκτοπα εἴδομεν,
κροκοδίλους τε καὶ στρουθούς. τέλος δὲ οἱ Πέρσαι, στρατὸν μέγιστον   35
συναγείραντες, ἡμῖν προσέβαλον· νῑκώμεθα οὖν καὶ ἐξ Αἰγύπτου
ἐξελαυνόμεθα. οὕτως οὖν συμφορὰν μεγίστην ἐπάθομεν· διᾱκοσίᾱς
γὰρ ναῦς ἀπολέσαντες μόλις ἡμεῖς αὐτοὶ ἐξεφύγομεν."

[ἔτη, years   θαύματα, wonders   πυραμίδας, pyramids   σήματα, tombs
ἀρχαίων, old, ancient   εἰκόνα, a statue   τὸ...ἥμισυ, half   λέαιναν, lioness
ζῷα, animals   ἔκτοπα, out of the way, unusual   κροκοδίλους, crocodiles
στρουθούς, ostriches   ἀπολέσαντες (from ἀπόλλῡμι), having lost]

WORD STUDY

*How are the following words derived from the Greek verb δύναμαι and the re-
lated noun δύναμις?*

1. dynamic 2. dynamo   3. dynamite 4. dynasty

GRAMMAR

1. The Passive Voice

For the concepts of active, passive, and middle voice, see Chapter 6, Grammar 2, pages 75–76.

In the present and imperfect tenses, the passive forms of verbs are spelled the same as middle voice forms. In the aorist and future tenses, the forms are different, and those forms will be introduced in Book II of this course. For the present and imperfect tenses, the context will make clear whether the verb is middle or passive in meaning, e.g.:

Active Voice:
ἡ γυνὴ τὸν ἄνδρα **ἐγείρει.**
The woman **wakes** *her husband.*

Middle Voice:
ὁ ἀνὴρ **ἐγείρεται.**
The husband **wakes himself up/wakes up**.

Passive Voice:
ὁ ἀνὴρ <u>ὑπὸ τῆς γυναικὸς</u> **ἐγείρεται.**
The husband **is woken up** <u>by his wife</u>.

Note that the *agent* by whom the action is performed is expressed with the preposition ὑπό + the genitive. The *thing* with which or by which the action is performed is expressed by a noun in the dative case (*dative of means or instrument*) without a preposition (see Chapter 6, Grammar 6d, page 88):

ὁ λύκος <u>μαχαίρᾱ</u> **τύπτεται** ὑπὸ τοῦ παιδός
The wolf **is struck** <u>with a knife</u> *by the boy.*

Here is a set of examples with the imperfect tense:

Active Voice:
ἡ μήτηρ τοὺς παῖδας **ἔλουεν.**
The mother **was washing** *her children.*

Middle Voice:
οἱ παῖδες **ἐλούοντο.**
The children **were washing themselves/were washing**.

Passive Voice:
οἱ παῖδες <u>ὑπὸ τῆς μητρὸς</u> **ἐλούοντο.**
The children **were being washed** <u>by their mother</u>.

Exercise 16α

Make four photocopies of the Verb Chart on page 282 and fill in the present and imperfect passive forms of λαμβάνω, φιλέω, τῑμάω, and δηλόω that you have learned to date. Translate each form. Keep these charts.

Exercise 16β

Read aloud and translate. Identify all passive verb forms (both indicatives and participles):

1. οἱ βόες πρὸς τὸν ἀγρὸν βραδέως ἐλαύνονται ὑπὸ τοῦ αὐτουργοῦ.

2. πᾶσαν τὴν ἡμέρᾱν ἐπόνει ὁ αὐτουργός, τῷ ἡλίῳ κατατρῑβόμενος (κατατρίβω, *I wear out*).

3. ἐπεὶ δὲ ἑσπέρᾱ γίγνεται, ὁ αὐτουργὸς παύεται ἐργαζόμενος· οἱ δὲ βόες λύονται καὶ τὸ ἄροτρον ἐν τῷ ἀγρῷ λείπεται.

4. ἐν ᾧ δὲ οἴκαδε ἠλαύνοντο οἱ βόες ὑπὸ τοῦ δούλου, ὁ αὐτουργὸς μάλα κάμνων πρὸς τῇ ὁδῷ ἐκαθίζετο.

5. ἐξαίφνης (*suddenly*) δὲ βοῇ ἐγείρεται καὶ τῶν παίδων ἀκούει ἑαυτὸν καλούντων.

6. ἐλθὲ δεῦρο, ὦ πάτερ, καὶ βοήθει· διωκόμεθα γὰρ ὑπὸ λύκου.

7. οἱ παῖδες ὑπὸ τοῦ λύκου διωκόμενοι μάλα ἐφοβοῦντο.

8. μὴ φοβεῖσθε, ὦ παῖδες· οὐδὲν γὰρ βλάπτεσθε ὑπὸ τοῦ λύκου.

9. οὕτως εἰπών, τὸν κύνα ἔλῡσεν· ὁ δὲ λύκος ὑπὸ τοῦ κυνὸς διωκόμενος ἀπέφυγεν.

10. οὕτως οὖν σῴζονται οἱ παῖδες καὶ μετὰ τοῦ πατρὸς οἴκαδε σπεύδουσιν.

Exercise 16γ

Translate the following pairs of sentences:

1. οἱ βάρβαροι ὑπὸ τῶν Ἑλλήνων νῑκώμενοι ἐτρέψαντο καὶ πρὸς τὴν γῆν ἔφυγον.
   The sailors, pursued by the pirates (ὁ λῃστής), raised their sails and fled to the harbor.

2. οἱ Ἕλληνες καίπερ ἐν ἀπορίᾳ ὄντες μεγίστῃ ὑπὸ τοῦ Θεμιστοκλέους πείθονται μὴ εἴκειν τοῖς βαρβάροις.
   The Persians, although having very many ships, are being defeated by the Greeks.

3. ἀναγκαζόμενοι ἐν τοῖς στενοῖς μάχεσθαι οὐκ ἐδύναντο πᾱ́σαις ταῖς ναυσὶ χρῆσθαι.
   They were being pursued by the Greeks, and all their ships were either being damaged or destroyed.

4. ὁ Δικαιόπολις ὑπὸ τῆς γυναικὸς ἐπείθετο πρὸς τὸ ἄστυ πορεύεσθαι.
   Philip was being pursued by a certain big wolf.

5. τῷ χειμῶνι ἀναγκαζόμεθα εἰς τὸν λιμένα ἐπανελθεῖν.
   We are ordered by our father to disembark from the ship.

Exercise 16δ

Translate into Greek:

1. The women are loved and honored by their husbands.
2. The girls, pursued by some young men, were hurrying home to their mothers.
3. Don't go away; we are ordered by the king to wait (*use present tense*) in the market place.
4. When evening was falling, a messenger arrived.
5. "Citizens," he said, "you are ordered to hurry (*use aorist*) home and return (*use aorist*) tomorrow."

The Athenian Empire

During the invasion of Xerxes, the loyal Greeks had accepted without question the leadership of Sparta by both land and sea; for she was still the dominant power in Greece. In spring of 479 B.C., the allied fleet, led by a Spartan general, was based at Delos and, invited by the Samians, sailed to Ionia, defeated the Persians at Mycale, and liberated the Ionians, who revolted from their Persian masters (see map, page 230). The following year the allied forces were led by Pausanias, the Spartan commander at Plataea. In a brilliant campaign he first liberated most of Cyprus from Persian rule and then sailed north and took Byzantium, the key to the Black Sea. Here he fell victim to *hubris*; he adopted Persian dress, intrigued with the Persian authorities, and alienated the allies by his outrageous and tyrannical behavior. In consequence, the allies appealed to the Athenians for protection, and Pausanias was recalled to Sparta and later executed.

Meanwhile the Athenians took over the leadership of the allies. Representatives met at Delos and agreed to form a voluntary league (the Delian League) to carry on the war against Persia under the leadership of Athens. Each member state was to provide ships or money in proportion to its means, of which an assessment was made. The representatives threw lumps of lead into the sea and swore to maintain the League until the lead swam.

Led by Cimon, their Athenian general, the fleet of the League had a series of very successful campaigns, expelling the Persian garrisons wherever they remained and finally defeating them in the great battle of the Eurymedon River on the southern coast of Asia Minor when they tried to make a comeback (ca. 467 B.C.). As the Persian danger receded, some members became less willing to contribute ships or money. Around 469 B.C. the important island of Naxos seceded from the League; the allied fleet blockaded the island and forced it back into the League on terms that made it a subject of Athens. This was the first step of the Athenians on the road to empire.

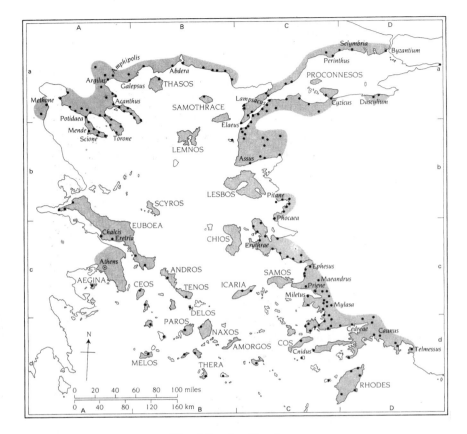

The Athenian Empire

As time went by, more and more members ceased to provide ships and contributed money instead, and soon only three large and wealthy islands (Lesbos, Chios, and Samos) were independent members contributing ships. The rest had become tributary allies, in whose internal affairs Athens began to interfere. In 454 B.C., a highly significant step was taken when the treasury of the League was transferred from Delos to Athens, ostensibly because the defeat of the Athenian expeditionary force in Egypt in 456 B.C. left the Aegean exposed to danger.

A number of inscriptions carved on stone have been found in Athens that throw much light on the development and organization of the Empire in these years. These include records of the annual tribute paid by each member from 454 B.C., when the treasury of the League was moved to Athens, until 415 B.C. We find that the Empire included nearly all the Aegean Sea and stretched from the coast of the Black Sea to the south of Asia Minor. In 449 B.C., the Athenians made peace with Persia; the purpose of the Delian League had come to an end. The following year the tribute list is very short; many members must have refused to pay. We then find a decree that introduced measures for tightening up the collection of the tribute, and the next year's tribute list is long; recalcitrant members had been forced to pay up. At the same time, evidence accumulates of Athenian interference in the internal affairs of League members. Uniform coinage, weights, and measures are imposed by decree; democracies are installed in some cities under the supervision of Athenian officials; garrisons of Athenian troops are stationed at some danger points; settlements of Athenian citizens are made on allied territory; and judicial cases involving an Athenian and an ally are referred to Athenian courts. All such measures infringed the sovereignty of "independent" allies, who were being reduced to the status of subjects in what the Athenians now openly called their Empire (ἡ ἀρχή).

These developments were inspired by Pericles, who dominated the Athenian democracy for nearly thirty years, until his death in 429 B.C. They were largely responsible for the great war between Athens and the Peloponnesian League led by Sparta, for the Peloponnesians not only feared the ever-growing power of Athens but also condemned the "enslavement" of fellow Greeks. The final ultimatum sent by Sparta to Athens said: "The Spartans want peace; and there would be peace, if you let the Greeks be independent." Even at Athens not all approved of the Empire, despite the economic and military advantages it brought. Not even Pericles himself sought moral justification for it. In a speech to the people shortly before his death, he said: "The Empire you hold is a tyranny, which you may think it was wrong to acquire, but it is dangerous to give it up."

Athenian tribute list
This fragment records the tribute paid in 440/439 B.C. by the Hellespontine district of the Empire. In the columns below the heading (ΗΕΛΛΕΣΠΟΝΤΙΟΣ ΦΟΡΟΣ) are listed on the left the amount of tribute and on the right the name of the city concerned.

ΜΕΤΑ ΤΗΝ ΕΝ ΤΗΙ ΣΑΛΑΜΙΝΙ ΜΑΧΗΝ (β)

τὸ Αἰτναῖον ὄρος εἶδον ποταμοὺς πυρὸς πρὸς τὸν οὐρανὸν ἐκβάλλον.

VOCABULARY

Verbs

λῡπέω, λῡπήσω, ἐλύπησα,
λῡπήσᾱς, *I grieve, vex, cause
pain to* X; *passive, I am
grieved, distressed*

πολιορκέω [= πόλις, *city* + ἕρκος,
wall], **πολιορκήσω, ἐπολιόρ-
κησα,** πολιορκήσᾱς, *I besiege*

Nouns

ὁ βίος, τοῦ βίου, *life*
ἡ εἰρήνη, τῆς εἰρήνης, *peace*
τὸ ἔτος, τοῦ ἔτους, *year*
ὁ θάνατος, τοῦ θανάτου, *death*
ὁ θῡμός, τοῦ θῡμοῦ, *spirit*
ὁ ποταμός, τοῦ ποταμοῦ, *river*
ἡ σπονδή, τῆς σπονδῆς, *libation*

(drink offering)

αἱ σπονδαί, τῶν σπονδῶν,
pl., *peace treaty*

Adjectives

ἄξιος, -ᾱ, -ον, *worthy;* + gen.,
worthy of

Expression

ἥκιστά γε, *least of all, not at all*
Cf. **μάλιστά γε,** *certainly,
indeed*

Proper Names

For the proper names in this
reading, see the Greek to English Vocabulary at the end of
the book.

ὁ δὲ Φίλιππος, "ἆρ' οὐ τοσαύτην συμφορὰν παθόντες τοῦ
πολέμου ἐπαύσασθε;"

ὁ δὲ ναύτης, "ἥκιστά γε," ἔφη· "οὐδὲν γὰρ ἐδύνατο τὸν τῶν Ἀθηναίων θῡμὸν καθαιρεῖν. δι' ὀλίγου οὖν ὁ Κίμων τῷ ναυτικῷ εἰς Κύπρον ἡγησάμενος τοὺς Πέρσᾱς αὖθις ἐνίκησεν, αὐτὸς δὲ πόλιν τινὰ πολιορκῶν ἀπέθανεν. ἡμεῖς οὖν λῡπούμενοι οἴκαδε ἀπεπλεύσαμεν. τῷ δὲ ἐπιγιγνομένῳ ἔτει σπονδαὶ ποιοῦνται ὑπὸ τοῦ δήμου πρὸς τοὺς Πέρσᾱς. τοσαῦτα οὖν εἰργασάμεθα πρὸς τοὺς βαρβάρους μαχόμενοι. ἀγὼν οὖν μέγιστος πρόκειταί σοι, ὦ παῖ· δεῖ γάρ σε ἄξιον γίγνεσθαι τῶν πατέρων."

[**καθαιρεῖν**, *to reduce*   **τῷ . . . ἐπιγιγνομένῳ ἔτει**, *the next year*   **πρός** + acc., *with* **πρόκειταί σοι**, *lies before you*]

ὁ δὲ Φίλιππος, "ἀληθῆ λέγεις, ὦ γέρον," ἔφη· "ἐὰν δὲ ἵλεως ᾖ ὁ θεός, ἐγὼ ἀνὴρ ἀγαθὸς γίγνεσθαι πειρᾱσομαι, ἄξιος τῶν πατέρων. ἀλλὰ τί ἐποίεις σὺ ἐν τῇ εἰρήνῃ;"

[**ἐὰν . . . ᾖ**, *if . . . is*]

ὁ δὲ γέρων, "οὐκέτι νεᾱνίᾱς ἦν ἐγώ," ἔφη, "οὐδὲ τοσαύτη ῥώμη ἐχρώμην ὥστε ἐν τῷ ναυτικῷ ἐρέσσειν. μισθοφορῶν οὖν ἐν ὁλκάσι πολλαχόσε τῆς γῆς ἔπλεον. εἴς τε γὰρ τὴν Σικελίᾱν ἦλθον, οὗπερ τὸ Αἰτναῖον ὄρος εἶδον ποταμοὺς πυρὸς πρὸς τὸν οὐρανὸν ἐκβάλλον, καὶ εἰς τὴν Σκυθίᾱν ἔπλευσα, οὗπερ τοῦ χειμῶνος τοσαῦτά ἐστιν τὰ ψύχη ὥστε πήγνυσθαι καὶ τὴν θάλατταν. νῦν δὲ μάλα γεραιὸς ὢν πλοῦς τινὰς μῑκροὺς ποιοῦμαι περὶ τὰς νήσους, καὶ θάνατον εὔκολος προσδέχομαι."

[**ῥώμη**, *strength*   **μισθοφορῶν**, *hiring myself out*   **οὗπερ**, *where*   **τοῦ χειμῶνος**, *in winter*   **τὰ ψύχη**, *the frosts*   **πήγνυσθαι** (present passive infinitive of πήγνῡμι, *I make solid, make stiff*), *freezes*   **πλοῦς**, *voyages*   **εὔκολος**, *contented(ly)*   **προσδέχομαι**, *I await*]

ὁ δὲ Φίλιππος, "πολλὰ μὲν εἶδες, ὦ γέρον," ἔφη, "ἐν τῷ μακρῷ βίῳ, πολλὰ δὲ καὶ ἔπαθες. οὐ γὰρ αὐτὸς ὁ Ὀδυσσεὺς πορρωτέρω ἐπλανᾶτο ἢ σύ."

[**πορρωτέρω**, *further*   **ἐπλανᾶτο** (from πλανάω, *I lead* X *astray, make* X *wander*; passive, *I wander*), *was used to wandering*]

ὁ δὲ γέρων πρὸς τὴν γῆν βλέψᾱς ἀνέστη καί, "ἰδού," ἔφη, "ἤδη γὰρ ἡ ναῦς ἀνέμῳ οὐρίῳ φερομένη τῷ λιμένι προσχωρεῖ. χαίρετε οὖν."

[**οὐρίῳ**, *favorable*]

οὕτως εἰπὼν ἀπέβη πρὸς τὴν πρῷραν, οἱ δὲ ἔμενον πάντα
ἐνθῡμούμενοι ἅπερ εἶπεν.

[τὴν πρῷραν, *the bow of the ship*   ἐνθῡμούμενοι, *thinking about, pondering*]

οἱ δ' ὅτε δὴ λιμένος πολυβενθέος ἐντὸς ἵκοντο,
ἱστία μὲν στείλαντο, θέσαν δ' ἐν νηὶ μελαίνῃ . . .   30
καρπαλίμως, τὴν δ' εἰς ὅρμον προέρεσσαν ἐρετμοῖς.

[πολυβενθέος, gen. sing., *very deep*   ἐντός + gen., *within*   ἵκοντο (unaugmented
aorist in Homer), *they arrived*   στείλαντο (unaugmented aorist in Homer; from
στέλλω, *I make ready; I send*; of sails, *I take down, furl*) *they took down*   θέσαν
(unaugmented aorist in Homer), *they put*   μελαίνῃ, *black*   καρπαλίμως, *quickly*
τὴν, *it*, i.e., the ship   ὅρμον, *anchorage*   προέρεσσαν ἐρετμοῖς (unaugmented
aorist in Homer), *they rowed . . . forward with the oars*   (The quotation is from *Iliad*
1.432, 433, and 435.)]

WORD BUILDING

The following adjectives, verbs, and nouns are related to the word ὁ θῡμός,
spirit, *with the prefixes* ἀ-, not, εὐ-, good, *and* προ-, before; forth (*often indi-
cating readiness*). *Deduce the meaning of the following compounds:*

1. ἄθῡμος, -ον   ἀθῡμέω   ἡ ἀθῡμίᾱ
2. εὔθῡμος, -ον   εὐθῡμέω   ἡ εὐθῡμίᾱ
3. πρόθῡμος, -ον   προθῡμέομαι   ἡ προθῡμίᾱ

GRAMMAR

2. Verbs with Athematic Presents and Imperfects: δύναμαι, κεῖμαι, and ἐπίσταμαι

The following common deponent verbs add personal endings directly to
the stem with no thematic vowel between the stem and the ending (note that
intervocalic σ remains except in the two alternative imperfect forms).
The verbs δύναμαι and ἐπίσταμαι do not have aorist middle forms; their
aorists will be introduced in Chapter 17 at the beginning of Book II. The
verb κεῖμαι was not used in the aorist.

Present

δύναμαι, δυνήσομαι
Stem: δυνα-, *be able*

Indicative	Imperative	Infinitive	Participle
δύνα-μαι		δύνα-σθαι	δυνά-μεν-ος, -η, -ον
δύνα-σαι	δύνα-σο		
δύνα-ται			
δυνά-μεθα			
δύνα-σθε	δύνα-σθε		
δύνα-νται			

κεῖμαι, κείσομαι
Stem: κει-, *lie*

Indicative	Imperative	Infinitive	Participle
κεῖ-μαι		κεῖ-σθαι	κεί-μεν-ος, -η, -ον
κεῖ-σαι	κεῖ-σο		
κεῖ-ται			
κεί-μεθα			
κεῖ-σθε	κεῖ-σθε		
κεῖ-νται			

ἐπίσταμαι, ἐπιστήσομαι
Stem: ἐπιστα-, *understand, know*

Indicative	Imperative	Infinitive	Participle
ἐπίστα-μαι		ἐπίστα-σθαι	ἐπιστά-μεν-ος, -η, -ον
ἐπίστα-σαι	ἐπίστα-σο		
ἐπίστα-ται			
ἐπιστά-μεθα			
ἐπίστα-σθε	ἐπίστα-σθε		
ἐπίστα-νται			

Imperfect Indicative

ἐ-δυνά-μην	ἐ-κεί-μην	ἠπιστά-μην
ἐ-δύνα-σο *or* ἐδύνω	ἔ-κει-σο	ἠπίστα-σο *or* ἠπίστω
ἐ-δύνα-το	ἔ-κει-το	ἠπίστα-το
ἐ-δυνά-μεθα	ἐ-κεί-μεθα	ἠπιστά-μεθα
ἐ-δύνα-σθε	ἔ-κει-σθε	ἠπίστα-σθε
ἐ-δύνα-ντο	ἔ-κει-ντο	ἠπίστα-ντο

Exercise 16ε

Read aloud and translate:

1. ὦ ξεῖν', ἀγγέλλειν Λακεδαιμονίοις ὅτι τῇδε
   κείμεθα τοῖς κείνων ῥήμασι πειθόμενοι. (See Chapter 14β, page 244.)
2. ἆρ' ἐπίστασθε τί οὐ δύνανται ἡμῖν βοηθεῖν οἱ σύμμαχοι;
3. ἡ γυνὴ οὐκ ἠπίστατο ὅτι ὁ ἀνὴρ ἐν ἐκείνῃ τῇ μάχῃ ἀπέθανεν.
4. αὕτη ἡ νῆσος οὕτως ἐγγὺς (*near*) ἔκειτο τῇ ἠπείρῳ (*mainland*) ὥστε
   ῥᾳδίως ἐκεῖσε διέβημεν.
5. ἐν οὐδεμιᾷ ναυμαχίᾳ ἐδύναντο οἱ βάρβαροι τοὺς Ἕλληνας νῑκῆσαι.
6. τέλος δὲ ὁ Ξέρξης ἠπίστατο ὅτι αἱ τῶν βαρβάρων νῆες ταῖς τῶν Ἑλλήνων οὐ δύνανται ἀντέχειν.
7. καίπερ ἄριστα μαχόμενοι, οὐκ ἐδύναντο οἱ Λακεδαιμόνιοι τοὺς βαρβάρους
   ἀμῦναι.
8. τί οὐκ ἐργάζει, ὦ νεᾱνίᾱ, ἀλλὰ οὕτω ἀργὸς κεῖσαι;
9. ἐπιστάμενοι ὅτι ὁ δεσπότης προσχωρεῖ, οἱ δοῦλοι, οἳ ἐν τῷ ἀγρῷ ἔκειντο,
   ἀνέστησαν καὶ εἰργάζοντο.
10. τοῦτο ἐπίστασο, ὅτι οὐ δύνασαι τοὺς θεοὺς ἐξαπατᾶν (*to deceive*).

Ο ΞΕΡΞΗΣ ΠΡΟΣ ΤΗΝ ΑΣΙΑΝ ΑΝΑΧΩΡΕΙ

Read the following passage (adapted from Herodotus 8.118) and answer the comprehension questions below:

After the defeat at Salamis, Xerxes accompanied his army on the retreat northwards. In Thessaly he left a large army under Mardonius to renew the attack the following year. Herodotus gives two versions of the rest of his journey home, of which this is the second.

ἔστι δὲ καὶ ὅδε ἄλλος λόγος, ὅτι, ἐπεὶ ὁ Ξέρξης ἀπελαύνων ἐξ Ἀθηνῶν ἀφίκετο εἰς Ἠϊόνα, οὐκέτι κατὰ γῆν ἐπορεύετο ἀλλὰ τὴν μὲν στρατιὰν Ὑδάρνει ἐπιτρέπει ἀπάγειν εἰς τὸν Ἑλλήσποντον, αὐτὸς δὲ εἰς ναῦν εἰσβὰς ἔπλει εἰς τὴν Ἀσίαν. πλέοντι δὲ αὐτῷ ἄνεμος μὲν μείζων ἐγίγνετο, ἡ δὲ θάλαττα ἐκύμαινεν. ἡ δὲ ναῦς πλείστους φέρουσα ἀνθρώπους τῶν Περσῶν, οἳ τῷ Ξέρξῃ ἠκολούθουν, ἐν κινδύνῳ ἦν. ὁ δὲ βασιλεὺς μάλα φοβούμενος τὸν κυβερνήτην ἤρετο εἴ τις σωτηρία ἐστὶν αὐτοῖς. ὁ δὲ εἶπεν· "ὦ δέσποτα, οὐκ ἔστιν οὐδεμία σωτηρία, ἐὰν μὴ ἀπαλλαγῶμέν τινων τῶν πολλῶν ἐπιβατῶν." 5

[ἀπελαύνων, *marching away* Ἠϊόνα, *Eion (a town in Thrace)* τὴν ... στρατιᾱν, *the army* Ὑδάρνει, *to Hydarnes* ἐπιτρέπει, *entrusts* ἀπάγειν, *to lead back* τὸν Ἑλλήσποντον, *the Hellespont* ἐκύμαινεν, *was becoming rough* ἠκολούθουν + dat., *were following, accompanying* τὸν κυβερνήτην, *the steers-*

man **σωτηρίᾱ,** *safety, salvation* **ἐὰν μὴ,** *unless* **ἀπαλλαγῶμέν** (from ἀπαλ-
λάττω) + gen., *get rid of* **ἐπιβατῶν,** *passengers*]

1. In this second version of the story of Xerxes' return to Asia, what did he do with his army and what did he do himself?
2. What happened during the voyage?
3. What did Xerxes ask his helmsman?
4. On what did the helmsman say their salvation depended?

καὶ Ξέρξης ταῦτα ἀκούσᾱς εἶπεν· "ὦ ἄνδρες Πέρσαι, νῦν δεῖ ῡμᾶς δηλοῦν εἰ
τὸν βασιλέᾱ φιλεῖτε· ἐν ῡμῖν γάρ, ὡς δοκεῖ, ἔστιν ἡ ἐμὴ σωτηρίᾱ." ὁ μὲν ταῦτα   10
εἶπεν, οἱ δὲ αὐτὸν προσκυνοῦντες ἔρρῑψαν ἑαυτοὺς εἰς τὴν θάλατταν, καὶ ἡ ναῦς
ἐπικουφισθεῖσα οὕτω δὴ ἔσωσε τὸν βασιλέᾱ εἰς τὴν Ἀσίᾱν. ὡς δὲ ἐξέβη εἰς τὴν
γῆν, ὁ Ξέρξης ἐποίησε τόδε· ὅτι μὲν ἔσωσε τὸν βασιλέᾱ, χρῡσοῦν στέφανον τῷ
κυβερνήτῃ ἔδωκεν, ὅτι δὲ Περσῶν πολλοὺς διέφθειρεν ἀπέταμε τὴν κεφαλὴν αὐτοῦ.

[**προσκυνοῦντες,** *bowing down to*   **ἔρρῑψαν** (from ῥίπτω),   *they threw*
ἐπικουφισθεῖσα (from ἐπικουφίζω), *lightened*   **ὅτι,** *because*   **χρῡσοῦν στέφανον,**
a golden crown   **ἔδωκεν** (from δίδωμι), *he gave*   **ἀπέταμε** (from ἀποτέμνω), *he cut
off*]

5. What does Xerxes say that the Persians must now show?
6. Upon whom does Xerxes say his salvation depends?
7. What two things do the Persians do?
8. What is the result of their action?
9. Why did Xerxes give his helmsman a golden crown?
10. Why did he cut off his head?

Exercise 16ζ

Translate into Greek:

1. After the battle, Xerxes and his generals, having stayed a certain few days in Attica, set out (*use aorist active*) toward Boeotia.
2. The king ordered Mardonius (*use* **ὁ Μαρδόνιος**) (on the one hand) to stay in Thessaly (*use* **ἡ Θετταλίᾱ**) during the winter, and (on the other hand) at the beginning of spring (**ἅμα ἦρι ἀρχομένῳ**) to advance against the Peloponnesus.
3. When they arrived in Thessaly, Mardonius (on the one hand) selected (**ἐξελέξατο**) the best of his soldiers, (on the other hand) Xerxes leaving them there marched as quickly as possible to the Hellespont.
4. We cannot trust the other story that they tell about the return (*use* **ὁ νόστος**) of Xerxes.
5. Those who understand the truth say that retreating to Asia by land he arrived at the Hellespont within forty-five (**πέντε καὶ τετταρά-κοντα**; *indeclinable*) days (*use genitive*).

Classical Greek

Sappho: Love's Power

The following two fragments (47 and 130, Campbell) of Sappho's poetry describe how love ("Ερος) affected her once in the past and how it affects her again in the present. For Sappho, see pages 131 and 202. The dialect is Aeolic.

"Ερος δ' ἐτίναξέ μοι

φρένας, ὡς ἄνεμος κὰτ ὄρος δρύσιν ἐμπέτων.

[ἐτίναξε, *shook*   μοι: take as possessive with φρένας   φρένας, *heart*   ὡς = ὡς, *as*
κὰτ = κατὰ + acc., *on*   δρύσιν, *oak trees*   ἐμπέτων = ἐμπεσών + dat, *falling on*]

"Ερος δηὖτέ μ' ὁ λῡσιμέλης δόνει,

γλυκύπικρον ἀμάχανον ὄρπετον.

[δηὖτε = δὴ αὖτε, *again*   ὁ λῡσιμέλης, *the limb-relaxing* (lit., *relaxing the limbs*, τὰ
μέλη)   δόνει, *shakes; excites*   γλυκύπικρον, *bitter-sweet* (lit., *sweet-bitter*)   ἀμάχανον = ἀμήχανον, *against whom or which one cannot fight; irresistible*   ὄρπετον =
ἐρπετόν, *creature*]

Temple of Athena Nike on the Acropolis
The Athenians built this temple in 427–424 B.C.
to commemorate their victories in the Persian Wars.

Classical Greek

Simonides

You have already read two epitaphs that Simonides wrote for the Athenians who died in the war against the Persians (pages 244 and 261); see also the epitaph on page 151. He wrote the following epitaph (no. IX, Campbell) for the Spartans who died at Plataea, where the Greeks defeated the Persian land army in 479 B.C. and ended Xerxes' attempt to conquer Greece.

ἄσβεστον κλέος οἵδε φίλῃ περὶ πατρίδι θέντες

κ̄υάνεον θανάτου ἀμφεβάλοντο νέφος·

οὐδὲ τεθνᾶσι θανόντες, ἐπεὶ σφ' ἀρετὴ καθύπερθε

κ̄υδαίνουσ' ἀνάγει δώματος ἐξ Ἀίδεω.

[ἄσβεστον κλέος, *inextinguishable / imperishable glory*   περὶ...θέντες, *putting* X (acc.) *around* Y (dat.), *crowning* Y *with* X   κ̄υάνεον...νέφος, *the dark cloud* ἀμφεβάλοντο, *they threw around themselves, clothed themselves in*   οὐδὲ τεθνᾶσι θανόντες, *and although having died they are not dead*   ἐπεί, *since*   σφ' = σφε = αὐτούς, *them*   καθύπερθε κ̄υδαίνουσα, *giving* (them) *glory* (τὸ κῦδος) *from* (the earth) *above*   δώματος...Ἀίδεω, *the house of Hades* (= death)]

New Testament Greek

Luke 2.15–20
The Birth of Jesus (concluded)

καὶ ἐγένετο ὡς ἀπῆλθον ἀπ' αὐτῶν εἰς τὸν οὐρανὸν οἱ ἄγγελοι, οἱ ποιμένες ἐλάλουν πρὸς ἀλλήλους, "διέλθωμεν δὴ ἕως Βηθλέεμ καὶ ἴδωμεν τὸ ῥῆμα τοῦτο τὸ γεγονὸς ὃ ὁ κύριος ἐγνώρισεν ἡμῖν. καὶ ἦλθαν σπεύσαντες καὶ ἀνεῦραν τήν τε Μαριὰμ καὶ τὸν Ἰωσὴφ καὶ τὸ βρέφος κείμενον ἐν τῇ φάτνῃ· ἰδόντες δὲ ἐγνώρισαν περὶ τοῦ ῥήματος τοῦ λαληθέντος αὐτοῖς περὶ τοῦ παιδίου τούτου. καὶ πάντες οἱ ἀκούσαντες ἐθαύμασαν περὶ τῶν λαληθέντων ὑπὸ τῶν ποιμένων πρὸς αὐτούς· ἡ δὲ Μαριὰμ πάντα συνετήρει τὰ ῥήματα ταῦτα συμβάλλουσα ἐν τῇ καρδίᾳ αὐτῆς. καὶ ὑπέστρεψαν οἱ ποιμένες δοξάζοντες καὶ αἰνοῦντες τὸν θεὸν ἐπὶ πᾶσιν οἷς ἤκουσαν καὶ εἶδον καθὼς ἐλαλήθη πρὸς αὐτούς.

[οἱ ἄγγελοι, *the angels*   οἱ ποιμένες, *the shepherds*   ἐλάλουν, *were saying* διέλθωμεν, *subjunctive, let us go*   ἕως, *to*   ἴδωμεν, *subjunctive, let us see*   τὸ ῥῆμα, *saying; event, happening*   γεγονὸς, *having happened, that has happened*   ὁ κύριος, *the Lord*   ἐγνώρισεν, *made known*   ἦλθαν...ἀνεῦραν = ἦλθον...ἀνεῦρον τὸ βρέφος, *baby, infant*   τῇ φάτνῃ, *manger, feeding-trough*   λαληθέντος, *that had been spoken*   τοῦ παιδίου, *child, infant*   συνετήρει, *was keeping, remembering* συμβάλλουσα, *thinking about, pondering*   τῇ καρδίᾳ, *the heart*   ὑπέστρεψαν, *turned back, returned home*   δοξάζοντες, *glorifying*   αἰνοῦντες, *praising*   ἐπὶ πᾶσιν οἷς, *for all the things that*   καθὼς, *just as*   ἐλαλήθη, *they had been spoken*]

VERB CHART: PRESENT AND IMPERFECT

Principal Parts of Verb: _____

Exercise Number: _____

Present

Indicative	Subjunctive	Optative	Imperative	Infinitive	Participle
_____	_____	_____	_____	_____	_____
_____	_____	_____	_____		_____
_____	_____	_____			_____
_____	_____	_____	_____		_____
_____	_____	_____	_____		

For participles, fill in the nominative singular, masculine, feminine, and neuter and the genitive singular masculine of participles having 3rd and 1st declension forms.

For middle voice participles, give the masculine nominative singular and the feminine and neuter endings.

Imperfect

_____	_____
_____	
_____	
_____	
_____	

VERB CHART: FUTURE AND AORIST

First Principal Part of Verb: _____

Exercise Number: _____

Future

Indicative	Subjunctive	Optative	Imperative	Infinitive	Participle

Aorist

Indicative	Subjunctive	Optative	Imperative	Infinitive	Participle

SYLLABLES AND ACCENTS

A Greek word has as many syllables as it has vowels and diphthongs, e.g.: ἄν-θρω-πος.

In dividing words into syllables, single consonants go with the following vowel (note -πος in ἄν-θρω-πος above); a group of consonants that cannot stand at the beginning of a word is divided between two syllables (note how the consonants νθρ are divided in ἄν-θρω-πος above); and double consonants are divided between syllables, e.g., θά-λατ-τα.

The final syllable is called the *ultima*, the next to the last, the *penult*, and the third from the end, the *antepenult*. These terms are useful in discussing the placement of accents.

A syllable is said to be long (1) if it contains a long vowel or diphthong or (2) if it contains a short vowel followed by two or more consecutive consonants or by one of the double consonants ζ, ξ, or ψ. Exceptions to these rules are the diphthongs αι and οι, which are regarded as short when they stand as the final element in a word (except in the optative mood, to be studied in Book II, and in a few words such as the adverb οἴκοι, *at home*, and the interjection οἴμοι, *alas!*). Note that η and ω are long vowels, ε and o are short vowels, and α, ι, and υ may be either long or short—when long they are marked with a macron in this book.

For the three types of accents, see Introduction, page xv. The acute accent can stand on any of the last three syllables of a word; the circumflex can stand on either of the last two syllables; and the grave can stand only on the ultima. The grave accent replaces an acute on the ultima when that word is followed immediately by another word with no intervening punctuation, except when the following word is an enclitic (see below).

The accent on finite forms of verbs is *recessive*, i.e., it is placed as far toward the beginning of the word as is allowed by the rule in d1 below. The accent on a noun, adjective, or participle is *persistent*, i.e., it remains as it is in the nominative case unless forced to change by one of the rules in d1 and d2 below. The placement of the accent in the nominative must be learned by observation, e.g.: ἄν-θρω-πος, ὀ-λί-γος, κα-λός, λῡ-ό-με-νος, λῡ́-ων, and λι-πών. In irregular comparative adjectives, the neuter nominative singular shows the natural syllable to be accented, e.g., ἀμείνων, ἄμεινον.

Placement of Accents

a. On the antepenult
   Only an acute accent may stand on the antepenult, e.g.: ἄν-θρω-πος.

b. On the penult
   If the penult is accented, it will have a circumflex if it contains a diphthong or a long vowel and if the vowel or diphthong of the final syllable is short, e.g.: οἶ-κος, οἶ-κοι. Otherwise, it will have an acute, e.g.: ἀν-θρώ-που, πό-νου.

c. On the ultima
   If the ultima is accented, its accent will be an acute (changed to a grave as noted above) or a circumflex (by special rules, particularly in contract verbs).

d. Shifts and changes of accent
   1. The acute cannot stand on the antepenult if the ultima is long. Therefore, ἄν-θρω-πος becomes ἀν-θρώ-που in the genitive case.
   2. Since the circumflex can stand on the accented penult only if the vowel or diphthong of the ultima is short, the circumflex on οἶ-κος changes to an acute in the genitive case (οἴ-κου).

ENCLITICS AND PROCLITICS

Enclitics lean upon the preceding word, and the two words taken together are accented to some extent as if they were one word. Enclitics met in Book I of *Athenaze* include the short forms of the personal pronouns (μου, μοι, με; σου, σοι, σε); the indefinite pronoun and adjective τις, τι; the indefinite adverbs που, πως, ποτέ, ποθέν, and ποι; the particle γε; the conjunction τε; and the forms of εἰμί and φημί in the present indicative (except for the 2nd person singular).

a. An acute accent on the ultima of a word preceding an enclitic does not change to a grave, and the enclitic has no accent, e.g.:

> ἀγρός τις
> ἀγροί τινες.

b. If a circumflex stands on the ultima of a word preceding an enclitic, the enclitic has no accent, e.g.:

> ἀγρῶν τινων

c. A word with an acute on its penult does not change its accent when followed by an enclitic, but a disyllabic enclitic will require an accent on its ultima (an acute accent if the ultima is short and a circumflex if it is long), e.g.:

> πόνος τις
> ἀνθρώπου τινός
> ἀνθρώπων τινῶν

The acute on the ultima of the enclitic will, of course, change to a grave if the enclitic is followed by another word with no intervening punctuation.

d. A word with an acute on its antepenult will need to add an acute to its ultima to support an enclitic, e.g.:

> ἄνθρωπός τις
> ἄνθρωποί τινες

The enclitics need no accents.

e. If a word has a circumflex on its penult, an acute accent is added to its ultima to support a following enclitic, e.g.:

> οἶκός τις
> οἶκοί τινες

f. If an enclitic is followed by another enclitic, the first receives an acute accent but the second does not, e.g.:

> δυνατόν ἐστί σοι

If an enclitic is followed by more than one enclitic, all but the last receive acute accents, e.g.:

> δυνατόν ἐστί σοί ποτε

g. The enclitic ἐστί(ν) receives an acute accent on its penult:
1. when it stands at the beginning of its sentence or clause, e.g., ἔστι λύκος ἐκεῖ. *There's a wolf there.*
2. when it follows οὐκ, e.g., οὐκ ἔστι λύκος ἐκεῖ. *There isn't a wolf there.*
3. when it means *it is possible*, e.g., σπεῦδε, ὦ πάτερ· οὐ γὰρ ἔστιν ἀπελαύνειν τὸν λύκον. *Hurry, father; for it's not possible to drive the wolf away.*

Note: the other enclitic forms of εἰμί retain their accents when they follow οὐκ, and the proclitic has no accent, e.g.: οὐκ εἰμὶ ἀργός. *I am not lazy.* See next page.

Proclitics

Proclitics are words of a single syllable that normally do not have accents, e.g., οὐ and εἰ. The following words are proclitic: the adverbs οὐ, οὐκ, οὐχ; the definite articles ὁ, ἡ, οἱ, and αἱ; the prepositions ἐν, εἰς, ἐκ, and ἐξ; the conjunctions εἰ and ὡς; and the adverb ὡς. When followed by enclitics, they must be accented, e.g.:

εἴ τις

οὔ τις

Exceptions: οὐκ followed by an enclitic form of εἰμί, e.g., οὐκ εἰμὶ ἀργός. *I am not lazy.* See the previous page for οὐκ followed by ἐστί(ν). Here is how the six forms of εἰμί are accented with οὐκ:

οὐκ εἰμί   οὐκ ἐσμέν

οὐκ εἶ   οὐκ ἐστέ

οὐκ ἔστι(ν)   οὐκ εἰσί(ν)

Greek warrior attacking a Persian archer

FORMS

1. THE DEFINITE ARTICLE (see page 50)

	Singular			Plural		
	M.	**F.**	**N.**	**M.**	**F.**	**N.**
N.	ὁ	ἡ	τό	οἱ	αἱ	τά
G.	τοῦ	τῆς	τοῦ	τῶν	τῶν	τῶν
D.	τῷ	τῇ	τῷ	τοῖς	ταῖς	τοῖς
A.	τόν	τήν	τό	τούς	τάς	τά

2. NOUNS OF THE 1ST DECLENSION

Feminine (see pages 40–42)

	Singular		Plural		Singular		Plural	
N.	ἡ	κρήνη	αἱ	κρῆναι	ἡ	ὑδρίᾱ	αἱ	ὑδρίαι
G.	τῆς	κρήνης	τῶν	κρηνῶν	τῆς	ὑδρίᾱς	τῶν	ὑδριῶν
D.	τῇ	κρήνῃ	ταῖς	κρήναις	τῇ	ὑδρίᾳ	ταῖς	ὑδρίαις
A.	τὴν	κρήνην	τὰς	κρήνᾱς	τὴν	ὑδρίᾱν	τὰς	ὑδρίᾱς
V.	ὦ	κρήνη	ὦ	κρῆναι	ὦ	ὑδρίᾱ	ὦ	ὑδρίαι

N.	ἡ	μέλιττᾰ	αἱ	μέλιτται	ἡ	μάχαιρᾰ	αἱ	μάχαιραι
G.	τῆς	μελίττης	τῶν	μελιττῶν	τῆς	μαχαίρᾱς	τῶν	μαχαιρῶν
D.	τῇ	μελίττῃ	ταῖς	μελίτταις	τῇ	μαχαίρᾳ	ταῖς	μαχαίραις
A.	τὴν	μέλιττᾰν	τὰς	μελίττᾱς	τὴν	μάχαιρᾰν	τὰς	μαχαίρᾱς
V.	ὦ	μέλιττᾰ	ὦ	μέλιτται	ὦ	μάχαιρᾰ	ὦ	μάχαιραι

Masculine (see pages 47–48)

	Singular		Plural		Singular		Plural	
N.	ὁ	δεσπότης	οἱ	δεσπόται	ὁ	νεᾱνίᾱς	οἱ	νεᾱνίαι
G.	τοῦ	δεσπότου	τῶν	δεσποτῶν	τοῦ	νεᾱνίου	τῶν	νεᾱνιῶν
D.	τῷ	δεσπότῃ	τοῖς	δεσπόταις	τῷ	νεᾱνίᾳ	τοῖς	νεᾱνίαις
A.	τὸν	δεσπότην	τοὺς	δεσπότᾱς	τὸν	νεᾱνίᾱν	τοὺς	νεᾱνίᾱς
V.	ὦ	δέσποτα*	ὦ	δεσπόται	ὦ	νεᾱνίᾱ	ὦ	νεᾱνίαι

*Irregular accent. Normally the accent is persistent as with the noun ὁ πολίτης, vocative, ὦ πολῖτα.

3. NOUNS OF THE 2ND DECLENSION

Masculine (see page 31)

	Singular		Plural	
N.	ὁ	ἀγρός	οἱ	ἀγροί
G	τοῦ	ἀγροῦ	τῶν	ἀγρῶν
D.	τῷ	ἀγρῷ	τοῖς	ἀγροῖς
A.	τὸν	ἀγρόν	τοὺς	ἀγρούς
V.	ὦ	ἀγρέ	ὦ	ἀγροί

Neuter (see page 31)

	Singular		Plural	
N.	τὸ	δένδρον	τὰ	δένδρα
G	τοῦ	δένδρου	τῶν	δένδρων
D.	τῷ	δένδρῳ	τοῖς	δένδροις
A.	τὸ	δένδρον	τὰ	δένδρα
V.	ὦ	δένδρον	ὦ	δένδρα

Feminine: e.g., ἡ ὁδός (see page 48)

Contract: Masculine (see page 263):

	Singular		Plural	
N.	ὁ	νοῦς	οἱ	νοῖ
G.	τοῦ	νοῦ	τῶν	νῶν
D.	τῷ	νῷ	τοῖς	νοῖς
A.	τὸν	νοῦν	τοὺς	νοῦς
V.	ὦ	νοῦ	ὦ	νοῖ

Attic Declension

	Singular		Plural	
N.	ὁ	λαγώς	οἱ	λαγώ
G.	τοῦ	λαγώ	τῶν	λαγών
D.	τῷ	λαγώ	τοῖς	λαγώς
A.	τὸν	λαγών/ώ	τοὺς	λαγώς
V.	ὦ	λαγώς	ὦ	λαγώ

Contract Neuter: τὸ κανοῦν (rare; not formally presented in this course; for an example, see κανᾶ, 9β:6)

4. NOUNS OF THE 3RD DECLENSION

Labial Stems (β, π, φ; see page 107)

	Singular		Plural	
N.	ὁ	κλώψ	οἱ	κλῶπες
G.	τοῦ	κλωπός	τῶν	κλωπῶν
D.	τῷ	κλωπί	τοῖς	κλωψί(ν)
A.	τὸν	κλῶπα	τοὺς	κλῶπας
V.	ὦ	κλώψ	ὦ	κλῶπες

Velar Stems (γ, κ, χ; see page 98)

	Singular		Plural			Singular		Plural	
N.	ὁ	φύλαξ	οἱ	φύλακες	ὁ	αἴξ	οἱ	αἶγες
G.	τοῦ	φύλακος	τῶν	φυλάκων	τοῦ	αἰγός	τῶν	αἰγῶν
D.	τῷ	φύλακι	τοῖς	φύλαξι(ν)	τῷ	αἰγί	τοῖς	αἰξί(ν)
A.	τὸν	φύλακα	τοὺς	φύλακας	τὸν	αἶγα	τοὺς	αἶγας
V.	ὦ	φύλαξ	ὦ	φύλακες	ὦ	αἴξ	ὦ	αἶγες

Dental Stems (δ, θ, τ; see page 99)

	Singular		Plural		Singular		Plural
N.	ὁ	παῖς	οἱ	παῖδες	τὸ	ὄνομα	τὰ	ὀνόματα
G.	τοῦ	παιδός	τῶν	παίδων	τοῦ	ὀνόματος	τῶν	ὀνομάτων
D.	τῷ	παιδί	τοῖς	παισί(ν)	τῷ	ὀνόματι	τοῖς	ὀνόμασι(ν)
A.	τὸν	παῖδα	τοὺς	παῖδας	τὸ	ὄνομα	τὰ	ὀνόματα
V.	ὦ	παῖ	ὦ	παῖδες	ὦ	ὄνομα	ὦ	ὀνόματα

Stems in -ντ- (see page 145)

	Singular		Plural	
N.	ὁ	γέρων	οἱ	γέροντες
G.	τοῦ	γέροντος	τῶν	γερόντων
D.	τῷ	γέροντι	τοῖς	γέρουσι(ν)
A.	τὸν	γέροντα	τοὺς	γέροντας
V.	ὦ	γέρον	ὦ	γέροντες

Liquid Stems (λ, ρ; see page 107)   Nasal Stems (ν; see pages 106–107)

	Singular		Plural		Singular		Plural	
N.	ὁ	ῥήτωρ	οἱ	ῥήτορες	ὁ	χειμών	οἱ	χειμῶνες
G.	τοῦ	ῥήτορος	τῶν	ῥητόρων	τοῦ	χειμῶνος	τῶν	χειμώνων
D.	τῷ	ῥήτορι	τοῖς	ῥήτορσι(ν)	τῷ	χειμῶνι	τοῖς	χειμῶσι(ν)
A.	τὸν	ῥήτορα	τοὺς	ῥήτορας	τὸν	χειμῶνα	τοὺς	χειμῶνας
V.	ὦ	ῥήτωρ	ὦ	ῥήτορες	ὦ	χειμών	ὦ	χειμῶνες

Stems in -ρ- (see pages 124–125)

Singular

N.	ὁ	ἀνήρ	ὁ	πατήρ	ἡ	μήτηρ	ἡ	θυγάτηρ
G.	τοῦ	ἀνδρός	τοῦ	πατρός	τῆς	μητρός	τῆς	θυγατρός
D.	τῷ	ἀνδρί	τῷ	πατρί	τῇ	μητρί	τῇ	θυγατρί
A.	τὸν	ἄνδρα	τὸν	πατέρα	τὴν	μητέρα	τὴν	θυγατέρα
V.	ὦ	ἄνερ	ὦ	πάτερ	ὦ	μῆτερ	ὦ	θύγατερ

Plural

N.	οἱ	ἄνδρες	οἱ	πατέρες	αἱ	μητέρες	αἱ	θυγατέρες
G.	τῶν	ἀνδρῶν	τῶν	πατέρων	τῶν	μητέρων	τῶν	θυγατέρων
D.	τοῖς	ἀνδράσι(ν)	τοῖς	πατράσι(ν)	ταῖς	μητράσι(ν)	ταῖς	θυγατράσι(ν)
A.	τοὺς	ἄνδρας	τοὺς	πατέρας	τὰς	μητέρας	τὰς	θυγατέρας
V.	ὦ	ἄνδρες	ὦ	πατέρες	ὦ	μητέρες	ὦ	θυγατέρες

Stems in -εσ- (see pages 226–227)

	Singular		Plural		Singular		Plural
N.	τὸ	τεῖχος	τὰ	τείχη	ἡ	τριήρης	αἱ	τριήρεις
G.	τοῦ	τείχους	τῶν	τειχῶν	τῆς	τριήρους	τῶν	τριήρων
D.	τῷ	τείχει	τοῖς	τείχεσι(ν)	τῇ	τριήρει	ταῖς	τριήρεσι(ν
A.	τὸ	τεῖχος	τὰ	τείχη	τὴν	τριήρη	τὰς	τριήρεις
V.	ὦ	τεῖχος	ὦ	τείχη	ὦ	τριῆρες	ὦ	τριήρεις

Also ὁ Θεμιστοκλῆς (see page 254)

N.	ὁ	Θεμιστοκλῆς
G.	τοῦ	Θεμιστοκλέους
D.	τῷ	Θεμιστοκλεῖ
A.	τὸν	Θεμιστοκλέᾱ
V.	ὦ	Θεμιστόκλεις

Stems Ending in a Vowel (see page 145)

	Singular		Plural		Singular		Plural	
N.	ἡ	πόλις	αἱ	πόλεις	τὸ	ἄστυ	τὰ	ἄστη
G.	τῆς	πόλεως	τῶν	πόλεων	τοῦ	ἄστεως	τῶν	ἄστεων
D.	τῇ	πόλει	ταῖς	πόλεσι(ν)	τῷ	ἄστει	τοῖς	ἄστεσι(ν)
A.	τὴν	πόλιν	τὰς	πόλεις	τὸ	ἄστυ	τὰ	ἄστη
V.	ὦ	πόλι	ὦ	πόλεις	ὦ	ἄστυ	ὦ	ἄστη

Stems in Diphthongs or Vowels (see page 146)

	Singular		Plural	
N.	ὁ	βασιλεύς	οἱ	βασιλῆς
G.	τοῦ	βασιλέως	τῶν	βασιλέων
D.	τῷ	βασιλεῖ	τοῖς	βασιλεῦσι(ν)
A.	τὸν	βασιλέᾱ	τοὺς	βασιλέᾱς
V.	ὦ	βασιλεῦ	ὦ	βασιλῆς

Irregular

	Singular		Plural		Singular		Plural	
N.	ἡ	ναῦς	αἱ	νῆες	ὁ	βοῦς	οἱ	βόες
G.	τῆς	νεώς	τῶν	νεῶν	τοῦ	βοός	τῶν	βοῶν
D.	τῇ	νηΐ	ταῖς	ναυσί(ν)	τῷ	βοΐ	τοῖς	βουσί(ν)
A.	τὴν	ναῦν	τὰς	ναῦς	τὸν	βοῦν	τοὺς	βοῦς
V.	ὦ	ναῦ	ὦ	νῆες	ὦ	βοῦ	ὦ	βόες

Irregular (see page 125)

	Singular	Plural		Singular	Plural
N.	ἡ γυνή	αἱ γυναῖκες	ἡ χείρ	αἱ χεῖρες
G.	τῆς γυναικός	τῶν γυναικῶν	τῆς χειρός	τῶν χειρῶν
D.	τῇ γυναικί	ταῖς γυναιξί(ν)	τῇ χειρί	ταῖς χερσί(ν)
A.	τὴν γυναῖκα	τὰς γυναῖκας	τὴν χεῖρα	τὰς χεῖρας
V.	ὦ γύναι	ὦ γυναῖκες	ὦ χείρ	ὦ χεῖρες

5. **ADJECTIVES AND PARTICIPLES OF THE 1ST AND 2ND DECLENSIONS**

Adjectives (see pages 48–49)

	Singular			Plural		
	M.	**F.**	**N.**	**M.**	**F.**	**N.**
N.	καλός	καλή	καλόν	καλοί	καλαί	καλά
G.	καλοῦ	καλῆς	καλοῦ	καλῶν	καλῶν	καλῶν
D.	καλῷ	καλῇ	καλῷ	καλοῖς	καλαῖς	καλοῖς
A.	καλόν	καλήν	καλόν	καλούς	καλάς	καλά
V.	καλέ	καλή	καλόν	καλοί	καλαί	καλά

	Singular			Plural		
	M.	**F.**	**N.**	**M.**	**F.**	**N.**
N.	ῥᾴδιος	ῥᾳδίᾱ	ῥᾴδιον	ῥᾴδιοι	ῥᾴδιαι	ῥᾴδια
G.	ῥᾳδίου	ῥᾳδίᾱς	ῥᾳδίου	ῥᾳδίων	ῥᾳδίων	ῥᾳδίων
D.	ῥᾳδίῳ	ῥᾳδίᾳ	ῥᾳδίῳ	ῥᾳδίοις	ῥᾳδίαις	ῥᾳδίοις
A.	ῥᾴδιον	ῥᾳδίᾱν	ῥᾴδιον	ῥᾳδίους	ῥᾳδίᾱς	ῥᾴδια
V.	ῥᾴδιε	ῥᾳδίᾱ	ῥᾴδιον	ῥᾴδιοι	ῥᾴδιαι	ῥᾴδια

Present or Progressive Middle Participles (see pages 115–116 and 262)

	Masculine	Feminine	Neuter
	Singular		
N.	λῡόμενος	λῡομένη	λῡόμενον
G.	λῡομένου	λῡομένης	λῡομένου
D.	λῡομένῳ	λῡομένῃ	λῡομένῳ
A.	λῡόμενον	λῡομένην	λῡόμενον
V.	λῡόμενε	λῡομένη	λῡόμενον
	Plural		
N., V.	λῡόμενοι	λῡόμεναι	λῡόμενα
G.	λῡομένων	λῡομένων	λῡομένων
D.	λῡομένοις	λῡομέναις	λῡομένοις
A.	λῡομένους	λῡομένᾱς	λῡόμενα

Singular

N.	φιλούμενος	φιλουμένη	φιλούμενον
G.	φιλουμένου	φιλουμένης	φιλουμένου
D.	φιλουμένῳ	φιλουμένῃ	φιλουμένῳ
A.	φιλούμενον	φιλουμένην	φιλούμενον
V	φιλούμενε	φιλουμένη	φιλούμενον

Plural

N., V.	φιλούμενοι	φιλούμεναι	φιλούμενα
G.	φιλουμένων	φιλουμένων	φιλουμένων
D.	φιλουμένοις	φιλουμέναις	φιλουμένοις
A.	φιλουμένους	φιλουμένᾱς	φιλούμενα

Exempli gratia:

| N. | τῑμώμενος | τῑμωμένη | τῑμώμενον |

Exempli gratia:

| N. | δηλούμενος | δηλουμένη | δηλούμενον |

Sigmatic 1st Aorist and Thematic 2nd Aorist Middle Participles (see pages 199 and 180)

Exempli gratia:

| N. | λῡσάμενος | λῡσαμένη | λῡσάμενον |

| N. | γενόμενος | γενομένη | γενόμενον |

6.   ADJECTIVES OF IRREGULAR DECLENSION (see page 49)

	Singular			**Plural**		
	M.	**F.**	**N.**	**M.**	**F.**	**N.**
N.	μέγας	μεγάλη	μέγα	μεγάλοι	μεγάλαι	μεγάλα
G.	μεγάλου	μεγάλης	μεγάλου	μεγάλων	μεγάλων	μεγάλων
D.	μεγάλῳ	μεγάλῃ	μεγάλῳ	μεγάλοις	μεγάλαις	μεγάλοις
A.	μέγαν	μεγάλην	μέγα	μεγάλους	μεγάλᾱς	μεγάλα
V.	μέγαλε	μεγάλη	μέγα	μεγάλοι	μεγάλαι	μεγάλα
N.	πολύς	πολλή	πολύ	πολλοί	πολλαί	πολλά
G.	πολλοῦ	πολλῆς	πολλοῦ	πολλῶν	πολλῶν	πολλῶν
D.	πολλῷ	πολλῇ	πολλῷ	πολλοῖς	πολλαῖς	πολλοῖς
A.	πολύν	πολλήν	πολύ	πολλούς	πολλάς	πολλά
V.	none					

7. ADJECTIVES OF THE 3RD DECLENSION

Adjectives with Stems in -ον- (see pages 107–108)

	Singular		**Plural**	
	M. & F.	**N.**	**M. & F.**	**N.**
N.	σώφρων	σῶφρον	σώφρονες	σώφρονα
G.	σώφρονος	σώφρονος	σωφρόνων	σωφρόνων
D.	σώφρονι	σώφρονι	σώφροσι(ν)	σώφροσι(ν)
A.	σώφρονα	σῶφρον	σώφρονας	σώφρονα
V.	σῶφρον	σῶφρον	σώφρονες	σώφρονα

Irregular comparative adjectives, such as ἀμείνων, ἄμεινον (see page 235), are declined like σώφρων, σῶφρον, but have some alternative forms that will be presented in Book II.

Adjectives with Stems in -εσ- (see page 227):

		M. & F.	**N.**
S.	**N.**	ἀληθής	ἀληθές
	G.	ἀληθοῦς	ἀληθοῦς
	D.	ἀληθεῖ	ἀληθεῖ
	A.	ἀληθῆ	ἀληθές
	V.	ἀληθές	ἀληθές
P.	**N.**	ἀληθεῖς	ἀληθῆ
	G.	ἀληθῶν	ἀληθῶν
	D.	ἀληθέσι(ν)	ἀληθέσι(ν)
	A.	ἀληθεῖς	ἀληθῆ
	V.	ἀληθεῖς	ἀληθῆ

8. ADJECTIVES AND PARTICIPLES OF 1ST AND 3RD DECLENSIONS

Adjectives

πᾶς, πᾶσα, πᾶν, *all; every; whole* (see page 126).

		Masculine	**Feminine**	**Neuter**
S.	**N., V.**	πᾶς	πᾶσα	πᾶν
	G.	παντός	πάσης	παντός
	D.	παντί	πάσῃ	παντί
	A.	πάντα	πᾶσαν	πᾶν
P.	**N., V.**	πάντες	πᾶσαι	πάντα
	G.	πάντων	πασῶν	πάντων
	D.	πᾶσι(ν)	πάσαις	πᾶσι(ν)
	A.	πάντας	πάσᾱς	πάντα

ταχύς, ταχεῖα, ταχύ, *quick, swift* (see pages 227–228)

		Masculine	Feminine	Neuter
S.	N.	ταχύς	ταχεῖα	ταχύ
	G.	ταχέος	ταχείᾱς	ταχέος
	D.	ταχεῖ	ταχείᾳ	ταχεῖ
	A.	ταχύν	ταχεῖαν	ταχύ
	V.	ταχύ	ταχεῖα	ταχύ
P.	N.	ταχεῖς	ταχεῖαι	ταχέα
	G.	ταχέων	ταχειῶν	ταχέων
	D.	ταχέσι(ν)	ταχείαις	ταχέσι(ν)
	A.	ταχεῖς	ταχείᾱς	ταχέα
	V.	ταχεῖς	ταχεῖαι	ταχέα

Present or Progressive Active Participles

		Masculine	Feminine	Neuter
εἰμί (see page 136):				
S.	N., V.	ὤν	οὖσα	ὄν
	G.	ὄντος	οὔσης	ὄντος
	D.	ὄντι	οὔσῃ	ὄντι
	A.	ὄντα	οὖσαν	ὄν
P.	N., V.	ὄντες	οὖσαι	ὄντα
	G.	ὄντων	οὐσῶν	ὄντων
	D.	οὖσι(ν)	οὔσαις	οὖσι(ν)
	A.	ὄντας	οὔσᾱς	ὄντα
λύω (see page 136):				
S.	N., V.	λύων	λύουσα	λῦον
	G.	λύοντος	λῡούσης	λύοντος
	D.	λύοντι	λῡούσῃ	λύοντι
	A.	λύοντα	λύουσαν	λῦον
P.	N., V.	λύοντες	λύουσαι	λύοντα
	G.	λῡόντων	λῡουσῶν	λῡόντων
	D.	λύουσι(ν)	λῡούσαις	λύουσι(ν)
	A.	λύοντας	λῡούσᾱς	λύοντα
φιλέω (see page 136):				
S.	N., V.	φιλῶν	φιλοῦσα	φιλοῦν
	G.	φιλοῦντος	φιλούσης	φιλοῦντος
	D.	φιλοῦντι	φιλούσῃ	φιλοῦντι
	A.	φιλοῦντα	φιλοῦσαν	φιλοῦν

P.	N., V.	φιλοῦντες	φιλοῦσαι	φιλοῦντα
	G.	φιλούντων	φιλουσῶν	φιλούντων
	D.	φιλοῦσι(ν)	φιλούσαις	φιλοῦσι(ν)
	A.	φιλοῦντας	φιλούσᾱς	φιλοῦντα

τῑμάω (see pages 136–137):

S.	N., V.	τῑμῶν	τῑμῶσα	τῑμῶν
	G.	τῑμῶντος	τῑμώσης	τῑμῶντος
	D.	τῑμῶντι	τῑμώσῃ	τῑμῶντι
	A.	τῑμῶντα	τῑμῶσαν	τῑμῶν
P.	N., V.	τῑμῶντες	τῑμῶσαι	τῑμῶντα
	G.	τῑμώντων	τῑμωσῶν	τῑμώντων
	D.	τῑμῶσι(ν)	τῑμώσαις	τῑμῶσι(ν)
	A.	τῑμῶντας	τῑμώσᾱς	τῑμῶντα

δηλόω (see page 262; declined like φιλῶν above; we give only the nominative):

	δηλῶν	δηλοῦσα	δηλοῦν

Sigmatic 1st Aorist Active Participles (see page 199)

S.	N., V.	λύσᾱς	λύσᾱσα	λῦσαν
	G.	λύσαντος	λῡσά̄σης	λύσαντος
	D.	λύσαντι	λῡσά̄σῃ	λύσαντι
	A.	λύσαντα	λύσᾱσαν	λῦσαν
P.	N., V.	λύσαντες	λύσᾱσαι	λύσαντα
	G.	λῡσάντων	λῡσά̄σῶν	λῡσάντων
	D.	λύσᾱσι(ν)	λῡσά̄σαις	λύσᾱσι(ν)
	A.	λύσαντας	λῡσά̄σᾱς	λύσαντα

Thematic 2nd Aorist Active Participles (see page 180)

S.	N., V.	λιπών	λιποῦσα	λιπόν
	G.	λιπόντος	λιπούσης	λιπόντος
	D.	λιπόντι	λιπούσῃ	λιπόντι
	A.	λιπόντα	λιποῦσαν	λιπόν
P.	N., V.	λιπόντες	λιποῦσαι	λιπόντα
	G.	λιπόντων	λιπουσῶν	λιπόντων
	D.	λιποῦσι(ν)	λιπούσαις	λιποῦσι(ν)
	A.	λιπόντας	λιπούσᾱς	λιπόντα

9. COMPARISON OF ADJECTIVES

Positive	Comparative	Superlative

Regular (see pages 234–235)

1st and 2nd Declension

ἀνδρεῖος	ἀνδρειότερος	ἀνδρειότατος
χαλεπός	χαλεπώτερος	χαλεπώτατος

3rd Declension

ἀληθής	ἀληθέστερος	ἀληθέστατος
σώφρων	σωφρονέστερος	σωφρονέστατος

Irregular (see page 235)

ἀγαθός, -ή, -όν	ἀμείνων, ἄμεινον	ἄριστος, -η, -ον
κακός, -ή, -όν	κακίων, κάκιον	κάκιστος, -η, -ον
καλός, -ή, -όν	καλλίων, κάλλιον	κάλλιστος, -η, -ον
μέγας, μεγάλη, μέγα	μείζων, μεῖζον	μέγιστος, -η, -ον
ὀλίγος, -η, -ον	ἐλάττων, ἔλαττον	ὀλίγιστος, -η, -ον
πολύς, πολλή, πολύ	πλείων/πλέων, πλεῖον/πλέον	πλεῖστος, -η, -ον

10. DEMONSTRATIVE ADJECTIVES

οὗτος, αὕτη, τοῦτο, *this* (see pages 244–245)

	Singular			Plural		
	M.	**F.**	**N.**	**M.**	**F.**	**N.**
N.	οὗτος	αὕτη	τοῦτο	οὗτοι	αὗται	ταῦτα
G.	τούτου	ταύτης	τούτου	τούτων	τούτων	τούτων
D.	τούτῳ	ταύτῃ	τούτῳ	τούτοις	ταύταις	τούτοις
A.	τοῦτον	ταύτην	τοῦτο	τούτους	ταύτᾱς	ταῦτα

ἐκεῖνος, ἐκείνη, ἐκεῖνο, *that* (see page 245):

	Singular			Plural		
	M.	**F.**	**N.**	**M.**	**F.**	**N.**
N.	ἐκεῖνος	ἐκείνη	ἐκεῖνο	ἐκεῖνοι	ἐκεῖναι	ἐκεῖνα
G.	ἐκείνου	ἐκείνης	ἐκείνου	ἐκείνων	ἐκείνων	ἐκείνων
D.	ἐκείνῳ	ἐκείνῃ	ἐκείνῳ	ἐκείνοις	ἐκείναις	ἐκείνοις
A.	ἐκεῖνον	ἐκείνην	ἐκεῖνο	ἐκείνους	ἐκείνᾱς	ἐκεῖνα

ὅδε, ἥδε, τόδε, *this here* (see page 245):

	Singular			Plural		
	M.	**F.**	**N.**	**M.**	**F.**	**N.**
N.	ὅδε	ἥδε	τόδε	οἵδε	αἵδε	τάδε
G.	τοῦδε	τῆσδε	τοῦδε	τῶνδε	τῶνδε	τῶνδε
D.	τῷδε	τῇδε	τῷδε	τοῖσδε	ταῖσδε	τοῖσδε
A.	τόνδε	τήνδε	τόδε	τούσδε	τάσδε	τάδε

11. THE ADJECTIVE αὐτός, -ή, -ό, -self, -selves; same (see pages 68–69)

		Masculine	Feminine	Neuter
S.	N.	αὐτός	αὐτή	αὐτό
	G.	αὐτοῦ	αὐτῆς	αὐτοῦ
	D.	αὐτῷ	αὐτῇ	αὐτῷ
	A.	αὐτόν	αὐτήν	αὐτό
P.	N.	αὐτοί	αὐταί	αὐτά
	G.	αὐτῶν	αὐτῶν	αὐτῶν
	D.	αὐτοῖς	αὐταῖς	αὐτοῖς
	A.	αὐτούς	αὐτάς	αὐτά

12. THE INTERROGATIVE ADJECTIVE (see page 108)

	Singular		Plural	
	M. & F.	N.	M. & F.	N.
N.	τίς	τί	τίνες	τίνα
G.	τίνος	τίνος	τίνων	τίνων
D.	τίνι	τίνι	τίσι(ν)	τίσι(ν)
A.	τίνα	τί	τίνας	τίνα

13. THE INDEFINITE ADJECTIVE (see page 109)

	Singular		Plural	
	M. & F.	N.	M. & F.	N.
N.	τις	τι	τινές	τινά
G.	τινός	τινός	τινῶν	τινῶν
D.	τινί	τινί	τισί(ν)	τισί(ν)
A.	τινά	τι	τινάς	τινά

14 NUMERICAL ADJECTIVES (see pages 128 and 263–264)

Cardinals

1	εἷς, μία, ἕν	11	ἕνδεκα
2	δύο	12	δώδεκα
3	τρεῖς, τρία	13	τρεῖς (τρία) καὶ δέκα or τρεισκαίδεκα
4	τέτταρες, τέτταρα	14	τέτταρες (τέτταρα) καὶ δέκα
5	πέντε	15	πεντεκαίδεκα
6	ἕξ	16	ἑκκαίδεκα
7	ἑπτά	17	ἑπτακαίδεκα
8	ὀκτώ	18	ὀκτωκαίδεκα
9	ἐννέα	19	ἐννεακαίδεκα
10	δέκα	20	εἴκοσι(ν)

	21	εἷς καὶ εἴκοσι(ν)
	100	ἑκατόν
	1,000	χίλιοι, -αι, -α
	10,000	μύριοι, -αι, -α

	M.	**F.**	**N.**
N.	εἷς	μία	ἕν
G.	ἑνός	μιᾶς	ἑνός
D.	ἑνί	μιᾷ	ἑνί
A.	ἕνα	μίαν	ἕν

	M. F. N.	**M. F.**	**N.**	**M. F.**	**N.**
N.	δύο	τρεῖς	τρία	τέτταρες	τέτταρα
G.	δυοῖν	τριῶν	τριῶν	τεττάρων	τεττάρων
D.	δυοῖν	τρισί(ν)	τρισί(ν)	τέτταρσι(ν)	τέτταρσι(ν)
A.	δύο	τρεῖς	τρία	τέτταρας	τέτταρα

Ordinals

1st	πρῶτος, -η, -ον	9th	ἔνατος, -η, -ον
2nd	δεύτερος, -ᾱ, -ον	10th	δέκατος, -η, -ον
3rd	τρίτος, -η, -ον	11th	ἑνδέκατος, -η, -ον
4th	τέταρτος, -η, -ον	12th	δωδέκατος, -η, -ον
5th	πέμπτος, -η, -ον	20th	εἰκοστός, -ή, -όν
6th	ἕκτος, -η, -ον	100th	ἑκατοστός, -ή, -όν
7th	ἕβδομος, -η, -ον	1,000th	χῑλιοστός, -ή, -όν
8th	ὄγδοος, -η, -ον	10,000th	μῡριοστός, -ή, -όν

15. PERSONAL PRONOUNS (see pages 64–65)

1st Person Singular

N.	ἐγώ		*I*
G.	ἐμοῦ	μου	*of me*
D.	ἐμοί	μοι	*to or for me*
A.	ἐμέ	με	*me*

1st Person Plural

ἡμεῖς	*we*
ἡμῶν	*of us*
ἡμῖν	*to or for us*
ἡμᾶς	*us*

2nd Person Singular

N.	σύ		*you*
G.	σοῦ	σου	*of you*
D.	σοί	σοι	*to or for you*
A.	σέ	σε	*you*

2nd Person Plural

ὑμεῖς	*you*
ὑμῶν	*of you*
ὑμῖν	*to or for you*
ὑμᾶς	*you*

3rd Person

		Masculine		**Feminine**		**Neuter**	
S.	G.	αὐτοῦ	of him or it	αὐτῆς	of her or it	αὐτοῦ	of it
	D.	αὐτῷ	to or for him or it	αὐτῇ	to or for her or it	αὐτῷ	to it
	A.	αὐτόν	him or it	αὐτήν	her or it	αὐτό	it
P.	G.	αὐτῶν	of them	αὐτῶν	of them	αὐτῶν	of them
	D.	αὐτοῖς	to or for them	αὐταῖς	to or for them	αὐτοῖς	to or for them
	A.	αὐτούς	them	αὐτάς	them	αὐτά	them

16. REFLEXIVE PRONOUNS (see pages 100–101)

		1st Person		**2nd Person**	
		Masculine	**Feminine**	**Masculine**	**Feminine**
S.	G.	ἐμαυτοῦ	ἐμαυτῆς	σεαυτοῦ	σεαυτῆς
	D.	ἐμαυτῷ	ἐμαυτῇ	σεαυτῷ	σεαυτῇ
	A.	ἐμαυτόν	ἐμαυτήν	σεαυτόν	σεαυτήν
P.	G.	ἡμῶν αὐτῶν	ἡμῶν αὐτῶν	ὑμῶν αὐτῶν	ὑμῶν αὐτῶν
	D.	ἡμῖν αὐτοῖς	ἡμῖν αὐταῖς	ὑμῖν αὐτοῖς	ὑμῖν αὐταῖς
	A.	ἡμᾶς αὐτούς	ἡμᾶς αὐτάς	ὑμᾶς αὐτούς	ὑμᾶς αὐτάς

		3rd Person		
		Masculine	**Feminine**	**Neuter**
S.	G.	ἐαυτοῦ	ἐαυτῆς	ἐαυτοῦ
	D.	ἐαυτῷ	ἐαυτῇ	ἐαυτῷ
	A.	ἐαυτόν	ἐαυτήν	ἐαυτό
P.	G.	ἐαυτῶν	ἐαυτῶν	ἐαυτῶν
	D.	ἐαυτοῖς	ἐαυταῖς	ἐαυτοῖς
	A.	ἐαυτούς	ἐαυτάς	ἐαυτά

17. THE RECIPROCAL PRONOUN

	Masculine	**Feminine**	**Neuter**
G.	ἀλλήλων	ἀλλήλων	ἀλλήλων
D.	ἀλλήλοις	ἀλλήλαις	ἀλλήλοις
A.	ἀλλήλους	ἀλλήλᾱς	ἄλληλα

18. POSSESSIVES (see pages 66–67)

Possessive Adjectives

	Singular	**Plural**
1st Person	ἐμός, -ή, -όν, *my, mine*	ἡμέτερος, -ᾱ, -ον, *our, ours*
2nd Person	σός, -ή, -όν, *your, yours*	ὑμέτερος, -ᾱ, -ον, *your, yours*

Possessive Pronouns (used for 3rd person possessives)

Singular

M.	αὐτοῦ, *of him, his; of it, its*
F.	αὐτῆς, *of her, her; of it, its*
N.	αὐτοῦ, *of it, its*

Plural

M., F., N.	αὐτῶν, *of them, their*

19.   THE INTERROGATIVE PRONOUN

For the interrogative pronoun τίς, τί, *who? what?* see page 108.   Its forms are the same as those of the interrogative adjective (see above) and are not repeated here; it always has an acute accent on the first syllable.

20.   THE INDEFINITE PRONOUN

For the indefinite pronoun τις, τι, *someone; something; anyone; anything,* see page 109.   This pronoun is enclitic, and it has the same forms as the indefinite adjective (see above).

21.   THE RELATIVE PRONOUN (see pages 224–225)

	Singular			**Plural**		
	M.	**F.**	**N.**	**M.**	**F.**	**N.**
N.	ὅς	ἥ	ὅ	οἵ	αἵ	ἅ
G.	οὗ	ἧς	οὗ	ὧν	ὧν	ὧν
D.	ᾧ	ᾗ	ᾧ	οἷς	αἷς	οἷς
A.	ὅν	ἥν	ὅ	οὕς	ἅς	ἅ

22   FORMATION OF ADVERBS (see page 50)

Adverbs regularly have the same spelling and accent as the genitive plural of the corresponding adjective, but with the final ν changed to ς:

Adjective καλός (genitive plural, καλῶν) > adverb καλῶς

Adjective σώφρων (genitive plural, σωφρόνων) > adverb σωφρόνως

Adjective ἀληθής (genitive plural, ἀληθῶν) > adverb ἀληθῶς

Adjective ταχύς (genitive plural, ταχέων) > adverb ταχέως

23. COMPARISON OF ADVERBS (see page 236)

For the comparative adverb the neuter singular of the comparative adjective is used, and for the superlative the neuter plural of the superlative adjective:

Regular

ἀνδρείως	ἀνδρειότερον	ἀνδρειότατα
χαλεπῶς	χαλεπώτερον	χαλεπώτατα
ἀληθῶς	ἀληθέστερον	ἀληθέστατα
σωφρόνως	σωφρονέστερον	σωφρονέστατα

Irregular

εὖ	ἄμεινον	ἄριστα
κακῶς	κάκῑον	κάκιστα
πόλυ	πλέον	πλεῖστα
μάλα	μᾶλλον	μάλιστα

Verbs

24. VERBS WITH THEMATIC PRESENTS, SIGMATIC FUTURES, AND SIGMATIC 1ST AORISTS

λύω, λύσω, ἔλῡσα, *I loosen, loose;* middle, *I ransom*

PRESENT ACTIVE (THEMATIC) (see pages 38 and 136)

Indicative	Imperative	Infinitive	Participle
λύω		λύειν	λύων,
λύεις	λῦε		λύουσα,
λύει			λῦον,
λύομεν			gen., λῦοντος, etc.
λύετε	λύετε		
λύουσι(ν)			

PRESENT MIDDLE/PASSIVE (THEMATIC) (see pages 77 and 115)

λύομαι		λύεσθαι	λῡόμενος, -η, -ον
λύει or λύῃ	λύου		
λύεται			
λῡόμεθα			
λύεσθε	λύεσθε		
λύονται			

IMPERFECT ACTIVE (THEMATIC) (see page 214)

ἔλῡον
ἔλῡες
ἔλῡε(ν)
ἐλύομεν
ἐλύετε
ἔλῡον

IMPERFECT MIDDLE/PASSIVE (THEMATIC) (see page 214)

Indicative

ἐλῡόμην
ἐλῡου
ἐλῡετο
ἐλῡόμεθα
ἐλῡεσθε
ἐλῡοντο

SIGMATIC FUTURE ACTIVE (THEMATIC) (see page 158; for consonant-stem verbs, see pages 158–159)

Indicative	**Infinitive**	**Participle**
λῡσω	λῡσειν	λῡσων,
λῡσεις		λῡσουσα,
λῡσει		λῦσον,
λῡσομεν		gen., λῡσοντος, etc.
λῡσετε		
λῡσουσι(ν)		

SIGMATIC FUTURE MIDDLE (THEMATIC) (see page 158; for consonant-stem verbs, see pages 158–159)

	Infinitive	**Participle**
λῡσομαι	λῡσεσθαι	λῡσόμενος, -η, -ον
λῡσει or λῡσῃ		
λῡσεται		
λῡσόμεθα		
λῡσεσθε		
λῡσονται		

SIGMATIC 1ST AORIST ACTIVE (see page 196; for consonant-stem verbs, see pages 197–198)

Indicative	**Imperative**	**Infinitive**	**Participle**
ἔλῡσα		λῦσαι	λῡσᾱς,
ἔλῡσας	λῦσον		λῡσᾱσα,
ἔλῡσε(ν)			λῦσαν,
ἐλῡσαμεν			gen., λῡσαντος, etc.
ἐλῡσατε	λῡσατε		
ἔλῡσαν			

SIGMATIC 1ST AORIST MIDDLE (see page 197; for consonant-stem verbs, see pages 197–198)

		Infinitive	**Participle**
ἐλῡσάμην		λῡσασθαι,	λῡσάμενος, -η, -ον
ἐλῡσω	λῦσαι,		
ἐλῡσατο			

ἐλῡσάμεθα
ἐλύσασθε   λύσασθε
ἐλύσαντο

25. VERBS WITH ATHEMATIC PRESENTS AND IMPERFECTS (see pages 276–277)

δύναμαι, δυνήσομαι, *I am able; I can*

PRESENT

Indicative	Imperative	Infinitive	Participle
δύναμαι		δύνασθαι	δυνάμενος, -η, -ον
δύνασαι	δύνασο		
δύναται			
δυνάμεθα			
δύνασθε	δύνασθε		
δύνανται			

IMPERFECT
ἐδυνάμην
ἐδύνασο or ἐδύνω
ἐδύνατο
ἐδυνάμεθα
ἐδύνασθε
ἐδύναντο

κεῖμαι, κείσομαι, *I lie*

PRESENT

κεῖμαι		κεῖσθαι	κείμενος, -η, -ον
κεῖσαι	κεῖσο		
κεῖται			
κείμεθα			
κεῖσθε	κεῖσθε		
κεῖνται			

IMPERFECT
ἐκείμην
ἔκεισο
ἔκειτο
ἐκείμεθα
ἔκεισθε
ἔκειντο

ἐπίσταμαι, ἐπιστήσομαι, *I understand; I know*

PRESENT

ἐπίσταμαι		ἐπίστασθαι	ἐπιστάμενος, -η, -ον
ἐπίστασαι	ἐπίστασο		
ἐπίσταται			

ἐπιστάμεθα
ἐπίστασθε   ἐπίστασθε
ἐπίστανται

IMPERFECT

Indicative

ἠπιστάμην
ἠπίστασο or ἠπίστω
ἠπίστατο
ἠπιστάμεθα
ἠπίστασθε
ἠπίσταντο

26. CONTRACT VERBS

φιλέω, φιλήσω, ἐφίλησα, *I love*

PRESENT ACTIVE (see pages 39 and 136)

Indicative	Imperative	Infinitive	Participle
φιλῶ		φιλεῖν	φιλῶν,
φιλεῖς	φίλει		φιλοῦσα,
φιλεῖ			φιλοῦν,
φιλοῦμεν			gen., φιλοῦντος, etc.
φιλεῖτε	φιλεῖτε		
φιλοῦσι(ν)			

PRESENT MIDDLE/PASSIVE (see pages 77 and 115–116)

φιλοῦμαι		φιλεῖσθαι	φιλούμενος, η, -ον
φιλεῖ or φιλῇ	φιλοῦ		
φιλεῖται			
φιλούμεθα			
φιλεῖσθε	φιλεῖσθε		
φιλοῦνται			

IMPERFECT ACTIVE (see page 214)

ἐφίλουν
ἐφίλεις
ἐφίλει
ἐφιλοῦμεν
ἐφιλεῖτε
ἐφίλουν

IMPERFECT MIDDLE/PASSIVE (see page 214)

ἐφιλούμην
ἐφιλοῦ
ἐφιλεῖτο

ἐφιλούμεθα
ἐφιλεῖσθε
ἐφιλοῦντο

FUTURE ACTIVE (see page 159)

φιλήσω, etc., like λύσω above

FUTURE MIDDLE (see page 159)

φιλήσομαι, etc., like λύσομαι above

AORIST ACTIVE (see page 198)

ἐφίλησα, etc., like ἔλῡσα above

AORIST MIDDLE (see page 198)

ἐφιλησάμην, etc., like ἐλῡσάμην above

τῑμάω, τῑμήσω, ἐτίμησα, *I honor*

PRESENT ACTIVE (see pages 56 and 136–137)

Indicative	Imperative	Infinitive	Participle
τῑμῶ		τῑμᾶν	τῑμῶν,
τῑμᾷς	τίμᾱ		τῑμῶσα,
τῑμᾷ			τῑμῶν,
τῑμῶμεν			gen., τῑμῶντος, etc.
τῑμᾶτε	τῑμᾶτε		
τῑμῶσι(ν)			

PRESENT MIDDLE/PASSIVE (see pages 77–78 and 116)

τῑμῶμαι		τῑμᾶσθαι	τῑμώμενος, -η, -ον
τῑμᾷ	τῑμῶ		
τῑμᾶται			
τῑμώμεθα			
τῑμᾶσθε	τῑμᾶσθε		
τῑμῶνται			

IMPERFECT ACTIVE (see page 214)

ἐτίμων
ἐτίμᾱς
ἐτίμᾱ
ἐτῑμῶμεν
ἐτῑμᾶτε
ἐτίμων

IMPERFECT MIDDLE/PASSIVE (see page 214)

ἐτῑμώμην
ἐτῑμῶ
ἐτῑμᾶτο
ἐτῑμώμεθα
ἐτῑμᾶσθε
ἐτῑμῶντο

FUTURE ACTIVE (see page 159)

τῑμήσω, etc., like λύσω above

FUTURE MIDDLE (see page 159)

τῑμήσομαι, etc., like λύσομαι above

AORIST ACTIVE (see page 198)

ἐτΐμησα, etc., like ἔλῡσα above

AORIST MIDDLE (see page 198)

ἐτῑμησάμην, etc., like ἐλῡσάμην above

δηλόω, δηλώσω, ἐδήλωσα, *I show*

PRESENT ACTIVE (see page 262)

Indicative	Imperative	Infinitive	Participle
δηλῶ		δηλοῦν	δηλῶν,
δηλοῖς	δήλου		δηλοῦσα,
δηλοῖ			δηλοῦν,
δηλοῦμεν			gen., δηλοῦντος, etc.
δηλοῦτε	δηλοῦτε		
δηλοῦσι(ν)			

PRESENT MIDDLE/PASSIVE (see page 262)

δηλοῦμαι		δηλοῦσθαι	δηλούμενος, -η, -ον
δηλοῖ	δηλοῦ		
δηλοῦται			
δηλούμεθα			
δηλοῦσθε	δηλοῦσθε		
δηλοῦνται			

IMPERFECT ACTIVE (see page 262)

ἐδήλουν
ἐδήλους
ἐδήλου

ἐδηλοῦμεν
ἐδηλοῦτε
ἐδήλουν

IMPERFECT MIDDLE/PASSIVE (see page 262)

Indicative

ἐδηλούμην
ἐδηλοῦ
ἐδηλοῦτο
ἐδηλούμεθα
ἐδηλοῦσθε
ἐδηλοῦντο

FUTURE ACTIVE (see page 262)

δηλώσω, etc., like λύσω above

FUTURE MIDDLE (see page 262)

δηλώσομαι, etc., like λύσομαι above

AORIST ACTIVE (see page 262)

ἐδήλωσα, etc., like ἔλῡσα above

AORIST MIDDLE (see page 262)

ἐδηλωσάμην, etc., like ἐλῡσάμην above

27. ASIGMATIC CONTRACT FUTURE OF VERBS IN -ίζω (see page 159)

κομίζω, κομιῶ, ἐκόμισα, *I bring; I take;* middle, *I get for myself, acquire*
FUTURE ACTIVE

Indicative	Infinitive	Participle
κομιῶ	κομιεῖν	κομιῶν,
κομιεῖς		κομιοῦσα,
κομιεῖ		κομιοῦν,
κομιοῦμεν		gen., κομιοῦντος, etc.
κομιεῖτε		
κομιοῦσι(ν)		

FUTURE MIDDLE

κομιοῦμαι	κομιεῖσθαι	κομιούμενος, -η, -ον
κομιεῖ or κομιῇ		
κομιεῖται		

κομιούμεθα
κομιεῖσθε
κομιοῦνται

28. ASIGMATIC CONTRACT FUTURE OF VERBS WITH LIQUID AND NASAL STEMS (see pages 166–167)

μένω, μενῶ, ἔμεινα, intransitive, *I stay* (in one place); *I wait;* transitive, *I wait for*

FUTURE ACTIVE

Indicative	Infinitive	Participle
μενῶ	μενεῖν	μενῶν,
μενεῖς		μενοῦσα,
μενεῖ		μενοῦν,
μενοῦμεν		gen., μενοῦντος, etc.
μενεῖτε		
μενοῦσι(ν)		

κάμνω, καμοῦμαι, ἔκαμον, *I am sick; I am tired*

FUTURE MIDDLE

καμοῦμαι	καμεῖσθαι	καμούμενος, -η, -ον
καμεῖ or καμῇ		
καμεῖται		
καμούμεθα		
καμεῖσθε		
καμοῦνται		

29. ASIGMATIC 1ST AORIST OF VERBS WITH LIQUID AND NASAL STEMS (see page 207)

αἴρω, ἀρῶ, ἦρα, *I lift;* with reflexive pronoun, *I get up*

AORIST ACTIVE

Indicative	Imperative	Infinitive	Participle
ἦρα		ἆραι	ἄρᾱς,
ἦρας	ἆρον		ἄρᾱσα,
ἦρε(ν)			ἆραν,
ἤραμεν			gen., ἄραντος, etc.
ἤρατε	ἄρατε		
ἦραν			

AORIST MIDDLE

ἠράμην		ἄρασθαι	ἀράμενος, -η, -ον
ἤρω	ἆραι		
ἤρατο			

ἠράμεθα
ἤρασθε   ἄρασθε
ἤραντο

30. THEMATIC 2ND AORISTS (see pages 177–178)

λείπω, λείψω, ἔλιπον, *I leave*

AORIST ACTIVE

Indicative	Imperative	Infinitive	Participle
ἔλιπον		λιπεῖν	λιπών,
ἔλιπες	λίπε		λιποῦσα,
ἔλιπε(ν)			λιπόν,
ἐλίπομεν			gen., λιπόντος, etc.
ἐλίπετε	λίπετε		
ἔλιπον			

γίγνομαι, γενήσομαι, ἐγενόμην, *I become*

AORIST MIDDLE

ἐγενόμην		γενέσθαι	γενόμενος, -η, -ον
ἐγένου	γενοῦ		
ἐγένετο			
ἐγενόμεθα			
ἐγένεσθε	γένεσθε		
ἐγένοντο			

31. ATHEMATIC 2ND AORISTS (see pages 252–253)

βαίνω, βήσομαι, ἔβην, *I step, walk, go*

ACTIVE

ἔβην		βῆναι	βάς,
ἔβης	βῆθι		βᾶσα,
ἔβη			βάν,
ἔβημεν			gen., βάντος, etc.
ἔβητε	βῆτε		
ἔβησαν			

γιγνώσκω, γνώσομαι, ἔγνων, *I come to know; I perceive; I learn*

ACTIVE

ἔγνων		γνῶναι	γνούς,
ἔγνως	γνῶθι		γνοῦσα,
ἔγνω			γνόν,
ἔγνωμεν			gen., γνόντος, etc.
ἔγνωτε	γνῶτε		
ἔγνωσαν			

ἔστην, *I stood; I stopped*

ACTIVE

Indicative	Imperative	Infinitive	Participle
ἔστην		στῆναι	στάς,
ἔστης	στῆθι		στᾶσα,
ἔστη			στάν,
ἔστημεν			gen., στάντος, etc.
ἔστητε	στῆτε		
ἔστησαν			

32. THE IRREGULAR VERB εἰμί, *I am*

εἰμί, ἔσομαι, *I am*

PRESENT (see pages 39 and 136)

Indicative	Imperative	Infinitive	Participle
εἰμί		εἶναι	ὤν,
εἶ	ἴσθι		οὖσα,
ἐστί(ν)			ὄν,
ἐσμέν			gen., ὄντος, etc.
ἐστέ	ἔστε		
εἰσί(ν)			

IMPERFECT (see page 215)

ἦ or ἦν
ἦσθα
ἦν
ἦμεν
ἦτε
ἦσαν

FUTURE (see page 160)

Indicative	Infinitive	Participle
ἔσομαι	ἔσεσθαι	ἐσόμενος, -η, -ον
ἔσει or ἔσῃ		
ἔσται		
ἐσόμεθα		
ἔσεσθε		
ἔσονται		

33. THE IRREGULAR VERB **εἶμι,** *I will go*

FUTURE/PRESENT (see pages 168–169)

Future	Present	Usually Present	Usually Present
Indicative	**Imperative**	**Infinitive**	**Participle**
εἶμι		ἰέναι	ἰών,
εἶ	ἴθι		ἰοῦσα,
εἶσι(ν)			ἰόν,
ἴμεν			gen., ἰόντος, etc.
ἴτε	ἴτε		
ἴᾱσι(ν)			

IMPERFECT (see page 215)

ἦα or ἦειν
ᾔεισθα or ᾔεις
ᾔειν or ᾔει
ᾖμεν
ᾖτε
ᾖσαν or ᾔεσαν

INDEX OF LANGUAGE AND GRAMMAR

This listing of topics will help you find information on language and grammar in this book.

GREEK TO ENGLISH VOCABULARY

We do not give principal parts of contract verbs except when they are irregular.

For the principal parts of most compound verbs, see the corresponding simple verb.

We give the principal parts of other regular and irregular verbs, with their stems when their stems are different from what is seen in the present indicative form and with their aorist participles.

For compound verbs we give in brackets the prefix and the simple verb when elision or elision and assimilation take place, e.g. ἀφικνέομαι [= ἀπο- + ἱκνέομαι].

Note: 5β means that the vocabulary item appears in the vocabulary list in the second half of Chapter 5, i.e., in 5β. A notation such as 14 Gr 2 refers to Chapter 14, Grammar 2.

Principal parts of model contract verbs:
φιλέω, φιλήσω, ἐφίλησα, φιλήσᾱς
τῑμάω, τῑμήσω, ἐτῑμησα, τῑμήσᾱς
δηλόω, δηλώσω, ἐδήλωσα, δηλώσᾱς

A

ἀγαθός, -ή, -όν, *good* (5β and 14 Gr 2)

   ἀμείνων, ἄμεινον, *better* (14 Gr 2)
   ἄριστος, -η, -ον, *best; very good; noble* (9β and 14 Gr 2)

'Αγαμέμνων, 'Αγαμέμνονος, ὁ, *Agamemnon* (7α)

ἄγᾱν, adv., *very much; too much; in excess*

ἀγγέλλω, [ἀγγελε-] **ἀγγελῶ,** [ἄγγειλ-] **ἤγγειλα,** ἀγγείλᾱς, *I announce; I tell* (14β)

ἄγγελος, ἀγγέλου, ὁ, *messenger* (4α)

ἄγε; pl., **ἄγετε,** *come on!* (9α)

ἀγείρω, [ἀγερε-] **ἀγερῶ,** [ἄγειρ-] **ἤγειρα,** ἀγείρᾱς, *I gather*

ἀγορά, ἀγορᾶς, ἡ, *agora, city center, market place* (8β)

ἄγριος, -ᾱ, -ον, *savage; wild; fierce* (5β)

   ἀγρίως, adv., *savagely; wildly; fiercely*

ἀγρός, ἀγροῦ, ὁ, *field* (1α and 3 Gr 2)
   ἐν τοῖς ἀγροῖς, *in the country*

ἄγω, ἄξω, [ἀγαγ-] **ἤγαγον,** ἀγαγών, *I lead; I take* (2β)

   ἄγε; pl., **ἄγετε,** *come on!* (9α)

ἀγών, ἀγῶνος, ὁ, *struggle; contest* (15β)

ἀδελφός, ἀδελφοῦ, ὁ, ὦ ἄδελφε, *brother* (11α)

ἀδύνατος, -ον, *impossible*

ἀεί, adv., *always* (4β)

ἀθάνατοι, ἀθανάτων, οἱ, *the Immortals*

'Αθηνᾶ, 'Αθηνᾶς, ἡ, τῇ 'Αθηνᾷ, τὴν 'Αθηνᾶν, ὦ 'Αθηνᾶ, *Athena* (daughter of Zeus) (9α)

'Αθήνᾱζε, adv., *to Athens* (12β)

'Αθῆναι, 'Αθηνῶν, αἱ, *Athens* (6α)
   'Αθήνησι, *at Athens*
   ἐν ταῖς 'Αθήναις, *in Athens* (1α)

'Αθηναῖος, -ᾱ, -ον, *Athenian* (1α)
   'Αθηναῖοι, 'Αθηναίων, οἱ, *the Athenians*

'Αθήνησι, *at Athens*

Αἰγαῖος πόντος, Αἰγαίου πόντου, ὁ, *Aegean Sea*

Αἰγεύς, Αἰγέως, ὁ, *Aegeus* (king of Athens) (6α)

Αἰγύπτιοι, Αἰγυπτίων, οἱ, *Egyptians*

Αἴγυπτος, Αἰγύπτου, ἡ, *Egypt*

αἴξ, αἰγός, ὁ or **ἡ,** *goat* (7α and 7 Gr 3a)

Αἴολος, Αἰόλου, ὁ, *Aeolus*

323

αἱρέω, αἱρήσω, [ἐλ-] εἷλον (irregular
augment), ἑλών, I take (7 α, 11β)

αἴρω, [ἀρε-] ἀρῶ, [ἀρ-] ἦρα, ἄρας, I
lift; with reflexive pronoun, I get up
(1β, 10β, and 12 Gr 3)

Αἰσχύλος, Αἰσχύλου, ὁ, Aeschylus
(15β)

αἰτέω, I ask; I ask for (11α)

αἴτιος, -ᾱ, -ον, responsible (for); to
blame (3α)

Αἰτναῖον ὄρος, Αἰτναίου ὄρους,
τό, Mount Etna (16β)

ἀκίνητος, -ον, motionless, unmoved

ἀκούω, ἀκούσομαι, ἤκουσα,
ἀκούσᾱς, intransitive, I listen; transitive
+ gen. of person, acc. of thing, I listen
to; I hear (4α)

'Ακρόπολις, 'Ακροπόλεως, ἡ, the
Acropolis (the citadel of Athens) (8β)

ἄκρος, -ᾱ, -ον, top (of) (5α)
ἄκρον τὸ ὄρος, the top of the moun-
tain/hill (5α)

ἀκτή, ἀκτῆς, ἡ, promontory

ἀληθής, ἀληθές, true (13β, 13 Gr 4,
and 14 Gr 1)
ἀληθῶς, adv., truly (14 Gr 3)
ἀληθέστερον, adv., more truly (14
Gr 3)
ἀληθέστατα, adv., most truly (14
Gr 3)
ἀληθῆ, ἀληθῶν, τά, the truth
(13β)

ἀλλά, conj., but (1α)

ἀλλᾱντοπώλης, ἀλλᾱντοπώλου, ὁ,
sausage-seller

ἀλλήλων, of one another (13α)

ἄλλος, -η, -ο, other, another (4β)

ἅμα, adv., together, at the same time
(13β)

ἅμα, prep. + dat., together with

ἅμαξα, ἁμάξης, ἡ, wagon

ἀμείνων, ἄμεινον, better (14 Gr 2)
ἄμεινον, adv., better (14 Gr 3)

ἀμῡνω, [ἀμυνε-] ἀμυνῶ, [ἀμῡν-]
ἤμῡνα, ἀμῡνᾱς, active, transitive, I
ward off X (acc.) from Y (dat.); middle,

transitive, I ward off X (acc.); I defend
myself against X (acc.) (13β)

ἀνά, prep. + acc., up (5α)

ἀναβαίνω, I go up, get up; + ἐπί + acc., I
climb, go up onto (8β)

ἀναβλέπω, I look up

ἀναγκάζω, ἀναγκάσω, ἠνάγκασα,
ἀναγκάσᾱς, I compel (15α)

ἀνάστηθι, stand up!

ἀναχωρέω, I retreat, withdraw (14β)

ἀνδρεῖος, -ᾱ, -ον, brave (3β, and 14 Gr
1)
ἀνδρείως, adv., bravely (14 Gr 3)
ἀνδρειότερον, adv., more bravely
(14 Gr 3)
ἀνδρειότατα, adv., most bravely
(14 Gr 3)

ἄνεμος, ἀνέμου, ὁ, wind (13α)

ἀνέστην, ἀναστάς, I stood up (15β)

ἀνήρ, ἀνδρός, ὁ, man; husband (4α
and 8 Gr 2)

ἄνθρωπος, ἀνθρώπου, ὁ, man; human being; person (1 α and 3 Gr 3)

ἀντέχω [= ἀντι- + ἔχω], imperfect,
ἀντεῖχον (irregular augment),
ἀνθέξω (irregular), [σχ-] ἀντέσχον,
ἀντισχών + dat., I resist (14β)

ἄντρον, ἄντρου, τό, cave

ἄξιος, -ᾱ, -ον, worthy; + gen., worthy
of (16β)

ἅπᾱς, ἅπᾱσα, ἅπᾱν, all; every; whole
(14β)

ἄπειμι [= ἀπο- + εἰμί], I am away (5α)

ἀπέκτονε (perfect of ἀποκτείνω), he/she
has killed

ἀπελαύνω [= ἀπο- + ἐλαύνω], I drive
away

ἀπέρχομαι [= ἀπο- + ἔρχομαι], I go
away (6α)

ἀπό, prep. + gen., from (4α)
ἀπο-, as a prefix in compound verbs,
away (4α)

ἀποβαίνω, I go away

ἀποθνῄσκω, [θανε-] ἀποθανοῦμαι,
[θαν-] ἀπέθανον, ἀποθανών, I die
(11α)

ἀποκρίνομαι, [κρινε-] ἀποκρινοῦμαι, [κρῖν-] ἀπεκρῑνάμην,
ἀποκρῑνάμενος, *I answer* (7β)

ἀποκτείνω, [κτενε-] ἀποκτενῶ,
[κτειν-] ἀπέκτεινα, ἀποκτείνᾱς, *I kill*
(6α, 10β)

ἀπόλλῡμι [= ἀπο- + ὄλλῡμι], [ὀλε-]
ἀπολῶ, ἀπώλεσα, ἀπολέσᾱς, *I destroy; I lose*

Ἀπόλλων, Ἀπόλλωνος, ὁ, *Apollo*

ἀποπέμπω, *I send away*

ἀποπλέω, *I sail away*

ἀπορέω, *I am at a loss* (12α)

ἀπορίᾱ, ἀπορίᾱς, ἡ, *perplexity; difficulty; the state of being at a loss* (15α)

ἀποφεύγω, *I flee (away), escape* (5β and
10β)

ἆρα, particle; introduces a question (4α
and 10 Gr 9)

Ἄργος, Ἄργου, ὁ, *Argus* (name of a
dog; cf. ἀργός, -ή, -όν, *shining; swift*)
(5α)

ἀργός [= ἀεργός = ἀ-, *not* + ἐργ-, *work*],
-όν, *not working, idle, lazy* (2α and 4α)

ἀργύριον, ἀργυρίου, τό, *silver;
money* (11β)

ἀρετή, ἀρετῆς, ἡ, *excellence; virtue;
courage* (15β)

Ἀριάδνη, -ης, ἡ, *Ariadne* (daughter
of King Minos) (6α)

ἀριστερά, ἀριστερᾶς, ἡ, *left hand*
(9α)

ἄριστος, -η, -ον, *best; very good;
noble* (9β)

ἄριστα, adv., *best* (14 Gr 3)

ἄροτος, ἀρότου, ὁ, *plowing*

ἄροτρον, ἀρότρου, τό, *plow* (2α)

ἀρόω, *I plow*

Ἀρτεμίσιον, Ἀρτεμισίου, τό,
Artemisium (14β)

ἀρχή, ἀρχῆς, ἡ, *beginning* (13β)

Ἀσίᾱ, Ἀσίᾱς, ἡ, *Asia* (i.e., Asia Minor)
(15β)

Ἀσκληπιός, Ἀσκληπιοῦ, ὁ, *Asclepius* (the god of healing) (11β)

ἀσκός, ἀσκοῦ, ὁ, *bag*

ἄστυ, ἄστεως, τό, *city* (8α and 9 Gr 3)

ἄτη, ἄτης, ἡ, *ruin*

ἀτραπός, ἀτραποῦ, ἡ, *path*

Ἀττική, Ἀττικῆς, ἡ, *Attica* (14β)

αὖθις, adv., *again* (3α)

αὔλιον, αὐλίου, τό, *sheepfold*

αὐξάνω, [αὐξε-] αὐξήσω, ηὔξησα,
αὐξήσᾱς, *I increase* (9β)

αὔριον, adv., *tomorrow* (11α)

αὐτήν, *her; it*

αὐτό, *it* (3)

αὐτόν, *him* (1β); *it* (3α)

αὐτός, -ή, -ό, intensive adjective, *-self,
-selves*; adjective, *same*; pronoun in
gen., dat., and acc. cases, *him, her, it,
them* (5β, 5 Gr 6, and 5 Gr 9)

αὐτουργός, αὐτουργοῦ, ὁ, *farmer*
(1α)

ἀφικνέομαι [= ἀπο- + ἱκνέομαι], [ἱκ-]
ἀφίξομαι, ἀφῑκόμην, ἀφῑκόμενος, *I
arrive; + εἰς + acc., I arrive at* (6α and
10α)

Ἀχαιοί Ἀχαιῶν, οἱ, *Achaeans;
Greeks* (7α)

B

βαδίζω, [βαδιε-] βαδιοῦμαι, [βαδι-]
ἐβάδισα, βαδίσᾱς, *I walk; I go* (1β)

βαίνω, [βη-] βήσομαι, ἔβην, βάς, *I
step; I walk; I go* (2β, 15 Gr 1)

βάλλω, [βαλε-] βαλῶ, [βαλ-] ἔβαλον,
βαλών, *I throw; I put; I pelt; I hit, strike*
(7β)

βάρβαρος, βαρβάρου, ὁ, *barbarian*
(13β)

βασιλεύς, βασιλέως, ὁ, *king* (6α and
9 Gr 4)

βασιλεύω, βασιλεύσω,
ἐβασίλευσα, βασιλεύσᾱς, *I rule* (6α)

βέβαιος, -ᾱ, -ον, *firm, steady* (13α)

βίος, βίου, ὁ, *life* (16β)

βλάπτω, [βλαβ-] βλάψω, ἔβλαψα,
βλάψᾱς, *I harm, hurt* (15β)

βλέπω, βλέψομαι, ἔβλεψα, βλέψᾱς,
usually intransitive, *I look; I see* (2β)

βοάω, βοήσομαι, ἐβόησα, βοήσᾱς, *I shout* (5α)

βοή, βοῆς, ἡ, *shout* (10β)

βοηθέω, *I come to the rescue;* + dat., *I come to X's aid; I come to rescue / aid X* (6α)

Βοιωτίᾱ, Βοιωτίᾱς, ἡ, *Boeotia* (14β)

βότρυες, βοτρύων, οἱ, *grapes*

βούλομαι, [βουλε-] βουλήσομαι, no aorist middle, + infin., *I want; I wish* (6α)

βοῦς, βοός, ὁ, *ox* (2β and 9 Gr 4)

βραδύς, βραδεῖα, βραδύ, *slow* (13 Gr 5)

βραδέως, adv., *slowly* (2β)

Βρόμιος, Βρομίου, ὁ, *the Thunderer* (a name of Dionysus) (9β)

βωμός, βωμοῦ, ὁ, *altar* (8β)

Γ

γάρ, postpositive conj., *for* (1α)

γε, postpositive enclitic; restrictive, *at least;* intensive, *indeed* (6β)

γέγονε (perfect of γίγνομαι), *he / she / it has become; he / she / it is*

γεραιός, -ά, -όν, *old* (12α)

γέρων, γέροντος, *old* (9β and 9 Gr 2)

γέρων, γέροντος, ὁ, *old man* (9β and 9 Gr 2)

γέφῡρα, γεφῡρᾱς, ἡ, *bridge*

γεωργέω, *I farm*

γῆ, γῆς, ἡ, *land; earth; ground* (4β)

κατὰ γῆν, *by land* (14α)

ποῦ γῆς; *where* (in the world)? (16α)

γίγᾱς, γίγαντος, ὁ, *giant*

γίγνομαι, [γενε-] γενήσομαι, [γεν-] ἐγενόμην, γενόμενος, *I become* (6α, 10α, 11 Gr 2, and 11 Gr 4)

γίγνεται, *he / she / it becomes; it happens* (6α)

γιγνώσκω, [γνω-] γνώσομαι, ἔγνων, γνούς, *I come to know; I perceive; I learn* (5β, 15 Gr 1)

γνῶθι, *know!*

γράφω, γράψω, ἔγραψα, γράψᾱς, *I write* (14β)

γυνή, γυναικός, ἡ, *woman; wife* (4α and 8 Gr 3)

Δ

δακρύω, δακρύσω, ἐδάκρῡσα, δακρύσᾱς, *I cry, weep* (11α)

δέ, postpositive particle, *and, but* (1α)

δεῖ, impersonal + acc. and infin., *it is necessary* (10β and 10 Gr 8)

δεῖ ἡμᾶς παρεῖναι, *we must be there* (10β and 10 Gr 8)

δεινός, -ή, -όν, *terrible* (6α)

δεινά, *terrible things*

δεινῶς, adv., *terribly, frightfully*

δειπνέω, *I eat*

δεῖπνον, δείπνου, τό, *dinner* (3β); *meal*

δέκα, indeclinable, *ten* (8 Gr 5)

δέκατος, -η, -ον, *tenth* (8 Gr 5)

Δελφοί, Δελφῶν, οἱ, *Delphi*

δένδρον, δένδρου, τό, *tree* (2β and 3 Gr 2)

δεξιός, -ά, -όν, *right* (i.e., on the right hand) (15β)

δεξιά, δεξιᾶς, ἡ, *right hand* (9α)

δεσμωτήριον, δεσμωτηρίου, τό, *prison*

δεσπότης, δεσπότου, ὁ, ὦ δέσποτα, *master* (2β and 4 Gr 4)

δεῦρο, adv., *here,* i.e., *hither* (3α)

δεύτερος, -ᾱ, -ον, *second* (8 Gr 5)

δέχομαι, δέξομαι, ἐδεξάμην, δεξάμενος, *I receive* (6α)

δή, postpositive particle; emphasizes that what is said is obvious or true, *indeed, in fact* (6β)

δηλόω, *I show* (15β and 15 Gr 3)

δῆμος, δήμου, ὁ, *the people* (9β)

διά, prep. + gen., *through* (9α)

δι᾽ ὀλίγου, *soon* (5α)

διαβαίνω, *I cross*

διαβιβάσαι (aorist infin. of διαβιβάζω), *to take across, transport*

διᾱκόσιοι, -αι, -α, *200* (15 Gr 5 and 16α)

διαλέγομαι, διαλέξομαι, διελεξάμην, διαλεξάμενος + dat., *I talk to, converse with* (8α)

διαφθείρω, [φθερε-] διαφθερῶ, [φθειρ-] διέφθειρα, διαφθείρᾱς, *I destroy* (15α)

διέρχομαι [= δια- + ἔρχομαι], *I come through; I go through* (14β)

Δικαιόπολις, Δικαιοπόλιδος, ὁ, τῷ Δικαιοπόλιδι, τὸν Δικαιόπολιν, ὦ Δικαιόπολι, *Dicaeopolis* (1α)

δίκαιος, -ᾱ, -ον, *just*

δι' ὀλίγου, *soon* (5α)

Διονύσια, Διονῡσίων, τά, *the festival of Dionysus* (4α)

    τὰ Διονύσια ποιῶ/ποιοῦμαι, *I celebrate the festival of Dionysus* (4α)

Διόνῡσος, Διονύσου, ὁ, *Dionysus* (8α)

διώκω, διώξομαι or διώξω, ἐδίωξα, διώξᾱς, *I pursue, chase* (5α)

δοκεῖ, impersonal, [δοκ-] δόξει, ἔδοξε(ν), δόξαν, *it seems (good);* + dat., e.g., δοκεῖ μοι, *it seems good to me; I think it best* (11α); + dat. and infin., e.g., δοκεῖ αὐτοῖς σπεύδειν, *it seems good to them to hurry, they decide to hurry* (11β)

    ὡς δοκεῖ, *as it seems* (13β)

δοῦλος, δούλου, ὁ, *slave* (2α)

δουλόω, *I enslave*

δραμεῖν (aorist infin. of τρέχω), *to run*

δραχμή, δραχμῆς, ἡ, *drachma (a silver coin worth six obols)* (11β)

δύναμαι, imperfect, ἐδυνάμην, δυνήσομαι, aorist middle not used in Attic Greek, *I am able; I can* (16α and 16 Gr 2)

δυνατός, -ή, -όν, *possible* (3α)

δύο, *two* (7β and 8 Gr 5)

δώδεκα, indeclinable, *twelve* (15 Gr 5)

    δωδέκατος, -η, -ον, *twelfth* (15 Gr 5)

E

ἑαυτοῦ: see ἐμαυτοῦ

ἑβδομήκοντα, indeclinable, *seventy* (15 Gr 5)

ἕβδομος, -η, -ον, *seventh* (8 Gr 5)

ἔβην: see βαίνω

ἐγγύη, ἐγγύης, ἡ, *pledge* (i.e., a promise of something as security)

ἐγγύς, adv., *nearl, near*

ἐγγύς, prep. + gen., *near* (13β)

ἐγείρω, [ἐγερε-] ἐγερῶ, [ἐγειρ-] ἤγειρα, ἐγείρᾱς, active, transitive, *I wake X up;* middle and passive, intransitive, *I wake up* (8β)

ἔγνων: see γιγνώσκω

ἐγώ, ἐμοῦ or μου, *I* (2α and 5 Gr 6)

    ἔγωγε, strengthened form of ἐγώ, *I indeed*

ἔδραμον: see τρέχω

ἐθέλω, [ἐθελε-] ἐθελήσω, ἠθέλησα, ἐθελήσᾱς + infin., *I am willing; I wish* (4α)

εἰ, conj., *if;* in indirect questions, *whether* (11α)

    εἰ μή, *unless*

    εἴ πως, *if somehow, if perhaps*

εἴκοσι(ν), indeclinable, *twenty* (15 Gr 5)

    εἰκοστός, -ή, -όν, *twentieth* (15 Gr 5)

εἴκω, εἴξω, εἶξα (no augment), εἴξᾱς + dat., *I yield* (15α)

εἰκών, εἰκόνος, ἡ, *statue*

εἶλον: see αἱρέω

εἰμί [ἐσ-], imperfect, ἦ or ἦν, ἔσομαι, *I am* (1α, 4 Gr 1, 10 Gr 1, and 13 Gr 1)

εἶμι [εἰ-/ἰ], imperfect, ᾖα or ᾔειν, *I will go* (10 Gr 6 and 13 Gr 1)

εἶπον (aorist of λέγω), *I/they said; I/they told; I/they spoke*

    εἰπέ; pl., εἴπετε, *tell!*

    εἰπεῖν, *to say; to tell*

    εἰπών, *having said, after saying,* sometimes, *saying; having told, after telling,* sometimes, *telling*

εἰρήνη, εἰρήνης, ἡ, *peace* (16β)

εἰς, prep. + acc., *into; to; at* (2β); *for*

    εἰς καιρόν, *at just the right time*

εἷς, μία, ἕν, *one* (7β and 8 Gr 5)

εἷς καὶ εἴκοσι(ν), *twenty-one* (15 Gr 5)

εἰσάγω, *I lead in; I take in* (2β and 11α)

εἰσβαίνω, *I go in; I come in*

εἰσβάντες, *having embarked*

εἰς ναῦν εἰσβαίνω, *I go on board ship, embark*

εἰσελαύνω, *I drive in*

εἰσέρχομαι, *I come in(to); I go in(to)*

εἴσελθε; pl., εἰσέλθετε (aorist imperative of εἰσέρχομαι), *come in(to)!*

εἰσελθών, *having come in(to), after coming in(to)*, sometimes, *coming in(to)*

εἰσιέναι (used as present infinitive of εἰσέρχομαι), *to go in(to)*

εἴσιθι; pl., εἴσιτε (used as present imperative of εἰσέρχομαι), *go in(to)!*

εἰσηγέομαι + dat., *I lead in*

εἰς καιρόν, *at just the right time*

εἰσκαλέω, *I call in(to)*

εἴσοδος, εἰσόδου, ἡ, *entrance*

εἰσπλέω, *I sail in(to)*

εἰσφέρω, *I bring in(to)*

ἐκ, ἐξ, before words beginning with vowels, prep. + gen., *out of* (3α)

ἐκ τοῦ ὄπισθεν, *from the rear*

ἐκατόν, indeclinable, *100* (15 Gr 5 and 16α)

ἐκατοστός, -ή, -όν, *hundredth* (15 Gr 5)

ἐκβαίνω, *I step out; I come out* (2α)

ἐκβαίνω ἐκ τῆς νεώς, *I disembark*

ἐκβάλλω, *I throw out*

ἐκεῖ, adv., *there* (6α)

ἐκεῖνος, ἐκείνη, ἐκεῖνο, *that*; pl., *those* (13β and 14 Gr 6)

ἐκεῖσε, adv., *to that place, thither* (8α)

ἐκκαλέω, *I call out*

ἐκπέμπω, *I send out*

ἐκπίπτω, *I fall out*

ἐκπλέω, *I sail out*

ἔκπλους, ἔκπλου, ὁ, *escape route*

ἔκτοπος, -ον, *out of the way, unusual*

ἕκτος, -η, -ον, *sixth* (8 Gr 5)

ἐκ τοῦ ὄπισθεν, *from the rear*

ἐκφέρω, *I carry out*

ἐκφεύγω, *I flee out, escape*

ἐλάττων, ἔλαττον, *smaller*, pl., *fewer* (14 Gr 2)

ἐλαύνω, [ἐλα-] ἐλῶ, ἐλᾶς, ἐλᾷ, etc., ἤλασα, ἐλάσᾱς, transitive, *I drive* (2α); intransitive, *I march*

ἐλεῖν (aorist infinitive of αἱρέω), *to take*

ἐλευθερίᾱ, ἐλευθερίᾱς, ἡ, *freedom* (13β)

ἐλεύθερος, -ᾱ, -ον, *free*

ἐλευθερόω, *I free, set free* (15β)

ἐλθέ; pl., ἔλθετε (aorist imperative of ἔρχομαι), *come!* (2α)

ἐλθεῖν (aorist infinitive of ἔρχομαι), *to come; to go*

ἕλκω, imperfect, εἷλκον (irregular augment), ἕλξω, [ἑλκυ-] εἵλκυσα (irregular augment), ἑλκύσᾱς, *I drag*

Ἑλλάς, Ἑλλάδος, ἡ, *Hellas, Greece* (13β)

Ἕλλην, Ἕλληνος, ὁ, *Greek*; pl., *the Greeks* (14α)

Ἑλλήσποντος, Ἑλλησπόντου, ὁ, *Hellespont*

ἐλπίζω, [ἐλπιε-] ἐλπιῶ, [ἐλπι-] ἤλπισα, ἐλπίσᾱς, *I hope; I expect; I suppose* (14α)

ἐμαυτοῦ, σεαυτοῦ, ἑαυτοῦ, *of myself, of yourself, of him-, her-, itself* (7α and 7 Gr 4)

ἐμός, -ή, -όν, *my, mine* (5 Gr 8)

ἐμπίπτω [= ἐν- + πίπτω] + dat., *I fall into; I fall upon; I attack* (15β)

ἐμποδίζω [ἐν- + πούς, ποδός, ὁ, *foot*), [ἐμποδιε-] ἐμποδιῶ, no aorist, *I obstruct*

ἔμπορος, ἐμπόρου, ὁ, *merchant* (12β)

ἐν, prep. + dat., *in; on* (3β); *among*

ἐν μέσῳ + gen., *between* (14α)

ἐν νῷ ἔχω + infin., *I have in mind; I intend* (4α)

ἐν ταῖς Ἀθήναις, *in Athens* (1α)

ἐν ... τούτῳ, *meanwhile* (8β)

ἐν ᾧ, *while* (8α)

ἐνακόσιοι, -αι, -α, *900* (15 Gr 5)

ἐναντίος, -ᾱ, -ον, *opposite*

ἔνατος, -η, -ον, *ninth* (8 Gr 5)

ἔνδεκα, indeclinable, *eleven* (15 Gr 5)

ἐνδέκατος, -η, -ον, *eleventh* (15 Gr 5)

ἔνδον, adv., *inside*

ἔνειμι, *I am in*

ἐνενήκοντα, indeclinable, *ninety* (15 Gr 5)

ἐνθάδε, adv., *here; hither; there; thither* (7 β)

ἐννέα, indeclinable, *nine* (8 Gr 5)

ἔνοικος, ἐνοίκου, ὁ, *inhabitant* (16α)

ἐνόπλιος, -ον, *in armor, fully armed*

ἐνταῦθα, adv., *then; here; hither; there; thither* (5 β)

ἐνταῦθα δή, *at that very moment, then* (5β)

ἐξ: *see* ἐκ

ἕξ, indeclinable, *six* (8 Gr 5)

ἐξάγω, *I lead out*

ἐξαιρέω, *I take out*

ἐξακόσιοι, -αι, -α, *600* (15 Gr 5)

ἐξελαύνω, *I drive out*

ἐξελθών (aorist participle of ἐξέρχομαι), *coming out, having come out*

ἐξέρχομαι + ἐκ + gen., *I come out of; I go out of* (6β)

ἔξεστι(ν), impersonal + dat. and infin., *it is allowed/possible* (10β and 10 Gr 8)

ἔξεστιν ἡμῖν μένειν, *we are allowed to stay, we may stay; we can stay* (10β and 10 Gr 8)

ἐξηγέομαι [ἐκ- + ἡγέομαι], *I relate* (12β)

ἐξήκοντα, *sixty* (15 Gr 5)

ἑορτή, ἑορτῆς, ἡ, *festival* (4α)

ἑορτὴν ποιῶ/ποιοῦμαι, *I celebrate a festival* (4β)

ἐπαίρω [ἐπι- + αἴρω], *I lift, raise* (7α)

ἐπαίρω ἐμαυτόν, *I get up* (7α)

ἐπανέρχομαι [= ἐπι- + ἀνα- + ἔρχομαι], infin., ἐπανιέναι, *I come back, return;* + εἰς or πρός + acc., *I return to* (9α)

ἐπάνελθε; pl., ἐπανέλθετε (aorist

imperative of ἐπανέρχομαι), *come back!*

ἐπανιέναι (used as present infinitive of ἐπανέρχομαι), *to come back, return* (9α)

ἐπεί, conj., *when* (3β); *since*

ἔπειτα, adv., *then, thereafter* (2β)

ἐπί, prep. + gen., *on;* + dat., *upon, on* (5β); + acc., *at; against* (5β); *onto, upon* (9α); *to*

Ἐπίδαυρος, Ἐπιδαύρου, ἡ, *Epidaurus* (11β)

ἐπίκειμαι + dat., *I lie near, lie off* (of islands with respect to the mainland)

ἐπιλανθάνομαι, [ληθ-] ἐπιλήσομαι, [λαθ-] ἐπελαθόμην, ἐπιλαθόμενος + gen., *I forget*

ἐπιπέμπω, *I send against; I send in* (14α)

ἐπιπλέω + dat. or + εἰς + acc., *I sail against* (15β)

ἐπίσταμαι, ἐπιστήσομαι, no aorist middle, *I understand; I know* (16α and 16 Gr 2)

ἕπομαι, imperfect, εἱπόμην (irregular augment), ἕψομαι, [σπ-] ἑσπόμην, σπόμενος + dat., *I follow* (8α)

ἑπτά, indeclinable, *seven* (8 Gr 5)

ἑπτακόσιοι, -αι, -α, *700* (15 Gr 5)

ἐράω, imperfect, ἤρων + gen., *I love*

ἐργάζομαι, imperfect, ἠργαζόμην or εἰργαζόμην, ἐργάσομαι, ἠργασάμην or εἰργασάμην, ἐργασάμενος, *I work; I accomplish* (8α)

ἔργον, ἔργου, τό, *work; deed* (8α)

ἐρέσσω, no future, [ἐρετ-] ἤρεσα, ἐρέσᾱς, *I row* (13α)

ἐρέτης, ἐρέτου, ὁ, *rower*

ἔρχομαι, [εἰ-/ἰ-] εἶμι (irregular), [ἐλθ-] ἦλθον, ἐλθών, *I come; I go* (6α, 11β, and 13 Gr 1b) For common compounds, *see page 169.*

ἐρωτάω, ἐρωτήσω, ἠρώτησα, ἐρωτήσᾱς or [ἐρ-] ἠρόμην, ἐρόμενος, *I ask* (12β)

ἐσθίω, [ἐδ-] ἔδομαι, [φαγ-] ἔφαγον, *I eat* (9α)

ἑσπέρᾱ, ἑσπέρᾱς, ἡ, *evening* (8a); *the west*

ἔστην, *I stood; I stopped* (15 Gr 1)

ἐστί(ν), *he/she/it is* (1α)

ἔστω, *let it be so! all right!*

ἑταῖρος, ἑταίρου, ὁ, *comrade, companion* (6α)

ἔτι, adv., *still* (3α)

ἔτοιμος, -η, -ον, *ready* (9β)

ἔτος, ἔτους, τό, *year* (16β)

εὖ, adv., *well* (8α and 14 Gr 3)
  ἄμεινον, adv., *better* (14 Gr 3)
  ἄριστα, adv., *best* (14 Gr 3)
  εὖ γε, *good! well done!* (8α)

Εὔβοια, Εὐβοίᾱς, ἡ, *Euboea* (14α)

εὐθύς, εὐθεῖα, εὐθύ, *straight*
  εὐθύς, adv., *straightway, immediately, at once* (10β)

εὐμενῶς, adv., *kindly*

εὑρίσκω, [εὑρε-] εὑρήσω, [εὑρ-]
  ηὗρον or εὗρον, εὑρών, *I find* (7α and 10α)

Εὐρύλοχος, Εὐρυλόχου, ὁ, *Eury-lochus*

Εὐρυμέδων ποταμός, Εὐρυμέδον-τος ποταμοῦ, ὁ, *the Eurymedon River*

εὔχομαι, εὔξομαι, ηὐξάμην,
  εὐξάμενος, *I pray;* + dat., *I pray to;* + acc. and infin., *I pray (that)* (8β)

ἔφη, *he/she said* (11α)
  ἔφασαν, *they said*

Ἐφιάλτης, Ἐφιάλτου, ὁ, *Ephialtes* (14β)

ἔχω, imperfect, εἶχον (irregular augment), ἕξω (irregular) (*I will have*) and [σχε-] σχήσω, (*I will get*), [σχ-] ἔσχον, σχών, *I have; I hold* (4α); middle + gen., *I hold onto*
  ἐν νῷ ἔχω, *I have in mind; I intend* (4α)
  καλῶς ἔχω, *I am well* (11α)
  πῶς ἔχεις; How are you? (11α)

ἕως, conj., *until* (14β)

Z

Ζεύς, ὁ, τοῦ Διός, τῷ Διί, τὸν Δία, ὦ

Ζεῦ, *Zeus* (king of the gods) (3α and 8β)

ζητέω, *I seek, look for* (5α)

ζῷον, ζῴου, τό, *animal*

Η

ἤ, conj., *or* (12α)
  ἤ ... ἤ, conj., *either ... or* (12α)
  ἤ, with comparatives, *than* (14α)

ἡγέομαι + dat., *I lead* (6β)

ἤδη, adv., *already; now* (2β)

ἥκιστα, adv., *least*
  ἥκιστά γε (the opposite of μάλιστά γε), *least of all, not at all* (16β)

ἥκω, *I have come;* imperfect, ἧκον, *I had come;* future, ἥξω, *I will have come* (5β)

ἥλιος, ἡλίου, ὁ, *sun* (1β)

ἡμεῖς, ἡμῶν, *we* (5β and 5 Gr 6)

ἡμέρᾱ, ἡμέρᾱς, ἡ, *day* (6α)
  καθ' ἡμέρᾱν, *every day*

ἡμέτερος, -ᾱ, -ον, *our* (5 Gr 8)

ἡμίονος, ἡμιόνου, ὁ, *mule* (12α)

ἦν, *he/she/it was*

ἡσυχάζω, ἡσυχάσω, ἡσύχασα,
  ἡσυχάσᾱς, *I keep quiet; I rest* (13α)

ἥσυχος, -ον, *quiet*

Θ

θάλαττα, θαλάττης, ἡ, *sea* (7α)
  κατὰ θάλατταν, *by sea* (11β)

θάνατος, θανάτου, ὁ, *death* (16β)

θαυμάζω, θαυμάσομαι, ἐθαύμασα,
  θαυμάσᾱς, intransitive, *I am amazed;* transitive, *I wonder at; I admire* (5β)

θαυμάσιος, -ᾱ, -ον, *wonderful, marvelous*

θεάομαι, θεάσομαι (note that because of the ε the α lengthens to ᾱ rather than η), ἐθεᾱσάμην, θεᾱσάμενος, *I see, watch, look at* (8α and 10α)

θέᾱτρον, θεάτρου, τό, *theater*

Θεμιστοκλῆς, Θεμιστοκλέους, ὁ, *Themistocles* (15α and 15 Gr 2)

θεός, θεοῦ, ἡ, *goddess* (9α)

θεός, θεοῦ, ὁ, *god* (8α)

θεράπων, θεράποντος, ὁ, *attendant; servant*

Θερμοπύλαι, Θερμοπυλῶν, αἱ, *Thermopylae* (14α)

θεωρέω, *I watch; I see* (4α)

θηρίον, θηρίου, τό, *beast, wild beast*

Θησεύς, Θησέως, ὁ, *Theseus* (son of King Aegeus) (6α)

θόρυβος, θορύβου, ὁ, *uproar, commotion* (15β)

θυγάτηρ, θυγατρός, ἡ, *daughter* (4α and 8 Gr 2)

θῡμός, θῡμοῦ, ὁ, *spirit* (16β)

θύρᾱ, θύρᾱς, ἡ, *door* (8α)

I

ἰᾱτρεύω, ἰᾱτρεύσω, ἰᾱτρευσα, ἰᾱτρεύσᾱς, *I heal*

ἰᾱτρός, ἰᾱτροῦ, ὁ, *doctor* (11α)

ἰδεῖν (aorist infinitive of ὁράω), *to see*

ἰδού, adv., *look!* (4α)

ἰέναι (infinitive of εἶμι, used as infinitive of ἔρχομαι), *to go* (7α)

ἱερεῖον, ἱερείου, τό, *sacrificial victim* (9β)

ἱερεύς, ἱερέως, ὁ, *priest* (9β)

ἱερόν, ἱεροῦ, τό, *temple* (9α)

ἴθι; pl., ἴτε (imperative of εἶμι, used as imperative of ἔρχομαι), *go!* (5α)

ἴθι δή, *go on!* (5α)

ἵλεως, acc., ἵλεων, *propitious* (9β)

ἵππος, ἵππου, ὁ, *horse*

ἴσθι; pl., ἔστε (imperative of εἰμί), *be!*

ἱστία, ἱστίων, τά, *sails* (13α)

ἰσχῡρός, -ά, -όν, *strong* (1β)

Ἴωνες, Ἰώνων, οἱ, *Ionians*

Ἰωνίᾱ, Ἰωνίᾱς, ἡ, *Ionia*

Κ

καθεύδω [= κατα- + εὕδω], imperfect, καθεῦδον or καθηῦδον, καθευδήσω, no aorist in Attic Greek, *I sleep* (2α)

καθ' ἡμέρᾱν, *every day*

καθίζω [= κατα- + ἵζω], [καθιε-] καθιῶ, [καθι-] ἐκάθισα, καθίσᾱς, active, transitive, *I make X sit down; I set; I place;* active, intransitive, *I sit* (1β); middle, intransitive, *I seat myself, sit down* (8β)

καί, adv., *even; also, too* (4α)

καί, conj., *and* (1α)

καὶ δὴ καί, *and in particular; and what is more* (16α)

καί . . . καί, conj., *both . . . and* (5β)

καίπερ + participle, *although* (12α)

καιρός, καιροῦ, ὁ, *time; right time* (4α)

εἰς καιρόν, *just at the right time*

καίω or κάω, κάεις, κάει, κάομεν, κάετε, κάουσι(ν), [καυ-] καύσω, ἔκαυσα, καύσᾱς, active, transitive, *I kindle, burn;* middle, intransitive, *I burn, am on fire* (9β)

κακός, -ή, -όν, *bad; evil* (12α and 14 Gr 2)

κακίων, κάκιον, *worse* (14 Gr 2)

κάκιστος, -η, -ον, *worst* (14 Gr 2)

κακῶς, adv., *badly* (14 Gr 3)

κάκιον, adv., *worse* (14 Gr 3)

κάκιστα, adv., *worst* (14 Gr 3)

κακόν τι, *something bad*

καλέω, καλῶ, ἐκάλεσα, καλέσᾱς, *I call* (2α)

καλός, -ή, -όν, *beautiful* (1α, 3 Gr 2, 4 Gr 3, 4 Gr 6, and 14 Gr 2)

καλλίων, κάλλιον, *more beautiful* (14 Gr 2)

κάλλιστος, -η, -ον, *most beautiful; very beautiful* (9α and 14 Gr 2)

καλῶς, adv., *well* (10α)

κάλλιον, adv., *better*

κάλλιστα, adv., *best*

καλῶς ἔχω, *I am well* (11α)

κάμνω, [καμε-] καμοῦμαι, [καμ-] ἔκαμον, καμών, *I am sick; I am tired* (9α)

κατά, prep. + acc., *down* (5α); distributive, *each; on; by* (11β)

καθ' ἡμέρᾱν, *every day*

κατὰ γῆν, *by land* (14α)

κατὰ θάλατταν, *by sea* (11β)

κατ᾽ εἰκός, *probably*
καταβαίνω, *I come down; I go down*
καταβάλλω, *I throw down; I drop*
κατάκειμαι, *I lie down* (16α)
καταλαμβάνω, *I overtake, catch* (16α)
καταλείπω, *I leave behind, desert* (10β)
καταπίπτω, *I fall down*
κατάρᾱτος, -ον, *cursed*
κατ᾽ εἰκός, *probably*
καττίτερος, καττιτέρου, ὁ, *tin*
κεῖμαι, imperfect, ἐκείμην, κείσομαι, no aorist, *I lie* (16α and 16 Gr 2)
κεῖνος = ἐκεῖνος
κελεύω, κελεύσω, ἐκέλευσα, κελεύσᾱς + acc. and infin., *I order, tell* (someone to do something) (7α)
κεφαλή, κεφαλῆς, ἡ, *head* (10β)
κῆπος, κήπου, ὁ, *garden*
κῆρυξ, κήρῡκος, ὁ, *herald* (9β)
Κίμων, Κίμωνος, ὁ, *Cimon*
κίνδῡνος, κινδῡνου, ὁ, *danger* (9α)
Κίρκη, Κίρκης, ἡ, *Circe*
κλῆρος, κλήρου, ὁ, *farm*
Κνωσός, Κνωσοῦ, ἡ, *Knossos* (6α)
κολάζω, κολάσω, ἐκόλασα, κολάσᾱς, *I punish*
κομίζω, [κομιε-] κομιῶ, [κομι-] ἐκόμισα, κομίσᾱς, *I bring; I take* (11α)
κόπτω, [κοπ-] κόψω, ἔκοψα, κόψᾱς, *I strike; I knock on* (a door) (11α)
κόρη, κόρης, ἡ, *girl*
Κόρινθος, Κορίνθου, ἡ, *Corinth* (14α)
κόσμος, κόσμου, ὁ, *good order* (15β)
κόσμῳ, *in order* (15β)
κρήνη, κρήνης, ἡ, *spring* (4α and 4 Gr 3)
Κρήτη, Κρήτης, ἡ, *Crete* (6α)
κυβερνήτης, κυβερνήτου, ὁ, *steersman*
Κύκλωψ, Κύκλωπος, ὁ, *Cyclops* (one-eyed monster) (7β)
κῦμα, κύματος, τό, *wave* (13β)
κῡμαίνω, [κῡμανε-] κῡμανῶ, [κῡμην-] ἐκύμηνα, κῡμήνᾱς, *I am rough* (of the sea)

Κύπρος, Κύπρου, ἡ, *Cyprus*
Κυρήνη, Κυρήνης, ἡ, *Cyrene*
κύων, κυνός, ὁ or ἡ, *dog* (5α)
κωμάζω, κωμάσω, ἐκώμασα, κωμάσᾱς, *I revel*

Λ

λαβύρινθος, λαβυρίνθου, ὁ, *labyrinth*
λαγώς, ὁ, acc., τὸν λαγών, *hare* (5α)
Λακεδαιμόνιοι, Λακεδαιμονίων, οἱ, *the Lacedaemonians, Spartans* (14α)
λαμβάνω, [ληβ-] λήψομαι, [λαβ-] ἔλαβον, λαβών, *I take* (2β); middle + gen., *I seize, take hold of* (11α)
λαμπρός, -ά, -όν, *bright; brilliant* (13α)
    λαμπρῶς, adv., *brightly; brilliantly*
λέγω, λέξω or [ἐρε-] ἐρῶ, ἔλεξα, λέξᾱς or [ἐπ-] εἶπον (irregular augment), εἰπών (augment retained), *I say; I tell; I speak* (1α, 11β)
λείπω, λείψω, [λιπ-] ἔλιπον, λιπών, *I leave* (3β, 11α, 11 Gr 2, and 11 Gr 4)
λέων, λέοντος, ὁ, *lion*
Λεωνίδης, Λεωνίδου, ὁ, *Leonidas* (14α)
λίθινος, -η, -ον, *of stone, made of stone*
λίθος, λίθου, ὁ, *stone* (3α)
λιμήν, λιμένος, ὁ, *harbor* (12α)
λῑμός, λῑμοῦ, ὁ, *hunger*
λίνον, λίνου, τό, *thread*
λόγος, λόγου, ὁ, *word; story* (11α); *reason*
λύκος, λύκου, ὁ, *wolf* (5α)
λῡπέω, *I grieve, vex, cause pain to* X; passive, *I am grieved, distressed* (16β)
λύω, λύσω, ἔλῡσα, λύσᾱς, *I loosen, loose* (3β, 4 Gr 1, 6 Gr 3, 9 Gr 1, 10 Gr 1, 12 Gr 1, 12 Gr 2, and 13 Gr 1)
    λύομαι, *I ransom* (6 Gr 2c, 6 Gr 3, 8 Gr 1, 10 Gr 1, 12 Gr 1, 12 Gr 2, and 13 Gr 1)

M

μακρός, -ά, -όν, *long; large* (1α)

μάλα, adv., *very* (4α and 14 Gr 3)

μᾶλλον, adv., *more; rather* (14 Gr 3)

μᾶλλον ἤ, *rather than* (14 Gr 3)

μάλιστα, adv., *most, most of all; very much; especially* (4β and 14 Gr 3)

μάλιστά γε, *certainly, indeed* (12β)

μανθάνω, [μαθε-] μαθήσομαι, [μαθ-] ἔμαθον, μαθών, *I learn; I understand* (11α)

μάχαιρα, μαχαίρας, ἡ, *knife* (4 Gr 3)

μάχη, μάχης, ἡ, *fight; battle* (13β)

μάχομαι, [μαχε-] μαχοῦμαι, ἐμαχεσάμην, μαχεσάμενος, *I fight* (6β); + dat., *I fight against*

μέγας, μεγάλη, μέγα, *big, large; great* (3α, 4 Gr 6, and 14 Gr 2)

μέγα, adv., *greatly; loudly* (12β)

μείζων, μεῖζον, *bigger, larger; greater* (14 Gr 2)

μέγιστος, -η, -ον, *biggest, largest; greatest* (7α and 14 Gr 2)

μεθύω, only present and imperfect, *I am drunk*

μείζων, μεῖζον, *bigger, larger; greater* (14 Gr 2)

μέλᾱς, μέλαινα, μέλαν, *black*

μελέτη, μελέτης, ἡ, *practice*

μέλιττα, μελίττης, ἡ, *bee* (4 Gr 3)

Μέλιττα, Μελίττης, ἡ, [= *bee*], *Melissa* (daughter of Dicaeopolis and Myrrhine) (4α)

μέλλω, [μελλε-] μελλήσω, ἐμέλλησα, μελλήσᾱς + infin., *I am about* (to); *I am destined* (to); *I intend* (to) (7β)

Μέμφις, Μέμφεως or Μέμφιδος or Μέμφιος, ἡ, *Memphis* (16α)

μέν . . . δέ . . ., postpositive particles, *on the one hand . . . and on the other hand . . .* or *on the one hand . . . but on the other hand* (2α)

μένω, [μενε-] μενῶ, [μειν-] ἔμεινα,

μείνᾱς, intransitive, *I stay* (in one place); *I wait;* transitive, *I wait for* (3α, 10β, and 10 Gr 5)

μέρος, μέρους, τό, *part* (15β)

μέσος, -η, -ον, *middle (of)* (9β)

ἐν μέσῳ + gen., *between* (14α)

μετά, prep. + gen., *with* (6α); + acc., of time or place, *after* (6α)

μέτρον, μέτρου, τό, *measure; due measure, proportion*

μή, adv., *not;* + imperative, *don't . . . !* (2α)

εἰ μή, *unless*

μηδείς, μηδεμία, μηδέν, used instead of οὐδείς with imperatives and infinitives, *no one, nothing; no* (13β)

μηκέτι, adv., + imperative, *don't . . . any longer!* (3β); + infin., *no longer* (15α)

μήτηρ, μητρός, ἡ, *mother* (4α and 8 Gr 2)

μῑκρός, -ά, -όν, *small* (1α)

Μίνως, Μίνω, ὁ, *Minos* (king of Crete) (6α)

Μῑνώταυρος, Μῑνωταύρου, ὁ, *Minotaur* (6α)

μισθός, μισθοῦ, ὁ, *reward; pay* (11β)

μνημεῖον, μνημείου, τό, *monument*

μόλις, adv., *with difficulty; scarcely; reluctantly* (4α)

μόνος, -η, -ον, *alone; only* (15α)

μόνον, adv., *only* (15α)

οὐ μόνον . . . ἀλλὰ καί, *not only . . . but also* (15α)

μόσχος, μόσχου, ὁ, *calf*

μοχλός, μοχλοῦ, ὁ, *stake*

μῦθος, μύθου, ὁ, *story* (5β)

Μυκαλή, Μυκαλῆς, ἡ, *Mycale*

μύριοι, -αι, -α, *10,000* (15 Gr 5)

μῡρίοι, -αι, -α, *numberless, countless* (15 Gr 5)

μῡριοστός, -ή, -όν, *ten thousandth* (15 Gr 5)

Μυρρίνη, Μυρρίνης, ἡ, [= *myrtle*], *Myrrhine* (wife of Dicaeopolis) (4α) μυχός, μυχοῦ, ὁ, *far corner*

N

ναύαρχος, ναυάρχου, ὁ, *admiral* (15α)

ναύκληρος, ναυκλήρου, ὁ, *ship's captain* (12β)

ναυμαχέω, *I fight by sea* (15β)

ναῦς, νεώς, ἡ, *ship* (6α and 9 Gr 4)

ναύτης, ναύτου, ὁ, *sailor* (12β)

ναυτικόν, ναυτικοῦ, τό, *fleet* (13β)

νεᾱνίᾱς, νεᾱνίου, ὁ, *young man* (4 Gr 4 and 8β)

Νεῖλος, Νείλου, ὁ, *Nile*

νεκρός, νεκροῦ, ὁ, *corpse* (15β)

νῆσος, νήσου, ἡ, *island* (4 Gr 5 and 6α)

νῑκάω, *I defeat; I win* (10α)

νίκη, νίκης, ἡ, *victory* (15β)
  Νίκη, Νίκης, ἡ, *Nike* (the goddess of victory) (9α)

νοσέω, *I am sick, ill* (11β)

νοστέω, *I return home*

νοῦς, νοῦ, ὁ, *mind* (15α and 15 Gr 4)
  ἐν νῷ ἔχω + infin., *I have in mind; I intend* (4α)

νύμφη, νύμφης, ἡ, *nymph*

νῦν, adv., *now* (5β)

νύξ, νυκτός, ἡ, *night* (6α)

Ξ

Ξανθίᾱς, Ξανθίου, ὁ, *Xanthias* (2α and 4 Gr 4)

ξένος, ξένου, ὁ, *foreigner; stranger* (7β)
  ξεῖνος = ξένος

Ξέρξης, Ξέρξου, ὁ, *Xerxes* (14α)

ξίφος, ξίφους, τό, *sword*

Ο

ὁ, ἡ, τό, *the* (4 Gr 8)
  ὁ δέ, *and he*

ὀβολός, ὀβολοῦ, ὁ, *obol* (a coin of slight worth) (11β)

ὀγδοήκοντα, indeclinable, *eighty* (15 Gr 5)

ὄγδοος, -η, -ον, *eighth* (8 Gr 5)

ὅδε, ἥδε (note the accent), τόδε, *this here*; pl., *these here* (14β and 14 Gr 5)

ὁδός, ὁδοῦ, ἡ, *road; way; journey* (4β and 4 Gr 5)

Ὀδυσσεύς, Ὀδυσσέως, ὁ, *Odysseus* (7α)

οἴκαδε, adv., *homeward, to home* (4β)

οἰκέω, *I live; I dwell* (1α)

οἰκίᾱ, οἰκίᾱς, ἡ, *house; home; dwelling* (5α)

οἶκος, οἴκου, ὁ, *house; home; dwelling* (1α and 3 Gr 3)
  κατ' οἶκον, *at home* (16α)
  οἴκοι, note the accent, adv., *at home* (8α)

οἴμοι, note the accent, interjection, *alas!* (11β)

οἶνος, οἴνου, ὁ, *wine* (7β)

ὀκνέω, *I shirk*

ὀκτακόσιοι, -αι, -α, *800* (15 Gr 5)

ὀκτώ, indeclinable, *eight* (8 Gr 5)

ὀλίγος, -η, -ον, *small*; pl., *few* (14α and 14 Gr 2)
  ἐλάττων, ἔλαττον, *smaller*; pl., *fewer* (14 Gr 2)
  ὀλίγιστος, -η, -ον, *smallest*; pl., *fewest* (14 Gr 2)

ὁλκάς, ὁλκάδος, ἡ, *merchant ship*

Ὀλύμπιοι, Ὀλυμπίων, οἱ, *the Olympian gods*

ὅμῑλος, ὁμίλου, ὁ, *crowd* (12α)

ὅμως, conj., *nevertheless* (8α)

ὄνομα, ὀνόματος, τό, *name* (7α and 7 Gr 3)

ὄπισθεν, adv. or prep. + gen., *behind*
  ἐκ τοῦ ὄπισθεν, *from the rear*

ὁπλίτης, ὁπλίτου, ὁ, *hoplite* (heavily-armed foot soldier) (14α)

ὅπου, adv., *where* (14β)

ὁράω, imperfect, ἑώρων (double augment), [ὀπ-] ὄψομαι, [ἰδ-] εἶδον (irregular augment), ἰδών, *I see* (5α, 11β)

ὀργίζομαι, [ὀργιε-] ὀργιοῦμαι, no aorist middle, *I grow angry; I am an-*

gry; + dat., *I grow angry at; I am angry at*

ὀρθός, -ή, -όν, *straight; right, correct* (12α)

ὁρμάω, active, transitive, *I set* X *in motion;* active, intransitive, *I start; I rush;* middle, intransitive, *I set myself in motion; I start; I rush; I hasten* (7β)

ὄρος, ὄρους, τό, *mountain; hill* (5α)

ὅς, ἥ, ὅ, relative pronoun, *who, whose, whom, which, that* (13β and 13 Gr 3)

ὅσπερ, ἥπερ (note the accent), ὅπερ, relative pronoun, emphatic forms, *who, whose, whom, which, that* (13β)

ὅτε, adv., *when* (13β)

ὅτι, conj., *that* (5β)

οὐ, οὐκ, οὐχ, οὐχί, adv., *not* (1α)

οὐ μόνον . . . ἀλλὰ καί, *not only . . . but also* (15α)

οὐδαμοῦ, adv., *nowhere* (16α)

οὐδαμῶς, adv., *in no way, no* (6β)

οὐδέ, conj., *and . . . not; nor; not even* (5α)

οὐδείς, οὐδεμία, οὐδέν, pronoun, *no one; nothing;* adjective, *no* (7α and 8 Gr 5)

οὐδέν, *nothing, no*

οὐκέτι, adv., *no longer* (3α)

οὖν, a connecting adverb, postpositive, *so* (i.e., because of this); *then* (i.e., after this) (1α)

οὐρανός, οὐρανοῦ, ὁ, *sky, heaven* (9β)

οὔτε . . . οὔτε, note the accent, conj., *neither . . . nor* (5α)

οὗτος, αὕτη, τοῦτο, *this;* pl., *these* (14α and 14 Gr 5)

οὕτως, adv., before consonants, οὕτω, *so, thus* (2α)

ὀφθαλμός, ὀφθαλμοῦ, ὁ, *eye* (7β)

ὀψέ, adv., *late; too late*

Π

παῖς, παιδός, ὁ or ἡ, *boy; girl; son; daughter; child* (3β and 7 Gr 3b)

πανήγυρις, πανηγύρεως, ἡ, *festival*

πάντα, *everything*

πανταχόσε, adv., *in all directions*

πανταχοῦ, adv., *everywhere* (15β)

πάππας, πάππου, ὁ, ὦ πάππα, *papa* (6α)

πάππος, πάππου, ὁ, *grandfather* (5α)

παρά, prep. + acc., of persons only, *to* (11α); *along, past*

πάρα = πάρεστι(ν), *is near at hand*

παραγίγνομαι, *I arrive* (14β)

παραπλέω, *I sail by; I sail past; I sail along*

παρασκευάζω, *I prepare* (7α)

πάρειμι [= παρα- + εἰμί], *I am present; I am here; I am there* (2α); + dat., *I am present at*

παρέχω [= παρα- + ἔχω], imperfect, παρεῖχον (irregular augment), παρασχήσω (irregular), [σχ-] παρέσχον, imperative, παράσχες, participle, παρασχών, *I hand over; I supply; I provide* (6β)

παρθένος, παρθένον, *virgin, chaste* παρθένος, παρθένου, ἡ, *maiden, girl* (6α)

Παρθένος, Παρθένου, ἡ, *the Maiden* (= the goddess Athena) (9α)

Παρθενών, Παρθενῶνος, ὁ, *the Parthenon* (the temple of Athena on the Acropolis in Athens) (8β)

πᾶς, πᾶσα, πᾶν, *all; every; whole* (7β and 8 Gr 4)

πάσχω, [πενθ-] πείσομαι, [παθ-] ἔπαθον, παθών, *I suffer; I experience* (5β and 11α)

πατήρ, πατρός, ὁ, *father* (3β and 8 Gr 2)

πατρίς, πατρίδος, ἡ, *fatherland* (15β)

παύω, παύσω, ἔπαυσα, παύσας, active, transitive, *I stop* X; middle, intransitive + participle, *I stop doing* X; + gen., *I cease from* (7β)

παῦε, *stop!* (7β)

πεζός, -ή, -όν, *on foot* (15β)

πείθω, πείσω, ἔπεισα, πείσᾱς, I persuade (4β)

πείθομαι, πείσομαι + dat., I obey (6α)

Πειραιεύς, Πειραιῶς, ὁ, τῷ Πειραιεῖ, τὸν Πειραιᾶ, the Piraeus (the port of Athens) (11β)

πειράω, πειράσω (note that because of the ρ the α lengthens to ᾱ rather than η), ἐπείρᾱσα, πειρᾱσᾱς, active or middle, I try, attempt (15β)

Πελοπόννησος, Πελοποννήσου, ἡ, the Peloponnesus (14β)

πέμπτος, -η, -ον, fifth (8 Gr 5)

πέμπω, πέμψω, ἔπεμψα, πέμψᾱς, I send (6α)

πεντακόσιοι, -αι, -α, 500 (15 Gr 5)

πέντε, indeclinable, five (8 Gr 5)

πεντήκοντα, indeclinable, fifty (15 Gr 5)

πέπλος, πέπλου, ὁ, robe; cloth (15β)

περί, prep. + gen., about, concerning (7α); + acc., around (7α)

Πέρσαι, Περσῶν, οἱ, the Persians (14α)

Περσικός, -ή, -όν, Persian (15β)

πεσεῖν (aorist infinitive of πίπτω), to fall

πίνω, [πῑ-] πίομαι, [πι-] ἔπιον, πιών, I drink (9α)

πίπτω, πεσοῦμαι (irregular), ἔπεσον (irregular), πεσών, I fall (3α)

πιστεύω, πιστεύσω, ἐπίστευσα, πιστεύσᾱς + dat., I trust, am confident (in); I believe; + ὡς or infin., I believe (that) (15β)

πλεῖστος, -η, -ον, most; very great; pl., very many (12β and 14 Gr 2)

πλεῖστα, adv., most (14 Gr 3)

πλείων/πλέων, alternative forms for either masculine or feminine, πλέον, neuter, more (12β)

πλέον, adv., more (14 Gr 3)

πλέω, [πλευ-] πλεύσομαι or [πλευσε-] πλευσοῦμαι, [πλευ-] ἔπλευσα, πλεύσᾱς, I sail (6α and 6 Gr 1)

πλῆθος, πλήθους, τό, number, multitude (14α)

πληρόω, I fill

πόθεν; adv., from where? whence? (7β, 10 Gr 9, and 14 Gr 6)

ποθέν, enclitic, from somewhere (14 Gr 6)

ποῖ; to where? whither? (10 Gr 9 and 14 Gr 6)

ποι, enclitic, to somewhere (14 Gr 6)

ποιέω, I make; I do (4α)

ποιητής, ποιητοῦ, ὁ, poet (8α)

πολέμιος, -ᾱ, -ον, hostile; enemy (14β)

πολέμιοι, πολεμίων, οἱ, the enemy (14β)

πόλεμος, πολέμου, ὁ, war (14β)

πολιορκέω [= πόλις, city + ἕρκος, wall], I besiege (16β)

πόλις, πόλεως, ἡ, city (7α and 9 Gr 3)

πολίτης, πολίτου, ὁ, citizen (8β)

πολλάκις, adv., many times, often (6β)

πολλαχόσε, adv., to many parts (16α)

πολύς, πολλή, πολύ, much (1α, 4 Gr 6, and 14 Gr 2); pl., many (3β)

πλείων/πλέων, alternative forms for either masculine or feminine, πλέον, neuter, more (12β and 14 Gr 2)

πλεῖστος, -η, -ον, most; very great; pl., very many (12β and 14 Gr 2)

πολύ, adv., much (14 Gr 3)

πλέον, adv., more (14 Gr 3)

πλεῖστα, adv., most (14 Gr 3)

πομπή, πομπῆς, ἡ, procession (9β)

πονέω, I work (1α)

πόνος, πόνου, ὁ, toil, work (1α)

Πόντος, Πόντου, ὁ, Pontus, the Black Sea

πορεύομαι, πορεύσομαι, ἐπορευσάμην (only in compounds), πορευσάμενος, I go; I walk; I march; I journey (6β)

Ποσειδῶν, Ποσειδῶνος, ὁ, Poseidon (13β)

πόσος; πόση; πόσον; *how much?* pl., *how many?* (16α)

ποταμός, ποταμοῦ, ὁ, *river* (16β)

πότε; adv., *when?* (10 Gr 9 and 14 Gr 6)

ποτέ, enclitic, *at some time, at one time, once, ever* (10β and 14 Gr 6)

ποῦ; adv., *where?* (5α and 14 Gr 6)

που, enclitic, *somewhere, anywhere* (10 Gr 9 and 14 Gr 6)

ποῦ γῆς; *where (in the world)?* (16α)

ποῦς, ποδός, ὁ, *foot*

πράττω, [πρᾱκ-] πράξω, ἔπρᾱξα, πράξᾱς, intransitive, *I fare;* transitive, *I do* X (14α)

πρό, prep. + gen., of time or place, *before* (10β)

πρόβατα, προβάτων, τά, *sheep* (5α)

πρόγονος, προγόνου, ὁ, *ancestor* (15β)

πρός, prep. + dat., *at, near, by* (4α); + acc., *to, toward* (1β); *upon, onto; against* (11β)

προσβάλλω + dat., *I attack* (14α)

προσέρχομαι + dat. or πρός + acc., *I approach* (11β)

προσπλέω, *I sail toward*

προστρέχω, *I run toward*

προσχωρέω + dat., *I go toward, approach* (3α)

προτεραίᾳ, τῇ, *on the day before* (14β)

προχωρέω, *I go forward; I come forward, advance* (6β); + ἐπί + acc., *I advance against*

πρῶτος, -η, -ον, *first* (5β and 8 Gr 5)

πρῶτοι, πρώτων, οἱ, *the leaders*

πρῶτον, adv., *first* (4α)

τὸ πρῶτον, *at first*

πύλη, πύλης, ἡ, *gate*

πύλαι, πυλῶν, αἱ, pl., *double gates* (6β); *pass* (through the mountains) (14β)

πῦρ, πυρός, τό, *fire* (7β)

πυραμίς, πυραμίδος, ἡ, *pyramid*

πῶς; adv., *how?* (7β, 10 Gr 9, and 14 Gr 6)

πῶς ἔχεις; *How are you?* (11α)

πως, enclitic adv., *somehow, in any way* (14 Gr 6)

Ρ

ῥάβδος, ῥάβδου, ἡ, *wand*

ῥάδιος, -ᾱ, -ον, *easy* (4β and 4 Gr 6)

ῥᾴθῡμος [= ῥᾷ, *easily* + θῡμός, *spirit*], -ον, *careless* (5α)

ῥῆμα, ῥήματος, τό, *word*

Σ

Σαλαμίς, Σαλαμῖνος, ἡ, *Salamis* (13α)

Σάμος, Σάμου, ἡ, *Samos*

σεαυτοῦ: see ἐμαυτοῦ

σῑγάω, *I am silent* (9β)

Σικελίᾱ, Σικελίᾱς, ἡ, *Sicily*

Σιμωνίδης, Σιμωνίδου, ὁ, *Simonides* (15β)

σῖτος, σίτου, ὁ, pl., τὰ σῖτα, *grain; food* (1α)

σκοπέω, [σκεπ-] σκέψομαι, ἐσκεψάμην, σκεψάμενος, *I look at, examine; I consider* (11α)

σκότος, σκότου, ὁ, *darkness*

Σκυθίᾱ, Σκυθίᾱς, ἡ, *Scythia*

σός, -ή, -όν, *your,* sing. (5 Gr 8)

σοφός, -ή, -όν, *skilled; wise; clever* (11α)

Σπαρτιάτης, Σπαρτιάτου, ὁ, *a Spartan* (14β)

σπείρω, [σπερε-] σπερῶ, [σπειρ-] ἔσπειρα, σπείρᾱς, *I sow*

σπέρμα, σπέρματος, τό, *seed*

σπεύδω, σπεύσω, ἔσπευσα, σπεύσᾱς, *I hurry* (2α)

σπονδή, σπονδῆς, ἡ, *libation* (drink offering) (16β)

σπονδαί, σπονδῶν, αἱ, pl., *peace treaty* (16β)

σπουδή, σπουδῆς, ἡ, *haste; eagerness* (15β)

στέλλω, [στελε-] στελῶ, [στειλ-] ἔστειλα, στείλᾱς, *I take down* (sails)

στενάζω, [στεναγ-] στενάξω, ἐστέναξα, στενάξᾱς, *I groan* (4β)

στενός, -ή, -όν, *narrow* (14α)
στενά, στενῶν, τά, *narrows, straits;
mountain pass* (13β)
στοά, στοᾶς, ἡ, *colonnade*
στόλος, στόλου, ὁ, *expedition; army;
fleet* (14α)
στρατεύω, στρατεύσω, ἐστρά-
τευσα, στρατεύσᾱς, active or middle, *I
wage war, campaign* (16α)
στρατηγός, στρατηγοῦ, ὁ, *general*
(15α)
στρατιώτης, στρατιώτου, ὁ, *soldier*
(14α)
στρατός, στρατοῦ, ὁ, *army* (14α)
στρογγύλος, -η, -ον, *round*
σύ, σοῦ or σου, *you*, sing. (3β and 5 Gr
6)
συλλαμβάνω [= συν- + λαμβάνω], *I
help* (2β); + dat., *I help* X (6 Gr 6g)
συμβάλλω [= συν- + βάλλω], *I join battle;* + dat., *I join battle with* (14α)
σύμμαχος, συμμάχου, ὁ, *ally* (16α)
συμπίπτω [= συν- + πίπτω], *I clash;*
+ dat., *I clash with* (15β)
συμφορά, συμφορᾶς, ἡ, *misfortune;
disaster* (16α)
συναγείρω, active, transitive, *I gather* X;
middle, intransitive, *I gather together*
(16α)
συνέρχομαι, *I come together* (14α)
συφεός, συφεοῦ, ὁ, *pigsty*
Σφίγξ, Σφιγγός, ἡ, *Sphinx*
σῴζω, σώσω, ἔσωσα, σώσᾱς, *I save*
(6α)
σώφρων, σῶφρον, *of sound mind; prudent; self-controlled* (7β, 7 Gr 7, and 14
Gr 1)

T

ταύτῃ, adv., *in this way; here* (14 Gr 5)
ταχύς, ταχεῖα, ταχύ, *quick, swift*
(13α and 13 Gr 5)
    ταχέως, *quickly; swiftly* (4α)
    τάχιστα, adv., *most quickly; most
swiftly* (12α)

ὡς τάχιστα, *as quickly as possible* (12α)
τε . . . καί or τε καί, the τε is postpositive and enclitic, particle and conjunction, *both . . . and* (3α)
τεῖχος, τείχους, τό, *wall* (12α and 13
Gr 4)
τεκόντες, τεκόντων, οἱ, *parents* (10β)
τελευτάω, *I end; I die* (16α)
τέλος, adv., *in the end, finally* (8β)
τέμενος, τεμένους, τό, *sacred
precinct*
τέρπομαι, τέρψομαι, ἐτερψάμην,
τερψάμενος, *I enjoy myself;* + dat., *I enjoy* X; + participle, *I enjoy doing* X (9β)
τέταρτος, -η, -ον, *fourth* (8 Gr 5)
τετρακόσιοι, -αι, -α, *400* (15 Gr 5)
τετταράκοντα, indeclinable, *forty* (15
Gr 5)
τέτταρες, τέτταρα, *four* (8 Gr 5)
τῇδε, adv., *in this way; here* (14 Gr 5)
τῇ προτεραίᾳ, *on the day before* (14β)
τῇ ὑστεραίᾳ, *on the next day* (8β)
τί; adv., *why?* (2α and 10 Gr 9)
τί; pronoun, *what?* (4β and 10 Gr 9)
τῑμάω, *I honor* (5α, 5 Gr 1, 6 Gr 3, 8 Gr 1,
9 Gr 1, and 13 Gr 1)
τίς; τί; gen., τίνος; interrogative adjective, *which . . . ? what . . . ?* (7α and 7
Gr 8)
τίς; τί; gen., τίνος; interrogative pronoun, *who? what?* (7α, 7 Gr 8, and 10
Gr 9)
τις, τι gen., τινός, enclitic indefinite
adjective, *a certain; some; a, an* (7α and
7 Gr 9)
τις, τι gen., τινός, enclitic indefinite
pronoun, *someone; something; anyone;
anything* (7α and 7 Gr 9)
τλήμων, τλήμονος, *poor; wretched*
τοσοῦτος, τοσαύτη, τοσοῦτο, *so
great;* pl., *so great; so many* (3β)
τότε, adv., *then* (12β)
τούτῳ, ἐν . . . , *meanwhile* (8β)
τραγῳδίᾱ, τραγῳδίᾱς, ἡ, *tragedy*
τρεῖς, τρία, *three* (8 Gr 5)

τρεῖς καὶ δέκα, *thirteen* (15 Gr 5)

τρέπω, τρέψω, ἔτρεψα, τρέψας, active, transitive, *I turn X;* middle, intransitive, *I turn myself, turn* (10β)

τρέχω, [δραμε-] δραμοῦμαι, [δραμ-] ἔδραμον, δραμών, *I run* (5α)

τριάκοντα, indeclinable, *thirty* (15 Gr 5)

τριᾱκόσιοι, -αι, -α, *300* (15 Gr 5)

τριήρης, τριήρους, ἡ, *trireme* (a warship) (13β and 13 Gr 4)

τρίτος, -η, -ον, *third* (8 Gr 5)

Τροίᾱ, Τροίᾱς, ἡ, *Troy* (7α)

τύπτω, [τυπτε-] τυπτήσω, no other principal parts of this verb in Attic, *I strike, hit* (5β and 10β)

τυφλός, -ή, -όν, *blind* (11α)

τύχη, τύχης, ἡ, *chance; luck; fortune* (15β)

τῷ ὄντι, *in truth* (13β)

Υ

ὑδρίᾱ, ὑδρίᾱς, ἡ, *water jar* (4α and 4 Gr 3)

ὕδωρ, ὕδατος, τό, *water* (10β)

ὑλακτέω, *I bark*

ὑμεῖς, ὑμῶν, *you,* pl. (5β and 5 Gr 6)

ὑμέτερος, -ᾱ, -ον, *your,* pl. (5 Gr 8)

ὑμνέω, *I hymn, praise*

ὑπέρ, prep. + gen., *on behalf of, for* (8β); *above*

ὑπηρέτης, ὑπηρέτου, ὁ, *servant; attendant*

ὑπό, prep. + gen., *under;* of agent, *by* (16α); + dat., *under* (5β); + acc., *under* (5β)

ὑστεραίᾳ, τῇ, *on the next day* (8β)

ὕστερον, adv., *later* (16α)

ὑφαίνω, *I weave*

Φ

φαίνομαι, [φανε-] φανήσομαι or φανοῦμαι, no aorist middle, *I appear* (12β)

Φάληρον, Φαλήρου, τό, *Phalerum* (the old harbor of Athens) (14β)

φᾱσί(ν), postpositive enclitic, *they say* (6β)

Φειδίᾱς, Φειδίου, ὁ, *Pheidias* (the great Athenian sculptor) (9α)

φέρω, [οἰ-] οἴσω, [ἐνεγκ-] ἤνεγκα, ἐνέγκᾱς or ἤνεγκον, ἐνεγκών, *I carry* (1β); of roads, *lead*

φεῦ, interjection, often used with gen. of cause, *alas!* (10α)

φεύγω, φεύξομαι, [φυγ-] ἔφυγον, φυγών, *I flee; I escape* (5α)

φησί(ν), postpositive enclitic, *he/she says* (3α)

ἔφη, *he/she said*

ἔφασαν, *they said*

φιλέω, *I love* (1α, 4 Gr 1, 6 Gr 3, 8 Gr 1, 9 Gr 1, and 13 Gr 1)

Φίλιππος, Φιλίππου, ὁ, *Philip* (3β)

φίλος, -η, -ον, *dear* (4α)

φίλος, φίλου, ὁ or φίλη, φίλης, ἡ, *friend* (4α)

φλυᾱρέω, *I talk nonsense*

φοβέομαι, imperfect, usually used for fearing in past time, ἐφοβούμην, φοβήσομαι, no aorist middle, intransitive, *I am frightened, am afraid;* transitive, *I fear, am afraid of* (something or someone) (6α)

φοβερός, -ά, -όν, *terrifying, frightening*

φορτία, φορτίων, τά, *cargoes; burdens*

φράζω, φράσω, ἔφρασα, φράσᾱς, *I show; I tell (of); I explain* (14β)

φροντίζω, [φροντιε-] φροντιῶ, [φροντι-] ἐφρόντισα, φροντίσᾱς, *I worry; I care* (12α)

φυγή, φυγῆς, ἡ, *flight* (15α)

φύλαξ, φύλακος, ὁ, *guard* (7 Gr 3)

φυλάττω, [φυλακ-] φυλάξω, ἐφύλαξα, φυλάξᾱς, *I guard* (5α)

Χ

χαίρω, [χαιρε-] χαιρήσω, ἐχαίρησα, χαιρήσᾱς, *I rejoice* (1α and 4α) χαῖρε; pl., χαίρετε, *greetings!* (4α)

χαίρειν κελεύω + acc., *I bid X farewell, I bid farewell to X* (12α)

χαλεπός, -ή, -όν, *difficult* (1β and 14 Gr 1)

χειμών, χειμῶνος, ὁ, *storm; winter* (7β and 7 Gr 5)

χείρ, χειρός, ἡ, *hand* (8β)

χίλιοι, -αι, -α, *1,000* (15 Gr 5)

χῑλιοστός, -ή, -όν, *thousandth* (15 Gr 5)

χορός, χοροῦ, ὁ, *dance; chorus* (4α)

χράομαι (present and imperfect have η where α would be expected: χρῶμαι, χρῇ, χρῆται, etc.), χρήσομαι (note that the α changes to η even after the ρ), ἐχρησάμην, χρησάμενος + dat., *I use; I enjoy* (14α)

χρόνος, χρόνου, ὁ, *time* (1β)

Ψ

ψευδής, -ές, *false* (13β)

ψευδῆ, ψευδῶν, τά, *lies* (13β)

ψόφος, ψόφου, ὁ, *noise*

Ω

ὦ, interjection, introducing a vocative

ὦ Ζεῦ, *O Zeus* (3α)

ᾧ, ἐν, *while* (8α)

ὠθίζομαι, no future or aorist, *I push*

ὤν, οὖσα, ὄν, participle of εἰμί, *being* (9 Gr 1)

ὤνια, ὠνίων, τά, *wares*

ὡς, adv., in exclamations, *how!* (6β and 15 Gr 6a)

ὡς, adv. + future participle to express purpose, *to* (10 Gr 7 and 15 Gr 6a)

ὡς, adv. + superlative adjective or adverb, e.g., ὡς τάχιστα, *as quickly as possible* (12α, 14 Gr 4d, and 15 Gr 6a)

ὡς, adv., *as* (13β and 15 Gr 6a)

ὡς δοκεῖ, *as it seems* (13β and 15 Gr 6a)

ὡς, conj., temporal, *when* (14β and 15 Gr 6b)

ὡς, conj., see πιστεύω, *that* (15β and 15 Gr 6b)

ὥσπερ, note the accent, adv., *just as* (8α and 15 Gr 6a)

ὥστε, note the accent, conj. + indicative or infinitive, introducing a clause that expresses result, *so that, that, so as to* (5α and 15 Gr 6b)

ὠφελέω, *I help; I benefit* (11β)

ENGLISH TO GREEK
VOCABULARY

This English to Greek vocabulary is provided merely as a reminder of Greek equivalents of English words. For further information about the Greek words, you must consult the Greek to English Vocabulary and the readings and grammar sections in the various chapters of this book.

A

a (certain), τις
able, I am, δύναμαι
about, περί
about (to), I am, μέλλω
accomplish, I, ἐργάζομαι
Achaeans, 'Αχαιοί
Acropolis, 'Ακρόπολις
admiral, ναύαρχος
admire, I, θαυμάζω
advance (against), I, προχωρέω
Aegean Sea, Αἰγαῖος
  πόντος
Aegeus, Αἰγεύς
Aeolus, Αἴολος
Aeschylus, Αἰσχύλος
afraid (of), I am, φοβέ-
  ομαι
after, μετά
again, αὖθις
against, ἐπί, πρός
Agamemnon, 'Αγαμέ-
  μνων
agora, ἀγορά
alas! οἴμοι, φεῦ
all, ἅπᾱς, πᾶς
all right! ἔστω
allowed, it is, ἔξεστι(ν)
ally, σύμμαχος
alone, μόνος
along, παρά
already, ἤδη
also, καί
altar, βωμός
although, καίπερ
always, ἀεί
am, I, εἰμί
amazed, I am, θαυμάζω
among, ἐν
an, τις

ancestor, πρόγονος
and, δέ, καί
and in particular, καὶ δὴ
  καί
and ... not, οὐδέ
and what is more, καὶ δὴ
  καί
angry (at), I grow/am,
  ὀργίζομαι
animal, ζῷον
announce, I, ἀγγέλλω
another, ἄλλος
answer, I, ἀποκρίνομαι
anyone, anything, τις, τι
anywhere, που
appear, I, φαίνομαι
approach, I, προσ-
  έρχομαι, προσχωρέω
Argus, "Αργος
Ariadne, 'Αριάδνη
army, στόλος, στρατός
around, περί
arrive (at), I, ἀφ-
  ικνέομαι, παρα-
  γίγνομαι
Artemisium, 'Αρτεμί-
  σιον
as, ὡς
as it seems, ὡς δοκεῖ
as quickly as possible, ὡ ς
  τάχιστα
Asclepius, 'Ασκληπιός
Asia (Minor), 'Ασίᾱ
ask, I, αἰτέω, ἐρωτάω
ask for, I, αἰτέω
at, εἰς, ἐπί, πρός
at a loss, I am, ἀπορέω
at home, κατ' οἶκον,
  οἴκοι
at just the right time, εἰς
  καιρόν

at least, γε
at once, εὐθύς
at one time, ποτέ
at some time, ποτέ
at that very moment, ἐν-
  ταῦθα δή
at the same time, ἅμα
Athena, 'Αθηνᾶ, Παρ-
  θένος
Athenian, 'Αθηναῖος
Athenians, 'Αθηναῖοι
Athens, 'Αθῆναι
Athens, at, 'Αθήνησι
Athens, in, ἐν ταῖς
  'Αθήναις
Athens, to, 'Αθήνᾱζε
attack, I, ἐμπίπτω,
  προσβάλλω
attempt, I, πειράω, πει-
  ράομαι
attendant, θεράπων,
  ὑπηρέτης
Attica, 'Αττική
away, I am, ἄπειμι

B

bad, κακός
bag, ἀσκός
barbarian, βάρβαρος
bark, I, ὑλακτέω
battle, μάχη
be! ἴσθι
be so! let it, ἔστω
beast, θηρίον
beautiful, καλός
beautiful, more, καλλίων
beautiful, most, κάλλισ-
  τος
become, I, γίγνομαι
bee, μέλιττα
before, πρό

beginning, ἀρχή
behind, ὄπισθεν
being, ὤν
believe (that), I, πιστεύω
benefit, I, ὠφελέω
besiege, I, πολιορκέω
best, ἄριστος
better, ἀμείνων
between, ἐν μέσῳ
bid X farewell, I, χαίρειν
   κελεύω
big, μέγας
bigger, μείζων
biggest, μέγιστος
black, μέλᾱς
Black Sea, the, Πόντος
blame, to (adj.), αἴτιος
blind, τυφλός
Boeotia, Βοιωτίᾱ
both . . . and, καί . . .
   καί, τε . . . καί
boy, παῖς
brave, ἀνδρεῖος
bravely, ἀνδρείως
bridge, γέφῡρα
bright, λαμπρός
brilliant, λαμπρός
bring, I, κομίζω
bring in(to), I, εἰσφέρω
brother, ἀδελφός
burn, I, καίω, κάω
but, ἀλλά, δέ
by, πρός, ὑπό
by land, κατὰ γῆν
by sea, κατὰ θάλατταν

C
calf, μόσχος
call, I, καλέω
call in(to), I, εἰσκαλέω
call out, I, ἐκκαλέω
called, ὀνόματι
campaign, I, στρατεύω
can, I, δύναμαι
captain: see ship's captain
care, I, φροντίζω
careless, ῥᾴθῡμος
carry, I, φέρω
carry out, I, ἐκφέρω
catch, I, καταλαμβάνω
cause pain to, I, λῡπέω

cave, ἄντρον
cease from, I, παύομαι
celebrate a festival, I, ἑορτὴν ποιῶ/ ποιοῦμαι
celebrate the festival of
   Dionysus, I, τὰ Διο-
   νύσια ποιῶ/ποιοῦμαι
certain, a, τις
certainly, μάλιστά γε
chance, τύχη
chase, I, διώκω
child, παῖς
chorus, χορός
Cimon, Κίμων
Circe, Κίρκη
citizen, πολίτης
city, ἄστυ, πόλις
city center, ἀγορᾱ́
clash (with), I, συμπῑ́πτω
clever, σοφός
climb, I, ἀναβαίνω
cloth, πέπλος
colonnade, στοά
come! ἐλθέ
come, I, ἔρχομαι
come, I have, ἥκω
come back! ἐπάνελθε
come back, I, ἐπαν-
   έρχομαι
come back, to, ἐπανιέναι
come down, I, κατα-
   βαίνω
come forward, I, προ-
   χωρέω
come in, I, εἰσβαίνω,
   εἰσέρχομαι
come on! ἄγε
come out (of), I, ἐκ-
   βαίνω, ἐξέρχομαι
come through, I, δι-
   έρχομαι
come to know, I, γιγνώ-
   σκω
come to rescue/aid X, I,
   βοηθέω
come to the rescue, I, βοηθέω
come to X's aid, I, βοηθέω
come together, I, συν-
   έρχομαι
coming out, ἐξελθών

commotion, θόρυβος
companion, ἑταῖρος
compel, I, ἀναγκάζω
comrade, ἑταῖρος
concerning, περί
confident (in), I am, πιστεύω
consider, I, σκοπέω
contest, ἀγών
converse with, I, δια-
   λέγομαι
Corinth, Κόρινθος
corpse, νεκρός
correct, ὀρθός
courage, ἀρετή
Crete, Κρήτη
cross, I, διαβαίνω
crowd, ὅμῑλος
cry, I, δακρῡ́ω
cursed, κατάρᾱτος
Cyclops, Κύκλωψ
Cyprus, Κύπρος
Cyrene, Κυρήνη

D
dance, χορός
danger, κίνδῡνος
darkness, σκότος
daughter, θυγάτηρ,
   παῖς
day, ἡμέρᾱ
day, on the next, τῇ
   ὑστεραίᾳ
day before, on the, τῇ
   προτεραίᾳ
dear, φίλος
death, θάνατος
decide, I, δοκεῖ μοι
deed, ἔργον
defeat, I, νῑκάω
defend myself (against), I,
   ἀμῡ́νομαι
desert, I, καταλείπω
destined (to), I am, μέλλω
destroy, I, ἀπόλλῡμι,
   διαφθείρω
Dicaeopolis, Δικαιό-
   πολις
die, I, ἀποθνῄσκω,
   τελευτάω
difficult, χαλεπός

difficulty, ἀπορίᾱ
difficulty, with, μόλις
dinner, δεῖπνον
Dionysus, Διόνῡσος
directions, in all, πανταχόσε
disaster, συμφορᾱ́
disembark, ἐκβαίνω ἐκ τῆς νεώς
distressed, I am, λῡπέομαι
do, I, ποιέω, πράττω
doctor, ἰᾱτρός
dog, κύων
don't, μή
don't . . . any longer, μηκέτι
door, θύρᾱ
down, κατά
drachma, δραχμή
drag, I, ἕλκω
drink, I, πίνω
drive, I, ἐλαύνω
drive away, I, ἀπελαύνω
drive in, I, εἰσελαύνω
drive out, I, ἐξελαύνω
drop, I, καταβάλλω
drunk, I am, μεθύω
during (use acc. of duration of time)
dwell, I, οἰκέω
dwelling, οἰκίᾱ, οἶκος

E
eagerness, σπουδή
earth, γῆ
easy, ῥᾴδιος
eat, I, δειπνέω, ἐσθίω
Egypt, Αἴγυπτος
Egyptians, Αἰγύπτιοι
eight, ὀκτώ
eighth, ὄγδοος
either . . . or, ἤ . . . ἤ
embark, I, εἰς ναῦν εἰσβαίνω
end, I, τελευτάω
enemy, πολέμιος
enemy, the, πολέμιοι
enjoy, I, χράομαι
enjoy (myself), I, τέρπομαι

enslave, I, δουλόω
entrance, εἴσοδος
Ephialtes, Ἐφιάλτης
Epidaurus, Ἐπίδαυρος
escape (from), I, ἀποφεύγω, ἐκφεύγω, φεύγω
escape route, ἔκπλους
especially, μάλιστα
Euboea, Εὔβοια
Eurylochus, Εὐρύλοχος
Eurymedon River, the, Εὐρυμέδων
even, καί
evening, ἑσπέρᾱ
ever, ποτέ
every, ἅπᾱς, πᾶς
every day, καθ' ἡμέρᾱν
everything, πάντα
everywhere, πανταχοῦ
evil, κακός
examine, I, σκοπέω
excellence, ἀρετή
expect, I, ἐλπίζω
expedition, στόλος
experience, I, πάσχω
explain, I, φράζω
eye, ὀφθαλμός

F
fall, I, πίπτω
fall down, I, καταπίπτω
fall into, I, ἐμπίπτω
fall (of evening, etc.), γίγνεται
fall out, I, ἐκπίπτω
fall (up)on, I, ἐμπίπτω
false, ψευδής
far corner, μυχός
fare, I, πράττω
farm, κλῆρος
farm, I, γεωργέω
farmer, αὐτουργός
father, πάππας, πατήρ
fatherland, πατρίς
fear, I, φοβέομαι
festival, ἑορτή, πανήγυρις

festival of Dionysus, Διονύσια
few, pl. of ὀλίγος
fewer, pl. of ἐλάττων
fewest, pl. of ὀλίγιστος
field, ἀγρός
fierce, ἄγριος
fifth, πέμπτος
fight, μάχη
fight (against), I, μάχομαι
fight by sea, I, ναυμαχέω
fill, I, πληρόω
finally, τέλος
find, I, εὑρίσκω
fire, πῦρ
fire, I am on, καίομαι, κάομαι
firm, βέβαιος
first, πρῶτον, πρῶτος
first, at, τὸ πρῶτον
five, πέντε
flee, I, φεύγω
flee (away), I, ἀποφεύγω
flee (out), I, ἐκφεύγω
fleet, ναυτικόν, στόλος
flight, φυγή
flow in, I, εἰσρέω
follow, I, ἕπομαι
food, σῖτος
foot, πούς
foot, on, πεζός
for, γάρ, εἰς, ὑπέρ
foreigner, ξένος
forget, I, ἐπιλανθάνομαι
fortune, τύχη
four, τέτταρες
fourth, τέταρτος
free, ἐλεύθερος
free, I, ἐλευθερόω
freedom, ἐλευθερίᾱ
friend, φίλη, φίλος
frightened, I am, φοβέομαι
frightening, φοβερός
frightfully, δεινῶς
from, ἀπό
from where? πόθεν;

G

garden, κῆπος
gates, double, πύλαι
gather (together), I, συναγείρω
general, στρατηγός
get (myself) up, I, *see*
αἴρω, ἐπαίρω
get up, I, ἀναβαίνω
giant, γίγᾱς
girl, κόρη, παῖς, παρ-
θένος
go! ἴθι
go, I, βαδίζω, βαίνω,
ἔρχομαι, πορεύομαι
go, to, ἰέναι
go away, I, ἀπέρχομαι
go down, I, καταβαίνω
go forward, I, προχωρέω
go in, I, εἰσβαίνω, εἰσ-
έρχομαι
go in, to, εἰσιέναι
go on! ἴθι δή
go on board ship, I, εἰς
ναῦν εἰσβαίνω
go out of, I, ἐκβαίνω,
ἐξέρχομαι
go through, I, διέρχομαι
go toward, I, προσχωρέω
go up (onto), I, ἀνα-
βαίνω
goat, αἴξ
god, θεός
goddess, θεός
good, ἀγαθός
good! εὖ γε
good order, κόσμος
grain, σῖτος
grandfather, πάππος
grapes, βότρυες
great, μέγας
greater, μείζων
greatest, μέγιστος
greatly, μέγα
Greece, Ἑλλάς
Greek(s), Ἕλλην(ες)
Greeks, Ἀχαιοί
greetings! χαῖρε
grieve, I, λῡπέω
grieved, I am, λῡπέομαι

groan, I, στενάζω
ground, γῆ
grow angry (at), I, ὀργί-
ζομαι
guard, φύλαξ
guard, I, φυλάττω

H

hand, χείρ
hand over, I, παρέχω
happens, it, γίγνεται
harbor, λιμήν
hare, λαγώς
harm, I, βλάπτω
has become, he/she/it,
γέγονε
haste, σπουδή
hasten, I, ὁρμάομαι
have, I, ἔχω
have come, I, ἥκω
have in mind, I, ἐν νῷ
ἔχω
having come out, ἐξ-
ελθών
he, and, ὁ δέ
head, κεφαλή
heal, I, ἰᾱτρεύω
hear, I, ἀκούω
heaven, οὐρανός
Hellas, Ἑλλάς
Hellespont, Ἑλλήσπον-
τος
help, I, συλλαμβάνω,
ὠφελέω
her, αὐτήν
herald, κῆρυξ
here, δεῦρο, ἐνθάδε,
ἐνταῦθα, ταύτῃ,
τῇδε
here, I am, πάρειμι
herself, of: *see* ἐμαυτοῦ
hill, ὄρος
him, αὐτόν
himself, of: *see* ἐμαυτοῦ
hit, I, βάλλω, τύπτω
hither, δεῦρο, ἐνθάδε,
ἐνταῦθα
hold, I, ἔχω
hold onto, I, ἔχομαι
home, οἰκίᾱ, οἶκος

home, at, κατ' οἶκον,
οἴκοι
home, to, οἴκαδε
homeward, οἴκαδε
honor, I, τῑμάω
hope, I, ἐλπίζω
hoplite, ὁπλίτης
horse, ἵππος
hostile, πολέμιος
house, οἰκίᾱ, οἶκος
how, ὡς
how? πῶς;
How are you? πῶς ἔχεις;
how many? pl. of πόσος;
how much? πόσος;
human being, ἄνθρωπος
hundred, a, ἑκατόν
hunger, λῑμός
hurry, I, σπεύδω
hurt, I, βλάπτω
husband, ἀνήρ
hymn, I, ὑμνέω

I

I, ἐγώ
I am, εἰμί
idle, ἀργός
if, εἰ
if perhaps, if somehow, εἰ
πως
ill, I am, νοσέω
immediately, εὐθύς
impossible, ἀδύνατος
in, ἐν
in, I am, ἔνειμι
in all directions, παντα-
χόσε
in any way, πως
in Athens, ἐν ταῖς
Ἀθήναις
in no way, οὐδαμῶς
in order, κόσμῳ
in the end, τέλος
in the field, ἐν τῷ ἀγρῷ
in this way, ταύτῃ, τῇδε
in truth, τῷ ὄντι
increase, I, αὐξάνω
indeed, γε, δή, μάλιστά
γε
inhabitant, ἔνοικος

intend (to), I, ἐν νῷ ἔχω, μέλλω
into, εἰς
Ionia, Ἰωνίᾱ
Ionians, Ἴωνες
is, he/she/it, ἐστί(ν)
island, νῆσος
it, αὐτόν, αὐτήν, αὐτό
it is necessary, δεῖ
itself: *see* ἐμαυτοῦ

J

jar, water, ὑδρίᾱ
join battle (with), I, συμβάλλω
journey, ὁδός
journey, I, πορεύομαι
just as, ὥσπερ

K

keep quiet, I, ἡσυχάζω
kill, I, ἀποκτείνω
killed, he/she has, ἀπέκτονε
kindle, I, καίω, κάω
kindly, εὐμενῶς
king, βασιλεύς
knife, μάχαιρα
knock on (a door), I, κόπτω
Knossos, Κνωσός
know, I, ἐπίσταμαι
know, come to, I, γιγνώσκω

L

labyrinth, λαβύρινθος
Lacedaemonians, the, Λακεδαιμόνιοι
land, γῆ
land, on *or* by, κατὰ γῆν
large, μακρός, μέγας
larger, μείζων
largest, μέγιστος
later, ὕστερον
lazy, ἀργός
lead, I, ἄγω, ἡγέομαι
lead in, I, εἰσάγω, εἰσηγέομαι
lead (of roads), I, φέρω

lead out, I, ἐξάγω
leaders, pl. of πρῶτος
learn, I, γιγνώσκω, μανθάνω
least of all, ἥκιστά γε
leave, I, λείπω
leave behind, I, καταλείπω
left hand, ἀριστερά
Leonidas, Λεωνίδης
libation, σπονδή
lie, I, κεῖμαι
lie down, I, κατάκειμαι
lie near, I, ἐπίκειμαι
lie off, I, ἐπίκειμαι
lies, ψευδῆ
life, βίος
lift, I, αἴρω, ἐπαίρω
lion, λέων
listen (to), I, ἀκούω
live, I, οἰκέω
long, μακρός
long (of time), πολύς
look! ἰδού
look, I, βλέπω
look at, I, θεάομαι, σκοπέω
look for, I, ζητέω
loose/loosen, I, λύω
lose, I, ἀπόλλῡμι
loss, I am at a, ἀπορέω
loss, state of being at a, ἀπορίᾱ
loudly, μέγα
love, I, ἐράω, φιλέω
luck, τύχη

M

made of stone, λίθινος
maiden, παρθένος
Maiden, the, Παρθένος
make, I, ποιέω
make X sit down, I, καθίζω
man, ἀνήρ, ἄνθρωπος
man, young, νεᾱνίας
many, pl. of πολύς
many times, πολλάκις
march, I, ἐλαύνω, πορεύομαι

market place, ἀγορᾱ́
master, δεσπότης
may, ἔξεστι(ν)
me, με
meal, δεῖπνον
meanwhile, ἐν . . . τούτῳ
Melissa, Μέλιττα
Memphis, Μέμφις
merchant, ἔμπορος
merchant ship, ὁλκάς
messenger, ἄγγελος
middle (of), μέσος
mind, νοῦς
mind, have in, I, ἐν νῷ ἔχω
mine, ἐμός
Minos, Μίνως
Minotaur, Μῑνώταυρος
misfortune, συμφορᾱ́
money, ἀργύριον
monument, μνημεῖον
more, μᾶλλον, πλείων/πλέων
more, and what is, καὶ δὴ καί
most, μάλιστα, πλεῖστος
most of all, μάλιστα
most swiftly/quickly, τάχιστα
mother, μήτηρ
motion, set in, I, ὁρμάω
motionless, ἀκίνητος
Mount Etna, Αἰτναῖον ὄρος
mountain, ὄρος
mountain pass, στενά
much, πολύς
mule, ἡμίονος
multitude, πλῆθος
must, δεῖ
my, ἐμός
Mycale, Μυκαλή
Myrrhine, Μυρρίνη
myself, of, ἐμαυτοῦ

N

name, ὄνομα
name, by, ὀνόματι

narrow, στενός
narrows, στενά
near, ἐγγύς, πρός
necessary, it is, δεῖ
neither . . . nor,
  οὔτε . . . οὔτε
nevertheless, ὅμως
next day, on the, τῇ
  ὑστεραίᾳ
night, νύξ
Nike, Νίκη
Nile, Νεῖλος
nine, ἐννέα
ninth, ἔνατος
no, μηδείς, οὐδαμῶς,
  οὐδείς, οὐδέν, οὐχί
no longer, μηκέτι, οὐ-
  κέτι
no one, μηδείς, οὐδείς
noble, ἄριστος
nor, οὐδέ
not, μή, οὐ, οὐκ, οὐχ,
  οὐχί
not, and, οὐδέ
not at all, ἥκιστά γε
not even, οὐδέ
not only . . . but also, οὐ
  μόνον . . . ἀλλὰ καί
not working, ἀργός
nothing, μηδέν, οὐδέν
now, ἤδη, νῦν
nowhere, οὐδαμοῦ
number, πλῆθος
nymph, νύμφη

O
obey, I, πείθομαι
obol, ὀβολός
obstruct, I, ἐμποδίζω
Odysseus, Ὀδυσσεύς
of one another, ἀλλήλων
of sound mind, σώφρων
often, πολλάκις
old, γεραιός, γέρων
old man, γέρων
on, ἐν, ἐπί, κατά, πρός
on behalf of, ὑπέρ
on fire, I am, καίομαι,
  κάομαι
on foot, πεζός

on the day before, τῇ
  προτεραίᾳ
on the next day, τῇ
  ὑστεραίᾳ
on the one hand . . . and on
  the other hand . . .; on the
  one hand . . . but on the
  other hand, μέν . . . δέ
  . . .
once, ποτέ
one, εἷς
one another, of,
  ἀλλήλων
only, μόνον, μόνος
onto, ἐπί, πρός
opposite, ἐναντίος
or, ἤ
order, I, κελεύω
order, in, κόσμῳ
other, ἄλλος
our, ἡμέτερος
out of, ἐκ, ἐξ
overtake, I, κατα-
  λαμβάνω
ox, βοῦς

P
pain to X, cause, I, λυπέω
papa, πάππας
parents, τεκόντες
part, μέρος
Parthenon, Παρθενών
particular, and in, καὶ δὴ
  καί
parts, to many, πολλα-
  χόσε
pass (through the
  mountains), πύλαι
past, παρά
path, ἀτραπός
pay, μισθός
peace, εἰρήνη
peace treaty, σπονδαί
Peloponnesus, the, Πελο-
  πόννησος
pelt, I, βάλλω
people, the, δῆμος
perceive, I, γιγνώσκω
perplexity, ἀπορίᾱ
Persian, Περσικός

Persians, the, Πέρσαι
person, ἄνθρωπος
persuade, I, πείθω
Phalerum, Φάληρον
Pheidias, Φειδίᾱς
Philip, Φίλιππος
pigsty, συφεός
Piraeus, the, Πειραιεύς
place, I, καθίζω
plow, ἄροτρον
plow, I, ἀρόω
plowing, ἄροτος
poet, ποιητής
Pontus, Πόντος
poor, τλήμων
Poseidon, Ποσειδῶν
possible, δυνατός
possible, it is, ἔξεστι(ν)
praise, I, ὑμνέω
pray (to), pray (that), I,
  εὔχομαι
precinct, sacred, τέμενος
prepare, I, παρα-
  σκευάζω, παρα-
  σκευάζομαι
present (at), I am, πάρ-
  ειμι
priest, ἱερεύς
prison, δεσμωτήριον
procession, πομπή
promontory, ἀκτή
propitious, ἵλεως
provide, I, παρέχω
prudent, σώφρων
punish, I, κολάζω
pursue, I, διώκω
push, I, ὠθίζομαι
put, I, βάλλω
pyramid, πυραμίς

Q
quick, ταχύς
quickly, ταχέως
quickly, most, τάχιστα
quiet, ἥσυχος
quiet, keep, I, ἡσυχάζω

R
raise, I, ἐπαίρω
ransom, I, λύομαι

rather, μᾶλλον
rather than, μᾶλλον ἤ
ready, ἕτοιμος
rear, from the, ἐκ τοῦ ὄπισθεν
reason, λόγος
receive, I, δέχομαι
rejoice, I, χαίρω
relate, I, ἐξηγέομαι
reluctantly, μόλις
resist, I, ἀντέχω
responsible (for), αἴτιος
rest, I, ἡσυχάζω
retreat, I, ἀναχωρέω
return, to, ἐπανιέναι
return home, I, νοστέω
return (to), I, ἐπανέρχομαι
revel, I, κωμάζω
reward, μισθός
right, δεξιός, ὀρθός
right hand, δεξιά
right time, καιρός
right time, just at the, εἰς καιρόν
river, ποταμός
road, ὁδός
robe, πέπλος
rough, I am, κῡμαίνω
round, στρογγύλος
route, escape, ἔκπλους
row, I, ἐρέσσω
rower, ἐρέτης
rule, I, βασιλεύω
run, I, τρέχω
run toward, I, προστρέχω
rush, I, ὁρμάομαι, ὁρμάω

S

sacrificial victim, ἱερεῖον
said, he/she, ἔφη
said, I/they, εἶπον
said, they, ἔφασαν
sail, I, πλέω
sail against, I, ἐπιπλέω
sail along, I, παραπλέω
sail away, I, ἀποπλέω
sail by, I, παραπλέω

sail in(to), I, εἰσπλέω
sail out, I, ἐκπλέω
sail past, I, παραπλέω
sail toward, I, προσπλέω
sailor, ναύτης
sails, ἱστία
Salamis, Σαλαμίς
same, αὐτός
same time, at the, ἅμα
Samos, Σάμος
sausage-seller, ἀλλᾱντοπώλης
savage, ἄγριος
save, I, σῴζω
say, I, λέγω
say, they, φᾱσί(ν)
say, to, εἰπεῖν
says, he/she, φησί(ν)
scarcely, μόλις
Scythia, Σκυθίᾱ
sea, θάλαττα
sea, by, κατὰ θάλατταν
seat myself, I, καθίζομαι
second, δεύτερος
see, I, βλέπω, θεάομαι, θεωρέω, ὁράω
seed, σπέρμα
seek, I, ζητέω
seems, as it, ὡς δοκεῖ
seems (good), it, δοκεῖ
seems good to me, it, δοκεῖ μοι
seize, I, λαμβάνομαι
-self, -selves, αὐτός
self-controlled, σώφρων
send, I, πέμπω
send against, I, ἐπιπέμπω
send away, I, ἀποπέμπω
send in, I, ἐπιπέμπω
send out, I, ἐκπέμπω
servant, θεράπων, ὑπηρέτης
set, I, καθίζω
set free, I, ἐλευθερόω
set myself in motion, I, ὁρμάομαι
set out, I, ὁρμάομαι, ὁρμάω
set X in motion, I, ὁρμάω
seven, ἑπτά

seventh, ἕβδομος
sheep, πρόβατα
sheepfold, αὔλιον
ship, ναῦς
ship, merchant, ὁλκάς
ship's captain, ναύκληρος
shirk, I, ὀκνέω
shout, βοή
shout, I, βοάω
show, I, δηλόω, φράζω
Sicily, Σικελίᾱ
sick, I am, κάμνω, νοσέω
silent, I am, σῑγάω
silver, ἀργύριον
Simonides, Σιμωνίδης
sit (down), I, καθίζω, καθίζομαι
sit down, I make X, καθίζω
six, ἕξ
sixth, ἕκτος
skilled, σοφός
sky, οὐρανός
slave, δοῦλος
sleep, I, καθεύδω
slow, βραδύς
slowly, βραδέως
small, μῑκρός, ὀλίγος
smaller, ἐλάττων, μῑκρότερος
smallest, μῑκρότατος, ὀλίγιστος
so, οὖν, οὕτω(ς)
so great, τοσοῦτος
so many, pl. of τοσοῦτος
so that, ὥστε
soldier, στρατιώτης
some, τις
somehow, πως
someone, something, τις, τι
something bad, κακόν τι
somewhere, που
somewhere, from, ποθέν
somewhere, to, ποι
son, παῖς
soon, δι᾽ ὀλίγου
sow, I, σπείρω

Spartan, Σπαρτιάτης
Spartans, the, Λακεδαι-
  μόνιοι
speak, I, λέγω
Sphinx, Σφίγξ
spirit, θῡμός
spoke, I/they, εἶπον
spring, κρήνη
stake, μοχλός
stand/stood, see ἔστην
stand up! ἀνάστηθι
start, I, ὁρμάομαι, ὁρ-
  μάω
state of being at a loss, the,
  ἀπορίᾱ
statue, εἰκών
stay, I, μένω
steady, βέβαιος
steersman, κυβερνήτης
step, I, βαίνω
step out, I, ἐκβαίνω
still, ἔτι
stone, λίθος
stone, of, λίθινος
stood, I, ἔστην
stood up, I, ἀνέστην
stop! παῦε
stop, I, παύω
stop (doing), I, παύομαι
stopped, I, ἔστην
storm, χειμών
story, λόγος, μῦθος
straight, ὀρθός
straightway, εὐθύς
straits, στενά
stranger, ξένος
strike, I, βάλλω, κόπτω,
  τύπτω
strong, ἰσχῡρός
struggle, ἀγών
suffer, I, πάσχω
sun, ἥλιος
supply, I, παρέχω
suppose, I, ἐλπίζω
swift, ταχύς
swiftly, ταχέως
sword, ξίφος

T
take, I, ἄγω, αἱρέω,
  κομίζω, λαμβάνω

take across, to, δια-
  βιβάσαι
take down (sails), I,
  στέλλω
take hold of, I, λαμβάνο-
  μαι
take in, I, εἰσάγω
take out, I, ἐξαιρέω
talk nonsense, I, φλυᾱρέω
talk to, I, διαλέγομαι
tell! εἰπέ
tell, I, ἀγγέλλω, λέγω
tell, to, εἰπεῖν
tell (of), I, φράζω
tell (someone to do some-
  thing), I, κελεύω
temple, ἱερόν
ten, δέκα
tenth, δέκατος
terrible, δεινός
terrible things, δεινά
terribly, δεινῶς
terrifying, φοβερός
than, ἤ
that, ἐκεῖνος, ὅς, ὅσ-
  περ, ὅτι, ὡς, ὥστε
the, ὁ, ἡ, τό
theater, θέᾱτρον
them: see αὐτός
Themistocles, Θεμισ-
  τοκλῆς
then, ἐνταῦθα (δή),
  ἔπειτα, οὖν, τότε
there, ἐκεῖ, ἐνθάδε,
  ἐνταῦθα
there, I am, πάρειμι
thereafter, ἔπειτα
Thermopylae, Θερμο-
  πύλαι
Theseus, Θησεύς
things: use neuter plural of
  adjective
think it best, I, δοκεῖ μοι
third, τρίτος
this, pl., these, οὗτος
this here, pl., these here,
  ὅδε
thither, ἐκεῖσε, ἐνθάδε,
  ἐνταῦθα
those, pl., of ἐκεῖνος

thread, λίνον
three, τρεῖς
three hundred, τριᾱ-
  κόσιοι
through, διά
throw, I, βάλλω
throw down, I,
  καταβάλλω
throw out, I, ἐκβάλλω
Thunderer, Βρόμιος
thus, οὕτω(ς)
time, χρόνος
time, (right), καιρός
tin, κασσίτερος
tired, I am, κάμνω
to, εἰς, παρά, πρός
to Athens, Ἀθήνᾱζε
to blame (adj.), αἴτιος
to home, οἴκαδε
to many parts, πολλα-
  χόσε
to that place, ἐκεῖσε
together, ἅμα
toil, πόνος
told, I/they, εἶπον
tomorrow, αὔριον
too, καί
top (of), ἄκρος
top of the mountain/hill,
  ἄκρον τὸ ὄρος
toward, πρός
tragedy, τραγῳδίᾱ
transport, to, δια-
  βιβάσαι
tree, δένδρον
trireme, τριήρης
Troy, Τροίᾱ
true, ἀληθής
trust, I, πιστεύω
truth, ἀληθῆ
truth, in, τῷ ὄντι
try, I, πειράομαι, πει-
  ράω
turn, I, τρέπω
turn (myself), I, τρέπο-
  μαι
two, δύο
two hundred, διᾱκόσιοι

U
under, ὑπό

understand, I, ἐπίσ-
ταμαι, μανθάνω
unless, εἰ μή
unmoved, ἀκίνητος
until, ἕως
up, ἀνά
upon, ἐπί, πρός
uproar, θόρυβος
us, ἡμῶν, ἡμῖν, ἡμᾶς
use, I, χράομαι

V

very, μάλα
very big, μέγιστος
very good, ἄριστος
very great, πλεῖστος
very many, pl. of πλεῖσ-
τος
very much, μάλιστα
vex, I, λῡπέω
victim, sacrificial, ἱερεῖον
victory, νίκη
virtue, ἀρετή

W

wage war, I, στρατεύω
wagon, ἅμαξα
wait (for), I, μένω
wake X up, I, ἐγείρω
walk, I, βαδίζω, βαίνω,
πορεύομαι
wall, τεῖχος
wand, ῥάβδος
want, I, βούλομαι
war, πόλεμος
ward off, I, ἀμύνω
wares, ὤνια
watch, I, θεάομαι, θεω-
ρέω

water, ὕδωρ
water jar, ὑδρίᾱ
wave, κῦμα
way, ὁδός
way, in any, πως
way, in this, ταύτῃ
we, ἡμεῖς
weep, I, δακρύω
well, εὖ, καλῶς
well, I am, καλῶς ἔχω
well done! εὖ γε
what? τί; τίς;
when, ἐπεί, ὅτε, ὡς
when? πότε;
whence? πόθεν;
where, ὅπου
where? ποῦ;
where?, from, πόθεν;
where (in the world)? ποῦ
γῆς;
where to? ποῖ;
whether, εἰ
which, ὅς, ὅσπερ
which? τί; τίς;
while, ἐν ᾧ
whither? ποῖ;
who? τίς;
who, whose, whom,
which, that, ὅς, ὅσπερ
whole, ἅπᾱς, πᾶς
why? τί;
wife, γυνή
wild, ἄγριος
wild beast, θηρίον
will go, I, εἶμι
willing, I am, ἐθέλω
win, I, νῑκάω
wind, ἄνεμος
wine, οἶνος

winter, χειμών
wise, σοφός
wish, I, βούλομαι,
ἐθέλω
with, μετά
with difficulty, μόλις
withdraw, I, ἀναχωρέω
wolf, λύκος
woman, γυνή
wonder at, I, θαυμάζω
word, λόγος
work, ἔργον, πόνος
work, I, ἐργάζομαι, πο-
νέω
worry, I, φροντίζω
worse, κακίων
worst, κάκιστος
worthy (of), ἄξιος
wretched, τλήμων
write, I, γράφω

X

Xanthias, Ξανθίᾱς
Xerxes, Ξέρξης

Y

year, ἔτος
yield, I, εἴκω
you, pl., ὑμεῖς
you, sing., σύ
young man, νεᾱνίᾱς
your, pl., ὑμέτερος
your, sing., σός,
yourself, of, σεαυτοῦ

Z

Zeus, Ζεύς
Zeus, O, ὦ Ζεῦ

GENERAL INDEX

This index is selective. It does not include the names of the family members when they appear in the stories, but it does include them when they appear in essays. Numbers in boldface refer to illustrations or maps.

A

Abraham, 93, 95, 105, 106, 200
Achaemenids, 219
Acharnians, Aristophanes', 7
Achilles, 102, 103
Acropolis, 117, **117**, 123, 133, 134, 139, 140, **141**, 264, 265, **280**
Aeaea, 149
Aegean Sea, 91, 110, 118, 119, 201, 220, 221, 268, 272
Aegeus, 73, 110, 111
Aegina, 201
Aeolia, 130
Aeolic dialect, 131, 280
Aeolus, 130, 131, 149
Aeschinus, 183
Aeschylus, 221
   Persae, 255–256, 259
Aetna, Mount, 275
Afghanistan, 220
Africa, 249
Agamemnon, 95, 102, 103
agora, 29, **138**, 139
Akkad, 220
Al Mina, 201
Alcaeus, 202
Alexander the Great, 219
alphabet, 201
altar of the ten eponymous heroes of Athens, 139
altar of Zeus, 139
Amasis, 201
Amazon, **83**
   Amazons, 82
Amphiaraus, 183
Anacreon, 71
Anacreontea, 71
animal sacrifice, 60
Antimenidas, 202

Aphrodite, 60, 81
Apollo, 60, 61, 151, 168, 219, 255
   Apollo Patroos, temple of, 139
   Apollo, sacrifice to, **168**
Archaic Greece, xi
Archilochus, 121, 173, 231, 241
archon, 118
Areopagus, 139, 264
Ares, 60
Argathonius, 210
Ariadne, 73, 85, 86, **91**, 91, **92**, 110
Aristagoras, 220, 239
aristocracy, 201
Aristophanes, x, 7, 16
   Acharnians, 7
Aristotle, 15, 16
army, the Persian, 260
Artemis, 60
Artemisium, 244
Asclepius, 188
Asia Minor, 117, 119, 219, 261, 272, 278, 279
Asopus River, 247
Assembly, Athenian, 29, 43, 118, 139
Assyria, 218
Assyrian Empire, 218
Athena, 60, 81, **81**, 140, 162
   Nike, temple of, **280**
   Parthenos, 134
   Parthenos, statue of, inside the Parthenon, **132**, 134, 140
   Promachos, statue of, 134, 139, 140, **141**
Athenian(s), 3, 6–7, 16, 29, 35, 37, 43, 44, 46, 51, 73, 84, 113, 118, 119, 120,

162, 163, 202, 220, 221, 224, 239, 240, **250**, 251, 255, 261, 264, 265, 267, 271, 272, 273, 275, 280, 281
   Assembly, 29, 43, 118, 139
   democracy, ix, 7, 29
   Empire, 119, 120, 271–273, **272**
   navy, 202
   tribute list, **273**
Athens, ix, 3, 6, 7, 15, 16, 28, 29, 35, 59, 70, 73, 74, 82, 85, 91, 110, 111, **117**, 117–120, **120**, 123, **132**, **138**, 139–140, 162, 202, 206, 213, 220, 224, 230, 238–240, 271–273, 278
   city of, 139–140
   rise of, 238–240
   history of, 117–120
athletic competitions, 163
Athos, Mount, 221, 240
Atlas, 131
Atossa, 255
Attic dialect, 131
Attica, 6, 28, 82, 117, 118, 119, 221, 239, 240, 243, 244, 251
Augustus Caesar, 257

B

Babylon, 202, 218, 219, 220
Babylonians, 218
Bacchylides, x
Bardiya, 220
Bay of Cadiz, 201
Bay of Naples, 201
Beatitudes, the, 185
Bethlehem, 257, 281
Bias of Priene, 70, 211
Birth of Jesus, 257, 281

LIST OF MAPS

ACKNOWLEDGMENTS

The material on writing Greek letters on pages xvi–xviii is taken from Eugene Van Ness Goetchius's *The Language of the New Testament*, originally published in 1965 by Charles Scribner's Sons, New York, and now available from Pearson Education, Inc., Upper Saddle River, NJ.

The Greek words and the names of the Muses, Graces, and Fates on pages xviii–xix are taken from Jane Gray Carter's *Little Studies in Greek*, published by Silver, Burdett and Company, New York, © 1927, pages 63–70 and 101–102.

Most of the passages in the Classical Greek readings and some of the quotations from Greek authors in the stories are taken from Loeb Classical Library editions (Cambridge, Mass.: Harvard University Press) with permission of the publishers and the Trustees of the Loeb Classical Library.

The selections from the Gospel of Luke are taken from *The Greek New Testament*, Fourth Revised Edition, edited by Barbara Aland, Kurt Aland, Johannes Karavidopoulos, Carlo M. Martini, and Bruce M. Metzger, © 1993 Deutsche Bibelgesellschaft, Stuttgart (available in the U.S.A. from the American Bible Society, 1865 Broadway, New York, NY 10023).

The passages from Aeschylus's *Persians* on pages 255–256 are taken from Anthony J. Podlecki, *The Persians by Aeschylus*, Upper Saddle River, NJ: Prentice Hall, © 1970.

LIST OF ILLUSTRATIONS

84 (Drawing: Catherine Balme).

91 Detail of an early Apulian red figure stamnos. Ht. 30 cm (11 13/16 in.). © 2002 Museum of Fine Arts, Boston 00.349a, Henry Lillie Pierce Fund. (Photo: Museum).

92 Detail of a Faliscan red figure calyx-krater. Ht. 49.1 cm. (19 5/16 in.). © 2002 Museum of Fine Arts, Boston 1970.487, John H. and Ernestine A. Payne Fund. (Photo: Museum).

94 (Drawing: Catherine Balme).

102 Bust of Homer. Sculpture 1825. Reproduced by courtesy of the Trustees of the British Museum, London. (Photo: Museum).

104 (Drawing: Catherine Balme).

112 (Drawing: Catherine Balme).

117 The Acropolis of Athens. (Photo: Alison Frantz).

119 Relief with Persian guards. Courtesy of the Oriental Institute of the University of Chicago P-848b/P. 58360/N. 38245. (Photo: Museum).

120 Bust of Pericles. Sculpture 549. Reproduced by courtesy of the Trustees of the British Museum, London. (Photo: Museum).

120 Reconstruction of house. From Peter Connolly and Hazel Dodge, *The Ancient City: Life in Classical Athens & Rome*, Oxford University Press, © 1998, page 49.

121 Floor plan of house. From Peter Connolly and Hazel Dodge, *The Ancient City: Life in Classical Athens & Rome*, Oxford University Press, © 1998, page 48.

122 (Drawing: Catherine Balme).

132 Model of Athena Parthenos. With permission of the Royal Ontario Museum, Toronto, Canada 962.228.16. © ROM. (Photo: Museum).

138 Model of the Agora. Athens, American School of Classical Studies at Athens.: Agora Excavations. (Photo: American School).

140 Relief of frieze from the Parthenon. Paris, Musée du Louvre. (Photo: Alison Frantz).

141 Model of the Athenian Acropolis. With permission of the Royal Ontario Museum, Toronto, Canada 956.118. © ROM. (Photo: Museum).

141 Parthenon. (Photo: Alison Frantz).

142 (Drawing: Catherine Balme).

144 Theater of Dionysus. (Photo: Alison Frantz).

151 Detail of Attic red figure calyx krater. All rights reserved, New York, The Metropolitan Museum of Art 41.83, gift of Amelia E. White, 1941. (Photo: Museum).

153 Boeotian skyphos. Oxford, Ashmolean Museum

156 (Drawing: Catherine Balme).

162 Relief of frieze from the Parthenon. West Frieze 1.2–3. Reproduced by courtesy of the Trustees of the British Museum, London. (Photo: Museum).

164 (Drawing: Catherine Balme).

168 Detail of Attic red figure bell krater. Frankfurt, Archäologisches Museum. (Photo: Museum).

174 (Drawing: Catherine Balme).

183 Relief. Deutsches Archäologisches Institut Athen NM 3312. (Photo: Wagner).

186 (Drawing: Catherine Balme).

194 (Drawing: Catherine Balme).

202 Detail of an Attic black figure cup. Vase B8436. Reproduced by courtesy of the Trustees of the British Museum, London. (Photo: Museum).

204 (Drawing: Catherine Balme).

206 Piraeus. © 1989 Loyola University Chicago. (Photo: R. V. Schoder, S.J.).